STATISTICAL MODELING USING LOCAL GAUSSIAN APPROXIMATION

STATISTICAL MODELING USING LOCAL GAUSSIAN APPROXIMATION

DAG TJØSTHEIM

HÅKON OTNEIM

BÅRD STØVE

ELSEVIER

ACADEMIC PRESS

An imprint of Elsevier

Academic Press is an imprint of Elsevier
125 London Wall, London EC2Y 5AS, United Kingdom
525 B Street, Suite 1650, San Diego, CA 92101, United States
50 Hampshire Street, 5th Floor, Cambridge, MA 02139, United States
The Boulevard, Langford Lane, Kidlington, Oxford OX5 1GB, United Kingdom

Notices

Knowledge and best practice in this field are constantly changing. As new research and experience broaden our understanding, changes in research methods, professional practices, or medical treatment may become necessary.

Practitioners and researchers must always rely on their own experience and knowledge in evaluating and using any information, methods, compounds, or experiments described herein. In using such information or methods they should be mindful of their own safety and the safety of others, including parties for whom they have a professional responsibility.

To the fullest extent of the law, neither the Publisher nor the authors, contributors, or editors, assume any liability for any injury and/or damage to persons or property as a matter of products liability, negligence or otherwise, or from any use or operation of any methods, products, instructions, or ideas contained in the material herein.

Library of Congress Cataloging-in-Publication Data
A catalog record for this book is available from the Library of Congress

British Library Cataloguing-in-Publication Data
A catalogue record for this book is available from the British Library

ISBN: 978-0-12-815861-6

For information on all Academic Press publications
visit our website at https://www.elsevier.com/books-and-journals

Publisher: Candice Janco
Acquisitions Editor: Brian Romer
Editorial Project Manager: Susan Ikeda
Production Project Manager: Surya Narayanan Jayachandran
Designer: Matthew Limbert

Typeset by VTeX

To our wives: Marit, Karina, Ellen Johanne

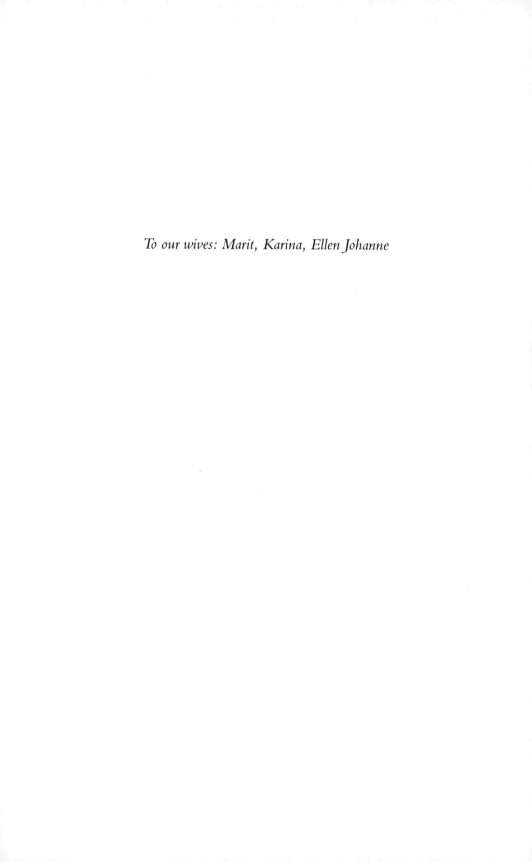

Contents

Biography *xi*
Preface *xiii*

1. Introduction **1**
1.1. Computer code 6
References 6

2. Parametric, nonparametric, locally parametric **7**
2.1. Introduction 7
2.2. Parametric density models 9
2.3. Parametric regression models 17
2.4. Time series 20
2.5. Nonparametric density estimation 23
2.6. Nonparametric regression estimation 29
2.7. Fighting the curse of dimensionality 33
2.8. Quantile regression 37
2.9. Semiparametric models 38
2.10. Locally parametric 40
References 43

3. Dependence **49**
3.1. Introduction 49
3.2. Weaknesses of Pearson's ρ 52
3.3. The copula 56
3.4. Global dependence functionals and tests of independence 61
3.5. Test functionals generated by local dependence relationships 80
References 81

4. Local Gaussian correlation and dependence **87**
4.1. Introduction 87
4.2. Local dependence 90
4.3. Local Gaussian correlation 94
4.4. Limit theorems 99
4.5. Properties 105
4.6. Examples 112
4.7. Transforming the marginals: Normalized local correlation 115
4.8. Some practical considerations 120
4.9. The p-dimensional case 123

4.10. Proof of asymptotic results 123
References 133

5. Local Gaussian correlation and the copula 135
5.1. Introduction 135
5.2. Local Gaussian correlation for copula models 136
5.3. Examples 142
5.4. Recognizing copulas by goodness-of-fit 148
5.5. A real-data study 157
References 159

6. Applications in finance 161
6.1. Introduction 161
6.2. Conditional correlation and the bias problem 164
6.3. Empirical analysis of dependence of financial returns 167
6.4. The portfolio allocation problem 182
6.5. Financial contagion 196
References 209

7. Measuring dependence and testing for independence 213
7.1. Introduction 213
7.2. Testing of independence in iid pairs of variables using local correlation functionals 214
7.3. Testing for serial independence in time series 224
7.4. Describing nonlinear dependence and tests of independence for two time series 235
7.5. Proofs 253
References 259

8. Time series dependence and spectral analysis 261
8.1. Introduction 261
8.2. Local Gaussian spectral densities 265
8.3. Visualizations and interpretations 280
References 297

9. Multivariate density estimation 301
9.1. Introduction 301
9.2. Description of the estimator 304
9.3. Asymptotic theory 308
9.4. Bandwidth selection 313
9.5. An example 316
9.6. Investigating performance in the multivariate case 318
9.7. A more flexible version of the LGDE 323

9.8. Proofs 327
References 333

10. Conditional density estimation **335**
10.1. Introduction 335
10.2. Estimating the conditional density 337
10.3. Asymptotic theory for dependent data 339
10.4. Examples 342
10.5. Proof of theorems 348
References 352

11. The local Gaussian partial correlation **353**
11.1. Introduction 353
11.2. The local Gaussian partial correlation 354
11.3. Properties 358
11.4. Estimation of the LGPC by local likelihood 360
11.5. Asymptotic theory 362
11.6. Examples 365
11.7. Testing for conditional independence 370
11.8. The multivariate LGPC 376
References 382

12. Regression and conditional regression quantiles **385**
12.1. Introduction 385
12.2. Comparison with additive regression modeling 387
12.3. Local Gaussian regression estimation 388
12.4. Asymptotic normality 390
12.5. Example 394
12.6. Conditional quantiles 396
12.7. Proof 398
References 401

13. A local Gaussian Fisher discriminant **403**
13.1. Introduction 403
13.2. A local Gaussian Fisher discriminant 408
13.3. Some asymptotics of Bayes risk 413
13.4. Choice of bandwidth 417
13.5. Illustrations 420
13.6. Summary remark 425
References 426

Author index *429*
Subject index *437*

Biography

Dag Tjøstheim

is Emeritus Professor, Department of Mathematics, University of Bergen. He has a PhD in applied mathematics from Princeton University (1974). He has authored more than 120 papers in international journals. He is a member of the Norwegian Academy of Sciences and has received several prizes for his scientific work. His main interests are in econometrics, nonlinear time series, nonparametric methods, modeling of dependence, spatial variables, and fishery statistics.

Håkon Otneim

is Associate Professor at the Norwegian School of Economics. He has a PhD in statistics from the University of Bergen (2016), and he has published papers in international journals about multivariate density estimation and conditional density estimation. His research interests include development and application of nonparametric and semiparametric statistics, statistical programming, and data visualization.

Bård Støve

is Professor of Statistics at the University of Bergen. He received his PhD degree in statistics, 2005. He was Assistant Professor at the Norwegian School of Economics (2007–2011), and worked as an Actuary in a consulting firm (2005–2007). He has been working on the development of nonparametric models and application of such models to finance and economics. He has published several research papers in such journals as *Econometric Theory* and *Scandinavian Journal of Statistics*.

Preface

The central idea of this book is the approximation of a general multivariate density f by a family of Gaussian distributions. Locally around a point x in the support of f, f is approximated by a multivariate Gaussian distribution. This makes it possible to define a local mean, a local variance, and a local correlation matrix.

This idea is powerful and can be applied to a number of tasks and problems for continuous stochastic variables. This has been done in several recent papers. These papers, thirteen altogether, form the basis of this book. In particular, following two introductory chapters, each of the main Chapters 3–11 and 13 is composed from one or more of these papers.

In Chapter 4 the emphasis is on the local correlation, its properties, and its use as a measure of dependence. It can be defined on the original x-scale, but also on a normalized z-scale obtained by transforming the marginals of f to the standard normal. This is in a way analogous to the transformation to uniform variables in a copula construction, and the relationship between the copula concept and the Gaussian approximation concept is explored in Chapter 5.

It has long been realized that a multivariate Gaussian distribution fitted to data in finance or econometrics may not be a good idea. In fact, data in finance and econometrics have thick tails, and a global Gaussian fit may lead to disastrous results with a large underestimation of economic risk. In Chapter 6, we apply local Gaussian approximation to financial data, including financial contagion and a preliminary attempt of portfolio construction.

With the establishment of local Gaussian correlation as a measure of local dependence, an obvious next step is employing this measure to testing of independence. This is done in Chapter 7 in three stages: testing of independence between two sequences, each consisting of independent identically distributed variables, testing of serial independence in a time series, and testing of independence between two stationary time series. This implies the introduction of a local autocorrelation and cross-correlation concept.

The locally Gaussian autocorrelation introduced in Chapter 7 is used in Chapter 8 to construct a locally Gaussian spectral density. It coincides with the ordinary power spectral density in the Gaussian time series case. For non-Gaussian data, the new local spectral concept can be used to pick up spectral peaks that may be hidden in a conventional spectral estimation.

Chapters 9 and 10 are devoted to estimation of multivariate density functions and to estimation of multivariate conditional densities. This is done by merging the Gaussian densities of the local approximating families. In the conditional case the unique properties of the conditional (global) Gaussian distribution is of crucial importance. Further, the curse of dimensionality is sought circumvented by a simplified Gaussian approximation, in a sense similar to the use of the additive simplification in nonparametric regression.

The local Gaussian approximation also makes it possible to introduce a local Gaussian partial correlation. In Chapter 11, it is shown how this can be used to construct a local measure of conditional dependence and to test for conditional independence. We believe that this idea has potential for network theory and causality.

Perhaps the most important use of nonparametric estimation methods is currently in nonparametric regression. The local Gaussian approximation concept is developed for multivariate statistical analysis, where all of the variables are, so to speak, on the same basis, in contradistinction to regression analysis, where one variable or a group of variables are dependent variables expressed as a function of another group of explanatory variables. Nevertheless, in Chapter 12, we make an attempt to apply local Gaussian approximation techniques to regression estimation and quantile regression estimation. More work is required to determine in what way local methods can complement nonparametric techniques like, for instance, additive modeling.

The local Gaussian approach can be applied to other fields of statistics as well. As an example of such an application, in Chapter 13, we look at applications to classification and discrimination, involving among other things a local Fisher discriminant.

To put local Gaussian approximation analysis into context with other methods, the book also contains three introductory chapters. Chapter 1 contains a general introduction explaining the overall features and concepts of our approach. Chapter 2 gives a brief but at the same time quite broad overview over parametric, nonparametric, and locally parametric approaches to statistics. Chapter 3, based on a very recent survey paper to appear in Statistical Science, contains an overview of the statistical concept of dependence, how it can be measured, and how we can test for independence. The survey concentrates on methods developed in the last two decades, going beyond the most used measure of dependence, the Pearson correlation. The local Gaussian correlation is put directly into this context in Chapter 4.

There is some overlap between the various chapters in the book. This has been done intentionally, so that a reader can single out the chapters of primary interest to her/him. Most chapters can be read independently of each other as the basic material from Chapter 4 is included briefly as an introductory material in each of the following chapters. The mathematical and technical level of each chapter is quite modest. For readers with more interest in technical details, we give references, often to supplementary material to the papers that the book is composed from.

There are three R-packages that have been developed for various types of analysis in the book. We do not present details of use of these packages in this book, but references to the packages are given in Chapter 1.

The local Gaussian approach is a recently developed methodology. Some of the chapters are based on papers that have just appeared or are in the process of appearing in journals. Putting this in a book, the emphasis is on presenting the fundamental concepts inherent in a local Gaussian approximation and in demonstrating their usefulness in several areas in statistics. At the same time, we hope that the book may serve as a starting point and inspiration for further research and applications in the subject matters taken up in each of the chapters of the book, as well as in new subject areas.

The chapters of the book have been primarily based on papers by the three authors of the book, but some chapters have also benefited from joint work and joint papers with others, namely Karl Ove Hufthammer (Chapters 4 and 6), Geir Berentsen (Chapters 5 and 7), Viginia Lacal (Chapter 7), Lars Arne Jordanger (Chapter 8), Martin Jullum (Chapter 13), and Anders Sleire (parts of Chapter 6). Without their contributions the book had not been possible in its present form, and we are very grateful to them for their good work and cooperation on these subjects.

Dag Tjøstheim
Håkon Otneim
Bård Støve
Bergen, May 2021

CHAPTER 1

Introduction

Contents

1.1. Computer code 6
References 6

The most important distribution in statistics is the Gaussian distribution. It has a number of very useful and special properties, particularly in the multivariate case. Just think about a normally distributed vector $\boldsymbol{X} = (X_1, \ldots, X_p)^T$ of dimension p, where T denotes transposed. Its distribution is given by the density function

$$f(\boldsymbol{x}) = \frac{1}{(2\pi)^{p/2}|\boldsymbol{\Sigma}|^{1/2}} \exp\{(\boldsymbol{x} - \boldsymbol{\mu})^T \boldsymbol{\Sigma}^{-1} (\boldsymbol{x} - \boldsymbol{\mu})\},$$

where $\boldsymbol{\mu} = \{\mu_i\}$ and $\boldsymbol{\Sigma} = \{\sigma_{ij}\}$, $i, j = 1, \ldots, p$, are the mean vector and covariance matrix of $\boldsymbol{X}$, respectively. Looking at this familiar expression, it is easy to forget its simplicity and elegance. Here we have a distribution whose location is completely determined by its means μ_i, the scale by the variances σ_{ii}, and whose dependence relations have the amazing property that they are completely determined by the pairwise covariances σ_{ij}.

Moreover, if $\boldsymbol{X}$ is subdivided into two components $\boldsymbol{X} = (\boldsymbol{X}_1, \boldsymbol{X}_2)$, then any linear combination of $\boldsymbol{X}_1$ and $\boldsymbol{X}_2$ is again Gaussian, and the conditional distribution $f_{\boldsymbol{X}_1|\boldsymbol{X}_2}(\boldsymbol{x}_1|\boldsymbol{x}_2)$ is Gaussian. The dependence properties of these derived distributions are again determined by the pairwise covariances, in the latter case, through the partial covariances. These properties make the Gaussian especially suitable for linear statistical modeling. Further, the properties of the conditional distribution imply that in a Gaussian system the optimal least squares predictor, given by the conditional mean, is linear and equals the optimal linear predictor. Finally, uncorrelatedness is equivalent to independence in the Gaussian distribution, that is, $\boldsymbol{X}_1$ and $\boldsymbol{X}_2$ are independent if and only if they are uncorrelated. In this case, we can test for independence by computing covariances.

Unfortunately, data are not always well described by a Gaussian distribution and a linear model. In particular, for data in economics and finance the data are usually governed by distributions having thicker tails, and the dependence properties are not well described by pairwise covariances only,

Statistical Modeling using Local Gaussian Approximation
https://doi.org/10.1016/B978-0-12-815861-6.00008-0

as is inherent in the Gaussian distribution. In fact, assuming a linear Gaussian model can lead to disastrous results with drastic underestimation of the risk involved in economic and financial transactions; see, for example, Taleb (2007).

To some degree, these problems can be avoided, or at least lessened, by trying to fit other parametric families to the data or by using a semiparametric or nonparametric approach. An important concept in a nonparametric methodology is the concept of a local approximation. In nonparametric density estimation, we may take as the starting point a locally smoothed version of a histogram of the available data. In a regression, the regression relationship may be approximated by locally fitted polynomials (the particular case of the locally constant case being the regression kernel estimator). What is local is determined by a bandwidth parameter, which for a given point $\boldsymbol{x}$, selects the neighboring points close to $\boldsymbol{x}$, "close" being determined by the bandwidth acting as a distance measure. A density, a conditional density, or a regression can be estimated nonparametrically in this manner. As the dimension p increases, the curse of dimensionality emerges, and simplifying assumptions, such as the additive model for regression, have to be introduced.

We are now ready to formulate the main idea of this book and of the papers it consists of. The idea is simply to approximate an arbitrary p-dimensional density function f locally by a family of Gaussians distributions. This can be viewed as an example of a semiparametric or a locally parametric approach. In principle, another family of parametric distributions could be used as a local approximant (as has been done by Hjort and Jones (1996), who considered the locally parametric density estimator), but we believe that the well-known simple and elegant properties of Gaussians makes this family of distributions the optimal choice. So, for a point $\boldsymbol{x}$, in a neighborhood of $\boldsymbol{x}$, we fit a Gaussian distribution, the neighborhood being determined by a bandwidth parameter. The parameters of this Gaussian distribution will be functions of the coordinates of the point $\boldsymbol{x}$. Moving to another point $\boldsymbol{y}$ and fitting another Gaussian in the neighborhood of $\boldsymbol{y}$ will in general result in another set of parameters depending on $\boldsymbol{y}$. The exception is when f itself is Gaussian. In that case, as the number of available observations tends to infinity at the same time as the bandwidth tends to zero, the estimated parameters at $\boldsymbol{x}$ and $\boldsymbol{y}$ will ultimately coincide and be equal to the parameters of the Gaussian f. The advantage of using the Gaussian distribution as an approximating family is that the unique properties of the Gaussian can be *locally* used for a general, possibly non-Gaussian, density f. For instance, for a thick-tailed distribution, it can be locally approximated in the tail by a Gaussian with large variance. In the multivariate case, we have the potential of approximating multivariate tail behavior locally by an appropriate multivariate Gaussian. This turns out to be useful for multivariate financial market data.

Using this idea as a statistical modeling philosophy has many ramifications and applications as we try to illustrate throughout the book. For example, we can define local covariances and correlations, and even local partial covariances. Local dependence and conditional dependence can be measured by these quantities, and local independence and conditional independence can be tested. Dependence properties may be analyzed by aggregation, and independence may be tested over larger regions, ultimately over the entire range of the data. Further, by using the same principle in approximating locally the joint distribution of time series variables, we can introduce concepts of local autocorrelation and cross-correlation. A local spectral density can be constructed, which makes it possible to derive one local spectral density describing the oscillatory properties at one level (e.g., close to extremes) and another local one describing the frequency distribution close to the center of the data.

Seen from this perspective, the unique properties of the Gaussian can be utilized in a non-Gaussian environment but, again, locally. In this book, we discuss many such examples, but there are other avenues that have not been explored so far. Local principal component analysis is one of them. The ordinary principal components are found by solving an eigenvalue problem involving the covariance matrix. Local principal components can be found by replacing the ordinary global covariance matrix by a matrix of local covariances. Another area where research has been initiated, is multiple spectral analysis, where a local amplitude spectrum and phase spectrum can be introduced. There are other possibilities as well, and we believe local Gaussian approximation to be a very comprehensive tool.

Another potential extension is to broaden the Gaussian family to a more general family like the family of elliptic distributions. Then we lose some of the simple properties of the Gaussian (e.g., independence is not equivalent to uncorrelatedness), but, on the other hand, a multivariate t-distribution, belonging to the elliptic family, is much easier to approximate. Other families are considered by Hjort and Jones (1996), but just in the situation of deriving an alternative density estimator to the kernel estimator.

Local quantities like the local correlation is sensitive to the curse of dimensionality as the dimension of $\boldsymbol{X}$ increases. Throughout the book, we discuss ways of bypassing it. Somewhat similarly to the additive approximation in regression analysis, we try to approximate the elements $\sigma_{ij}(\boldsymbol{x})$ of the covariance matrix by a function of two coordinates $\sigma_{ij}(x_i, x_j)$. Still we have to be careful at the edges of the data set where there are few observations. Another device that has been much used in this book is transforming the data to a standard normal marginal scale by using the marginal empirical distribution function. A very different approach, which may deserve a closer examination, is trying to fit a parametric model to the local quantities.

Here is a brief overview of the contents of the book:

To put our method into perspective, we summarize briefly traditional parametric, semiparametric, nonparametric, and locally parametric modeling in Chapter 2. Very briefly, properties of the Gaussian and elliptic distribution are also included.

Local correlation represents one way of measuring dependence as a local version of the traditional Pearson correlation. Chapter 3 presents a fairly self-contained review of recent developments in nonlinear dependence analysis, among them, the Brownian distance covariance and reproducing kernel Hilbert space measures, both having received considerable attention lately.

In Chapter 4, we contrast the dependence measures of Chapter 3 with the local Gaussian correlation (LGC). We define this concept as well as the concept of local Gaussian approximation. Two versions are described, one on the original $\boldsymbol{x}$-scale and one on the $\boldsymbol{z}$-scale obtained by transforming the marginals to standard normals. We give a number of properties and illustrate these on simulated and financial real data.

The connection to description of dependence by means of copulas is explored in Chapter 5. We compute the local correlation for traditional copulas like the Clayton, Gumbel, and Frank copulas.

Much of what we do is motivated by problems met in the description of financial markets. Chapter 6 contains a number of applications to financial and econometric data. It is shown that key "typical" dependence properties of such markets are well described by the local Gaussian correlation, and we also look at applications to financial contagion, portfolio analysis, and value at risk.

In Gaussian distributions, independence and uncorrelatedness are equivalent, so it is natural to use the local Gaussian correlation to test for local and nonlinear independence. In Chapter 7, we extend this to tests of serial dependence in a univariate time series and to independence testing between two time series. We compare to other tests like the Brownian distance covariance for both simulated and real data.

In Chapter 8 the time series frame is kept, but here we focus on the local autocorrelation and the local spectrum that can be derived from it. It is shown that frequency behavior that cannot be detected by ordinary spectral analysis can be detected by the local spectrum. The chapter also contains a brief review of alternative nonlinear spectral techniques.

Chapters 9 and 10 are devoted to density estimation and conditional density estimation, respectively. The density estimation is the aspect stressed by Hjort and Jones (1996) in their local parametric analysis. We carry this through for the local Gaussian approximation of a density and compare with other methods as the dimension increases. In the conditional density estimation, we exploit locally the fact that the conditional density in a joint Gaussian density framework is again a Gaussian density, where the local mean vector and covariance matrix can be found by explicit formulas.

In a sense testing for *conditional* independence is more important than testing for independence. This is due to the applications to causality analysis among other things. For globally Gaussian data, the partial correlation coefficient is an important tool, for example, in path analysis. In Chapter 11, we introduce the local partial correlation and use it both for measuring conditional dependence and for testing of conditional independence. We compare with alternative tests and give applications to testing Granger causality.

Regression and conditional quantile estimation is covered in Chapter 12. We note that the local Gaussian approach is primarily suited to a situation where all the variables are treated on the same basis. It is perhaps less well suited to a situation where there is one dependent variable and one or several explanatory variables. Nevertheless, we show in this chapter that the local Gaussian approximation can be applied and that in particular cases it may offer an alternative to the additive approximation in regression models.

The traditional Fisher discriminant for discriminating between two or more populations is based on a Gaussian assumption. In Chapter 13, we make the parameters of the Gaussian local and derive a local Gaussian Fisher discriminant, which is applied to simulated and real data. It is easy to find examples where the global Fisher discriminant does not work, whereas the local one does.

1.1 Computer code

The package `lg`, see Otneim (2021), for the R programming language (see R Core Team, 2017) provides implementations of most of the methodological advances on applications of the local Gaussian approximation presented in this book. This includes estimation of the local Gaussian correlation itself, multivariate density estimation, conditional density estimation, various tests for independence, conditional independence and financial contagion (cf. Chapter 6), and a graphical module for creating dependence maps; see Otneim (2019). Note that the use of local Gaussian correlation in spectral analysis of time series, presented in Chapter 8, has its own computational ecosystem in the `localgaussSpec`-package[1] for R. The R package `localgauss` (see Berentsen et al., 2014) provided the first publicly available implementation of the LGC and a test for independence. Note that the `lg`-package depends on the `localgauss`-package.

We refer to the R documentation of the mentioned packages and Otneim (2021) for the direct use of various available functions, as this will not be covered in the book.

References

Berentsen, G.D., Kleppe, T., Tjøstheim, D., 2014. Introducing localgauss, an R package for estimating and visualizing local Gaussian correlation. Journal of Statistical Software 56 (12), 1–18.

Hjort, N., Jones, M., 1996. Locally parametric nonparametric density estimation. Annals of Statistics 24 (4), 1619–1647.

Otneim, H., 2019. lg: Locally Gaussian distributions: estimation and methods. https://CRAN.R-project.org/package=lg. R package version 0.4.1.

Otneim, H., 2021. lg: an R package for local Gaussian approximations. To appear, The R Journal. URL: https://journal.r-project.org/archive/2021/RJ-2021-079/index.html.

R Core Team, 2017. R: A Language and Environment for Statistical Computing. R Foundation for Statistical Computing, Vienna, Austria.

Taleb, N.N., 2007. The Black Swan: The Impact of the Highly Improbable. Random House.

[1] See `https://github.com/LAJordanger/localgaussSpec` for details.

CHAPTER 2

Parametric, nonparametric, locally parametric

Contents

2.1. Introduction 7
2.2. Parametric density models 9
2.2.1 The Gaussian distribution 9
2.2.2 The elliptical distribution 11
2.2.3 The exponential family 15
2.3. Parametric regression models 17
2.3.1 Linear regression 17
2.3.2 Nonlinear regression and some further modeling aspects 19
2.4. Time series 20
2.5. Nonparametric density estimation 23
2.5.1 Nonparametric kernel density estimation 24
2.5.2 Bandwidth selection 26
2.5.3 Multivariate and conditional density estimation 27
2.6. Nonparametric regression estimation 29
2.6.1 Kernel regression estimation 29
2.6.2 Local polynomial estimation 31
2.6.3 Choice of bandwidth in regression 32
2.7. Fighting the curse of dimensionality 33
2.7.1 Additive models 34
2.7.2 Regression trees, splines, and MARS 37
2.8. Quantile regression 37
2.9. Semiparametric models 38
2.9.1 Partially linear models 39
2.9.2 Index models and projection pursuit 39
2.10. Locally parametric 40
References 43

2.1 Introduction

In statistical modeling, we have to choose between a parametric model and the use of nonparametric statistics. A compromise is a semiparametric model, where both aspects of modeling are taken into consideration.

For a parametric model, the mathematical form of the model and relationships between stochastic variables entering the model and their distributions are explicitly stated and generally assumed to be known except

Statistical Modeling using Local Gaussian Approximation
https://doi.org/10.1016/B978-0-12-815861-6.00009-2

for a set of parameters. The parameters may, for instance, appear as coefficients in a linear regression or as parameters of a distribution function from a certain class. Strictly speaking, a parametric model is never true, or in the words of Box and Draper (1987, p. 424), "All models are wrong, but some are useful." A parametric model is often quite simple and has a straightforward interpretation. In certain situations, however, parametric models may lead astray. When the model is seriously wrong, the accuracy of parameter estimates does not help. One well-known example is the estimation of value-at-risk for financial markets. Sometimes, financial crises have been blamed on using Gaussian models in the tail of a distribution when financial objects quite clearly have thicker tails. Using the Gaussian distribution may lead to a disastrous underestimation of the risk; see Taleb (2007). In such situations a parametric model works as an extremely inconvenient strait jacket.

The purpose of a nonparametric approach is letting the data speak for themselves and thereby preventing such situations from occurring. However, this approach also has its disadvantages. First, the convergence rate of nonparametric estimates is slower than the parametric rate. But perhaps the most important obstacle is the curse of dimensionality: when we have a moderate or large number of variables, the nonparametric approach does not work in practice. It may still be possible to state theorems of convergence rates for nonparametric estimates, but these are so slow that we need astronomically large sample sizes to come close to the true values, which we typically do not have. There are various ways of trying to get around the *curse*. This can be done by assuming further restrictive assumptions such as an additive model in a regression context. We will come back to this on several occasions later in this chapter and in later chapters of the book.

Another way of tackling the curse of dimensionality is using a semiparametric model, that is, a model where some parts of the model are treated parametrically and other parts of the model are treated nonparametrically. The implicit understanding is that the nonparametric part is specified in such a way that we avoid the curse of dimensionality. However, it may not be obvious which parts of the model should be specified parametrically and which parts should be treated in a nonparametric fashion.

The main philosophy of this book is to try to take advantage of the best features of the nonparametric and parametric methodologies. We do this by letting the parameters of a parametric model depend on the variables involved, which is a local parametric approach advocated by, for example, Hjort and Jones (1996) and Loader (1996). These two references treat localization of parameters for a quite general parametric family. On the other hand, we concentrate on localizing the Gaussian parametric family. It turns out that this has some great potential advantages, and we are not only able to use the local Gaussian structure to lessen the curse of dimensionality, but we are also able to generalize and extend models where the correlation or autocorrelation function plays a natural role. A brief introduction to the idea of local parametric estimation is given in Section 2.10 of this chapter, and a much more detailed account of the local Gaussian approach follows in Chapter 4.

In the present chapter we will give a brief overview of the two main approaches, parametric and nonparametric, and mention the semiparametric hybrid. The overview will be rather subjective in its choice of topics and emphasis. Some special topics are given more coverage than in most reviews of this sort. We do this in such a manner because we not only motivate local Gaussian modeling in its present state, but also briefly include topics that may serve as extensions of the local modeling as presented in this book. There are no data illustrations in this chapter as such illustrations can be found in numerous other books on these topics.

2.2 Parametric density models

Motivated by their use later in the book, as possible candidates for extensions of local Gaussian models, we discuss three types of distributions: the Gaussian, elliptic, and exponential families.

2.2.1 The Gaussian distribution

The Gaussian, or normal, distribution is probably the most used distribution in statistics. There are several reasons for this, but the most important one is probably the central limit theorem, which states that averages are (approximately) normally distributed if we have fairly many observations. Moreover, the normal distribution has a number of attractive and simple mathematical properties, not the least that it can be generalized very easily to the multivariate case. This is one reason why many books on multivariate statistics to a large part are based on the multivariate normal distribution; see, for example, Anderson (2003) and Johnson and Wichern (2007).

In applications, however, and perhaps particularly in finance, the normal distribution does not always give a good approximation to the data and may in fact lead to very wrong and even catastrophic results. The main idea of this book is to use the Gaussian distribution as a local approximation.

We are seeking to replace a given distribution, univariate or multivariate, by a family of Gaussian distributions, where each member of the family approximates the properties of the given distribution locally in a neighborhood surrounding a given point. The motivation is that we hope to avoid the inaccuracy of using the pure Gaussian distribution and at the same time retain simple and unique properties of the Gaussian distribution locally.

The Gaussian is of course a prime example of a parametric model in statistics, and in this section, we very briefly survey some fundamental facts of this distribution that we will use in later chapters. The multivariate normal density function $f(\boldsymbol{x})$ for a continuous stochastic variable $\boldsymbol{X} = (X_1, \ldots, X_p)^T$ of dimension p is given by

$$f(\boldsymbol{x}) = (2\pi)^{-p/2}|\boldsymbol{\Sigma}|^{-1/2} \exp\left\{(\boldsymbol{x} - \boldsymbol{\mu})^T \boldsymbol{\Sigma}^{-1}(\boldsymbol{x} - \boldsymbol{\mu})\right\}, \tag{2.1}$$

where $\boldsymbol{\mu} = (\mu_1, \ldots, \mu_p)^T$ with $\mathrm{E}(X_i) = \mu_i$, and $\boldsymbol{\Sigma}$ is the covariance matrix of $\boldsymbol{X}$ given by $\boldsymbol{\Sigma} = \{\sigma_{ij}\}$ with $\sigma_{ij} = \mathrm{Cov}(X_i, X_j) = \mathrm{E}\left((X_i - \mu_i)(X_j - \mu_j)\right)$ for $i \neq j$ and $\sigma_{ii} = \sigma_i^2$, the variance of X_i. Moreover, $|\boldsymbol{\Sigma}|$ is the determinant of $\boldsymbol{\Sigma}$, and T denotes transpose. We write $\boldsymbol{X} \sim \mathcal{N}(\boldsymbol{\mu}, \boldsymbol{\Sigma})$. A fantastic property of this multivariate distribution is that it is composed of pairwise dependencies only. It suffices to compute the means, variances, and pairwise covariances to obtain the whole distribution. This is a fact that we will use later in our local Gaussian analysis.

In the bivariate case ($p = 2$), we write

$$f(\boldsymbol{x}) = \frac{1}{2\pi\sigma_1\sigma_2\sqrt{1-\rho_{12}^2}} \exp\left\{-\frac{1}{2(1-\rho_{12}^2)} \times \left[\left(\frac{x_1-\mu_1}{\sigma_1}\right)^2 - 2\rho_{12}\left(\frac{x_1-\mu_1}{\sigma_1}\frac{x_2-\mu_2}{\sigma_2}\right) + \left(\frac{x_2-\mu_2}{\sigma_2}\right)^2\right]\right\},$$

where $\rho_{12} = \sigma_{12}/\sigma_1\sigma_2$ is the correlation between X_1 and X_2. It is well known that uncorrelatedness does not imply independence in general, but for the Gaussian, as is easy to check from the form of the distribution function, uncorrelatedness and independence are equivalent. In a local Gaussian approximation, this property is used to asses dependence by means of the *local* correlation, and tests of independence are constructed by accumulating the local Gaussian correlation, see Chapter 7.

Another very important property of the Gaussian distribution is that marginal distributions and conditional distributions are again Gaussian. Let $\boldsymbol{X} \sim \mathcal{N}(\boldsymbol{\mu}_{\boldsymbol{X}}, \boldsymbol{\Sigma}_{\boldsymbol{XX}})$ be a p-dimensional column vector, and let $\boldsymbol{Y}$ be a q-dimensional column vector with mean $\boldsymbol{\mu}_{\boldsymbol{Y}} = \mathrm{E}(\boldsymbol{Y})$ and covariance matrix

$\boldsymbol{\Sigma}_{YY}$. Assume that the covariance matrix $\boldsymbol{\Sigma}_{XX} = \mathrm{E}(\boldsymbol{X} - \boldsymbol{\mu}_X)(\boldsymbol{X} - \boldsymbol{\mu}_X)^T$ is nonsingular, and assume that $(\boldsymbol{X}, \boldsymbol{Y})$ is jointly $(p+q)$-variate normally distributed. Then the conditional distribution of $\boldsymbol{Y}$ given $\boldsymbol{X}$ is Gaussian with mean

$$\boldsymbol{\mu}_{Y|X=x} = \boldsymbol{\mu}_Y + \boldsymbol{\Sigma}_{YX}\boldsymbol{\Sigma}_{XX}^{-1}(\boldsymbol{x} - \boldsymbol{\mu}_X) \tag{2.2}$$

with $\boldsymbol{\Sigma}_{YX} = \mathrm{E}(\boldsymbol{Y} - \boldsymbol{\mu}_Y)(\boldsymbol{X} - \boldsymbol{\mu}_X)^T$, and with covariance matrix

$$\boldsymbol{\Sigma}_{Y|X} = \boldsymbol{\Sigma}_{YY} - \boldsymbol{\Sigma}_{YX}\boldsymbol{\Sigma}_{XX}^{-1}\boldsymbol{\Sigma}_{XY}. \tag{2.3}$$

In the bivariate case $\boldsymbol{X} = (X_1, X_2)$, this reduces to

$$\mu_{2|1} = \mu_2 + \rho_{21}\frac{\sigma_2}{\sigma_1}(x_1 - \mu_1)$$

and

$$\Sigma_{2|1} = (1 - \rho_{21}^2)\sigma_2^2.$$

These formulas are starting points for defining the partial correlation function of two vectors $\boldsymbol{X}$ and $\boldsymbol{Y}$ given a third vector $\boldsymbol{Z}$. In Chapter 11, we will introduce local versions of these quantities by straight analogy and use them in a description of conditional density functions and tests for conditional independence. The local partial correlation function derived from the formulas for the global Gaussian will play an essential role in these derivations.

Other useful properties of a multivariate Gaussian are its simple transformation rules. If $\boldsymbol{X}$ is a multivariate Gaussian of dimension p, $\boldsymbol{c}$ is a vector of scalars having dimension q, $\boldsymbol{B}$ is a $q \times p$ matrix of scalars, and if $\boldsymbol{X} \sim \mathcal{N}(\boldsymbol{\mu}, \boldsymbol{\Sigma})$, then $\boldsymbol{Y} = \boldsymbol{c} + \boldsymbol{B}\boldsymbol{X} \sim \mathcal{N}(\boldsymbol{c} + \boldsymbol{B}\boldsymbol{\mu}, \boldsymbol{B}\boldsymbol{\Sigma}\boldsymbol{B}^T)$. In particular, any linear combination of the components of $\boldsymbol{X}$ is again normally distributed. We will make use of this in Section 6.4 on nonlinear local portfolio construction.

The estimation of the parameters $\boldsymbol{\mu}$ and $\boldsymbol{\Sigma}$ in (2.1) can be done by maximizing the log likelihood function, which becomes very simple for the density function (2.1). The analogue for estimating a local mean and a local covariance is a local log likelihood function as explained in some detail in Chapter 4.

2.2.2 The elliptical distribution

The normal distribution plays a very central role in this book, since it forms the basis for a local Gaussian representation. For a distribution that is not normal but belongs to a specific class of distributions, say the t-distribution, it may of course be a disadvantage to try to approximate it with a family of Gaussian distributions. Then the question arises whether we should try to use a family of more general distributions. In particular, we might be interested in distributions that retain as many as possible of the very simple properties of Gaussian distributions and that are easily extendable to the multivariate case. A natural class for this purpose is the elliptical distributions. This class of distributions is also of interest in its own right when it comes to applications in finance, since it contains several heavy-tailed distributions. A classic paper in this context is by Owen and Rabinovitch (1983). A more recent contribution is by Landsman and Valdez (2003). There is also a separate chapter on elliptical distributions in McNeil et al. (2005).

There are several ways to define an elliptic distribution, which can be defined for both discrete and continuous variables. Perhaps the simplest definition is taking as a starting point the class of spherical distributions. The random q-dimensional variable $\boldsymbol{X}'$ is said to have a spherical distribution if its characteristic function $\phi_{\boldsymbol{X}'}(\boldsymbol{t})$ can be written as

$$\phi_{\boldsymbol{X}'}(\boldsymbol{t}) = \mathrm{E}\left(\exp(i\boldsymbol{t}^T\boldsymbol{X}')\right) = \psi\left(\boldsymbol{t}^T\boldsymbol{t}\right) = \psi\left(t_1^2 + \cdots + t_q^2\right)$$

for some function ψ, which is called the characteristic generator. We write $\boldsymbol{X}' \sim S_q(\psi)$. A particular case of spherical multivariate distributions is obtained by taking $\psi(\boldsymbol{t}) = \exp(-\boldsymbol{t}^T\boldsymbol{t}/2)$, which is the multivariate normal $\boldsymbol{X}' \sim \mathcal{N}(0, \boldsymbol{I}_q)$ with $\boldsymbol{I}_q$ being the q-dimensional identity matrix.

Then the general p-dimensional distribution is defined by the distribution of a stochastic variable $\boldsymbol{X}$ of dimension p given by

$$\boldsymbol{X} = \boldsymbol{\mu} + \boldsymbol{A}\boldsymbol{X}',$$

where $\boldsymbol{\mu}$ is a p-dimensional vector of real numbers, $\boldsymbol{A}$ is a $p \times q$ matrix, and $\boldsymbol{X}' \sim S_q(\psi)$.

Hence we obtain elliptical distributions by multivariate affine transformations of spherical distributions. The characteristic function is

$$\begin{aligned}\phi_{\boldsymbol{X}}(\boldsymbol{t}) &= \mathrm{E}\exp\left(i\boldsymbol{t}^T\boldsymbol{X}\right) \\ &= E\left(\exp\left(i\boldsymbol{t}^T\left(\boldsymbol{\mu} + \boldsymbol{A}\boldsymbol{X}'\right)\right)\right) \\ &= \exp(i\boldsymbol{t}^T\boldsymbol{\mu})\mathrm{E}(\exp(i(\boldsymbol{A}^T\boldsymbol{t})^T)\boldsymbol{X}') \\ &= e^{i\boldsymbol{t}^T\boldsymbol{\mu}}\psi(\boldsymbol{t}^T\boldsymbol{\Sigma}\boldsymbol{t}), \qquad (2.4)\end{aligned}$$

where $\mathbf{\Sigma} = \mathbf{A}\mathbf{A}^T$. Denote the elliptic distribution by $\mathbf{X} \sim E_p(\boldsymbol{\mu}, \mathbf{\Sigma}, \psi)$, where $\boldsymbol{\mu}$ is the location vector, $\mathbf{\Sigma}$ is the dispersion matrix, and ψ is the characteristic generator of the distribution.

Note that the representation in (2.4) is not unique. Even though the location vector $\boldsymbol{\mu}$ is uniquely determined, the dispersion matrix $\mathbf{\Sigma}$ and the characteristic generator ψ are only determined up to a multiplicative constant c. If $\mathbf{X} \sim E_p(\boldsymbol{\mu}, \mathbf{\Sigma}, \psi(\cdot))$, then we also have that $\mathbf{X} \sim E_p(\boldsymbol{\mu}, c\mathbf{\Sigma}, \psi(\cdot/c))$. This implies that if $\mathbf{X} \sim E_p(\boldsymbol{\mu}, \mathbf{\Sigma}, \psi(\cdot))$, then $\mathbf{\Sigma}$ may not necessarily be directly identified with the covariance matrix of $\mathbf{X}$. Provided that all variances are finite, however, it is always possible to find a representation where $\mathbf{\Sigma}$ *can* be identified with the covariance matrix, but this may not be the standard representation of the distribution; see McNeil et al. (2005, p. 93).

It is possible to find a representation of $\mathbf{X}$ in terms of the density function, if it exists, by taking the inverse Fourier transform. Let g be a non-negative function on $(0, \infty)$ such that

$$\int_0^\infty x^{\frac{p}{2}-1} g(x)\,\mathrm{d}x < \infty,$$

where $p = \dim(\mathbf{X})$. Further, let $\boldsymbol{\mu} \in \mathbb{R}^p$, and let $\mathbf{\Sigma}$ be a positive definite $p \times p$ matrix. Then an elliptic density function parameterized by $g(\cdot)$, $\boldsymbol{\mu}$, and $\mathbf{\Sigma}$ is given by

$$f(\mathbf{x}; \boldsymbol{\mu}, \mathbf{\Sigma}, g) = c_p |\mathbf{\Sigma}|^{-1/2} g\left((\mathbf{x} - \boldsymbol{\mu})^T \mathbf{\Sigma}^{-1} (\mathbf{x} - \boldsymbol{\mu})\right), \tag{2.5}$$

where c_p is a normalizing factor given by

$$c_p = \frac{\Gamma(p/2)}{(2\pi)^{p/2}} \left[\int_0^\infty x^{\frac{p}{2}-1} g(x)\,\mathrm{d}x\right].$$

There is exactly the same type of scaling non-uniqueness in this representation as for the representation in terms of a characteristic function, and $\mathbf{\Sigma}$ cannot necessarily be identified with the covariance matrix of $\mathbf{X}$. One case in which $\mathbf{\Sigma}$ can be identified with the covariance matrix is the multivariate t-distribution. The density of this distribution is given by

$$f(\mathbf{x}) = \frac{\Gamma(\frac{p+\nu}{2})}{(\pi\nu)^{p/2}\Gamma(\frac{\nu}{2})|\mathbf{\Sigma}|^{1/2}} \left[1 + \frac{(\mathbf{x} - \boldsymbol{\mu})^T \mathbf{\Sigma}^{-1} (\mathbf{x} - \boldsymbol{\mu})}{\nu}\right]^{-\frac{p+\nu}{2}}, \tag{2.6}$$

where the parameter ν is known as the number of degrees of freedom. There are various generalizations of the t-distribution to include asymmetry and alternative tail behavior; see, for example, Nadarajah and Dey (2005).

We now turn to consider whether we loose some of the attractive statistical and mathematical properties of the multivariate normal distributions by considering the broader family of elliptical distributions instead. One striking fact is that uncorrelatedness is not equivalent with independence for the general elliptical family. This is clear from the functional form (2.6) of the t-distribution, because this density does not factor into separate components, each containing only one component of $\boldsymbol{x}$, even if the dispersion matrix $\boldsymbol{\Sigma}$ is diagonal. Hence zero correlation in a t-distribution does not imply independence. See also Leipnik (1961).

Furthermore, it may appear that the elliptical distribution is determined for a given characteristic generator ψ (or g) and thus may be estimated by pairwise relationships. This is not generally true, because ψ (or g) may contain extraneous parameters in addition to $\boldsymbol{\mu}$ and $\boldsymbol{\Sigma}$. An example of such a parameter is ν, the degrees of freedom in a t-distribution.

Elliptic distributions are invariant to linear transformations. It is easy to check that if $\boldsymbol{X} \sim E_p(\boldsymbol{\mu}, \boldsymbol{\Sigma}, \psi)$, then $\boldsymbol{c} + \boldsymbol{A}\boldsymbol{X} \sim E_p(\boldsymbol{c} + \boldsymbol{A}\boldsymbol{\mu}, \boldsymbol{A}\boldsymbol{\Sigma}\boldsymbol{A}^T, \psi)$. In particular, this implies that a linear combination of the components of an elliptically distributed vector $\boldsymbol{X}$ is again elliptically distributed. A particular case of this statement is that marginals of an elliptic distribution are again elliptic.

Distributional invariance of the conditional distribution in the multinormal case does, unfortunately, not quite hold for the general elliptical family. The conditional distribution of $\boldsymbol{Y}$ given $\boldsymbol{X}$ for an elliptically distributed vector $(\boldsymbol{X}, \boldsymbol{Y})$ is still elliptically distributed but in general with a different characteristic generator. This is in particular true for the multivariate t-distribution, which has a conditional distribution similar to the t-distribution but with a different characteristic generator. For this and other properties of the multivariate t-distribution, we refer to McNeil et al. (2005, p. 95).

When estimating elliptical distributions, we may at first think that the average and product moment estimator for $\boldsymbol{\mu}$ and $\boldsymbol{\Sigma}$ can be used, at least for a distribution with known characteristic generator. This is not entirely the case, however, because $\boldsymbol{\Sigma}$ is not uniquely determined, and also because the characteristic generator may contain extra parameters, the estimation of which is intertwined with the estimation of $\boldsymbol{\mu}$ and $\boldsymbol{\Sigma}$. This is well illustrated in the case of the t-distribution as laid out in more detail by Liu and Rubin (1995) and Nadarajah and Kotz (2008). The relevant part of the log-likelihood for a t-distribution with a fixed number of degrees of freedom ν is

$$L(\boldsymbol{\mu}, \boldsymbol{\Sigma}, \nu) = -\frac{n}{2}\log|\boldsymbol{\Sigma}| - \frac{\nu+p}{2}\sum_{i=1}^{n}\log(\nu+s_i)$$

with $s_i = (\boldsymbol{X}_i - \boldsymbol{\mu})^T\boldsymbol{\Sigma}^{-1}(\boldsymbol{X}_i - \boldsymbol{\mu})$, where $\boldsymbol{X}_i$ is the ith observation, and n is the number of observations. Differentiating with respect to $\boldsymbol{\mu}$ and $\boldsymbol{\Sigma}$ leads to the estimators

$$\widehat{\boldsymbol{\mu}} = \text{ave}\{w_i\boldsymbol{X}_i\}/\text{ave}\{w_i\} \qquad \text{and} \qquad \widehat{\boldsymbol{\Sigma}} = \text{ave}\left\{w_i(\boldsymbol{X}_i - \boldsymbol{\mu})(\boldsymbol{X}_i - \boldsymbol{\mu})^T\right\},$$

where $w_i = (\nu + p)/(\nu + s_i)$, and "ave" means taking the average. These equations can be adapted to an iterative procedure, as done by Liu and Rubin (1995) using the EM algorithm. They also present extensions of the EM algorithm, which may be used in the case of an unknown ν.

When the characteristic generator is known, we can use a similar procedure for quite general elliptic distributions; see, for example, McNeil et al. (2005, pp. 96–99). However, in a specific empirical problem, we may be unwilling to assume a specific ψ. We then face the problem of estimating both this function and the parameters $\boldsymbol{\mu}$ and $\boldsymbol{\Sigma}$. This is an example of a semiparametric estimation problem, which will be treated in more generality in Section 2.9. This problem was approached by Battey and Linton (2014) for a subclass of elliptic distributions satisfying a consistency property. We refer to that paper for details and additional references.

2.2.3 The exponential family

Many distributional parametric models belong to the exponential family of distributions. Let $\boldsymbol{\theta}$ be a one-dimensional or multidimensional parameter, and let $f(\boldsymbol{x}, \boldsymbol{\theta})$ be a general multivariate density function or a discrete distribution function of a random vector $\boldsymbol{X}$. Then the probability density (or mass) function $f(\boldsymbol{x}, \boldsymbol{\theta})$ is said to belong to the exponential family if it can be written as

$$f(\boldsymbol{x}) = h(\boldsymbol{x})\exp\{\boldsymbol{\eta}(\boldsymbol{\theta}) \cdot \boldsymbol{T}(\boldsymbol{x}) + A(\boldsymbol{\theta})\},$$

where h is a real-valued function; see, for example, Lehmann and Casella (2006). The vector functions $\boldsymbol{\eta}(\cdot)$ and $\boldsymbol{T}(\cdot)$ are of the same dimension and such that their inner product, denoted by "$\cdot$", is a real number. Moreover, A is a real-valued function. There are other ways in which the exponential property can be stated as well. A distribution of the exponential family is said to be *curved* if $\dim(\boldsymbol{\eta}) > \dim(\boldsymbol{\theta})$, but most distributions used in practice are not curved. Furthermore, the parameterization $\boldsymbol{\eta}(\boldsymbol{\theta})$ is said to be *canonical*, but the canonical parameterization is not unique in general, as they can be multiplied and divided by the same number.

The quantity $\boldsymbol{T}(\boldsymbol{X})$ is a sufficient statistic. We obtain its moments by differentiating the *partition function*

$$\log \int h(\boldsymbol{x}) \exp(\boldsymbol{\eta}(\boldsymbol{\theta}) \cdot \boldsymbol{T}(\boldsymbol{x}))\, \mathrm{d}\boldsymbol{x}.$$

The exponential family of distributions enjoys several important properties, for instance, the existence of a sufficient statistic, its use in Bayesian analysis via the existence of conjugate priors, and the subsequent computation of a closed-form posterior predictive distribution. The student t-distribution in fact does *not* belong to the exponential family, but it can nevertheless be obtained as a posterior predictive density.

A great number of well-known parametric families of distributions belong to the exponential family: the Gaussian, exponential, log-normal, gamma, chi-squared, beta, Dirichlet, Bernoulli, Poisson, geometric, inverse Gaussian, and von Mises distributions, to mention some. The Gaussian is by far the most used of these distributions.

It may be problematic to find a natural multivariate extension within, or even outside, the exponential family for many of the distributions mentioned above. In this regard, we can safely state that the Gaussian distribution is in a division by itself: It is straightforward to formulate a multivariate extension, which is well known and noted in Section 2.2.1.

The Gaussian enjoys a very special position among multivariate distributions. Attempts of generalizing a univariate distribution to the multivariate case in some cases lead to artificial restrictions. An example of this is the univariate Poisson distribution. Its bivariate version, as defined, for instance, by Karlis (2003), has a complicated likelihood function, and its components cannot be negatively correlated. We can easily think of models for count variables where this restriction is problematic. Fokianos et al. (2020) do in fact introduce a more general count model with Poisson marginals via a copula construction, which allows for negative dependence between variables as well. The difficulty of extending a distribution to a multivariate version, of course, leads to difficulties in finding useful expressions and parametric models for conditional distributions. However, the Gaussian is again a noteworthy important exception.

One important reason for the massive attention directed toward the exponential family within the field of mathematical statistics is the ease in which the asymptotic maximum likelihood theory can be established. Under independence or weak dependence conditions, and relatively mild additional regularity conditions, one can prove the uniqueness and asymptotic normality for parameter estimates. For many of the examples of distributions mentioned above, we can even obtain explicit expressions for the maximum likelihood estimates in the case of independent observations. For the dependent data case, this is far more difficult, and often one has to resort to numerical optimization methods to obtain parameter estimates.

2.3 Parametric regression models

2.3.1 Linear regression

Regression is a method for predicting one variable Y, say, given a set of explanatory variables $\boldsymbol{X} = (X_1, \ldots, X_p)^T$. The most used model is the linear regression model

$$Y_j = a_0 + \sum_{i=1}^{p} a_i X_{ij} + \varepsilon_j \tag{2.7}$$

for $j = 1, \ldots, n$, where n is the number of observations. Here $a_0, a_1, \ldots, a_p$ are unknown parameters, $\{Y_j\}$ and $\{X_{ij}\}$ are observations for Y and X_i, and $\{\varepsilon_j\}$ are random noise variables. The variables $X_1, \ldots, X_p$ are assumed to be deterministic in the simplest fixed design version of the regression model. Moreover, the noise variables $\{\varepsilon_j\}$ are typically assumed to be a set of independent identically distributed (iid) variables having a zero-mean Gaussian distribution such that $\varepsilon_j \sim \mathcal{N}(0, \sigma^2)$. In this case, we have fully specified a parametric linear model. The unknown parameters $a_0, a_1, \ldots, a_p$ and σ^2 can be estimated by least squares or maximum likelihood, which coincide for this particular model. If we do not want to assume the normality of the noise variables, we can estimate the density function of $\{\varepsilon_j\}$ nonparametrically, resulting in a semiparametric model, where some interesting issues of efficiency of the parameter estimates arise; see Kreiss (1987).

The explanatory variables $\boldsymbol{X}$ are typically random variables in practical applications, and they may depend on each other. They may, for instance, be normally distributed with mean vector $\boldsymbol{\mu}$ and covariance matrix $\boldsymbol{\Sigma}$. We can still estimate the regression coefficients $a_0, a_1, \ldots, a_p$ by means of least squares estimation, which, again, provides identical estimates as maximum likelihood estimation if $\varepsilon_j \sim \mathcal{N}(0, \sigma^2)$. Conditioning techniques can be used to derive the asymptotic properties of these estimates. The literature on regression models and their estimation is very rich, and there are several books devoted exclusively to regression techniques. A classic text is by Harrell (2001); a more recent is by Draper and Smith (2014), and the topic is fundamental to many texts on econometrics as well; see, for example, Greene (2003).

Assuming the normality for $\boldsymbol{X}$ is critical neither for establishing estimation theory nor for independence of the residuals, but least squares estimates of the regression coefficients $\boldsymbol{a} = (a_0, a_1, \ldots, a_p)^T$ may not be efficient under a milder set of conditions. However, we will typically be able to prove the following limiting behavior of parameter estimates $\widehat{\boldsymbol{a}}$ in fairly general settings:

$$\sqrt{n}(\widehat{\boldsymbol{a}} - \boldsymbol{a}) \xrightarrow{d} \mathcal{N}\left(\mathbf{0}, \sigma^2 \boldsymbol{\Sigma}_{\boldsymbol{X}}^{-1}\right),$$

where $\boldsymbol{\Sigma}_{\boldsymbol{X}}$ is the covariance matrix of $\boldsymbol{X}$, assumed to be invertible. For more detail, we refer to Greene (2003).

Nowadays, we readily encounter data sets with a large or even a very large number of explanatory variables. When the number of explanatory variables increases, the risk of multicolinearity increases as well, which happens if sets of variables are strongly correlated, positively or negatively, which again leads to a covariance matrix $\boldsymbol{\Sigma}_{\boldsymbol{X}}$ that is close to being singular. There are several techniques for circumventing this problem, two of which are the ridge regression and the lasso (least absolute shrinkage and selection operator). The lasso was introduced by Tibshirani (1996), and an adaptive version proposed by Zou (2006) has better consistency properties. Consider again the linear model (2.7). Then the ordinary least squares estimator of $\boldsymbol{a} = (a_0, a_1, \ldots, a_p)^T$ is defined by

$$\widehat{\boldsymbol{a}} = \arg\min_{\boldsymbol{a}} \sum_{j=1}^{n} \left(Y_i - a_0 - \sum_{i=1}^{p} a_i X_{ij} \right)^2 . \tag{2.8}$$

For large p, this estimator may suffer from large variance due to multicolinearity as explained above. Ridge and lasso regression works by imposing size constraints on the parameter estimates. In ridge regression the size constraint takes the form $\sum_{i=1}^{p} a_i^2 \leq t$, where t is a regularization parameter that must be chosen by the user, and where this constraint can be formulated as a penalty term in the minimization problem (2.8). The lasso imposes a constraint of the form $\sum_{i=1}^{p} |a_i| \leq t$. There is a very large literature on properties and extensions of these important constrained estimation methods, as well as on their applications to sparse data and time series models. The essentials of the ridge and lasso are explored in detail by Hastie et al. (2009).

2.3.2 Nonlinear regression and some further modeling aspects

So far, we have only considered linear models. However, the essence of this book is treating nonlinear models. The easiest way of making the linear regression (2.7) nonlinear is introducing a *link* function where Y is modified by a nonlinear function $g(Y)$, which is then linked to the linear explanatory variables as before. This approach is known as the *generalized* linear model (GLM). Another simple modification is allowing powers of the explanatory variables to appear in the model, resulting in polynomial regression. The asymptotic theory for these modes is identical to that for the basic linear regression (2.7), because the models are still linear in the parameters. A disadvantage of all these models (including the linear one) is that they cannot be true (or even approximately true) for large values of the explanatory variables. The response variable Y will not continue to grow without limits as the components of $\boldsymbol{X}$ increase. It may therefore be necessary to introduce a nonlinearity such that the response stays linear for moderate values of $\boldsymbol{X}$ but then reaches a horizontal asymptote as the components of $\boldsymbol{X}$ become large (positive or negative). There are many functions that achieve this, such as sigmoidal functions or hyperbolic tangent functions, which are extensively used in neural network modeling; see Ripley (2007) and Cybenko (1989).

A general nonlinear scalar regression model can be expressed as

$$Y_j = f(\boldsymbol{X}_j, \boldsymbol{\theta}) + \varepsilon_j, \tag{2.9}$$

where f is a known function, and $\boldsymbol{\theta}$ is an unknown parameter to be estimated. Least squares, conditional least squares, maximum likelihood, and the method of moments have been applied to this problem. It is usually not possible to obtain explicit expressions for such estimators, but numerical solutions can often be found. There are a number of papers on asymptotic properties under a variety of assumptions. Many of them are based on the technique of conditional least squares as described in the time series case by Klimko and Nelson (1978). For more recent contributions with extensions to the nonlinear nonstationary case, see Park and Phillips (1999), Park and Phillips (2001), and more recently Li et al. (2016).

One important stage of the analysis when using a linear or nonlinear regression model is model validation. For linear models, this is most often done by checking the estimated residuals $\{\widehat{\varepsilon}_j\}$ for independence, homogeneity, and normality. For nonlinear models, the same checks can be applied, but there are also general tests available for checking the functional form of $f(\cdot,\boldsymbol{\theta})$. We can do this by comparing the estimated regression function $f(\cdot,\widehat{\boldsymbol{\theta}})$ against a nonparametric estimate $\widehat{f}$ of f, where no functional form of f is assumed. We refer to Section 2.6 for the construction of nonparametric estimates of f and to Härdle and Mammen (1993) for details on constructing a test functional. The latter reference has in fact spawned numerous other papers within the field of goodness-of-fit testing.

Much of the motivation for estimating regression models revolves around constructing predictions of the response variable Y. For a given set of values of $\boldsymbol{X}$, we are interested in finding an optimal predictor $\widehat{Y}$ of Y. Given a set of estimated regression coefficients $\widehat{\boldsymbol{a}}$, a natural predictor is given by $\widehat{Y} = \widehat{a_0} + \sum_{i=1}^{p} \widehat{a_i} X_i$ or $\widehat{Y} = f(X,\widehat{\boldsymbol{\theta}})$. The estimate of $\boldsymbol{a}$ in the linear model is essentially based on the correlation between the components in $\boldsymbol{X}$ and on the correlation between Y and $\boldsymbol{X}$, and we can estimate the correlations independently from whatever dependence structure the data may or may not have, resulting in a *linear* predictor. A linear predictor will naturally not perform very well if the nonlinear model $f(\cdot,\boldsymbol{\theta})$ is approximately true and if the nonlinearity is strong.

It is well known that the optimal predictor based on least squares is given by $Y^{\text{pred}} = E(Y|\boldsymbol{X})$, which is the conditional mean of Y given $\boldsymbol{X}$. In the nonlinear case and if ε is uncorrelated with $\boldsymbol{X}$, it is trivial to see that $E(Y|\boldsymbol{X}) = f(\boldsymbol{X},\boldsymbol{\theta})$, and an optimal implementable predictor is obtained by replacing $\boldsymbol{\theta}$ by an estimate $\widehat{\boldsymbol{\theta}}$. If $(Y,\boldsymbol{X})$ is Gaussian, then the optimal predictor $E(Y|\boldsymbol{X})$ coincides with the optimal linear predictor. We will consider nonparametric regression estimation in Section 2.6, and we will develop some new nonparametric estimates of the conditional mean based on local Gaussian approximations in Chapter 12.

2.4 Time series

Consider a time series $\{X_t, t \geq 0\}$. Corresponding to the parametric regression models that we discussed above, the simplest time series model is the autoregressive (AR) model, where X_t is modeled linearly on p previous lags, so that

$$X_t = a_0 + \sum_{i=1}^{p} a_i X_{t-i} + \varepsilon_t, \qquad t \geq 0,$$

where, as in the regression models, $\{\varepsilon_t\}$ is often assumed to be a sequence of iid random variables, and the model is causal if ε_t is uncorrelated with $\{X_s, s < t\}$. A well-known condition for causality is that the characteristic polynomial $A(z) = 1 - \sum_{i=1}^{p} a_i z^i$ has its roots outside the unit circle in the complex z-plane.

A time series $\{X_t, t \geq 0\}$ is strictly stationary (abbreviated to only "stationary" in the following) if for all $m \geq 1$, $0 \leq t_1 \leq \cdots \leq t_m$, and $h \geq 0$, the joint distribution of $(X_{t_1+h}, \ldots, X_{t_m+h})$ is the same as that of $(X_{t_1}, \ldots, X_{t_m})$. The above condition on the characteristic polynomial is also a stationarity condition. If it holds and $\{\epsilon_t\}$ consists of iid variables, then there exists a distribution on some initial variables $(X_{-1}, \ldots, X_{-p})$ such that the process is stationary when it has been started with this initial condition. If the second moment exists, then we can formulate a weaker definition of stationarity, usually referred to as weak stationarity, only requiring that $\mathrm{E}(X_t) = \mu =$ constant and that $\mathrm{Cov}(X_t, X_s)$ is only a function of the difference between t and s.

The ARMA model extends the AR model, and is given by

$$X_t - a_0 - \sum_{i=1}^{p} a_i X_{t-i} = \varepsilon_t + \sum_{i=1}^{q} b_i \varepsilon_{t-i}.$$

ARMA models are treated in any standard textbook on time series, such as Brockwell and Davis (2013) and Shumway and Stoffer (2006), as is the ARIMA model, which is an extension that allows us to model so-called integrated non-stationary time series in the ARMA framework. As when working with regression problems, we are primarily interested in estimating the coefficients $(a_0, a_1, \ldots, a_p; b_1, \ldots, b_q)$ and the residual variance σ_ε^2.

In classic time series analysis (see, e.g., Box and Jenkins (1970) and Granger and Newbold (1977)), the concept of autocorrelation (the correlation between X_t and X_{t+h}) plays a major role, both in model identification and when constructing predictions, for example, in the ARIMA model. The traditional model fitting task involves looking for a model having uncorrelated estimated residuals. However, in finance, it was discovered that such uncorrelated residuals potentially contain essential information about the volatility structure. This was particularly highlighted by Engle (1982), for which he was awarded the Nobel Memorial Prize in Economics, and later by Engle and Bollerslev (1986).

The GARCH model class (generalized autoregressive conditional heteroskedastic) was introduced in these papers and is by now well known and much used. A time series $\{X_t\}$ is said to be a GARCH process if

$$X_t = \sqrt{h_t}\varepsilon_t; \quad h_t = a_0 + \sum_{i=1}^{p} a_i h_{t-i} + \sum_{i=1}^{q} b_i X_{t-i}^2, \qquad t \geq 0,$$

where $\{\varepsilon_t\}$ is a set of iid zero-mean random variables independent of $\{h_t\}$, and the variable h_t is a measure of the instantaneous volatility at time t. It is easy to check that the process has zero autocorrelation and thus generally would pass unnoticed in a classic ARMA time series goodness-of-fit test. Francq and Zakoian (2011) have written a textbook on GARCH time series that covers all the important aspects of the theory and to which we refer for regularity and stationarity conditions. Fokianos et al. (2009) study a somewhat similar construction for univariate count time series and provide an extension to the bivariate case in Fokianos et al. (2020). An earlier paper in this regard is by Rydberg and Shephard (2000).

The estimation theory for ARMA time series and for GARCH models is well developed. Estimates are usually based on likelihood or quasi-likelihood procedures. If $\{\varepsilon_t\}$ is a Gaussian process, then the ARMA process $\{X_t\}$ is a Gaussian process as well. The Gaussian specification is, however, often untenable in both ARMA and GARCH models due to thickness of tail distributions, a problem that may be alleviated by replacing the Gaussian assumption with a distribution with thicker tails, such as the multivariate t, or by using a local Gaussian approach as advocated in this book.

There has been a surge of interest in nonlinear time series in the last couple of decades, to which the appearance of several new books will testify: Tong (1990), Fan and Yao (2003), De Gooijer (2017), Douc et al. (2014), and Teräsvirta et al. (2010), as well as a large number of papers, particularly in econometric journals. The first-order nonlinear analogue to the regression model (2.9) can be stated as

$$X_t = f(X_{t-1}, \boldsymbol{\theta}) + \varepsilon_t, \ t \geq 0, \tag{2.10}$$

where, again, the function f is known, but the parameter $\boldsymbol{\theta}$ is unknown and must be estimated from data. There is, however, at least one added difficulty of formulating the nonlinear time series model (2.10) compared to the nonlinear regression model (2.9). To avoid that realizations from the model grow without bounds, we must introduce conditions on f to guarantee stationarity, which is essential in many estimation problems. For example, we cannot allow the function f to grow (uniformly) faster than a linear stationary first-order AR model at infinity. Such conditions have been systematically examined in a Markov chain context in the book by Meyn and Tweedie (2009). See also Teräsvirta et al. (2010, Chapter 3) and Fokianos et al. (2020) for the bivariate count time series case. Once stationarity is obtained, the estimation can proceed, for instance, by nonlinear least square or conditional least squares.

Financial time series are often nonstationary, and ARIMA type models have been popular in analyzing them. There is a vast literature on this, including work on cointegration for multivariate time series by Hamilton (1994, Chapter 19). Clive Granger received the Nobel Memorial Prize in Economics for his work on cointegration, but linearity is still assumed in this context. The next step in this line of research is to allow nonlinearity and nonstationarity. Park and Phillips (1999) study parametric models such as (2.10), and Park and Phillips (2001) consider models with regression structure. This work is followed up, among others, by Li et al. (2016). Tjøstheim (2020) proposes a way to extend to the general nonstationary case with autocorrelation structure and indicates the possible use of the local Gaussian method. Clearly, if $\mathcal{F}_t$ is the σ-algebra formed by $\{X_s, s \leq t\}$, then $E(X_{t+1}|\mathcal{F}t) = f(X_t, \boldsymbol{\theta})$, so that a one-step predictor can be computed once $\boldsymbol{\theta}$ is estimated. In Section 2.6, we will look at the case where f is unknown, and we will briefly comment on the nonparametric estimation in both stationary and non-stationary cases.

2.5 Nonparametric density estimation

We stressed the salient aspects of parametric statistical models in the introduction of this chapter, but we also stated that a parametric model is always wrong. This is not so serious in the sense that all parametric models are approximations to a "true" model and that an approximation can be adequate even if it is wrong, but situations exist in which choosing the wrong parametric model leads to seriously wrong results, which in turn may have grave consequences.

We avoid this, at least to a certain degree, by choosing a nonparametric approach to modeling. However, there is a price to be paid. Nonparametric estimates converge more slowly than parametric estimates, and even if we have a moderate number of variables, the curse of dimensionality is a very serious obstacle. Various strategies of trying to avoid the curse exist, but inevitably this leads to certain simplifications and restrictions in the modeling process.

We treat density estimation and regression estimation separately in the following and then explore the curse of dimensionality in more detail in a separate section. We will highlight the potential and applicability of constructing local Gaussian estimates as we go along and refer to forthcoming chapters for details. A brief introduction to nonparametric density estimation given below is to a large degree a drastic concentration of material that can be found in much more detail in dedicated books, such as Silverman (1986), Härdle (1990), and Wand and Jones (1995).

2.5.1 Nonparametric kernel density estimation

We start with the scalar case. Assume that we have observations $\{X_1, \ldots, X_n\}$ from a scalar stochastic variable X with density function $f(x)$. If f is smooth in a neighborhood $[x - b, x + b]$ of a point x ($b > 0$), then as b becomes smaller and smaller, we obtain the following approximation from the mean value theorem:

$$\int_{x-b}^{x+b} f(u)\,\mathrm{d}u = P(X \in [x - b, x + b]) \approx 2bf(x).$$

The probability $P(X \in [x - b, x + b])$ can be estimated by the relative frequency $n_{x,b}/n$, where $n_{x,b}$ is the number of observations in $[x - b, x + b]$. If we define the *kernel* function K by $K(u) = (1/2)I(|u| \leq 1)$, where I is the indicator function, then we can express this estimator of $f(x)$ as

$$\widehat{f}(x) = n^{-1} \sum_{i=1}^{n} K_b(X_i - x), \tag{2.11}$$

with $K_b(\cdot) = b^{-1}K(\cdot/b)$, and this is quite simply the histogram estimator of $f(x)$ with bin center x and binwidth $2b$. The function K has the advantage of being simple, but it is discontinuous, and we notice further that this particular estimator gives equal weight to all observations in $[x - b, x + b]$. It might be better to assign more weight to the observations closer to x than to those farther away. We achieve this by replacing the indicator function by a smooth function having its maximum at zero. Estimator (2.11) is in general referred to as the *kernel density estimator*. The idea of estimating probability density functions by nonparametric smoothing dates back at least to the fundamental papers by Rosenblatt (1956) and Parzen (1962).

The Gaussian density function

$$K(u) = \frac{1}{\sqrt{2\pi}} \exp(-u^2/2)$$

is widely used as the kernel function, and another example is the so-called quartic kernel

$$K(u) = (15/16)(1 - u^2)^2 I(|u| \leq 1),$$

which is continuous on a compact support. Here 15/16 is a normalization factor making K a probability density function. In fact, we always require $\int K(u)\,du = 1$ and usually, but not always, that $K(u) \geq 0$. As $n \to \infty$, more observations fall into the neighborhood $[x - b, x + b]$, and we can allow the bandwidth b to approach zero in such a way that $nb \to \infty$. By heuristic arguments (that can easily be made rigorous; see Silverman (1986, Chapter 3)), assuming iid or stationary observations $\{X_i\}$, we compute the asymptotic bias and variance of the smoothed estimator $\widehat{f}(x)$. A standard Taylor expansion provides the following expression as $n \to \infty$:

$$\begin{aligned}
\mathrm{E}\left(\widehat{f}(x)\right) &= (nb)^{-1}\sum_{i=1}^{n}\mathrm{E}\left\{K\left(\frac{X_i - x}{b}\right)\right\} \\
&= \frac{1}{b}\int K\{(u - x)/b\}f(u)\,du \\
&= f(x)\int K(u)\,du + f'(x)b\int uK(u)\,du \\
&\quad + \frac{1}{2}f''(x)b^2\int u^2K(u)\,du + o(b^2). \qquad (2.12)
\end{aligned}$$

If K is an even function, then $\int uK(u)\,du = 0$, and using $\int K(u)du = 1$, it follows that

$$\mathrm{E}\{\widehat{f}(x)\} = f(x) + (1/2)f''(x)b^2\int u^2K(u)\,du + o(b^2),$$

so that the bias is of order b^2. Using similar arguments, we can show that under weak regularity conditions, including a condition of dependence in the time series case,

$$\mathrm{Var}\{\widehat{f}(x)\} \sim \frac{f(x)}{nb}\int K^2(u)\,du;$$

see, for example, Silverman (1986, Chapter 3) for the iid case and Fan and Yao (2003, Chapter 5) for the time series case. These references establish the asymptotic normality for $\widehat{f}(x)$ as well. It is important to note that the kernel density estimator converges with rate $(nb)^{-1/2}$, which is slower than the standard parametric convergence rate of $n^{-1/2}$.

There are many other ways to approach density estimation. In this book, we pursue local parametric density estimation as briefly outlined in Section 2.10 of this chapter. We will in particular use a local Gaussian density approach, and Chapter 9 is devoted to this approach.

By using higher-order kernels having the property $\int u^j K(u)\,\mathrm{d}u = 0$ for $1 \le j \le m$ for an integer m, the kernel density estimator achieves bias of order h^{m+1}, and we can, in principle, obtain an expected squared error approaching the parametric rate of n^{-1} by increasing m. This requires that a kernel K can take negative value, however. Furthermore, we cannot get anywhere close to the theoretical asymptotic error in practice unless n is extremely large. Also, higher-order kernel density estimates have a tendency to be hampered with negativity, and this problem tends to become more severe as the order m increases.

2.5.2 Bandwidth selection

Much research has gone into the problem of choosing the bandwidth parameter b in all areas of nonparametric estimation. It is generally recognized as the most important design problem of nonparametric statistics, much more important than the choice of a kernel function K. Cross-validation is probably the strategy that is most used in practice (see, e.g., Silverman (1986), Härdle (1990), and Fan and Gijbels (1996)), but it is also possible to derive simple bandwidth selection rules based on asymptotic derivations, in particular, for density estimation. Observe first, by ignoring higher-order bias correction, that in order for the variance and the squared bias to be of the same order of magnitude, we must require that $b = cn^{-1/5}$ as $n \to \infty$. The proportionality factor c can be chosen by minimizing the integrated mean square error

$$\mathrm{IMSE} = \int \mathrm{E}\{\widehat{f}(u) - f(u)\}^2\,\mathrm{d}u.$$

If f is a Gaussian density function, then the bandwidth

$$b = \left[\frac{8\sqrt{\pi}\int K^2(u)du}{3(\int u^2 K(u)du)^2}\right]^{1/5} \widehat{\sigma} n^{-1/5} \tag{2.13}$$

minimizes the IMSE. Here $\widehat{\sigma}$ is the estimated standard deviation of $\{X_1, \ldots, X_n\}$ given by

$$\widehat{\sigma} = \sqrt{\frac{1}{n-1}\sum_i (X_i - \bar{X})^2}.$$

Silverman (1986) computes the leading constant of (2.13) in the particular case where K is the standard Gaussian density, resulting in the simple rule-of-thumb bandwidth $b = 1.06\widehat{\sigma}n^{-1/5}$. For more detail on bandwidth selection, see Fan and Gijbels (1996), Härdle (1990), and Silverman (1986). Optimal choice of bandwidth in a time series case is discussed by Hart and Vieu (1990). Their results are recently generalized and extended to a spatial framework by Jiang et al. (2020). Similar problems to the bandwidth choice arise in discrete models and in models where the data are mixtures of discrete and continuous values. Such problems are treated extensively by Hayfield and Racine (2008).

It may be argued that one should not use the same bandwidth for every x-value in the kernel estimator (2.11). For regions with few data points, it may be sensible to use more smoothing (larger b) than for regions with many data points. This principle is implemented in the nearest-neighbor estimate. The m-nearest neighborhood of the point x is defined as the collection of data points X_i that constitutes the m nearest neighbors of x. Then we can define the kernel with varying bandwidth starting from the function $K(u) = (1/2)I(|u| \leq 1)$ by

$$K_b(u) = \frac{1}{R(m)}\frac{1}{2}I\left(\frac{|u|}{R(m)}\right)$$

where $b = R(m)$ is the distance between x and its farthest m-nearest neighbor. This results in the following variable-bandwidth (adaptive) density estimate:

$$\widehat{f}(x) = \frac{1}{nR(m)}\frac{1}{2}\sum_{i=1}^{n} I\left(\frac{|X_i - x|}{R(m)}\right).$$

It corresponds to a histogram with variable bin width, and its asymptotic properties can be found as $n \to \infty$, which implies that $R(m) \to 0$. A basic reference is again Silverman (1986, Chapter 5), where we can also find other density estimates with adaptive bandwidth. A much extended version of the problem of adaptive estimation for densities for spatial variables can be found in Jiang et al. (2020).

2.5.3 Multivariate and conditional density estimation

The histogram was used as a motivation for the univariate ($p = 1$) kernel density estimator (2.11). Extending this idea to the multivariate case, we face two problems: First, a histogram is not easy to visualize if $p > 2$. Second, as p increases, there will be many empty cells in the p-dimensional histogram for a fixed sample size n. This happens because the number of bins N^p quickly becomes a very big number compared to N, which is the number of bins in the one-dimensional case. The corresponding smoothed kernel estimator will clearly also suffer from this problem, and this is one expression of the well-known curse of dimensionality. Hayfield and Racine (2008) lessen the curse of dimensionality by clever bandwidth selection algorithms that work for discrete and mixed data types as well as in the continuous case.

It is in fact impossible to avoid the curse of dimensionality unless we want to make some additional restricting assumptions. One such set of assumptions is made in Chapter 9, where a simplified local Gaussian framework is used based on Otneim and Tjøstheim (2017). Other ways of avoiding the curse of dimensionality in density estimation are discussed by Nagler and Czado (2016) using a pair copula construction and by Friedman et al. (1984) using projection pursuit. In all these approaches the problem is to find a point of balance to strike a compromise between accuracy and feasibility.

It is more difficult to estimate conditional densities in both parametric and nonparametric cases, not in the least because simple expressions of conditional densities are not available for most parametric families of distributions. Even for the general elliptic family, the question of forming a conditional distribution is not trivial, since in general different generators have to be involved. The exception is, predictably, the multivariate normal, for which the conditional distribution has straightforward expressions, as seen in (2.2) and (2.3), and even stays within the same family of multivariate normal distributions.

The obvious way to proceed in the nonparametric case is to use the definition of the conditional density as $f_{Y|X}(y|x) = f_{X,Y}(x,y)/f_X(x)$, where X and Y may be vector variables in general. Here $f_{X,Y}(x,y)$ and $f_X(x)$ may be estimated by kernel estimation, but for moderate and large dimensions of X and/or Y, the curse of dimensionality comes into play. The density $f_X(x)$ is in addition close to zero in its tails, so the kernel estimate will be expected to be close to zero as well. This leads to instability in the ratio used to define the kernel estimate.

The above facts make it demanding to estimate conditional densities, and much theory and applications have been limited to the Gaussian case. This is also the case for derived quantities like the partial correlation function. Such conditional concepts are important, for instance, in causal networks. We approach these problems using the local Gaussian approximation in Chapters 10 and 11. Again, simplifications are needed as the dimensions of $\boldsymbol{X}$ and/or $\boldsymbol{Y}$ increase.

2.6 Nonparametric regression estimation

In a similar fashion as for the parametric case, we assume that our dependent variable Y is given by

$$Y_j = g(X_j) + \varepsilon_j \tag{2.14}$$

for $j = 1, \ldots, n$. At the outset, we assume that the variables $\{X_j\}$ and $\{\varepsilon_j\}$ are independent and that they are iid. For now, we will also assume that all stochastic variables involved are scalars. Many generalizations exist, and in Section 2.6.2, we will very briefly mention the time series case. If the dimension of X is moderate or large, then we must once again suffer the consequences of the curse of dimensionality, which that can be evaded in various ways, as will become clear in Section 2.7.

2.6.1 Kernel regression estimation

Given observations $\{X_j, Y_j, 1 \le j \le n\}$, we are faced with the problem of estimating the unknown function g, a function that we immediately identify as $g(x) = \mathrm{E}(Y|X = x)$. It should be noted that the arguments presented below for estimating $\mathrm{E}(Y|X = x)$ do not really require a regression relationship like (2.14). They are equally valid if the pairs $\{X_i, Y_i\}$ are iid or indeed if $\{X_t, Y_t\}$ are pairs of observations from a jointly stationary time series, although some additional regularity conditions are required to make the asymptotic arguments go through in that case.

Given that $\mathrm{E}(Y|X = x) = \int y f(y|x)\,\mathrm{d}y$, where $f(y|x)$ is the conditional density of Y given $X = x$, a natural estimator might be

$$\widehat{g}(x) = \int y \widehat{f}(y|x)\,\mathrm{d}y,$$

where the integral can be computed numerically, by means of the law of large numbers, or, as we will argue in Chapter 12, using local Gaussian approximations.

The standard nonparametric method for obtaining this estimate is, however, the Nadaraya–Watson estimator. By using that $f(y|x) = f_{X,Y}(x, y)/f_X(x)$, write

$$g(x) = \mathrm{E}(Y|X = x) = \int y \frac{f_{Y,X}(y, x)}{f_X(x)}\,\mathrm{d}y$$

$$= \frac{1}{f_X(x)} \int y f_{Y,X}(y, x)\, dy \stackrel{\text{def}}{=} \frac{M(x)}{f_X(x)}, \tag{2.15}$$

where all densities are assumed to exist. Introducing kernel estimators, in view of the developments of the previous sections, it is natural to estimate $M(x)$ in (2.15) by

$$\widehat{M}(x) = \frac{1}{n} \sum_{j=1}^{n} \int y K_b(X_j - x) K_b(Y_j - y)\, dy,$$

But assuming that $\int K(u)\, du = 1$ and $\int uK(u)\, du = 0$ it follows that

$$\int y K_b(Y_j - y)\, dy = \int (Y_j + ub) K(u)\, du = Y_j$$

and furthermore that

$$\widehat{g}(x) = \frac{\widehat{M}(x)}{\widehat{f}(x)} = \frac{\sum_{j=1}^{n} Y_j K_b(X_j - x)}{\sum_{j=1}^{n} K_b(X_j - x)}, \tag{2.16}$$

which is the Nadaraya–Watson kernel estimator. The expression for $\widehat{g}(x)$ is a ratio, and stability problems may be expected close to the tails of $f_X(x)$. Moreover, contrary to density estimation, it is not entirely unproblematic to establish the existence of $\mathrm{E}\left(\widehat{g}(x)\right)$ and $\mathrm{Var}\left(\widehat{g}(x)\right)$. Formally, computations can be carried out in the same way as for the density estimation case, resulting in

$$\begin{aligned} \mathrm{E}\left(\widehat{g}(x)\right) &= g(x) + \frac{b^2}{2} \left\{ g''(x) + 2g'(x) \frac{f'(x)}{f(x)} \right\} \int u^2 K(u)\, du + o(b^2) \\ &\stackrel{\text{def}}{=} g(x) + B(x) + o(b^2). \end{aligned} \tag{2.17}$$

Under weak regularity conditions, we can prove the asymptotic normality with asymptotic variance

$$\mathrm{Var}\{\widehat{g}(x)\} \sim \frac{1}{nb} \frac{V(x)}{f(x)} \int K^2(u) du, \tag{2.18}$$

where $V(x) = \mathrm{Var}(Y|X = x)$. See Robinson (1983) and Masry and Tjøstheim (1995) for the time series case.

It is often necessary to estimate the conditional variance $V(x) = \mathrm{Var}(Y|X = x)$, for example, in the evaluation of asymptotic confidence intervals. Generally, using kernel estimation for a given function G, the conditional expectation $\mathrm{E}\{G(Y)|X = x\}$ is estimated by

$$\sum_{j=1}^{n} G(Y_j)K_b(X_j - x)/\sum_{j=1}^{n} K_b(X_j - x), \tag{2.19}$$

and properties are evaluated analogously to those for the estimator $\widehat{g}(x)$. We refer again to Robinson (1983) and Masry and Tjøstheim (1995) for more detail and proofs, valid even in the time series case. Karlsen and Tjøstheim (2001) and Karlsen et al. (2007) have generalized these results to null recurrent Markov chains.

The bias $B(x)$ depicted in (2.17) can be reduced by using higher-order kernels as explained for the density estimation case, but such amendments would require very large sample sizes to be effective also in the regression problem.

2.6.2 Local polynomial estimation

Local polynomials are very flexible and widely used as alternatives to kernel estimation, not in the least because they have superior bias properties compared to ordinary kernel estimation. Note that the Nadaraya–Watson estimator (2.16) can be regarded as the solution of the minimization problem

$$\widehat{g}(x) = \arg\min_{\gamma} \sum_{j=1}^{n} (Y_i - \gamma)^2 K_b(X_i - x).$$

This means that the curve $g(x) = \mathrm{E}\{Y|X = x\}$ is approximated by the constant γ locally at x. It is also possible to approximate the curve by other functions such as polynomials, and this motivates the class of locally polynomial estimators. To consider this, let $\widehat{\gamma_0}, \ldots, \widehat{\gamma_k}$ minimize

$$\widehat{p_k}(x) = \sum_{j=1}^{n} K_b(X_j - x)\left\{Y_j - \gamma_0 - \gamma_1(X_j - x) - \cdots - \gamma_k \frac{(X_j - x)^k}{k!}\right\}. \tag{2.20}$$

It is not difficult to show that $\widehat{\gamma_0}$ is a natural estimator of $g(x)$, whereas $\widehat{\gamma_i}$ estimates the ith derivative $g^{(i)}(x)$ of g at x. The order of the bias for $\widehat{g}^{(i)}$ is b^2, the same as for $\widehat{g}(x)$, but the order of the variance is increased to $\left(nb^{2i+1}\right)^{-1}$; see Fan and Gijbels (1995). Local polynomial estimators constitute very flexible tools, and they contain the Nadaraya–Watson (locally constant) estimator as a particular case.

The asymptotic variance of the general local polynomial estimator is identical to that of the Nadaraya–Watson estimator, but its asymptotic bias is different. In the local linear case ($k = 1$ in (2.20)) the asymptotic bias is given by

$$\frac{b^2}{2} g''(x) \int u^2 K(u)\,\mathrm{d}u + o(b^2).$$

This implies that if $g(x)$ itself is linear, then the bias of $\widehat{g}(x)$ has order $o(b^2)$, in contrast to the Nadaraya–Watson bias formula (2.17).

Another distinct difference between local polynomials and kernel estimators are their global properties. The kernel estimator converges to the mean $\overline{X}$ as the bandwidth b tends to infinity, whereas the local polynomial estimator converges to a polynomial of the corresponding degree.

The local approximation provided by $\widehat{\gamma}_0$ can alternatively be obtained by other parametric functions than polynomials. See, for instance, Tibshirani and Hastie (1987) and Kauermann and Opsomer (2003) for a local likelihood procedure. For an example where local polynomials are replaced by local exponentials, we refer the reader to Linton et al. (2001).

2.6.3 Choice of bandwidth in regression

When choosing the bandwidth in nonparametric regression problems, we are faced with much of the same problems, and we can use many of the same results, as when smoothing a density estimate. The bandwidth can be selected either locally (adaptively) by choosing $b = b(x)$ to minimize the mean square error MSE of $\widehat{g}(x)$ or globally by minimizing the integrated mean square error

$$\mathrm{IMSE} = \int \mathrm{MSE}\{\widehat{g}(x)\} w(x) f(x)\,\mathrm{d}x$$

for some weighting function $w(x)$. Here

$$\mathrm{MSE}\{\widehat{g}(x)\} \stackrel{\mathrm{def}}{=} \mathrm{E}\{\widehat{g}(x) - g(x)\}^2.$$

Again, the optimal order for b is given by $b = O(n^{-1/5})$. Letting $b = cn^{-1/5}$, the optimal local value $c = c(x)$ at x in the kernel estimation case can be found by minimizing the approximate mean square error

$$\mathrm{MSE}\{\widehat{g}(x)\} \sim (nb)^{-1}\sigma^2(x) + b^4 B^2(x),$$

where $B(x)$ and $\sigma^2(x)$ are given in (2.17) and (2.18). This leads to the optimal bandwidth

$$b(x) = \left\{ \frac{\sigma^2(x)}{4B(x)} \right\}^{1/5} n^{-1/5}. \tag{2.21}$$

We see that the bandwidth may vary considerably with x. As $x \to \pm\infty$, in general, $b(x) \to \infty$, which has as a natural consequence that more smoothing is used as the data become sparser. For the IMSE criterion, the same line of reasoning yields the following optimal b:

$$b = \left\{ \frac{\int \sigma^2(x) w(x) f(x)\,\mathrm{d}x}{\int B^2(x) w(x) f(x)\,\mathrm{d}x} \right\}^{1/5} n^{-1/5}. \tag{2.22}$$

In expressions (2.21) and (2.22) the quantities $\sigma^2(x)$, $B(x)$, and $f(x)$ are unknown, and estimates must be computed. If we use plug-in estimates, we must first choose an initial bandwidth to obtain the subsequent optimal plug-in bandwidth. Choosing this initial bandwidth, we have to estimate $\sigma(x)$, $B(x)$, and $f(x)$, which in turn require estimates of $g''(x)$, $g'(x)$, $V(x)$, $f(x)$, and $f'(x)$. Obtaining such estimates are cumbersome tasks, and as in the case of density estimation, we can, as an alternative to the plug-in approach, turn to cross-validation. We refer to Section 2.5 for relevant references.

Choosing adaptive bandwidths depending on x leads naturally to nearest-neighbor estimation. The principles are the same as for kernel density estimates, and we refer to Section 2.5 and to the general references Silverman (1986) and Fan and Gijbels (1996) for more detail. Note that the nearest-neighbor estimator is not limited to the Nadaraya–Watson kernel estimator. A local polynomial nearest-neighbor estimator can be constructed. This is the so-called LOWESS estimator introduced by Cleveland (1979). It has been used quite heavily in practice.

2.7 Fighting the curse of dimensionality

The curse of dimensionality comes into play quite soon in multivariate problems when using kernel estimation. There is still a way out. However, restrictions must be made, so there is a price to be paid. In this section, we explore various alternatives for avoiding the curse of dimensionality.

2.7.1 Additive models

The most common alternative is the class of additive regression models. In this case, $g(x) = \mathrm{E}(Y|X = x)$ is approximated by an additive function. If $\mathbf{X} = (X_1, \ldots X_p)^T$ is a p-dimensional explanatory variable, assuming an additive model means that

$$g(\mathbf{x}) = \mathrm{E}(Y|\mathbf{X} = \mathbf{x}) = g_0 + \sum_{i=1}^{p} g_i(x_i), \tag{2.23}$$

where g_0 is a constant, and g_i, $i = 1, \ldots, p$, are real-valued functions of one argument. For ease of presentation, we will assume that the variables $(X_{1j}, \ldots, X_{pj})$, $j = 1, \ldots, n$, are iid, but the time series case has been treated with appropriate modifications by Mammen et al. (1999), Tjøstheim and Auestad (1994), and Chen and Tsay (1993), and even in the spatial case as in Lu et al. (2007a).

One option is taking representation (2.23) as a theoretical point of departure. However, more often, a noise-driven additive model is assumed, so that

$$Y_j = g_0 + \sum_{i=1}^{p} g(X_{ij}) + \varepsilon_j, \;\; j = 1, \ldots, n, \tag{2.24}$$

where the residual variables $\{\varepsilon_j, j = 1, \ldots\}$ are assumed to be iid.

Additive models have a long history in statistics and econometrics. They were discussed already by Leontief (1947), who analyzed so-called separable functions. Today, additive models are widely used in both theoretical economics and empirical data analysis. Additive models constitute a reasonable compromise between the somewhat conflicting requirements of flexibility, dimensionality, and interpretability.

The dominant method of estimating additive models such as (2.24) is backfitting, a method that is included in many software libraries. The theory is relatively complicated, partly because it depends on recursions. A more straightforward estimation method is marginal integration; see Newey (1994), Tjøstheim and Auestad (1994), and Linton and Nielsen (1995). This method delivers consistent estimates with the same convergence rate as for the backfitting method, but they are in general not efficient.

We briefly explain the backfitting procedure. Taking the conditional expectations with respect to X_{ij} in (2.24) yields

$$\mathrm{E}(Y_j|X_{ij}=x_i)=g_0+g_i(x_i)+\sum_{k\neq i}\mathrm{E}(g_k(X_{kj})|X_{ij}=x_i)$$

for $i=1,\ldots,p$. Here $m_i(x_i)=\mathrm{E}(Y_j|X_{ij}=x_i)$ can be estimated by the Nadaraya–Watson estimator

$$\widehat{m}_i(x_i)=\frac{\sum_j Y_j K_b(X_{ij}-x_i)}{\sum_j K_b(X_{ij}-x_i)},$$

where the kernel function K_b has been introduced earlier in Section 2.5. Moreover, $\mathrm{E}(g_k(X_{kj})|X_{ij}=x_i)$ can be estimated by the Nadaraya–Watson estimator

$$\frac{\sum_j \widehat{g}_k(X_{kj})K_b(X_{ij}-x_i)}{\sum_j K_b(X_{ij}-x_i)}.$$

If the initial estimates $\widehat{g}_i^{(0)}$ of g_i, $i=1,\ldots,p$, are available, then an updated estimate of $g_i(x_i)$ can be found using the relationship

$$g_i(x_i)=\mathrm{E}(Y_j|X_{ij}=x_i)-g_0-\sum_{k\neq i}\mathrm{E}(g_k(X_{kj})|X_{ij}=x_i),\quad i=1,\ldots,p.$$

This leads to the recursive estimation algorithm

$$\widehat{g}_i^{(r)}(x_i)=\widehat{m}(x_i)-\widehat{g}_0-\sum_{k<i}\widehat{g}_k^{(r)}(x_k)-\sum_{k>i}\widehat{g}_k^{(r-1)}(x_k),$$

where $\widehat{g}_0=\overline{Y}$. See Hastie and Tibshirani (1990, p. 108) for details. The curse of dimensionality is avoided using backfitting because only conditional expectations with one-dimensional arguments are used, and the resulting estimates are consistent and converge at the one-dimensional rate of $(nb)^{-1/2}$. Its asymptotic theory is given by Opsomer and Ruppert (1997) and with weaker sufficient conditions for a smoothed version by Mammen et al. (1999) using a projection argument.

Tjøstheim and Auestad (1994) propose to use the marginal integration estimates as initial estimates in a backfitting algorithm. Linton (1997) in fact formalizes this and shows that one step of the backfitting algorithm is sufficient to obtain efficiency.

The projection argument by Mammen et al. (1999) remains valid also in the absence of an additive noise-driven model (2.24). Eq. (2.23) can be taken as a starting point. In the more general case the estimated projection $\tilde{g}_0 + \sum_i \tilde{g}_i(x_i)$ is the best additive approximation to $\mathrm{E}(Y|X = x)$. This approach is very useful in situations where models of type (2.24) are difficult to establish. An example for spatial variables is given by Lu et al. (2007a).

The additive model may be extended to allow for (pairwise) interaction between the explanatory variables, so that

$$Y_j = g_0 + \sum_{i=1}^{p} g_i(X_{ij}) + \sum_{i \neq k} g_{ik}(X_{ij}, X_{kj}) + \varepsilon_j,\ \ j = 1, \dots, n.$$

The estimation theory becomes more complicated, and several identifiability conditions are needed. We refer to Sperlich et al. (2002) for details. They use marginal integration as an estimation technique, and also the interaction model is used to test the null hypothesis of a "pure" additive model on the form (2.24).

The additive modeling can of course proceed for other quantities than the conditional mean, such as the conditional variance. In this context, we should also mention that a widely used modification of the additive model (2.24) is the generalized additive model (GAM), which is treated extensively in the book by Hastie and Tibshirani (1990) and in the paper by Hastie and Tibshirani (1993). A link function makes additive models available for discrete-valued variables Y. The logit function, for instance, is suitable if the response variable Y is binary. This results in the generalized additive model

$$\log \frac{p(\boldsymbol{x})}{1 - p(\boldsymbol{x})} = g_0 + \sum_{i=1}^{p} g_i(x_i),$$

where $p(\boldsymbol{x}) = P(Y = 1|\boldsymbol{X} = \boldsymbol{x})$. Obviously, this is a generalization of the logistic regression model.

The dependent variable Y and the explanatory variables $\boldsymbol{X} = (X_1, \dots, X_p)^T$ play distinctly different roles in additive regression models. Sometimes, it is advantageous to treat these variables on a more equal footing (in fact, we will argue for such a view in several instances in this book). The ACE (alternating conditional expectations) algorithm by Breiman and Friedman (1985) is designed for a situation in which both the dependent and explanatory variables may be transformed. Thus

$$h(Y_j) = g_0 + \sum_{i=1}^{p} g_i(X_{ij}) + \varepsilon_j.$$

Some curious aspects of the ACE algorithm are highlighted by Hastie and Tibshirani (1990, pp. 84–86).

We will present another way of eluding the curse of dimensionality for nonparametric regression estimation in Chapter 12. This will be based on a simplification of the local Gaussian conditional density estimator.

2.7.2 Regression trees, splines, and MARS

There are several other alternatives to the additive decomposition of g in the model $Y_j = g(\boldsymbol{X}_j) + \varepsilon_j$ when $\boldsymbol{X}_j$ is the jth observation of a p-dimensional random variable $\boldsymbol{X}$. The function g may be approximated in terms of simple basis functions A_k so that g is written as $g(\boldsymbol{x}) = \sum_k c_k A_k(\boldsymbol{x})$. The single-hidden layer neural networks constitute an example of this. In the regression tree approach of Breiman et al. (1984) the approximation is built up recursively from indicator functions $A_k(\boldsymbol{x}) = I(\boldsymbol{x} \in R_k)$, and the regions R_k are partitioned in the next "parent–child" step of the algorithm according to a certain pattern. However, the indicator function is somewhat cumbersome in approximating simple smooth functions such as the linear model.

Friedman (1991) made at least two important new contributions in his MARS (Multivariate Adaptive Regression Splines) paper. First, to overcome the difficulty in fitting simple smooth functions, Friedman proposed to not automatically eliminate the parent region in the above recursion scheme for creating subregions. In subsequent iterations, both the parent region and its subregions are eligible for further partitioning, which increases the flexibility of the model. The second contribution was replacing step functions by products of linear left- and right-truncated regression splines. These products make it possible to include interaction terms.

There has recently been an almost explosive development within the topic of multivariate nonparametric regression and related fields. The book by Hastie et al. (2009) surveys some of the developments that happened before 2009. After that, further advances have taken place, such as deep learning in neural network analysis; see, for example, Schmidhuber (2015).

2.8 Quantile regression

Thus far, we have been concerned with modeling the conditional mean $\mathrm{E}(Y|\boldsymbol{X})$ and partly the conditional variance $\mathrm{Var}(Y|\boldsymbol{X})$ nonparametrically. This is restrictive in the sense that it only gives the mean and variance of the conditional distribution of Y given X. We may of course want to estimate the conditional distribution itself, and we have already briefly mentioned conditional probability density estimation.

Instead of the conditional distribution, there has been much focus on the quantiles of the conditional distribution. The task is to estimate the $(1-\alpha)$ quantile $q_{1-\alpha}$, where $P(Y \leq q_{1-\alpha}|\boldsymbol{X}=\boldsymbol{x}) = 1-\alpha$ as a function of $\boldsymbol{X}$. The most obvious solution is perhaps to estimate the conditional distribution and then to invert it. This is a rather non-trivial extension of kernel estimation. For example, we have to be careful to prevent quantile curves from crossing each other as $\boldsymbol{X}$ varies. In the time series case the problem has been studied by Cai (2002). We will return to this problem in Chapters 10 and 12.

Modeling the quantiles directly as functions of $\boldsymbol{X}$ has given rise to the field of quantile regression. This goes back at least to Koenker and Bassett (1978), and has been much developed since then. For comprehensive accounts of the theory and practice of quantile regression, see Koenker (2005) and an easy-to-read survey article by Yu et al. (2003). Here we will just mention a few facts, including the curse of dimensionality, to put the concept into the context of the main nonparametric topics treated here.

The 0.5-quantile is the median, and it is well known in the scalar x-case that it is obtained by minimizing the expected least absolute deviation $\mathrm{E}|Y - m(X)|$ given $X = x$. Similarly, other α-quantiles may be found by minimizing an absolute deviation function weighted by α and $1-\alpha$.

The curse of dimensionality arises in quantile regression as well. It has already been demonstrated that for the conditional mean and variance, there are number of ways of getting around this problem. Additive modeling is one of them, and it has been extended to quantile regression; see Horowitz and Lee (2005) and a number of follow-up articles. For a multidimensional $\boldsymbol{X}$, it is not so easy to make interpretable plots of the quantile function. However, this does not prevent us from studying the quantiles separately, given each of the one-dimensional components X_i of $\boldsymbol{X}$. They may give valuable extra information compared to the estimated conditional mean and conditional variance.

2.9 Semiparametric models

The field of semiparametric modeling is large, even though there is no exact agreement on how a semiparametric model should be defined. Here we consider a semiparametric model as a model where some component(s) of the data-generating process is (are) treated nonparametrically, whereas the rest of the model is parametric. This is a rather loose definition. A review of econometric applications of these models can be found in Powell (1994). Much of the statistical theory is presented by Bickel et al. (1998); see also Gao (2007). Spatial variables are treated by Gao et al. (2006).

As semiparametric modeling is a hybrid of the parametric and non-parametric approaches and shares the advantages and disadvantages of each. Schematically, a semiparametric model may be written as

$$Y_j = g(\mathbf{X}_j; \boldsymbol{\theta}, \varepsilon),$$

where the partially unknown function g contains a nonparametric part, $\boldsymbol{\theta}$ is an unknown parameter or parameter vector, and $\{\varepsilon_j\}$ are the generating innovations. Quite often, we are able to prove the $\sqrt{n}$ consistency for the estimator of $\boldsymbol{\theta}$, whereas the rate for the estimate of the nonparametric part of g would generally be $(nb^m)^{-1/2}$, where m is the dimension of the argument $\mathbf{X}$ of the nonparametric part of g, and b is a smoothing bandwidth.

2.9.1 Partially linear models

Fitting and estimating partially linear models represent the most common uses of semiparametrics in a nonlinear regression context. If we have reason to believe that Y_j depends linearly on some of the explanatory variables and possibly nonlinearly on the others, we may choose the model

$$Y_j = \boldsymbol{\theta}^T \mathbf{X}_{1j} + g(\mathbf{X}_{2j}) + \varepsilon_j, \quad j = 1, \ldots, n.$$

An illustrative example can be found in Engle et al. (1986), who modeled electricity sales using a number of explanatory variables. It is natural to assume that the impact of temperature on electricity consumption is non-linear, as both high and low temperatures lead to increased consumption, whereas other regressors enter the model linearly. A similar situation can be found in Shumway et al. (1988), who studied mortality as a function of weather and pollution variables in the Los Angeles region. More details in both theory and applications can be found in Gao (2007).

2.9.2 Index models and projection pursuit

An index model for the relationship between the response variable Y and the explanatory variables $\mathbf{X}$ is a model of type

$$Y_j = g(\boldsymbol{\theta}^T \mathbf{X}_j) + \varepsilon_j, \quad j = 1, \ldots, n, \tag{2.25}$$

where both g and the parameter vector $\boldsymbol{\theta}$ are unknown. In principle, even the dimension of the parameter vector $\boldsymbol{\theta}$ may be unknown. For example, the inner product $\boldsymbol{\theta}^T\mathbf{X}_t$ may be equal to $\sum_{i=1}^{p}\theta_i Y_{t-i}$ in a time series context, and the maximum lag p may not be known. In a regression problem, $\boldsymbol{\theta}^T\mathbf{X}$ may be thought of as a principal component-type variable or an index, and for interpretation reasons, the parameter vector $\boldsymbol{\theta}$ may be of greater interest than the function g. Fan et al. (2003) and Lu et al. (2007b) coupled the index model with the time series functional coefficient model of Chen and Tsay (1993). Estimates are often found using an iterative method, where the emphasis is alternating between estimating g and estimating $\boldsymbol{\theta}$. We refer to Dong et al. (2016) for a recent account in the nonstationary time series case.

The projection pursuit regression analysis was introduced by Friedman and Stuetzle (1981). Main asymptotic properties were derived by Hall (1989). Both papers considered a set of iid explanatory variables. The arguments and results of Hall were carried over to the nonlinear autoregressive time series case by Xia and An (1999). In the projection pursuit setup, the model (2.25) is extended as follows:

$$Y_j = \sum_{i=1}^{L} g_i(\boldsymbol{\theta}_i^T\mathbf{X}_j) + \varepsilon_j, \;\; j = 1, \ldots, n,$$

where the right-hand side contains L latent variables or factors $\boldsymbol{\theta}_i^T\mathbf{X}_j$, $i = 1, \ldots, L$. The functions g_i and parameters $\boldsymbol{\theta}_i$ can be estimated one at a time, and we refer to Hastie et al. (2009) for some more details. The latter authors also stress that projection pursuit models may be looked at as a forerunner to the far more popular neural network models, where the functions g_i are usually taken to be known and of sigmoidal type, and where the approximation is done in several layers.

2.10 Locally parametric

The idea behind locally parametric density estimation is that an unknown density function f is sought approximated locally by a family of parametric densities $\{p(\cdot, \boldsymbol{\theta}), \boldsymbol{\theta} = \boldsymbol{\theta}(\boldsymbol{x})\}$. More precisely, for a given point $\boldsymbol{x}$, we try to find a member $p(\cdot, \boldsymbol{\theta}(\boldsymbol{x}))$, where $\boldsymbol{\theta} = \boldsymbol{\theta}(\boldsymbol{x})$ is now allowed to depend on $\boldsymbol{x}$ so that the member $p(\boldsymbol{v}, \boldsymbol{\theta}(\boldsymbol{x}))$ of the family gives a good approximation to f for $\boldsymbol{v}$ in a neighborhood of $\boldsymbol{x}$. Moving to another point $\boldsymbol{y}$ means that we have to find another member $p(\boldsymbol{v}, \boldsymbol{\theta}(\boldsymbol{y}))$ giving a good approximation to f

for $\boldsymbol{v}$ in a neighborhood of $\boldsymbol{y}$, unless f is identical to $p(\cdot, \boldsymbol{\theta})$ for all $\boldsymbol{x}$. Hjort and Jones (1996) and Loader (1996) elaborated this idea for quite general families of distributions.

The basic idea of this book is to use this local family representation for a general density f in the particular case where $p(\cdot, \boldsymbol{\theta})$ is assumed to be a univariate or multivariate normal distribution. Using very favorable properties of the multivariate normal distribution locally, we are able to obtain a number of results related to such topics as dependence, density estimation, conditional density estimation, nonlinear spectral distribution, and quite a few more. They will be described in due course throughout this book.

We conclude this chapter by presenting a few general features of this representation based on Hjort and Jones (1996), Loader (1996), and Tjøstheim and Hufthammer (2013).

In the general local likelihood framework, we estimate the parameter $\boldsymbol{\theta} = \boldsymbol{\theta}(\boldsymbol{x})$ by maximizing the local log likelihood function at each location $\boldsymbol{x}$ for vector observations $\boldsymbol{X}_1, \ldots, \boldsymbol{X}_n$,

$$L_n(\boldsymbol{X}, \boldsymbol{\theta}) = L(\boldsymbol{X}_1, \ldots, \boldsymbol{X}_n) = n^{-1} \sum_{j=1}^{n} K_{\boldsymbol{b}}(\boldsymbol{X}_j - \boldsymbol{x}) \log(p(\boldsymbol{X}_j, \boldsymbol{\theta})) - \int K_{\boldsymbol{b}}(\boldsymbol{v} - \boldsymbol{x}) p(\boldsymbol{v}, \boldsymbol{\theta}) \, \mathrm{d}\boldsymbol{v}, \quad (2.26)$$

where $\boldsymbol{X}$, $\boldsymbol{x}$, and $\boldsymbol{\theta}$ in general are vectors, $K_{\boldsymbol{b}}$ is defined in the same way as before (see, e.g., a multivariate generalization of Eq. (2.11)), and $\boldsymbol{b}$ is a bandwidth vector or possibly a matrix of bandwidths. One may well wonder why the last term is included in the local likelihood, since the first term localizes the ordinary likelihood function in a seemingly intuitive fashion. However, we immediately see that omission of this term leads to nonsensical results. For example, if $X \sim \mathcal{N}(\mu, \sigma^2)$, so that $\boldsymbol{\theta} = (\mu, \sigma^2)$, then we easily show that maximizing just the first term leads to $\widehat{\mu}(x) = x$ and $\widehat{\sigma}^2(x) = \infty$. We obtain a more constructive explanation by taking the partial derivatives with respect to $\boldsymbol{\theta}$. Then for $\boldsymbol{\theta}(\boldsymbol{x}) = \boldsymbol{\theta} = (\theta_1, \ldots, \theta_m)^T$,

$$\frac{\partial L_n(\boldsymbol{X}, \boldsymbol{\theta})}{\partial \theta_i} = n^{-1} \sum_{j=1}^{n} K_{\boldsymbol{b}}(\boldsymbol{X}_j - \boldsymbol{x}) u_i(\boldsymbol{X}_j, \boldsymbol{\theta}) - \int K_{\boldsymbol{b}}(\boldsymbol{v} - \boldsymbol{x}) u_i(\boldsymbol{X}_j, \boldsymbol{\theta}) p(\boldsymbol{v}, \boldsymbol{\theta}) \, \mathrm{d}\boldsymbol{v}, \quad (2.27)$$

where $u_i(\boldsymbol{v}, \boldsymbol{\theta}) = \partial \log(p(\boldsymbol{v}, \boldsymbol{\theta}))/\partial\theta_i$. By the law of large numbers or by the ergodic theorem in the stationary time series case it follows that the expression on the right-hand side of (2.27) converges almost surely to the quantity

$$\int K_{\boldsymbol{b}}(\boldsymbol{v}-\boldsymbol{x})u_i(\boldsymbol{v}, \boldsymbol{\theta})[f(\boldsymbol{v}) - p(\boldsymbol{v}, \boldsymbol{\theta})]\,\mathrm{d}\boldsymbol{v}. \tag{2.28}$$

Requiring $\partial \log L/\partial\theta_i = 0$, we see that the second term in the local likelihood function forces $f(\boldsymbol{x}) - p(\boldsymbol{x}; \boldsymbol{\theta})$ to be zero as $\boldsymbol{b} \to \boldsymbol{0}$ under the weak assumption that $u_i(\boldsymbol{v}, \boldsymbol{\theta})$ is not equal to zero for $\boldsymbol{v} = \boldsymbol{x}$. In fact, a Taylor expansion of the integral (2.28) reveals that letting $\boldsymbol{b} \to 0$ (componentwise) and requiring that $\partial L/\partial\theta_i = 0$ lead to

$$u_i(\boldsymbol{x}, \boldsymbol{\theta})\{f(\boldsymbol{x}) - p(\boldsymbol{x}, \boldsymbol{\theta})\} + O(\boldsymbol{b}^T\boldsymbol{b}) = 0,$$

where we have used the symmetry of the kernel function K. This can also be used to show that the bias of the corresponding estimate is of order $\boldsymbol{b}^T\boldsymbol{b}$. As $\boldsymbol{b} \to \infty$ (again, componentwise), we see that the second term in (2.26) tends to $\int p(\boldsymbol{v}, \boldsymbol{\theta}) = 1$ since $p(\boldsymbol{v}, \boldsymbol{\theta})$ is a density function, and this in turn means that (2.27) is consistent with global maximum likelihood estimation. This is discussed more fully, including another type of additional term, by Hjort and Jones (1996).

Hjort and Jones (1996) also justify the modified log likelihood from the point of view of minimizing a localized Kullback–Leibler distance between the unknown density function f and the chosen parametric family of densities $p(\cdot, \boldsymbol{\theta})$. To see this, note that by the law of large numbers (or ergodic theorem),

$$L_n(\boldsymbol{X}, \boldsymbol{\theta}) \xrightarrow{P} \lambda(\boldsymbol{x}, \boldsymbol{\theta}) = \int K_b(\boldsymbol{v}-\boldsymbol{x})\{f(\boldsymbol{v})\log p(\boldsymbol{v}; \boldsymbol{\theta}) - p(\boldsymbol{v}, \boldsymbol{\theta})\}\,\mathrm{d}\boldsymbol{v}$$

as n becomes large. The maximizer of L_n in terms of $\boldsymbol{\theta} = \boldsymbol{\theta}(\boldsymbol{x})$ aims at the parameter value $\boldsymbol{\theta}_0(\boldsymbol{x})$ that maximizes $\lambda(\boldsymbol{x}, \boldsymbol{\theta})$ This is equivalent to minimizing the distance function

$$d[f(\cdot), p(\cdot, \boldsymbol{\theta})] = \int K_{\boldsymbol{b}}(\boldsymbol{v}-\boldsymbol{x})\left[f(\boldsymbol{v})\log\frac{f(\boldsymbol{v})}{p(\boldsymbol{v}, \boldsymbol{\theta})} - \{f(\boldsymbol{v}) - p(\boldsymbol{v}, \boldsymbol{\theta})\}\right]\mathrm{d}\boldsymbol{v}. \tag{2.29}$$

Noting that the Kullback–Leibler distance between f and $p(\cdot, \boldsymbol{\theta})$ can be written as (using that densities integrate to one)

$$\int f(\boldsymbol{v})\log\{f(\boldsymbol{v})/p(\boldsymbol{v}, \boldsymbol{\theta})\}\,\mathrm{d}\boldsymbol{v} = \int \left[f(\boldsymbol{v})\log\frac{f(\boldsymbol{v})}{p(\boldsymbol{v}, \boldsymbol{\theta})} - \{f(\boldsymbol{v}) - p(\boldsymbol{v}, \boldsymbol{\theta})\}\right]\mathrm{d}\boldsymbol{v},$$

we see that (2.29) is a version of the same, locally weighted distance function around $\boldsymbol{x}$.

The asymptotic theory of this local parametric estimate $\widehat{\boldsymbol{\theta}}(\boldsymbol{x})$ for a fixed set of bandwidths $\boldsymbol{b}$ is derived by Hjort and Jones (1996) in the iid case. Similar estimates have been defined by Loader (1996) using densities on the form $\exp\{w(\boldsymbol{x}, \boldsymbol{\theta})\}$, where $w(\boldsymbol{x})$ typically is a polynomial function. The leading term in the asymptotic variance is the same as for the kernel density estimator; see Hjort and Jones (1996). They also prove the asymptotic normality in a vector parameter situation and for a scalar x and indicate extensions to the multivariate case, where, again, the curse of dimensionality occurs as an obstacle. We refer to their paper for details and to the specific chapters in this book pertaining to the various applications we consider, all of which employ the multivariate normal distribution to play the role of the parametric family $p(\cdot, \boldsymbol{\theta})$.

Hjort and Jones (1996) also discuss the case of asymptotic bias and variance in the case $\boldsymbol{b} \to 0$. This leads to consistency requirements in terms of smoothness of the functions f and $p(\cdot, \boldsymbol{\theta})$ at the point $\boldsymbol{x}$. When these conditions are fulfilled, we can obtain explicit but complex bias expressions in the simplest cases after some quite heavy computations. The results are comparable to the bias in the local linear estimation of Section 2.6.2. This has also been examined in the local Gaussian case by Berentsen et al. (2017).

References

Anderson, T.W., 2003. An Introduction to Multivariate Statistical Analysis. Wiley-Interscience.

Battey, H., Linton, O., 2014. Nonparametric estimation of multivariate elliptic densities via finite mixture sieves. Journal of Multivariate Analysis 123, 43–67.

Berentsen, G.D., Cao, R., Francisco-Fernández, M., Tjøstheim, D., 2017. Some properties of local Gaussian autocorrelation and other nonlinear dependence measures. Journal of Time Series Analysis 38 (2), 352–380.

Bickel, P., Klaasen, C.A.G., Ritov, Y., Wellner, J.A., 1998. Efficient and Adaptive Estimation in Semiparametric Models, 2nd edition. Springer Verlag, New York.

Box, G.E., Draper, N.R., 1987. Empirical Model-Building and Response Surfaces. John Wiley & Sons.

Box, G.E.P., Jenkins, G.M., 1970. Time Series Analysis, Forecasting and Control. Holden Day, San Francisco.

Breiman, L., Friedman, J.H., 1985. Estimating optimal transformations for multiple regression and correlation (with discussion). Journal of the American Statistical Association 80 (391), 580–619.

Breiman, L., Friedman, J.H., Olshen, R.A., Stone, C.J., 1984. Classification and Regression Trees. Chapman and Hall, New York.

Brockwell, P., Davis, R.A., 2013. Time Series: Theory and Methods. Springer Science & Business Media.

Cai, Z., 2002. Regression quantiles for time series. Econometric Theory 18 (1), 169–192.
Chen, R., Tsay, R.S., 1993. Functional coefficient autoregressive models. Journal of the American Statistical Association 88, 298–308.
Cleveland, W.S., 1979. Robust locally weighted regression and smoothing scatterplots. Journal of the American Statistical Association 74 (368), 829–836.
Cybenko, G., 1989. Approximation by superpositions of a sigmoidal function. Mathematics of Control, Signals and Systems 2 (4), 303–314.
De Gooijer, J.G., 2017. Elements of Nonlinear Time Series Analysis and Forecasting. Springer.
Dong, C., Gao, J., Tjøstheim, D., 2016. Estimation for single-index and partially linear single-index integrated models. Annals of Statistics 44 (1), 425–453.
Douc, R., Moulines, E., Stoffer, D., 2014. Nonlinear Time Series: Theory, Methods and Applications With R Examples. Chapman and Hall/CRC.
Draper, N.R., Smith, H., 2014. Applied Regression Analysis, vol. 326. John Wiley & Sons.
Engle, R.F., 1982. Autoregressive conditional heteroscedasticity with estimates of variance of U.K. inflation. Econometrica 50 (4), 987–1008.
Engle, R.F., Bollerslev, T., 1986. Modelling the persistence of conditional variances. Econometric Reviews 5 (1), 1–50.
Engle, R.F., Granger, C.W.J., Rice, J., Weiss, A., 1986. Semiparametric estimates of the relation between weather and electricity sales. Journal of the American Statistical Association 81 (394), 310–320.
Fan, J., Gijbels, I., 1995. Data-driven bandwidth selection in local polynomial fitting: variable bandwidth and spatial adaptation. Journal of the Royal Statistical Society Series B 57 (2), 371–394.
Fan, J., Gijbels, I., 1996. Local Polynomial Modelling and Its Application, Theory and Methodologies. Chapman and Hall, London.
Fan, J., Yao, Q., 2003. Nonlinear Time Series. Nonparametric and Parametric Methods. Springer.
Fan, J., Yao, Q., Cai, Z., 2003. Adaptive varying-coefficient linear models. Journal of the Royal Statistical Society Series B 65 (1), 57–80.
Fokianos, K., Rahbek, A., Tjøstheim, D., 2009. Poisson autoregression. Journal of the American Statistical Association 104 (488), 1430–1439.
Fokianos, K., Støve, B., Tjøstheim, D., Doukhan, P., 2020. Multivariate count autoregression. Bernoulli 26 (1), 471–499.
Francq, C., Zakoian, J.-M., 2011. GARCH Models: Structure, Statistical Inference and Financial Applications. John Wiley & Sons.
Friedman, J.H., 1991. Multivariate adaptive regression splines (with discussion). Annals of Statistics 19 (1), 79–141.
Friedman, J.H., Stuetsle, W., Schroeder, A., 1984. Projection pursuit density estimation. Journal of the American Statistical Association 79, 599–608.
Friedman, J.H., Stuetzle, W., 1981. Projection pursuit regression. Journal of the American Statistical Association 76 (376), 817–823.
Gao, J., 2007. Nonlinear Time Series: Semiparametric Methods. Chapman and Hall, London.
Gao, J., Lu, Z., Tjøstheim, D., 2006. Estimation in semiparametric spatial regression. Annals of Statistics 34 (3), 1395–1435.
Granger, C.W., Newbold, P., 1977. Forecasting Economic Time Series. Academic Press, New York.
Greene, W.H., 2003. Econometric Analysis, 5th edition. Prentice Hall, New York.
Hall, P., 1989. On projection pursuit regression. Annals of Statistics 17 (2), 573–588.
Hamilton, J.D., 1994. Time Series Analysis. Princeton University Press.
Härdle, W., 1990. Applied Nonparametric Regression. Oxford University Press.

Härdle, W., Mammen, E., 1993. Comparing nonparametric versus parametric regression fits. Annals of Statistics 21 (4), 1926–1947.

Harrell, F.E., 2001. Regression Modeling Strategies, With Applications to Linear Models, Survival Analysis and Logistic Regression. Springer.

Hart, J.D., Vieu, P., 1990. Data-driven bandwidth choice for density estimation based on dependent data. Annals of Statistics 18 (2), 873–890.

Hastie, T., Tibshirani, R., 1990. Generalized Additive Models. Chapman and Hall, London.

Hastie, T., Tibshirani, R., 1993. Varying-coefficient models. Journal of the Royal Statistical Society Series B 55 (4), 757–796.

Hastie, T., Tibshirani, R., Friedman, J., 2009. The Elements of Statistical Learning. Data Mining, Inference, and Prediction, 2nd edition. Springer, New York.

Hayfield, T., Racine, J.S., 2008. Nonparametric econometrics: the np package. Journal of Statistical Software 27, 1–32.

Hjort, N., Jones, M., 1996. Locally parametric nonparametric density estimation. Annals of Statistics 24 (4), 1619–1647.

Horowitz, J.L., Lee, S., 2005. Nonparametric estimation of an additive quantile regression model. Journal of the American Statistical Association 100 (472), 1238–1249.

Jiang, Z., Ling, N., Lu, Z., Tjøstheim, D., Zhang, Q., 2020. On bandwidth choice for spatial data density estimation. Journal of the Royal Statistical Society: Series B (Statistical Methodology) 82 (3), 817–840.

Johnson, R.A., Wichern, D.W., 2007. Applied Multivariate Statistical Analysis. Pearson Education.

Karlis, D., 2003. An EM algorithm for multivariate Poisson distribution and related models. Journal of Applied Statistics 30 (1), 63–77.

Karlsen, H.A., Myklebust, T., Tjøstheim, D., 2007. Nonparametric estimation in a nonlinear cointegration type model. Annals of Statistics 35 (1), 252–299.

Karlsen, H.A., Tjøstheim, D., 2001. Nonparametric estimation in null recurrent time series models. Annals of Statistics 29 (2), 372–416.

Kauermann, G., Opsomer, J., 2003. Local likelihood estimation in generalized additive models. Scandinavian Journal of Statistics 30 (2), 317–337.

Klimko, L.A., Nelson, P.I., 1978. On conditional least squares estimation for stochastic processes. Annals of Statistics 6 (3), 629–642.

Koenker, R., 2005. Quantile Regression. Cambridge University Press.

Koenker, R., Bassett, G., 1978. Regression quantiles. Econometrica 46 (1), 33–50.

Kreiss, J.-P., 1987. On adaptive estimation in stationary ARMA processes. Annals of Statistics 15 (1), 112–133.

Landsman, Z.M., Valdez, E.A., 2003. Tail conditional expectations for elliptical distributions. North American Actuarial Journal 7 (4), 55–71.

Lehmann, E.L., Casella, G., 2006. Theory of Point Estimation. Springer Science & Business Media.

Leipnik, R., 1961. When does zero correlation imply independence? The American Mathematical Monthly 68 (6), 563–565.

Leontief, W., 1947. Introduction to a theory of the internal structure of functional relationships. Econometrica 15 (4), 361–373.

Li, D., Tjøstheim, D., Gao, J., et al., 2016. Estimation in nonlinear regression with Harris recurrent Markov chains. Annals of Statistics 44 (5), 1957–1987.

Linton, O., 1997. Efficient estimation of additive nonparametric regression models. Biometrika 84 (2), 469–473.

Linton, O., Mammen, E., Nielsen, J.P., Tanggaard, C., 2001. Yield curve estimation by kernel smoothing methods. Journal of Econometrics 105 (1), 185–223.

Linton, O., Nielsen, J.P., 1995. A kernel method for estimating structured nonparametric regression based on marginal integration. Biometrika 82 (1), 93–100.

Liu, C., Rubin, D.B., 1995. ML estimation of the t distribution using EM and its extensions, ECM and ECME. Statistica Sinica 5 (1), 19–39.

Loader, C.R., 1996. Local likelihood density estimation. Annals of Statistics 24 (4), 1602–1618.

Lu, Z., Lundervold, A., Tjøstheim, D., Yao, Q., 2007a. Exploring spatial nonlinearity using additive approximation. Bernoulli 13 (2), 447–472.

Lu, Z., Tjøstheim, D., Yao, Q., 2007b. Adaptive varying-coefficient linear models for stochastic processes. Statistica Sinica 17 (1), 177–197.

Mammen, E., Linton, O., Nielsen, J.P., 1999. The existence and asymptotic properties of a backfitting projection algorithm under weak conditions. Annals of Statistics 27 (5), 1443–1490.

Masry, E., Tjøstheim, D., 1995. Nonparametric estimation and identification of ARCH non-linear time series: strong convergence and asymptotic normality. Econometric Theory 11 (2), 258–289.

McNeil, A.J., Frey, R., Embrechts, P., 2005. Quantitative Risk Management: Concepts, Techniques and Tools. Princeton University Press, Princeton.

Meyn, S.P., Tweedie, R.L., 2009. Markov Chains and Stochastic Stability. Springer.

Nadarajah, S., Dey, D.K., 2005. Multitude of multivariate t-distributions. Statistics 39 (2), 149–181.

Nadarajah, S., Kotz, S., 2008. Estimation methods for the multivariate t distribution. Acta Applicandae Mathematicae 102 (1), 99–118.

Nagler, T., Czado, C., 2016. Evading the curse of dimensionality in nonparametric density estimation with simplified vine copulas. Journal of Multivariate Analysis 151, 69–89.

Newey, W.K., 1994. Kernel estimation of partial means and a general variance estimator. Econometric Theory 10 (2), 1–21.

Opsomer, J.D., Ruppert, D., 1997. Fitting a bivariate additive model by local polynomial regression. Annals of Statistics 25 (1), 186–211.

Otneim, H., Tjøstheim, D., 2017. The locally Gaussian density estimator for multivariate data. Statistics and Computing 27 (6), 1595–1616.

Owen, J., Rabinovitch, R., 1983. On the class of elliptical distributions and their applications to the theory of portfolio choice. Journal of Finance 38 (3), 745–752.

Park, J.Y., Phillips, P.C.B., 1999. Asymptotics for nonlinear transformations of integrated time series. Econometric Theory 15 (3), 269–298.

Park, J.Y., Phillips, P.C.B., 2001. Nonlinear regression with integrated time series. Econometrica 69 (1), 117–161.

Parzen, E., 1962. On estimation of a probability density function and mode. Annals of Mathematical Statistics 33 (3), 1065–1076.

Powell, J.L., 1994. Estimation of semiparametric models. In: Engle, R.F., McFadden, D. (Eds.), Handbook of Econometrics, vol. 4. Elsevier, Amsterdam, pp. 2444–2524.

Ripley, B.D., 2007. Pattern Recognition and Neural Networks. Cambridge University Press.

Robinson, P.M., 1983. Nonparametric estimators for time series. Journal of Time Series Analysis 4, 185–207.

Rosenblatt, M., 1956. Remarks on some nonparametric estimates of a density function. Annals of Mathematical Statistics 27 (3), 832–837.

Rydberg, T.H., Shephard, N., 2000. A modelling framework for the prices and times of trades made on the New York stock exchange. Nonlinear and Nonstationary Signal Processing, 217–246.

Schmidhuber, J., 2015. Deep learning in neural networks. Neural Networks 61 (61), 85–117.

Shumway, R., Azari, A., Pawitan, Y., 1988. Modeling mortality fluctuations in Los Angeles as functions of pollution and weather effects. Environmental Research 45 (2), 224–241.

Shumway, R.H., Stoffer, D.S., 2006. Time Series Analysis and Its Applications: With R Examples. Springer-Verlag, New York.
Silverman, B.W., 1986. Density Estimation for Statistics and Data Analysis. Chapman and Hall, London.
Sperlich, S., Tjøstheim, D., Yang, L., 2002. Nonparametric estimation and testing of interaction in additive models. Econometric Theory 18 (2), 197–251.
Taleb, N.N., 2007. The Black Swan: The Impact of the Highly Improbable. Random House.
Teräsvirta, T., Tjøstheim, D., Granger, C.W., 2010. Modelling Nonlinear Economic Time Series. Oxford University Press.
Tibshirani, R., 1996. Regression shrinkage and selection via the lasso. Journal of the Royal Statistical Society Series B 58 (1), 267–288.
Tibshirani, R., Hastie, T., 1987. Local likelihood estimation. Annals of Statistics 182 (398), 717–741.
Tjøstheim, D., 2020. Some notes on nonlinear cointegration: a partial review with some novel perspectives. Econometric Reviews 39 (7), 655–673.
Tjøstheim, D., Auestad, B., 1994. Nonparametric identification of nonlinear time series: projections. Journal of the American Statistical Association 89 (428), 1398–1409.
Tjøstheim, D., Hufthammer, K.O., 2013. Local Gaussian correlation: a new measure of dependence. Journal of Econometrics 172 (1), 33–48.
Tong, H., 1990. Non-Linear Time Series: A Dynamical System Approach. Oxford University Press, Oxford.
Wand, M.P., Jones, M.C., 1995. Kernel Smoothing. Chapman and Hall, London.
Xia, X., An, H.Z., 1999. Projection pursuit autoregression in time series. Journal of Time Series Analysis 20 (6), 693–714.
Yu, K., Lu, Z., Stander, J., 2003. Quantile regression: applications and current research areas. Journal of the Royal Statistical Society Series D 52 (3), 331–350.
Zou, H., 2006. The adaptive lasso and its oracle properties. Journal of the American Statistical Association 101 (476), 1418–1429.

CHAPTER 3

Dependence

Contents

3.1. Introduction 49
3.2. Weaknesses of Pearson's ρ 52
 3.2.1 The non-Gaussianity issue 52
 3.2.2 The robustness issue 53
 3.2.3 The nonlinearity issue 54
3.3. The copula 56
3.4. Global dependence functionals and tests of independence 61
 3.4.1 Maximal correlation 63
 3.4.2 Measures and tests based on the distribution function 64
 3.4.3 Distance covariance 67
 3.4.4 The HSIC measure of dependence 72
 3.4.5 Density-based tests of independence 77
3.5. Test functionals generated by local dependence relationships 80
References 81

3.1 Introduction

Dependence is a basic concept in statistics. In this chapter, we give a survey of existing dependence measures and tests for statistical independence. We do this partly to put our subsequent treatment of local Gaussian correlation in perspective and partly to review other recent development within dependence modeling. This field has seen important progress in the last couple of decades, not the least in the modeling of nonlinear dependence using the distance covariance function, as well as related techniques in the machine learning community such as the HSIC measure. The material in this chapter is to a large degree based on Tjøstheim et al. (2021).

The modeling of statistical dependence started with the introduction of the so-called Pearson product moment correlation ρ more than 100 years ago. If X and Y are two random variables with finite second moments, then the product moment correlation is defined by

$$\rho = \rho(X, Y) = \frac{\sigma(X, Y)}{\sigma_X \sigma_Y}$$

with $\sigma(X, Y) = \mathrm{E}\{(X - \mathrm{E}(X))(Y - \mathrm{E}(Y))\}$ being the covariance between X and Y and with $\sigma_X = \sqrt{\sigma_X^2} = \sqrt{\mathrm{E}(X - \mathrm{E}(X))^2}$ being the standard deviation

Statistical Modeling using Local Gaussian Approximation
https://doi.org/10.1016/B978-0-12-815861-6.00010-9

for X, and similarly for σ_Y. It takes values between and including -1 and $+1$. For a given set of pairs of observations $(X_1, Y_1), \ldots, (X_n, Y_n)$ of X and Y, an estimate of ρ is

$$r = \hat{\rho} = \frac{\sum_{j=1}^{n} \left(X_j - \overline{X}\right)\left(Y_j - \overline{Y}\right)}{\sqrt{\sum_{j=1}^{n} \left(X_j - \overline{X}\right)^2}\sqrt{\sum_{j=1}^{n} \left(Y_j - \overline{Y}\right)^2}} \tag{3.1}$$

with $\overline{X} = \frac{1}{n}\sum_{j=1}^{n} X_j$, and similarly for $\overline{Y}$. The consistency and asymptotic normality of estimate (3.1) can be proved using a law of large numbers and a central limit argument.

On a historic note, we may remark that Pearson's ρ, the product moment correlation, was not invented by Pearson, but rather by Francis Galton. Galton, a cousin of Charles Darwin, needed a measure of association in his hereditary studies; see Galton (1888, 1890). This was formulated in a scatter diagram and regression context, and he chose the letter r (for regression) as the symbol for his measure of association. Pearson (1896) gave a more precise mathematical development and used ρ as a symbol for the population value and r for its estimated value. The product moment correlation is now universally referred to as Pearson's ρ. Galton died in 1911, and Karl Pearson became his biographer, resulting in a massive 4-volume biography; see Pearson (1922, 1930). All this and much more is detailed by Stigler (1989) and Stanton (2001). Some other relevant historical references are Fisher (1915, 1921), von Neumann (1941, 1942), and the survey paper by King (1987).

The correlation coefficient ρ has been, and probably still is, the most used measure for statistical association, and it is generally accepted as *the* measure of dependence, not only in statistics, but in most applications of statistics to the natural and social sciences. There are several reasons for this.

(i) It is easy to compute (estimate).

(ii) Linear models are much used, and in a linear regression model of Y on X, say, ρ is proportional to the slope of the regression line. This also means that ρ and its estimate $\widehat{\rho}$ appear naturally in a linear least squares analysis.

(iii) In the bivariate Gaussian density

$$f(x, y) = \frac{1}{2\pi\sqrt{1-\rho^2}\sigma_X\sigma_Y} \times \exp\left\{-\frac{1}{2(1-\rho^2)}\left(\frac{(x-\mu_X)^2}{\sigma_X^2} - 2\rho\frac{(x-\mu_X)(y-\mu_Y)}{\sigma_X\sigma_Y} + \frac{(y-\mu_Y)^2}{\sigma_Y^2}\right)\right\},$$

the dependence between X and Y is completely characterized by ρ. In particular, two jointly Gaussian variables (X, Y) are independent if and only if they are uncorrelated (see, e.g., Billingsley (2008, pp. 384–385) for a formal proof of this statement). For a considerable number of data sets, the Gaussian distribution works at least as a fairly good approximation. Moreover, joint asymptotic normality often appears as a consequence of the central limit theorem for many statistics, and the joint asymptotic behavior of such statistics is therefore generally well defined by the correlation coefficient.

(iv) The product moment correlation is easily generalized to the multivariate case. For p stochastic variables $X_1, \ldots, X_p$, their joint dependencies can simply (but not always accurately) be characterized by their covariance matrix $\mathbf{\Sigma} = \{\sigma_{ij}\}$ with σ_{ij} being the covariance between X_i and X_j. Similarly, the correlation matrix is defined by $\mathbf{\Lambda} = \{\rho_{ij}\}$ with ρ_{ij} being the correlation between X_i and X_j. Again, for a column vector $\boldsymbol{x} = (x_1, \ldots, x_p)^T$, the joint normality density is defined by

$$f(\boldsymbol{x}) = \frac{1}{(2\pi)^{p/2}|\mathbf{\Sigma}|^{1/2}} \exp\left\{-\frac{1}{2}(\boldsymbol{x}-\boldsymbol{\mu})^T \mathbf{\Sigma}^{-1}(\boldsymbol{x}-\boldsymbol{\mu})\right\},$$

where $|\mathbf{\Sigma}|$ is the determinant of the covariance matrix $\mathbf{\Sigma}$ (whose inverse $\mathbf{\Sigma}^{-1}$ is assumed to exist), and $\boldsymbol{\mu} = \mathrm{E}(\boldsymbol{X})$. Then the complete dependence structure of the Gaussian vector is given by the *pairwise* covariances σ_{ij} or, equivalently, the *pairwise* correlations ρ_{ij}. This is remarkable: the entire dependence structure is determined by pairwise dependencies. We will make good use of this fact later when we get to the local Gaussian dependence measure in Chapter 4 and subsequently in later chapters.

(v) It is easy to extend the correlation concept to time series. For a time series $\{X_t\}$, the autocovariance and autocorrelation functions, respectively, are defined assuming the stationarity and existence of second moments by $c(t) = \sigma(X_{t+s}, X_s)$ and $\rho(t) = \rho(X_{t+s}, X_s)$ for arbitrary integers s and t. For a Gaussian time series, the dependence structure is completely determined by $\rho(t)$. For linear (say ARMA) type series, the analysis, as a rule, is based on the autocovariance function, even though the entire joint probability structure cannot be captured by this in the non-Gaussian case. Even for nonlinear time series and nonlinear regression models, the autocovariance function has often been made to play a major role. In the frequency domain, all the traditional spectral analysis is based again on the autocovariance function. Similar considerations have been made in spatial models such as in linear Kriging models; see Stein (1999).

In spite of these assets, there are several serious weaknesses of Pearson's ρ. These will be briefly reviewed in Section 3.2. In the remaining sections of this chapter a number of alternative dependence measures going beyond the Pearson's ρ will be described.

3.2 Weaknesses of Pearson's ρ

We have subsumed, somewhat arbitrarily, the problems of ρ under three issues described in the following three subsections. The local Gaussian correlation introduced in Chapter 4 is a local version of the Pearson's ρ, where we try to retain the positive features mentioned above and, at the same time, attempt to avoid the weaknesses mentioned below.

3.2.1 The non-Gaussianity issue

A relevant question to ask is whether the close connection between Gaussianity and correlation/covariance properties can be extended to larger classes of distributions. The family of distributions being the most natural extension of the Gaussian family is probably the family of elliptical distributions, already briefly discussed in Chapter 2.2.2. At first glance the defining expression (2.5) of the elliptical class in Chapter 2.2.2 appears to be close to the Gaussian with the location parameter $\boldsymbol{\mu}$ and scale parameter $\boldsymbol{\Sigma}$. However, these parameters cannot be identified with the mean $\mathrm{E}(\boldsymbol{X})$ and covariance matrix $\mathrm{Cov}(\boldsymbol{X})$ in general. In fact, the parameters $\boldsymbol{\mu}$ and $\boldsymbol{\Sigma}$ in that expression may remain meaningful even if the mean and covariance matrix do not exist. If they do exist, then $\boldsymbol{\mu}$ can be identified with the mean and $\boldsymbol{\Sigma}$ is proportional to the covariance matrix, the proportionality factor generally depending on the dimension p.

A number of additional properties of elliptical distributions, among other things, pertaining to linear transformations, marginal distributions, and conditional distributions are surveyed by Gómez et al. (2003) and Landsman and Valdez (2003). Many of these properties are analogous to those of the multivariate normal distribution, which is an elliptical distribution; see Chapter 2.2.2.

Unfortunately, the equivalence between uncorrelatedness and independence is generally not true for elliptical distributions. Consider, for instance, the multivariate t-distribution with ν degrees of freedom

$$f(\boldsymbol{x}) = \frac{\Gamma(\frac{p+\nu}{2})}{(\pi\nu)^{p/2}\Gamma(\nu/2)|\boldsymbol{\Sigma}|^{1/2}}\left(1+\frac{(\boldsymbol{x}-\boldsymbol{\mu})^T\boldsymbol{\Sigma}^{-1}(\boldsymbol{x}-\boldsymbol{\mu})}{\nu}\right)^{-\frac{p+\nu}{2}}. \tag{3.2}$$

Unlike the multinormal distribution, where the exponential form of the distribution forces the distribution to factor if $\boldsymbol{\Sigma}$ is a diagonal matrix (uncorrelatedness), this is not true for the t-distribution defined in Eq. (3.2) if $\boldsymbol{\Sigma}$ is diagonal. In other words, if two components of a bivariate t-distribution are uncorrelated, then they are not necessarily independent. This pinpoints a serious deficiency of the Pearson's ρ in measuring dependence in t-distributions and indeed in general elliptical distributions.

3.2.2 The robustness issue

As is the case for regression, it is well known that the product moment estimator is sensitive to outliers. Even just one single outlier may be very damaging. There are therefore several robustified versions of ρ, primarily based on ranks. The idea of rank correlation goes back at least to Spearman (1904), and it is most easily explained through its sample version. Given scalar observations $\{X_1, \ldots, X_n\}$, we denote by $R_{i,X}^{(n)}$ the rank of X_i among $X_1, \ldots, X_n$. (There are various rules for treating ties). The estimated Spearman rank correlation function given n pairwise observations of two random variables X and Y is given by

$$\widehat{\rho}_S = \frac{n^{-1}\sum_{i=1}^n R_{i,X}^{(n)}R_{i,Y}^{(n)} - (n+1)^2/4}{(n^2-1)/12}.$$

If X and Y have continuous cumulative distribution functions F_X and F_Y, and joint distribution function $F_{X,Y}$, then the population value of Spearman's ρ_S is given by

$$\rho_S = 12\int F_X(x)F_Y(y)\,\mathrm{d}F_{X,Y}(x,y) - 3 = \rho(F_X(X), F_Y(Y)), \tag{3.3}$$

and hence it is the Pearson correlation between the two uniform variables $F_X(X)$ and $F_Y(Y)$. The rank correlation is thought to be especially effective in picking up linear trends in the data, but it suffers in a very similar way as Pearson's ρ to certain nonlinearities of the data, which are treated in the next subsection. Spearman's ρ may be modified to a rank autocorrelation measure for time series in the obvious way; see Knoke (1977), Bartels (1982), Hallin and Mélard (1988), and Ferguson et al. (2000).

Another way of using the ranks is the Kendall τ rank correlation coefficient given by Kendall (1938). Again, consider the situation of n pairs (X_i, Y_i) of the random variables X and Y. Two pairs of observations (X_i, Y_i) and (X_j, Y_j), $i \neq j$, are said to be concordant if the ranks for both elements agree; that is, if both $X_i > X_j$ and $Y_i > Y_j$ or if both $X_i < X_j$ and $Y_i < Y_j$. Similarly, they are said to be discordant if $X_i > X_j$ and $Y_i < Y_j$ or if $X_i < X_j$ and $Y_i > Y_j$. If one has equality, they are neither concordant nor discordant, even though there are various rules for treating ties in this case as well. Then the estimated Kendall τ is given by

$$\widehat{\tau} = \frac{(\text{number of concordant pairs}) - (\text{number of discordant pairs})}{n(n-1)/2}.$$

The population value can be shown to be

$$\tau = 4 \int F_{X,Y}(x, y)\, \mathrm{d}F_{X,Y}(x, y) - 1. \tag{3.4}$$

Both ρ_s and τ are expressible in terms of the copula (see Section 3.3) associated with $F_{X,Y}$. It is then perhaps not surprising that both ρ_s and τ are bivariate measures of monotone dependence. This means that (i) they are invariant with respect to strictly increasing (decreasing) transformations of both variables, and (ii) they are equal to 1 (or -1) if one of the variables is an increasing (or decreasing) transformation of the other one. Property (i) does not hold for Pearson's ρ, and ρ is not directly expressible in terms of the copula of $F_{X,Y}$ either. The invariance property (i) is also shared by the van der Waerden (1952) correlation based on normal scores. Some will argue that this invariance property make them more desirable as dependence measures in case X and Y are non-Gaussian.

The asymptotic normality of Spearman's ρ_S and Kendall's τ was established early. Some of the theory is reviewed by Kendall (1970), and these results can be viewed as particular cases of much more general results obtained by Ferguson et al. (2000). For some details in the time series case, we refer to Tjøstheim (1996). A more recent account from the copula point of view is given by Genest and Rémillard (2004).

3.2.3 The nonlinearity issue

This is probably the most serious issue with Pearson's ρ, and it is an issue also for the rank-based correlations of Spearman and Kendall. All these (and similar measures) are designed to detect rather specific types of statistical dependencies, namely those for which large values of X tend to be associated with large values of Y and small values of X with small values of Y (positive dependence), or the opposite case of negative dependence in which large values of one variable tend to be associated with small values of the other variable. It is easy to find examples where this is not the case, but where nevertheless there is strong dependence. A standard introductory text book example is the case where

$$Y = X^2. \tag{3.5}$$

Here, Y is uniquely determined once X is given, that is, basically the strongest form of dependence one can have. However, if $\mathrm{E}(X) = \mathrm{E}(X^3) = 0$, then it is trivial to show that $\rho(X, Y) = 0$ and, moreover, that ρ_s and τ will also fail.

The same problem occurs if $X = UW$ and $Y = VW$, where U and V are independent of each other and independent of W. It is trivial to show that $\rho(X, Y) = 0$ if $\mathrm{E}(U) = \mathrm{E}(V) = 0$, whereas X and Y are clearly dependent. This example typifies the kind of dependence we have in ARCH/GARCH time series models: If $\{\varepsilon_t\}$ is a time series of zero-mean iid variables, the time series $\{h_t\}$ is independent of $\{\varepsilon_t\}$, and $\{X_t\}$ and $\{h_t\}$ are given by the recursive relationship

$$X_t = \varepsilon_t h_t^{1/2}, \qquad h_t = \alpha + \beta h_{t-1} + \gamma X_{t-1}^2, \tag{3.6}$$

where the stochastic process $\{h_t\}$ is the so-called volatility process, then the resulting model is a GARCH(1,1) model; see also Chapter 2.4. Further, $\alpha > 0$, $\beta \geq 0$, and $\gamma \geq 0$ are constants satisfying $\beta + \gamma < 1$. This model can be extended in many ways, and the ARCH/GARCH models are extremely important in finance. The work on these models was initiated by Engle (1982), and he was awarded the Nobel Memorial Prize in Economics for his work. The point as far as Pearson's ρ is concerned, is that X_t and X_s are uncorrelated for $t \neq s$, but they are in fact strongly dependent through the volatility process $\{h_t\}$, which can be taken to measure financial risk. This is probably the best known and most important model class where the dependence structure of the process is not at all revealed by the autocorrelation function. The variables are uncorrelated but contain a dependence structure that is very important from an economic point of view.

The nonlinearity issue will be analyzed extensively and quite systematically in the following sections, but there have also been various more ad hoc solutions to this problem. Here we just briefly mention two of them. Slightly more details are given in the early survey paper by Tjøstheim (1996) and the references therein.

(a) Higher moments: An "obvious" ad hoc solution in the nonlinear GARCH case is to compute the product moment correlation on squares $\{X_t^2\}$ instead of $\{X_t\}$ themselves. It is easily seen that the squares are autocorrelated. This is the idea behind the McLeod and Li (1983) test of independence. It requires the existence of fourth moments, though, which will not always be fulfilled for models of financial time series that typically have heavy tails; see, for example, Teräsvirta et al. (2010, Chapter 8).

(b) Frequency-based tests: These are also based on higher product moments, but in this instance one takes the Fourier transform of these to obtain the so-called bi-spectrum and tri-spectrum, on which in turn independence tests can be based (Subba Rao and Gabr, 1980; Hinich, 1982).

In the next sections, we will look at ways of detecting nonlinear and non-Gaussian structures by going beyond Pearson's ρ.

3.3 The copula

For two variables, we may ask why not just take the joint density function $f(x, y)$ or the cumulative distribution function $F(x, y)$ as a descriptor of the joint dependence? The answer is quite obvious. If a parametric density model is considered, then it is usually quite difficult to give an interpretation of the parameters in terms of the strength of dependence. An exception is the multivariate normal distribution of course, but even for elliptical distributions, the "correlation" parameter ρ is not, as we have seen, necessarily a good measure of dependence. If we look at nonparametric estimates for multivariate density functions, then to a certain degree we may get an informal indication of strength of dependence in certain regions from a display of the density, but the problems increase quickly with dimension due both to difficulties of producing a graphical display and to the lack of precision of the estimates due to the curse of dimensionality.

Another problem in analyzing a joint density function is that it may be difficult to disentangle effects due to the shape of marginal distributions and effects due to dependence among the variables involved. This last problem is resolved by the copula construction. Sklar's (1959) theorem states that a multivariate cumulative distribution function $F(\mathbf{x}) = F(x_1, \ldots, x_p)$ with marginals $F_i(x_i)$, $i = 1, \ldots, p$, can be decomposed as

$$F(x_1, \ldots, x_p) = C(F_1(x_1), \ldots, F_p(x_p)), \tag{3.7}$$

where $C(u_1, \ldots u_p)$ is a distribution function over the unit cube $[0, 1]^p$. Klaassen and Wellner (1997) point out that Hoeffding (1940) had the basic idea of summarizing the dependence properties of a multivariate distribution by its associated copula, but he chose to define the corresponding function on the interval $[-1/2, 1/2]$ instead of on the interval $[0, 1]$. In the continuous case, C is a function of uniform variables $U_1, \ldots, U_p$ by the well-known fact that for a continuous random variable X_i, $F_i(X_i)$ is uniform on $[0, 1]$. Further, in the continuous case, C is uniquely determined by Sklar's (1959) theorem.

The theorem continues to hold for discrete variables under certain weak regularity conditions securing uniqueness. We refer to Nelsen (1999) and Joe (2014) for extensive treatments of the copula, the latter of which, in particular, contains a large section on copulas in the discrete case. See also Genest and Nešlehová (2007). For simplicity and in keeping with the assumptions in the rest of this book, we will mostly limit ourselves to the continuous case from now on in this section.

Decomposition (3.7) very effectively disentangles the distributional properties of a multivariate distribution into a dependence part measured by the copula C and a marginal part described by the univariate marginals. Note that C is invariant with respect to one-to-one transformations of the marginal variables X_i. In this respect, it is analogous to the invariance of the Kendall and Spearman rank-based correlation coefficients.

A representation in terms of uniform variables can be said to be in accord with a statistical principle that complicated models should preferably be represented in terms of the most simple variables possible, in this case, uniform random variables. A possible disadvantage of the multivariate uniform distribution is that tail behavior of distributions may be difficult to discern on the uniform scale, as it may result in a singular-type behavior in the corners of the uniform distribution with accumulations of observations there in a scatter diagram on $[0, 1]^2$ or $[0, 1]^p$. It is therefore sometimes an advantage to change the scale to a standard normal scale, where the uniform scores U_i are replaced by standard normal scores $\Phi^{-1}(U_i)$ with Φ being the cumulative distribution of the standard normal distribution. This leads to a more clear representation of tail properties. This scale is sometimes used in copula theory (see, e.g., Joe, 2014), and we have used it systematically in our work on local Gaussian approximation in this book. We refer to Chapter 4 for some more basic facts of this representation.

Decomposition (3.7) is very useful in that it leads to large classes of models that can be specified by defining the marginals and the copula function separately. It has great flexibility in that very different models can be chosen for the marginal distribution, and there is a large catalog of possible parametric models available for the copula function C; it can also be estimated nonparametrically. The simplest one is the Gaussian copula. It is constructed from a multivariate Gaussian distribution $\Phi_{\boldsymbol{\Sigma}}$ with correlation matrix $\boldsymbol{\Sigma}$ and is defined by

$$C_{\boldsymbol{\Sigma}}(\boldsymbol{u}) = \Phi_{\boldsymbol{\Sigma}}\left(\Phi^{-1}(u_1), \ldots, \Phi^{-1}(u_p)\right) \tag{3.8}$$

such that $Z_i = \Phi^{-1}(U_i)$ are standard normal variables for $i = 1, \ldots, p$. It should be carefully noted that if we use (3.8) in model building, then we can still put in a marginal cumulative distribution functions of our own choice, resulting in a joint distribution that is not Gaussian. A multivariate Gaussian distribution with correlation matrix $\boldsymbol{\Sigma}$ is obtained if the marginals are univariate Gaussians. If the marginals are not Gaussians, then the correlation matrix in the distribution obtained by (3.7) will not in general be $\boldsymbol{\Sigma}$. Klaassen and Wellner (1997) present an interesting optimality property of the normal scores rank correlation coefficient, the van der Waerden correlation, as an estimate of $\boldsymbol{\Sigma}$.

A similar construction taking as its departure the multivariate t-distribution can be used to obtain a t-copula.

A general family of copulas is the family of Archimedean copulas. It is useful because it can be defined in an arbitrary dimension p with only one parameter θ belonging to some parameter space Θ. A copula C is called Archimedean if it has the representation

$$C(\boldsymbol{u}, \theta) = \psi^{[-1]}(\psi(u_1, \theta) + \cdots + \psi(u_p, \theta); \theta), \tag{3.9}$$

where $\psi : [0, 1] \times \Theta \to [0, \infty)$ is a continuous strictly decreasing convex function such that $\psi(1, \theta) = 0$. Moreover, θ is a parameter within some parameter space Θ. The function ψ is called the generator function, and $\psi^{[-1]}$ is the pseudo-inverse of ψ. We refer to Joe (2014) and Nelsen (1999) for more detail and further regularity conditions. Copulas have in practice been used mostly in the bivariate situation, in which case there are many particular cases of the Archimedean copula (3.9), such as the Clayton, Gumbel, and Frank copulas. In particular, the Clayton copula is important in economics and finance. It is defined by

$$C_C(u_1, u_2) = \max\{u_1^{-\theta} + u_2^{-\theta} - 1; 0\}^{-1/\theta} \quad \text{with} \quad \theta \in [-1, \infty) \setminus 0. \tag{3.10}$$

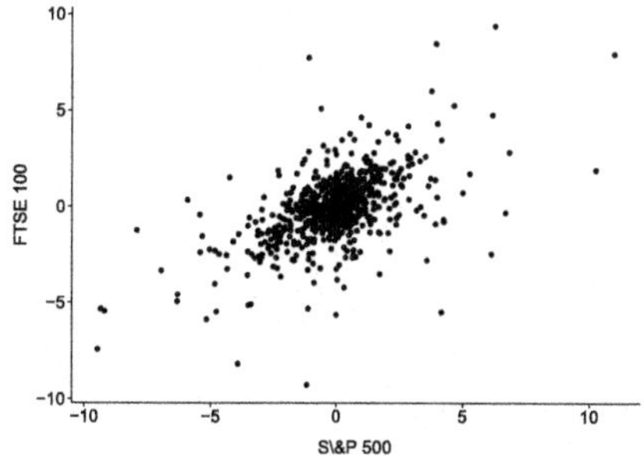

(a) The observed log-returns of the daily data

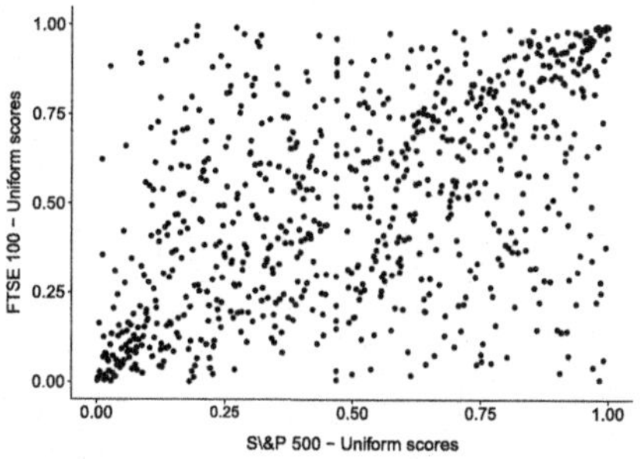

(b) Uniform scores of the financial returns data set

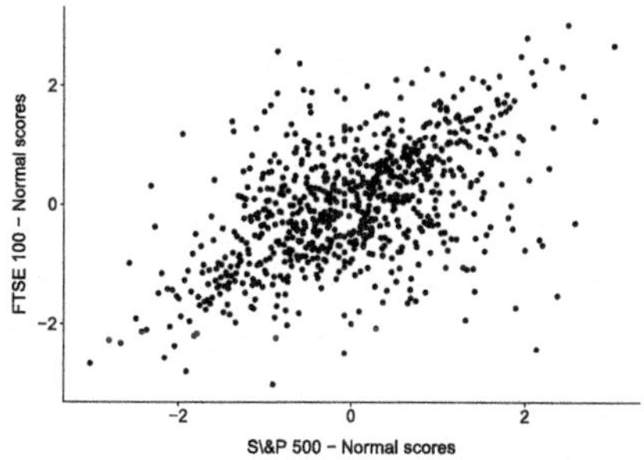

(c) Normal scores of the financial returns data set

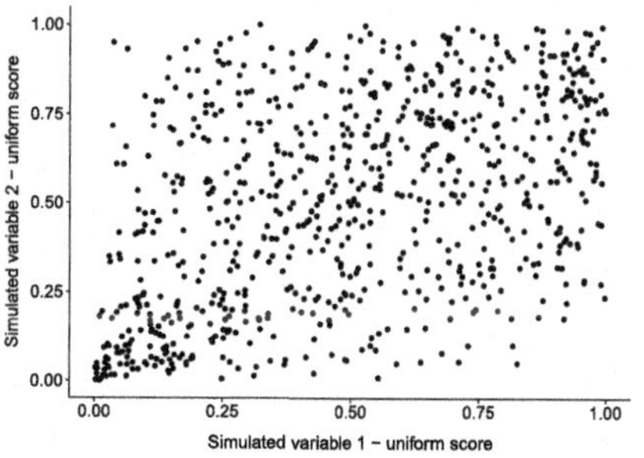

(d) Simulated data from a Clayton copula fitted to the financial returns data set

Figure 3.1 Illustrations using the financial returns data set.

We will throughout this book illustrate several points using a bivariate data set on some financial returns. We use daily international equity price index data for the United States (i.e., S&P 500) and the United Kingdom (i.e., FTSE 100). The data are obtained from Datastream (2018), and the returns are defined as

$$r_t = 100 \times \left(\log(p_t) - \log(p_{t-1})\right),$$

where p_t is the price index at time t. The observation span covers the period from January 1, 2007, through December 31, 2009, in total 784 observations.

In Fig. 3.1, four scatterplots are presented. Fig. 3.1a displays a scatterplot of the observed log-returns, with S&P 500 on the horizontal axis and FTSE 100 on the vertical axis. Fig. 3.1b displays the uniform scores of the same data, that is, $(\widehat{U}_{1i}, \widehat{U}_{2i}) = (\widehat{F}_1(X_{1i}), \widehat{F}_2(X_{2i}))$, where $\widehat{F}_1$ and $\widehat{F}_2$ are the empirical distribution functions of X_1: S&P500 and X_2: FTSE100, and we see indications of a singular behavior of the copula density in the lower left and upper right corners of the unit square. In Fig. 3.1c the observations have been transformed to normal scores, which more clearly reveals the tail properties of the underlying distribution. Finally, Fig. 3.1d shows the scatter plot of 784 simulated pairs of variables, on uniform scale, from a Clayton copula fitted to the return data. This plot partially resembles Fig. 3.1b, in particular, in the lower left corner. However, there are some differences in the upper right corner. We will look at this discrepancy in Chapter 5.

In Fig. 3.1a, and perhaps more clearly in Fig. 3.1c, we see that there seems to be stronger dependence between the variables when the market is going either up or down, which is very sensible from an economic point of view, but it is not easy to give an interpretation of the parameter θ of the Clayton copula in terms of such type of dependence. In fact, in this particular case, $\widehat{\theta} = 0.96$. The difficulty of giving a clear and concrete interpretation of copula parameters in terms of measuring strength of dependence can be stated as a potential issue of the copula representation. In this respect, it is very different from Pearson's ρ. We will return to this point in Chapter 4, where we define a local correlation, and in Chapter 5, where the local correlation is applied to copula examples.

Another issue of the original copula approach has been the lack of good practical models as the dimension increases, as it would for example in a portfolio problem in finance. This has recently been addressed by the so-called pair copula construction. For example, a trivariate density $f(x_1, x_2, x_3)$ can, by conditioning, be written as $f(x_1, x_2, x_3) = f_1(x_1)f_{23|1}(x_2, x_3|x_1)$, and a bivariate copula construction, for example, a Clayton copula, can be applied to the conditional density $f_{23|1}(x_2, x_3|x_1)$ with x_1 fixed. Then this conditioning can be extended to higher dimensions under a few simplifying assumptions, resulting in a so-called vine pair copula, of which there are several types. The procedure is well described by Aas et al. (2009) and has found a number of applications. The Clayton canonical vine copula, for instance, allows for the occurrence of very strongly correlated downside events and has been successfully applied in portfolio choice and risk management operations. The model is able to reduce the effects of extreme downside correlations and produces improved statistical and economical performance compared to elliptical type copulas such as the Gaussian copula (3.8) and the t-copula; see Low et al. (2013).

Other models developed for risk management applications are so-called panic copulas to analyze the effect of panic regimes in the portfolio profit and loss distribution; see, for example, Meucci (2011). A panic reaction is taken to mean that a number of investors react in the same way, such that the statistical dependence becomes very strong between financial returns from various financial objects, in this way rendering the risk spreading of the portfolio illusory. We will return to this situation in Chapters 5 and 6, where among other things we can show that in a panic situation the local correlation increases and may approach one. The copula has also been used directly for independence testing; see, for example, Genest and Rémillard (2004) and Mangold (2017).

Most of the copula theory and also most of the applications are to vector variables, which are assumed to be iid, but there is also a growing literature on stochastic processes such as Markov chains. The existence of both auto-dependence and cross-dependence in a multivariate stochastic process is quite challenging. Some of the mathematical difficulties in the Markov chain case is clearly displayed by Darsow et al. (1992). They used the ordinary copula, but it is not obvious how the theory of Markov processes can be assisted by the concept of a copula. That work was limited to a first-order Markov chain. The pair copula has also been introduced in a Markov theory framework and then in higher-order Markov processes by Ibragimov (2009). Again, so far, the impact on Markov theory has not been overwhelming. This may partly be due to complicated technical conditions.

Two other papers using copulas (and pair copulas) in serial dependence are Beare (2010) and Smith et al. (2010). In the context of parametric time series analysis, especially for multivariate time series, it has been easier to implement the copula concept as developed for iid variables. This is well documented by Patton (2012). Modeling both cross- and auto-dependence, including use of vine copulas, in a multivariate time series or Markov process setting is done by Smith (2015). Time-dependent risk is treated using a dynamic copula model by Oh and Patton (2018).

3.4 Global dependence functionals and tests of independence

Studies of statistical dependence may be said to center mainly around two problems: (i) definition and estimation of measures of dependence and (ii) tests of independence. Of course, these two themes are closely related. Measures of association such as Pearson's ρ can also be used in tests of independence, or more precisely, tests of uncorrelatedness. On the other hand, test functionals for tests of independence can also in many cases, but not all, be used as a measures of dependence. A disadvantage with measures derived from tests is that they are virtually always based on a distance function and therefore non-negative. This means that they cannot distinguish between negative and positive dependence. We will return to this later in this chapter and in Chapter 7.

In this section, we review some basic concepts in the construction of dependence functionals and their use in independence testing. In the next chapter, we will present the local Gaussian correlation (LGC), and then, in Chapter 7, we will develop a theory for dependence functionals based on the LGC. Such dependence functionals can take both positive and negative values, and we will make comparisons with some of the functionals treated in the present chapter.

Most of the test functionals are based on the definition of independence in terms of cumulative distribution functions or density functions. Consider p stochastic variables $X_1, \ldots, X_p$. These variables are independent if and only if their joint cumulative distribution function is the product of the marginal distribution functions: $F_{X_1,\ldots,X_p}(x_1, \ldots, x_p) = F_1(x_1) \cdots F_p(x_p)$; the same is true for all subsets of variables of $(X_1, \ldots, X_p)$. If the variables are continuous, then this identity can be phrased in terms of the corresponding density functions instead. A typical test functional is then designed to measure the distance between the estimated joint distributions/densities and the product of the estimated marginals. This is not so easily done for parametric densities, since the dependence on parameters in the test functional may be very complex, and tests of independence may be more sensibly stated in terms of the parameters themselves, as is certainly the case for the Gaussian distribution. Therefore, in general, we would usually estimate the involved distributions nonparametrically, which, for joint distributions, may be problematic for moderate and large p due to the curse of dimensionality. We will treat these problems in some detail in Chapters 7 and 9–11.

Before starting on the description of the various dependence measures, let us remark that Rényi (1959) proposed that a measure $\delta(X, Y)$ of dependence between two stochastic variables X and Y should ideally have the following seven properties:

(i) $\delta(X, Y)$ is defined for any X, Y neither of which is constant with probability 1.

(ii) $\delta(X, Y) = \delta(Y, X)$.

(iii) $0 \leq \delta(X, Y) \leq 1$.

(iv) $\delta(X, Y) = 0$ if and only if X and Y are independent.

(v) $\delta(X, Y) = 1$ if either $X = g(Y)$ or $Y = f(X)$, where f and g are measurable functions.

(vi) If the Borel-measurable functions f and g map the real axis in a one-to-one way to itself, then $\delta(f(X), g(Y)) = \delta(X, Y)$.

(vii) If the joint distribution of X and Y is normal, then $\delta(X, Y) = |\rho(X, Y)|$, where $\rho(X, Y)$ is Pearson's ρ.

The product moment correlation ρ satisfies only (ii) and (vii).

Some can argue that the rules (i)–(vii) do not take into account the difference between positive and negative dependence; it only looks at the strength of the measured dependence. If this wider point of view were to be taken into account, (iii) could be changed into (iii'): $-1 \le \delta(X, Y) \le 1$, (v) into (v'): $\delta(X, Y) = 1$ or $\delta(X, Y) = -1$ if there is a deterministic relationship between X and Y. Finally, (vii) should be changed into (vii') requiring $\delta(X, Y) = \rho(X, Y)$. Moreover, some will argue that property (vi) may be too strong to require. It means that the strength of dependence is essentially independent of the marginals as for the copula case.

We will discuss these properties as we proceed in this chapter and in more detail for the local Gaussian correlation in Chapter 4. Before we begin surveying the test functionals as announced above, we start with the maximal correlation, which, as we will see, is intertwined with at least one of the test functionals to be presented further; see Section 3.4.4.

3.4.1 Maximal correlation

The maximal correlation is based on Pearson's ρ. It is constructed to avoid the problem demonstrated in Section 3.2.3 that Pearson's ρ can easily be zero even if there is strong dependence.

It seems that the maximal correlation was first introduced by Gebelein (1941). He introduced it as

$$S(X, Y) = \sup_{f,g} \rho(f(X), g(Y)),$$

where ρ is Pearson's ρ. Here the supremum is taken over all Borel-measurable functions f, g with finite and positive variance for $f(X)$ and $g(Y)$. The measure S gets rid of the nonlinearity issue of ρ. It is not difficult to check that $S = 0$ if and only if X and Y are independent, and in fact all seven Rényi's criteria hold for the maximal correlation; see Lancaster (1957) for property (vii). On the other hand, S cannot distinguish between negative and positive dependence, and it is in general difficult to compute.

The maximal correlation $S(X, Y)$ cannot be evaluated explicitly except in particular cases, not the least because there do not always exist functions f_0 and g_0 such that $S(X, Y) = \rho(f_0(X), g_0(Y))$. If this equality holds for some

f_0 and g_0, it is said that the maximal correlation between X and Y is attained. Rényi (1959) gave a characterization of attainability.

Czáki and Fischer (1963) studied mathematical properties of the maximal correlation and computed it for a number of examples. Abrahams and Thomas (1980) considered maximal correlation in the context of stochastic processes. A multivariate version of maximal correlation was proposed by Koyak (1987). In a rather influential paper, at least at the time, Breiman and Friedman (1985) presented the ACE (alternating conditional expectation) algorithm for estimating the optimal functions f and g in the definition of the maximal correlation. They applied it both to correlation and regression. Some curious aspects of the ACE algorithm are highlighted in Hastie and Tibshirani (1990, pp. 84–86).

Two more recent publications are Huang (2010), where the maximal correlation is used to test for conditional independence, and Yenigün et al. (2011), where it is used to test for independence in contingency tables. The latter paper introduces a new example where $S(X, Y)$ can be explicitly computed. See also Yenigün and Rizzo (2014).

3.4.2 Measures and tests based on the distribution function

We start with, and in fact put the main emphasis on, the bivariate case. Let X and Y be stochastic variables with cumulative distribution functions F_X and F_Y. Then the problem of measuring the dependence between X and Y can be formulated as a problem of measuring the distance between the joint cumulative distribution function $F_{X,Y}$ of (X, Y) and the distribution function F_XF_Y formed by taking the product of the marginals. Let $\Delta(\cdot,\cdot)$ be a candidate for such a distance functional. We will assume that Δ is a metric, and it is natural to require (Skaug and Tjøstheim, 1996) that

$$\Delta(F_{X,Y}, F_XF_Y) \geq 0$$

and

$$\Delta(F_{X,Y}, F_XF_Y) = 0 \quad \text{if and only if} \quad F_{X,Y} = F_XF_Y. \tag{3.11}$$

Clearly, such a measure is capable only of measuring the strength of dependence, not its direction.

A natural estimate $\widehat{\Delta}$ of a distance functional Δ is obtained by setting

$$\widehat{\Delta}(F_{X,Y}, F_XF_Y) = \Delta(\widehat{F}_{X,Y}, \widehat{F}_X\widehat{F}_Y),$$

where $\widehat{F}$ may be taken to be the empirical distribution functions given by

$$\widehat{F}_X(x) = \frac{1}{n}\sum_{j=1}^{n} 1(X_j \leq x) \quad \text{and} \quad \widehat{F}_Y(y) = \frac{1}{n}\sum_{j=1}^{n} I(Y_j \leq y),$$

where I is the indicator function, and

$$F_{X,Y}(x, y) = \frac{1}{n}\sum_{j=1}^{n} I(X_j \leq x)I(Y_j \leq y)$$

(or a normalized version with n^{-1} replaced by $(n+1)^{-1}$) for given observations $\{(X_1, Y_1), \ldots, (X_n, Y_n)\}$. Similarly, for a stationary time series $\{X_t\}$ at lag k,

$$\widehat{F}_k(x_1, x_2) \stackrel{\text{def}}{=} \widehat{F}_{X_t, X_{t-k}}(x_1, x_2) = \frac{1}{n-k}\sum_{t=k+1}^{n} I(X_t \leq x_1)I(X_{t-k} \leq x_2).$$

Conventional distance measures between two distribution functions F and G are the Kolmogorov–Smirnov distance

$$\Delta_1(F, G) = \sup_{(x,y)} |F(x, y) - G(x, y)|$$

and the Cramér–von Mises-type distance of a distribution G from a distribution F

$$\Delta_2(F, G) = \int \{F(x, y) - G(x, y)\}^2 \, dF(x, y).$$

Here both Δ_1 and Δ_2 satisfy (3.11).

Most of the work pertaining to measuring dependence and testing independence has been done in terms of the Cramér–von Mises distance. This work started already by Hoeffding (1948), who looked at iid pairs (X_i, Y_i) and studied finite sample distributions in some particular cases. With considerable justification, it has been named the Hoeffding functional by some. This work was continued by Blum et al. (1961), who provided an asymptotic theory, still for the iid case. It was extended to the time series case with a resulting test of serial independence by Skaug and Tjøstheim (1993a). A brief summary of the time series case is given in the supplement of Tjøstheim et al. (2021). The results of Skaug and Tjøstheim (1993a) were very considerably extended and improved by Hong (1998).

Under the hypothesis of $\{X_t\}$ being iid, the bootstrap is a natural tool to use for constructing the null distribution and critical values. For moderate and large k, the bootstrapping yields a substantially better approximation to the level.

Under the alternative hypothesis that X_t and X_{t-k} are dependent, the test statistic of Skaug and Tjøstheim (1993a) and Hong (1998) are in general asymptotically normal, but the power function is complicated; see, for example, Hong (2000).

As mentioned in the beginning of this section, an independence test for $p > 2$ should test the cumulative distribution functions for all subsets of $X_1, \ldots, X_p$. Deheuvels (1981a,b) does exactly that using the Möbius transformation. A recent follow-up is Ghoudi and Rémillard (2018).

Instead of stating independence in terms of cumulative distribution functions, this can alternatively be expressed in terms of the characteristic function. Székely et al. (2007) and Székely and Rizzo (2009), as we will see in Section 3.4.3, make systematic use of this in their introduction of the distance covariance test. Two random variables X and Y are independent if and only if the characteristic functions satisfy

$$\phi_{X,Y}(u,v) = \phi_X(u)\phi_Y(v), \quad \forall (u,v),$$

where

$$\phi_{X,Y}(u,v) = \mathrm{E}\left(e^{iuX+ivY}\right), \quad \phi_X(u) = \mathrm{E}\left(e^{iuX}\right), \quad \phi_Y(v) = \mathrm{E}\left(e^{ivY}\right).$$

This was exploited by Csörgö (1985) and Pinkse (1998) to construct tests for independence based on the characteristic function in the iid and time series case, respectively. Further work on testing of conditional independence was done by Su and White (2007). See also Fan et al. (2017). Hong (1999) put this into a much more general context by focusing on

$$\sigma_k(u,v) = \phi_{X_t, X_{t-|k|}}(u,v) - \phi_{X_t}(u)\phi_{X_{t-|k|}}(v).$$

By taking the Fourier transform of this quantity we obtain

$$f(\omega,u,v) = \frac{1}{2\pi}\sum_{k=-\infty}^{\infty} \sigma_k(u,v)e^{-ik\omega}. \tag{3.12}$$

Hong (1999) called (3.12) the generalized spectral density function. Here $f(\omega,u,v)$ can be estimated by

$$\widehat{f}_n(\omega,u,v) = \frac{1}{2\pi}\sum_{k=-n+1}^{n-1} (1-|k|/n)^{1/2} w(k/b)\widehat{\sigma}_k(u,v)e^{-ik\omega},$$

where w is a kernel weight function, b is a bandwidth or lag order, and

$$\widehat{\sigma}_k(u,v) = \widehat{\phi}_k(u,v) - \widehat{\phi}_k(u,0)\widehat{\phi}_k(0,v)$$

with

$$\widehat{\phi}_k(u,v) = (n-|k|)^{-1} \sum_{t=|k|+1}^{n} e^{i(uX_t+vX_{t-|k|})}.$$

Under the null hypothesis of serial independence, $f(\omega, u, v)$ becomes a constant function of frequency ω:

$$f_0(\omega, u, v) = \frac{1}{2\pi}\sigma_0(u,v)$$

with $\sigma_0(u,v) = \phi(u+v) - \phi(u)\phi(v)$, where $\phi(\cdot) = \phi_{X_t}(\cdot)$. To test for independence, we can compare $\widehat{f_n}(\omega, u, v)$ and $\widehat{f_0}(\omega, u, v)$ using, for example, an L^2-functional. More work related to this has been done by Hong and Lee (2003) and Escanciano and Velasco (2006), and more recently by Escanciano and Hualde (2019).

3.4.3 Distance covariance

We have seen that there are at least two ways of constructing functionals that are consistent against all forms of dependence, namely those based on the empirical distribution function initiated by Hoeffding (1948) and briefly reviewed above, and those based on the characteristic function represented by Csörgö (1985) in the iid case and Pinkse (1998) in the serial dependence case, and treated in Hong (1999, 2000) in a time series spectrum approach. See also Fan et al. (2017). Both Pinkse and Hong use a kernel-type weight function in their functionals. Thus Pinkse uses a weight function g in the functional

$$\int g(u)g(v)|\phi(u,v)|^2 \,du\,dv,$$

where for a pair of two random variables (X, Y),

$$\phi(u,v) = \mathrm{E}\left(e^{i(uX+vY)}\right) - \mathrm{E}\left(e^{iuX}\right)\mathrm{E}\left(e^{ivY}\right).$$

Let $h(x) = \int e^{iux}g(u)\,du$. Pinkse in his simulation experiments chose the weight functions $h(x) = \exp(-\frac{1}{2}x^2)$ and $h(x) = 1/(1+x^2)$.

The authors of two remarkable papers, Székely et al. (2007) and Székely and Rizzo (2009), take up the characteristic function test statistic again in the non-time series case. The difference from earlier papers is an especially judicious choice of weight function reducing the empirical characteristic function functional to empirical moments of differences between the variables, or distances in the vector case, which leads to the covariance of distances. Some of these ideas go back to what the authors term an "energy statistic"; see Székely (2002), Székely and Rizzo (2013), and also Székely and Rizzo (2012). It has been extended to time series and multiple dependencies by Davis et al. (2018), Fokianos and Pitsillou (2017), Zhou (2012), Dueck et al. (2014), Dueck et al. (2015), and Yao et al. (2018). In the locally stationary time series case, there is also a theory; see Jentsch et al. (2020). The distance covariance dcov seems to work well in a number of situations, and it has been used as a yardstick by several authors writing on dependence and tests of independence. In particular, it has been used as a measure of comparison in the work on local Gaussian correlation to be detailed in Chapter 7. There are also points of contacts, as we will see in Section 3.4.4, with the HSIC measure of dependence popular in the machine learning community.

The central ideas and derivations are more or less all present in Székely et al. (2007). The framework is that of pairs of iid vector variables $(\boldsymbol{X}, \boldsymbol{Y})$ in $\mathbb{R}^p$ and $\mathbb{R}^q$, respectively, and the task is to construct a test functional for independence between $\boldsymbol{X}$ and $\boldsymbol{Y}$. Let $\phi_{\mathbf{X},\mathbf{Y}}(\boldsymbol{u}, \boldsymbol{v}) = \mathrm{E}\left(e^{i(\langle \mathbf{X},\boldsymbol{u}\rangle + \langle \boldsymbol{Y},\boldsymbol{v}\rangle)}\right)$, $\phi_{\mathbf{X}}(\boldsymbol{u}) = \mathrm{E}\left(e^{i\langle \mathbf{X},\boldsymbol{u}\rangle}\right)$ and $\phi_{\mathbf{Y}}(\boldsymbol{v}) = \mathrm{E}\left(e^{i\langle \boldsymbol{Y},\boldsymbol{v}\rangle}\right)$ be the characteristic functions involved, where $\langle \cdot, \cdot \rangle$ is the inner product in $\mathbb{R}^p$ and $\mathbb{R}^q$, respectively. The starting point is again the weighted characteristic functional

$$\mathcal{V}^2(\boldsymbol{X}, \boldsymbol{Y}; w) = \int_{\mathbb{R}^{p+q}} |\phi_{\mathbf{X},\mathbf{Y}}(\boldsymbol{u}, \boldsymbol{v}) - \phi_{\mathbf{X}}(\boldsymbol{u})\phi_{\mathbf{Y}}(\boldsymbol{v})|^2 w(\boldsymbol{u}, \boldsymbol{v})\, \mathrm{d}\boldsymbol{u}\, \mathrm{d}\boldsymbol{v}, \tag{3.13}$$

where w is a weight function to be chosen, Note that it is easy to choose w so that $\mathcal{V}^2(\boldsymbol{X}, \boldsymbol{Y}) = 0$ if and only if $\boldsymbol{X}$ and $\boldsymbol{Y}$ are independent. Similarly, we define

$$\mathcal{V}^2(\boldsymbol{X}; w) = \int_{\mathbb{R}^{2p}} |\phi_{\mathbf{X},\mathbf{X}}(\boldsymbol{u}, \boldsymbol{v}) - \phi_{\mathbf{X}}(\boldsymbol{u})\phi_{\mathbf{X}}(\boldsymbol{v})|^2 w(\boldsymbol{u}, \boldsymbol{v})\, \mathrm{d}\boldsymbol{u}\, \mathrm{d}\boldsymbol{v} \tag{3.14}$$

and $\mathcal{V}^2(\boldsymbol{Y}; w)$. Assuming $\mathcal{V}^2(\boldsymbol{X})\mathcal{V}^2(\boldsymbol{Y}) > 0$, the distance correlation dcor is defined by

$$\mathcal{R}^2(\boldsymbol{X}, \boldsymbol{Y}) = \frac{\mathcal{V}^2(\boldsymbol{X}, \boldsymbol{Y})}{\sqrt{\mathcal{V}^2(\boldsymbol{X})\mathcal{V}^2(\boldsymbol{Y})}}.$$

These quantities can be estimated by the empirical counterparts given n observations of the vector pair $(\boldsymbol{X}, \boldsymbol{Y})$ with

$$\mathcal{V}_n^2(\boldsymbol{X}, \boldsymbol{Y}; w) = \int_{\mathbb{R}^{p+q}} |\widehat{\phi}_{\boldsymbol{X},\boldsymbol{Y}}(\boldsymbol{u}, \boldsymbol{v}) - \widehat{\phi}_{\boldsymbol{X}}(\boldsymbol{u})\widehat{\phi}_{\boldsymbol{Y}}(\boldsymbol{v})|^2 w(\boldsymbol{u}, \boldsymbol{v})\, \mathrm{d}\boldsymbol{u}\, \mathrm{d}\boldsymbol{v}, \tag{3.15}$$

where, for a set of observations $\{(\boldsymbol{X}_1, \boldsymbol{Y}_1), \ldots, (\boldsymbol{X}_n, \boldsymbol{Y}_n)\}$, the empirical characteristic functions are given by

$$\widehat{\phi}_{\boldsymbol{X},\boldsymbol{Y}}(\boldsymbol{u}, \boldsymbol{v}) = \frac{1}{n}\sum_{k=1}^{n} \exp\{i(\langle \boldsymbol{X}_k, \boldsymbol{u}\rangle + \langle \boldsymbol{Y}_k, \boldsymbol{v}\rangle)\}$$

and

$$\widehat{\phi}_{\boldsymbol{X}}(\boldsymbol{u}) = \frac{1}{n}\sum_{k=1}^{n} \exp\{i\langle \boldsymbol{X}_k, \boldsymbol{u}\rangle\}, \quad \widehat{\phi}_{\boldsymbol{Y}}(\boldsymbol{v}) = \frac{1}{n}\sum_{k=1}^{n} \exp\{i\langle \boldsymbol{Y}_k, \boldsymbol{v}\rangle\}.$$

It turns out that it is easier to handle the weight function in the framework of the empirical characteristic functions. We will see below that

$$w(\boldsymbol{u}, \boldsymbol{v}) = (c_p c_q |\boldsymbol{u}|_p^{1+p} |\boldsymbol{v}|_q^{1+q})^{-1} \tag{3.16}$$

is a good choice. Here $|\cdot|_p$ is the Euclidean norm in $\mathbb{R}^p$, and similarly for $|\cdot|_q$. Moreover, the normalizing constants are given by $c_j = \pi^{(1+j)/2}/\Gamma((1+j)/2)$, $j = p, q$. For it to make sense to introduce the weight function on the empirical characteristic function, we must show that the empirical functionals $\mathcal{V}_n$ converge to the theoretical functionals $\mathcal{V}$ for this weight function. This is not trivial because of the singularity at 0 for w given by (3.16). A detailed argument is given in the proof of Theorem 2 in Székely et al. (2007).

The advantage of introducing the weight function for the empirical characteristic functions is that we can compute the squares in (3.15) and then interchange summation and integration. The resulting integrals can be computed using trigonometric identities, in particular, the odd symmetry of products of cosines and sines, which makes the corresponding integrals disappear. The details are given in the proof of Theorem 1 in Székely et al. (2007) and in Lemma 1 of the Appendix of Szekely and Rizzo (2005), who in turn refer to Prudnikov et al. (1986) for the fundamental lemma

$$\int_{\mathbb{R}^d} \frac{1 - \cos\langle \boldsymbol{x}, \boldsymbol{u}\rangle}{|\boldsymbol{u}|_d^{d+\alpha}}\, \mathrm{d}\boldsymbol{u} = C(d, \alpha)|\boldsymbol{x}|_d^{\alpha}$$

for $0 < \alpha < 2$ with

$$C(d, \alpha) = \frac{2\pi^{d/2}\Gamma(1-\alpha/2)}{\alpha 2^{\alpha}\Gamma((d+\alpha)/2)}, \tag{3.17}$$

and where the weight function considered above corresponds to $\alpha = 1$ and $d = p$ or $d = q$ in (3.16). The general α-case corresponds to the weight function

$$w(\boldsymbol{u}, \boldsymbol{v}; \alpha) = (C(p, \alpha)C(q, \alpha)|\boldsymbol{u}|_p^{p+\alpha}|\boldsymbol{v}|_q^{q+\alpha})^{-1}.$$

With the simplification $\alpha = 1$, all this implies that $\mathcal{V}_n^2$ defined in (3.15) can be computed as

$$\mathcal{V}_n^2(\boldsymbol{u}, \boldsymbol{v}) = S_1 + S_2 - 2S_3,$$

where

$$S_1 = \frac{1}{n^2}\sum_{k,l=1}^{n} |\boldsymbol{X}_k - \boldsymbol{X}_l|_p |\boldsymbol{Y}_k - \boldsymbol{Y}_l|_q,$$

$$S_2 = \frac{1}{n^2}\sum_{k,l=1}^{n} |\boldsymbol{X}_k - \boldsymbol{X}_l|_p \frac{1}{n^2}\sum_{k,l=1}^{n} |\boldsymbol{Y}_k - \boldsymbol{Y}_l|_q,$$

$$S_3 = \frac{1}{n^3}\sum_{k=1}^{n}\sum_{l,m=1}^{n} |\boldsymbol{X}_k - \boldsymbol{X}_l|_p |\boldsymbol{Y}_k - \boldsymbol{Y}_m|_q, \tag{3.18}$$

which explains the appellation distance covariance. In fact, it is possible to further simplify this by introducing

$$a_{kl} = |\boldsymbol{X}_k - \boldsymbol{X}_l|_p, \quad \overline{a}_{k.} = \frac{1}{n}\sum_{l=1}^{n} a_{kl}, \quad \overline{a}_{.l} = \frac{1}{n}\sum_{k=1}^{n} a_{kl},$$

$$\overline{a}_{..} = \frac{1}{n^2}\sum_{k,l=1}^{n} a_{kl}, \quad A_{kl} = a_{kl} - \overline{a}_{k.} - \overline{a}_{.l} + a_{..}$$

for $k, l = 1, \ldots, n$. Similarly, we can define $b_{kl} = |\boldsymbol{Y}_k - \boldsymbol{Y}_l|_q$, $B_{kl} = b_{kl} - \overline{b}_{k.} - \overline{b}_{.l} + \overline{b}_{..}$,

$$\mathcal{V}_n^2(\boldsymbol{X}, \boldsymbol{Y}) = \frac{1}{n^2}\sum_{k,l=1}^{n} A_{kl}B_{kl},$$

and

$$\mathcal{V}_n^2(\boldsymbol{X}) = \mathcal{V}_n^2(\boldsymbol{X}, \boldsymbol{X}) = \frac{1}{n^2}\sum_{k,l=1}^{n} A_{kl}^2,$$

and similarly for $\mathcal{V}_n^2(\boldsymbol{Y})$. From this we can easily compute $\mathcal{R}_n^2(\boldsymbol{X}, \boldsymbol{Y})$. The computations are available in an R package by Rizzo and Szekely (2018).

As is the case of the empirical joint distribution functional, we can expect that the curse of dimensionality will influence the result for large and moderate values of p and q. Obviously, in the time series case, it is possible to base ourselves on pairwise distances as in (3.13) or (3.15), which has been done by Yao et al. (2018).

Letting $n \to \infty$, it is not difficult to prove that an alternative expression for $\mathcal{V}(\boldsymbol{X}, \boldsymbol{Y})$ is given by (assuming $\mathrm{E}|\boldsymbol{X}|_p < \infty$ and $\mathrm{E}|\boldsymbol{Y}|_q < \infty$)

$$\begin{aligned}\mathcal{V}^2(\boldsymbol{X}, \boldsymbol{Y}) = &\, \mathrm{E}_{\boldsymbol{X},\boldsymbol{X}',\boldsymbol{Y},\boldsymbol{Y}'}\{|\boldsymbol{X}-\boldsymbol{X}'|_p|\boldsymbol{Y}-\boldsymbol{Y}'|_q\}\\ &+ \mathrm{E}_{\boldsymbol{X},\boldsymbol{X}'}\{|\boldsymbol{X}-\boldsymbol{X}'|_p\}\mathrm{E}_{\boldsymbol{Y},\boldsymbol{Y}'}\{|\boldsymbol{Y}-\boldsymbol{Y}'|_q\}\\ &- 2\mathrm{E}_{\boldsymbol{X},\boldsymbol{Y}}\{\mathrm{E}_{\boldsymbol{X}'}|\boldsymbol{X}-\boldsymbol{X}'|_p\mathrm{E}_{\boldsymbol{Y}'}|\boldsymbol{Y}-\boldsymbol{Y}'|_q\},\end{aligned} \tag{3.19}$$

where $(\boldsymbol{X}, \boldsymbol{Y})$ and $(\boldsymbol{X}', \boldsymbol{Y}')$ are iid. This expression will be useful later in Section 3.4.4 in a comparison with the HSIC statistic. Properly scaled $\mathcal{V}_n^2$ has a limiting behavior under independence somewhat similar to that described in Theorem 2 of Skaug and Tjøstheim (1993b). Namely, under the condition of existence of the first moment, $Q_n = n\mathcal{V}_n^2/S_2$ converges in distribution to a quadratic form,

$$Q_n \xrightarrow{d} \sum_{j=1}^{\infty}\lambda_j Z_j^2$$

where $\{Z_j\}$ are independent standard normal variables, and $\{\lambda_j\}$ are non-negative constants that depend on the distribution of $(\boldsymbol{X}, \boldsymbol{Y})$. We can also obtain an empirical process limit theorem, Theorem 5 of Székely et al. (2007). In the R package, as for the case of the empirical distribution function, it has been found advantageous to rely on re-sampling via permutations. This is quite fast since the algebraic formulas (3.18) are especially amenable to permutations. Both Székely et al. (2007) and Székely and Rizzo (2009) in their experiments only treat the case of $\alpha = 1$ in (3.17).

Turning to properties (i)–(vii) of Rényi (1959) listed in the beginning of this section, it is clear that (i)–(iv) are satisfied by $\mathcal{R}$. Moreover, according to Székely et al. (2007), if $\mathcal{R}(\boldsymbol{X}, \boldsymbol{Y}) = 1$, then there exists a vector α, a non-zero real number β, and an orthogonal matrix $\boldsymbol{C}$ such that $\boldsymbol{Y} = \alpha + \beta \boldsymbol{X}\boldsymbol{C}$, which is not quite the same as Rényi's requirement (v). Also, the general invariance in his property (vi) does not hold in general; see also Berrett and Samworth (2019). The final criterion (vii) of Rényi is that the dependent measure should reduce to the absolute value of Pearson's ρ in the bivariate normal case. This is not quite the case for the dcov, but it comes close, as is seen from Theorem 6 of Székely and Rizzo (2009). In fact, if (X, Y) is bivariate normal with $\mathrm{E}(X) = \mathrm{E}(Y) = 0$, $\mathrm{Var}(X) = \mathrm{Var}(Y) = 1$, and correlation ρ, then $\mathcal{R}(X, Y) \leq |\rho|$, and

$$\inf_{\rho \neq 0} \frac{\mathcal{R}(X, Y)}{|\rho|} = \lim_{\rho \to 0} \frac{\mathcal{R}(X, Y)}{|\rho|} = \frac{1}{2(1 + \pi/3 - \sqrt{3})^{1/2}} \approx 0.891.$$

3.4.4 The HSIC measure of dependence

Recall the definition and formula for the maximal correlation. This, as stated in Section 3.4.1, gives rise to a statistic $S(X, Y)$, where $S(X, Y) = 0$ if and only if X and Y are independent. However, it is difficult to compute since it requires the supremum of the correlation $\rho(f(X), g(Y))$ taken over Borel-measurable f and g. In the framework of reproducing kernel Hilbert spaces (RKHS), it is possible to pose this problem or an analogous one, much more general, and we can compute an analogue of S quite easily. This is the so-called HSIC (Hilbert–Schmidt independence criterion).

Reproducing kernel Hilbert spaces are very important tools in mathematics and statistics. A general reference to applications in statistics is Berlinet and Thomas-Agnan (2004). In the last decade or so, there has also been a number of uses of RKHS in dependence modeling. These have often been published in the machine learning literature. See, for example, Gretton et al. (2005b), Gretton and Györfi (2010), Gretton and Györfi (2012), Sejdinovic et al. (2013), and Pfister et al. (2018).

We have found the quite early paper by Gretton et al. (2005a) useful both for a glimpse of the general theory and for the HSIC criterion in particular.

A reproducing kernel Hilbert space is a separable Hilbert space $\mathcal{F}$ of functions f on a set $\mathcal{X}$ such that the evaluation functional $f \to f(x)$ is a continuous linear functional on $\mathcal{F}$ for every $x \in \mathcal{X}$. Then by the Riesz representation theorem (see, e.g., Muscat (2014), Chapter 10) there exists an element $k_x \in \mathcal{F}$ such that $\langle f, k_x \rangle = f(x)$, where $\langle \cdot, \cdot \rangle$ is the inner product in $\mathcal{F}$. Applying this to $f = k_x$ and another point $y \in \mathcal{X}$, we have $\langle k_x, k_y \rangle = k_x(y)$. The function $(x, y) \to k_x(y)$ from $\mathcal{X} \times \mathcal{X}$ to $\mathbb{R}$ is the kernel of the

RKHS $\mathcal{F}$. It is symmetric and positive definite because of the symmetry and positive definiteness of the inner product in $\mathcal{F}$. We use the notation $k(x, y)$ for the kernel.

The next step is to introduce another set $\mathcal{Y}$ with a corresponding RKHS $\mathcal{G}$ and to introduce a probability structure and probability measures p_X, p_Y, and $p_{X,Y}$ on $\mathcal{X}$, $\mathcal{Y}$, and $\mathcal{X} \times \mathcal{Y}$, respectively. With these probability measures and function spaces $\mathcal{F}$ and $\mathcal{G}$, we can introduce the correlation functions of stochastic variables on $\mathcal{X}$, $\mathcal{Y}$, and $\mathcal{X} \times \mathcal{Y}$. This is an analogy of the functions used in the definition of the maximal correlation. In the RKHS setting the covariance (or cross-covariance) is an *operator* on the function space $\mathcal{F}$. Note also that this has a clear analogy in functional statistics; see, for example, Ferraty and Vieu (2006).

It is time to introduce the Hilbert–Schmidt operator: A linear operator $C : \mathcal{G} \to \mathcal{F}$ is called a Hilbert–Schmidt operator if its Hilbert–Schmidt (HS) norm $||C||_{HS}$

$$||C||_{HS}^2 \stackrel{\text{def}}{=} \sum_{i,j} \langle Cv_j, u_i \rangle_{\mathcal{F}}^2 < \infty,$$

where $\{u_i\}$ and $\{v_j\}$ are orthonormal bases of $\mathcal{F}$ and $\mathcal{G}$, respectively. The HS-norm generalizes the Froebenius norm $||\boldsymbol{A}||_F = (\sum_i \sum_j a_{ij}^2)^{1/2}$ for a matrix $\boldsymbol{A} = (a_{ij})$. Finally, we need to define the tensor product in this context: If $f \in \mathcal{F}$ and $g \in \mathcal{G}$, then the tensor product operator $f \otimes g : \mathcal{G} \to \mathcal{F}$ is defined by

$$(f \otimes g)h \stackrel{\text{def}}{=} f \langle g, h \rangle_{\mathcal{G}}, \quad h \in \mathcal{G}.$$

Moreover, by using the definition of the HS norm it is not difficult to show that

$$||f \otimes g||_{HS}^2 = ||f||_{\mathcal{F}}^2 ||g||_{\mathcal{G}}^2.$$

We can now introduce an expectation and a covariance on these function spaces. Again, the analogy with corresponding quantities in functional statistics will be clear. We assume that $(\mathcal{X}, \Gamma)$ and $(\mathcal{Y}, \Lambda)$ are furnished with probability measures p_X and p_Y, and with σ-algebras Γ and Λ of sets on $\mathcal{X}$ and $\mathcal{Y}$. The expectations $\mu_X \in \mathcal{F}$ and $\mu_Y \in \mathcal{G}$ defined by X and Y are stochastic variables in $(\mathcal{X}, \Gamma)$ and $(\mathcal{Y}, \Lambda)$, respectively,

$$\langle \mu_X, f \rangle_{\mathcal{F}} = \mathrm{E}_X(f(X))$$

and

$$\langle \mu_Y, g \rangle_{\mathcal{G}} = \mathrm{E}_Y(g(Y)),$$

where μ_X and μ_Y are well-defined as elements in $\mathcal{F}$ and $\mathcal{G}$ because of the Riesz representation theorem. The norm is obtained by

$$||\mu_X||_{\mathcal{F}}^2 = \mathrm{E}_{X,X'}(k(X, X')),$$

where, as before, X and X' are independent but have the same distribution p_X, and $||\mu_Y||$ is defined in the same way. With given $\phi \in \mathcal{F}$ and $\psi \in \mathcal{G}$, we can now define the cross covariance operator as

$$C_{X,Y} \stackrel{\text{def}}{=} \mathrm{E}_{X,Y}((\phi(X) - \mu_X) \otimes (\psi(Y) - \mu_Y)) = \mathrm{E}_{X,Y}(\phi(X) \otimes \phi(Y)) - \mu_X \otimes \mu_Y.$$

Now take $\phi(X)$ to be identified with $k_X \in \mathcal{F}$ defined above as a result of the Riesz representation theorem, and let $\psi(Y) \in \mathcal{G}$ be defined in exactly the same way. The Hilbert–Schmidt information criterion (HSIC) is then defined as the squared HS norm of the associated cross-covariance operator

$$\mathrm{HSIC}(p_{XY}, \mathcal{F}, \mathcal{G}) \stackrel{\text{def}}{=} ||C_{XY}||_{HS}^2.$$

Let $k(x, x')$ and $l(y, y')$ be kernel functions on $\mathcal{F}$ and $\mathcal{G}$. Then (Gretton et al., 2005a, Lemma 1), the HSIC can be written in terms of these kernels as

$$\begin{aligned} \mathrm{HSIC}(p_{XY}, \mathcal{F}, \mathcal{G}) = {} & E_{X,X',Y,Y'}(k(X, X')l(Y, Y')) \\ & + \mathrm{E}_{X,X'}(k(X, X'))\mathrm{E}_{Y,Y'}(l(Y, Y')) \\ & - 2\mathrm{E}_{X,Y}\Big(\mathrm{E}_{X'}[k(X, X')]\mathrm{E}_{Y'}[l(Y, Y')]\Big). \quad (3.20) \end{aligned}$$

The existence is guaranteed if the kernels are bounded. The similarity in structure to (3.19) for the distance covariance should be noted (partly due to the identity $(a - b)^2 = a^2 + b^2 - 2ab$ but going deeper as we will see below when HSIC is compared to dcov). Note that the kernel functions depend on the way the spaces $\mathcal{F}$ and $\mathcal{G}$ and their inner products are defined. In fact, it follows from a famous result by Moore–Aronszajn (see Aronszajn, 1950) that if k is a symmetric positive definite kernel on a set $\mathcal{X}$, then there is a unique Hilbert space of functions on $\mathcal{X}$ for which k is a reproducing kernel. Hence, as we will see next, in practice, when applying the HSIC criterion, the user has to choose a kernel.

With some restrictions, the HSIC measure is a proper measure of dependence in the sense of Rényi (1959) criterion (iv): From Theorem 4 of Gretton et al. (2005a) we have that if the kernels k and l are universal (universal kernel requires a mild continuity requirement on the kernel) on compact domains $\mathcal{X}$ and $\mathcal{Y}$, then $||C_{XY}||_{HS} = 0$ if and only if X and Y are independent. The compactness assumption results from the application of an equality for bounded random variables taken from Hoeffding (1963), which is actively used in the proof.

A big asset of the HSIC measure it that its empirical version is easily computable. In fact, if we have independent observations $X_1, \ldots, X_n$ and independent observations $Y_1, \ldots, Y_n$, then

$$\widehat{\text{HSIC}}(X, Y, \mathcal{F}, \mathcal{G}) = (n-1)^{-2}\text{tr}\{\boldsymbol{KHLH}\}, \tag{3.21}$$

where tr is the trace operator, and the $n \times n$ matrices $\boldsymbol{H}, \boldsymbol{K}, \boldsymbol{L}$ are defined by

$$\boldsymbol{K} = \{K_{ij}\} = \{k(X_i, X_j)\},\ \ \boldsymbol{L} = \{L_{ij}\} = \{l(Y_i, Y_j)\},\ \ \boldsymbol{H} = \{H_{ij}\} = \{\delta_{ij} - n^{-1}\},$$

where δ_{ij} is the Kronecker delta. It is shown by Gretton et al. (2005a) that this estimator converges toward $||C_{XY}||^2_{HS}$. The convergence rate is $n^{-1/2}$. There is also a limit theorem for the asymptotic distribution, which under the null hypothesis of independence and scaled with n, converges in distribution to the random variable $Q = \sum_{i,j=1}^{\infty} \lambda_i \eta_j N_{ij}^2$, where N_{ij} are independent standard normal variables, and λ_i and η_j are the eigenvalues of integral operators associated with centralized kernels derived from k and l by integrating using the probability measures p_X and p_Y, respectively. Again, this can be compared to the limiting variable for the statistic in the Cramér–von Mises functional as stated in Theorem 2 in Skaug and Tjøstheim (1993b). We can obtain critical values for Q, but, as a rule, but one seems to rely more on resampling as is the case for most independence test functionals.

We see from (3.21) that computation of the empirical HSIC criterion requires the evaluation of $k(X_i, X_j)$ and $l(Y_i, Y_j)$. Then appropriate kernels have to be chosen. Two commonly used kernels are the Gaussian kernel given by

$$k(x, y) = e^{\frac{|x-y|^2}{2\sigma^2}}, \quad \sigma > 0,$$

and the Laplace kernel

$$k(x, y) = e^{\frac{|x-y|}{\sigma}}, \quad \sigma > 0.$$

Pfister and Peters (2017) describe a recent R package involving HSIC. Gretton et al. (2005a) use these kernels in comparing the HSIC test with several other tests, including the dcov test in, among other cases, an independent component setting. Both of these tests do well, and one of these tests does not decisively out-compete the other one. This is perhaps not so unexpected, because there is a strong relationship between these two tests. This is demonstrated by Sejdinovic et al. (2013). They look at both the dcov test and the HSIC test in a generalized setting of semi-metric spaces, that is, with kernels and distances defined on such spaces $\mathcal{X}$ and $\mathcal{Y}$. For a given distance function, they introduce a distance-induced kernel, and under certain regularity conditions, they establish a relationship between these two quantities. There is a related paper by Lyons (2013), who obtains similar results not in an explicit RKHS context, but in fact in a general dcov context.

Let $d_{\mathcal{X}}$ and $d_{\mathcal{Y}}$ be distance measures on the semi-metric spaces $\mathcal{X}$ and $\mathcal{Y}$, respectively. Then a generalized dcov distançe functional can be defined as (cf. again to (3.19))

$$\begin{aligned}\mathcal{V}^2_{d_{\mathcal{X}},d_{\mathcal{Y}}}(X,Y) = \\ &\mathrm{E}_{XY}\mathrm{E}_{X'Y'}d_{\mathcal{X}}(X,X')d_{\mathcal{Y}}(Y,Y') + \mathrm{E}_X\mathrm{E}_{X'}d_{\mathcal{X}}(X,X')\mathrm{E}_Y\mathrm{E}_{Y'}d_{\mathcal{Y}}(Y,Y') \\ &\qquad - 2\mathrm{E}_{XY}\{\mathrm{E}_{X'}d_{\mathcal{X}}(X,X')\mathrm{E}_{Y'}d_{\mathcal{Y}}(Y,Y')\}.\end{aligned}$$

This distance covariance in metric spaces characterizes independence, that is, $\mathcal{V}_{d_{\mathcal{X}},d_{\mathcal{Y}}}(X,Y) = 0$ if and only if X and Y are independent and if the metrics $d_{\mathcal{X}}$ and $d_{\mathcal{Y}}$ satisfy an additional property termed strong "negative type". See Sejdinovic et al. (2013) for more detail. An asset of the RKHS formulation is that it is very general. As was seen from the introduction of HSIC above, the sets $\mathcal{X}$ and $\mathcal{Y}$ can have a metric space structure, probability measures p_X, p_Y, and $p_{X,Y}$ can still be introduced, and the definition of HSIC given in the beginning of this section and the accompanying decomposition (3.20) still make sense in this generalized framework. Then one can show (Theorem 24 in Sejdinovic et al. (2013)) the following equivalence: Let $k_{\mathcal{X}}$ and $k_{\mathcal{Y}}$ be any two kernels on $\mathcal{X}$ and $\mathcal{Y}$ that generate $d_{\mathcal{X}}$ and $d_{\mathcal{Y}}$, respectively, and let $k((x,y),(x',y')) = k_{\mathcal{X}}(x,x')k_{\mathcal{Y}}(y,y')$. Then $\mathcal{V}^2_{d_{\mathcal{X}},d_{\mathcal{Y}}} = 4\mathrm{HSIC}^2(p_{XY},\mathcal{F},\mathcal{G})$. Among the regularity conditions required for this result, there is an assumption of negative type, which is satisfied in standard Euclidean spaces.

Lately there have been other extensions of both the dcov and HSIC to conditional dependence, partial distance and time series. A few references are Szekely and Rizzo (2014), Chwialkowski and Gretton (2014), Zhang et al. (2012), and Pfister et al. (2018). A recent tutorial on RKHS is Gretton (2019).

Further, the generalization of the distance covariance to more than two vectors have independently been shown by Bilodeau and Nangue (2017), building on Bilodeau and de Micheaux (2009), and Böttcher et al. (2019). More specifically, Bilodeau and Nangue (2017) use the Möbius transformation of characteristic functions to characterize independence, and a generalization to p vectors of distance covariance and the Hilbert–Schmidt independence criterion (HSIC) is proposed. The consistency and weak convergence of both types of statistics are established. We also refer to the note on p. 2787 in Böttcher et al. (2019), explaining the relationship between the results from these two papers.

3.4.5 Density-based tests of independence

Intuitively, one may think that knowing that the density exists should lead to increased power of the independence tests due to more information. This is true, at least for some examples (see, e.g., Teräsvirta et al. (2010), Chapter 7.7). As in the preceding sections, we can construct distance functionals between the joint density under dependence and the product density under independence. A number of authors have considered such an approach; both in the iid and time series case; see, for example, Rosenblatt (1975), Robinson (1991), Skaug and Tjøstheim (1993b, 1996), Granger et al. (2004), Hong and White (2005), Su and White (2007), and Berrett and Samworth (2019). For two random variables X and Y having the joint density $f_{X,Y}$ and marginals f_X and f_Y, the degree of dependence can be measured by $\Delta(f_{X,Y}, f_X f_Y)$, where Δ is now the distance measure between two bivariate density functions. The variables are normalized with $\mathrm{E}(X) = \mathrm{E}(Y) = 0$ and $\mathrm{Var}(X) = \mathrm{Var}(Y) = 1$. It is natural to consider the Rényi (1959) requirements again, in particular, requirements (iv) and (vi).

All the distance functionals considered will be of type

$$\Delta = \int B\{f_{X,Y}(x, y), f_X(x), f_Y(y)\} f_{X,Y}(x, y)\, \mathrm{d}x\, \mathrm{d}y, \tag{3.22}$$

where B is a real-valued function such that the integral exists. If B is of the form $B(z_1, z_2, z_3) = D(z_1/z_2 z_3)$, then we have

$$\Delta = \int D\left\{\frac{f_X(x) f_Y(y)}{f_{X,Y}(x, y)}\right\} f_{X,Y}(x, y)\, \mathrm{d}x\, \mathrm{d}y, \tag{3.23}$$

which by the change-of-variable formula for integrals is seen to have Rényi property (vi). Moreover, if $D(w) = 0$ if and only if $w = 1$, then Rényi property (iv) is fulfilled. If $D(1) = 0$ and D is convex, then D is a so-called f-divergence (Csiszár, 1967) measure with $f = D$. Several well-known distance measures for density functions are of this type. For instance, letting $D(w) = 2(1 - w^{1/2})$, we obtain the Hellinger distance

$$H = \int \left\{ \sqrt{f_{X,Y}(x, y)} - \sqrt{f_X(x) f_Y(y)} \right\}^2 \mathrm{d}x\, \mathrm{d}y$$
$$= 2 \int \left\{ 1 - \sqrt{\frac{f_X(x) f_Y(y)}{f_{X,Y}(x, y)}} \right\} f_{X,Y}(x, y)\, \mathrm{d}x\, \mathrm{d}y$$

between $f_{X,Y}$ and $f_X f_Y$. The Hellinger distance is a metric and hence satisfies Rényi property (iv).

The familiar Kullback–Leibler information (entropy) distance is obtained by taking $D(w) = -\ln w$:

$$I = \int \ln \left\{ \frac{f_{X,Y}(x, y)}{f_X(x) f_Y(y)} \right\} f_{X,Y}(x, y)\, \mathrm{d}x\, \mathrm{d}y. \tag{3.24}$$

Since this distance is of type (3.23), it satisfies (vi). A recent paper linking I with other recent approaches to independence testing is by Berrett and Samworth (2019). Taking $D(w) = w^2 - 1$ yields the χ^2-divergence; see also the test-of-fit distance in Bickel and Rosenblatt (1973).

All of the above measures are trivially extended to two arbitrary multivariate densities. However, estimating such densities in high or moderate dimensions may be difficult due to the curse of dimensionality. A functional built up from pairwise dependencies can be considered instead.

For a given functional $\Delta = \Delta(f, g)$ depending on two densities f and g, Δ may be estimated by $\widehat{\Delta} = \Delta(\widehat{f}, \widehat{g})$. There are several ways of estimating the densities, for example, by the kernel density estimator

$$\widehat{f}_X(x) = \frac{1}{n} \sum_{i=1}^{n} K_b(x - X_i)$$

for given scalar observations $\{X_1, \ldots, X_n\}$. Here $K_b(x - X_i) = b^{-1} K\{b^{-1}(x - X_i)\}$, where b is the bandwidth (generally, a matrix in the multivariate case), and K is the kernel function. In the vector case the kernel function is usually taken to be a product of one-dimensional kernels, that is, $K(\boldsymbol{x}) =$

$\prod K_i(x_i)$, where each K_i generally is non-negative and satisfies

$$\int K_i(u)\,du = 1, \quad \int u^2 K_i(u)\,du < \infty.$$

Once estimators for $f_{X,Y}$, f_X, and f_Y in the integral expression (3.22) for Δ have been obtained, the integral can be computed by numerical integration or by empirical averages using the ergodic theorem (or law of large numbers in the iid case). Consequently, for a given lag k in the time series case,

$$\widehat{\Delta}_k = \frac{1}{n-k} \sum_{t=k+1}^{n} B\{\widehat{f}_k(X_t, X_{t-k}), \widehat{f}(X_t), \widehat{f}(X_{t-k})\} w(X_t, X_{t-k}).$$

Here f_k is the joint density of (X_t, X_{t-k}), and w is a weight function, for example, $w(u, v) = I\{|u| \leq c\sigma_X\} I\{|v| \leq c\sigma_X\}$ for some chosen constant c. It should be pointed out that there are often different estimators of $\Delta(f, g)$ that are much easier to calculate and have better theoretical properties. For example, in the case of $\Delta = I$ as in (3.24), we can consider the KSG-estimator; see Kraskov et al. (2004).

Under regularity conditions (see, e.g., Skaug and Tjøstheim, 1996), the consistency and asymptotic normality can be obtained for the estimated test functionals. It should be noted that the leading term in an asymptotic expansion of the standard deviation of $\widehat{\Delta}$ for the estimated Kullback–Leibler functional $\widehat{I}$ and the estimated Hellinger functional $\widehat{H}$ is of order $O(n^{-1/2})$. This is of course the same as for the standard deviation of a parametric estimate in a parametric estimation problem. In that situation the next term of the Edgeworth expansion is of order $O(n^{-1})$, and for moderately large values of n, the first-order term $n^{-1/2}$ will dominate. However, for the functionals considered above, due to the presence of an n-dependent bandwidth, the next terms in the Edgeworth expansion are much closer, being of order $O(n^{-1/2}b)$ and $O(\{nb\}^{-1})$, and since typically $b = O(n^{-1/6})$ or $O(n^{-1/5})$, n must indeed be very large to have the first term dominate in the asymptotic expansion. As a consequence, first-order asymptotics in terms of the normal approximation cannot be expected to work well unless n is exceedingly large. Hence basing a test of independence directly on the asymptotic theory may be hazardous as the real test size will typically deviate substantially from the nominal size. In this sense the situation is quite different from the empirical functionals treated in the previous sections, where there is no bandwidth parameter involved.

All this suggests the use of the bootstrap or permutations as an alternative for constructing the null distribution. We may anticipate that it picks up higher-order terms of the Edgeworth expansion (Hall, 1992, Chapters 3 and 4) although no rigorous analysis confirming this has been carried out for the functionals discussed here.

It is quite difficult to undertake local asymptotic power analysis for the functionals based on estimated density functions. For reasons mentioned above, asymptotic studies can be expected to be unreliable unless n is very large. It has therefore been found more useful to carry out comparative simulation studies against a wide choice of alternatives using a modest sample size; see, for example, Skaug (1993), Skaug and Tjøstheim (1996), and Hong and White (2005). These references also contain applications to real data.

3.5 Test functionals generated by local dependence relationships

If we have bivariate normal data with standard normal marginals and $\rho = 0$, then we get observations scattered in a disc-like region around zero, and most test functionals will easily recognize this as a situation of independence. However, as pointed out by Heller et al. (2013), if data are generated along a circle with radius r, for example, $X^2 + Y^2 = r^2 + \epsilon$ for some stochastic noise variable ϵ, then X and Y are dependent, but as reported by Heller et al. (2013), in practice, the dcov and some other nonlinear global test functionals do not work well. Heller et al. (2013) point a way out of this difficulty, namely, looking at dependence locally (along the circle) and then aggregating the dependence by integrating, or by other means, over the local regions. There are of course several ways of measuring local dependence, and we will approach this problem more fundamentally in Chapter 4.

Another paper in this category, Reshef et al. (2011), is published in Science. The idea behind their MIC (maximal information coefficient) statistic consists in computing the mutual information I as defined in (3.24) *locally* over a grid in the data set and then taking as statistic the maximum value of these local information measures obtained by maximizing over a suitable choice of grid. Some limitations of the method are identified in a later paper by Reshef et al. (2013), and we should also point out that Kinney and Atwal (2014) have found serious problems with the paper. See also Gorfine et al. (2012).

Finally, we should mention the so-called BDS test, named after its originators Brock, Dechert, and Scheinkman (1996). This test has a local flavor at its basis, but the philosophy is a bit different from the other tests presented here. The BDS test attracted much attention among econometricians in the 1990s, and it was improved by Genest et al. (2007).

References

Aas, K., Czado, C., Frigessi, A., Bakken, H., 2009. Pair-copula constructions of multiple dependence. Insurance: Mathematics and Economics 44 (2), 182–198.

Abrahams, J., Thomas, J.B., 1980. Properties of the maximal correlation function. Journal of the Franklin Institute 310 (6), 317–323.

Aronszajn, N., 1950. Theory of reproducing kernels. Transactions of the American Mathematical Society 68 (3), 337–404.

Bartels, R., 1982. The rank version of von Neumann's ratio test for randomness. Journal of the American Statistical Association 77 (377), 40–46.

Beare, B.K., 2010. Copulas and temporal dependence. Econometrica 78 (1), 395–410.

Berlinet, A., Thomas-Agnan, C., 2004. Reproducing Kernel Hilbert Spaces in Probability and Statistics. Springer.

Berrett, T.B., Samworth, R.J., 2019. Nonparametric independence testing via mutual information. Biometrika 106 (3), 547–566.

Bickel, P.J., Rosenblatt, M., 1973. On some global measures of the deviations of density function estimators. Annals of Statistics 1, 1071–1095.

Billingsley, P., 2008. Probability and Measure. John Wiley & Sons.

Bilodeau, M., de Micheaux, P.L., 2009. A-dependence statistics for mutual and serial independence of categorical variables. Journal of Statistical Planning and Inference 139 (7), 2407–2419.

Bilodeau, M., Nangue, A.G., 2017. Tests of mutual or serial independence of random vectors with applications. The Journal of Machine Learning Research 18 (1), 2518–2557.

Blum, J.R., Kiefer, J., Rosenblatt, M., 1961. Distribution free tests of independence based on the sample distribution function. Annals of Mathematical Statistics 32 (2), 485–498.

Böttcher, B., Keller-Ressel, M., Schilling, R.L., et al., 2019. Distance multivariance: new dependence measures for random vectors. Annals of Statistics 47 (5), 2757–2789.

Breiman, L., Friedman, J.H., 1985. Estimating optimal transformations for multiple regression and correlation (with discussion). Journal of the American Statistical Association 80 (391), 580–619.

Chwialkowski, K., Gretton, A., 2014. A kernel independence test for random processes. In: Proceedings of the 31st International Conference on Machine Learning, vol. 32, pp. 1422–1430.

Csiszár, I., 1967. Information-type measures of difference of probability distributions and indirect observation. Studia Scientiarum Mathematicarum Hungarica 2, 229–318.

Csörgö, S., 1985. Testing for independence by the empirical characteristic function. Journal of Multivariate Analysis 16, 290–299.

Czáki, P., Fischer, J., 1963. On the general notion of maximal correlation. Magyar tudományos Akad. Mat. Kutató Intézetenk Közlemenényei (Publ. Math. Inst. Hungar. Acad. Sci. 8, 27–51.

Darsow, W.F., Nguyen, B., Olsen, E.T., 1992. Copulas and Markov processes. Illinois Journal of Mathematics 36 (4), 600–642.

Datastream, 2018.

Davis, R., Matsui, M., Mikosch, T., Wan, P., 2018. Applications of distance correlation to time series. Bernoulli 24 (4A), 3087–3116.

Deheuvels, P., 1981a. An asymptotic decomposition for multivariate distribution-free tests of independence. Journal of Multivariate Analysis 11 (1), 102–113.

Deheuvels, P., 1981b. A Kolmogorov–Smirnov type test for independence and multivariate samples. Revue Roumaine de Mathemátiques Pures et Appliquées 26 (2), 213–226.

Dueck, J., Edelman, D., Gneiting, T., Richards, D., 2014. The affinely invariant distance correlation. Bernoulli 20 (4), 2305–2330.

Dueck, J., Edelman, D., Richards, D., 2015. A generalization of an integral arising in the theory of distance correlation. Statistics and Probability Letters 97, 116–119.

Engle, R.F., 1982. Autoregressive conditional heteroscedasticity with estimates of variance of U.K. inflation. Econometrica 50 (4), 987–1008.

Escanciano, J.C., Hualde, J., 2019. Measuring asset market linkages: nonlinear dependence and tail risk. Journal of Business & Economic Statistics, 1–25.

Escanciano, J.C., Velasco, C., 2006. Generalized spectral tests for the martingale difference hypothesis. Journal of Econometrics 134 (1), 151–185.

Fan, Y., de Micheaux, P.L., Penev, S., Sapolek, D., 2017. Multivariate nonparametric tests of independence. Journal of Multivariate Analysis 153, 189–210.

Ferguson, T.S., Genest, C., Hallin, M., 2000. Kendall's tau for serial dependence. Canadian Journal of Statistics 28 (3), 587–604.

Ferraty, F., Vieu, P., 2006. Nonparametric Functional Data Analysis: Theory and Practice. Springer, New York.

Fisher, R.A., 1915. Frequency distribution of the values of the correlation coefficient in samples of an indefinitely large population. Biometrika 10 (4), 507–521.

Fisher, R.A., 1921. On the probable error of a coefficient of correlation deduced from a small sample. Metron 1, 3–32.

Fokianos, K., Pitsillou, M., 2017. Consistent testing for pairwise dependence in time series. Technometrics 59 (2), 262–270.

Galton, F., 1888. Co-relations and their measurement, chiefly from anthropometric data. Proceedings of the Royal Society, London 45 (273–279), 135–145.

Galton, F., 1890. Kinship and correlation. North American Review 150 (401), 419–431.

Gebelein, H., 1941. Das statistische Problem der Korrelation als Variations- und Eigenwertproblem und sein Zusammenhang mit der Ausgleichsrechnung. ZAMM-Journal of Applied Mathematics and Mechanics/Zeitschrift für Angewandte Mathematik und Mechanik 21 (6), 364–379.

Genest, C., Ghoudi, K., Rémillard, B., 2007. Rank-based extensions of the Brock, Dechert, Scheinkman test. Journal of the American Statistical Association 102 (480), 1363–1376.

Genest, C., Nešlehová, J., 2007. A primer on copulas for count data. ASTIN Bulletin 37 (2), 475–515.

Genest, C., Rémillard, B., 2004. Tests of independence and randomness based on the empirical copula process. TEST 13 (2), 335–369.

Ghoudi, K., Rémillard, B., 2018. Serial independence tests for innovations of conditional mean and variance models. TEST 27 (1), 3–26.

Gómez, E., Gómez-Villegas, M.A., Mari'in, J., 2003. A survey on continuous elliptical vector distributions. Revista Matemática Computense 16, 345–361.

Gorfine, M., Heller, R., Heller, Y., 2012. Comment on "Detecting novel associations in large data sets" by Reshef et al., Science, Dec. 16, 2011.

Granger, C., Maasoumi, E., Racine, J., 2004. A dependence metric for possible nonlinear processes. Journal of Time Series Analysis 25 (5), 649–670.

Gretton, A., 2019. Introduction to RKHS, and some simple kernel algorithms. Unpublished Manuscript.

Gretton, A., Bousquet, O., Smola, A., Schölkopf, B., 2005a. Measuring statistical dependence with Hilbert-Schmidt norms. In: Jain, S., Simon, U., Tomita, E. (Eds.), International Conference on Algorithmic Learning Theory. Springer, Berlin, pp. 63–77.

Gretton, A., Györfi, L., 2010. Consistent nonparametric tests of independence. Journal of Machine Learning Research 11, 1391–1423.

Gretton, A., Györfi, L., 2012. Strongly consistent nonparametric test of conditional independence. Journal of Multivariate Analysis 82 (6), 1145–1150.

Gretton, A., Herbrich, R., Smola, A., Bousquet, O., Schölkopf, B., 2005b. Kernel methods for measuring independence. Journal of Machine Learning Research 6, 2075–2129.

Hall, P., 1992. The Bootstrap and Edgeworth Expansion. Springer, New York.

Hallin, M., Mélard, G., 1988. Rank based tests for randomness against first order serial dependence. Journal of the American Statistical Association 83 (404), 1117–1129.

Hastie, T., Tibshirani, R., 1990. Generalized Additive Models. Chapman and Hall, London.

Heller, R., Heller, Y., Gorfine, M., 2013. A consistent multivariate test of association based on ranks of distances. Biometrika 100 (2), 503–510.

Hinich, M.J., 1982. Testing for Gaussianity and linearity of a stationary time series. Journal of Time Series Analysis 3 (3), 169–176.

Hoeffding, W., 1940. Mass-stabinvariante Korrelationstheorie. Schriften des Mathematischen Seminars und des Instituts für Angewandte Mathematik der Universität Berlin 5 (3), 179–233. Translated in: Fisher, N.I., Sen, P.K. (Eds.), 1994. The Collected Work of Wassily Hoeffding. Springer, New York.

Hoeffding, W., 1948. A nonparametric test of independence. Annals of Mathematical Statistics 19 (4), 546–557.

Hoeffding, W., 1963. Probability inequalities for sums of bounded random variables. Journal of the American Statistical Association 58 (301), 13–30.

Hong, Y., 1998. Testing for pairwise serial independence via the empirical distribution function. Journal of the Royal Statistical Society Series B 60 (2), 429–460.

Hong, Y., 1999. Hypothesis testing in time series via the empirical characteristic function: a generalized spectral density approach. Journal of the American Statistical Association 94 (448), 1201–1220.

Hong, Y., 2000. Generalized spectral tests for serial dependence. Journal of the Royal Statistical Society Series B 62 (3), 557–574.

Hong, Y., Lee, T.-H., 2003. Inference on predictability of foreign exchange rates via generalized spectrum and nonlinear time series models. Review of Economics and Statistics 80 (4), 188–201.

Hong, Y., White, H., 2005. Asymptotic distribution theory for nonparametric entropy measures of serial dependence. Econometrica 73 (3), 837–901.

Huang, T.-M., 2010. Testing conditional independence using maximal nonlinear conditional correlation. Annals of Statistics 38 (4), 2047–2091.

Ibragimov, R., 2009. Copula based characterizations for higher-order Markov processes. Econometric Theory 25 (3), 819–846.

Jentsch, C., Leucht, A., Meyer, M., Beering, C., 2020. Empirical characteristic functions-based estimation and distance correlation for locally stationary processes. Journal of Time Series Analysis 41 (1), 110–133.

Joe, H., 2014. Dependence Modeling with Copulas. Chapman and Hall, London.

Kendall, M.G., 1938. A new measure of rank correlation. Biometrika 30 (1/2), 81–89.

Kendall, M.G., 1970. Rank Correlation Methods, 4th edition. Griffin, London.

King, M.L., 1987. Testing for autocorrelation in linear regression models: a survey. In: King, M., Giles, D. (Eds.), Specification Analysis in the Linear Regression Model. Rutledge and Kegan Paul, London, pp. 19–73.

Kinney, J.B., Atwal, G.S., 2014. Equitability, mutual information, and the maximal information coefficient. Proceedings National Academy of Science USA 111, 3354–3359.

Klaassen, C.A., Wellner, J.A., 1997. Efficient estimation in the bivariate normal copula model: normal margins are least favorable. Bernoulli 3 (1), 55–77.

Knoke, J.D., 1977. Testing for randomness against autocorrelation: alternative tests. Biometrika 64 (3), 523–529.

Koyak, R., 1987. On measuring internal dependence in a set of random variables. Annals of Statistics 15 (3), 1215–1228.

Kraskov, A., Stögbauer, H., Grassberger, P., 2004. Estimating mutual information. Physical Review E 69 (6), 066138.

Lancaster, H.O., 1957. Some properties of the bivariate normal distribution considered in the form of a contingency table. Biometrika 44 (1/2), 289–292.

Landsman, Z.M., Valdez, E.A., 2003. Tail conditional expectations for elliptical distributions. North American Actuarial Journal 7 (4), 55–71.

Low, R.K.Y., Alcock, J., Faff, R., Brailsford, T., 2013. Canonical vine copulas in the context of modern portfolio management: are they worth it? Journal of Banking and Finance 37 (8), 3085–3099.

Lyons, R., 2013. Distance covariance in metric spaces. Annals of Probability 41 (5), 3284–3305.

Mangold, B., 2017. A multivariate rank test of independence based on a multiparametric polynomial copula. Discussion paper.

McLeod, A.I., Li, W.K., 1983. Diagnostic checking ARMA time series models using squared residuals and autocorrelations. Journal of Time Series Analysis 4 (4), 269–273.

Meucci, A., 2011. A new breed of copulas for risk and portfolio management. Risk 24 (9), 122–126.

Muscat, J., 2014. Functional Analysis: An Introduction to Metric Spaces, Hilbert Spaces and Banach Algebras. Springer, New York.

Nelsen, R.B., 1999. An Introduction to Copulas. Springer, New York.

Oh, D.H., Patton, A.J., 2018. Time-varying systemic risk from a dynamic copula model of cds spreads. Journal of Business and Economic Statistics 36 (2), 181–195.

Patton, A.J., 2012. A review of copula models for economic time series. Journal of Multivariate Analysis 110, 4–18.

Pearson, K., 1896. Mathematical contributions to the theory of evolution. III. Regression, heredity and panmixia. Philosophical Transactions of the Royal Society of London 187, 253–318.

Pearson, K., 1922. Francis Galton: A Centenary Appreciation. Cambridge University Press, Cambridge.

Pearson, K., 1930. The Life, Letters and Labors of Francis Galton. Cambridge University Press, Cambridge.

Pfister, N., Bühlmann, P., Schölkopf, B., Peters, J., 2018. Kernel-based tests for joint independence. Journal of the Royal Statistical Society Series B 80 (1), 5–31.

Pfister, N., Peters, J., 2017. dHSIC: Independence Testing via Hilbert Schmidt Independence Criterion. R package version 2.0.

Pinkse, J., 1998. Consistent nonparametric testing for serial independence. Journal of Econometrics 84 (2), 205–231.

Prudnikov, A., Brychkov, A., Marichev, O., 1986. Integrals and Series. Gordon Breach Science Publisher, New York.

Rényi, A., 1959. On measures of dependence. Acta Mathematica Hungarica 10 (3–4), 441–451.

Reshef, D., Reshef, Y., Mitzenmacher, M., Sabeti, P., 2013. Equitability analysis of the maximal information coefficient, with comparisons. arXiv:1301.6314.

Reshef, D.N., Reshef, Y.A., Finucane, H.K., Grossman, S.R., McVean, G., Turnbaugh, P.J., Lander, E.S., Mitzenmacher, M., Sabeti, P.C., 2011. Detecting novel associations in large datasets. Science 334 (6062), 1518–1524.

Rizzo, M.L., Szekely, G.J., 2018. energy: E-Statistics: Multivariate Inference via the Energy of Data. R package version 1.7-4.
Robinson, P.M., 1991. Consistent nonparametric entropy-based testing. Review of Economic Studies 58 (3), 437–453.
Rosenblatt, M., 1975. A quadratic measure of deviation of two-dimensional density estimates and a test of independence. Annals of Statistics 3 (1), 1–14.
Sejdinovic, D., Sriperumbudur, B., Gretton, A., Fukumizu, K., 2013. Equivalence of distance-based and RKHS-based statistics in hypothesis testing. Annals of Statistics 41 (5), 2263–2291.
Skaug, H.J., 1993. The limit distribution of the Hoeffding statistic for tests of serial independence.
Skaug, H.J., Tjøstheim, D., 1993a. A nonparametric test of serial independence based on the empirical distribution function. Biometrika 80 (3), 591–602.
Skaug, H.J., Tjøstheim, D., 1993b. Nonparametric tests for serial independence. In: Rao, T.S. (Ed.), Developments in Time Series Analysis, The Priestley Birthday Volume. Chapman and Hall, London, pp. 207–230.
Skaug, H.J., Tjøstheim, D., 1996. Testing for serial independence using measures of distance between densities. In: Robinson, P.M., Rosenblatt, M. (Eds.), Athens Conference on Applied Probability and Time Series, Vol. II, in memory of E.J. Hannan. In: Springer Lecture Notes in Statistics, vol. 115. Springer, Berlin, pp. 363–378.
Sklar, A., 1959. Fonctions de répartition à n dimensions et leurs marges. Université Paris 8.
Smith, M., Min, A., Almeida, C., Czado, C., 2010. Modeling longitudinal data using a pair-copula decomposition of serial dependence. Journal of the American Statistical Association 61 (492), 1467–1479.
Smith, M.S., 2015. Copula modelling of dependence in multivariate time series. International Journal of Forecasting 31 (3), 815–833.
Spearman, C., 1904. The proof and measurement of association between two things. American Journal of Psychology 15 (1), 72–101.
Stanton, J.M., 2001. Galton, Pearson, and the peas: a brief history of linear regression for statistics instructors. Journal of Statistical Education 9 (3), 1–13.
Stein, M.L., 1999. Interpolation of Spatial Data: Some Theory for Kriging. Springer, New York.
Stigler, S.M., 1989. Francis Galton's account of the invention of correlation. Statistical Science 4 (2), 73–86.
Su, L., White, H., 2007. A consistent characteristic-function-based test for conditional independence. Journal of Econometrics 141 (2), 807–837.
Subba Rao, T., Gabr, M.M., 1980. A test for linearity of stationary time series. Journal of Time Series Analysis 1 (2), 145–158.
Székely, G.J., 2002. *E*-statistics: the energy of statistical samples. Technical report, Technical report 02-16. Bowling Green State University.
Szekely, G.J., Rizzo, M.L., 2005. Hierarchical clustering via joint between-within distances: extending Ward's minimum variance method. Journal of Classification 22 (2), 151–183.
Székely, G.J., Rizzo, M.L., 2009. Brownian distance covariance. Annals of Applied Statistics 3 (4), 1236–1265.
Székely, G.J., Rizzo, M.L., 2012. On the uniqueness of distance correlation. Statistics and Probability Letters 82 (12), 2278–2282.
Székely, G.J., Rizzo, M.L., 2013. Energy statistics: a class of statistics based on distances. Journal of Statistical Planning and Inference 143 (8), 1249–1272.
Szekely, G.J., Rizzo, M.L., 2014. Partial distance correlation with methods for dissimilarities. Annals of Statistics 42 (6), 2382–2412.
Székely, G.J., Rizzo, M.L., Bakirov, N.K., 2007. Measuring and testing dependence by correlation of distances. Annals of Statistics 35 (6), 2769–2794.

Teräsvirta, T., Tjøstheim, D., Granger, C.W., 2010. Modelling Nonlinear Economic Time Series. Oxford University Press.

Tjøstheim, D., 1996. Measures of dependence and tests of independence. Statistics 28 (3), 249–284.

Tjøstheim, D., Otneim, H., Støve, B., 2021. Statistical dependence: beyond Pearson's ρ. Statistical Science. In press.

van der Waerden, B.L., 1952. Order tests for the two-sample problem and their power. Idagationes Mathematicae 55, 453–458.

von Neumann, J., 1941. Distribution of the ratio of mean square successive differences to the variance. Annals of Mathematical Statistics 12 (4), 367–395.

von Neumann, J., 1942. A further remark concerning the distribution of the ratio of mean square difference to the variance. Annals of Mathematical Statistics 13 (1), 86–88.

Yao, S., Zhang, X., Shao, X., 2018. Testing mutual independence in high dimension via distance covariance. Journal of the Royal Statistical Society Series B 80 (3), 455–480.

Yenigün, C.D., Rizzo, M.L., 2014. Variable selection in regression using maximal correlation and distance correlation. Journal of Statistical Computation and Simulation 85 (8), 1692–1705.

Yenigün, C.D., Székely, G.J., Rizzo, M.L., 2011. A test of independence in two-way contingency tables based on maximal correlation. Communications in Statistics – Theory and Methods 40 (12), 2225–2242.

Zhang, K., Peters, J., Janzing, D., Schölkopf, B., 2012. Kernel-based conditional independence test and applications in causal discovery. In: Proceedings of the Uncertainty in Artificial Intelligence. AUAI Press, Corvallis, Oregon, pp. 804–813.

Zhou, Z., 2012. Measuring nonlinear dependence in time series, a distance correlation approach. Journal of Time Series Analysis 33 (3), 438–457.

CHAPTER 4

Local Gaussian correlation and dependence

Contents

4.1. Introduction 87
4.2. Local dependence 90
  4.2.1 Quadrant dependence 90
  4.2.2 Local measures of dependence 91
4.3. Local Gaussian correlation 94
4.4. Limit theorems 99
  4.4.1 Asymptotic theory for $\boldsymbol{b}$ fixed 99
  4.4.2 Asymptotic theory as $\boldsymbol{b} \to \mathbf{0}$ 102
4.5. Properties 105
  4.5.1 Some general properties of the local Gaussian correlation 105
  4.5.2 Independence and functional dependence 105
  4.5.3 The Rényi criteria 106
  4.5.4 Linear transformation and symmetries 107
4.6. Examples 112
  4.6.1 Simulated examples 112
  4.6.2 A real-data example 114
4.7. Transforming the marginals: Normalized local correlation 115
  4.7.1 Examples of the normalized LGC 119
4.8. Some practical considerations 120
  4.8.1 Estimating the standard error of estimates 120
  4.8.2 Choosing the bandwidth 122
4.9. The p-dimensional case 123
4.10. Proof of asymptotic results 123
  4.10.1 Non-normalized 123
  4.10.2 Normalized 127
  4.10.3 Proof of the linear transformation result 131
References 133

4.1 Introduction

Most of the discussion in Chapter 3 has been about global measures of dependence where the dependence is characterized by one single number. For the Pearson correlation, this number is between -1 and $+1$ with -1 expressing the extreme case of negative dependence and with $+1$ the same

Statistical Modeling using Local Gaussian Approximation
https://doi.org/10.1016/B978-0-12-815861-6.00011-0

for positive dependence. The weaknesses of Pearson's ρ have been pointed out in Chapter 3.2.

Alternative nonlinear and non-Gaussian measures were introduced in Chapters 3.3–3.5. These work in many cases where the Pearson's ρ does not work in the sense that they are able to detect dependence in the cases where $\rho = 0$ and are typically based on tests of independence measuring the *strength* of dependence only, in general being unable to distinguish positive and negative dependence. In fact, it has not been clear how negative and positive dependence should be defined in the general nonlinear case, a possible exception being the paper by Lehmann (1966), which will be briefly discussed in Section 4.2.1, as well as some other perspectives in Section 4.2.2.

Characterizing dependence between stochastic variables by one single number is rather crude. For instance, in economic markets, it is well understood that dependence between financial objects varies with the state of the market. If the market is going down, in particular, if there is an extreme downturn, then this typically influences shares in the same direction, and the dependence is expected to increase. The same, but perhaps not quite to the same degree, can be said if the market has an upturn. This demonstrates that there is need for a dependence measure that depends on the state of the market. This is an important motivation for using a local dependence measure, where the dependence is allowed to depend on the value of the stochastic variables involved. The local Gaussian correlation $\rho(\boldsymbol{x})$ to be introduced in this chapter is such a measure based on a local Gaussian description of the market, so that different pairs of Gaussian variables are used to approximate the distributional properties of the market in a downturn and in an upturn. We present an example in Fig. 4.4a. A more precise definition and more examples will be given later in this chapter, and in Chapter 6, several applications within finance will be given.

The local Gaussian correlation was introduced in Tjøstheim and Hufthammer (2013), but other local dependence measures had been introduced before that. In Section 4.2.2, we give a brief review of these historic developments. Note also the more ad hoc use of local dependence in the nonlinear dependence measures constructed in Chapter 3.5.

The local Gaussian measure of dependence is formally introduced in this book in Section 4.3, which also includes a number of its properties. The Rényi criteria of Chapter 3.4 can again be used as a yardstick. Estimation will be based on local likelihood arguments, and several asymptotic results are presented, whose proofs are outlined in Section 4.10. A number of simulated and real data examples are furnished in Section 4.6.

The local Gaussian correlation does depend on the marginal distributions, as does the Pearson's ρ. As mentioned in Chapter 3, this is sometimes pointed out as a problematic issue. There is a normal score-based version of ρ, the van der Waerden correlation, where this problem is eliminated. Moreover, this difficulty is certainly removed in a copula description of dependence, which is sometimes cited as a crucial advantage of that construct. It is possible to remove the dependence on marginals for the local Gaussian correlation as well by transforming the marginals to standard normal distributions. This corresponds to using uniform $U[0, 1]$ variables in the copula construction (see Chapter 5). Next, we can obtain a local Sklar-type theorem where the local dependence is decomposed in a margin free part based on the joint distribution of normal score variables and a marginal distribution part. The corresponding local correlation $\rho_Z(\boldsymbol{z})$ (called the normalized local correlation) is treated in Section 4.7. It is different from $\rho(\boldsymbol{x})$ except in the Gaussian copula case. The asymptotic distribution is stated in Section 4.7 with proofs in Section 4.10 and examples in Section 4.6. A simplified version is introduced in Section 4.9. It will be used in later chapters to circumvent the curse of dimensionality.

The connection to the copula construction is investigated much more closely in Chapter 5, where we also give a characterization of various copulas in terms of local dependence.

In the rest of the book the local Gaussian correlation $\rho(\boldsymbol{x})$ and the local correlations $\rho_Z(\boldsymbol{z})$ play a fundamental role. The idea is to try to exploit the uniquely simple properties of the Gaussian distribution locally. This is quite a powerful tool, which has a number of applications. Hence in Chapter 6, we give applications to finance and econometrics. Tests of independence are treated in Chapter 7, including the time series case. In Chapter 8 the local autocorrelation and local spectral densities are introduced. The local Gaussian approximation can be used for density and conditional density estimation as demonstrated in Chapters 9 and 10. The estimation of conditional quantities such as a local Gaussian partial correlation is also used for conditional independence testing in Chapter 11. Regression and conditional quantiles are taken up in Chapter 12, whereas applications to discrimination are treated in Chapter 13.

4.2 Local dependence

The main purpose of the present chapter is to introduce local Gaussian correlation, but let us first go back to some other attempts to define signed nonlinear dependence measures and local dependence starting with the remarkable paper by Lehmann (1966), who manages to define positive and negative dependence in a quite general nonlinear situation.

4.2.1 Quadrant dependence

Lehmann's theory is based on the concept of quadrant dependence. Consider two random variables X and Y with cumulative distribution $F_{X,Y}$. Then the pair (X, Y) or its distribution function $F_{X,Y}$ is said to be positively quadrant dependent if

$$P(X \leq x, Y \leq y) \geq P(X \leq x)P(Y \leq y) \quad \text{for all} \quad (x, y). \tag{4.1}$$

Similarly, (X, Y) or $F_{X,Y}$ is said to be negatively quadrant dependent if (4.1) holds with the reversed central inequality.

The connection between quadrant dependence and Pearson's ρ is secured through a lemma of Hoeffding (1940). The lemma is a general result and resembles the result by Székely (2002) in his treatment of the so-called Cramér functional, a forerunner of the Cramér–von Mises functional. If $F_{X,Y}$ denotes the joint distribution and F_X and F_Y denote the marginal distributions, then assuming that the necessary moments exist, we have

$$\mathrm{E}(XY) - \mathrm{E}(X)\mathrm{E}(Y) = \int_{-\infty}^{\infty}\int_{-\infty}^{\infty} \left(F_{X,Y}(x, y) - F_X(x)F_Y(y)\right) \mathrm{d}x\,\mathrm{d}y.$$

It follows immediately from the definitions that if (X, Y) is positively quadrant dependent (negatively quadrant dependent), then Pearson's $\rho \geq 0$ ($\rho \leq 0$). Similarly, it is shown by Lehmann that if $F_{X,Y}$ is positively quadrant dependent, then Kendall's τ, Spearman's ρ_S, and the quadrant measure q defined by Blomqvist (1950) are all non-negative. The paper by Blomqvist is an even earlier paper where positive and negative dependence were considered in a nonlinear case using quadrants centered at the median. An analogous result holds in the negatively quadrant dependent case.

Lehmann (1966) introduces two additional and stronger concepts of dependence. The first is regression dependence. Definition (4.1) can be written

$$P(Y \leq y | X \leq x) \geq P(Y \leq y),$$

but following Lehman, we may argue that the intuitive concept of positive dependence is better represented by the stronger condition

$$P(Y \le y | X \le x) \ge P(Y \le y | X \le x') \quad \text{for all} \quad x < x' \quad \text{and} \quad y. \tag{4.2}$$

Rather than (4.2), Lehmann considers the stronger condition

$$P(Y \le y | X = x) \quad \text{is non-increasing in} \quad x,$$

which was discussed earlier by Tukey (1958).

The concept of negative regression dependence is defined by an obvious analog. Lehmann finally introduces a stronger type of dependence still by requiring the conditional density of y given x to have a monotone likelihood ratio. Assuming the existence of a density $f = f_{X,Y}$, the condition may be formally written as

$$f(x, y')f(x', y) \le f(x, y)f(x', y') \quad \text{for all} \quad x < x', \ y < y'.$$

If we reverse the inequality, then (X, Y) is said to be negatively likelihood ratio dependent. The bivariate normal distribution is positively or negatively likelihood ratio dependent according to $\rho \ge 0$ or $\rho \le 0$. We will briefly return to these dependence concepts when we get to the local Gaussian correlation in Section 4.3.

4.2.2 Local measures of dependence

As already mentioned, econometricians have long looked for a formal statistical way of describing the shifting region-like dependence structure of financial markets. It is obvious that when the market is going down, there is a stronger dependence between financial objects, and very strong if there is panic. Similar effects, but perhaps not quite so strong, appear when the market is going up. But how should it be quantified and measured? It is important to finance, not the least in portfolio theory, where it is well known (see, e.g., Taleb, 2007) that the ordinary Gaussian model of uncertainty does not work and, if used, may lead to catastrophic results. Mainly two approaches are used among econometricians. The first is non-local and consists simply in using copula theory, but it may not always be so easy to implement in a time series and portfolio context. We will return to the copula construction and outline some relationships with local Gaussian correlation in Chapter 5.

The other local approach is to use "conditional correlations" as in Silvapulle and Granger (2001) and Forbes and Rigobon (2002). Estimates as in Eq. (3.1) of Pearson's ρ are computed, but in various regions of the sample space, for example, in the tail of two distributions. Let R be such a region. A conditional correlation estimate is then given by (we let n_R be the number of observed pairs $(X_i, Y_i) \in R$ and $\overline{X}_R = \frac{1}{n_R}\sum_{(X_i, Y_i)\in R} X_i$, and similarly for $\overline{Y}_R$)

$$\widehat{\rho}_R = \frac{\sum_{(X_i, Y_i)\in R}(X_i - \overline{X}_R)(Y_i - \overline{Y}_R)}{\sqrt{\sum_{(X_i, Y_i)\in R}(X_i - \overline{X}_R)^2}\sqrt{\sum_{(X_i, Y_i)\in R}(Y_i - \overline{Y}_R)^2}}. \tag{4.3}$$

However, this estimate suffers from a serious bias, which is obvious by using the ergodic theorem or the law of large numbers in the sense that for a Gaussian distribution, it does not converge to ρ. This is unfortunate, because if the data indeed happens to be Gaussian, then we would like it to approximate the classic Gaussian portfolio theory of Markowitz (1952). This bias is examined by Boyer et al. (1999).

Consider, as an example, a bivariate Gaussian distribution with correlation $\rho = 0.5$. The conditional correlation when one of the variables is large, for example, larger than its 75% quantile, $X > q_{75}$, is reduced to 0.27, and as the quantile increases, ρ_R converges to zero. In the finance literature, there are tries to correct this, for example, in contagion studies by Forbes and Rigobon (2002). We may think that here it is wrong to try using a product moment estimator, which is a linear Gaussian concept, on a quantity ρ that in the nonlinear case is better thought of as a distributional parameter. We will return to this in Section 4.3, where a distributional approach yields an estimate without bias.

Statisticians have also tried various other ways of describing local dependence. We will report on two such attempts. Bjerve and Doksum (1993) extend the relationship between correlation and regression coefficients in a linear regression model to a nonlinear situation. Recall that in a linear model $Y = \alpha + \beta X + \varepsilon$,

$$\rho = \beta\frac{\sigma_X}{\sigma_Y} = \frac{\beta\sigma_X}{\sqrt{(\beta\sigma_X)^2 + \sigma_\varepsilon^2}},$$

where σ_X^2, σ_Y^2, and σ_ε^2 are the variances of X, Y, and ε. Based on this formula, Bjerve and Doksum suggested a local measure of dependence, the correlation curve, based on localizing ρ by conditioning on X. Consider a generalization of the linear model to $Y = f(X) + g(X)\varepsilon$, where f and g are continuous functions, f is in addition continuously differentiable, and ε has zero mean and is independent of X. The correlation curve is defined by

$$\rho(x) = \rho_{X,Y}(x) = \frac{\beta(x)\sigma_X}{\sqrt{(\beta(x)\sigma_X)^2 + \sigma_\varepsilon^2(x)}},$$

where

$$\beta(x) = \mu'(x) \quad \text{with} \quad \mu(x) = \mathrm{E}(Y|X = x),$$

and $\sigma_\varepsilon^2(x) = \mathrm{Var}(Y|X = x)$. It is trivial to check that $\rho(x)$ reduces to ρ in the linear case. The quantities $\beta(x)$ and $\sigma_\varepsilon^2(x)$ can be estimated by standard nonparametric methods. The correlation curve inherits many properties of ρ, but it succeeds in several cases where ρ fails to detect dependence, such as the parabola in Eq. (3.5). However, unlike ρ, it is not symmetric in (X, Y). In fact, it depends only on x, whereas we may want it to depend on (x, y) in such a way that $\rho_{X,Y}(x, y) = \rho_{Y,X}(y, x)$. This is of course due to the conditioning and regression on X. Conditioning and regression on Y would in general produce a different result. This brings out the difference between regression analysis and multivariate analysis, where ρ is a concept of the latter, which accidentally enters into the first. Bjerve and Doksum propose a solution to this dilemma, but it is an ad hoc one. Moreover, it is not so difficult to find examples where the correlation curve is zero even though there is dependence. Some further references are Wilcox (2005) and Wilcox (2007).

We noted in Chapter 3.5 that Heller et al. (2013) used local contingency-type arguments to construct a global test functional. Such contingency reasoning goes further back in time. Holland and Wang (1987) consider continuous stochastic variables (X, Y) defined on $\mathbb{R}^2$. Let $R_{x,y}$ denote the rectangle containing the point (x, y) having sides of lengths Δx and Δy. Then, approximately as the sides become small,

$$P_{x,y} \stackrel{\text{def}}{=} P((X, Y) \in R_{x,y}) \approx f(x, y)\Delta x \Delta y,$$

where f is the joint density function. We now imagine that the sample space of (X, Y) is covered by such non-overlapping rectangles (cells). For each cell, we pick one point (x, y) contained in that cell. Based on all these pairs (x, y), construct a contingency table with indices (i, j) with elements $P_{x,y} = P_{ij}$. Now consider four neighboring cells (i, k), (i, l), (j, k), and (j, l)

with $i < j$ and $k < l$ and with (x, y) in the cell defined by (i, k) and using the simplified notation Δi for Δx_i. The cross-product ratio is

$$\alpha((i,k),(j,l)) = \frac{P_{ik}P_{jl}}{P_{il}P_{jk}} \approx \frac{f(i,k)\Delta i \Delta k \cdot f(j,l)\Delta j \Delta l}{f(i,l)\Delta i \Delta l \cdot f(j,k)\Delta j \Delta k} = \frac{f(i,k)f(j,l)}{f(i,l)f(j,k)}.$$

Let $\theta((i,k),(j,l)) = \log \alpha((i,k),(j,l))$. Letting the sides of all four cells tend to zero and then taking limits, we obtain

$$\gamma(x,y) = \lim_{\Delta x \to 0, \Delta y \to 0} \frac{\theta[(x,y),(x+\Delta x, y+\Delta y)]}{\Delta x \Delta y} = \frac{\partial^2}{\partial x \partial y} \log f(x,y),$$

which is the local dependence function. It is implicitly assumed here that both mixed second-order partial derivatives exist and are continuous.

For an alternative derivation based on limiting arguments of local covariance functions and for properties and extensions, we refer to Jones (1996), Jones (1998), Jones and Koch (2003), Sankaran and Gupta (2004), and Inci et al. (2011).

The conditional dependence function does not take values between -1 and $+1$, and it does not reduce to ρ in the Gaussian bivariate case. In fact, then

$$\gamma(x,y) = \frac{\rho}{1-\rho^2}\frac{1}{\sigma_X \sigma_Y}.$$

Both the correlation curve and local dependence function works well for the example $Y = X^2 + \varepsilon$, where $\rho = 0$ (see Eq. (3.5)), producing dependence proportional to x and producing a sign of the dependence in accordance with intuition.

4.3 Local Gaussian correlation

Pearson's ρ gives a complete characterization of dependence in a bivariate Gaussian distribution, but, as we saw in Chapter 3, this is not true in general for two random variables X and Y with density function $f(x, y)$. The motivation for introducing the local Gaussian correlation (LGC) by Tjøstheim and Hufthammer (2013) was to approximate f locally in a neighborhood of a point (x, y) by a bivariate Gaussian distribution $\psi_{x,y}(u, v)$, where (u, v) are running variables. In this neighborhood, we get a nearly complete local characterization of dependence, its precision depending on the size of the neighborhood and of course on the properties of the density at the point (x, y). In practice, it has to be reasonably smooth.

For notational convenience, we write (x_1, x_2) instead of (x, y) in this section, and by a slight inconsistency of notation, we let $\boldsymbol{x} = (x_1, x_2)$. In the same way, we replace (u, v) by $\boldsymbol{v} = (v_1, v_2)$. Then letting $\boldsymbol{\mu}(\boldsymbol{x}) = (\mu_1(\boldsymbol{x}), \mu_2(\boldsymbol{x}))$ be the mean vector in the normal distribution with density $\psi_{\boldsymbol{x}}$, the vector of standard deviations $\boldsymbol{\sigma}(\boldsymbol{x}) = (\sigma_1(\boldsymbol{x}), \sigma_2(\boldsymbol{x}))$, and the correlation coefficient $\rho(\boldsymbol{x})$ in the normal distribution $\psi_{\boldsymbol{x}}$, the approximating density is given as

$$\psi_{\boldsymbol{x}} = \psi(\boldsymbol{v}, \mu_1(\boldsymbol{x}), \mu_2(\boldsymbol{x}), \sigma_1^2(\boldsymbol{x}), \sigma_2^2(\boldsymbol{x}), \rho(\boldsymbol{x})) = \frac{1}{2\pi\sigma_1(\boldsymbol{x})\sigma_2(\boldsymbol{x})\sqrt{1-\rho^2(\boldsymbol{x})}}$$
$$\times \exp\left[-\frac{1}{2}\frac{1}{1-\rho^2(\boldsymbol{x})}\left(\frac{(v_1-\mu_1(\boldsymbol{x}))^2}{\sigma_1^2(\boldsymbol{x})} - 2\rho(\boldsymbol{x})\frac{(v_1-\mu_1(\boldsymbol{x}))(v_2-\mu_2(\boldsymbol{x}))}{\sigma_1(\boldsymbol{x})\sigma_2(\boldsymbol{x})}\right.\right.$$
$$\left.\left. + \frac{(v_2-\mu_2(\boldsymbol{x}))^2}{\sigma_2^2(\boldsymbol{x})}\right)\right]. \tag{4.4}$$

An alternative parameterization is given by $(\boldsymbol{\mu}(\boldsymbol{x}), \boldsymbol{\Sigma}(\boldsymbol{x}))$, where $\boldsymbol{\mu}(\boldsymbol{x})$ and $\boldsymbol{\Sigma}(\boldsymbol{x})$ are the local mean and local covariance matrix, respectively. Moving to another point $\boldsymbol{y} = (y_1, y_2)$ gives another approximating normal distribution $\psi_{\boldsymbol{y}}$ depending on a new set of parameters $(\mu_1(\boldsymbol{y}), \mu_2(\boldsymbol{y}), \sigma_1(\boldsymbol{y}), \sigma_2(\boldsymbol{y}), \rho(\boldsymbol{y}))$. One exception to this is the case where f itself is Gaussian with parameters $(\mu_1, \mu_2, \sigma_1, \sigma_2, \rho)$, in which case $(\mu_1(\boldsymbol{x}), \mu_2(\boldsymbol{x}), \sigma_1(\boldsymbol{x}), \sigma_2(\boldsymbol{x}), \rho(\boldsymbol{x})) \equiv (\mu_1, \mu_2, \sigma_1, \sigma_2, \rho)$. This means that we avoid the bias of the conditional correlation described in Section 4.2.2, and this also means that property (vii) in Rényi's (1959) scheme, stated in Chapter 3.4, is satisfied by the LGC.

To make this into a construction that can be used in practice, we define the vector parameter $\boldsymbol{\theta}(\boldsymbol{x}) \stackrel{\text{def}}{=} (\mu_1(\boldsymbol{x}), \mu_2(\boldsymbol{x}), \sigma_1(\boldsymbol{x}), \sigma_2(\boldsymbol{x}), \rho(\boldsymbol{x}))$ and derive its estimators. Fortunately, this problem has been treated more generally by Hjort and Jones (1996) and Loader (1996). They consider the problem of approximating f locally with a general parametric family of densities, the Gaussians being only one such family. They allow in principle $\boldsymbol{x}$ to have an arbitrary dimension p but mostly cover the univariate case $p = 1$ in those publications. The focus of Hjort and Jones (1996) and Loader (1996) was the estimation of the unknown density function f rather than of the local parameters, but their estimation method using local likelihood is applicable also for estimating local parameters directly, which we will make use of in the following.

First, however, we need a more precise definition of $\boldsymbol{\theta}(\boldsymbol{x})$, which we obtain in two stages using a neighborhood defined by bandwidths $\boldsymbol{b} = (b_1, b_2)$

in the (x_1, x_2) direction and then let $\boldsymbol{b} \to \mathbf{0}$ componentwise. We could, as an alternative, use a set of smoothness conditions requiring not only f and ψ to coincide at x, but also first- and second-order derivatives, as indicated by Berentsen et al. (2017), but the resulting equations are in general difficult to solve.

A suitable function measuring the difference between f and ψ is given by

$$q = \int K_{\boldsymbol{b}}(\boldsymbol{v} - \boldsymbol{x})[\psi(\boldsymbol{v}, \boldsymbol{\theta}(\boldsymbol{x})) - \log \psi\{\boldsymbol{v}, \boldsymbol{\theta}(\boldsymbol{x})\} f(\boldsymbol{v})] \, \mathrm{d}\boldsymbol{v}, \tag{4.5}$$

where $K_{\boldsymbol{b}}(\boldsymbol{v} - \boldsymbol{x}) = (b_1 b_2)^{-1} K_1(b_1^{-1}(v_1 - x_1)) K_2(b_2(v_2 - x_2))$ is a product kernel. See also Chapter 2.5 and 2.10 for some general properties of kernel functions. As noted by Hjort and Jones (1996), (4.5) can be interpreted as a locally weighted Kullback–Leibler distance from $f(\boldsymbol{x})$ to $\psi(\boldsymbol{x}, \boldsymbol{\theta}(\boldsymbol{x}))$. We then obtain that the minimizer $\boldsymbol{\theta}(\boldsymbol{x}) = \boldsymbol{\theta}_{\boldsymbol{b}}(\boldsymbol{x})$ (also depending on K) should satisfy

$$\int K_{\boldsymbol{b}}(\boldsymbol{v} - \boldsymbol{x}) \frac{\partial}{\partial \theta_j} (\log\{\psi(\boldsymbol{v}, \boldsymbol{\theta}(\boldsymbol{x}))\})[f(\boldsymbol{v}) - \psi(\boldsymbol{v}, \boldsymbol{\theta}(\boldsymbol{x}))] \, \mathrm{d}\boldsymbol{v} = 0, \;\; j = 1, \ldots, 5. \tag{4.6}$$

In the first stage, we define the population value $\boldsymbol{\theta}_{\boldsymbol{b}}(\boldsymbol{x})$ as the minimizer of (4.5), assuming that there is a unique solution to (4.6). The definition of $\boldsymbol{\theta}_{\boldsymbol{b}}(\boldsymbol{x})$ and the assumption of uniqueness are essentially identical to those used by Hjort and Jones (1996) for more general parametric families of densities. A trivial example where (4.6) is satisfied with a unique $\boldsymbol{\theta}_{\boldsymbol{b}}(\boldsymbol{x})$ is when $\boldsymbol{X} \sim \mathcal{N}(\boldsymbol{\mu}, \boldsymbol{\Sigma})$, where $\boldsymbol{\Sigma}$ is the covariance matrix of $\boldsymbol{X}$.

In the next stage, we let $\boldsymbol{b} \to \mathbf{0}$ componentwise. This is in fact considered indirectly by Hjort and Jones (1996) on pp. 1627–1630 and more directly by Tjøstheim and Hufthammer (2013), both using Taylor expansion arguments. In the following, we will assume that such a unique $\boldsymbol{\theta}(\boldsymbol{x}) = \lim_{\boldsymbol{b} \to \mathbf{0}} \boldsymbol{\theta}_b(\boldsymbol{x})$ independent of $\boldsymbol{b}$ and K exists. (It is possible to avoid the problem of a population value altogether if we take the view of some of the authors cited in Chapter 3.5, who just estimate a suitable dependence function.) Excepting the Gaussian or the Gaussian step model, to be discussed next, it is not straightforward to find analytic expressions for $\boldsymbol{\theta}(\boldsymbol{x})$. We will return, however, to this problem in Chapter 5 when treating the copula and exchangeable distributions.

The next stage up from the Gaussian consists in defining a step function of a Gaussian variable $\boldsymbol{Z} \sim \mathcal{N}(\boldsymbol{\mu}, \boldsymbol{\Sigma})$, where we will take $\boldsymbol{\mu} = \mathbf{0}$ and $\boldsymbol{\Sigma} = \boldsymbol{I}_2$, and where $\boldsymbol{I}_2$ is the identity matrix of dimension 2. Let $R_i, i = 1, \ldots, K$, be a set of non-overlapping regions of $\mathbb{R}^2$ such that $\mathbb{R}^2 = \cup_{i=1}^K R_i$. Further, let $\{\boldsymbol{a}_i\}$ and $\{\boldsymbol{A}_i\}$ be the corresponding sets of vectors and matrices in $\mathbb{R}^2$ such that each $\boldsymbol{A}_i$ is non-singular, and define the piecewise linear function

$$\boldsymbol{X} = g_S(\boldsymbol{Z}) = \sum_{i=1}^{K} (\boldsymbol{a}_i + \boldsymbol{A}_i \boldsymbol{Z}) I(\boldsymbol{Z} \in R_i), \tag{4.7}$$

where I is the indicator function. Let S_i be the region defined by $S_i = \{\boldsymbol{x} : \boldsymbol{x} = \boldsymbol{a}_i + \boldsymbol{A}_i \boldsymbol{z}, \boldsymbol{z} \in R_i\}$. We assume that mapping (4.7) is one-to-one in the sense that $S_i \cap S_j = \phi$ for $i \neq j$ and $\cup_{i=1}^K S_i = \mathbb{R}^2$. To see that the linear step function (4.7) can be used to obtain a solution of (4.6), let $\boldsymbol{x}$ be a point in the interior of S_i, and let the kernel function K have a compact support. By choosing $\boldsymbol{b}$ small enough, all $\boldsymbol{v}$ for which $\boldsymbol{v} - \boldsymbol{x}$ is in the support of $K_{\boldsymbol{b}}$ will be in S_i. Under this restriction on $\boldsymbol{b}$, $\boldsymbol{\theta}_{\boldsymbol{b}}(\boldsymbol{x}) = \boldsymbol{\theta}(\boldsymbol{x}) \equiv \boldsymbol{\theta}_i = (\boldsymbol{\mu}_i, \boldsymbol{\Sigma}_i)$, where $\boldsymbol{\mu}_i = \boldsymbol{a}_i$ and $\boldsymbol{\Sigma}_i = \boldsymbol{A}_i \boldsymbol{A}_i^T$, as defined in (4.7). Thus, in this sense, for a fixed but small $\boldsymbol{b}$, there exists a local Gaussian approximation $\psi(\boldsymbol{x}, \boldsymbol{\theta}_{\boldsymbol{b}})$ of f with corresponding local means $\mu_{j,\boldsymbol{b}}(\boldsymbol{x})$, variances $\sigma_{j,\boldsymbol{b}}(\boldsymbol{x}), j = 1, 2$, and correlation $\rho_{\boldsymbol{b}}(\boldsymbol{x})$. We will see in Section 4.4 that for these points, the local likelihood estimates $\widehat{\boldsymbol{\theta}}(\boldsymbol{x}) = (\widehat{\boldsymbol{\mu}}_{\boldsymbol{b}}(\boldsymbol{x}), \widehat{\boldsymbol{\Sigma}}(\boldsymbol{x}))$ converge toward $\boldsymbol{\theta}_{\boldsymbol{b}}(\boldsymbol{x}) = (\boldsymbol{\mu}_{\boldsymbol{b}}(\boldsymbol{x}), \boldsymbol{\Sigma}_{\boldsymbol{b}}(\boldsymbol{x}))$ as the number of observations tends to infinity and the bandwidth $\boldsymbol{b}$ is kept fixed, and toward a population parameter $\boldsymbol{\theta}(\boldsymbol{x})$ as $n \to \infty$ and $\boldsymbol{b} \to \boldsymbol{0}$. (The local parameters at the boundary of the regions can be defined by some convention, these boundaries having zero measure in $\mathbb{R}^2$.)

In general, estimating $\boldsymbol{\theta}(\boldsymbol{x})$ and $\boldsymbol{\theta}_{\boldsymbol{b}}(\boldsymbol{x})$, a neighborhood with finite bandwidth of course has to be used in analogy with nonparametric density estimation. The estimate $\widehat{\boldsymbol{\theta}}(\boldsymbol{x}) = \widehat{\boldsymbol{\theta}}_{\boldsymbol{b}}(\boldsymbol{x})$ is obtained from maximizing a local likelihood. Given observations $\boldsymbol{X}_1, \ldots, \boldsymbol{X}_n$, the local log likelihood is defined by

$$L(\boldsymbol{X}_1, \ldots, \boldsymbol{X}_n, \boldsymbol{\theta}(\boldsymbol{x})) = n^{-1} \sum_i K_{\boldsymbol{b}}(\boldsymbol{X}_i - \boldsymbol{x}) \log \psi(\boldsymbol{X}_i, \boldsymbol{\theta}(\boldsymbol{x})) - \int K_{\boldsymbol{b}}(\boldsymbol{v} - \boldsymbol{x}) \psi(\boldsymbol{v}, \boldsymbol{\theta}(\boldsymbol{x}))\, \mathrm{d}\boldsymbol{v} \tag{4.8}$$

almost surely. As $\boldsymbol{b} \to \infty$, the last term has a constant limiting value, and the likelihood reduces to the ordinary global likelihood. However, this last (and perhaps somewhat unexpected term) is essential as it implies that $\psi(\boldsymbol{x}, \boldsymbol{\theta}_{\boldsymbol{b}}(\boldsymbol{x}))$ is not allowed to stray far away from $f(\boldsymbol{x})$ as $\boldsymbol{b} \to \boldsymbol{0}$. It is discussed at length by Hjort and Jones (1996). Indeed, using the notation

$$u_j(\cdot, \boldsymbol{\theta}) \stackrel{\text{def}}{=} \frac{\partial}{\partial \theta_j} \log \psi(\cdot, \boldsymbol{\theta}), \tag{4.9}$$

by the law of large numbers or by the ergodic theorem in the time series case, assuming that $\mathrm{E}(K_{\boldsymbol{b}}(\boldsymbol{X}_i - \boldsymbol{x}) \log \psi(\boldsymbol{X}_i, \boldsymbol{\theta}_{\boldsymbol{b}}(\boldsymbol{x}))) < \infty$, we have almost surely

$$\begin{aligned} \frac{\partial L}{\partial \theta_j} &= n^{-1} \sum_i K_{\boldsymbol{b}}(\boldsymbol{X}_i - \boldsymbol{x}) u_j(\boldsymbol{X}_i, \boldsymbol{\theta}_{\boldsymbol{b}}(\boldsymbol{x})) \\ &\quad - \int K_{\boldsymbol{b}}(\boldsymbol{v} - \boldsymbol{x}) u_j(\boldsymbol{v}, \boldsymbol{\theta}_{\boldsymbol{b}}(\boldsymbol{x})) \psi(\boldsymbol{v}, \boldsymbol{\theta}_{\boldsymbol{b}}(\boldsymbol{x}))\, \mathrm{d}\boldsymbol{v} \\ &\to \int K_{\boldsymbol{b}}(\boldsymbol{v} - \boldsymbol{x}) u_j(\boldsymbol{v}, \boldsymbol{\theta}_{\boldsymbol{b}}(\boldsymbol{x}))[f(\boldsymbol{v}) - \psi(\boldsymbol{v}, \boldsymbol{\theta}_{\boldsymbol{b}}(\boldsymbol{x}))]\, \mathrm{d}\boldsymbol{v}. \end{aligned} \tag{4.10}$$

Putting the expression in the first line of (4.10) equal to zero yields the local maximum likelihood estimate $\widehat{\boldsymbol{\theta}}_{\boldsymbol{b}}(\boldsymbol{x})$ $(= \widehat{\boldsymbol{\theta}}(\boldsymbol{x}))$ of the population value $\boldsymbol{\theta}_{\boldsymbol{b}}(\boldsymbol{x})$ (and $\boldsymbol{\theta}(\boldsymbol{x})$, which satisfies (4.6)).

To see the importance of the additional last term in the local likelihood, let $\boldsymbol{b} \to \boldsymbol{0}$. Then by Taylor expansion and requiring $\partial L / \partial \theta_j = 0$, we have that

$$u_j(\boldsymbol{x}, \boldsymbol{\theta}_{\boldsymbol{b}}(\boldsymbol{x}))[f(\boldsymbol{x}) - \psi(\boldsymbol{x}, \boldsymbol{\theta}_{\boldsymbol{b}}(\boldsymbol{x}))] + O(\boldsymbol{b}^T \boldsymbol{b}) = 0,$$

where $\boldsymbol{b}^T$ is the transposed of $\boldsymbol{b}$. By ignoring solutions that yield $u_j(\boldsymbol{x}, \boldsymbol{\theta}_{\boldsymbol{b}}(\boldsymbol{x})) = 0$ it follows that $\psi(\boldsymbol{x}, \boldsymbol{\theta}_{\boldsymbol{b}}(\boldsymbol{x}))$ is close to $f(\boldsymbol{x})$.

Another important motivation for introducing a local Gaussian correlation is to be able to handle auto-dependence in a time series, such as financial returns. One example would be $\{\boldsymbol{X}_t\} = \{Y_t, Y_{t-j}\}$ for a univariate time series $\{Y_t\}$ for modeling auto-dependence for lag j. The local likelihood function of (4.8) can be used for dependent data in that it can be maximized using the same algorithm as in the iid case, resulting in the same expression for $\widehat{\boldsymbol{\theta}}_{\boldsymbol{b}}(\boldsymbol{x})$ in terms of the variables $\{\boldsymbol{X}_t\}$. However, when $\boldsymbol{X}_t$ are dependent, it cannot really be thought of as a local Gaussian log likelihood. A local likelihood can be constructed by approximating the dependence between the variables $\{\boldsymbol{X}_t\}$ by a multivariate Gaussian, but in general, this will lead to a drastic increase in the number of local parameters, and we prefer instead to use the marginal Gaussian penalty function

$$Q_n(\boldsymbol{X}_1, \ldots, \boldsymbol{X}_n; \boldsymbol{\theta}_{\boldsymbol{b}}(\boldsymbol{x})) = -nL(\boldsymbol{X}_1, \ldots, \boldsymbol{X}_n, \boldsymbol{\theta}_{\boldsymbol{b}}(\boldsymbol{x}))$$

$$= -\sum K_b(\mathbf{X}_t - \mathbf{x}) \log \psi(\mathbf{X}_t, \boldsymbol{\theta}_b(\mathbf{x})) \\ + n \int K_b(\mathbf{v} - \mathbf{x}) \psi(\mathbf{v}, \boldsymbol{\theta}_b(\mathbf{x}))\, \mathrm{d}\mathbf{v}, \quad (4.11)$$

which is proportional to a local Gaussian likelihood in the independent case and can be interpreted as an M-estimation penalty function in the more general case. For a bivariate time series, we can still approximate the marginal distribution of $\{X_{1t}, X_{2t}\}$ by a local Gaussian distribution if we assume stationarity, and we can model the local Gaussian cross-correlation structure for $\{X_{1t}, X_{2,t-j}\}$ for each j. A natural next step is to use this as a first stage in a local autocorrelation and cross-correlation analysis of time series, leading to the concepts of a local spectral density function and local cross-spectral density that can describe periodicities on several scales. We refer to Chapter 8 for details.

We see that the expected value for the function $n^{-1}Q(\mathbf{x})$ for a fixed bandwidth vector $\boldsymbol{b}$ is given by the penalty function q defined in (4.5). Eq. (4.5) is identical to the equation used by Hjort and Jones (1996) to define a population value $\boldsymbol{\theta}_b(\mathbf{x})$ under some regularity conditions.

4.4 Limit theorems

4.4.1 Asymptotic theory for b fixed

After having defined the population values, we are in a position to discuss local likelihood estimates of these and prove the consistency and asymptotic normality. We define the local likelihood estimate $\widehat{\boldsymbol{\theta}}_b(\mathbf{x})$ as an estimate maximizing the local log likelihood in (4.8). With a sufficient number of observations, we can estimate the population value for different bandwidths, thereby getting several measures of correlation, each measuring the correlation at the specified degree of locality. For the extreme case of $\boldsymbol{b} = \infty$, the local Gaussian likelihood reduces to the global Gaussian quasi-likelihood, and we easily see that by maximizing this, we get an estimated parameter vector $\widehat{\boldsymbol{\theta}}$ of the vector $\boldsymbol{\theta}$ composed of the global means, global variances, and global correlation of (X_1, X_2).

In the asymptotic theory below, we will first look at the case where the bandwidth vector $\boldsymbol{b}$ is fixed, that is, estimating $\boldsymbol{\theta}_b(\mathbf{x})$ of (4.6). In the next subsection, we let $\boldsymbol{b} \to \mathbf{0}$ componentwise, estimating $\boldsymbol{\theta}(x)$ as defined in Section 4.3.

Asymptotic theory for a fixed $\boldsymbol{b}$ in the iid case is covered by Hjort and Jones (1996). Our contribution in this section is in allowing dependence in time as formulated in Theorem 4.1 taken from Tjøstheim and Hufthammer (2013).

A basic assumption of Hjort and Jones (1996) is the existence of a unique solution $\boldsymbol{\theta}_b(\boldsymbol{x})$ of (4.6) for every bandwidth vector $\boldsymbol{b} > 0$ (componentwise). Under this assumption, they state the following result, which is used as an instrument of density estimation in their paper. (We will cover local Gaussian density estimation in Chapter 9.)

Proposition 4.1 (Hjort and Jones, 1996). *Let $\{\boldsymbol{X}_t\}$ be iid. Under the existence and uniqueness assumption on $\boldsymbol{\theta}_b(\boldsymbol{x})$, letting $\widehat{\boldsymbol{\theta}}_{n,b}(\boldsymbol{x})$ be the local likelihood estimate of $\boldsymbol{\theta}_b(\boldsymbol{x})$,*

$$(nb_1b_2)^{1/2}\left(\widehat{\theta}_{n,b}(\boldsymbol{x}) - \theta_b(\boldsymbol{x})\right) \xrightarrow{d} \mathcal{N}(\boldsymbol{0}, \boldsymbol{J}_b^{-1}\boldsymbol{M}_b(\boldsymbol{J}_b^{-1})^T), \tag{4.12}$$

where $\boldsymbol{J}_b = \boldsymbol{J}_b(\boldsymbol{x})$ is given by

$$\begin{aligned}\boldsymbol{J}_b = &\int K_b(\boldsymbol{v}-\boldsymbol{x})\boldsymbol{u}(\boldsymbol{v},\boldsymbol{\theta}_b(\boldsymbol{x}))\boldsymbol{u}^T(\boldsymbol{v},\boldsymbol{\theta}_b(\boldsymbol{x}))\psi(\boldsymbol{v},\boldsymbol{\theta}_b(\boldsymbol{x}))\,d\boldsymbol{v}\\ &-\int K_b(\boldsymbol{v}-\boldsymbol{x})\nabla\boldsymbol{u}(\boldsymbol{v},\boldsymbol{\theta}_b(\boldsymbol{x}))\Big(f(\boldsymbol{v})-\psi(\boldsymbol{v},\boldsymbol{\theta}_b(\boldsymbol{x}))\Big)\,d\boldsymbol{v}\end{aligned} \tag{4.13}$$

with $\boldsymbol{u}(\boldsymbol{x},\boldsymbol{\theta}) = \nabla\log\psi(\boldsymbol{x},\boldsymbol{\theta})$, and where $\boldsymbol{M}_b = \boldsymbol{M}_b(\boldsymbol{x})$ is given by

$$\begin{aligned}\boldsymbol{M}_b &= \lim_{n\to\infty} Var((nb_1b_2)^{1/2}\boldsymbol{V}_n(\boldsymbol{\theta}_b))\\ &= b_1b_2\int K_b^2(\boldsymbol{v}-\boldsymbol{x})\boldsymbol{u}(\boldsymbol{v},\boldsymbol{\theta}_b(\boldsymbol{x}))\boldsymbol{u}^T(\boldsymbol{v},\boldsymbol{\theta}_b(\boldsymbol{x}))f(\boldsymbol{v})\,d\boldsymbol{v}\\ &\quad - b_1b_2\int K_b(\boldsymbol{v}-\boldsymbol{x})\boldsymbol{u}(\boldsymbol{v},\boldsymbol{\theta}_b(\boldsymbol{x}))f(\boldsymbol{v})\,d\boldsymbol{v}\int K_b(\boldsymbol{v}-\boldsymbol{x})\boldsymbol{u}^T(\boldsymbol{v},\boldsymbol{\theta}_b(\boldsymbol{x}))f(\boldsymbol{v})\,d\boldsymbol{v}\end{aligned} \tag{4.14}$$

with $\boldsymbol{V}_n(\theta) = \partial L(\boldsymbol{\theta})/\partial\boldsymbol{\theta}$.

The use of the scaling factor $(nb_1b_2)^{1/2}$ is perhaps slightly deceptive, because the limit result holds for a fixed $\boldsymbol{b}$. The local likelihood algorithm works by fitting a Gaussian surface to the surface of f at any neighborhood of finite size $\boldsymbol{b}$, and if f is Gaussian or stepwise Gaussian, then its parameter vector is uniquely determined by any finite portion $f(\boldsymbol{x}), \boldsymbol{x} \in \mathcal{N}(\boldsymbol{x})$, of its surface, where $\mathcal{N}(\boldsymbol{x})$ is a neighborhood of $\boldsymbol{x}$.

As mentioned in Section 4.3, an important motivation for introducing a local Gaussian correlation is to be able to handle time series, such as financial returns. In the following theorem, we extend the above result to the time series case using (4.11) as a local penalty function. A proof can be found in Section 4.10.1.

Theorem 4.1. *Let $\{\mathbf{X}_t\}$ be a stationary bivariate time series with $\mathbf{X}_t$ having a bivariate density f. Assume that*

(i) *$\{\mathbf{X}_t\}$ is geometrically ergodic;*

(ii) *f has support on all of $\mathbb{R}^2$ and is such that*

$$E|K_{\boldsymbol{b}}(\mathbf{X}_t - \boldsymbol{x})\partial/\partial\theta_j \log\psi(\mathbf{X}_t, \boldsymbol{\theta})|^\gamma < \infty, \quad j = 1, \ldots, 5,$$

for some $\gamma > 2$, where $|\cdot|$ is the Euclidean norm; and

(iii) *For a fixed bandwidth $\boldsymbol{b}$, there is a unique solution $\boldsymbol{\theta}_{\boldsymbol{b}}(\boldsymbol{x})$ of* (4.6).

Then, for every $\varepsilon > 0$, there is a possibly $\boldsymbol{x}$-dependent event A with $P(A^c) < \varepsilon$, A^c being the complement of A, such that there exists a sequence $\{\widehat{\theta}_{n,\boldsymbol{b}}(\boldsymbol{x})\}$ that minimizes Q in (4.11) *and such that $\widehat{\boldsymbol{\theta}}_{n,\boldsymbol{b}}(\boldsymbol{x})$ converges almost surely to $\boldsymbol{\theta}_{\boldsymbol{b}}(\boldsymbol{x})$ on A. Moreover, the central limit result in Proposition 4.1 continues to hold, with the integral expression in the first part of* (4.14) *as the leading part of $\boldsymbol{M}_b$.*

Remark 1. The condition that f has support on all of $\mathbb{R}^2$ can be weakened, but with this assumption, we do not need to discuss what happens with $\boldsymbol{\theta}_{\boldsymbol{b}}$ at the boundary of the support. Estimation has been tried on a restricted support with good results. Another way of avoiding this condition is transforming to standard normal marginals as discussed in Section 4.7.

Remark 2. The condition of geometric ergodicity is quite standard in time series analysis; see, for example, Meyn and Tweedie (2009). Condition (ii) is fulfilled under weak conditions on f because of the presence of the kernel function. In fact, the finiteness condition in (ii) can be expressed as

$$\int K_{\boldsymbol{b}}^\gamma(\boldsymbol{v} - \boldsymbol{x})\left[\frac{\partial}{\partial\theta_j}\left\{\frac{1}{2}\log|\boldsymbol{\Sigma}(\boldsymbol{x})| \right.\right.$$
$$\left.\left. - \frac{1}{2}(\boldsymbol{v} - \boldsymbol{\mu}(\boldsymbol{x}))^T\boldsymbol{\Sigma}^{-1}(\boldsymbol{x})(\boldsymbol{v} - \boldsymbol{\mu}(\boldsymbol{x}))\right\}\right]^\gamma f(\boldsymbol{v})\,d\boldsymbol{v} < \infty,$$

where $\theta_j, j = 1, \ldots, 5$, correspond to the components of $\boldsymbol{\mu}(\boldsymbol{x})$ and $\boldsymbol{\Sigma}(\boldsymbol{x})$ in the definition of $\psi(\boldsymbol{x}, \boldsymbol{\theta})$. Clearly, for a fixed $\boldsymbol{x}$, this integral exists by choosing the tail behavior of the kernel K to decrease sufficiently fast compared to the tail behavior of f. In particular, K can be chosen to have a compact support.

Condition (iii) (in a slightly stronger version) is left unverified by Hjort and Jones (1996) but was discussed in Section 4.3. It seems quite reasonable from a practical point of view, and it holds for the step function (4.7), which in turn can be taken as an approximation for more general models. This condition is in a way analogous to a condition of existence and uniqueness for a maximum likelihood estimate. Note that the assumption is made for a fixed $\boldsymbol{x}$ and does not hold necessarily for every $\boldsymbol{x}$.

Remark 3. The question remains how $\boldsymbol{J}_b$ in (4.13) and $\boldsymbol{M}_b$ in (4.14) should be evaluated for a given data set. We will return to this question in Section 4.8.

Remark 4. The set A mentioned in the theorem is due to the use of a result by Egorov, in turn used by Klimko and Nelson (1978), on which our asymptotic analysis is based. In fact, much of our asymptotic analysis is based on this approach, and when we talk about consistency, it is with the above proviso on a set A.

4.4.2 Asymptotic theory as $\boldsymbol{b} \to 0$

The main difficulty in extending Theorem 4.1 to the present situation of $\boldsymbol{b} \to \boldsymbol{0}$ is that the matrices $\boldsymbol{J}_b$ in (4.13) and $\boldsymbol{M}_b$ in (4.14) are no longer positive definite as $\boldsymbol{b} \to \boldsymbol{0}$. In fact, with $\boldsymbol{J}_b$ and $\boldsymbol{M}_b$ defined by the integral expressions in (4.13) and (4.14) but with the parameter $\boldsymbol{\theta}_b(\boldsymbol{x})$ replaced by $\boldsymbol{\theta}(\boldsymbol{x})$, we have $\boldsymbol{J}_b \to \boldsymbol{J} \stackrel{\text{def}}{=} \boldsymbol{u}(\boldsymbol{x}, \boldsymbol{\theta}(\boldsymbol{x}))\boldsymbol{u}^T(\boldsymbol{x}, \boldsymbol{\theta}(\boldsymbol{x}))\psi(\boldsymbol{x}, \boldsymbol{\theta}(\boldsymbol{x}))$ and $\boldsymbol{M}_b \to \boldsymbol{M} \stackrel{\text{def}}{=} \boldsymbol{u}^T(\boldsymbol{x}, \boldsymbol{\theta}(\boldsymbol{x}))\boldsymbol{u}(\boldsymbol{x}, \boldsymbol{\theta}(\boldsymbol{x}))f(\boldsymbol{x}) \int K^2(\boldsymbol{v})\, d\boldsymbol{v}$ (the last term of (4.14) is of smaller order as $\boldsymbol{b} \to \boldsymbol{0}$). Both these matrices are non-negative definite but not positive definite because the matrix $\boldsymbol{u}(\boldsymbol{x}, \boldsymbol{\theta}(\boldsymbol{x}))\boldsymbol{u}^T(\boldsymbol{x}, \boldsymbol{\theta}(\boldsymbol{x}))$ is of rank 1. The matrices $\boldsymbol{J}$ and $\boldsymbol{M}$ are obtained by only retaining the first-order term in a Taylor expansion in terms of $\boldsymbol{b}$. To obtain the positive definiteness or rather avoid non-singularity, higher-order terms must be included, and these are picked up by a scaling that is changed accordingly.

We illustrate this by looking at the Taylor expansion of the term

$$\boldsymbol{I}_M \sim \int K_b^2(\boldsymbol{v} - \boldsymbol{x})\boldsymbol{u}(\boldsymbol{v}, \boldsymbol{\theta}(\boldsymbol{x}))\boldsymbol{u}^T(\boldsymbol{v}, \boldsymbol{\theta}(\boldsymbol{x}))f(\boldsymbol{v})\, d\boldsymbol{v}$$

corresponding to $\boldsymbol{M}_b$ and looking at the general (possibly non-Gaussian) case of a parameter vector $\boldsymbol{\theta}(\boldsymbol{x})$, the existence of which was assumed in Section 4.3. The other terms are treated in an identical manner. Substituting $w_i = b_i^{-1}(v_i - x_i)$ and letting $\boldsymbol{w} = (w_1, w_2)$, we have, by retaining two more terms of the Taylor expansion,

$$\boldsymbol{I}_M \sim \int K^2(w_1, w_2)\boldsymbol{A}\boldsymbol{b}_w\boldsymbol{b}_w^T\boldsymbol{A}^T f(\boldsymbol{x} + b_1w_1 + b_2w_2)\, dw_1\, dw_2,$$

where typically K is a product kernel, $\boldsymbol{b}_w$ is the six-dimensional vector defined by $\boldsymbol{b}_w^T = (1\ b_1w_1\ b_2w_2\ b_1^2w_1^2\ b_1w_1b_2w_2\ b_2^2w_2^2)$, and $\boldsymbol{A}$ is the 5×6 matrix $(\boldsymbol{u}\ u_{x_1}\ \boldsymbol{u}_{x_2}\ \frac{1}{2}\boldsymbol{u}_{x_1^2}\ \boldsymbol{u}_{x_1x_2}\ \frac{1}{2}\boldsymbol{u}_{x_2^2})$, with

$$\boldsymbol{u}_{x_1} = \frac{\partial \boldsymbol{u}}{\partial x_1},\ \boldsymbol{u}_{x_2} = \frac{\partial \boldsymbol{u}}{\partial x_2},\ \boldsymbol{u}_{x_1^2} = \frac{\partial^2 \boldsymbol{u}}{\partial x_1^2},\ \boldsymbol{u}_{x_2^2} = \frac{\partial^2 \boldsymbol{u}}{\partial x_2^2},\ \boldsymbol{u}_{x_1x_2} = \frac{\partial^2 \boldsymbol{u}}{\partial x_1 \partial x_2}.$$

Computing $\int K^2(w_1, w_2)\boldsymbol{b}_w\boldsymbol{b}_w^T\, dw_1\, dw_2$ and omitting multiplicative factors consisting of integral expressions in terms of the kernel function, we obtain the following 6×6 matrix:

$$\boldsymbol{H} = \begin{pmatrix} 1 & 0 & 0 & b_1^2 & b_2^2 & 0 \\ 0 & b_1^2 & 0 & 0 & 0 & 0 \\ 0 & 0 & b_2^2 & 0 & 0 & 0 \\ b_1^2 & 0 & 0 & b_1^4 & b_1^2b_2^2 & 0 \\ b_2^2 & 0 & 0 & b_1^2b_2^2 & b_2^4 & 0 \\ 0 & 0 & 0 & 0 & 0 & b_1^2b_2^2 \end{pmatrix}.$$

Assuming that the local Gaussian at the point $\boldsymbol{x}$ is non-degenerate, the matrix $\boldsymbol{A}$ is of rank 5, and consequently, since $\boldsymbol{H}$ is at least (depending on the choice of bandwidth) of rank 5, $\boldsymbol{AHA}^T$ is of rank 5. It follows that the second-order Taylor expansion $\boldsymbol{M}_{b,2}$ of $\boldsymbol{M}_b$ is positive definite (non-singular) of order $(b_1b_2)^2$ in the sense that $(b_1b_2)^{-2}\boldsymbol{M}_{b,2}$ exists and is positive definite in the limit. Similarly, whereas the matrix $\boldsymbol{J}$ is singular, $(b_1b_2)^{-2}\boldsymbol{J}_{b,2}$ is non-singular and positive definite as $b_1, b_2 \to 0$. We can get an explicit expression for the leading term of $(b_1b_2)^2\boldsymbol{J}_b^{-1}\boldsymbol{M}_b\boldsymbol{J}_b^{-1}$ by symbol manipulation software, for example, the software package Maple. The coefficient associated with the leading term is very complicated and not useful as it runs over several pages of computer output.

We will see that the above matrix terms enter into the asymptotic expressions in the following theorem. For evaluating the covariances in practice, we refer to Section 4.8.

We can now formulate a theorem in the case where $\boldsymbol{b} \to \boldsymbol{0}$. We require that the kernel function K is Lipschitz, that is, there exists a positive constant C such that $|K(\boldsymbol{x}) - K(\boldsymbol{y})| \leq C|\boldsymbol{x} - \boldsymbol{y}|$ for any $\boldsymbol{x}$ and $\boldsymbol{y}$ in the support of K. Its proof is given in Section 4.10.1. (Note that there are a couple of typos in the formulation of the corresponding theorem in Tjøstheim and Hufthammer (2013).)

Theorem 4.2. *Let $\{\mathbf{X}_t\}$ be a bivariate stationary time series with bivariate density f having support on all of $\mathbb{R}^2$. Assume that*

(i) *$\{\mathbf{X}_t\}$ is geometrically ergodic,*

(ii) *$n \to \infty$ and $b_1, b_2 \to 0$ so that $\log n/n(b_1b_2)^3 \to 0$,*

(iii) *the kernel function K is Lipschitz,*

(iv) *f is such that at the fixed point $\boldsymbol{x}$, there exists a non-degenerate local Gaussian approximation $\psi(\boldsymbol{v}, \boldsymbol{\theta}(\boldsymbol{x}))$ as given in Section 4.3 such that $E(K_{\boldsymbol{b}}(\mathbf{X}_t - \boldsymbol{x})|\partial/\partial\theta_j \log \psi(\mathbf{X}_t, \boldsymbol{\theta}(\boldsymbol{x}))|^\gamma) < \infty, j = 1, \ldots, 5$, for some $\gamma > 2$,*

(v) *there exists a bandwidth vector $\boldsymbol{b}_0$ such that there is a unique solution $\boldsymbol{\theta}_{\boldsymbol{b}}(\boldsymbol{x})$ of (4.6) for every $\mathbf{0} < \boldsymbol{b} < \boldsymbol{b}_0$ (component-wise).*

Then for every $\varepsilon > 0$, there is a possibly $\boldsymbol{x}$-dependent event A with $P(A^c) < \varepsilon$ such that there exists a sequence $\{\widehat{\boldsymbol{\theta}}_{\boldsymbol{b},n}(\boldsymbol{x})\}$ that minimizes Q in (4.11) and such that $\widehat{\boldsymbol{\theta}}_{n,\boldsymbol{b}}(\boldsymbol{x})$ for a fixed $\boldsymbol{x}$ converges almost surely to the true value $\boldsymbol{\theta}(\boldsymbol{x}) = \boldsymbol{\theta}_0(\boldsymbol{x})$ on A. Moreover,

$$(n(b_1b_2)^3)^{1/2}(\widehat{\boldsymbol{\theta}}_{n,\boldsymbol{b}}(\boldsymbol{x}) - \boldsymbol{\theta}_0(\boldsymbol{x})) \xrightarrow{d} \mathcal{N}(\mathbf{0}, (b_1b_2)^2\boldsymbol{J}_{\boldsymbol{b}}^{-1}\boldsymbol{M}_{\boldsymbol{b}}\boldsymbol{J}_{\boldsymbol{b}}^{-1}),$$

this meaning that the left-hand side is asymptotically normal with limiting covariance as obtained from $(b_1b_2)^2\boldsymbol{J}_{\boldsymbol{b}}^{-1}\boldsymbol{M}_{\boldsymbol{b}}\boldsymbol{J}_{\boldsymbol{b}}^{-1}$ as $b_1, b_2 \to 0$ at the appropriate rate or, alternatively,

$$(nb_1b_2)^{1/2}\boldsymbol{M}_{\boldsymbol{b}}^{-1/2}\boldsymbol{J}_{\boldsymbol{b}}(\widehat{\boldsymbol{\theta}}_{n,\boldsymbol{b}}(\boldsymbol{x}) - \boldsymbol{\theta}_0(\boldsymbol{x})) \xrightarrow{d} \mathcal{N}(\mathbf{0}, \boldsymbol{I}), \tag{4.15}$$

where $\boldsymbol{I}$ is the identity matrix of dimension 5.

Remark 1. The convergence rate can be compared to the results of Jones (1996), where the convergence is of the same order. The convergence is much slower than in the standard bivariate nonparametric case, which means that for a given number of observations, we must use a much larger bandwidth, which again means that if we are interested in details of a non-smooth $\boldsymbol{\theta}(\boldsymbol{x})$ in the non-Gaussian case, then we must have rather large samples. For a reasonable smooth density, $\boldsymbol{\theta}(\boldsymbol{x})$ will typically be smooth. Note that in Section 4.7 we point out an approximation that converges much faster, in fact, with a rate that equals the standard bivariate nonparametric rate. As is seen in Berentsen et al. (2014b), Berentsen and Tjøstheim (2014), Støve et al. (2014), and Section 4.6, we get good results for $n = 500$ and in some cases for n considerably smaller.

Remark 2. The almost sure nonparametric convergence in fact may yield the uniform convergence on a compact set. We refer to Hansen (2008) for a possibly expanding set. Such results are of interest in the construction of test functionals for independence and goodness-of-fit tests.

4.5 Properties

4.5.1 Some general properties of the local Gaussian correlation

Before stating particular properties of the LGC, we should remark that the family of Gaussian distributions is of course especially attractive for multivariate analysis because of its extensive and elegant theory. Most statisticians will agree that the Gaussian distribution is in a class of itself regarding transparency and simplicity of multivariate theory, and this is the main reason why it has been so much used in applications, not only in finance, but in a host of multivariate problems. Sometimes, however, and this is certainly the case in econometrics and finance, data do not follow a multivariate Gaussian, and applications based on it can give very misleading and even catastrophic results; see for example, Taleb (2007). The point of using the local Gaussian approximation is that then we can move away from Gaussian distributions and describe much more general situations, in particular, multivariate thick-tailed distributions like those we otherwise see in finance. At the same time, we can exploit much of the multivariate Gaussian theory locally. We have found this very useful in a number of papers extending in various directions, such as Støve et al. (2014), Støve and Tjøstheim (2014), Berentsen and Tjøstheim (2014), Berentsen et al. (2014a), Berentsen et al. (2014b), Berentsen et al. (2017), Lacal and Tjøstheim (2017), Lacal and Tjøstheim (2019), Otneim and Tjøstheim (2017), Otneim and Tjøstheim (2018), Otneim and Tjøstheim (2021), and Jordanger and Tjøstheim (2020). Much of the rest of the book is based on these papers.

4.5.2 Independence and functional dependence

First note that from the form of the local likelihood it follows that $-1 \leq \widehat{\rho}(\boldsymbol{x}) \leq 1$. Since, by Theorems 4.1 and 4.2, $\widehat{\rho}(\boldsymbol{x}) \to \rho(\boldsymbol{x})$ almost surely, this implies that $-1 \leq \rho(\boldsymbol{x}) \leq 1$.

The (global) correlation between two independent variables is equal to zero, but the converse statement does not hold. Moreover, if X_1 and X_2 are linearly related (not necessarily Gaussian) with $X_2 = a + bX_1$, then $\rho = 1$ if

$b > 0$ and $\rho = -1$ if $b < 0$, but if $X_2 = \alpha(X_1)$ for some function α, then the value of ρ will depend on α. For instance, if $X_2 = X_1^2$, then $\rho = 0$ under weak assumptions.

If X_1 and X_2 are independent, then their joint density function (if it exists) satisfies $f(x_1, x_2) = f_1(x_1)f_2(x_2)$. As $\boldsymbol{b} \to \mathbf{0}$ in (4.10), then $\boldsymbol{\theta}_b(\boldsymbol{x}) \to \boldsymbol{\theta}(\boldsymbol{x})$, and independence forces $\psi(\boldsymbol{x}, \theta(\boldsymbol{x}))$ to factor, and hence $\rho(\boldsymbol{x}) \equiv 0$.

However, a necessary and sufficient condition for independence is that $\rho(\boldsymbol{x}) \equiv 0$, $\mu_i(\boldsymbol{x}) \equiv \mu_i(x_i)$, $\sigma_i(\boldsymbol{x}) = \sigma_i(x_i)$, $i = 1, 2$. Functionals based on $\rho(\boldsymbol{x})$ for measuring dependence and for testing independence are given in Chapter 7. An advantage of the LGC approach is that we can distinguish between positive and negative dependence in a nonlinear situation, which does not seem to be the case for other commonly used nonlinear dependence measures; see Chapter 3.4.

The other extreme is where $|\rho(\boldsymbol{x})| \equiv 1$. This is connected to functional dependence in much the same way as linear dependence is connected to $\rho = 1$. Assume that $X_2 = \alpha(X_1)$ with differentiable α. Let $Z_1 = \Phi^{-1}(F_{X_1}(X_1))$, where Φ is the cumulative distribution function of a standard normal variable, and F_{X_1} is the cumulative distribution function of X_1. Then $Z_1 \sim \mathcal{N}(0, 1)$ and $X_1 = F_{X_1}^{-1}(\Phi(Z_1)) \stackrel{\text{def}}{=} g(Z_1)$; see also Section 4.7. Hence X_1 can be represented by a local Gaussian representation, so that $X_1 = g(Z_1)$. Then $X_2 = \alpha(g(Z_1))$. There is only one variable involved, and any Gaussian approximation must also collapse to one variable. This is only possible if there are two Gaussian variables $(Y_1(\boldsymbol{x}), Y_2(\boldsymbol{x}))$ having bivariate density $\psi(\boldsymbol{v}, \boldsymbol{\mu}(\boldsymbol{x}), \boldsymbol{\Sigma}(\boldsymbol{x}))$ such that $Y_1(\boldsymbol{x}) = a + bY_2(\boldsymbol{x})$ for some scalars a and b at the point $\boldsymbol{x}$, which in turn implies that $\rho(\boldsymbol{x}) = +1$ or $\rho(\boldsymbol{x}) = -1$, depending on whether the sign of $\alpha'(\boldsymbol{x})$ is positive or negative. The same reasoning can be carried out if $\{(x_1, x_2)\}$ defines a closed curve, such as $\alpha(x_1) + \beta(x_2) = c$. Then $\rho(\boldsymbol{x})$ is equal to $+1$ or -1 along the curve, depending on whether the tangent at the point $\boldsymbol{x}$ has positive or negative slope.

4.5.3 The Rényi criteria

The Rényi properties are seven desirable properties for a dependence measure to have. We stated them in Chapter 3.4 and discussed several dependence measures in light of these criteria. We will now look at them in the context of the local Gaussian correlation $\rho(\boldsymbol{x})$:

(i) $\rho(\boldsymbol{x})$ is a local measure, but it is defined for any X_1 and X_2 under the regularity conditions discussed when defining the population value.

(ii) Because $\rho(\boldsymbol{x})$ is a local measure, we generally have $\rho(x_1, x_2) \neq \rho(x_2, x_1)$, but $\rho_{X_1,X_2}(x_1, x_2) = \rho_{X_2,X_1}(x_2, x_1)$.

(iii) We have that $-1 \leq \rho(\boldsymbol{x}) \leq 1$ and $-1 \leq \widehat{\rho}(\boldsymbol{x}) \leq 1$. We believe the possibility to measure negative and positive dependence to be one of the main assets of the local Gaussian correlation.

(iv) As we discussed in the preceding subsection, the independence between X_1 and X_2 implies $\rho(x_1, x_2) \equiv 0$. For the opposite to be true, we must require in addition that $\mu_i(x_1, x_2) \equiv \mu_i(x_i)$ and $\sigma_i(x_1, x_2) \equiv \sigma_i(x_i)$ for $i = 1, 2$. In the global Gaussian case, this is trivially fulfilled since all x-dependence disappears.

(v) If $X_1 = f(X_2)$ or $X_2 = g(X_1)$, then again see the preceding subsection: the limiting value $\rho(x_1, x_2)$ as the neighborhood shrinks to the point (x_1, x_2) is equal to 1 or -1, according to f or g having a positive or negative slope at x_2 or x_1. The same is true for the closed curve relationship $g(X_1) + f(X_2) = c$ for a constant c; then $\rho(\boldsymbol{x})$ is equal to 1 or -1 along the curve, depending on whether the tangent at the point $\boldsymbol{x}$ has positive or negative slope.

(vi) Like Pearson's ρ, the LGC $\rho(\boldsymbol{x})$ depends on the marginals, but the normalized correlation $\rho_{\boldsymbol{Z}}(\boldsymbol{z})$, to be introduced in Section 4.7, is independent of marginals.

(vii) In the Gaussian case, we have $\rho(\boldsymbol{x}) \equiv \rho_{\boldsymbol{Z}}(\boldsymbol{z}) \equiv \rho$ by construction. Note that this is also true for the Gaussian copula (under monotone transformations of the marginals from normal distributions). See Chapter 5.3.2.

We cover general transformation properties in the next subsection but note first the connection with the quadrant dependence of Lehmann (1966). Using the results from that paper, we can show that if $\rho(\boldsymbol{x}) \geq 0$ or $\rho(\boldsymbol{x}) \leq 0$ for all $\boldsymbol{x}$, then (X_1, X_2) belongs to the class $\mathcal{F}$ defined in Lehmann's paper. Moreover, if the second moments exist, then $\rho(\boldsymbol{x}) \geq 0$ for all $\boldsymbol{x}$ implies that the global correlation $\rho \geq 0$, and $\rho(\boldsymbol{x}) \leq 0$ for all $\boldsymbol{x}$ implies $\rho \leq 0$.

4.5.4 Linear transformation and symmetries

A very useful feature of the ordinary global correlation is that it is scale invariant in the sense that $\rho_{\alpha_1+\beta_1 X_1, \alpha_2+\beta_2 X_2} = \rho_{X_1,X_2}$. There is a corresponding scale invariance for the LGC, but with the proviso that the point (x_1, x_2) is moved to the point $(\alpha_1 + \beta_1 x_1, \alpha_2 + \beta_2 x_2)$. To analyze this and to analyze symmetry, we need to study the effect of a linear transformation. We assume that $\boldsymbol{X}$ has a local Gaussian representation $\psi(\boldsymbol{x}, \theta(\boldsymbol{x}))$ with $\boldsymbol{\theta}(\boldsymbol{x}) = (\boldsymbol{\mu}(\boldsymbol{x}), \boldsymbol{\Sigma}(\boldsymbol{x}))$, and we look at the transformation $\boldsymbol{Y} = \boldsymbol{\alpha} + \boldsymbol{A}\boldsymbol{X}$, where

$\boldsymbol{\alpha}$ is a two-dimensional vector, and $\boldsymbol{A}$ is a non-singular 2×2 matrix. We know (Theorems 4.1 and 4.2) that under mild regularity conditions, $\widehat{\boldsymbol{\theta}}(\boldsymbol{x})$ converges toward $\boldsymbol{\theta}(\boldsymbol{x})$ almost surely. We will use local likelihood theory to establish the following proposition.

Proposition 4.2. *For $\boldsymbol{X}$ and $\boldsymbol{Y}$ as defined above and with $\boldsymbol{y} = \boldsymbol{\alpha} + \boldsymbol{A}\boldsymbol{x}$, $\boldsymbol{\theta}(\boldsymbol{y}) = (\boldsymbol{\mu}(\boldsymbol{y}), \boldsymbol{\Sigma}(\boldsymbol{y}))$, we have $\boldsymbol{\mu}(\boldsymbol{y}) = \boldsymbol{\alpha} + \boldsymbol{A}\boldsymbol{\mu}(\boldsymbol{x})$ and $\boldsymbol{\Sigma}(\boldsymbol{y}) = \boldsymbol{A}\boldsymbol{\Sigma}(\boldsymbol{x})\boldsymbol{A}^T$.*

A proof is given in Section 4.10.3, and from that proof we see that these transformation results are also true for a population parameter $\boldsymbol{\theta}_b(\boldsymbol{x})$ for a fixed bandwidth.

We will look at bivariate densities f having the following types of symmetries (we may assume that the global mean $\boldsymbol{\mu} = \mathrm{E}(\boldsymbol{X}) = \boldsymbol{0}$, because otherwise we may just center the density at $\boldsymbol{\mu}$ and discuss symmetry around $\boldsymbol{\mu}$):

(i) Radial symmetry, where $f(-\boldsymbol{x}) = f(\boldsymbol{x})$,

(ii) reflection symmetry, where $f(-x_1, x_2) = f(x_1, x_2)$ and/or $f(x_1, -x_2) = f(x_1, x_2)$,

(iii) exchange symmetry, where $f(x_1, x_2) = f(x_2, x_1)$, and

(iv) rotation symmetry, where $f(\boldsymbol{x}) = r(|\boldsymbol{x}|)$ for some function r.

We will examine how the corresponding local Gaussian correlation $\rho(\boldsymbol{x})$ behaves. All the symmetries can be described by linear transformations, and we use the facts already established in Proposition 4.2 that if $\boldsymbol{y} = g(\boldsymbol{x}) = \boldsymbol{A}\boldsymbol{x}$, then $\boldsymbol{\Sigma}_Y(\boldsymbol{y}) = \boldsymbol{A}\boldsymbol{\Sigma}_X(\boldsymbol{x})\boldsymbol{A}^T$ and $\boldsymbol{\mu}_Y(\boldsymbol{y}) = \boldsymbol{A}\boldsymbol{\mu}(\boldsymbol{x})$ with $\boldsymbol{x} = \boldsymbol{A}^{-1}\boldsymbol{y}$. Symmetry properties of $\boldsymbol{\Sigma}(\boldsymbol{x})$ and $\boldsymbol{\mu}(\boldsymbol{x})$ can conceivably be used to obtain more precise estimates and increased power of tests.

(i) Radial symmetry: If $\boldsymbol{X}$ has radial symmetry, then $\boldsymbol{X}$ and

$$-\boldsymbol{X} = \begin{pmatrix} -1 & 0 \\ 0 & -1 \end{pmatrix} \boldsymbol{X}$$

have the same density. It follows that

$$\boldsymbol{\Sigma}(-\boldsymbol{x}) = \begin{pmatrix} -1 & 0 \\ 0 & -1 \end{pmatrix} \boldsymbol{\Sigma}(\boldsymbol{x}) \begin{bmatrix} -1 & 0 \\ 0 & -1 \end{bmatrix} = \boldsymbol{\Sigma}(\boldsymbol{x}),$$

so that $\boldsymbol{\Sigma}(\boldsymbol{x})$ and hence $\rho(\boldsymbol{x})$ have radial symmetry. However, for the local mean, $\boldsymbol{\mu}(-\boldsymbol{x}) = -\boldsymbol{\mu}(\boldsymbol{x})$. Examples of densities having radial symmetry are all elliptical distributions. If we let X_1 and X_2 represent Y_t and Y_{t-1} in a GARCH model, then $(-Y_t, -Y_{t-1})$ has the same GARCH structure, and GARCH densities have radial symmetry.

See Chapter 2.4 for a definition of the GARCH model. Consequently, the local covariance and local correlation have radial symmetry. Figs. 4.1 and 4.2 show estimates of $\rho(\boldsymbol{x})$ for a t-distribution with 4 degrees of freedom and global $\rho = 0$ and for a GARCH(1, 1) model, respectively. The radial symmetry of $\rho(\boldsymbol{x})$ emerges clearly from the estimated values in the figures, but note that the values at the boundaries of the plot carry larger uncertainty; see also Sections 4.6.2 and 4.8 for confidence intervals.

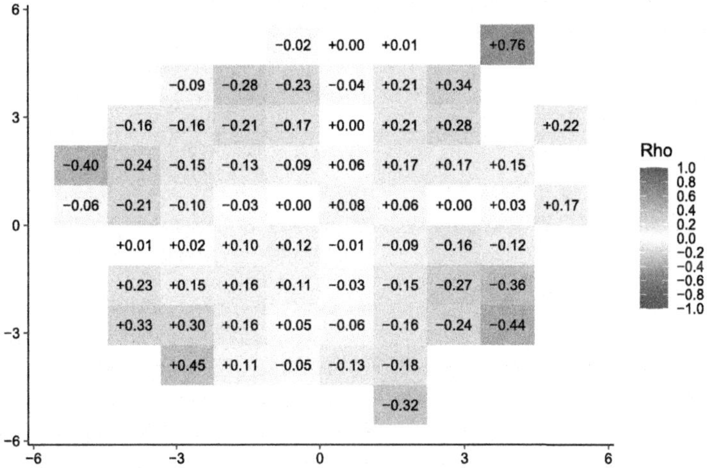

Figure 4.1 Estimate of the LGC for 10 000 observations generated from a t-distribution with 4 degrees of freedom using bandwidths $b_1 = b_2 = 1$.

(ii) Reflection symmetry: Reflection symmetry around the x_1 and x_2 axes is described by the matrices

$$\boldsymbol{A}_1 = \begin{pmatrix} 1 & 0 \\ 0 & -1 \end{pmatrix} \quad \text{and} \quad \boldsymbol{A}_2 = \begin{pmatrix} -1 & 0 \\ 0 & 1 \end{pmatrix},$$

so that

$$\begin{pmatrix} x_1 \\ -x_2 \end{pmatrix} = \boldsymbol{A}_1 \begin{pmatrix} x_1 \\ x_2 \end{pmatrix} \quad \text{and} \quad \begin{pmatrix} -x_1 \\ x_2 \end{pmatrix} = \boldsymbol{A}_2 \begin{pmatrix} x_1 \\ x_2 \end{pmatrix}.$$

We have

$$\boldsymbol{\Sigma}(x_1, -x_2) = \boldsymbol{A}_1 \boldsymbol{\Sigma}(\boldsymbol{x}) \boldsymbol{A}_1^T = \begin{pmatrix} \sigma_{11}(\boldsymbol{x}) & -\sigma_{12}(\boldsymbol{x}) \\ -\sigma_{12}(\boldsymbol{x}) & \sigma_{22}(\boldsymbol{x}) \end{pmatrix}.$$

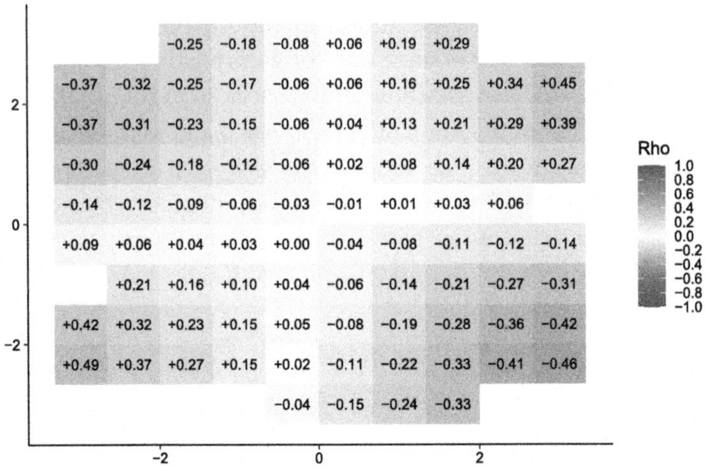

Figure 4.2 Estimate of the LGC for 10 000 observations (X_t, X_{t-1}), where X_t is generated from the GARCH(1,1)-model defined in Section 4.6.1 using bandwidths $b_1 = b_2 = 1$.

We see that $\sigma_{ii}(x_1, -x_2) = \sigma_{ii}(x_1, x_2)$, $i = 1, 2$, and $\rho(x_1, -x_2) = -\rho(x_1, x_2)$. Similarly, if there is reflection symmetry around the x_2 axis, then $\sigma_{ii}(-x_1, x_2) = \sigma_{ii}(x_1, x_2)$, $i = 1, 2$, and $\rho(-x_1, x_2) = -\rho(x_1, x_2)$, that is, odd reflection symmetry for the local correlation. Moreover, $\mu_1(x_1, -x_2) = \mu_1(x_1, x_2)$, $\mu_2(x_1, -x_2) = -\mu_2(x_1, x_2)$, and $\mu_1(-x_1, x_2) = -\mu_1(x_1, x_2)$, $\mu_2(-x_1, x_2) = \mu_2(x_1, x_2)$. Examples of densities having reflection symmetry are the spherical densities, for example, the t-distribution with 4 degrees of freedom with global $\rho = 0$. The odd reflection symmetry of the local correlation in this case is brought out by the estimated $\widehat{\rho}(x)$ in Fig. 4.1. A general consequence of the odd reflection symmetry derived above is that $\rho(\boldsymbol{x})$ is zero along the coordinate axes, that is, $\rho(x_1, 0) \equiv \rho(0, x_2) \equiv 0$. Again, this is roughly confirmed by the estimates in Fig. 4.1. In the GARCH model, $(-Y_t, Y_{t-1})$ have the same distribution as (Y_t, Y_{t-1}), meaning that in this example the local correlation also has odd reflection symmetry (see Fig. 4.2).

(iii) Exchange symmetry: Let

$$\boldsymbol{A} = \begin{pmatrix} 0 & 1 \\ 1 & 0 \end{pmatrix}.$$

If we have exchange symmetry, then $\boldsymbol{\Sigma}(x_2, x_1) = \boldsymbol{A}\boldsymbol{\Sigma}(x_1, x_2)\boldsymbol{A}^T$, and exchange symmetry of $f(\boldsymbol{x})$ implies exchange symmetry of $\boldsymbol{\Sigma}(\boldsymbol{x})$ and hence of $\rho(x)$. Many copula models have exchange symmetry. An example is given in Fig. 4.3d. Elliptical distributions with a principal axis along $x_1 = x_2$ have exchange symmetry. On the other hand, for a GARCH model, we cannot in general exchange Y_t and Y_{t-1} and still obtain the same bivariate distribution. This implies that the local correlation for GARCH models does not in general have exchange symmetry (although this is not very clear for the model in Fig. 4.2). For an exchange-symmetric density, the local mean is exchange symmetric.

(iv) Rotations: The rotation matrix is given by

$$\boldsymbol{A} = \begin{pmatrix} \cos\alpha & -\sin\alpha \\ \sin\alpha & \cos\alpha \end{pmatrix}.$$

For a given vector $\boldsymbol{x}$, $\boldsymbol{A}\boldsymbol{x}$ is rotated counter-clockwise through an angle α. We consider an arbitrary spherical density f. Then f is rotation symmetric in addition to being radial and reflection and exchange symmetric. The corresponding local correlation is radial and exchange symmetric, but it is odd reflection symmetric. We start rotation from a point $\boldsymbol{x} = (x_1, 0)$ on the positive x_1 axis. Then $\rho(x_1, 0) = 0$, so that

$$y = \begin{pmatrix} y_1 \\ y_2 \end{pmatrix} = \boldsymbol{A}\begin{pmatrix} x_1 \\ 0 \end{pmatrix} = \begin{pmatrix} x_1\cos\alpha \\ x_1\sin\alpha \end{pmatrix}.$$

Further, noting that $\boldsymbol{\Sigma}(\boldsymbol{x})$ is diagonal, since $\rho(\boldsymbol{x}) = 0$,

$$\begin{aligned}\boldsymbol{\Sigma}(\boldsymbol{y}) &= \boldsymbol{A}\boldsymbol{\Sigma}(\boldsymbol{x})\boldsymbol{A}^T \\ &= \begin{pmatrix} \sigma_{11}(\boldsymbol{x})\cos^2\alpha + \sigma_{22}(\boldsymbol{x})\sin^2\alpha & (\sigma_{11}(\boldsymbol{x}) - \sigma_{22}(\boldsymbol{x}))\sin\alpha\cos\alpha \\ (\sigma_{11}(\boldsymbol{x}) - \sigma_{22}(\boldsymbol{x}))\sin\alpha\cos\alpha & \sigma_{11}(\boldsymbol{x})\sin^2\alpha + \sigma_{22}(\boldsymbol{x})\cos^2\alpha \end{pmatrix}.\end{aligned}$$

It follows that

$$\rho^2(\boldsymbol{y}) = \rho^2(\alpha) = \frac{(\sigma_{11}(\boldsymbol{x}) - \sigma_{22}(\boldsymbol{x}))^2}{\sigma_{11}^2(\boldsymbol{x}) + \sigma_{22}^2(\boldsymbol{x}) + \sigma_{11}(\boldsymbol{x})\sigma_{22}(\boldsymbol{x})(\tan^2\alpha + \frac{1}{\tan^2\alpha})},$$

which has its maximum for $\tan^2\alpha = 1$, that is, $\alpha = \pm\pi/4$. This is consistent with Fig. 4.1, where we see that $\rho(\alpha)$ has maxima/minima along $\alpha = \pi/4$ and $\alpha = -\pi/4$, and similarly for the other quadrants. Moreover, we can show that $\rho(\alpha)$ is positive in the first and third quadrants and negative in the second and fourth quadrants. For an elliptical distribution (again assuming that $\boldsymbol{\mu} = \mathbf{0}$), let $\boldsymbol{\Sigma}$ be the global covariance of $\mathbf{X}$. Then the elliptic density can be written as $f(\boldsymbol{x}) = |\boldsymbol{\Sigma}^{-1/2}| g(\boldsymbol{x}^T \boldsymbol{\Sigma}^{-1} \boldsymbol{x})$ for a function g. If the global standard deviations σ_1 and σ_2 are equal, then $(x_1, x_2)\boldsymbol{\Sigma}^{-1}(x_1, x_2)^T = (x_2, x_1)\boldsymbol{\Sigma}^{-1}(x_2, x_1)^T$, and $f(\boldsymbol{x})$ and $\rho(\boldsymbol{x})$ are exchange symmetric. This in turn implies that $f(\boldsymbol{x})$ and $\rho(\boldsymbol{x})$ are reflection symmetric along the line $x_1 = x_2$. A similar argument leads to reflection symmetry around the line $x_1 = -x_2$. This means that as we approach the diagonals along the density contours, which are ellipses, these are axes of local maxima and minima (for $\rho > 0$, we have local maxima along the diagonals in the first and third quadrants and minima along the axes in the second and fourth quadrants; for $\rho < 0$, the role of the axes are reversed). If $\sigma_1 \neq \sigma_2$, the same reasoning can be carried through for the scaled variables X_i/σ_i, the axes (x_1, x_1) and $(x_1, -x_1)$ now corresponding to $(x_1, (\sigma_1/\sigma_2)x_1)$ and $(x_1, -(\sigma_1/\sigma_2)x_1)$.

4.6 Examples

In this subsection, we give some examples of estimated LGC maps of simulated and real data sets. Many more examples will be provided throughout the book.

4.6.1 Simulated examples

Figs. 4.3a–4.3d show some examples of estimated LGC maps, using bandwidths determined by the cross-validation procedure proposed in Section 4.8.2 (see also Berentsen and Tjøstheim (2014)) on the original non-normalized scale, that is, $\widehat{\rho}(\boldsymbol{x})$, for the following simulated data:

(i) Simulations from a bivariate standard normal distribution with correlation -0.5.

(ii) Simulations from a bivariate t-distribution with 4 degrees of freedom and a global correlation 0.

(iii) Simulations from the GARCH(1,1) model $X_t = \varepsilon_t h_t^{1/2}$, where $h_t = \alpha + \beta h_{t-1} + \gamma X_{t-1}^2$ with parameters $\alpha = 0.1$, $\beta = 0.7$, $\gamma = 0.2$, and $\epsilon_t \sim$ iid $\mathcal{N}(0, 1)$.

(iv) Simulations from a Clayton copula, defined in Eq. (3.10), with parameter $\theta = 2$ and standard Gaussian marginals.

We use the same sample size $n = 784$ in the simulations as we have for the log-return data examined in Chapter 3.3. The results are given in Fig. 4.3, where we have used the same color code as in Figs. 4.1 and 4.2.

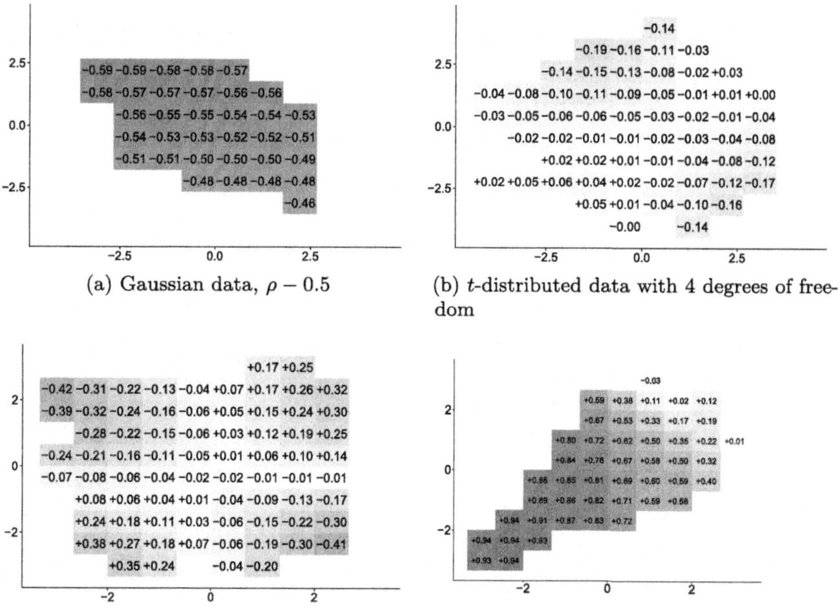

(a) Gaussian data, $\rho - 0.5$

(b) t-distributed data with 4 degrees of freedom

(c) X_t vs. X_{t-1} where X_t is generated from a GARCH(1,1)-model

(d) A bivariate distribution with standard Gaussian marginals and a Clayton copula

Figure 4.3 Some examples of local Gaussian correlation maps; $n = 784$ in all cases.

For the first example in Fig. 4.3a, we see that the estimated LGC is close to the constant true value across all points (in fact, the sample Pearson correlation is $\widehat{\rho} = -0.53$ for these data).

The symmetry pattern of the local Gaussian correlation for the t- distribution with 4 degrees of freedom with global $\rho = 0$ (see Fig. 4.3b) has already been explained in Section 4.5.4. Note that the LGC map reveals the well-known fact that even though we have zero global correlation in this example, the marginal distributions do not agree with statistical independence.

Although X_t and X_{t-1} are uncorrelated in the GARCH model, Fig. 4.3c shows strong local dependence with much the same, although much stronger, pattern as for the t-distribution, that is, positive dependence in the first and third quadrants and negative dependence in the second and fourth quadrants, with increasing dependence away from the center.

Fig. 4.3d clearly picks up the lower tail dependence from generated observations from the Clayton copula, as the estimated LGC is above 0.9 for large negative observations, and then gradually decreases as the observations turn positive.

We will return to the construction of confidence intervals in due course.

4.6.2 A real-data example

We briefly explore the local Gaussian correlation structure for a real bivariate financial data set introduced in Chapter 3.3. Several other financial data sets will be examined in Chapter 6. We recall that this is the daily international equity price index data for the United States (S&P 500) and the United Kingdom (FTSE 100) and that the returns are defined as

$$r_t = 100 \times \left(\log(p_t) - \log(p_{t-1})\right),$$

where p_t is the price index at time t. The observation span covers the period from January 1, 2007, through December 31, 2009, in total 784 observations.

For the return data in Fig. 4.4a, we clearly see that the bivariate return distribution is not Gaussian, since, in particular, there are large local correlations for both large negative and large positive returns. Hence this LGC map shows that when the market is going down, in particular, if there is an extreme downturn, then the dependence increases. The same, but perhaps not quite to the same degree, can be said when the market has an upturn. Such detected differences have direct implications for portfolios where these indices are involved. An increase of dependence when the market is going down leads to a deterioration of the classical diversification protection; see more in Chapter 6.

In many cases, we are mainly interested in data for fixed quantiles of the series, and returns data are basically measured on the same scale. For greater clarity, we may restrict ourselves to looking at the local Gaussian correlation $\widehat{\rho}(x, y)$ at values at the diagonal, that is, for $x = y$. This is shown in Fig. 4.4b. Here we have also plotted the approximate 95% confidence intervals obtained by bootstrapping using 500 realizations, as explained in Section 4.8.1.

We further mention that for this example, we have disregarded a GARCH filtering of the returns, which otherwise we will usually perform for financial data. Such a filtering has the effect of reducing the kurtosis and transforming the data to being closer to independence. The filtering option is discussed in Chapter 6.4.

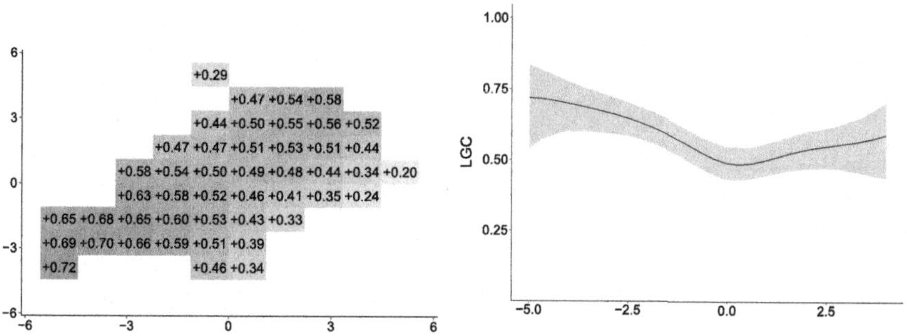

(a) Local Gaussian correlation map

(b) Diagonal local Gaussian correlation values with approximate 95% confidence intervals

Figure 4.4 Local Gaussian correlations of the log-returns data, S&P 500 vs. FTSE 100.

4.7 Transforming the marginals: Normalized local correlation

The local correlation is clearly dependent on the marginal distributions of X_1 and X_2, as is Pearson's ρ. In this section, this marginal dependence will be removed by scaling the observations to a standard normal scale. As mentioned in Chapter 3.3 about the copula, the dependence structure is disentangled from the marginals by Sklar's theorem (3.7) using uniform variables $U_i = F_i(X_i)$, $i = 1, 2$, as basic variables. For measuring local dependence in terms of the LGC, for a number of purposes, it is advantageous to replace the scaling of uniform variables $U_i = F_i(X_i)$ by standard normal variables

$$\boldsymbol{Z} = (Z_1, Z_2) = (\Phi^{-1}(F_1(X_1)), \Phi^{-1}(F_2(X_2))), \tag{4.16}$$

where Φ is the cumulative distribution function of the standard normal distribution. The local Gaussian correlation on the Z-scale will be denoted by $\rho_Z(\boldsymbol{z})$. The normalized measure $\rho_Z(\boldsymbol{z})$ is arguably a better measure of the dependence between X_1 and X_2. Properties (i)–(iii), (v), and (vii) of the Rényi criteria in Chapter 3.4 go through without changes. For (iv), note that even if $Z_i \sim \mathcal{N}(0, 1)$ for $i = 1, 2$, then this does not necessarily imply that in a bivariate local framework $\mu_i(\boldsymbol{z}) \equiv 0$ and $\sigma_i(\boldsymbol{z}) \equiv 1$. For distributions where this is true, X_1 and X_2 are independent if and only if $\rho_Z(\boldsymbol{z}) \equiv 0$. As already mentioned and as is easily checked for the Rényi criterion (vi), $\rho_Z(\boldsymbol{z})$ is invariant with respect to transformations of the marginals. Note that the Pearson's ρ reduces to the van der Waerden (1952) rank correlation in the global case if the margins are transformed to standard normals.

The variable $\boldsymbol{Z}$ cannot of course be observed via transformation (4.16) without knowledge of the margins F_1 and F_2, but these can be estimated by the empirical distribution function. We have made extensive use of $\rho_{\boldsymbol{Z}}(z_1, z_2)$ or rather $\rho_{\widehat{\boldsymbol{Z}}}(z_1, z_2)$ with $\widehat{Z}_i = \Phi^{-1}(\widehat{F}_i(X_i))$. Under certain regularity conditions, the difference between $\boldsymbol{Z}$ and $\widehat{\boldsymbol{Z}}$ can be ignored in limit theorems; see Theorem 4.5. Using the sample of pairs of Gaussian pseudo-observations $\left\{\Phi^{-1}(\widehat{F}_1(X_{1i})), \Phi^{-1}(\widehat{F}_2(X_{2i}))\right\}$, $i = 1, \ldots, n$, we can estimate $\rho_{\boldsymbol{Z}}(z_1, z_2)$ by local log likelihood as described in Section 4.3. Under regularity conditions, as we will see further, the asymptotic theory will be the same as in Section 4.4.

The choice of Gaussian margins in transformation (4.16) is not arbitrary. Since the copula of (X_1, X_2) is defined as the distribution function of $(U_1, U_2) = (F_1(X_1), F_2(X_2))$, we could in principle consider the local Gaussian correlation $\rho_U(u_1, u_2)$ of the variable (U_1, U_2) (or the corresponding pseudo-uniforms). However, fitting a family of Gaussian density functions to uniform variables requires special considerations of boundary effects, which makes this approach unpractical and illogical. The choice of Gaussian margins is much more natural since we are dealing with local Gaussian approximations.

The local normalized correlation can be introduced in the stationary time series case as well for the local autocorrelation and local cross-correlation for a bivariate time series. In the univariate time series case, $F_1 = F_2 = F$, the cumulative distribution function for a stationary time series $\{X_t\}$. The normalized correlation in addition to being invariant to monotone transformations of the marginals is computationally easier to handle because of the standardized marginals. We will give a number of examples of its use in this chapter and in others chapters of the book. The relationship to the copula construction is further explored in Chapter 5.

Even though the variables Z_1 and Z_2 are standard normal, as mentioned, that does not necessarily imply $\mu_i(z_1, z_2) \equiv 0$ and $\sigma_i(z_1, z_2) \equiv 1$ for $i = 1, 2$ in a bivariate local Gaussian approximation to the distribution of (Z_1, Z_2). It does hold, of course, if (Z_1, Z_2) are jointly Gaussian, but in general, assuming this would imply a more restrictive class of approximations.

Otneim and Tjøstheim (2017, 2018) have made the simplification $\mu_{Z_i}(\boldsymbol{z}) \equiv 0$ and $\sigma_{Z_i}(\boldsymbol{z}) \equiv 1$, in which case the asymptotic theory simplifies, and we obtain the familiar nonparametric rate of $O((nb_1b_2)^{-1/2})$ for $\widehat{\rho}_{\widehat{\boldsymbol{Z}}}(\boldsymbol{z})$. It has been used with good results in a multivariate approach to density and conditional density estimation. We will come back to this in

Chapters 9 and 10. In Section 4.7.1, we compare normalized estimates with corresponding unnormalized ones of Section 4.6.

In this section, we consider the asymptotic theory for Z-scaled variables and compare it to the asymptotic theory in Section 4.3. We will discuss the asymptotic theory for the restricted (Z_1, Z_2)-case with $\mu_i(\boldsymbol{z}) \equiv 0$ and $\sigma_i(\boldsymbol{z}) \equiv 1$ in Chapters 9 and 10.

The main difficulty in transferring the asymptotic theory in Section 4.4 along with the corresponding proofs in Section 4.10.1 is that $F_i(x_i)$ is not known, so we have to depend on the pseudo-variables

$$\widehat{Z}_i = \Phi^{-1}\left(\widehat{F}_i(X_i)\right), \tag{4.17}$$

where the $\widehat{F}_i = F_{i,n}$ are the empirical distribution functions given by

$$F_{i,n} = \frac{1}{n}\sum_{t=1}^{n} I(X_{it} \leq x), \qquad i = 1, 2.$$

(Sometimes, $1/n$ is replaced by $1/(n+1)$ to secure better stability for small samples.) The idea in deriving an asymptotic theory for $\widehat{\rho}_{\widehat{\boldsymbol{Z}}}(\boldsymbol{z})$ is to first derive an asymptotic theory in the case where $\boldsymbol{Z}$ is known and then show that using $\widehat{\boldsymbol{Z}}$ instead leads to an additional term that can be neglected because it converges faster to zero in probability than the main term in the asymptotics.

The unrealistic case of known $\boldsymbol{Z}$ is in fact very easy to treat since it is essentially just a particular case of Theorems 4.1 and 4.2. We restate these theorems in terms of the $\boldsymbol{Z}$-notation. First, for a fixed bandwidth $\boldsymbol{b}$:

Theorem 4.3. *Let $\{\boldsymbol{Z}_t\}$ be a stationary bivariate time series obtained from a stationary bivariate time series $\{\boldsymbol{X}_t\}$ with $Z_{it} = \Phi^{-1}(F_i(X_{it}))$ for $i = 1, 2$ and with $\boldsymbol{Z}_t$ having bivariate density g. Assume that*

(i) *$\{\boldsymbol{Z}_t\}$ is geometrically ergodic,*

(ii) *g has support on all of $\mathbb{R}^2$, and*

(iii) *for a fixed bandwidth $\boldsymbol{b}$, there is a unique solution $\boldsymbol{\theta}_{\boldsymbol{b}}(\boldsymbol{z})$ of (4.6) stated in terms of $\boldsymbol{Z}$-variables.*

Then, for every $\varepsilon > 0$, there is a possibly $\boldsymbol{z}$-dependent event A with $P(A^c) < \varepsilon$ such that there exists a sequence $\{\widehat{\boldsymbol{\theta}}_{n,\boldsymbol{b}}(\boldsymbol{z})\}$ that minimizes Q in (4.11), again formulated in terms of $\boldsymbol{Z}$-variables, and such that $\widehat{\boldsymbol{\theta}}_{n,\boldsymbol{b}}(\boldsymbol{z})$ converges almost surely to $\boldsymbol{\theta}_{\boldsymbol{b}}(\boldsymbol{z})$ on A. Moreover, the central limit result in Theorem 4.1 formulated in terms of $\boldsymbol{Z}$-variables continues to hold with the first integral part of Theorem 4.1 as the leading part of $\boldsymbol{M}_b$.

Remark. Note that condition (i) follows from condition (i) in Theorem 4.1. The same is true for the support part of condition (ii); the moment part of that condition formulated in Theorem 4.1 is automatically fulfilled in the present case due to the transformation to standard normal margins.

Second, for $\boldsymbol{b} \to \boldsymbol{0}$:

Theorem 4.4. *Let $\{\boldsymbol{Z}_t\}$ be a bivariate stationary time series derived from the bivariate stationary time series $\{\boldsymbol{X}_t\}$ having components $Z_{it} = \Phi^{-1}(F_i(X_{it}))$ for $i = 1, 2$ with bivariate density g having support on all of $\mathbb{R}^2$. Assume that*

- **(i)** *$\{\boldsymbol{Z}_t\}$ is geometrically ergodic, $n \to \infty$ and $b_1, b_2 \to 0$ so that $\log n / n(b_1 b_2)^3 \to 0$,*
- **(ii)** *the kernel function K is Lipschitz,*
- **(iii)** *g is such that at each fixed point $\boldsymbol{z}$ and for every $\boldsymbol{b} > \boldsymbol{0}$, there exists a non-degenerate local Gaussian approximation $\psi(\boldsymbol{v}, \boldsymbol{\theta}(\boldsymbol{z}))$ as given in Section 4.3, and*
- **(iv)** *there exists a bandwidth vector $\boldsymbol{b}_0$ such that there is a unique solution $\boldsymbol{\theta}_{\boldsymbol{b}}(\boldsymbol{z})$ of (4.6) stated in terms of $\boldsymbol{Z}$-variables for every $\boldsymbol{b} < \boldsymbol{b}_0 < \boldsymbol{0}$, taken componentwise.*

Then, for every $\varepsilon > 0$, there is a possibly $\boldsymbol{z}$-dependent event A with $P(A^c) < \varepsilon$ such that there exists a sequence $\{\widehat{\boldsymbol{\theta}}_{\boldsymbol{b},n}(\boldsymbol{z})\}$ that minimizes Q in (4.11) in Z-variable notation and such that $\widehat{\boldsymbol{\theta}}_{n,\boldsymbol{b}}(\boldsymbol{z})$ for a fixed $\boldsymbol{z}$ converges almost surely to the true value $\boldsymbol{\theta}(\boldsymbol{z}) = \boldsymbol{\theta}_0(\boldsymbol{z})$ on A. Moreover,

$$(n(b_1 b_2)^3)^{1/2}(\widehat{\boldsymbol{\theta}}_{n,\boldsymbol{b}}(\boldsymbol{z}) - \boldsymbol{\theta}_0(\boldsymbol{z})) \xrightarrow{d} \mathcal{N}(0, (b_1 b_2)^2 \boldsymbol{J}_{\boldsymbol{b}}^{-1} \boldsymbol{M}_{\boldsymbol{b}} \boldsymbol{J}_{\boldsymbol{b}}^{-1}), \tag{4.18}$$

this meaning that the left-hand side is asymptotically normal with limiting covariance as obtained from $(b_1 b_2)^2 \boldsymbol{J}_{\boldsymbol{b}}^{-1} \boldsymbol{M}_{\boldsymbol{b}} \boldsymbol{J}_{\boldsymbol{b}}^{-1}$ as $b_1, b_2 \to 0$ at the appropriate rate or, alternatively,

$$(n b_1 b_2)^{1/2} \boldsymbol{M}_{\boldsymbol{b}}^{-1/2} \boldsymbol{J}_{\boldsymbol{b}}(\widehat{\boldsymbol{\theta}}_{n,\boldsymbol{b}}(\boldsymbol{z}) - \boldsymbol{\theta}_0(\boldsymbol{z})) \xrightarrow{d} \mathcal{N}(0, \boldsymbol{I}),$$

where $\boldsymbol{I}$ is the identity matrix of dimension 5, and $\boldsymbol{J}_{\boldsymbol{b}}$ and $\boldsymbol{M}_{\boldsymbol{b}}$ are defined in (4.13) and (4.14) with $\boldsymbol{x}$ replaced by $\boldsymbol{z}$.

Exactly the same remark can be made as for Theorem 4.3.

We are now in a position to state a version of Theorem 4.4 in the realistic case where Z_i are unknown and need to be replaced by $\widehat{Z}_i$ as defined in (4.17) and where $\boldsymbol{b}$ is allowed to tend to zero.

Theorem 4.5. *Let $\{\widehat{\boldsymbol{Z}}_t\}$ be the estimated bivariate time series derived from the bivariate stationary time series $\{\boldsymbol{X}_t\}$ having components $\widehat{\boldsymbol{Z}}_{it} = \Phi^{-1}(F_{i,n}(X_{it}))$ for*

$i = 1, 2$. *Assume that conditions* (i)–(iv) *of Theorem 4.4 are fulfilled. Then for every* $\varepsilon > 0$, *there is a possibly* $\boldsymbol{z}$*-dependent event* A *with* $P(A^c) < \varepsilon$ *such that there exists a sequence* $\{\widehat{\boldsymbol{\theta}}_{\widehat{Z},\boldsymbol{b}}(\boldsymbol{z})\}$ *that minimizes* Q *in* (4.11), *formulated in terms of* $\widehat{\boldsymbol{Z}}$*-variables, and such that* $\widehat{\boldsymbol{\theta}}_{\widehat{Z},\boldsymbol{b}}(\boldsymbol{z})$ *for a fixed* $\boldsymbol{z}$ *converges almost surely to the true value* $\boldsymbol{\theta}(\boldsymbol{z}) = \boldsymbol{\theta}_0(\boldsymbol{z})$ *on* A. *Moreover,*

$$(n(b_1 b_2)^3)^{1/2}(\widehat{\boldsymbol{\theta}}_{\widehat{Z},\boldsymbol{b}}(\boldsymbol{z}) - \boldsymbol{\theta}_0(\boldsymbol{z})) \xrightarrow{d} \mathcal{N}(\boldsymbol{0}, (b_1 b_2)^2 \boldsymbol{J}_{\boldsymbol{b}}^{-1} \boldsymbol{M}_{\boldsymbol{b}} \boldsymbol{J}_{\boldsymbol{b}}^{-1}), \tag{4.19}$$

this meaning that the left-hand side is asymptotically normal with limiting covariance as obtained from $(b_1 b_2)^2 \boldsymbol{J}_{\boldsymbol{b}}^{-1} \boldsymbol{M}_{\boldsymbol{b}} \boldsymbol{J}_{\boldsymbol{b}}^{-1}$ *as* $b_1, b_2 \to \boldsymbol{0}$ *at the appropriate rate or, alternatively,*

$$(n b_1 b_2)^{1/2} \boldsymbol{M}_{\boldsymbol{b}}^{-1/2} \boldsymbol{J}_{\boldsymbol{b}} (\widehat{\boldsymbol{\theta}}_{\widehat{Z},\boldsymbol{b}}(\boldsymbol{z}) - \boldsymbol{\theta}_0(\boldsymbol{z})) \xrightarrow{d} \mathcal{N}(\boldsymbol{0}, \boldsymbol{I}),$$

where $\boldsymbol{I}$ *is the identity matrix of dimension 5.*

The proof of Theorem 4.5 can be found in the Section 4.10.2. There are corresponding results for the simplified model discussed above where $\mu_i(\boldsymbol{z}) \equiv 0$ and $\sigma_i(\boldsymbol{z}) \equiv 1$. The proof of those results is postponed until Chapter 9, where they are actively used. The asymptotic distribution is simpler in that case.

4.7.1 Examples of the normalized LGC

In this section, we revisit the examples from Section 4.6, more precisely those depicted in Figs. 4.3 and 4.5, but now the same observations are scaled to the normal scale as explained earlier in this section.

Fig. 4.5 shows the estimated normalized LGC maps $\widehat{\rho}_{\boldsymbol{Z}}(\boldsymbol{z})$ by again using the cross-validated bandwidth procedure of Section 4.8.2. For the Gaussian data in Fig. 4.5a, the normal scale is almost identical to the LGC map on the original scale (Fig. 4.3a), subject only to the estimation error in the marginal distribution functions. This is also the case for the example with the Clayton copula; see Fig. 4.5d. For the t-distributed and GARCH-data, in Figs. 4.5b and 4.5c, respectively, the pattern in the LGC maps is as for the original data (Figs. 4.3b and 4.3c), albeit slightly more clearly for the normalized data. Hence these examples show that in many cases, it can be beneficial working on data that is transformed to normal scale, for instance, during hypothesis testing; see Chapter 7. Similar conclusions are drawn in Chapter 8.

The normalized LGC map and the corresponding diagonal curve with approximate 95% confidence intervals obtained by 500 bootstrap realizations for the financial data set are shown in Fig. 4.6. Also in this case, the

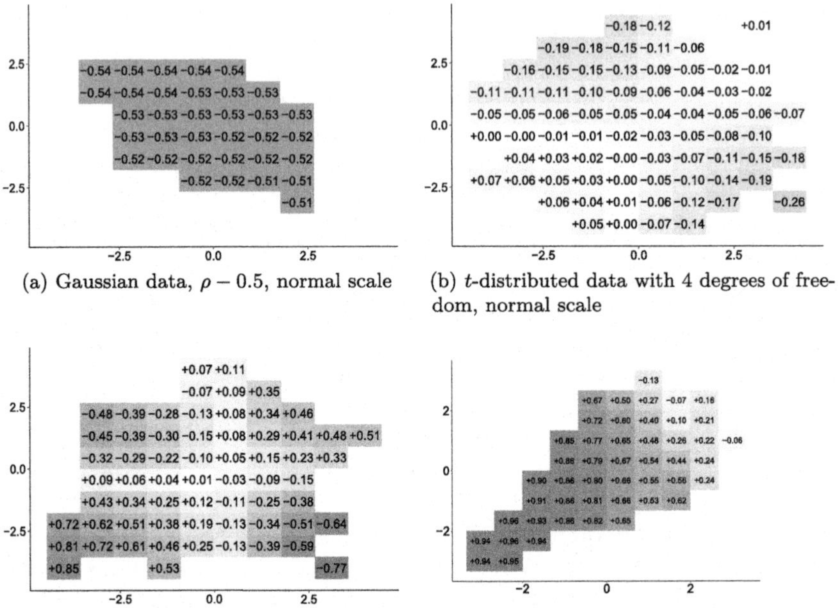

(a) Gaussian data, $\rho - 0.5$, normal scale

(b) t-distributed data with 4 degrees of freedom, normal scale

(c) X_t vs. X_{t-1} where X_t is generated from a GARCH(1,1)-model, normal scale

(d) A bivariate distribution with standard Gaussian marginals and a Clayton copula, normal scale

Figure 4.5 Some examples of local Gaussian correlation maps; $n = 784$ in all cases, normalized scale. The color codes are the same as in Figs. 4.1 and 4.2.

pattern in the LGC map (Fig. 4.6a) is more visible for the transformed data than in the original case; cf. Fig. 4.4a. Further, we note from Fig. 4.6b that the estimated local Gaussian correlations for large negative returns are significantly different from the local Gaussian correlations for returns around 0, based on the non-overlapping confidence intervals, documenting the increase in dependence during market downturns compared to more normal market conditions. Further studies of financial returns are found in Chapter 6.

4.8 Some practical considerations

4.8.1 Estimating the standard error of estimates

As seen in Sections 4.4 and 4.7, it may be difficult to obtain explicit and useful expressions for the standard error of $\widehat{\boldsymbol{\theta}}_{b,n}(\boldsymbol{x})$ in the general formulas (4.12), (4.15), (4.18), and (4.19). Tjøstheim and Hufthammer (2013) have used two alternative methods. The first one is the bootstrap, which is valid

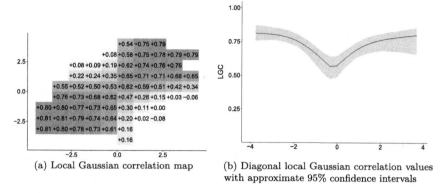

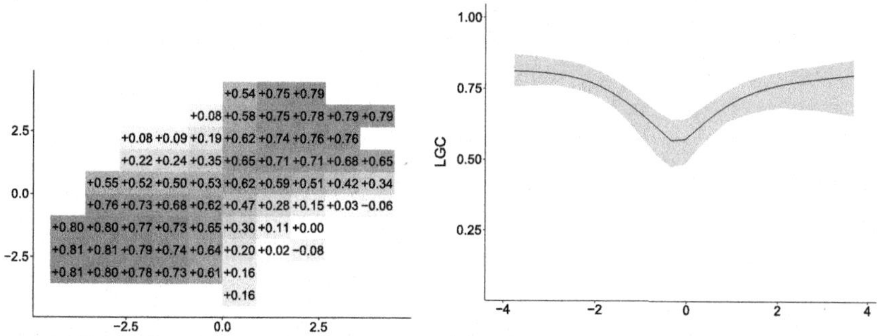

(a) Local Gaussian correlation map

(b) Diagonal local Gaussian correlation values with approximate 95% confidence intervals

Figure 4.6 Local Gaussian correlations of the log-returns data, S&P 500 vs. FTSE 100, normalized scale.

only for the case where $\{X_t\}$ consists of iid variables, and this approach has been used in a number of papers on local Gaussian approximation and in several chapters of this book. For the dependent case, the block bootstrap has been used, as can be seen in Chapters 7, 8, and 11, its validity being discussed in Chapters 7 and 11. However, bootstrapping is quite time consuming, since for each bootstrap realization, the local likelihood has to be optimized numerically over a grid of points.

The second alternative is to first note that $\boldsymbol{M}_b$ in (4.14) can be approximated by

$$\widehat{\boldsymbol{M}}_b = b_1 b_2 \Bigg[\frac{1}{n} \sum_{t=1}^{n} K_b^2(\boldsymbol{X}_t - \boldsymbol{x}) \boldsymbol{u}(\boldsymbol{X}_t, \boldsymbol{\theta}_b(\boldsymbol{x})) \boldsymbol{u}^T(\boldsymbol{X}_t, \boldsymbol{\theta}_b(\boldsymbol{x})) \\ - \frac{1}{n} \sum_{t=1}^{n} K_b(\boldsymbol{X}_t - \boldsymbol{x}) \boldsymbol{u}(\boldsymbol{X}_t, \boldsymbol{\theta}_b(\boldsymbol{x})) \frac{1}{n} \sum_{t=1}^{n} K_b(\boldsymbol{X}_t - \boldsymbol{x}) \boldsymbol{u}^T(\boldsymbol{X}_t, \boldsymbol{\theta}_b(\boldsymbol{x})) \Bigg],$$

where $\widehat{\boldsymbol{M}}_b \to \boldsymbol{M}_b$ almost surely (for a fixed bandwidth vector $\boldsymbol{b}$) by the strong law of large numbers or the ergodic theorem. We must in practice replace $\boldsymbol{\theta}_b(\boldsymbol{x})$ by the estimate $\widehat{\boldsymbol{\theta}}_b(\boldsymbol{x})$. Similarly, in (4.13) the term containing $f(\boldsymbol{v})$ can be approximated by the law of large numbers (or ergodic theorem), whereas the other integral terms can be computed analytically if K is a Gaussian kernel. If K is not Gaussian, then these latter integrals can be computed by Monte Carlo sampling from $\psi(\boldsymbol{v}, \widehat{\boldsymbol{\theta}}_b(\boldsymbol{x}))$. In case a Gaussian kernel is used, this method is much faster than the bootstrap, and it gave very similar results for some examples in the thesis of Hufthammer (2009).

4.8.2 Choosing the bandwidth

The choice of bandwidth depends to a large extent on the purpose of the analysis. If the goal is to examine the local dependence structure in a data set, then it can be quite informative to compute $\widehat{\rho}_{\boldsymbol{b}}(\boldsymbol{x})$ for several bandwidths. In this way, we can obtain information about the dependence structure on several scales of locality. However, in many situations, it would be beneficial to have a data-driven bandwidth choice similar to a bandwidth choice for a kernel density estimate.

Likelihood cross-validation is a well-known method for model selection. For a general framework, we refer to Stone (1974), and in the particular case of bandwidth selection for the kernel estimator, an overview can be found in Silverman (1986, Section 3.4.4). The methodology of likelihood cross-validation can be used for selecting the bandwidth $\boldsymbol{b}$ as follows. Let $\widehat{\boldsymbol{\theta}}_{n,\boldsymbol{b}}^{-i}(\boldsymbol{x})$ estimate $\boldsymbol{\theta}(\boldsymbol{x})$ (or $\boldsymbol{\theta}_{\boldsymbol{b}}(\boldsymbol{x})$) when the ith observation is omitted; that is, the result of maximizing

$$\frac{1}{n-1}\sum_{j\neq i} K_{\boldsymbol{b}}(\boldsymbol{X}_j-\boldsymbol{x})\log\psi(\boldsymbol{X}_j,\boldsymbol{\theta}_{\boldsymbol{b}}(\boldsymbol{x}))-\int K_{\boldsymbol{b}}(\boldsymbol{v}-\boldsymbol{x})\psi(\boldsymbol{v},\boldsymbol{\theta}_{\boldsymbol{b}}(\boldsymbol{x}))\,\mathrm{d}\boldsymbol{v},$$

where $\{\boldsymbol{X}_j\}$ is assumed to consist of iid observations (in the time series case, it may be natural to leave out more than one observation). Then, assuming $\{\boldsymbol{X}_i\}$ to be iid, $\boldsymbol{b}=(b_1,b_2)$ is chosen such that

$$\mathrm{CV}(\boldsymbol{b})=\frac{1}{n}\sum_i \log\psi(\boldsymbol{X}_i,\widehat{\boldsymbol{\theta}}_{\boldsymbol{b}}^{-i}(\boldsymbol{X}_i)) \tag{4.20}$$

is maximized. In the sense of Stone (1974), this can be viewed as minimizing $n^{-1}\sum_i R(\widehat{\boldsymbol{\theta}}_{n,\boldsymbol{b}}(\boldsymbol{X}_i),\boldsymbol{\theta}(\boldsymbol{X}_i))$, where $R(\widehat{\boldsymbol{\theta}}_{n,\boldsymbol{b}}(\boldsymbol{X}_i),\boldsymbol{\theta}(\boldsymbol{X}_i))=-\log(\psi(\boldsymbol{X}_i,\widehat{\boldsymbol{\theta}}_{n,\boldsymbol{b}}^{-i}(\boldsymbol{X}_i)))$ is a loss function of $\widehat{\theta}_{n,\boldsymbol{b}}(\boldsymbol{X}_i)$ as a predictor of $\boldsymbol{\theta}(\boldsymbol{X}_i)$.

We will see in later chapters of this book that the cross-validation method has been used in many of our experiments. Clearly, there is room for more research here; an $\boldsymbol{x}$-dependent bandwidth being an obvious candidate to try, not in the least since we may be especially interested in tails of distributions. Combined with the bootstrap algorithm, the cross-validation algorithm may considerably slow down the estimation or testing methodology. Therefore, in some cases, we have also considered much simpler plug-in bandwidths of the type $b_1=b_2=cn^{-1/6}$, where the factor c is determined through an empirical experiment; see Chapter 9 for more detail about this approach.

4.9 The p-dimensional case

We have thus far concentrated on the bivariate case, in which we estimate a single local Gaussian correlation based on a bivariate sample. We will later use locally Gaussian approximations to consider several basic statistical tasks such as probability density estimation, conditional density estimation, testing for conditional independence, classification, and regression. In all these tasks, it is far too limiting to restrict oneself to the bivariate case only.

The treatment so far in this book is, in principle, straightforward to extend to the case of more than two variables. Assume that we observe a multivariate sample $\boldsymbol{X}_i = \{X_{1i}, \ldots, X_{pi}\}$, $i = 1, \ldots, n$, with dimension $p > 2$. Then we can estimate the $p \times p$ local correlation *matrix* $\boldsymbol{R}(\boldsymbol{x}) = \{\rho_{k\ell}(\boldsymbol{x})\}$, $1 \leq k < \ell \leq p$, $\boldsymbol{x} = (x_1, \ldots, x_p)$, and p local means $\boldsymbol{\mu}(\boldsymbol{x}) = \{\mu_1(\boldsymbol{x}), \ldots, \mu_p(\boldsymbol{x})\}$ and local variances $\boldsymbol{\sigma}(\boldsymbol{x}) = \{\sigma_1(\boldsymbol{x}), \ldots, \sigma_p(\boldsymbol{x})\}$ by maximizing the local likelihood function (4.8). Moreover, we can transform to a $\boldsymbol{z} = (z_1 \ldots, z_p)$-scale as in Section 4.7. However, the precision of such estimates deteriorates quickly as the dimension p grows due to the curse of dimensionality.

We introduce a simplifying technique that reduces the complexity of this estimation problem in Chapter 9. The basic idea is that we first transform the data toward marginal standard normality as described in Section 4.7 and then fix all the local means and local standard deviations at the values 0 and 1, respectively (a less drastic simplification would be putting $\mu_i(\boldsymbol{z}) = \mu_i(z_i)$ and $\sigma_i^2(\boldsymbol{z}) = \sigma_i^2(z_i)$). We then estimate each local correlation $\rho_{k\ell}(\boldsymbol{z})$ as a bivariate problem by only considering the corresponding *pair* of observation vectors $\{X_{ik}, X_{i\ell}\}$, $i = 1, \ldots, n$. Thus we reduce the p-variate problems of estimating the local parameters depending on all coordinates to a series of bivariate problems of estimating pairwise local correlations depending on their respective *pairs* of coordinates. In this way, we obtain a simplification that can be thought of as being analogous to an additive approximation in nonparametric regression.

We present the details of use of this construction and relevant estimation theory in Chapters 6 and 9–13.

4.10 Proof of asymptotic results

4.10.1 Non-normalized

Proof of Theorem 4.1. We will use the approach formalized by Klimko and Nelson (1978) and Tjøstheim (1986) (see also Taniguchi and Kakizawa (2000, pp. 96–100)). This is an approach for obtaining asymptotic properties of estimates using Taylor expansion of a general penalty function Q.

We denote the minimizer of (4.11) by $\widehat{\boldsymbol{\theta}}_b(\boldsymbol{x}) = \widehat{\boldsymbol{\theta}}_b = \widehat{\boldsymbol{\theta}}_{n,b}$. We further omit the $\boldsymbol{x}$-dependence as $\boldsymbol{x}$ is fixed. By Taylor expansion we have in a neighborhood $\mathcal{N} = \{\boldsymbol{\theta} : |\boldsymbol{\theta} - \boldsymbol{\theta}_b| < \delta\}$ of $\boldsymbol{\theta}_b$ (noting that $Q_n(\boldsymbol{\theta})$ is twice continuously differentiable with respect to $\boldsymbol{\theta}$) that

$$
\begin{aligned}
Q_n(\boldsymbol{\theta}) &= Q_n(\boldsymbol{\theta}_b) + (\boldsymbol{\theta} - \boldsymbol{\theta}_b)^T \frac{\partial}{\partial \boldsymbol{\theta}} Q_n(\boldsymbol{\theta}_b) + \frac{1}{2}(\boldsymbol{\theta} - \boldsymbol{\theta}_b)^T \frac{\partial^2}{\partial \boldsymbol{\theta} \partial \boldsymbol{\theta}^T} Q_n(\boldsymbol{\theta}_b)(\boldsymbol{\theta} - \boldsymbol{\theta}_b) \\
&\quad + \frac{1}{2}(\boldsymbol{\theta} - \boldsymbol{\theta}_b)^T \left\{ \frac{\partial^2}{\partial \boldsymbol{\theta} \partial \boldsymbol{\theta}^T} Q_n(\boldsymbol{\theta}^*) - \frac{\partial^2}{\partial \boldsymbol{\theta} \partial \boldsymbol{\theta}^T} Q_n(\boldsymbol{\theta}_b) \right\} (\boldsymbol{\theta} - \boldsymbol{\theta}_b) \\
&\overset{\text{def}}{=} Q_n(\boldsymbol{\theta}_b) + (\boldsymbol{\theta} - \boldsymbol{\theta}_b)^T \frac{\partial}{\partial \boldsymbol{\theta}} Q_n(\boldsymbol{\theta}_b) + \frac{1}{2}(\boldsymbol{\theta} - \boldsymbol{\theta}_b)^T \boldsymbol{W}_n(\boldsymbol{\theta}_b)(\boldsymbol{\theta} - \boldsymbol{\theta}_b) \\
&\quad + \frac{1}{2}(\boldsymbol{\theta} - \boldsymbol{\theta}_b)^T \boldsymbol{T}_n(\boldsymbol{\theta}^*, \boldsymbol{\theta}_b)(\boldsymbol{\theta} - \boldsymbol{\theta}_b),
\end{aligned}
$$

where $\boldsymbol{\theta}^*$ is an intermediate point between $\boldsymbol{\theta}$ and $\boldsymbol{\theta}_b$. It should be carefully noted that we do our analysis for fixed $\boldsymbol{b}$, so the true value of $\boldsymbol{\theta}$ is identified with $\boldsymbol{\theta}_b$ satisfying Eq. (4.6). To obtain the consistency statement via Egorov's theorem, we have to show (see Klimko and Nelson (1978, Theorem 2.1) or Taniguchi and Kakizawa (2000, Theorem 3.2.23))

(i) $n^{-1} \frac{\partial}{\partial \boldsymbol{\theta}} Q_n(\boldsymbol{\theta}_b) \overset{\text{a.s}}{\to} \boldsymbol{0}$,

(ii) $n^{-1} \boldsymbol{W}_n(\boldsymbol{\theta}_b) \overset{\text{a.s}}{\to} \boldsymbol{W}_b$, where $\boldsymbol{W}_b$ is a 5×5 positive definite matrix, which can be identified with $\boldsymbol{J}_b$ of (4.13),

(iii) For $j, k = 1, \ldots, 5$, $\lim_{n\to\infty} \sup_{\delta\to 0} (n\delta)^{-1} |\boldsymbol{T}_n(\boldsymbol{\theta}^*, \boldsymbol{\theta}_b)_{jk}| < \infty$ a.s., where $\boldsymbol{T}_n(\boldsymbol{\theta}^*, \boldsymbol{\theta}_b)_{jk}$ is the (j, k)th element of $\boldsymbol{T}_n(\boldsymbol{\theta}^\star, \boldsymbol{\theta}_b)$.

Because of the ergodic assumption on $\{X_t\}$,

$$
\begin{aligned}
-n^{-1} \frac{\partial}{\partial \boldsymbol{\theta}} Q_n(\boldsymbol{\theta}_b) &= \frac{\partial L}{\partial \boldsymbol{\theta}} (\boldsymbol{X}_1, \ldots, \boldsymbol{X}_n, \boldsymbol{\theta}_b) \\
&\overset{\text{a.s.}}{\to} \int K_b(\boldsymbol{v} - \boldsymbol{x}) \frac{\partial}{\partial \boldsymbol{\theta}} \log(\psi(\boldsymbol{v}, \boldsymbol{\theta}_b)) f(\boldsymbol{v})\, d\boldsymbol{v} \\
&\quad - \int K_b(\boldsymbol{v} - \boldsymbol{x}) \frac{\partial}{\partial \boldsymbol{\theta}} \log(\psi(\boldsymbol{v}, \boldsymbol{\theta}_b)) \psi(\boldsymbol{v}, \boldsymbol{\theta}_b)\, d\boldsymbol{v} = \boldsymbol{0}
\end{aligned}
$$

due to the requirement on $\boldsymbol{\theta}_b$ in (4.6). Similarly, using ergodicity, we can show that

$$
n^{-1} \boldsymbol{W}_n(\boldsymbol{\theta}_b) = -\frac{\partial^2 L(\boldsymbol{X}_1, \ldots, \boldsymbol{X}_n, \boldsymbol{\theta}_b)}{\partial \boldsymbol{\theta} \partial \boldsymbol{\theta}^T} \overset{\text{a.s}}{\to} \boldsymbol{J}_b.
$$

Since $\boldsymbol{\theta}_b$ is a global minimizer of the function $\int K_b(\boldsymbol{v} - \boldsymbol{x})[\psi(\boldsymbol{v}, \boldsymbol{\theta}) - \log(\psi(\boldsymbol{v}, \boldsymbol{\theta})) f(\boldsymbol{v})]\, d\boldsymbol{v}$, this means that the second-order derivative matrix of the function must be positive definite at $\boldsymbol{\theta}_b$, but this derivative matrix is

$\boldsymbol{J}_b = \boldsymbol{W}_b$, so that (ii) above is fulfilled. Finally, the third-order derivative of $\psi(\boldsymbol{x}, \boldsymbol{\theta})$ is bounded on $\mathcal{N}$, and (iii) is implied by the mean value theorem.

Theorem 2.2 of Klimko and Nelson (1978) or the last part of Theorem 3.2.23 of Taniguchi and Kakizawa (2000) can now be used to prove the asymptotic normality of $\widehat{\boldsymbol{\theta}}_b$. In addition to (i)–(iii), we need to verify the condition

(iv) $n^{-1/2}\frac{\partial}{\partial \boldsymbol{\theta}} Q_n(\boldsymbol{\theta}_b) \xrightarrow{d} \mathcal{N}(0, \boldsymbol{S}_b)$,

where $\boldsymbol{S}_b$ is a positive definite matrix, which can be identified with $(b_1 b_2)^{-1}\boldsymbol{M}_b$ in (4.14). The expression for $\boldsymbol{M}_b$ is positive definite since it can be expressed as the covariance matrix of the stochastic vector variable $\sqrt{b_1 b_2}\boldsymbol{u}(\boldsymbol{X}_t, \boldsymbol{\theta}_b)$ ($\boldsymbol{u}$ cannot be degenerate due to the uniqueness condition). To prove (iv) in our case, we can use a mixing CLT; see, for instance, Theorems 2.20(i) and 2.21(i) of Fan and Yao (2003). Those theorems are formulated for a scalar process, whereas $n^{-1/2}\frac{\partial}{\partial \boldsymbol{\theta}} Q_n(\boldsymbol{\theta}_b)$ is a five-dimensional quantity. However, Theorem 2.20(i) of Fan and Yao (2003) can be applied component-wise, and by a Cramèr–Wold argument Theorem 2.21(i) can be used. Those theorems assume an α-mixing process $\{\boldsymbol{X}_t\}$ with certain mixing rate, but this is fulfilled by our assumption of geometric ergodicity (in fact, a slower rate would suffice). In addition, it is required that $\mathrm{E}|K_b(\boldsymbol{X}_t - \boldsymbol{x})\partial/\partial\boldsymbol{\theta}_j \log\psi(\boldsymbol{X}_t, \boldsymbol{\theta})|^\gamma < \infty$ for some $\gamma > 2$, which is condition (ii) in the statement of Theorem 4.1. □

Proof of Theorem 4.2. The proof follows the same pattern as the proof of Theorem 4.1, but we introduce the new penalty function

$$Q_n' = (b_1 b_2)^{-2} Q_n \tag{4.21}$$

with Q_n as in (4.11). Further, $\boldsymbol{\theta}_0$ denotes the true value of $\boldsymbol{\theta}(\boldsymbol{x})$. Instead of relying on the ergodic theorem and CLT for a fixed $\boldsymbol{b}$ in the proof of Theorem 4.1, we now have to utilize an ergodic theorem where smoothing is involved. It turns out that we can use standard theorems of this type. For example, we can use the nonparametric ergodic Theorem 4.1 of Masry and Tjøstheim (1995). In the proof of that theorem, $\widehat{h}_n(y)$ is replaced by $n^{-1}\sum_t K_b(\boldsymbol{X}_t - \boldsymbol{x})\boldsymbol{u}(\boldsymbol{X}_t, \boldsymbol{\theta})$, where $\boldsymbol{u}(\boldsymbol{X}_t, \boldsymbol{\theta}) = \partial \log\psi(\boldsymbol{X}_t, \boldsymbol{\theta})/\partial\boldsymbol{\theta}$, and $\mathrm{E}(h_n(y))$ is replaced by the corresponding expectation $\int K_b(\boldsymbol{v} - \boldsymbol{x})\boldsymbol{u}(\boldsymbol{v}, \boldsymbol{\theta})\psi(\boldsymbol{v}, \boldsymbol{\theta})\,\mathrm{d}\boldsymbol{v}$. We use the truncation argument of that proof with $\bar{s} > 2$ replaced by $\gamma > 2$ of condition (ii) of Theorem 4.1. Moreover, we use geometric ergodicity instead of the weaker mixing condition in the proof by Masry and Tjøstheim (1995). The conclusion of that proof is that for a compact subset D of $\mathbb{R}^2$,

$$\sup_{x\in D}\left|\frac{1}{n}\sum_t K_b(\boldsymbol{X}_t-\boldsymbol{x})\boldsymbol{u}(\boldsymbol{X}_t,\boldsymbol{\theta})-\int K_b(\boldsymbol{v}-\boldsymbol{x})\boldsymbol{u}(\boldsymbol{v},\boldsymbol{\theta})\psi(\boldsymbol{v},\boldsymbol{\theta})\,\mathrm{d}\boldsymbol{v}\right| = O\left(\frac{\log n}{nb_1b_2}\right)^{1/2}$$

almost surely. It follows that for a fixed $\boldsymbol{x}$ and with the bandwidth condition (ii),

$$n^{-1}\frac{\partial Q_n'(\theta_0)}{\partial\boldsymbol{\theta}}=\frac{1}{(b_1b_2)^2}\left[\int K_b(\boldsymbol{v}-\boldsymbol{x})\boldsymbol{u}(\boldsymbol{v},\boldsymbol{\theta}_0)\psi(\boldsymbol{v},\boldsymbol{\theta}_0)\,\mathrm{d}\boldsymbol{v} - n^{-1}\sum K_b(\boldsymbol{X}_t-\boldsymbol{x})\frac{\partial\log\psi(\boldsymbol{X}_t,\boldsymbol{\theta}_0)}{\partial\boldsymbol{\theta}}\right]\overset{\text{a.s.}}{\to}\boldsymbol{0}.$$

Moreover,

$$n^{-1}\frac{\partial^2 Q_n'(\boldsymbol{\theta}_0)}{\partial\boldsymbol{\theta}\partial\boldsymbol{\theta}^T}=\frac{1}{(b_1b_2)^2}\left[\int K_b(\boldsymbol{v}-\boldsymbol{x})\boldsymbol{u}(\boldsymbol{v},\boldsymbol{\theta}_0)\boldsymbol{u}^T(\boldsymbol{v},\boldsymbol{\theta}_0)\,\mathrm{d}\boldsymbol{v} + \int K_b(\boldsymbol{v}-\boldsymbol{x})\nabla\boldsymbol{u}(\boldsymbol{v},\boldsymbol{\theta}_0)\psi(\boldsymbol{v},\boldsymbol{\theta}_0)\,\mathrm{d}\boldsymbol{v} - n^{-1}\sum_t K_b(\boldsymbol{X}_t-\boldsymbol{x})\nabla\boldsymbol{u}(\boldsymbol{X}_t,\boldsymbol{\theta}_0)\right].$$

The last two terms cancel almost surely, again using the nonparametric ergodic theorem and the bandwidth condition. The first term has the positive definite matrix $\boldsymbol{J}_2=\lim_{\boldsymbol{b}\to 0}(b_1b_2)^{-2}\boldsymbol{J}_{\boldsymbol{b},2}$ as a limit, which means that $\boldsymbol{J}_2$ has positive eigenvalues and that an inverse exists. Finally, we look at

$$(\delta n)^{-1}\left[\frac{\partial^2 Q_n'(\boldsymbol{\theta}_0)}{\partial\boldsymbol{\theta}\partial\boldsymbol{\theta}^T}-\frac{\partial^2 Q_n'(\boldsymbol{\theta})}{\partial\boldsymbol{\theta}\partial\boldsymbol{\theta}^T}\right] = (b_1b_2)^{-2}\left[(\delta n)^{-1}\left(\frac{\partial^2 Q_n(\boldsymbol{\theta}_0)}{\partial\boldsymbol{\theta}\partial\boldsymbol{\theta}^T}-\frac{\partial^2 Q_n(\boldsymbol{\theta})}{\partial\boldsymbol{\theta}\partial\boldsymbol{\theta}^T}\right)\right],$$

where $|\boldsymbol{\theta}-\boldsymbol{\theta}_0|<\delta$. From the existence and continuity of the third-order derivative we have that, element-wise, $|\partial^2 Q_n'/\partial\boldsymbol{\theta}\partial\boldsymbol{\theta}^T(\boldsymbol{\theta})-\partial^2 Q_n'/\partial\boldsymbol{\theta}\partial\boldsymbol{\theta}^T(\theta_0)|$ $\leq c\delta$ for some constant c. Using the bandwidth condition, it follows that, element-wise,

$$\lim_{n\to\infty}\limsup_{\delta\to 0}\left|(\delta n)^{-1}\left(\frac{\partial^2 Q_n'(\boldsymbol{\theta}_0)}{\partial\boldsymbol{\theta}^2}-\frac{\partial^2 Q_n'(\boldsymbol{\theta})}{\partial\boldsymbol{\theta}^2}\right)\right|<\infty,$$

and as in the proof of Theorem 4.1, the almost sure part of Theorem 4.2 follows. We then look at

$$((b_1b_2)^3n)^{1/2}n^{-1}\frac{\partial Q_n'(\boldsymbol{\theta}_0)}{\partial\boldsymbol{\theta}} = (nb_1b_2)^{1/2}\left[n^{-1}(b_1b_2)^{-1}\frac{\partial Q_n(\boldsymbol{\theta}_0)}{\partial\boldsymbol{\theta}}\right].$$

The quantity in brackets has the covariance matrix $\boldsymbol{M}_b/(b_1b_2)^2$, which tends to a positive definite matrix $\boldsymbol{M}_2$. The asymptotic normality can then be shown using a standard nonparametric CLT; see, for example, Masry and Tjøstheim (1995, Theorem 4.4), where $Z^\star_{n,t}$ in (4.47) and (4.48) of the proof of that theorem was replaced by

$$(b_1b_2)^{3/2}\left[K_{\boldsymbol{b}}(\boldsymbol{X}_t-\boldsymbol{x})\frac{\partial\log\psi(\boldsymbol{X}_t,\boldsymbol{\theta})}{\partial\boldsymbol{\theta}} - \mathrm{E}\left\{K_{\boldsymbol{b}}(\boldsymbol{X}_t-\boldsymbol{x})\frac{\partial\log\psi(\boldsymbol{X}_t,\boldsymbol{\theta})}{\partial\boldsymbol{\theta}}\right\}\right],$$

and then the "big block–small block" technique was used. Assumptions (4.6a) and (4.7) of Masry and Tjøstheim (1995) follow from the Gaussianity of the local approximation and condition (i), whereas (4.6b) and (4.6c) are trivially fulfilled by the definition of $Z^\star_{n,t}$. The claimed result then follows from that theorem and Theorem 2.2 of Klimko and Nelson (1978). □

4.10.2 Normalized

The proofs of Theorems 4.3 and 4.4 are identical to the proofs of Theorems 4.1 and 4.2 with obvious notational changes. However, to prove Theorem 4.5, changes are necessary to take into account that only estimated $\widehat{\boldsymbol{Z}}_t$, that is, estimated $\widehat{F}_i$ are available, not the variables $\boldsymbol{Z}_t$. This proof in turn is essentially taken from Appendix D in the supplementary material of Otneim and Tjøstheim (2021). To ease the steps of the proof, we start as if the bandwidth $\boldsymbol{b}$ is fixed and then at the end let $\boldsymbol{b}$ tend to zero to use the slower convergence rate than that obtained from Theorem 4.4.

Proof of Theorem 4.5. The basic idea is still using the Klimko–Nelson approach but now with the penalty function ($\boldsymbol{b}$ fixed for the moment)

$$Q_n(\widehat{\boldsymbol{Z}}_1,\ldots,\widehat{\boldsymbol{Z}}_n;\boldsymbol{\theta}_{\boldsymbol{b}}(\boldsymbol{z})) = -\sum K_{\boldsymbol{b}}(\widehat{\boldsymbol{Z}}_t-\boldsymbol{z})\log\psi(\widehat{\boldsymbol{Z}}_t,\theta_{\boldsymbol{b}}(\boldsymbol{z})) + n\int K_{\boldsymbol{b}}(\boldsymbol{v}-\boldsymbol{z})\psi(\boldsymbol{v},\boldsymbol{\theta}_{\boldsymbol{b}}(\boldsymbol{z}))\,\mathrm{d}\boldsymbol{v}. \quad (4.22)$$

This is still a penalty function for $(\boldsymbol{X}_1,\ldots,\boldsymbol{X}_n)$ (or $(\boldsymbol{Z}_1,\ldots,\boldsymbol{Z}_n)$) using the relationship $X_{it}=\widehat{F}_i^{-1}(\Phi(\widehat{Z}_{it}))$, or $Z_{it}=\Phi^{-1}(F_i(\widehat{F}_i^{-1}(\Phi(\widehat{Z}_{it}))))$. The idea of the proof is showing that the penalty function in terms of the $\widehat{\boldsymbol{Z}}_t$ can be written as a penalty function in terms of $\boldsymbol{Z}_t$ plus a term that can be neglected in the limit.

According to the proof of Theorem 4.1 (or Theorem 4.3), we have to prove that for $\boldsymbol{\theta}_b = \boldsymbol{\theta}_b(\boldsymbol{z})$ defined in Section 4.7 and now treated as a target in terms of the new penalty function Q_n of (4.22), we have that in a neighborhood $\mathcal{N} = \{\boldsymbol{\theta} : |\boldsymbol{\theta} - \boldsymbol{\theta}_b| < \delta\}$ of $\boldsymbol{\theta}_b$ and in the scheme of the proof of Theorem 4.1 (and using the notation of that proof),

(i) $n^{-1}\frac{\partial}{\partial\boldsymbol{\theta}}Q_n(\boldsymbol{\theta}_b) \overset{\text{a.s.}}{\to} \boldsymbol{0}$.

(ii) $n^{-1}\boldsymbol{W}_n(\boldsymbol{\theta}_b) \overset{\text{a.s.}}{\to} \boldsymbol{W}_b$, where $\boldsymbol{W}_b$ is a 5×5 positive definite matrix that can be identified with $\boldsymbol{J}_b$ of (4.13) with $\boldsymbol{x}$ replaced by $\boldsymbol{z}$.

(iii) For $j, k = 1, \ldots, 5$, $\lim_{n\to\infty}\sup_{\delta\to 0}(n\delta)^{-1}|\boldsymbol{T}_n(\boldsymbol{\theta}^\star, \boldsymbol{\theta}_b)_{jk}| < \infty$ a.s., where $\boldsymbol{T}_n(\boldsymbol{\theta}^\star, \boldsymbol{\theta}_b)_{jk}$ is the (j, k)th element of $\boldsymbol{T}_n(\boldsymbol{\theta}^\star, \boldsymbol{\theta}_b)$.

(iv) $n^{-\frac{1}{2}}\frac{\partial}{\partial\boldsymbol{\theta}}Q_n(\boldsymbol{\theta}_b) \overset{d}{\to} \mathcal{N}(\boldsymbol{0}, \boldsymbol{S}_b)$, where $\boldsymbol{S}_b$ is the positive definite matrix that can be identified with $(b_1b_2)^{-1}\boldsymbol{M}_b$ in (4.14) with $\boldsymbol{x}$ replaced by $\boldsymbol{z}$.

Note that the derivative with respect to $\boldsymbol{\theta}$ of the first term of (4.22) (neglecting the minus sign) can be written as

$$\widehat{\boldsymbol{Y}}_n(\boldsymbol{z}) = \frac{1}{n}\sum_{t=1}^{n} K_b(\widehat{\boldsymbol{Z}}_t - \boldsymbol{z})\boldsymbol{u}(\widehat{\boldsymbol{Z}}_t, \boldsymbol{\theta}_b), \tag{4.23}$$

where $\boldsymbol{u}(\widehat{\boldsymbol{Z}}_t, \boldsymbol{\theta}_b) = \frac{\partial}{\partial\boldsymbol{\theta}}\log\psi(\widehat{\boldsymbol{Z}}_t, \boldsymbol{\theta}_b)$. We write $\widehat{\boldsymbol{Y}}_n(\boldsymbol{z}) = \boldsymbol{Y}_n(\boldsymbol{z}) - (\boldsymbol{Y}_n(\boldsymbol{z}) - \widehat{\boldsymbol{Y}}_n(\boldsymbol{z}))$, where

$$\boldsymbol{Y}_n(\boldsymbol{z}) = \frac{1}{n}\sum_{t=1}^{n} K_b(\boldsymbol{Z}_t - \boldsymbol{z})\boldsymbol{u}(\boldsymbol{Z}_t, \boldsymbol{\theta}_b). \tag{4.24}$$

By checking the proof of Theorem 4.1 (and Theorem 4.3) we see that Theorem 4.5 can be proved if we show that $|\boldsymbol{Y}_n(\boldsymbol{z}) - \widehat{\boldsymbol{Y}}_n(\boldsymbol{z})|$ converges to zero at appropriate mode and rate. We will accomplish this by Taylor expansion of $\boldsymbol{Y}_n(\boldsymbol{z})$ around $F_{in}(X_{it})$ for $i = 1, 2$.

At this point, we introduce some simplifying notations: We let $y_i = F_i(x_i)$, $\boldsymbol{y} = (y_1, y_2)$ and $b_1 = b_2 = b$, use that K is a product kernel $K = K(\cdot)K(\cdot)$ with $K(-x) = K(x)$, and let $\boldsymbol{w}_i = \partial\boldsymbol{u}/\partial y_i$. Further, write $\Phi^{-1}(\boldsymbol{y}) = \{\Phi^{-1}(y_1), \Phi^{-1}(y_2)\}$. Then let

$$\boldsymbol{U}_{\boldsymbol{z},b} = \boldsymbol{U}_{\boldsymbol{z},b,K} = K\left(\frac{z_1 - \Phi^{-1}(y_1)}{b}\right)K\left(\frac{z_2 - \Phi^{-1}(y_2)}{b}\right)\boldsymbol{u}(\Phi^{-1}(\boldsymbol{y}), \boldsymbol{\theta}_b).$$

The quantity $U_{\boldsymbol{z},b} = U_{\boldsymbol{z},b}(\boldsymbol{y})$ depends on two variables $\boldsymbol{y} = (y_1, y_2)$. We need the derivatives with respect to y_1 and y_2 in the Taylor expansion. Using the chain rule, we have

$$\frac{\partial \boldsymbol{U}_{z,b}}{\partial y_1} = k\Big(\frac{z_1 - \Phi^{-1}(y_1)}{b}\Big)K\Big(\frac{z_2 - \Phi^{-1}(y_2)}{b}\Big)\frac{\boldsymbol{u}(\Phi^{-1}(\boldsymbol{y}), \boldsymbol{\theta}_b)}{b\phi(\Phi^{-1}(y_1))} + K\Big(\frac{z_1 - \Phi^{-1}(y_1)}{b}\Big)K\Big(\frac{z_2 - \Phi^{-1}(y_2)}{b}\Big)\frac{\boldsymbol{w}_1(\Phi^{-1}(\boldsymbol{y}))}{\phi(\Phi^{-1}(y_1))} \tag{4.25}$$

with $k = K'$ and

$$\frac{\partial \boldsymbol{U}_{z,b}}{\partial y_2} = K\Big(\frac{z_1 - \Phi^{-1}(y_1)}{b}\Big)k\Big(\frac{z_2 - \Phi^{-1}(y_2)}{b}\Big)\frac{\boldsymbol{u}(\Phi^{-1}(\boldsymbol{y}), \boldsymbol{\theta}_b)}{b\phi(\Phi^{-1}(y_2))} + K\Big(\frac{z_1 - \Phi^{-1}(y_1)}{b}\Big)K\Big(\frac{z_2 - \Phi^{-1}(y_2)}{b}\Big)\frac{\boldsymbol{w}_2(\Phi^{-1}(\boldsymbol{y}))}{\phi(\Phi^{-1}(y_2))}. \tag{4.26}$$

A typical term in the Taylor expansion of $Y_n(\boldsymbol{z})$ takes the form

$$\begin{aligned}
&K_{\boldsymbol{b}}\left(\Phi^{-1}(F(\boldsymbol{X}_t)) - \boldsymbol{z}\right)\boldsymbol{u}\left(\Phi^{-1}(F(\boldsymbol{X}_t)), \boldsymbol{\theta}_b\right)\\
&\quad = K_{\boldsymbol{b}}\left(\Phi^{-1}(F_n(\boldsymbol{X}_t)) - \boldsymbol{z}\right)\boldsymbol{u}\left(\Phi^{-1}(F_n(\boldsymbol{X}_t)), \boldsymbol{\theta}_b\right)\\
&\quad + k\left(\frac{z_1 - \Phi^{-1}(F_n^*(X_{1t}))}{b}\right)K\left(\frac{z_2 - \Phi^{-1}(F_n^*(X_{2,t}))}{b}\right)\\
&\qquad \times \frac{v(\Phi^{-1}(F_n^*(\boldsymbol{X}_t)))}{b\phi(\Phi^{-1}(F_n^*(X_{1t})))}(F(X_{1t}) - F_n(X_{1t}))\\
&\quad + K\left(\frac{z_1 - \Phi^{-1}(F_n^*(X_{1t}))}{b}\right)K\left(\frac{z_2 - \Phi^{-1}(F_n^*(X_{2,t}))}{b}\right)\\
&\qquad \times \frac{\boldsymbol{w}_1(\Phi^{-1}(F_n^*(\boldsymbol{X}_t)))}{\phi(\Phi^{-1}(F_n^*(X_{1t})))}(F(X_{1t}) - F_n(X_{1t}))\\
&\quad + \text{ analogous terms for the second index involving } \left(F(X_{2,t}) - F_n(X_{2,t})\right),
\end{aligned} \tag{4.27}$$

where F_n^* is determined by the mean value theorem. The challenge in proving the desired result is control of the behavior of quantities on the form $1/\phi(\Phi^{-1}(F(x)))$, because this fraction tends to infinity as $|x| \to \infty$. The key to this problem is the assumption that the kernel function K and thus its derivative $k = K'$ have compact support. This means that in the expressions above, $K = k = 0$ if for some $M > 0$,

$$\frac{|z_1 - \Phi^{-1}(F_n^*(X_{1t}))|}{b} \geq M,$$

or

$$|z_1 - \Phi^{-1}(F_n^*(X_{1t}))| \geq Mb,$$

or, by removing the absolute value signs,

$$\Phi^{-1}(F_n^*(X_{1t})) \leq z_1 - Mb \quad \text{or} \quad \Phi^{-1}(F_n^*(X_{1t})) \geq z_1 + Mb,$$

where M may be large. The same reasoning applies of course to the second index as well. Letting $n \to \infty$ and using the consistency of the empirical distribution function, it follows that the kernel function term is zero if

$$X_{1t} \leq F^{-1}(\Phi(z_1 - Mb)) \quad \text{or} \quad X_{1t} \geq F^{-1}(\Phi(z_1 + Mb)).$$

The same reasoning applies to the derivative of the kernel function, where we consider the function k/b instead of K. All this implies that the challenge of controlling the magnitude of the Taylor terms above as $|x| \to \infty$ disappears, since taking the boundedness of the other terms into account,

$$k\left(\frac{z_1 - \Phi^{-1}(F_n^*(X_{1t}))}{b}\right) K\left(\frac{z_2 - \Phi^{-1}(F_n^*(X_{2t}))}{b}\right) \frac{\boldsymbol{u}(\Phi^{-1}(F_n^*(\boldsymbol{X}_t)))}{b\phi(\Phi^{-1}(F_n^*(X_{1t})))}$$

and

$$K\left(\frac{z_1 - \Phi^{-1}(F_n^*(X_{1t}))}{b}\right) K\left(\frac{z_2 - \Phi^{-1}(F_n^*(X_{2t}))}{b}\right) \frac{\boldsymbol{w}_1(\Phi^{-1}(F_n^*(\boldsymbol{X}_t)))}{\phi(\Phi^{-1}(F_n^*(X_{1t})))}$$

are bounded almost surely as $n \to \infty$ (and $b \to 0$).

All this means that if we can prove that for $i = 1, 2$,

$$\frac{1}{n}\sum_{t=1}^{n}(F_n(X_{it}) - F(X_{it})) \xrightarrow{P} 0$$

at an appropriate rate, then we are done by Slutsky's theorem. Using a U-statistic decomposition for a strongly mixing process for $i = 1, 2$, we have

$$\begin{aligned}
\frac{1}{n}\sum_{t=1}^{n}(F_n(X_{it}) - F(X_{it})) &= \frac{1}{n^2}\sum_{t=1}^{n}\sum_{s\neq t}^{n}(I(X_{is} \leq X_{it}) - F(X_{it})) \\
&\quad + \frac{1}{n^2}\sum_{t=1}^{n}(1 - F(X_{it})) \\
&= \frac{1}{n}\sum_{t=1}^{n}(0.5 - F(X_{it})) + O_P\left(n^{-1}\right)
\end{aligned}$$

$$= O_P\left(n^{-1/2}\right) + O_P\left(n^{-1}\right)$$
$$= O_P\left(n^{-1/2}\right).$$

Now we are ready to introduce $\boldsymbol{b} \to \mathbf{0}$. Inspecting the proof of Theorems 4.2 and 4.4 in conjunction with the above result, we will see that the above reasoning can be transferred to those proofs as well. In this case, there is a multiplicative factor $(b_1 b_2)^{-2}$ in the penalty function Q_n' of (4.21). The bandwidth b appearing in the denominator of (4.25) and (4.26) now tends to zero but can be absorbed in the boundedness argument related to (4.27). See also Section D of the supplement of Otneim and Tjøstheim (2021). Assuming that $b_1 = b_2 = b$, this results in a faster convergence rate for the additional term in (4.27) than the rate $O_P[(b_1 b_2)^{-3} n^{-1}]^{1/2}$ of the leading terms in Theorems 4.2 and 4.4, from which the conclusion of Theorem 4.5 follows. □

4.10.3 Proof of the linear transformation result

Proof of Proposition 4.2. Let $(\boldsymbol{X}_1, \ldots, \boldsymbol{X}_n)$, with $\boldsymbol{X}_t = (X_{1t}, X_{2t})$ be observations from the density $f(\boldsymbol{x})$ having the local Gaussian representation $\psi(\boldsymbol{x}, \boldsymbol{\theta}(\boldsymbol{x}))$, and let $\boldsymbol{Y}_t = \boldsymbol{\alpha} + \boldsymbol{A}\boldsymbol{X}_t$, $t = 1, \ldots, n$. We introduce non-singular bandwidth matrices $\boldsymbol{B}_x$ and $\boldsymbol{B}_y$ (see Fan and Gijbels (1996)), and we have

$$L_{\boldsymbol{X}}(\boldsymbol{X}_1, \ldots, \boldsymbol{X}_n, \boldsymbol{\mu}(\boldsymbol{x}), \boldsymbol{\Sigma}(\boldsymbol{x})) = n^{-1} \sum_{t=1}^{n} K_{\boldsymbol{B}_x}(\boldsymbol{X}_t - \boldsymbol{x}) \log \psi(\boldsymbol{X}_t, \boldsymbol{\theta}(\boldsymbol{x})) - \int K_{\boldsymbol{B}_x}(\boldsymbol{v} - \boldsymbol{x}) \psi(\boldsymbol{v}, \boldsymbol{\theta}(\boldsymbol{x}))\, \mathrm{d}\boldsymbol{v},$$

where $K_{\boldsymbol{B}_x}(\boldsymbol{X}_t - \boldsymbol{x}) = |\boldsymbol{B}_x^{-1}| K(\boldsymbol{B}_x^{-1}(\boldsymbol{X}_t - \boldsymbol{x}))$, and $|\cdot|$ is the determinant. Let $\boldsymbol{B}_x$ be diagonal with $\boldsymbol{b}_x = (b_{x1}, b_{x2})$ along the diagonal, and let $K(\boldsymbol{x}) = K_1(x_1)K_2(x_2)$ be the familiar product kernel representation. Analogously,

$$L_{\boldsymbol{Y}}(\boldsymbol{Y}_1, \ldots, \boldsymbol{Y}_n) = n^{-1} \sum_{t=1}^{n} K_{\boldsymbol{B}_y}(\boldsymbol{Y}_t - \boldsymbol{y}) \log \psi(\boldsymbol{Y}_t, \boldsymbol{\theta}(\boldsymbol{y})) - \int K_{\boldsymbol{B}_y}(\boldsymbol{w} - \boldsymbol{y}) \psi(\boldsymbol{w}, \boldsymbol{\theta}(\boldsymbol{y}))\, \mathrm{d}\boldsymbol{w}$$

with $\boldsymbol{\theta}(\boldsymbol{y}) = (\boldsymbol{\mu}(\boldsymbol{y}), \boldsymbol{\Sigma}(\boldsymbol{y}))$. We will now assume that $\boldsymbol{\mu}(\boldsymbol{y}) = \boldsymbol{\alpha} + \boldsymbol{A}\boldsymbol{\mu}(\boldsymbol{x})$ and $\boldsymbol{\Sigma}(\boldsymbol{y}) = \boldsymbol{A}\boldsymbol{\Sigma}(\boldsymbol{x})\boldsymbol{A}^T$ and show that this parameterization is consistent with the local likelihood procedure. With this parameterization it follows at once that

$$(\boldsymbol{Y}_t - \boldsymbol{\mu}(\boldsymbol{y}))^T \boldsymbol{\Sigma}^{-1}(\boldsymbol{y})(\boldsymbol{Y}_t - \boldsymbol{\mu}(\boldsymbol{y})) = (\boldsymbol{X}_t - \boldsymbol{\mu}(\boldsymbol{x}))^T \boldsymbol{\Sigma}^{-1}(\boldsymbol{x})(\boldsymbol{X}_t - \boldsymbol{\mu}(\boldsymbol{x})),$$

and hence

$$\begin{aligned}\log \psi(\boldsymbol{Y}_t, \boldsymbol{\theta}(\boldsymbol{y})) &= -\log 2\pi - \log|\boldsymbol{A}| - \frac{1}{2}\log|\boldsymbol{\Sigma}(\boldsymbol{x})| \\ &\quad - (\boldsymbol{Y}_t - \boldsymbol{\mu}(\boldsymbol{y}))^T \boldsymbol{\Sigma}^{-1}(\boldsymbol{y})(\boldsymbol{Y}_t - \boldsymbol{\mu}(\boldsymbol{y})) \\ &= -\log|\boldsymbol{A}| + \log \psi(\boldsymbol{X}_t, \boldsymbol{\theta}(\boldsymbol{x})).\end{aligned}$$

We need to let $\boldsymbol{B_x}$ and $\boldsymbol{B_y}$ tend to zero at different rates, which is not unnatural given the possibly different metric structure of two neighborhoods $\mathcal{N}(\boldsymbol{x})$ and $\mathcal{N}(\boldsymbol{y})$ around $\boldsymbol{x}$ and $\boldsymbol{y}$, respectively. We let $\boldsymbol{B}_{\boldsymbol{y}}^{-1} = \boldsymbol{B}_{\boldsymbol{x}}^{-1}\boldsymbol{A}^{-1}$ and then $|\boldsymbol{B}_{\boldsymbol{y}}^{-1}| = |\boldsymbol{B}_{\boldsymbol{x}}^{-1}||\boldsymbol{A}^{-1}|$. Hence

$$K_{\boldsymbol{B_y}}(\boldsymbol{Y}_i - \boldsymbol{y}) = |\boldsymbol{B}_{\boldsymbol{y}}^{-1}|K(\boldsymbol{B}_{\boldsymbol{y}}^{-1}(\boldsymbol{Y}_t - \boldsymbol{y})) = |\boldsymbol{A}^{-1}||\boldsymbol{B}_{\boldsymbol{x}}^{-1}|K(\boldsymbol{B}_{\boldsymbol{x}}^{-1}\boldsymbol{A}^{-1}(\boldsymbol{Y}_t - \boldsymbol{y})),$$

and, consequently,

$$K_{\boldsymbol{B_y}}(\boldsymbol{Y}_t - \boldsymbol{y}) \log \psi(\boldsymbol{Y}_t, \boldsymbol{\theta}(\boldsymbol{y})) = |\boldsymbol{A}^{-1}|K_{\boldsymbol{B_x}}(\boldsymbol{X}_t - \boldsymbol{x})[-\log|\boldsymbol{A}| + \log \psi(\boldsymbol{X}_t, \boldsymbol{\theta}(\boldsymbol{x}))].$$

In the same manner with $\boldsymbol{w} = \boldsymbol{\alpha} + \boldsymbol{A}\boldsymbol{v}$,

$$\int K_{\boldsymbol{B_y}}(\boldsymbol{w} - \boldsymbol{y})\psi(\boldsymbol{w}, \boldsymbol{\theta}(\boldsymbol{y}))\, d\boldsymbol{w} = |\boldsymbol{A}^{-1}| \int K_{\boldsymbol{B_x}}(\boldsymbol{v} - \boldsymbol{x})\psi(\boldsymbol{v}, \boldsymbol{\theta}(\boldsymbol{x}))\, d\boldsymbol{v},$$

and hence

$$\begin{aligned}L_{\boldsymbol{Y}}(\boldsymbol{Y}_1, \ldots, \boldsymbol{Y}_n, \boldsymbol{\mu}(\boldsymbol{y}), \boldsymbol{\Sigma}(\boldsymbol{y})) &= |\boldsymbol{A}^{-1}|L_{\boldsymbol{X}}(\boldsymbol{X}_1, \ldots, \boldsymbol{X}_n, \boldsymbol{\mu}(\boldsymbol{x}), \boldsymbol{\Sigma}(\boldsymbol{x})) - \\ &\quad |\boldsymbol{A}^{-1}| \log|\boldsymbol{A}| n^{-1} \sum_{i=1}^{n} K_{\boldsymbol{B_x}}(\boldsymbol{X}_i - \boldsymbol{x}).\end{aligned}$$

The last term and the multiplicative factor $|\boldsymbol{A}^{-1}|$ do not depend on local parameters. Hence, as $\boldsymbol{B_x}$ and $\boldsymbol{B_y}$ tend to zero at their different rates, there will be a one-to-one correspondence between the local likelihood estimates. The estimates $\widehat{\boldsymbol{\theta}}_{\boldsymbol{B_x},n}(\boldsymbol{x})$ are associated with $\boldsymbol{\theta}(\boldsymbol{x})$, and the estimates $\widehat{\boldsymbol{\theta}}_{\boldsymbol{B_y},n}(\boldsymbol{y})$ are associated with $\boldsymbol{\theta}(\boldsymbol{y}) = (\boldsymbol{\mu}(\boldsymbol{y}), \boldsymbol{\Sigma}(\boldsymbol{y})) = (\boldsymbol{\alpha} + \boldsymbol{A}\boldsymbol{\mu}(\boldsymbol{x}), \boldsymbol{A}\boldsymbol{\Sigma}(\boldsymbol{x})\boldsymbol{A}^T)$. Here $\widehat{\boldsymbol{\theta}}_{\boldsymbol{B_x},n}(\boldsymbol{x})$ converges to $\boldsymbol{\theta}(\boldsymbol{x})$, and $\widehat{\boldsymbol{\theta}}_{\boldsymbol{B_y},n}(\boldsymbol{y})$ converges to $\boldsymbol{\theta}(\boldsymbol{y})$, as was shown in Theorem 4.2, and Proposition 4.2 is proved. □

Going through the steps of the proof, we see that the same proof holds for $\boldsymbol{\theta}_b(\boldsymbol{x})$ and $\boldsymbol{\theta}_b(\boldsymbol{y})$. Tjøstheim and Hufthammer (2013) show an additional alternative route to these results.

References

Berentsen, G.D., Cao, R., Francisco-Fernández, M., Tjøstheim, D., 2017. Some properties of local Gaussian autocorrelation and other nonlinear dependence measures. Journal of Time Series Analysis 38 (2), 352–380.

Berentsen, G.D., Kleppe, T., Tjøstheim, D., 2014a. Introducing localgauss, an R-package for estimating and visualizing local Gaussian correlation. Journal of Statistical Software 56 (12), 1–18.

Berentsen, G.D., Støve, B., Tjøstheim, D., Nordbø, T., 2014b. Recognizing and visualizing copulas: an approach using local Gaussian approximation. Insurance: Mathematics and Economics 57, 90–103.

Berentsen, G.D., Tjøstheim, D., 2014. Recognizing and visualizing departures from independence in bivariate data using local Gaussian correlation. Statistics and Computing 24 (5), 785–801.

Bjerve, S., Doksum, K., 1993. Correlation curves: measures of association as function of covariate values. Annals of Statistics 21 (2hol), 890–902.

Blomqvist, N., 1950. On a measure of dependence between two random variables. Annals of Mathematical Statistics 21 (4), 593–600.

Boyer, B.H., Gibson, M.S., Loretan, M., 1999. Pitfalls in tests for changes in correlation. Discussion Paper 597. Federal Reserve Government Papers.

Fan, J., Gijbels, I., 1996. Local Polynomial Modelling and Its Application, Theory and Methodologies. Chapman and Hall, London.

Fan, J., Yao, Q., 2003. Nonlinear Time Series. Nonparametric and Parametric Methods. Springer.

Forbes, K.J., Rigobon, R., 2002. No contagion, only interdependence: measuring stock market comovements. The Journal of Finance 57 (5), 2223–2261.

Hansen, B.E., 2008. Uniform convergence rates for kernel estimation with dependent data. Econometric Theory 24 (3), 726–748.

Heller, R., Heller, Y., Gorfine, M., 2013. A consistent multivariate test of association based on ranks of distances. Biometrika 100 (2), 503–510.

Hjort, N., Jones, M., 1996. Locally parametric nonparametric density estimation. Annals of Statistics 24 (4), 1619–1647.

Hoeffding, W., 1940. Mass-stabinvariante Korrelationstheorie. Schriften des Mathematischen Seminars und des Instituts für Angewandte Mathematik der Universität Berlin 5 (3), 179–233. Translated in: Fisher, N.I., Sen, P.K. (Eds.), 1994. The Collected Work of Wassily Hoeffding. Springer, New York.

Holland, P.W., Wang, Y.J., 1987. Dependence functions for continuous bivariate densities. Communications in Statistics 16 (3), 863–876.

Hufthammer, K.O., 2009. Local Gaussian correlation. PhD thesis. Department of Mathematics, University of Bergen.

Inci, A.C., Li, H.-C., McCarthy, J., 2011. Financial contagion: a local correlation analysis. Research in International Business and Finance 25 (1), 11–25.

Jones, M.C., 1996. The local dependence function. Biometrika 83 (4), 899–904.

Jones, M.C., 1998. Constant local dependence. Journal of Multivariate Analysis 64 (2), 148–155.

Jones, M.C., Koch, I., 2003. Dependence maps: local dependence in practice. Statistics and Computing 13 (3), 241–255.

Jordanger, L.A., Tjøstheim, D., 2020. Nonlinear spectral analysis: a local Gaussian approach. Journal of the American Statistical Association, 1–55.

Klimko, L.A., Nelson, P.I., 1978. On conditional least squares estimation for stochastic processes. Annals of Statistics 6 (3), 629–642.

Lacal, V., Tjøstheim, D., 2017. Local Gaussian autocorrelation and tests of serial dependence. Journal of Time Series Analysis 38 (1), 51–71.

Lacal, V., Tjøstheim, D., 2019. Estimating and testing nonlinear local dependence between two time series. Journal of Business and Economic Statistics 37 (4), 648–660.
Lehmann, E.L., 1966. Some concepts of dependence. Annals of Mathematical Statistics 37 (5), 1137–1153.
Loader, C.R., 1996. Local likelihood density estimation. Annals of Statistics 24 (4), 1602–1618.
Markowitz, H., 1952. Portfolio selection. Journal of Finance 7 (1), 77–91.
Masry, E., Tjøstheim, D., 1995. Nonparametric estimation and identification of ARCH non-linear time series: strong convergence and asymptotic normality. Econometric Theory 11 (2), 258–289.
Meyn, S.P., Tweedie, R.L., 2009. Markov Chains and Stochastic Stability. Springer.
Otneim, H., Tjøstheim, D., 2017. The locally Gaussian density estimator for multivariate data. Statistics and Computing 27 (6), 1595–1616.
Otneim, H., Tjøstheim, D., 2018. Conditional density estimation using the local Gaussian correlation. Statistics and Computing 28 (2), 303–321.
Otneim, H., Tjøstheim, D., 2021. The locally Gaussian partial correlation. Journal of Business & Economic Statistics, 1–33.
Rényi, A., 1959. On measures of dependence. Acta Mathematica Hungarica 10 (3–4), 441–451.
Sankaran, P., Gupta, R., 2004. Characterizations using local dependence function. Communications in Statistics. Theory and Methods 33 (12), 2959–2974.
Silvapulle, P., Granger, C.W., 2001. Large returns, conditional correlation and portfolio diversification: a value-at-risk approach. Quantitative Finance 1 (5), 542–551.
Silverman, B.W., 1986. Density Estimation for Statistics and Data Analysis. Chapman and Hall, London.
Stone, M., 1974. Cross-validatory choice and assessment of statistical predictions. Journal of the Royal Statistical Society Series B 36 (2), 111–147.
Støve, B., Tjøstheim, D., 2014. Measuring asymmetries in financial returns: an empirical investigation using local Gaussian correlation. In: Haldrup, N., Meitz, M., Saikkonen, P. (Eds.), Essays in Nonlinear Time Series Econometrics. Oxford University Press, Oxford, pp. 307–329.
Støve, B., Tjøstheim, D., Hufthammer, K., 2014. Using local Gaussian correlation in a nonlinear re-examination of financial contagion. Journal of Empirical Finance 25, 785–801.
Székely, G.J., 2002.]-statistics: the energy of statistical samples. Technical report. Technical report 02-16. Bowling Green State University.
Taleb, N.N., 2007. The Black Swan: The Impact of the Highly Improbable. Random House.
Taniguchi, M., Kakizawa, Y., 2000. Asymptotic Theory of Statistical Inference for Time Series. Springer-Verlag, New York.
Tjøstheim, D., 1986. Estimation in nonlinear time series models. Stochastic Processes and Their Application 21 (2), 251–273.
Tjøstheim, D., Hufthammer, K.O., 2013. Local Gaussian correlation: a new measure of dependence. Journal of Econometrics 172 (1), 33–48.
Tukey, J.W., 1958. A problem of Berkson, and minimum variance orderly estimators. Annals of Mathematical Statistics 29 (2), 588–592.
van der Waerden, B.L., 1952. Order tests for the two-sample problem and their power. Idagationes Mathematicae 55, 453–458.
Wilcox, R.R., 2005. Estimating the conditional variance of y, given x, in a simple regression model. Journal of Applied Statistics 32 (5), 495–502.
Wilcox, R.R., 2007. Local measures of association: estimating the derivative of the regression line. British Journal of Mathematical and Statistical Psychology 60 (1), 107–117.

CHAPTER 5

Local Gaussian correlation and the copula

Contents

5.1. Introduction 135
5.2. Local Gaussian correlation for copula models 136
 5.2.1 Tail behavior 140
 5.2.2 Normalized local Gaussian correlation 141
5.3. Examples 142
 5.3.1 Archimedean copulas 143
 5.3.2 Elliptical copulas 146
5.4. Recognizing copulas by goodness-of-fit 148
 5.4.1 Uniform pseudo-observations 149
 5.4.2 Gaussian pseudo-observations 149
 5.4.3 A goodness-of-fit test based on local Gaussian correlation 150
 5.4.4 Choice of bandwidth 152
 5.4.5 Simulation study 153
 5.4.6 Visualizing departures from H_0 156
5.5. A real-data study 157
References 159

5.1 Introduction

In this chapter, we compare the local Gaussian representation with the copula. Most of the material is taken from Berentsen et al. (2014).

Some basic properties of the copula were given in Chapter 3.3. The main asset of the copula is the disentanglement of effects due to the shape of the marginal distributions and effects due to the dependence between the variables involved. This is expressed in the Sklar formula (3.7), a representation that can also be made to be valid in the discrete case. It is a representation in terms of uniform variables, where these uniform variables U_i are obtained from the marginal distribution functions F_i in Sklar's formula, so that $U_i = F_i(X_i)$. This can be compared to the normalized representation of the local Gaussian representation in Chapter 4.7, which requires continuity and where standard normal variables Z_i are given by $Z_i = \Phi^{-1}(F_i(X_i))$.

As we saw in Chapter 3.3, parametric copula functions determine classes of copulas. The parametric representation means that estimates of the pa-

Statistical Modeling using Local Gaussian Approximation
https://doi.org/10.1016/B978-0-12-815861-6.00012-2

rameters can typically be obtained with convergence rate $n^{-1/2}$, but these parameters are not always easy to interpret as measures of dependence. Moreover, we have to identify a "correct" copula class. This identification problem is the main issue of the present chapter, and we will demonstrate how the local Gaussian correlation can contribute to its solution and, in addition, that it can be used to obtain a straightforward interpretation of the local dependence structure of copulas. This is in spite of the slower convergence rate of its estimate. Its fastest rate is $(nb^2)^{-1/2}$, where b is a bandwidth parameter in the simplified bivariate model of Chapter 4.7 (see also, in particular, Chapters 9–11), and in the general bivariate case the rate is significantly slower.

Examples of copula identification for some well-known copula classes with accompanying hypotheses tests are given in Sections 5.3 and 5.4.3.

One way of examining the relationships between the copula and the local Gaussian concept is proceeding via the so-called Rosenblatt (1952) transformation. We do this in Section 5.2, where it is also shown that this can be employed to obtain at least a partially explicit expression for the local Gaussian correlation for exchangeable copulas and, as a consequence, for exchangeable distributions. This can be used to get a better understanding of local dependence properties of a number of standard copula models, in particular, in the tail. In practice the tail behavior can be coupled to the observed behavior of financial indexes.

This chapter is restricted to the bivariate case. For a very brief discussion of the multivariate case including the vine copula, we refer to Berentsen et al. (2014).

5.2 Local Gaussian correlation for copula models

We start by a generalization of the so-called Rosenblatt (1952) transformation:

Lemma 5.1. *Let $\boldsymbol{X}$ have a density $f_{\boldsymbol{X}}(\boldsymbol{x})$ on $\mathbb{R}^2$ with cumulative distribution function*

$$F_{\boldsymbol{X}}(\boldsymbol{x}) = \int_{-\infty}^{x_1}\int_{-\infty}^{x_2} f_{\boldsymbol{X}}(w_1, w_2)\, dw_1\, dw_2.$$

Then there exists a one-to-one function $\boldsymbol{g}$ such that $\boldsymbol{X} = \boldsymbol{g}(\boldsymbol{Z})$, where $\boldsymbol{Z} \sim \mathcal{N}(0, \boldsymbol{I}_2)$.

This is not difficult to prove. We have $f_{\boldsymbol{X}}(\boldsymbol{x}) = f_{X_1}(x_1) f_{X_2|X_1}(x_2|x_1)$. Then $U_1 = F_{X_1}(X_1)$ is uniform. There also exists a standard normal variable $Z_1 =$

$\Phi^{-1}(U_1)$ such that $U_1 = \Phi(Z_1)$, where Φ is the cumulative distribution function of the standard normal density. Hence $X_1 = F_{X_1}^{-1}(\Phi(Z_1))$. In the same manner, there exists a uniform variable U_2 independent of U_1 (see Rosenblatt (1952)) such that $U_2 = F_{X_2|X_1}(X_2|X_1)$, and there exists $Z_2 \sim \mathcal{N}(0,1)$ independent of Z_1 such that $U_2 = \Phi(Z_2)$, and hence

$$\begin{pmatrix} X_1 \\ X_2 \end{pmatrix} = \begin{pmatrix} F_{X_1}^{-1}(\Phi(Z_1)) \\ F_{X_2|X_1}^{-1}(\Phi(Z_2))|F_{X_1}^{-1}(\Phi(Z_1)) \end{pmatrix} \stackrel{\text{def}}{=} \boldsymbol{g}(\boldsymbol{Z}), \tag{5.1}$$

where $F_{X_2|X_1}^{-1}$ is interpreted as the inverse of $F_{X_2|X_1}$ with fixed X_1 (i.e., with fixed U_1 and Z_1). Here g is one-to-one due to the strict monotonicity of $F_{\boldsymbol{X}}$.

As pointed out by Rosenblatt (1952), this representation is non-unique, since we also have

$$\begin{pmatrix} X_1 \\ X_2 \end{pmatrix} = \begin{pmatrix} F_{X_1|X_2}^{-1}(\Phi(Z_1))|F_{X_2}^{-1}(\Phi(Z_2)) \\ F_{X_2}^{-1}(\Phi(Z_2)) \end{pmatrix} \stackrel{\text{def}}{=} \boldsymbol{g}'(\boldsymbol{Z}'), \tag{5.2}$$

where, in general, $\boldsymbol{g} \neq \boldsymbol{g}'$ and $\boldsymbol{Z} \neq \boldsymbol{Z}'$.

Assuming $\boldsymbol{g}$ to be continuously differentiable at $\boldsymbol{z}$, by Taylor expansion we have $\boldsymbol{X} = \boldsymbol{g}(\boldsymbol{Z}) = \boldsymbol{g}(\boldsymbol{z}) + \frac{\partial \boldsymbol{g}}{\partial \boldsymbol{z}}(\boldsymbol{z})(\boldsymbol{Z} - \boldsymbol{z}) + o_P(|\boldsymbol{Z} - \boldsymbol{z}|)$, where $\frac{\partial \boldsymbol{g}}{\partial \boldsymbol{z}}$ is the Jacobi matrix. For this representation, it may be tempting to define a local mean and local covariance of the density of $\boldsymbol{X}$ at the point $\boldsymbol{x}$ as the mean and covariance of the Gaussian variable $\boldsymbol{V}_{\boldsymbol{z}}(\boldsymbol{Z}) = \boldsymbol{g}(\boldsymbol{z}) + \frac{\partial \boldsymbol{g}}{\partial \boldsymbol{z}}(\boldsymbol{z})(\boldsymbol{Z} - \boldsymbol{z})$, where $\boldsymbol{z} = \boldsymbol{g}^{-1}(\boldsymbol{x}) \stackrel{\text{def}}{=} \boldsymbol{h}(\boldsymbol{x})$. Since $\mathrm{E}(\boldsymbol{Z}) = 0$ and $\boldsymbol{\Sigma}(\boldsymbol{Z}) = \boldsymbol{I}_2$, this results in

$$\boldsymbol{\mu}_1(\boldsymbol{x}) = \boldsymbol{g}(\boldsymbol{z}) - \frac{\partial \boldsymbol{g}(\boldsymbol{z})}{\partial \boldsymbol{z}}\boldsymbol{z} = \boldsymbol{x} - \left(\frac{\partial \boldsymbol{h}(\boldsymbol{x})}{\partial \boldsymbol{x}}\right)^{-1} \boldsymbol{h}(\boldsymbol{x}) \tag{5.3}$$

and

$$\boldsymbol{\Sigma}_1(\boldsymbol{x}) = \frac{\partial \boldsymbol{g}(\boldsymbol{z})}{\partial \boldsymbol{z}}\left(\frac{\partial \boldsymbol{g}(\boldsymbol{z})}{\partial \boldsymbol{z}}\right)^T = \left(\frac{\partial \boldsymbol{h}(\boldsymbol{x})}{\partial \boldsymbol{x}}\right)^{-1}\left(\left(\frac{\partial \boldsymbol{h}(\boldsymbol{x})}{\partial \boldsymbol{x}}\right)^{-1}\right)^T. \tag{5.4}$$

This can also be done for $\boldsymbol{g}'$ and a Gaussian variable $\boldsymbol{V}_{\boldsymbol{Z}'}(\boldsymbol{Z}') = \boldsymbol{g}'(\boldsymbol{z}') + \frac{\partial \boldsymbol{g}'}{\partial \boldsymbol{z}'}(\boldsymbol{z}')(\boldsymbol{Z}' - \boldsymbol{z}')$ with resulting parameters $\boldsymbol{\mu}_2(\boldsymbol{x})$ and $\boldsymbol{\Sigma}_2(\boldsymbol{x})$. It is easy to verify that $f_{\boldsymbol{V}_{\boldsymbol{z}}(\boldsymbol{Z})}(\boldsymbol{v}) \stackrel{\text{def}}{=} \psi(\boldsymbol{v}, \boldsymbol{\mu}_1(\boldsymbol{x}), \boldsymbol{\Sigma}_1(\boldsymbol{x}))$ and $f_{\boldsymbol{V}_{\boldsymbol{z}'}(\boldsymbol{Z}')}(v) \stackrel{\text{def}}{=} \psi(\boldsymbol{v}, \boldsymbol{\mu}_2(\boldsymbol{x}), \boldsymbol{\Sigma}_2(\boldsymbol{x}))$ yield representations similar to a local Gaussian one as in Section 4.3, but, in fact, they cannot be identified with such a representation. This is clearly seen from the non-uniqueness of the Rosenblatt representation resulting, in general, in $\boldsymbol{\mu}_2(\boldsymbol{x}) \neq \boldsymbol{\mu}_1(\boldsymbol{x})$, $\boldsymbol{\Sigma}_2(\boldsymbol{x}) \neq \boldsymbol{\Sigma}_1(\boldsymbol{x})$, and $\rho_2(\boldsymbol{x}) \neq \rho_1(\boldsymbol{x})$.

We now look at (5.1) and (5.2) and examine under what conditions these two transformations give rise to a unique local correlation that can be expressed analytically and can be used to recognize copulas. Concentrating first on representation (5.1), by (5.1) and (5.4) the matrix

$$\frac{\partial \boldsymbol{h}}{\partial \boldsymbol{x}}(\boldsymbol{x}) = \begin{bmatrix} \frac{\partial h_1}{\partial x_1} & \frac{\partial h_1}{\partial x_2} \\ \frac{\partial h_2}{\partial x_1} & \frac{\partial h_2}{\partial x_2} \end{bmatrix} \tag{5.5}$$

is lower triangular, and

$$\left(\frac{\partial \boldsymbol{h}}{\partial \boldsymbol{x}}(\boldsymbol{x})\right)^{-1} = \left(\frac{\partial h_1}{\partial x_1} \cdot \frac{\partial h_2}{\partial x_2}\right)^{-1} \begin{bmatrix} \frac{\partial h_2}{\partial x_2} & 0 \\ \frac{-\partial h_2}{\partial x_1} & \frac{\partial h_1}{\partial x_1} \end{bmatrix},$$

which, using (5.4), results in the following local correlation-like quantity:

$$\rho_1(\boldsymbol{x}) = \rho_1(x_1, x_2) = \frac{\boldsymbol{\Sigma}_{12}(\boldsymbol{x})}{\sqrt{\boldsymbol{\Sigma}_{11}(\boldsymbol{x})\boldsymbol{\Sigma}_{22}(x)}} = \frac{-\frac{\partial h_2}{\partial x_1}}{\sqrt{\left(\frac{\partial h_1}{\partial x_1}\right)^2 + \left(\frac{\partial h_2}{\partial x_1}\right)^2}}, \tag{5.6}$$

and to its validity and uniqueness we return below. Now, consider a continuous random variable $\boldsymbol{X} = (X_1, X_2)$ with joint cumulative distribution function F and margins $F_{X_1}(x_1) = F_1(x_1)$ and $F_{X_2}(x_1) = F_2(x_2)$. Due to the representation theorem of Sklar (1959), F can be written as

$$F(x_1, x_2) = C(F_1(x_1), F_2(x_2)), \tag{5.7}$$

where the copula $C: [0,1]^2 \to [0,1]$ is a unique bivariate distribution function with uniform margins. Since any continuous distribution function F has representation (5.7), we may re-express (5.1) and thus $\rho_1(x_1, x_2)$ in terms of the copula C and the margins F_1 and F_2. By standard theory, $F_{2|1}^{-1}(x_2|x_1)$ may be written as

$$F_{2|1}^{-1}(x_2|x_1) = F_2^{-1}\left(C_1^{-1}(F_1(x_1), x_2)\right),$$

where $C_1^{-1}(u_1, u_2)$ is interpreted as the inverse of $C_1(u_1, u_2) = \frac{\partial}{\partial u_1} C(u_1, u_2)$ with fixed u_1. It follows that (5.1) may be written as

$$\boldsymbol{g}(\boldsymbol{Z}) = \begin{bmatrix} F_1^{-1}(\Phi(Z_1)) \\ F_2^{-1}\left(C_1^{-1}(\Phi(Z_1), \Phi(Z_2))\right) \end{bmatrix}. \tag{5.8}$$

Note that this transformation, only with $\Phi(Z_1)$ and $\Phi(Z_2)$ replaced by two independent uniform $[0, 1]$ variables, is a standard way of sampling from the distribution $C(F_1(x_1), F_2(x_2))$ (see, e.g., Nelsen (1999, pp. 35–37)). In the continuous case, $\boldsymbol{g}$ is one-to-one if the copula density $c(u_1, u_2)$ satisfies $c(u_1, u_2) > 0$ for all $(u_1, u_2) \in [0, 1]^2$. This guarantees the invertibility of $C_1(u_1, u_2)$ with respect to u_2. Then the inverse $\boldsymbol{h} = \boldsymbol{g}^{-1}$ is given by

$$\boldsymbol{h}(\boldsymbol{X}) = \begin{bmatrix} h_1(X_1, X_2) \\ h_2(X_1, X_2) \end{bmatrix} = \begin{bmatrix} \Phi^{-1}(F_1(X_1)) \\ \Phi^{-1}(C_1(F_1(X_1), F_2(X_2))) \end{bmatrix}. \tag{5.9}$$

To find an expression for $\rho_1(x_1, x_2)$ using (5.6), let ϕ denote the standard normal density function, and let $C_{11}(u_1, u_2) = \frac{\partial^2}{\partial u_1^2} C(u_1, u_2)$. Then by using the two partial derivatives of $\boldsymbol{h}$, $\rho_1(\boldsymbol{x})$ of (5.6) for model (5.7) may be written as

$$\rho_1(x_1, x_2) = \frac{-C_{11}(F_1(x_1), F_2(x_2))\phi\left(\Phi^{-1}(F_1(x_1))\right)}{\sqrt{\phi^2\left(\Phi^{-1}(C_1(F_1(x_1), F_2(x_2)))\right) + C_{11}^2(F_1(x_1), F_2(x_2))\phi^2\left(\Phi^{-1}(F_1(x_1))\right)}}. \tag{5.10}$$

However, repeating the above argument with the Rosenblatt representation (5.2) as a starting point leads to another local correlation-like quantity $\rho_2(x_1, x_2)$ given by

$$\rho_2(x_1, x_2) = \frac{-C_{22}(F_1(x_1), F_2(x_2))\phi\left(\Phi^{-1}(F_2(x_2))\right)}{\sqrt{\phi^2\left(\Phi^{-1}(C_2(F_1(x_1), F_2(x_2)))\right) + C_{22}^2(F_1(x_1), F_2(x_2))\phi^2\left(\Phi^{-1}(F_2(x_2))\right)}}, \tag{5.11}$$

where $C_2(u_1, u_2) = \frac{\partial}{\partial u_2} C(u_1, u_2)$ and $C_{22}(u_1, u_2) = \frac{\partial^2}{\partial u_2^2} C(u_1, u_2)$.

Since the two Rosenblatt representations are bases for any representation of $f_X(\boldsymbol{x})$ (including the density generated by a general functional relationship $\boldsymbol{X} = \boldsymbol{g}(\boldsymbol{Z})$), we have the uniqueness at points where they coincide. The local parameters in such a set of points are consistent with the local parameters derived from the local penalty function q in Eq. (4.5) in Chapter 4. Indeed, for a point $\boldsymbol{x}$ where the Rosenblatt representations give a unique $\boldsymbol{\gamma}(\boldsymbol{x}) = (\mu(\boldsymbol{x}), \boldsymbol{\Sigma}(\boldsymbol{x}))$ such that $f(\boldsymbol{x}) = \psi(\boldsymbol{x}, \boldsymbol{\gamma}(\boldsymbol{x}))$, we can find a local Gaussian approximation with $\boldsymbol{\gamma}_{\boldsymbol{b}}(\boldsymbol{x})$ that satisfies Eqs. (4.6) and converges to $\boldsymbol{\gamma}(\boldsymbol{x})$. Simply choose a linear stepwise representation (4.7) such that $\boldsymbol{x} \in S_i$ for some i and take $\boldsymbol{A}_i = \boldsymbol{\Sigma}^{1/2}(\boldsymbol{x})$ and $\boldsymbol{a}_i = \boldsymbol{\mu}(\boldsymbol{x})$. Then with a small enough bandwidth, $\boldsymbol{\gamma}_{\boldsymbol{b}}(\boldsymbol{x}) = \boldsymbol{\gamma}_i = (\boldsymbol{a}_i, \boldsymbol{A}_i\boldsymbol{A}_i^T) = (\boldsymbol{\mu}(\boldsymbol{x}), \boldsymbol{\Sigma}(\boldsymbol{x}))$, and $\boldsymbol{\gamma}_{\boldsymbol{b}}(\boldsymbol{x}) \to \boldsymbol{\gamma}(\boldsymbol{x})$ trivially as $\boldsymbol{b} \to \boldsymbol{0}$. If for a point $\boldsymbol{x}$, there is no unique Rosenblatt representation, then such an approach is not possible since there is no unique $\boldsymbol{\gamma}(\boldsymbol{x})$ that could serve as a starting point for the construction. Nevertheless, for such points $\boldsymbol{x}$, under the regularity conditions mentioned by Tjøstheim and Hufthammer (2013) (or see Chapter 4), there does exist a limiting unique minimizer $\boldsymbol{\gamma}(\boldsymbol{x})$ and resulting $\rho(\boldsymbol{x})$ of solving (4.6) such that the local likelihood estimate $\widehat{\boldsymbol{\gamma}}_{n,\boldsymbol{b}}(\boldsymbol{x})$ (or $\widehat{\rho}_{n,\boldsymbol{b}}(\boldsymbol{x})$) converges toward $\boldsymbol{\gamma}(\boldsymbol{x})$ (or $\rho(\boldsymbol{x})$) (see Tjøstheim and Hufthammer (2013, Theorems 1–3) or Theorems 4.1 and 4.2 in Chapter 4).

Inspecting (5.10) and (5.11), we see that in the copula case, when the copula is exchangeable (i.e., $C(u_1, u_2) = C(u_2, u_1)$), the points where $\rho_2(x_1, x_2) = \rho_1(x_1, x_2)$ are found along the curve defined by $F_1(x_1) = F_2(x_2)$. In the particular case of identical margins, which is true when X_1 and X_2 are exchangeable, we have equality along the diagonal $x_1 = x_2$.

Our identification and testing procedure in Sections 5.2.2 and 5.4 will be based on the properties of $\rho_1(x_1, x_2)$ on the diagonal where $x_1 = x_2 = d$ and $\rho_1(d, d) = \rho_2(d, d)$. This produces tests with good power properties.

5.2.1 Tail behavior

Tjøstheim and Hufthammer (2013) consider the connection between $\rho(x_1, x_2)$ and the upper and lower tail dependence indices defined by

$$\lambda_u = \lim_{q \to 1^-} P(F_2(X_2) > q | F_1(X_1) > q), \tag{5.12}$$

$$\lambda_l = \lim_{q \to 0+} P(F_2(X_2) \leq q | F_1(X_1) \leq q). \tag{5.13}$$

It is known that the tail indices for a Gaussian distribution are zero, which is one of the arguments raised vigorously against the Gaussian as a model for tail dependence for financial variables.

Let $\psi_{\boldsymbol{x}} = \psi(\cdot, \mu(\boldsymbol{x}), \boldsymbol{\Sigma}(\boldsymbol{x}))$ be the local Gaussian approximation of $f(\boldsymbol{x})$ at the point $\boldsymbol{x}$. Letting $\boldsymbol{x}$ be on the diagonal with $x_1 = x_2 = d$. Then the lower tail dependence index of the Gaussian distribution $\psi_{\boldsymbol{x}}$ is given by McNeil et al. (2005, Chapter 5.3):

$$\lambda_l = \lambda_l(d, d) = 2 \lim_{u \to -\infty} \Phi\left(u\sqrt{\frac{1-\rho(d,d)}{1+\rho(d,d)}}\right)$$

for a fixed d. Since the lower tail index for a Gaussian variable is zero, this means that if $f(x)$ has a tail index different from zero and $\psi(\cdot, \mu(\boldsymbol{x}), \boldsymbol{\Sigma}(\boldsymbol{x}))$ should approximate f as $\boldsymbol{x} = (d, d) \to -\infty$, then this would require that $\rho(d, d) \to 1$ as $d \to -\infty$. Thus, by (5.10), on the diagonal, where for an exchangeable copula, $\rho_1(d, d) = \rho_2(d, d) = \rho(d, d)$, $\rho(d, d)$ for copula models with non-zero lower tail dependence should satisfy

$$\lim_{d\to-\infty} \rho(d,d) = \lim_{q\to 0^+} \frac{-C_{11}(q,q)\phi\left(\Phi^{-1}(q)\right)}{\sqrt{\phi^2\left(\Phi^{-1}\left(C_1(q,q)\right)\right) + C_{11}^2(q,q)\phi^2\left(\Phi^{-1}(q)\right)}} = 1. \tag{5.14}$$

This, for example, can be verified for the Clayton copula. For the speed at which $\rho(d, d) \to 1$ for the Clayton copula, we refer to Fig. 5.1 in the case of standard normal margins.

5.2.2 Normalized local Gaussian correlation

The variables $\boldsymbol{Z}$ of the preceding section obtained from the Rosenblatt transformation must be carefully distinguished from the normalized variables

$$\boldsymbol{Z} = (Z_1, Z_2) = (\Phi^{-1}(F_1(X_1)), \Phi^{-1}(F_2(X_2))) \tag{5.15}$$

obtained from the transformations of the marginal distributions $F_i, i = 1, 2$. The latter variables were introduced and discussed in Chapter 4.7. These standard normals are in general dependent and can themselves be used as a starting point for the Rosenblatt transformation and for obtaining the local correlations ρ_1, ρ_2, and ρ as in the preceding section. In this section and in the rest of the chapter, the $\boldsymbol{Z}$- and z-notation will be reserved for these normalized variables. Since the copula C of a continuous random variable $\boldsymbol{X} = (X_1, X_2)$ is invariant to any continuous strictly increasing transformations of X_1 and X_2, $\boldsymbol{Z}$ and $\boldsymbol{X}$ share the same copula. Moreover, since $F_1(X_1)$ and $F_2(X_2)$ are both marginally uniformly distributed, Z_1 and Z_2 are marginally standard normal distributed. It follows that the distribution function of $\boldsymbol{Z}$ is given by $F(z_1, z_2) = C(\Phi(z_1), \Phi(z_2))$. For a random variable $\boldsymbol{Z} = (Z_1, Z_2)$ with distribution function $C(\Phi(z_1), \Phi(z_2)) =$

$C_\theta(\Phi(z_1), \Phi(z_2))$ with a scalar parameter θ, Eqs. (5.10) and (5.11) simplify to

$$\rho_{\theta,1}(z_1, z_2) \stackrel{\text{def}}{=} \frac{-C_{11}(\Phi(z_1), \Phi(z_2))\phi(z_1)}{\sqrt{\phi^2\left(\Phi^{-1}\left(C_1(\Phi(z_1), \Phi(z_2))\right)\right) + C_{11}^2(\Phi(z_1), \Phi(z_2))\phi^2(z_1)}} \tag{5.16}$$

and

$$\rho_{\theta,2}(z_1, z_2) \stackrel{\text{def}}{=} \frac{-C_{22}(\Phi(z_1), \Phi(z_2))\phi(z_2)}{\sqrt{\phi^2\left(\Phi^{-1}\left(C_2(\Phi(z_1), \Phi(z_2))\right)\right) + C_{22}^2(\Phi(z_1), \Phi(z_2))\phi^2(z_2)}}. \tag{5.17}$$

The subscript θ emphasizes that the above local correlations depend on a parameter θ characterizing the copula C.

For the variable $\boldsymbol{Z}$ defined by (5.15), the local Gaussian correlation is independent of the margins F_1 and F_2, and we define (5.16) and (5.17) as the normalized local Gaussian correlations for the copula C. Of course, the variable $\boldsymbol{Z}$ cannot be observed via transformation (5.15) without knowledge of the margins F_1 and F_2. Nevertheless, as we will see in Section 5.4 (see also Chapter 4.7), given observations $X_1, \ldots, X_n$, we can obtain an approximate sample from $C(\Phi(z_1), \Phi(z_2))$ via an empirical version of transformation (5.15). Using this sample of Gaussian pseudo-observations, we can estimate ρ_θ by the local likelihood method described in Chapter 4.7 and subsequently compare this estimate with the analytic expression for ρ_θ obtained in (5.16)–(5.17) for different copulas. This is the theme of Section 5.3.

5.3 Examples

All copulas considered in the following examples are exchangeable, and since Z_1 and Z_2 are standard normals, that is, $F_1 = F_2 = \Phi$, we have that $\rho_{\theta,1}(z_1, z_2)$, $\rho_{\theta,2}(z_1, z_2)$, and $\rho_\theta(z_1, z_2)$ are all well defined and give the same result along the diagonal $z_1 = z_2 = d$. In much of the following the emphasis will be on $\rho_{\theta,1}(d, d)$ in the computations, but we will write $\rho_\theta(d, d)$. In practice, given a copula, formula (5.16) often becomes quite complicated. As a consequence, for the examples in Sections 5.3.1 and 5.3.2, only the functions C_1 and C_{11} are computed, and the reader is referred to Figs. 5.1–5.4 for the characteristics of $\rho_\theta(z_1, z_2)$ for each copula. The left plots in Figs. 5.1–5.4 are plots of $\rho_\theta(d, d)$ against d. The copula parameters in these plots are chosen so that they correspond to a specific value of Kendall's tau ($\tau = 0.2, 0.4, 0.6, 0.8$), defined in Chapter 3.2.2, which in general is uniquely related to the one-parameter copula C by the formula (cf. formula (3.4) in Section 3.2.2)

$$\tau = m(\theta) = 4 \int\int_{[0,1]^2} C(u, v)\, \mathrm{d}C(u, v) - 1. \tag{5.18}$$

Using the local likelihood algorithm, we can estimate the local correlation, defined by minimizing the penalty function (4.5) for all (z_1, z_2) for which there are sufficient data. The right plots of Figs. 5.1–5.4 display this estimate based on one realization of $n = 1000$ samples from each of the copula models $C(\Phi(z_1), \Phi(z_2))$ considered with copula parameter corresponding to $\tau = 0.4$ and with bandwidth b chosen according to the procedure outlined in Section 5.4.4. There is some expected boundary bias in the estimation due to few observations and a fairly large bandwidth, but the estimated dependence patterns revealed in the right plots of Figs. 5.1–5.4 are consistent with the theoretical ones along the diagonal in the left plots of Figs. 5.1–5.4.

5.3.1 Archimedean copulas

An important class of copulas is the class of Archimedean copulas, which have been extensively studied. These copulas are completely defined by their so-called generator function ψ; see its properties in, for example, Nelsen (1999). See also Chapter 3.3 for definitions. In the following three examples, we consider the commonly used Clayton, Gumbel, and Frank Archimedean copulas.

Example 5.1. The Clayton copula. The Clayton copula is an asymmetric copula, exhibiting greater dependence in the negative tail than in the positive one (i.e., lower tail dependence and no upper tail dependence).

$$C_\theta^{Cl}(u_1, u_2) = \max\{(u_1^{-\theta} + u_2^{-\theta} - 1); 0\}^{-1/\theta}, \quad \text{where} \quad \theta \in [-1, \infty) \setminus 0,$$

with derivatives

$$C_1(u_1, u_2) = \left(1 + u_1^{\theta}(u_2^{-\theta} - 1)\right)^{-\frac{\theta+1}{\theta}},$$
$$C_{11}(u_1, u_2) = (\theta + 1)u_2^{\theta-1}(1 - u_2^{-\theta})(1 + u_1^{\theta}(u_2^{-\theta} - 1))^{-1/\theta-2}.$$

This implies, using formula (5.16) (or (5.17)), that $\rho_\theta(d, d) \to 0$ as $d \to \infty$ and that $\rho_\theta(d, d) \to 1$ as $d \to -\infty$. These features can be seen in the left plot of Fig. 5.1 for θ-values corresponding to the chosen values of Kendall's tau. This plot and the subsequent plots for the other copulas give a precise and interpretable characterization of the local dependence of the Clayton copula. It replaces an informal scatter plot. It also gives a vastly more detailed picture of the (asymmetric) dependence properties than the one-number characterization of the Kendall's tau. The same values of Kendall's tau are used in Figs. 5.2–5.4, but the other copulas have very different local correlation curves associated with them, this difference forming the basis for the formal goodness-of-fit test in Section 5.4.

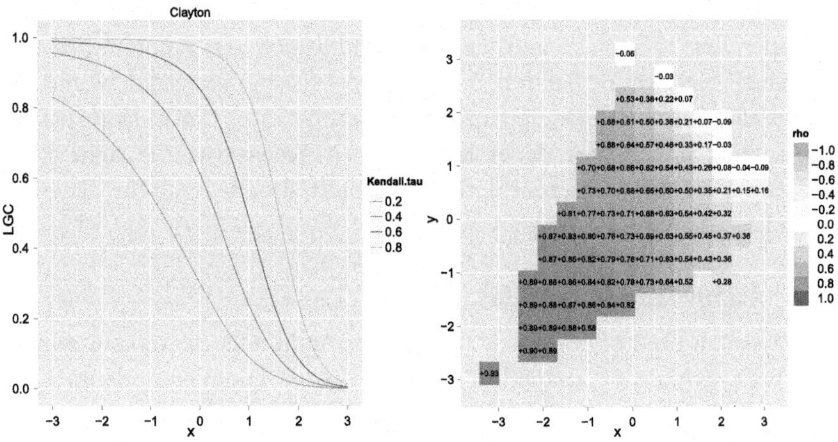

Figure 5.1 Local Gaussian correlation for $C(\Phi(z_1), \Phi(z_2))$, where C is the Clayton copula: left plot along the diagonal $z_1 = z_2$ with lower curve corresponding to $\tau = 0.2$, upper curve to $\tau = 0.8$; right plot is estimated based on $n = 1000$ observations with $\tau = 0.4$.

Example 5.2. The Gumbel copula. The Gumbel copula is also an asymmetric copula exhibiting greater dependence in the positive tail than in the negative one (i.e., upper tail dependence and no lower tail dependence). The Gumbel copula can be written as

$$C_\theta^{Gu}(u_1, u_2) = \exp\left[- ((-\ln u_1)^\theta + (-\ln u_2)^\theta)^{1/\theta} \right] \quad \text{with} \quad \theta \in [1, \infty).$$

The functions C_1 and C_{11} are quite complicated and therefore are not given here. The characteristics of $\rho_\theta(z_1, z_2)$ for the Gumbel copula can be seen in Fig. 5.2, where we clearly see the upper tail dependence numerically quantified in terms of the local correlation.

An alternative to modeling variables (X_1, X_2) with upper tail dependence by the Gumbel copula is modeling $(-X_1, -X_2)$ by the Clayton copula. What separates the resulting dependence structure in these two approaches? From the left plots of Figs. 5.1 and 5.2 we see that the dependence structure in the "non-dependent" tail of these two copulas is quite different. For the Clayton copula, $\rho_\theta(z_1, z_2)$ in the upper tail approaches zero faster than in the lower tail of the Gumbel copula with corresponding values of τ. This is consistent with a plot (not shown) of the upper tail dependence coefficient λ_u given by (5.12) for the Clayton copula together with the lower tail coefficient λ_l given by (5.13) for the Gumbel copula, where both copula parameters are chosen to correspond to $\tau = 0.4$ (there are known formulas in terms of copula limiting values for these indices). Then $\lambda_u < \lambda_l$, indicating that the upper tail dependence in the Clayton copula vanishes faster than the lower tail dependence in the Gumbel copula. This distinction plays an important role in analyzing the empirical example of Section 5.5.

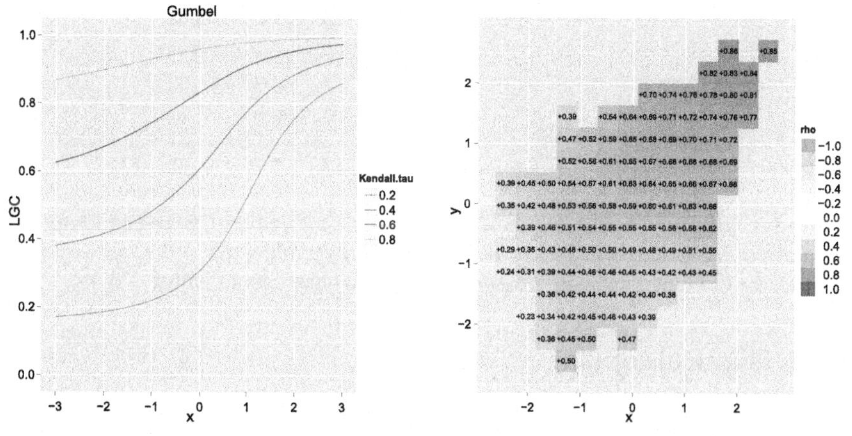

Figure 5.2 Local Gaussian correlation for $C(\Phi(z_1), \Phi(z_2))$, where C is the Gumbel copula: left plot along the diagonal $z_1 = z_2$, lower curve corresponding to $\tau = 0.2$, upper curve to $\tau = 0.8$; right plot is estimated based on $n = 1000$ observations with $\tau = 0.4$.

Example 5.3. The Frank copula. Define $q_t = e^{-\theta t} - 1$. The Frank copula may be written as

$$C_\theta^{Fr}(u_1, u_2) = -\theta^{-1} \ln\left\{1 + q_{u_1} q_{u_2} / q_1\right\} \quad \text{with} \quad \theta \in \mathbb{R} \setminus 0.$$

The derivatives C_1 and C_{11} are

$$C_1(u_1, u_2) = \frac{q_{u_1} q_{u_2} + q_{u_2}}{q_{u_1} q_{u_2} + q_1},$$
$$C_{11}(u_1, u_2) = \frac{q'_{u_1} q_{u_2}(q_1 - q_{u_2})}{\left(q_{u_1} q_{u_2} + q_1\right)^2}.$$

Thus $\rho_\theta(z_1, z_2)$ goes to zero in both upper and lower tails. This feature is reflected in Fig. 5.3; close to constant dependence in the center, which vanishes in the tails.

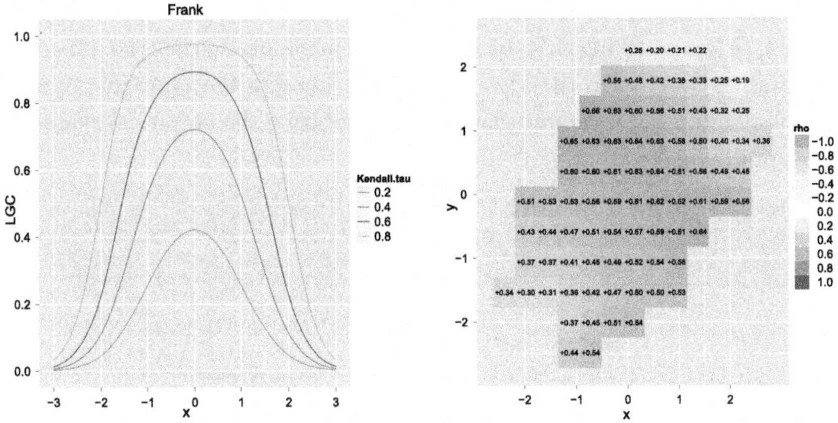

Figure 5.3 Local Gaussian correlation for $C(\Phi(z_1), \Phi(z_2))$, where C is the Frank copula: left plot along the diagonal $z_1 = z_2$, lower curve corresponding to $\tau = 0.2$, upper curve to $\tau = 0.8$; right plot is estimated based on $n = 1000$ observations with $\tau = 0.4$.

5.3.2 Elliptical copulas

Elliptical copulas are the copulas of elliptical distributions. The key advantage of elliptical copulas is that we can specify different levels of global correlation between the marginals, but a disadvantage is that elliptical copulas typically have no simple closed-form expressions. The most commonly used elliptical distributions are the Gaussian and Student-t distributions.

Example 5.4. Gaussian copula. For a given correlation matrix $\mathbf{\Sigma} = \begin{bmatrix} 1 & \rho \\ \rho & 1 \end{bmatrix}$, the Gaussian copula with correlation matrix $\mathbf{\Sigma}$ can be written as

$$C_{\mathbf{\Sigma}}^{Gauss}(u_1, u_2) = \Phi_{\mathbf{\Sigma}}(\Phi^{-1}(u_1), \Phi^{-1}(u_2)),$$

where $\Phi_{\mathbf{\Sigma}}$ is the joint bivariate distribution function of a Gaussian variable with mean vector zero and correlation matrix $\mathbf{\Sigma}$. In general, when (Z_1, Z_2) is Gaussian with mean vector zero and correlation matrix $\mathbf{\Sigma}$, $Z_1|Z_2 = z_2 \sim \mathcal{N}(\rho z_2, 1-\rho^2)$. It follows that for the Gaussian copula,

$$\begin{aligned} C_1(u_1, u_2) &= P(U_2 \le u_2 | U_1 = u_1) \\ &= P(\Phi^{-1}(U_2) \le \Phi^{-1}(u_2) | \Phi^{-1}(U_1) = \Phi^{-1}(u_1)) \\ &= \Phi\left(\frac{\Phi^{-1}(u_2) - \rho\Phi^{-1}(u_1)}{\sqrt{1-\rho^2}}\right). \end{aligned}$$

Letting $R = \frac{\Phi^{-1}(u_2) - \rho\Phi^{-1}(u_1)}{\sqrt{1-\rho^2}}$ and differentiating this expression once more with respect to u_1, we obtain

$$C_{11}(u_1, u_2) = \frac{-\rho}{\sqrt{1-\rho^2}\phi(\Phi^{-1}(u_1))}\phi(R).$$

Thus for a Gaussian copula model $C^{\text{Gauss}}(F_1(x_1), F_2(x_2))$ with arbitrary margins F_1 and F_2, the local Gaussian correlation is given by (5.10) and reduces to

$$\rho(x_1, x_2) = \frac{\rho}{\sqrt{1-\rho^2+\rho^2}} = \rho. \tag{5.19}$$

This is of course valid for all (x_1, x_2), not only on a curve $F_1(x_1) = F_2(x_2)$, and shows that a constant local Gaussian correlation is a feature of the Gaussian copula, that is, more general than for the bivariate Gaussian distribution. It is in fact a consequence of the invariance noted for (5.16). Note that the local mean and local variance are not in general constant for non-Gaussian marginals. It remains to prove the converse statement that $\rho(\mathbf{x}) = c$ $(-1 < c < 1,\ c \neq 0)$ implies the Gaussian copula.

Example 5.5. ***t*-copula.** In the case where (X_1, X_2) is t-distributed with ν degrees of freedom and correlation coefficient ρ, we have that $X_1|X_2 = x_2$ is t-distributed with $\nu+1$ degrees of freedom, expected value ρx_2, and variance $\left(\frac{\nu + x_2^2}{\nu+1}\right)(1-\rho^2)$. With t_ν as the standard t-distribution function, a similar argument as for the Gaussian copula leads to

$$C_1(u_1, u_2) = t_{\nu+1}\left(\frac{t_\nu^{-1}(u_2) - \rho t_\nu^{-1}(u_1)}{\sqrt{\frac{(\nu + t_\nu^{-1}(u_1)^2)(1-\rho^2)}{\nu+1}}}\right) \stackrel{\text{def}}{=} t_{\nu+1}(R),$$

and with f_{t_ν} as the standard t-density function and $s=\sqrt{\frac{(\nu+t_\nu^{-1}(u_1)^2)(1-\rho^2)}{\nu+1}}$, to

$$C_{11}(u_1,u_2)=\frac{\partial R}{\partial u_1}f_{t_{\nu+1}}(R)=\frac{-f_{t_{\nu+1}}(R)}{f_{t_\nu}(t_\nu^{-1}(u_1))s^2}\left(\rho s+\frac{1-\rho^2}{\nu+1}t_\nu^{-1}(u_1)R\right).$$

No simple formula for $\rho_\theta(z_1,z_2)$ computed from (5.16) comes as a result of this. In Fig. 5.4, left, we see that $\rho_\theta(d,d)$ increases toward each tail that is consistent with the t-copula having both upper and lower tail-dependence.

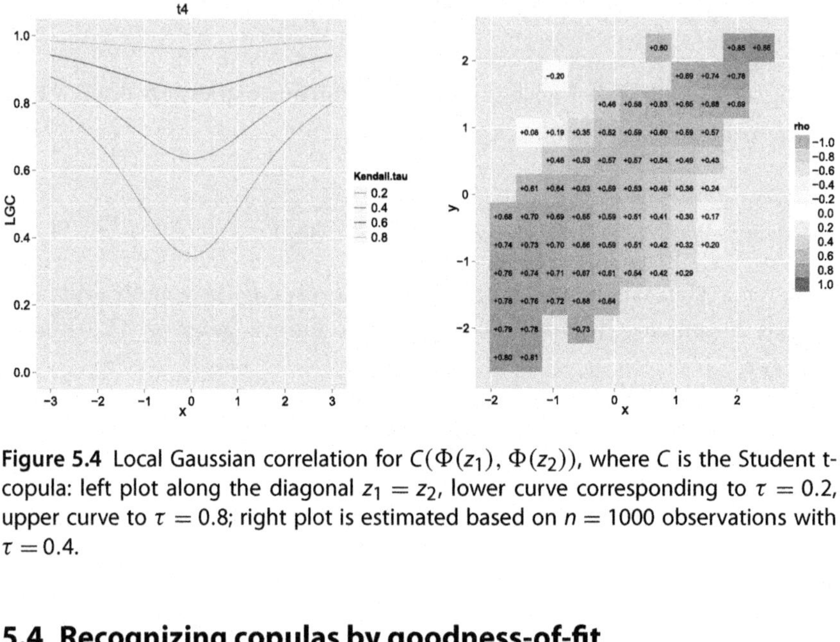

Figure 5.4 Local Gaussian correlation for $C(\Phi(z_1),\Phi(z_2))$, where C is the Student t-copula: left plot along the diagonal $z_1=z_2$, lower curve corresponding to $\tau=0.2$, upper curve to $\tau=0.8$; right plot is estimated based on $n=1000$ observations with $\tau=0.4$.

5.4 Recognizing copulas by goodness-of-fit

Given iid observations $\boldsymbol{X}_1,\ldots,\boldsymbol{X}_n$ from $F(x_1,x_2)=C(F_1(x_1),F_2(x_1))$, consider the issue of using local Gaussian correlation to test the null hypothesis

$$H_0: C\in\mathcal{C},\quad \mathcal{C}=\{C_\theta:\theta\in\Theta\},$$

where Θ is the parameter space. This null hypothesis should not be confused with the compound null hypothesis $H_0\cap H_0'$, where H_0' is the additional parametric assumption

$$H_0': F_1\in\mathcal{F}_1,\ F_2\in\mathcal{F}_2,$$

that is, the margins also belong to some parametric class. In classical goodness-of-fit testing for copulas, H_0' is avoided by considering (uniform) pseudo-observations. In our approach, we avoid the additional assumption H_0' by considering a rank-based transformation of the observations to Gaussian pseudo-observations.

5.4.1 Uniform pseudo-observations

Since we only consider one-parameter copulas, here we emphasize that the copula parameter θ is a scalar. When estimating θ under H_0, a full maximum likelihood approach or the "Inference Functions for Margins" (IFM) approach (see Joe, 1997) requires the additional assumption H_0'. This assumption can be avoided by replacing F_i in the likelihood by the empirical distribution function (X_{ij} being the jth observation of X_i, $i = 1, 2$)

$$F_{i,n}(\boldsymbol{x}) = \frac{1}{n}\sum_{j=1}^{n} I(X_{ij} \leq \boldsymbol{x}), \quad i = 1, 2, \tag{5.20}$$

where I is the indicator function. This method is called the pseudo-likelihood (McNeil, 1997) or the canonical maximum likelihood (Romano, 2002). To avoid the blowup of the copula density at the boundary of $[0, 1]^2$, one typically bases the pseudo-likelihood estimation on the scaled ranks $\widehat{\boldsymbol{U}}_1 = (\hat{U}_{11}, \hat{U}_{21}) \ldots, \widehat{\boldsymbol{U}}_n = (\hat{U}_{1n}, \hat{U}_{2n})$, where $\hat{U}_{ij} = nF_{i,n}(X_{ij})/(n+1)$. This transformation can be seen as an empirical version of the marginal probability integral transformation given by $U_{ij} = F_i(X_{ij})$. Since the distribution function of $\boldsymbol{U} = (F_1(X_1), F_2(X_2))$ is the very definition of the copula C, we can interpret $\widehat{\boldsymbol{U}}_1, \ldots, \widehat{\boldsymbol{U}}_n$ approximately as a sample from the underlying copula C. The observations $\widehat{\boldsymbol{U}}_1, \ldots, \widehat{\boldsymbol{U}}_n$ are therefore often referred to as (uniform) pseudo-observations. By using pseudo-observations we could also estimate the copula parameter using the relation to Kendall's tau given by Eq. (5.18). For other rank-based estimators, see Tsukahara (2005) and Chen et al. (2006).

5.4.2 Gaussian pseudo-observations

Most copula goodness-of-fit tests are carried out using the pseudo-observations described above to avoid the additional assumption H_0'. See, for example, Genest et al. (2009) for an overview. In our approach, we first obtain "Gaussian pseudo-observations" $\widehat{\boldsymbol{Z}}_1 = (\hat{Z}_{11}, \hat{Z}_{21}) \ldots, \widehat{\boldsymbol{Z}}_n = (\hat{Z}_{1n}, \hat{Z}_{2n})$ by applying Φ^{-1} to the pseudo-observations $\widehat{\boldsymbol{U}}_1, \ldots, \widehat{\boldsymbol{U}}_n$, that is,

$$\hat{Z}_{ij} = \Phi^{-1}\left(nF_{i,n}(X_{ij})/(n+1)\right) = \Phi^{-1}(\hat{U}_{ij}).$$

In the same sense that the pseudo-observations $\widehat{\boldsymbol{U}}_1, \ldots, \widehat{\boldsymbol{U}}_n$ can be interpreted as a sample from the underlying copula C, the Gaussian pseudo-observations $\widehat{\boldsymbol{Z}}_1, \ldots, \widehat{\boldsymbol{Z}}_n$ can be interpreted as a sample from $C(\Phi(z_1), \Phi(z_2))$, for which we have defined the normalized local Gaussian correlation $\rho_\theta(z_1, z_2)$ by (5.16)–(5.17). Again, since we will only be concerned with values of ρ_θ along the diagonal, in computations, we will just use formula (5.16) and will not distinguish $\rho_{\theta,1}$ and ρ_θ in our notations. Then a nonparametric estimate of $\rho_\theta(z_1, z_2)$ can be obtained by replacing $\boldsymbol{X}_1, \ldots, \boldsymbol{X}_n$ by $\widehat{\boldsymbol{Z}}_1, \ldots, \widehat{\boldsymbol{Z}}_n$ in the local likelihood described in formula (4.8). As before, we denote this estimate $\widehat{\rho}_{n,b}(z_1, z_2)$, for a point (z_1, z_2). From the results of Section 5.3 and the fact that $\widehat{\boldsymbol{Z}}_1, \ldots, \widehat{\boldsymbol{Z}}_n$ approach a real sample from $C(\Phi(z_1), \Phi(z_2))$ as $n \to \infty$ it follows that $\widehat{\rho}_{n,b}(z_1, z_2)$ is consistent estimating $\rho_\theta(z_1, z_2)$ along the line $z_1 = z_2$ for an exchangeable copula C. A parametric estimate $\widehat{\rho}_{\theta_n}(z_1, z_2)$ of $\rho_\theta(z_1, z_2)$ can be obtained by replacing θ in (5.16) with θ_n, where $\theta_n = \theta_n(\widehat{\boldsymbol{U}}_1, \ldots, \widehat{\boldsymbol{U}}_n)$ is an estimate of the copula parameter under H_0 based on the pseudo-observations $\widehat{\boldsymbol{U}}_1, \ldots, \widehat{\boldsymbol{U}}_n$. Note that both $\widehat{\rho}_{n,b}$ and $\widehat{\rho}_{\theta_n}$ are based on the pseudo-observations and thus (for any fixed bandwidth b) only depend on the ranks of the original observations. This means that a copula goodness-of-fit test based on $\widehat{\rho}_{n,b}$ and $\widehat{\rho}_{\theta_n}$ requires no additional assumption about the marginal distributions F_1 and F_2 other than continuity.

5.4.3 A goodness-of-fit test based on local Gaussian correlation

Having established a nonparametric and parametric estimate of the canonical local Gaussian correlation, we propose to base a goodness-of-fit test on the process

$$P_n = \widehat{\rho}_{n,b} - \widehat{\rho}_{\theta_n}. \tag{5.21}$$

(An alternative would have been to smooth $\widehat{\rho}_{\theta_n}$ with a kernel operator as in Härdle and Mammen (1993).) Recall that $\widehat{\rho}_{n,b}$ is consistent for ρ_θ along the curve defined by $z_1 = z_2$ (cf. Theorem 4.5). We therefore aggregate P_n^2 along the diagonal by

$$T_n = \int_{z_{\alpha/2}}^{z_{1-\alpha/2}} P_n^2(t, t)\,\mathrm{d}t, \tag{5.22}$$

where $z_{\alpha/2}$ and $z_{1-\alpha/2}$ are the $\alpha/2$ and $1-\alpha/2$ quantiles of the standard normal distribution (we typically use $\alpha = 0.05$). Here large values of T_n

lead to the rejection of H_0. There has been much work on the asymptotic theory of test functionals such as T_n in a goodness-of-fit context (see, e.g., Härdle and Mammen (1993) and Gao et al. (2009)), but we do not pursue this theory in this chapter. An asymptotic theory for a similar functional is given in Chapters 7.2 and 7.3. If desired that theory can be adapted to the T_n in (5.22). There are several reasons why the asymptotic theory for the test functional is of limited practical value. By the construction of T_n it is clear that its asymptotic distribution, when scaled properly by some function $\delta(n, b)$, depends on the underlying copula and the parameter θ, which in turn means that critical values are difficult to tabulate by means of the asymptotic properties. Moreover, it is known (see, e.g., Härdle and Mammen (1993), Gao et al. (2009), and Teräsvirta et al. (2010, Chapter 7.7)) that the asymptotics of functional tests like T_n are not very accurate and much better results are obtained by bootstrapping. In this chapter, we therefore directly adopt the parametric bootstrap proposed by Genest et al. (2009) (see also Stute et al. (1993)) to obtain approximate p-values. The validity of the bootstrap for test functionals such as T_n is discussed in Chapter 7.

Parametric bootstrap:

1. Convert the observations $\boldsymbol{X}_1, \dots, \boldsymbol{X}_n$ into pseudo-observations $\widehat{\boldsymbol{U}}_1, \dots, \widehat{\boldsymbol{U}}_n$.
2. Estimate θ under H_0 by a pseudo-observation-based estimator $\hat{\theta}_n = \theta_n(\widehat{\boldsymbol{U}}_1, \dots, \widehat{\boldsymbol{U}}_n)$. Obtain $\widehat{\rho}_{\theta_n}$ by replacing θ in (5.16) with $\hat{\theta}_n$.
3. Convert the pseudo-observations into Gaussian pseudo-observations $\widehat{\boldsymbol{Z}}_1 = \Phi^{-1}(\widehat{\boldsymbol{U}}_1), \dots, \widehat{\boldsymbol{Z}}_n = \Phi^{-1}(\widehat{\boldsymbol{U}}_n)$. Obtain $\widehat{\rho}_{n,b}$ by local likelihood using the Gaussian pseudo-observations $\hat{Z}_1, \dots, \hat{Z}_n$ as observations.
4. Compute the value of T_n.
5. For some large integer R, repeat the following steps for every $k \in \{1, \dots, R\}$:
   a. Generate a random sample $\boldsymbol{U}^*_{1k}, \dots, \boldsymbol{U}^*_{nk}$ from the copula C_{θ_n} and compute the associated pseudo-observations $\widehat{\boldsymbol{U}}^*_{1k}, \dots, \widehat{\boldsymbol{U}}^*_{nk}$.
   b. Compute $T^*_{n,k}$ by repeating steps 2–4 for the new pseudo-observations $\widehat{\boldsymbol{U}}^*_{1k}, \dots, \widehat{\boldsymbol{U}}^*_{nk}$.

The p-value for this test can then be approximated by $R^{-1} \sum_{k=1}^{R} I(T^*_{n,k} > T_n)$.

In the Monte Carlo study in Section 5.4.5, we only consider one-parameter copulas, so we have chosen to estimate θ by $\widehat{\theta}_n = m^{-1}(\hat{\tau})$, where $\hat{\tau}$ is the sample Kendall's tau, and m is defined by (5.18). A general framework for the validity of the parametric bootstrap can be found in Genest et al. (2009). It is clear, however, that the process P_n given by (5.21) does not fall into the category of processes considered there due to the bandwidth parameter b involved in the estimation of $\widehat{\rho}_{n,b}$. To establish a theoretical framework for the validity in our case, we should have to proceed using arguments similar to those of Chapters 7.3 and 7.4, where a bandwidth is involved in the bootstrap operations. The results of the Monte Carlo study in Section 5.4.5 for the level of the test empirically indicate the validity for our approach. See also Berg (2009), where the parametric bootstrap has been used successfully in a number of different approaches.

The method described above can only be used when the analytic expression (5.16) is available as in the examples considered in this chapter, but this is not always the case. There exists a second bootstrap procedure that does not rely on the analytical expression (5.16), but where we instead estimate ρ_θ by Monte Carlo approximation. We refer to Berentsen et al. (2014) and Genest et al. (2009).

5.4.4 Choice of bandwidth

When testing $H_0 : C \in \mathcal{C}$, we may choose a bandwidth that is optimal if H_0 is true. In general, for a variable $\boldsymbol{Z}$ with distribution function $C(\Phi(z_1), \Phi(z_2))$, the mean integrated squared error of the local likelihood estimate $\widehat{\rho}_{n,b}$ along $z_1 = z_2$ is given by

$$\text{MISE}(\widehat{\rho}_{n,b}(\cdot)) = \text{E}\left(\int \left(\widehat{\rho}_{n,b}(t,t) - \rho_\theta(t,t)\right)^2 \text{d}t\right), \tag{5.23}$$

where the expectation is with respect to the distribution function $F(\boldsymbol{z}) = C_\theta(\Phi(z_1), \Phi(z_2))$. Since $\widehat{\rho}_{\theta_n}$ has the ordinary parametric convergence rate, it converges faster than $\widehat{\rho}_{n,b}$ (under H_0). It therefore seems reasonable to choose b as the minimizer of

$$\widehat{\text{MISE}}(\widehat{\rho}_{n,b}(\cdot)) = \text{E}^*\left(\int \left(\widehat{\rho}_{n,b}(t,t) - \widehat{\rho}_{\theta_n}(t,t)\right)^2 \text{d}t\right), \tag{5.24}$$

where the expectation E^* is with respect to the bootstrap distribution estimated under H_0. The bandwidth b is chosen as the minimizer of (5.24), which can be approximated by Monte Carlo integration. These bandwidths are subsequently used in the simulation experiments in Section 5.4.5. Note that another possibility is choosing b by likelihood cross-validation as outlined in Section 4.8.2, Chapter 7, and Chapter 9.

Table 5.1 reports bandwidth estimates based on minimizing (5.24). For simplicity, we take $b_1 = b_2 = b$. The copula parameter and the re-sampling distribution $F_n^*(z)$ is estimated from the associated pseudo-observations of a single sample from five different copulas. We considered two different sample sizes ($n = 250, 500$) and two degrees of global dependence (Kendall's tau $\tau = 0.2, 0.4$). For comparison, the minimizer of (5.23) (which can be computed knowing the real value of θ) is given in parentheses. To avoid unreliable estimates of $\widehat{\rho}_{n,b}$ in the tails, finite integration limits were used in (5.23) and (5.24), the limit $(-1.8, 1.8)$ for $n = 250$ and $(-2, 2)$ for $n = 500$.

Not surprisingly, neither (5.23) nor (5.24) has a minimum for the Gaussian copula (both decrease as b increases). This is a result of the equivalence of the local Gaussian likelihood and the global Gaussian likelihood as $b \to \infty$. However, we do not recommend to use a very large bandwidth when testing for the Gaussian copula, since too much smoothing results in poor power when the null hypothesis is false. In the simulation experiments to be described next, $b_1 = b_2 = 1$ in the Gaussian case. See Berentsen et al. (2014) for more detail.

Table 5.1 Estimated bandwidth based on minimizing $\widehat{\text{MISE}}(\widehat{\rho})$ for a single sample from each copula model for $n = 250, 500$ and $\tau = 0.2, 0.4$. The minimizer of $\text{MISE}(\widehat{\rho}_{n,b})$ is given in the parentheses.

Copula	$\tau = 0.2$		$\tau = 0.4$	
	$n = 250$	$n = 500$	$n = 250$	$n = 500$
Clayton	0.9731(1.0536)	0.9710(0.9515)	0.8465(0.8525)	0.8116(0.7955)
Gumbel	1.1030(1.0674)	0.9198(0.9350)	1.0084(0.9602)	0.9116(0.8896)
Frank	1.4065(1.7846)	1.0166(1.0423)	0.8545(0.7824)	0.7165(0.7122)
Gaussian	∞	∞	∞	∞
t4	0.9176(0.8728)	0.8290(0.7778)	0.8786(0.7977)	0.7675(0.7055)

5.4.5 Simulation study

Berentsen et al. (2014) perform a Monte Carlo study to assess the finite-sample properties of the proposed goodness-of-fit test (5.22) based on the one-level parametric bootstrap. To examine its performance, they compared it with a much used test proposed by Genest and Rémillard (2008). This test is chosen because of its very good overall performance in the simulation studies of Genest et al. (2009) and Berg (2009). It stands out as one of the best. Their test is based on the empirical copula process

$$C_n(u) = \frac{1}{n}\sum_{j=1}^{n} I(\hat{U}_{1j} \le u_1, \hat{U}_{2j} \le u_2),$$

where $\widehat{\boldsymbol{U}}_j = (\hat{U}_{1j}, \hat{U}_{2j})$ $j = 1, \ldots, n$, are the pseudo-observations, and $\boldsymbol{u} = (u_1, u_2) \in [0, 1]^2$. A natural test consists in comparing a distance between C_n and an estimate C_{θ_n} of C obtained under H_0. Then a goodness-of-fit test may be based on the Cramer–von Mises-type statistic

$$A_n = n \int_{[0,1]^2} \{C_n(\boldsymbol{u}) - C_{\theta_n}(\boldsymbol{u})\}^2 \, \mathrm{d}C_n(\boldsymbol{u}). \tag{5.25}$$

Further, we proceed by a parametric bootstrap analogue to the procedure described in Section 5.4.3 to find an approximate p-value for the test. For a more detailed description of these test procedures, we refer to Genest et al. (2009) or Berg (2009). The test based on (5.25) and similar tests are good in discriminating between copulas with different asymmetries. They are not so good in discriminating between copulas whose main difference is expressed in the tail structure, such as a Gaussian copula versus a Student t_4-copula. We believe that the reason for this is that the tail behavior in (5.25) is measured on a $[0, 1]$ scale where tail differences are compressed. This is very different if Gaussian pseudo-observations and the local correlation are used. Tail differences are expressed much more clearly and in fact lead to a very dramatic increase of discriminatory power, as will be seen in the simulation experiment reported in Table 5.2. Possibly, the use of an analogue version of (5.25) with Gaussian pseudo-observations instead of traditional pseudo-observations may also lead to an increase of power, but we have not examined this.

In particular, we are interested in the ability of a test to maintain its prescribed level (arbitrarily fixed at 5% throughout the study) and the power against a variety of fixed alternatives. The simulation design is as follows:

- Five H_0 copulas: Clayton, Gumbel, Frank, Gaussian, and Student t with 4 degrees of freedom
- Five H_1 copulas: Clayton, Gumbel, Frank, Gaussian, and Student t with 4 degrees of freedom
- Two degrees of global dependence: Kendall's tau $\tau = \{0.2, 0.4\}$
- Two sample sizes: $n = \{250, 500\}$

For every combination of the above setup, 1000 samples of size n are drawn from the copula C under H_1 with dependence parameter corresponding to τ. Then the test statistic (5.22) and the alternative test statistic (5.25) are computed under H_0, and p-values are estimated using the parametric bootstrap procedure described in Section 5.4.3. The number of bootstrap realizations was fixed at $R = 1000$. In the estimation of (5.22) the

Table 5.2 Percentage of rejection of H_0 by the T_n-based test and the A_n-based test (in parentheses) for data sets of different sizes arising from different copula models with dependence $\tau = 0.2$ or $\tau = 0.4$.

Copula under H_0	True copula	$\tau = 0.2$		$\tau = 0.4$	
		$n = 250$	$n = 500$	$n = 250$	$n = 500$
Clayton	Clayton	**5.9(4.6)**	**5.4(5.0)**	**5.3(5.2)**	**4.1(5.0)**
	Gumbel	97.3(90.0)	100.0(99.8)	100.0(100.0)	100.0(100.0)
	Frank	77.4(60.3)	95.9(88.8)	96.7(97.6)	99.6(100.0)
	Gaussian	74.8(58.2)	93.4(77.8)	97.4(95.4)	100.0(100.0)
	Student 4 dof	83.3(69.2)	98.2(84.6)	99.5(97.8)	100.0(100.0)
Gumbel	Clayton	98.3(81.2)	100.0(99.0)	100.0(99.8)	100.0(100.0)
	Gumbel	**6.1(5.8)**	**6.1(5.2)**	**6.1(5.2)**	**5.2(4.8)**
	Frank	65.7(20.2)	90.7(49.0)	90.9(50.2)	99.9(92.2)
	Gaussian	55.6(11.4)	81.6(36.0)	76.2(27.8)	96.4(69.0)
	Student 4 dof	43.5(20.2)	74.0(54.6)	75.1(36.6)	97.8(80.4)
Frank	Clayton	74.4(50.6)	94.0(85.6)	98.8(95.8)	100.0(100.0)
	Gumbel	56.5(40.4)	90.2(62.8)	92.3(76.0)	99.8(97.4)
	Frank	**3.1(4.8)**	**3.8(4.6)**	**4.7(4.6)**	**4.6(5.0)**
	Gaussian	11.4(8.0)	25.1(15.6)	49.7(19.2)	76.3(49.6)
	Student 4 dof	84.4(27.8)	99.7(52.0)	97.2(46.0)	100.0(87.0)
Gaussian	Clayton	66.0(44.2)	91.7(73.6)	98.4(93.4)	100.0(100.0)
	Gumbel	31.1(33.2)	67.4(42.8)	56.0(58.2)	92.8(82.4)
	Frank	7.7(7.6)	14.6(7.0)	29.5(21.4)	65.6(35.4)
	Gaussian	**6.3(5.2)**	**6.2(4.8)**	**5.8(5.0)**	**6.3(5.4)**
	Student 4 dof	35.0(20.6)	82.5(26.6)	14.5(21.2)	66.2(23.8)
Student 4 dof	Clayton	81.8(35.8)	97.8(69.8)	98.9(88.4)	100.0(99.6)
	Gumbel	55.7(23.0)	81.9(34.0)	67.5(45.8)	95.2(63.4)
	Frank	81.6(9.2)	98.3(16.8)	94.1(26.8)	100.0(48.4)
	Gaussian	72.4(5.2)	93.8(7.8)	66.3(4.0)	94.6(2.8)
	Student 4 dof	**6.5(5.4)**	**5.7(5.0)**	**6.2(4.8)**	**7.6(4.8)**

bandwidth $b = b_1 = b_2$ is taken from Table 5.1, except when H_0 is Gaussian, in which case we put $b_1 = b_2 = 1$.

Table 5.2 reports the level and power of the test (5.22) and the A_n-based test (5.25) in parentheses. Each line of the table shows the percentage of rejections of H_0 associated with the two tests for the different combinations described above. The nominal levels match relatively well the prescribed size of 5% but seem to be a little more volatile compared to the nominal level of the A_n-based test. A rerun of the level was done for the Student test for $n = 500$ and $\tau = 0.4$ (the case where the nominal level deviated the most from the prescribed level) but based on 5000 test decisions and with $R = 2000$ bootstrap replicas for each test. For prescribed levels 1%, 5%, and 10%, the corresponding nominal levels where 1.36%, 6.12%, and 10.84%.

This indicates that 1000 bootstrap replicas may not quite be sufficient for constructing the null distribution of P_n.

The power of the proposed test is very good compared to the A_n-based test, and the power of the A_n-based test in our simulation study corresponds very well with the power found in similar studies by Genest et al. (2009) and Berg (2009). Note that for testing the Gaussian and Student hypotheses, powers are in general lower than for testing the Clayton, Gumbel, and Frank hypotheses. This is also in line with the previously mentioned studies.

There were only two cases where the power did not increase with the level of dependence. This happened when H_0 was the Gaussian copula and H_1 was the t-copula with 4 degrees of freedom, and when H_0 was the t-copula with 4 degrees of freedom and H_1 was the Gaussian copula. This can be explained by Fig. 5.4, where we see that the local Gaussian correlation for the Student t-copula becomes more constant as the level of dependence increases, thus resembling more the Gaussian structure.

5.4.6 Visualizing departures from H_0

An advantage of using the local correlation is that if the null is rejected, then the cause of the rejection can be investigated by visually comparing the nonparametric estimate of ρ_θ with the corresponding estimate under the null hypothesis. Deviations between these estimates can easily be interpreted since both measure local dependence. Two types of diagnostic plots, being based on the Gaussian pseudo-observations $\widehat{\boldsymbol{Z}}_1, \ldots, \widehat{\boldsymbol{Z}}_n$, are presented by Berentsen et al. (2014). This means that local dependence properties of an approximate sample from the distribution $C(\Phi(z_1), \Phi(z_2))$ are compared with the local dependence properties of the corresponding distribution $C_\theta(\Phi(z_1), \Phi(z_2))$ under the null hypothesis. The goal is to identify which regions of the Gaussian pseudo-observations deviate from H_0, but also to pinpoint *how* the local dependence in these regions deviates from H_0.

The simplest of the two approaches, depending on the parametric bootstrap and comparing values along the diagonal, is presented in Fig. 5.5. This depicts a situation of the evaluation of H_0: t-copula with 4 degrees of freedom when Clayton with $\theta = 0.5$ is the true copula. There are 500 data points, and on the plot, we also added standard 95% bootstrap confidence intervals. We clearly see why H_0 is rejected. The second approach also includes off-diagonal points, and we refer to Berentsen et al. (2014) for more detail.

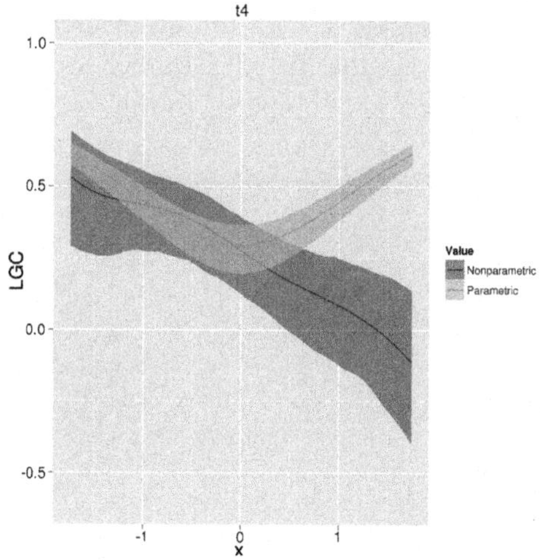

Figure 5.5 Evaluation of H_0: t-copula when Clayton is the true copula by a diagonal plot with confidence intervals of $\widehat{\rho}_{n,b}$ and $\widehat{\rho}_{\theta_n}$ where $\widehat{\rho}_{\theta_n}$ is estimated under H_0: t-copula.

5.5 A real-data study

The Danish fire insurance claims data have been studied in actuarial science and extreme value theory (see, e.g., McNeil, 1997). The data consist of 2167 losses over one million DKK from the years 1980 to 1990 inclusive. There were registered in total 604 cases where a loss in both contents and profits occurred, and the log-transformed values of these claims can be seen in the left plot of Fig. 5.6. There were some ties present in the data, so before the analysis the observations were jittered randomly by a small amount to break the ties. The corresponding Gaussian pseudo-observations and the estimated values of $\widehat{\rho}_{n,b}$ based on the Gaussian pseudo observations can be seen in the right plot of Fig. 5.6. From the latter figure we see that the dependence increases toward the upper tail. Indeed, in terms of AIC (Akaike information criteria), the best ranked copula amongst Clayton, Frank, Gumbel, Gaussian, and Student-t was the Gumbel copula (−379.6), followed by the Gaussian copula (−327.9). Nevertheless, the null hypothesis that the copula of the data is the Gumbel copula was rejected by the goodness-of-fit test proposed in Section 5.4.3 (p-value ≈ 0) and also by an alternative test discussed by Berentsen et al. (2014). However, by using the diagnostic diagonal plot proposed in Section 5.4.6 we now has the possibility to investigate the characteristics of the discrepancy between the data and the null hypothesis. In Fig. 5.7 the parametric estimate of the local Gaussian correlation is plotted together with the nonparametric estimate along the curve $z_1 = z_2$. We see that the (fitted) Gumbel copula assigns too large local correlation in the lower tail compared to the data.

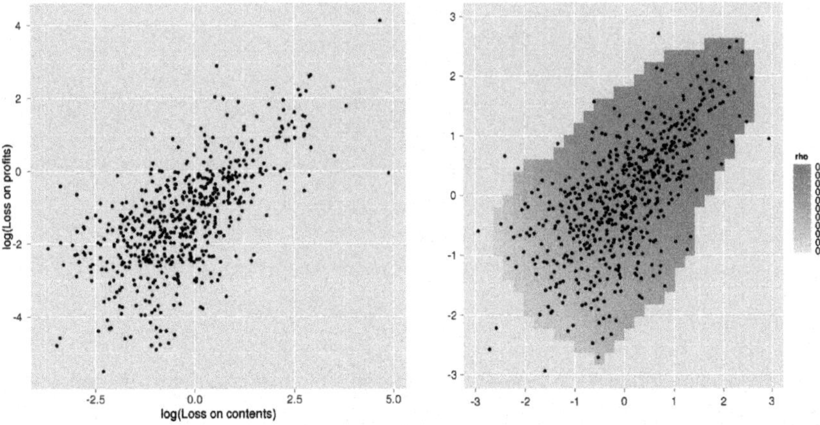

Figure 5.6 Left plot: Scatter plot of log-transformed values of loss on contents and loss on profits; right plot: Gaussian pseudo-observations overlain the estimated local correlation $\widehat{\rho}_{n,b}$.

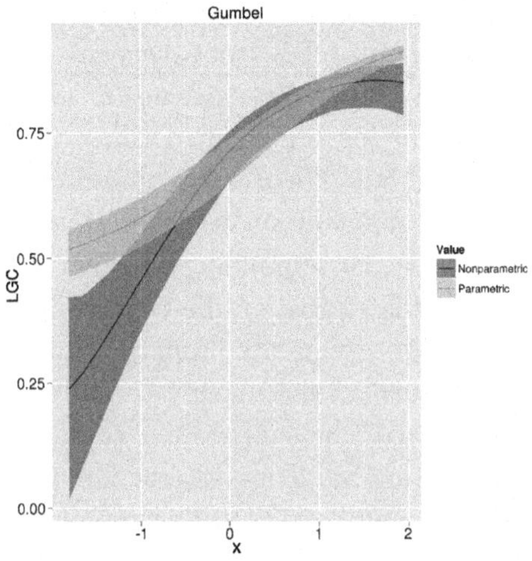

Figure 5.7 Diagnostic plot: Parametric versus non-parametric estimate of ρ_θ.

In Section 5.3.1, we investigated the differences between modeling (X_1, X_2) with upper tail dependence by the Gumbel copula with the alternative of modeling $(-X_1, -X_2)$ by the Clayton copula. The conclusion was that ρ_θ in the "non-dependent" tail approaches zero faster with the Clayton copula than with the Gumbel copula. From the diagnostic plot (Fig. 5.7) we see that this approach could be useful since the Gumbel copula assigns too large local correlation in the lower tail compared to the data. Indeed, the goodness-of-fit test proposed in Section 5.4.3 did not reject the Clayton copula for the negative observations (p-value $= 0.56$). Neither did the alternative test discussed by Berentsen et al. (2014). This illustrates the usefulness of pinpointing the discrepancies between the null-hypothesis and the data: It can help toward selecting a better model.

References

Berentsen, G.D., Støve, B., Tjøstheim, D., Nordbø, T., 2014. Recognizing and visualizing copulas: an approach using local Gaussian approximation. Insurance: Mathematics and Economics 57, 90–103.

Berg, D., 2009. Copula goodness-of-fit testing: an overview and power comparison. European Journal of Finance 15, 675–701.

Chen, X., Fan, Y., Tsyrennikov, V., 2006. Efficient estimation of semiparametric multivariate copula models. Journal of the American Statistical Association 101 (475), 1228–1240.

Gao, J., King, M., Lu, Z., Tjøstheim, D., 2009. Specification testing in nonlinear and nonstationary time series autoregression. Annals of Statistics 37 (6B), 3893–3928.

Genest, C., Rémillard, B., 2008. Validity of the parametric bootstrap for goodness-of-fit testing in semiparametric models. Annales Henri Poincaré 44, 1096–1127.

Genest, C., Rémillard, B., Beaudoin, D., 2009. Goodness-of-fit tests for copulas: a review and a power study. Insurance: Mathematics and Economics 44 (2), 199–213.

Härdle, W., Mammen, E., 1993. Comparing nonparametric versus parametric regression fits. Annals of Statistics 21 (4), 1926–1947.

Joe, H., 1997. Multivariate Models and Dependence Concepts. Chapman and Hall, London.

McNeil, A.J., 1997. Estimating the tails of loss severity distributions using extreme value theory. ASTIN Bulletin 27 (1), 117–132.

McNeil, A.J., Frey, R., Embrechts, P., 2005. Quantitative Risk Management: Concepts, Techniques and Tools. Princeton University Press, Princeton.

Nelsen, R.B., 1999. An Introduction to Copulas. Springer, New York.

Romano, C., 2002. Calibrating and simulating copula functions: an application to the Italian stock market. In: Risk Management Function. Capitalia, Viale U. Tupini.

Rosenblatt, M., 1952. Remarks on a multivariate transformation. Annals of Mathematical Statistics 23 (3), 470–472.

Sklar, A., 1959. Fonctions de répartition à n dimensions et leurs marges. Université Paris 8.

Stute, W., Manteiga, W.G., Quindimil, M.P., 1993. Bootstrap based goodness-of-fit tests. Metrika 40 (1), 243–256.

Teräsvirta, T., Tjøstheim, D., Granger, C.W., 2010. Modelling Nonlinear Economic Time Series. Oxford University Press.

Tjøstheim, D., Hufthammer, K.O., 2013. Local Gaussian correlation: a new measure of dependence. Journal of Econometrics 172 (1), 33–48.

Tsukahara, H., 2005. Semiparametric estimation in copula models. Canadian Journal of Statistics 33 (3), 357–375.

CHAPTER 6

Applications in finance

Contents

6.1. Introduction 161
6.2. Conditional correlation and the bias problem 164
    6.2.1 Why local Gaussian correlation is better 165
6.3. Empirical analysis of dependence of financial returns 167
    6.3.1 Daily stock index returns 168
    6.3.2 Monthly stock index returns 175
    6.3.3 Dependence between commodities, bonds, and stocks 178
6.4. The portfolio allocation problem 182
    6.4.1 Portfolio allocation using the LGC 183
    6.4.2 Empirical example 186
6.5. Financial contagion 196
    6.5.1 A review of measures of interdependence and contagion 198
    6.5.2 A bootstrap test for contagion based on the LGC 202
    6.5.3 Example: Testing for contagion in the 1987 US stock market crash 204
References 209

6.1 Introduction

In finance, dependence between asset returns is important, in particular, for portfolio theory, where the aim is to allocate assets by maximizing the expected return of the portfolio while minimizing its risk, measured, for instance, by the standard deviation. The rule is simple: low correlated assets are good for diversification, but highly correlated assets should be avoided. Markowitz (1952) provides the foundation for this mean-variance (MV) approach, where the crucial assumption is that the asset returns follow a joint Gaussian distribution, and hence the aforementioned rule. The advantage of the Gaussian approach is that it is straightforward, being based on means and covariances, leading to a complete theoretical framework, also in the multivariate case.

There are other methods within finance, which also rest on the Gaussian distribution assumption; for instance, the Black–Scholes formula for pricing options introduced by Black and Scholes (1973) and Merton (1973) and the capital asset pricing model (CAPM) (see Sharpe (1964), Lintner (1965), and Mossin (1966)), used to determine a theoretically appropriate required rate of return of an asset and, to some degree, the calculation of the risk of loss

Statistical Modeling using Local Gaussian Approximation
https://doi.org/10.1016/B978-0-12-815861-6.00013-4

for investments, for instance, measured by the value at risk (VaR) (see, e.g., Jorion, 2006). It estimates how much a set of investments might lose with a given probability in a set time period such as a day. The calculation of VaR is typically significantly simplified by assuming the Gaussian distribution.

However, the restrictive nature of the Gaussian distribution approach is well documented, as asymmetries can be found in the distribution of financial returns; see, for example, Silvapulle and Granger (2001), Longin and Solnik (2001), Ang and Chen (2002), Hong et al. (2007), Okimoto (2008), Chollete et al. (2009), Aas et al. (2009), Støve and Tjøstheim (2014), and BenSaïda et al. (2018). One of the key findings opposing the Gaussian assumption is the often stronger dependence between returns of financial assets during periods of market downturn or crashes (often called "bear markets") and weaker dependence in stable or increasing markets (often called "bull markets"). Another well-known asymmetry is the skewness in the distribution of individual asset returns. This has led to the conclusion that the Gaussian distribution is not well founded empirically; see, for example, Rydberg and Shephard (2000). More recently, in the financial crisis of 2007–2008, it became clear that certain asset returns related to housing and mortgage defaults moved stronger together than assumed in the models used in the financial industry to price, for instance, mortgage derivatives. Indeed, poor modeling of such dependencies is thought to be one of the causes of the collapse in these markets; see, for example, Zimmer (2012).

There are several alternative methods of studying asymmetry of financial returns. Silvapulle and Granger (2001) have looked at various quantile estimation methods (see Chapter 4.2.2), and Longin and Solnik (2001) have used extreme value theory to show that for monthly data, there is a bear market effect but no bull effect. Okimoto (2008) and Rodriguez (2007) have employed regime-switching copulas to study asymmetric dependence for various international stock indices, whereas Aas et al. (2009) and Nikoloulopoulos et al. (2012) have used vine copulas (also called the pair-copula construction) to model multivariate financial return data. In a related works, Ang and Bekaert (2002) and Ang and Chen (2002) have based themselves on Markov regime structures with ARCH/GARCH (see Chapter 2.4) modeling. Recently, factor copulas were introduced for modeling dependence in high dimensions; see, for example, Oh and Patton (2017). Also, Christoffersen et al. (2012) model the correlation among a large set of countries with a dynamic asymmetric copula (or DAC), concluding that correlations have increased markedly in both developed markets and emerging markets. Another way of modeling time-varying correlations, is using the very popular dynamic conditional correlation (DCC) estimators, which have the flexibility of univariate GARCH but not the complexity of conventional multivariate GARCH; see Engle (2002).

Finally, recent papers have examined jumps in the asset return process and its relation to correlation; see, for instance, Pukthuanthong and Roll (2014) and Aït-Sahalia et al. (2015). Solnik and Watewai (2016) develop a regime-switching model to study the correlation asymmetries in international equity markets. They decompose returns into frequent-but-small diffusion and infrequent-but-large jumps and derive an estimation method, finding that correlations due to jumps markedly increase in bad markets, leading to correlation breaks during crises.

A common feature for many alternative approaches is that one ends up with one or more parameters that have a rather indirect interpretation as a measure of dependence. In this respect, correlation has a more natural basis, and thus the local Gaussian correlation (LGC) is a dependence measure that is easier to interpret. Since the well-known bias effect, to be explained in the next subsection, is avoided by the LGC, we can safely state expressions like "correlations tend to 1 during crisis" by using the LGC instead of the ordinary global correlation. Further, by certain simplifying assumptions (cf. Chapter 4.9) the LGC can be used to model high-dimensional dependencies, which may be important in asset allocation problems. This will be elaborated on in Section 6.4.

In this chapter, we present some applications of the local Gaussian correlation concept in finance. These applications include a) the estimation of asset return dependence, b) how to do portfolio allocation using the LGC, and c) how to test for financial contagion.

We will also briefly mention other (competing) approaches, but we will not go into detail of each one of these methods, but rather give some appropriate references.

Recall from Chapter 4 that it is possible to estimate the local Gaussian correlation in several ways. A main option is transforming the variables to marginal standard normality and then estimating the local correlations pairwise, thus resulting in the normalized local Gaussian correlation; cf. Chapters 4.7 and 4.9. Another option is to do a full nonparametric local Gaussian fit of bivariate densities, estimating both local means and local variances, in addition to the local Gaussian correlations. In this chapter, we mainly use this option, but with a filtering of the observations. As the conditional variance of financial returns typically are dependent in time (see, e.g., Engle and Bollerslev, 1986), we calculate filtered returns obtained by filtration of the original return series by fitting GARCH(1, 1) models and then analyzing the residuals (i.e., the filtered returns). Of course, even more complex filtration could be used, for example, AR(1)-GARCH(p, q) models (or your own personal favorite model). However, as we will demonstrate for some data in this chapter, the filtering has only a moderate impact on the main dependency patterns.

6.2 Conditional correlation and the bias problem

One popular approach to analyzing the aforementioned asymmetric dependence between asset returns has been to use the conditional correlation. This was mentioned briefly in Chapter 4.2.2. For time series $\{X_t\}$ and $\{Y_t\}$ of two (log) returns, the *conditional correlation* between X and Y when they are restricted to a set R is

$$\rho_R = \text{corr}(X_t, Y_t \mid (X_t, Y_t) \in R), \tag{6.1}$$

where we assume at least stationarity for the series. See Eq. (4.3) for the conditional correlation estimator.

We define the *exceedance correlation* as the conditional correlation with $R = (-\infty, -c] \times (-\infty, -c]$ or $R = [c, \infty) \times [c, \infty)$, where $c > 0$ is the exceedance level, and define *truncated correlations* similarly, but where R only restricts one of the returns.

The set R can be, and has been, chosen in many ways, and rather different results are obtained depending on the conditioning set used; see, for instance, Campbell et al. (2008). The multitude of conditioning methods used and corresponding differences in interpretation have contributed to conditional correlation analysis being looked upon as somewhat problematic despite its immediate intuitive appeal.

Consider, as an example, a bivariate Gaussian distribution with correlation $\rho = 0.5$, also mentioned briefly in Chapter 4.2.2. Using the results of Boyer et al. (1999) on truncated correlations and conditioning on one of the variables being large, for example, larger than its 75% quantile, $X > q_{75}$, the conditional correlation is reduced to 0.27, and as the quantile increases, ρ_R converges to zero. Such an effect is known as the "bias effect" of the conditional correlation. When analyzing (Gaussian) returns data and detecting such correlation values, we might be tempted to incorrectly conclude that the dependence has been lower in periods of large X-returns and that it goes to zero as $X \to \infty$.

Conditioning on *both* returns being large or small (exceedance correlation), or lying in various finite sets, again leads to different correlation values; see Campbell et al. (2008). As remarked by Longin and Solnik (2001), "[i]t would be wrong to infer from this large difference in conditional correlation that correlation differs between volatile and tranquil periods, as correlation is constant and equal to ρ by assumption".

In an attempt to meet the interpretational difficulties, the bias effect has been sought adjusted for by Campbell et al. (2002), and it is possible to construct useful tests of asymmetry in terms of conditional correlation; see Ang and Chen (2002). The test used in that paper was model-dependent, but Hong et al. (2007) have designed a test based on a model-free approach and have put it to effective use in a number of applications. Still, the conditional correlation does not furnish a measure that is easy to interpret. In the next section, we will argue for why we believe that the local Gaussian correlation is a better measure for understanding and describing asymmetric dependence patterns for financial returns.

6.2.1 Why local Gaussian correlation is better

The bivariate return density f for two (log) returns X and Y is never Gaussian, at least for monthly and daily observed data, and in the conditional correlation approach, one tries to take care of this by computing the ordinary (sample) correlation restricted to a set R, as described in the last section, but we believe that it is better to start with the density f itself and approximate *it*, not the correlation, locally. This local approximation is done with a family of Gaussian distributions such that at each point (x, y), the density $f(x, y)$ is approximated by a Gaussian bivariate density, as introduced in Chapter 4.3. This is a distributional approach to nonlinearity and non-Gaussianity rather than a moment-based approach.

We note the following advantages of applying the local Gaussian correlation model as a description of asymmetries in financial data.

1. The dependence measure, the local Gaussian correlation (LGC) $\rho(x, y)$, is based on a family of Gaussian distributions and describes the dependence relation for $\psi_{x,y}$ (defined in Eq. (4.4), where the notation (x, y) is replaced by $\boldsymbol{x} = (x_1, x_2)$) and hence approximately for f around the point (x, y), since $\psi_{x,y}$ approximates f around that point. Moreover, properties that are true for global Gaussian dependence can be transferred locally to a neighborhood of (x, y).
2. Using local Gaussian likelihood theory (summarized in Chapters 4.3, 4.4, and 4.7), we can construct asymptotic confidence intervals for

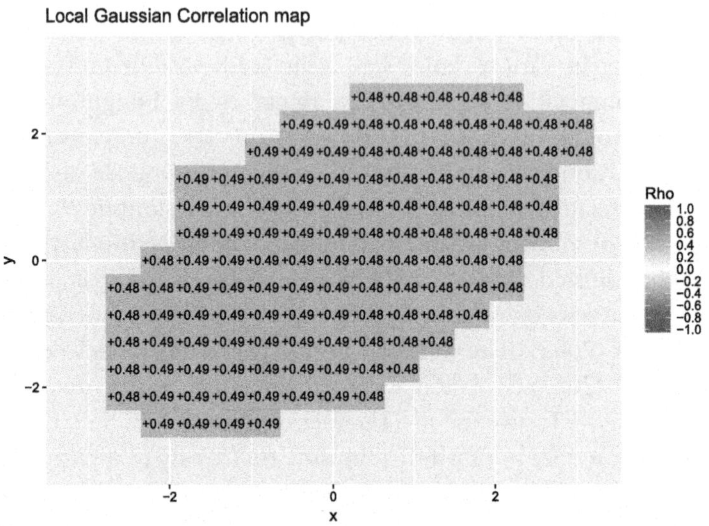

Figure 6.1 Local Gaussian correlation map for a bivariate Gaussian distribution with correlation $\rho = 0.5$ based on 3500 observations.

$\rho(x, y)$, allowing us to judge whether an observed asymmetry for financial returns measured by $\widehat{\rho}(x, y)$ is statistically significant.

3. Unlike the conditional correlation and similar local dependence measures, in the case where f itself is Gaussian, $\rho(x, y) \equiv \rho$ everywhere, where ρ is the ordinary correlation implied by f. This follows from the definition of $\rho(x, y)$ (and $\rho_b(x, y)$) via the minimization of the penalty function q defined in Eq. (4.5), and it is demonstrated for one realization of 3500 bivariate Gaussian observations with standard normal marginals and global correlation $\rho = 0.5$ in Fig. 6.1. Here $\rho(x, y)$ was estimated by the local likelihood procedure of Chapter 4 using the cross-validation for bandwidth selection; cf. Chapter 4.8.2. Thus $\rho(x, y)$ does not suffer from the bias problem of the conditional correlation described in the last section. However, there is some boundary bias in the estimated local Gaussian correlation, but this bias is similar to that in ordinary kernel estimation. The bias problem for the conditional correlation is further illustrated in Table 6.1. In this table, estimates for the conditional correlation are given for several sets R, for example, for $X < 0$ and $Y > 0$, based on the same simulated observations. Clearly, for all sets, the conditional correlations estimated are not equal to the true correlation of 0.5 and in most cases far from it.

Table 6.1 The estimated conditional correlation for several subsets of 3500 simulated observations from a bivariate Gaussian distribution with correlation 0.5.

Conditioning set R	Conditional correlation
$X > 0, Y > 0$	0.21
$X < 0, Y > 0$	0.15
$X < 0, Y < 0$	0.30
$X > 0, Y < 0$	0.18
$X < -1.5, Y < -1.5$	0.31
$X > 1.5, Y > 1.5$	0.09

4. As we will see in the next section, the local Gaussian correlation $\rho(x, y)$ is capable of detecting and quantifying asymmetries in financial returns such as bull and bear effects. Moreover, a quantitative interpretation can be given in terms of the strength of the correlation of the approximating local Gaussian distribution, and $\rho(x, y)$ is invariant in a specific sense to linear scaling, as demonstrated in Chapter 4.5.4.
5. It is possible to generalize the local Gaussian approach to a set of p variables, financial returns $(X_1, \ldots, X_p)$, having a joint density function f. Then the localized correlation $\rho(x, y)$ is replaced by a local covariance matrix $\mathbf{\Sigma} = [\sigma_{ij}(x_i, x_j)]$ for $i, j = 1, \ldots, p$. Note that to avoid the curse of dimensionality in the estimation procedure, for each pair of variables (X_i, X_j), the local covariance at the point $(X_1 = x_1, \ldots, X_p = x_p)$ is restricted to depend only on (x_i, x_j), as outlined in Chapter 4.9 and used extensively in Chapters 9 and 10.

6.3 Empirical analysis of dependence of financial returns

In this section, we apply the local Gaussian correlation to describe daily and monthly returns from financial markets. As mentioned in the introduction of this chapter, we will do a full nonparametric locally Gaussian fit of bivariate densities, estimating both local means and local variances, in addition to the local Gaussian correlations, that is, we estimate the unnormalized $\rho(x, y)$ as introduced in Chapter 4.3. However, we will mainly use filtered returns obtained by a GARCH(1, 1) filtration of the original data. The cross-validated bandwidth selector has been tried, but in many cases with financial data, this selector often gives too small bandwidths in the sense of wiggly plots. We will therefore mainly use a much simpler bandwidth selector, that is, the standard deviation of the observations times a constant close to 1. Further details will be given in each subsection.

6.3.1 Daily stock index returns

We use daily international equity price index data for the United States (S&P 500), the United Kingdom (FTSE 100), Germany (DAX 30), and Japan (TOPIX) in local currency. The data are obtained from Datastream, and the returns are defined as 100 times the change in the natural logarithm of each market price index, that is, as $r_t = 100 \times \big(\log(p_t) - \log(p_{t-1})\big)$, where p_t is the index from Datastream.

We use the observation span from October 10, 1987, to March 2, 2018, a total of 7996 daily observations. As a first step, we treat these return data pairwise as coming from the same bivariate density f, that is, stationarity. Stationarity, of course, depends on the nature of the time scale and the length of the time period involved, but assuming stationarity for such a long time interval, even if allowing for a stationary model with several regimes, is hardly realistic. In fact, at the end of this section, when the time period is divided into four different time periods of roughly the same length, significant differences in the shape of the local Gaussian correlation will arise.

The daily returns for the entire period are shown in Fig. 6.2, and the summary statistics for the returns are shown in Table 6.2. We use the skewness

$$\gamma = \mathrm{E}\Big[\Big(\frac{X-\mu}{\sigma}\Big)^3\Big] \tag{6.2}$$

and kurtosis

$$\kappa = \mathrm{E}\Big[\Big(\frac{X-\mu}{\sigma}\Big)^4\Big] \tag{6.3}$$

of a stochastic variable X with mean μ and standard deviation σ.

The daily returns range from -22.9% to almost 13%. All series have a small negative skewness, and the kurtosis is generally high, between 9 and 33. The high kurtosis values indicate a departure from the Gaussian distribution, and in these cases the global correlation may not be a good measure of dependence (see Campbell et al., 2008). The global correlations are given in Table 6.3, and for the returns between S&P 500 and two European indices, both are around 0.5, whereas the correlation between the European indices is 0.72. The correlation between the TOPIX and the three other indices are much lower, ranging from around 0.1 to 0.3.

Table 6.2 Summary index statistics for daily data from October 1987 to March 2018.

Statistic	Mean	St. Dev.	Min	Pctl(25)	Pctl(75)	Max	Skewness	Kurtosis
S&P 500	0.027	1.130	−22.900	−0.413	0.532	10.957	−1.315	32.645
FTSE 100	0.014	1.096	−13.029	−0.508	0.572	9.384	−0.483	12.970
DAX 30	0.027	1.406	−13.710	−0.611	0.730	10.797	−0.326	9.443
TOPIX	−0.002	1.296	−15.810	−0.609	0.639	12.865	−0.341	12.026

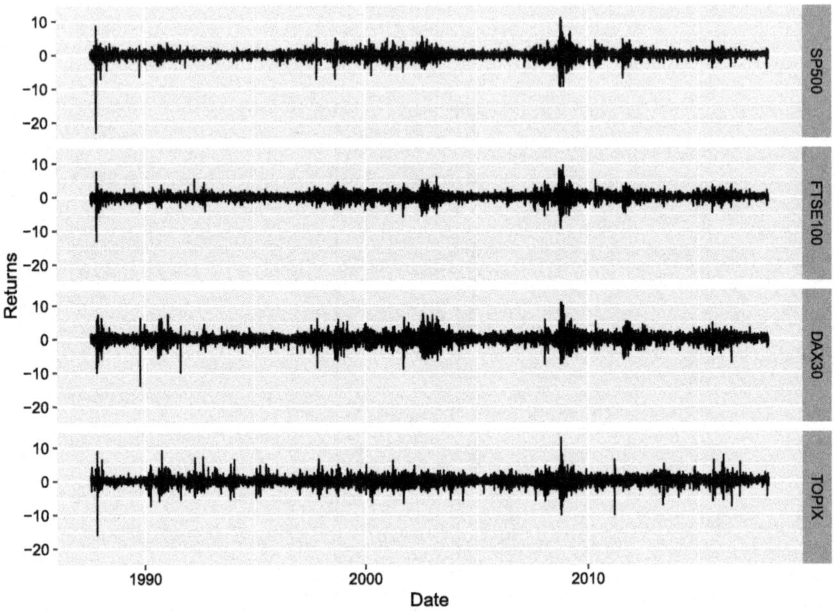

Figure 6.2 Non-filtered returns for the market indices for the United States, the United Kingdom, Germany, and Japan (in this order, from top to bottom).

Table 6.3 Correlation matrix for the daily return series.

	S&P 500	FTSE 100	DAX 30	TOPIX
S&P 500	1			
FTSE 100	0.495	1		
DAX 30	0.500	0.719	1	
TOPIX	0.118	0.289	0.258	1

We next turn to estimates of the local Gaussian correlation on the original observations. We first examine the full LGC map for the returns from S&P 500 and FTSE 100; see Fig. 6.3. We see that the bivariate return distribution is not Gaussian, since, in particular, there are large local correlations for both large negative and large positive returns. The large local correlations for negative returns imply that diversification opportunities would erode in bear markets (e.g., a downward price trend), which is when they are most needed. As a final remark, note the scale on both axes on Fig. 6.3, ranging from approximately -4 to $+4$. The reason for limiting the LGC map to this region is that there are too few observations outside this region, and hence the estimated local Gaussian correlations will be very uncertain.

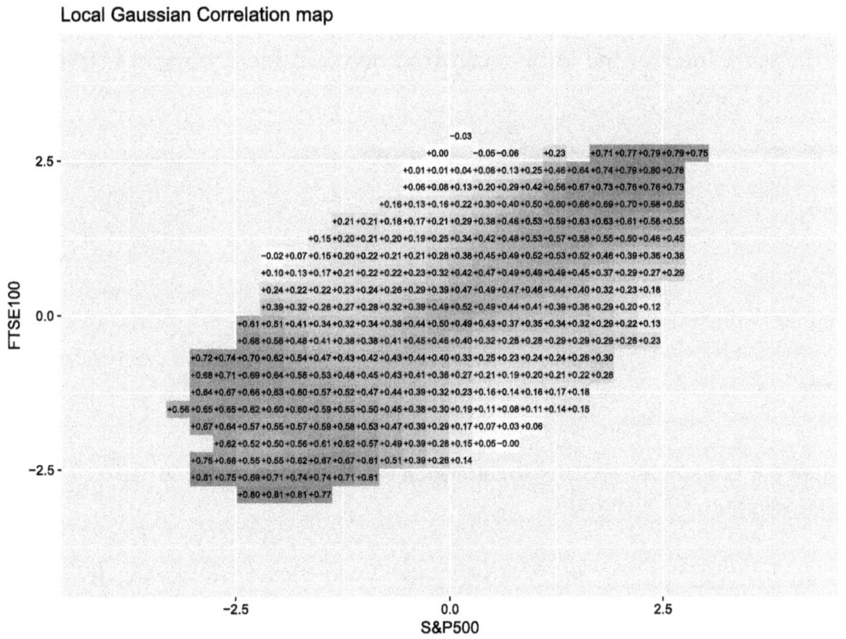

Figure 6.3 Local Gaussian correlation map for S&P500 against FTSE100 daily non-filtered returns.

Since we are mainly interested in data for fixed quantiles of the series, and returns data are basically measured on the same scale, for greater clarity, we may restrict ourselves to looking at the local Gaussian correlation $\rho(x, y)$ at values at the diagonal, that is, for $x = y$; see Fig. 6.4.

In the left plot of Fig. 6.4 the estimated LGCs between the European and the US index are shown, and the curve for the two European indices is at the top. Note that the local Gaussian correlation properties in fact seem to be symmetric as far as bear and bull (e.g., upward price trend) market is concerned. Further, the local correlations are very high between the UK and German index. A possible reason for the U-shaped local Gaussian correlation curves between the US market and the European markets is that during time periods with a bear market, even though the price trend is falling, for some days, we actually will see quite large positive daily returns, for example, a bear market rally (also known as "sucker's rally"). This may explain why we observe the high local correlation also for positive returns, and not just for negative returns, when examining daily data. However, this explanation is rather tentative, since it is not always present when we look at sub-periods, as will be seen below. Moreover, we see that the plots where the S&P500 is involved is almost symmetric between −2 and +2, whereas in the same interval the local correlation between the European markets is closer to linear.

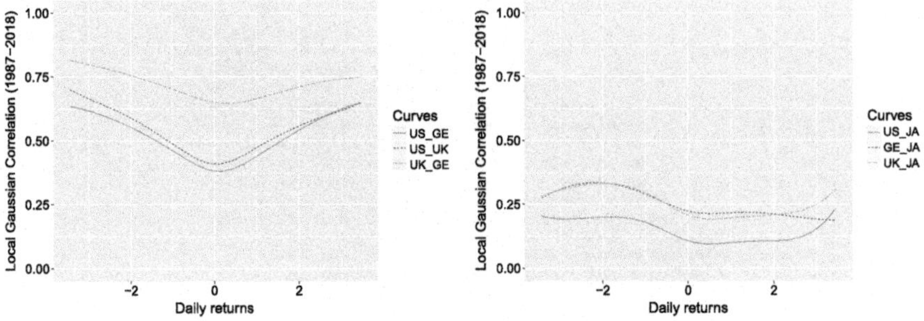

Figure 6.4 Diagonal local Gaussian correlation values between pairwise market indices using daily non-filtered returns.

In the right plot of Fig. 6.4 the estimated LGCs between the Japanese markets and the other markets are shown, and the US–Japan curve is at the bottom. These curves have a completely different shape; they are close to a horizontal line for positive returns, centering around a correlation of 0.25 for the Japanese index toward the European indices, and even lower versus the US index. An explanation for this relatively low correlation is that the Japanese index has been slightly unsynchronized with the US and European indices. Japan experienced an economic bubble in the late 1980s, whereas the US stock market boom occurred during the 1990s and ended in 2000. The economic bubble in Japan came to an abrupt end as the Tokyo Stock Exchange crashed in 1990–1992 and real estate prices peaked in 1991. Growth in Japan throughout the 1990s and 2000s was slower than global growth, and this has naturally been reflected in the development of the Japanese stock index and hence results in lower dependencies between the Japanese and other markets.

Again, we mention that in this analysis, we have implicitly assumed stationarity between these long time series, and thus these interpretations should be considered in that light. As indicated as an option in the introduction to this chapter, the bandwidth is equal to the standard deviation of the observations times a constant close to 1 (usually, we choose the constant equal to 1.1); the reason is that we prefer to oversmooth, so that we smooth slightly toward a constant local correlation. Our experience is that with returns data, a bandwidth selected by the cross-validation procedure, introduced in Chapter 4.8.2, typically produces wiggly estimates of the LGC when looking at diagonal plots, as in Fig. 6.4.

Much of the variation in local Gaussian correlation in Figs. 6.3 and 6.4 could be expected to be due to volatility, since we have daily data. As already mentioned, we therefore filter the log returns with univariate GARCH(1, 1) models with a skewed Student t error distribution and then compute the filtered residuals. The GARCH(1, 1) parameters are statistically significant for the return series, and the Ljung–Box statistics calculated for squared and non-squared residuals indicate that the fitted models are adequate; however, we do not report the parameters of these filtrations.

The correlations between the filtered returns are given in Table 6.4. Comparing this table with the correlations of the original data, we see that most of correlations based on the filtered returns are marginally smaller than those on the original scale.

Table 6.4 Correlation matrix for the daily filtered return series.

	S&P 500	FTSE 100	DAX 30	TOPIX
S&P 500	1			
FTSE 100	0.467	1		
DAX 30	0.436	0.661	1	
TOPIX	0.124	0.260	0.259	1

In Fig. 6.5 the diagonal pairwise local Gaussian correlation values using the filtered returns are given. We see that the general pattern is almost the same as for the nonfiltered returns, but, as expected, removing volatility reduces the local correlation effects somewhat.

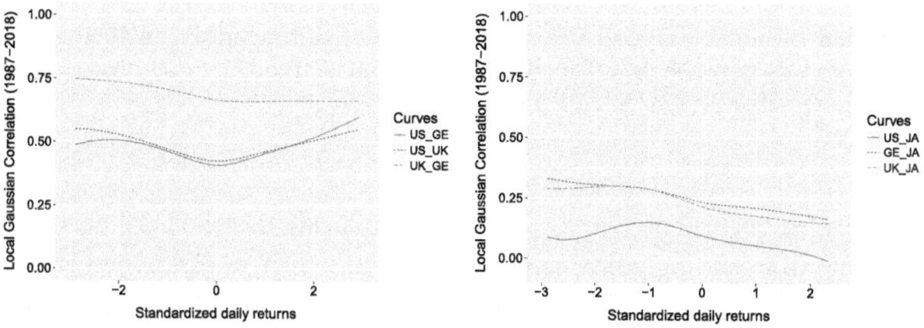

Figure 6.5 Diagonal local Gaussian correlation values between pairwise market indices using daily filtered returns.

We have also computed the local Gaussian correlations between the filtered returns from S&P 500 and FTSE 100 on different sub-periods of

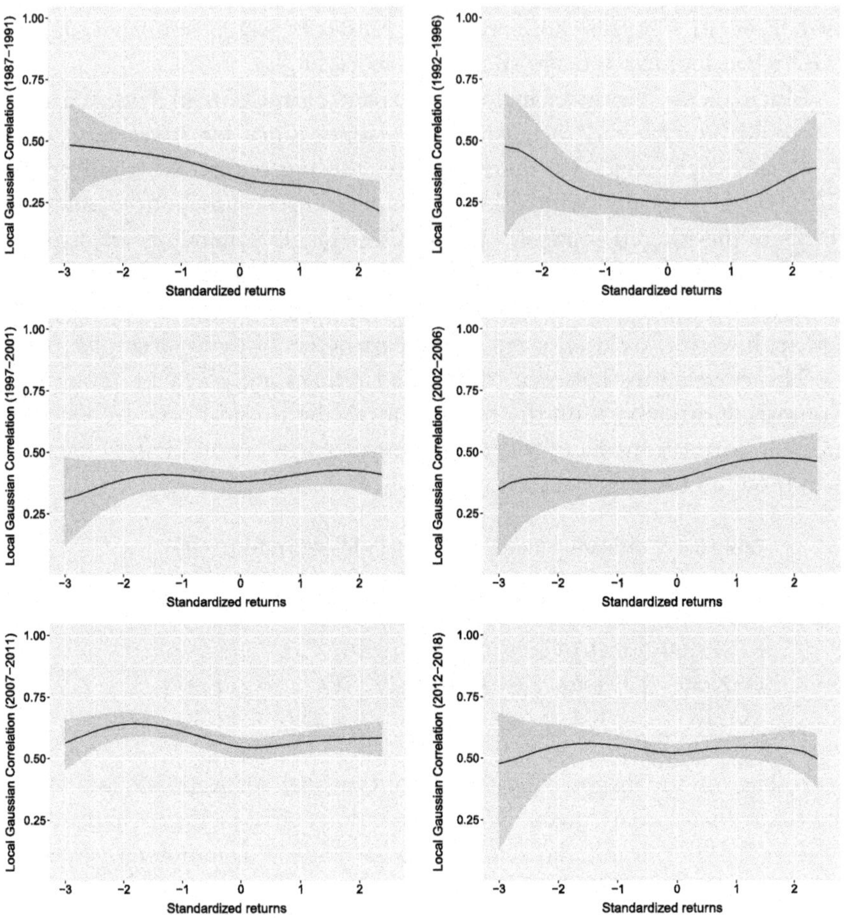

Figure 6.6 Diagonal local Gaussian correlation values with approximate 90% confidence intervals, between daily filtered returns from S&P 500 and FTSE 100, divided into six time intervals from 1987 to 2018.

five-year intervals, shown in Fig. 6.6. These indicate that the local correlations are time-varying, with statistical significant changes from one period to another, consistent with similar results for classical global correlation; see, for example, Longin and Solnik (2001). There are also statistically significant differences in curve shape. The confidence intervals are pointwise confidence intervals, not confidence bands, and they are obtained by 1000 bootstrap replications. They can be used to pinpoint significant pointwise differences for given returns. Validity of using the bootstrap in such situations has been demonstrated by Lacal and Tjøstheim (2019); see also Chapter 7.

Now looking closer at the six time periods, in the first time period from 1987 to 1991 the market crash of October 1987 may explain the high local correlations we observe for negative returns. All major world markets declined sharply, many over 20% in just one month. A period of relatively calm US and UK markets then followed, with an overall low local correlation 1992–1996, but the burst of the dotcom-bubble from early 2000 and lasting to 2002 can explain the increased local correlations observed from 1997 and onward. The years from the late 2002 until mid-2007 were characterized by a booming US and UK market, which may explain the large local correlations for positive returns in the plot. The period 2007–2011 has been dominated by the financial crisis and has caused ever more increased local correlations. Finally, in the last period 2012–2018 the local correlations are still quite high, compared to the first couple of time periods. Putting all these periods together, we see that the symmetry patterns of Fig. 6.5 could easily emerge in a composite plot.

The findings in this section are mainly identical to findings by Støve and Tjøstheim (2014). There are also a few other papers studying financial returns using the LGC; see Bampinas and Panagiotidis (2017), Bouri et al. (2020), and Nguyen et al. (2020).

6.3.2 Monthly stock index returns

We would expect the bear market (occasional) rally effect to vanish when looking at returns over a longer period than one day, say weekly or monthly, since the weekly or monthly returns in a bear market would per definition be negative. Therefore, in this section, we will study monthly returns. As for the daily stock returns, we use the international equity price index data for the United States (S&P 500), the United Kingdom (FTSE 100), Germany (DAX 30), and Japan (TOPIX) in local currency and calculate the returns as for the daily data, that is, as 100 times the change in the natural logarithm of each market price index. The data range from October 1987 to February 2018, in total 365 observations.

Descriptive statistics are given in Table 6.5, again with the definition of skewness and kurtosis given in Eqs. (6.2) and (6.3), respectively. In particular, we see that the maximum and minimum returns are somewhat larger than for the daily returns, and again, the kurtosis for all series is high, indicating a departure from the Gaussian distribution. The global correlations between the returns are given in Table 6.6. Note the differences from the

Table 6.5 Summary index statistics for monthly data from October 1987 to February 2018.

Statistic	Mean	St. Dev.	Min	Pctl(25)	Pctl(75)	Max	Skewness	Kurtosis
S&P 500	0.584	4.315	−24.543	−1.755	3.301	10.579	−1.172	7.049
FTSE 100	0.306	4.404	−30.170	−1.853	2.968	13.477	−1.210	9.066
DAX 30	0.579	6.208	−29.333	−2.317	4.300	19.374	−0.957	5.862
TOPIX	−0.052	5.575	−22.837	−3.504	3.484	16.681	−0.413	4.223

correlations in Table 6.3. The monthly based correlations are much higher than the corresponding daily based.

Table 6.6 Correlation matrix for the monthly return series.

	S&P 500	FTSE 100	DAX 30	TOPIX
S&P 500	1			
FTSE 100	0.803	1		
DAX 30	0.730	0.721	1	
TOPIX	0.488	0.446	0.468	1

The estimate of the local Gaussian correlation (on the diagonal) between the non-filtered returns from the different markets are shown in Fig. 6.7. In the left plot, the estimated LGCs between the European and the US index are shown (again the curve for the two European indices at the top), whereas the right plot shows the estimated LGCs between the Japanese market and the US and European markets (with the curve for the US–Japan overall slightly below). Clearly, we have evidence of strong asymmetric dependence in both plots, in particular, larger local correlations in bear markets. Further, the local correlations decrease from the left of the plot to the right, implying that diversification opportunities would be largest in a bull market, or rather erode in bear markets, which is when they are most needed. The results thus support our intuition from the beginning of this section that the U-shaped local correlation patterns usually disappear when looking at returns over a longer period than one day, that is, since high local correlations for large daily positive returns usually occur due to bear markets rallies (i.e., sucker's rallies).

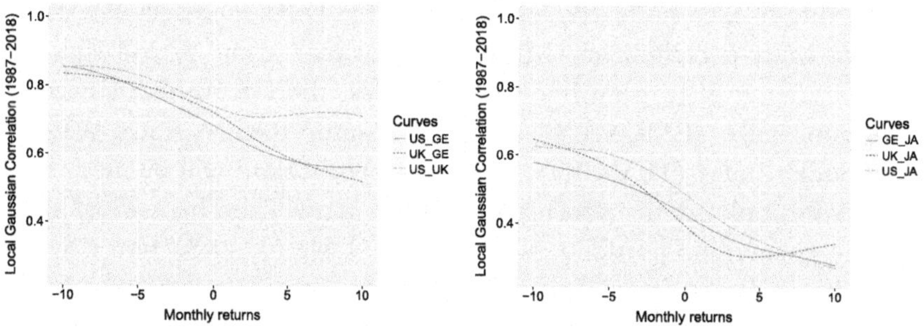

Figure 6.7 Diagonal local Gaussian correlation values between pairwise market indices using monthly non-filtered returns.

Further, GARCH(1, 1) filtrations with skewed t-distributed error terms are undertaken on the monthly returns, and filtered residuals are calculated. (Tables of these filtrations are not shown, but all GARCH-parameters are significant, and the models are reasonable when measured by goodness-of-fit.) The corresponding diagonal plot is not shown, but the same pattern as before is present, that is, strong asymmetric dependence. Although these estimates are subject to relatively large estimation errors due to the limited number of observations, especially for extreme values (see Fig. 6.8 for approximate 90% confidence intervals, obtained by bootstrapping, for the local correlation between the US–UK filtered returns), we do see that the local correlation estimates decrease in normal and bull markets, compared to the bear market correlations, as we observed for the unfiltered log returns.

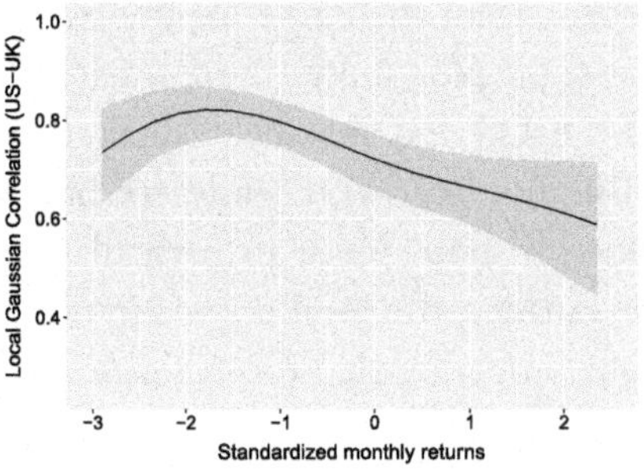

Figure 6.8 Diagonal local Gaussian correlation values between US and UK market indices using monthly filtered returns with approximate 90% confidence intervals.

6.3.3 Dependence between commodities, bonds, and stocks

In this section, the dependence relationships between stock, bond, and commodity indices are briefly examined by the LGC approach. We stress that this study is preliminary. Monthly return data in the period January 1980 to August 2018 from the S&P500 index, the US 10 Year Government bond index (BMUS10Y), and the Thomson Reuters Equal Weight Commodity Index (TRCCI), totaling 464 observations will be used. See Fig. 6.9 for a plot of the return data. These data will also be used in Section 6.4 concerning portfolio allocation; see Table 6.8 in Section 6.4 for some descriptive statistics. Again, these statistics confirm departure from the Gaussian distribution. The global correlation is given in that same table. The correlation between the stock and bond returns is slightly negative, but close to zero, whereas the correlation between the stock and commodity returns is positive, around 0.3. Finally, the correlation between the bond and commodity returns is negative, around −0.2.

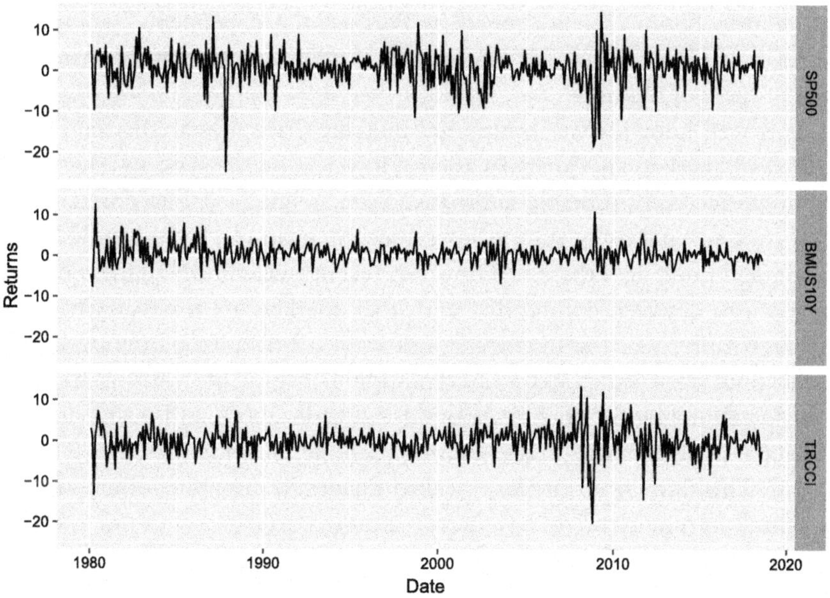

Figure 6.9 Monthly non-filtered returns from S&P500, US10Y treasury bonds, and the TRCCI-commodity index, from top to bottom.

The dependence relationships between these asset classes, that is, stocks, bonds, and commodities, have been widely studied. The main reason for studying the relationships is that the three asset classes typically represent the building blocks of most investment portfolios because of their different risk-return characteristics, and in particular the stocks and bonds linkage is important in this respect.

The current knowledge on the stock–bond returns relation is that this relation is time-varying; see, for example, Ilmanen (2003), Connolly et al. (2005), and Dajcman (2012). In particular, several studies have documented a positive relation during the 1990s, which is in line with the conventional view that common macroeconomic variables, such as expected inflation or economic prospects, drive both stock and bond markets. However, from the early 2000s a negative stock–bond relation is observed, which could be caused by the strengthened role of flight-to-quality episodes, that is, that investors move capital away from "risky" investments, such as stocks, and toward "safer" investments, such as bonds, due to uncertainty about the overall economy. Some papers have also used a copula approach, for instance, Jammazi et al. (2015). They document a lack of tail dependence in the stock–bond relation, which suggests that stock and bond markets do not tend to boom or crash together. Further, the dependence seems not especially strong during extreme market conditions, but rather that it is present most of the time.

It is well known that commodity markets share several characteristics with stock markets and financial assets. However, many investors have used commodities as a profitable alternative asset, relying on low correlations with conventional assets, such as stocks; see, for example, Chong and Miffre (2010) and references therein. However, recent research has suggested that correlations between commodity and stock markets are time-varying and highly volatile; see, for instance, Creti et al. (2013). In particular, most correlations between stocks and commodities begin the 1990s near zero, but closer integration emerges around the early 2000s and peaks during the 2007–2008 financial crisis, see, for example, Silvennoinen and Thorp (2013). This thus confirms the so-called financialization phenomenon, the fact that commodity prices have become more correlated with prices of financial assets and with each other; see Tang and Xiong (2012) and Nguyen et al. (2020).

The typical explanation of the relationship between commodities and bonds is that with an increase in commodity prices, the cost of goods for companies increases. This increase in commodity prices causes a rise in inflation. Inflation reduces the value of money over the term of a loan, so the interest rates rise to compensate for the loss of value. This increase in interest rate makes a bond issue undesirable (at least for companies), which potentially pulls down the bond prices. Thus we should expect to see an inverse relationship between commodity prices and bond prices (at least issued by companies). However, Silvennoinen and Thorp (2013) documents increasing correlations between commodities and bonds since around 2000.

To illustrate the use of the LGC measure when examining the above relationships, we use the non-filtered returns and again a simple bandwidth selector of 1.1 times the standard deviations of the observations. In Fig. 6.10 the resulting LGC maps of the three relations (stock–bond, stock–commodity, and commodity–bond) are given. Note that in this case, it is *not* sufficient to study only the diagonals, as we may expect to see some negative relationships and also positive and negative returns at the same time for different asset classes, as commented on above.

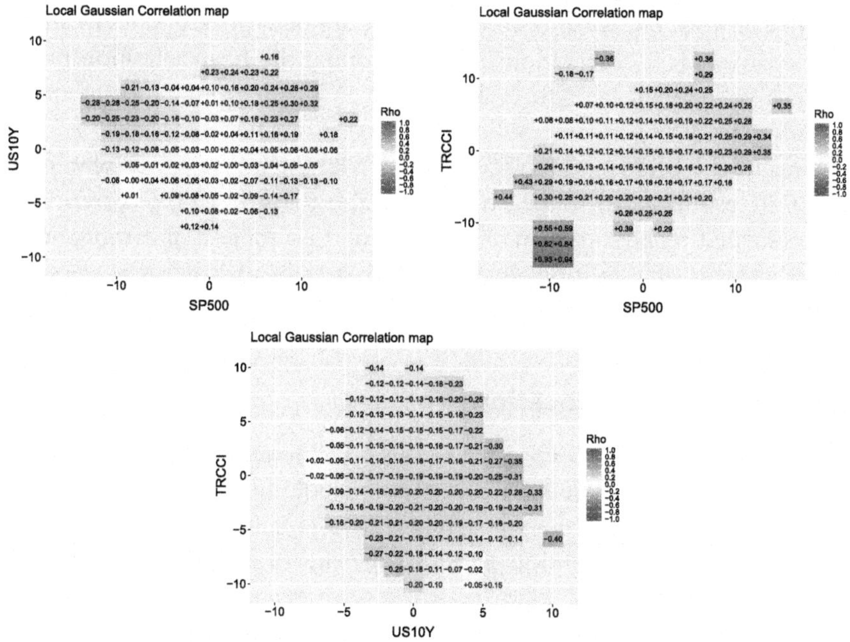

Figure 6.10 Local Gaussian correlation maps for the monthly non-filtered returns from S&P500, US10Y treasury bonds, and the TRCCI-commodity index.

Examining the stock–bond map (upper left plot), we can see that there actually seems to be an asymmetric dependence relationship, somewhat in contrast to the findings of Jammazi et al. (2015). However, we agree with that paper that it seems that stock and bonds do not crash together; see the close to zero estimated LGCs in the third quadrant. There does, however, appear to be an indication that the markets boom together; see the positive LGCs in the first quadrant. In the last quadrants (i.e., two and four), we see negative estimated correlations. In particular, when stock markets fall, the estimated LGCs are below -0.2, an indication of the flight-to-quality effect. We repeat, however, that the observations are monthly returns from 1980 until 2018, and thus we are really not able to pick up any time-varying LGCs.

Looking at the stock–commodity relation (upper right plot), there seems to be some evidence of an asymmetric relationship, that is, relative low correlations under normal market conditions, when returns center around zero, but larger correlations under market booms, and in particular when markets crash. We observe very high correlations for very large negative returns, but we also note that there are high uncertainties in areas with relatively few observations. For confirming the financialization phenomena, we should have to look into the LGC maps for different time periods.

Finally, the bond–commodity relation is given in the lower plot. All LGCs are estimated to be negative; recall also that the global correlation was estimated to be -0.2, and we conclude that there is not substantial asymmetries in this relation, but rather an overall small negative dependence.

6.4 The portfolio allocation problem

In this subsection, we present results from ongoing research. Although the results are preliminary, we have chosen to include them here as they indicate that the local Gaussian approach may have potential for the important problem of portfolio allocation. Most of the material in this section is based on Sleire et al. (2021).

As already mentioned in the introduction of this chapter, in portfolio theory the aim is allocating assets by maximizing the expected return of the portfolio while minimizing its risk, for instance, measured by the standard deviation. Markowitz (1952) provides the foundation for this mean-variance (MV) approach, where the crucial assumption is that the asset returns follow a jointly Gaussian distribution and hence that the dependence between these returns is fully described by the linear correlation coefficient. The idea is simple: low correlated assets are good for diversification, whereas highly correlated assets should be avoided.

However, as shown by numerous empirical studies, there are asymmetries in the distribution of financial returns. An implication of the asymmetric dependence is that the classical mean-variance optimized portfolios are not efficient with respect to their risk profile, and thus the benefit of diversification will erode if the correlations are asymmetric. Several studies have sought to overcome this shortcoming by modeling the dependence structure using copula theory and employing it in the optimization of a portfolio. Amongst the first papers introducing such an idea, was Patton (2004), who examines whether the asymmetries are predictable and if portfolio decisions are improved by forecasting such asymmetries. He finds that for investors with no short-sales constraints, the knowledge of these asymmetries leads to economic gains. Hatherley and Alcock (2007) finds that managing asymmetric dependence using a Clayton copula against the multivariate Gaussian model results in reduced downside exposure. Low et al. (2013) use the bivariate Clayton and Clayton canonical vine (CVC) copulas to address the asset allocation for loss-averse investors through the minimization of CVaR (Conditional Value at Risk) in portfolios of up to 12 constituents and conclude that using CVC copulas is valuable when managing larger portfolios. Kakouris and Rustem (2014) employ a mixture of copulas to derive CVaR and the worse case CVaR used for the optimization of a convex portfolio of stock indices. Bekiros et al. (2015) use pair-vine copula models and minimum risk optimal portfolios applied to mining stock portfolios. Finally, Han et al. (2017) use a copula-GARCH and DCC copulas approach, and extend Kakouris and Rustem (2014) to dynamic portfolio optimization models.

However, these procedures are in most cases quite complicated, if done properly, and there is still no guarantee that portfolio allocations based on complicated models will perform better; see, for example, DeMiguel et al. (2009) and Low et al. (2016), who find that outperforming the naive $1/N$, that is, the equally weighted portfolio, remains an elusive task. A non-technical asset manager might be overwhelmed by such choices.

We propose a much simpler approach. Without making assumptions about the nature of the underlying probability model, we present an adjustment to the correlation matrix of the assets, which takes the current state of the market into account by using the local Gaussian correlation. In other words, if the market is going down and correlations increase as is often loosely stated as a fact, this effect, being a consequence of the non-linearity/asymmetry of the dependence between assets, will be captured by the LGC. It will thus provide an updated correlation matrix to be used in the portfolio allocation problem. Thus the main goal of this section is an extension of the classical MV framework by using the theory of local Gaussian correlation.

6.4.1 Portfolio allocation using the LGC

Mean-variance-based portfolio construction is a common approach for asset management, where the measures of return and risk are the mean and variance of the portfolio returns, respectively. In this section, we adopt the general formulation for portfolio optimization, which consists of minimization of a risk measure given a target reward and operational constraints. We assume that there are p risky assets. The returns on the risky assets are denoted by $\boldsymbol{r}_t \in \mathbb{R}^p$, which are assumed to have the expected values $\boldsymbol{\mu}_t \in \mathbb{R}^p$ and covariance matrix $\boldsymbol{\Sigma}_t \in \mathbb{R}^p \times \mathbb{R}^p$ of the portfolio of asset returns at time t.

Further, let $\boldsymbol{w}_t \in \mathbb{R}^p$ be the unknown vector of optimal portfolio weights at time t.

The MV optimization problem is defined as follows. The weights of the chosen portfolio are given by a vector $\boldsymbol{w}_t$ invested in p risky assets. The investor selects $\boldsymbol{w}_t$ to maximize the expected quadratic utility function at each time t, that is,

$$\max_{\boldsymbol{w}_t} U = \boldsymbol{w}_t^T \boldsymbol{\mu}_t - \frac{\gamma}{2} \boldsymbol{w}_t^T \boldsymbol{\Sigma}_t \boldsymbol{w}_t, \tag{6.4}$$

where U is the investor's utility, and γ represents the investor's degree of risk aversion. Hence, for a range of different risk aversion levels, the MV optimization will produce the corresponding optimal portfolios with a trade-off between the expected volatility and expected return. However, throughout this section, for simplicity, we fix the risk aversion coefficient $\gamma = 1$.

There are three different ways of formulating the MV optimization problem: First, minimize the risk subject to a lower bound on the expected return (which results in the minimum variance portfolio); second, maximize the expected return subject to an upper bound on the risk; and the third option that optimizes the corresponding ratio between risk and return subject to a given level of risk aversion. We assume that $w_1 + \cdots + w_p = 1$. This constraint states that all capital must be invested in the portfolio (*full investment* constraint), where the weights correspond to portions of the capital allocated to a given component. Another type of constraints is related to *long only* positions, which specify that we can only buy shares and therefore only have position-related weights in contrast to the case of short positions, in which the selling positions would be reflected as negative weights. In the empirical example that follows, we examine both cases. Further, we do not include a risk-free asset in our treatment of the portfolio allocation problem.

The optimization problem with additional non-negativity constraints cannot be solved by the method of Lagrange multipliers because of the inequality constraints; it must be represented as a quadratic programming problem. Furthermore, the theory is unable to account for the presence of higher moments beyond the mean and variance in both the portfolio returns distributions or investor preferences, such as skewness and kurtosis. See, for example, Francis and Kim (2013) or Fan and Yao (2015) for a more detailed treatment of modern portfolio theory.

The typical portfolio allocation problem that arises in practice is described below. In the empirical analysis, we use monthly return data, but of course, shorter or longer time horizons are possible. As data of returns become available in time, we follow the approach of DeMiguel et al. (2009), Tu and Zhou (2011), and Low et al. (2016), where rolling sampling windows of historical returns are used to estimate the expected return vector $\boldsymbol{\mu}_t$ and covariance matrix $\boldsymbol{\Sigma}_t$ required as inputs into the Markowitz model. More specifically, the process is given as follows:

1. At time t, a rolling sampling window of M trading months is selected.
2. During each month at time t, starting from $t = M + 1$, the return data for the M previous months are used to estimate the one month ahead expected return vector $\boldsymbol{\mu}_t$ and the covariance matrix $\boldsymbol{\Sigma}_t$ by the standard empirical versions. As new information arrives at month $t + 1$, these estimates are updated. This process is repeated by incorporating the return for each month going forward and ignoring the earliest one, until the end of the sample.
3. Based upon these estimates, various optimization problems are solved. and the updated portfolio weights are calculated at every first trading day of each month, and the rebalancing is done to construct a portfolio that achieves the desired investment objective.
4. The estimates of $\boldsymbol{w}$ are then used to calculate out-of-sample returns $\hat{r}_{t+1}$ and portfolio performance over the next month. A total of $n - M$ out-of-sample returns are produced for each model, with n being the total number of observations.
5. These out-of-sample returns and portfolio weights are analyzed using a range of performance metrics and statistical measures that are reported for each model, respectively. For example, we can examine the cumulative returns resulting from a one dollar initial investment after a specified end date.

In this standard procedure, we note that as the covariance matrices $\boldsymbol{\Sigma}_t$ are calculated globally, no explicit consideration is taken of any potential asymmetries in the return distribution. Our idea is now utilizing the local Gaussian correlation in the following way: All steps above are equal, except that in step 2, the rolling sampling windows of historical returns are used to estimate a local covariance matrix $\boldsymbol{\Sigma}_t(\boldsymbol{x})$ in the gridpoint $\boldsymbol{x} = (x_1, ..., x_p)$ by using the pairwise approach of Chapter 4.9. More specifically, step 2 is replaced by the following:

2'. During each month t, starting from $t = M + 1$, returns from the M previous months are used to calculate the one month ahead local covariance matrix $\boldsymbol{\Sigma}_t(\boldsymbol{x})$, consisting of the pairwise local covariances and local standard deviations $\hat{\Sigma}_b(x_i, x_j) = \hat{\rho}_b(x_i, x_j)\hat{\sigma}_{i,b}(x_i)\hat{\sigma}_{j,b}(x_j)$,

$i, j = 1, \ldots, p$, in the gridpoint $\boldsymbol{x}$ with b being the bandwidth in the local Gaussian approximation. As new information arrives at month $t+1$, we update these estimates. This process is repeated by incorporating the return for each month going forward and ignoring the earliest one, as previously mentioned.

Thus our model is specified to account for asymmetries by specifying the gridpoint $\boldsymbol{x}$ to use. But then the key question is what gridpoint and hence which corresponding local covariance matrix should be used for solving the optimization problem in finding the optimal weights for the different asset classes for each time period? In practice, a regular grid is placed across the area of interest, and then an investor is able to pick any gridpoint of her own interest, respectively, for instance, a subjective meaning of where she thinks the market of a particular asset is going to be in the following trading month.

However, in the empirical analysis in the next section, we propose one main procedure. The procedure is that we chose the gridpoint to be based upon an average of the three last months recorded return observations, and thus the gridpoint will potentially change from one month to the next. More specifically, the "moving-grid" point at time t is defined for all pairs of assets i, j as

$$(x_i, x_j) = \text{moving-grid} = \left(\frac{1}{3}\sum_{k=1}^{3} r_{t-k}^{i}, \frac{1}{3}\sum_{k=1}^{3} r_{t-k}^{j}\right). \tag{6.5}$$

In this way, we are hopefully able to pick the "most likely" covariance matrix in the following trading month, based on a predicted return of an asset in month t equal to its three months moving average of observed previous returns. This procedure should produce smoother portfolio weights than, for instance, only using the last months observed return as the prediction. Clearly, this should just be taken as a point of departure for future research.

6.4.2 Empirical example

Our data set consists of monthly closing prices on six US dollar denominated indices sourced from Thompson Reuters Datastream. The sample period extends from February 1980 to August 2018, yielding 463 monthly returns observations. The included time series are FTSE Actuaries All Share Index (FTALLSH), Standard and Poor's 500 Index (S&P500), UK Benchmark 10 Year DS government bond Index (BMUK10Y), US Benchmark 10 Year DS government bond Index (BMUS10Y), Thomson Reuters Equal Weight Commodity Index (EWCI), and Standard and Poor's GSCI Gold Index (GSGCSPT) (see Table 6.7).

Table 6.7 Data.

Name	Description
FTALLSH	FTSE Actuaries All Share Index
S&P500	Standard and Poor's 500 Index
BMUK10Y	UK Benchmark 10 Year DS government bond Index
BMUS10Y	US Benchmark 10 Year DS government bond Index
EWCI	Thomson Reuters Equal Weight Commodity Index
GSGCSPT	Standard and Poor's GSCI Gold Index

From: '*Portfolio Allocation under Asymmetric Dependence in Asset Returns using Local Gaussian Correlations*', to appear in '*Finance Research Letters*'.

From the descriptive statistics in Table 6.8 we note that all the returns are skewed and show relatively high kurtosis. The normality is rejected with the Jarque–Bera test, which is significant on the 1% level for all series. A departure from the Gaussian assumption suggests that the multivariate normal distribution with a global covariance matrix may not be a sufficient description of the dependence structure, in particular, in the tails of the distribution.

The two top panels in Table 6.8 show the global and local correlation matrices over the entire sampling period. The latter is constructed for a *bear market* scenario by using the lower 5% percentiles for the grid point selection in the pairwise calculation approach described above. Globally, the strongest positive correlation $\rho = 0.76$ can be found between the stock indices FTALLSH and S&P500, and the strongest negative $\rho = -0.185$ between EWCI and BMUS10Y. Both stock indices show a positive but close to zero correlation with gold. Locally, in the bear market scenario the positive stock market correlation is larger, $\rho = 0.843$, and the negative relation between commodities and US interest rate markets enhanced to $\rho = -0.224$. Here both stock indices are negatively correlated with gold, with $\rho = -0.135$ and $\rho = -0.131$ for FTALLSH and S&P500, respectively. Intuitively, this seems reasonable, as gold historically has been considered a safe haven in times of turmoil. Such asymmetries in the returns data will be accounted for by calculating local covariance matrices with the moving-grid approach at each time step for the asset allocation below.

Our analysis compares the portfolio performance for all MV strategies listed in Table 6.9 by evaluating outcomes when the optimization is performed with (a) the global covariance matrix and (b) the local covariance

Table 6.8 Correlations and descriptive statistics.

	FTALLSH	S&P500	BMUK10Y	BMUS10Y	EWCI	GSGCSPT
Global correlation matrix						
FTALLSH	1					
S&P500	0.760	1				
BMUK10Y	0.184	0.017	1			
BMUS10Y	−0.067	−0.029	0.489	1		
EWCI	0.246	0.288	−0.094	−0.185	1	
GSGCSPT	0.038	0.031	0.080	0.077	0.483	1
Local correlation matrix, bear market (lower 5% percentiles)						
FTALLSH	1					
S&P500	0.843	1				
BMUK10Y	0.174	−0.017	1			
BMUS10Y	0.020	0.034	0.635	1		
EWCI	0.161	0.185	−0.140	−0.224	1	
GSGCSPT	−0.135	−0.131	0.204	0.215	0.480	1
Descriptive statistics						
Observations	463	463	463	463	463	463
Mean	0.628	0.704	0.769	0.583	0.079	0.177
Std. Dev.	4.588	4.406	2.376	2.417	3.511	5.211
Variance	21.050	19.413	5.643	5.839	12.326	27.159
Skewness	−1.300	−0.968	−0.128	0.453	−0.592	0.026
Kurtosis	6.288	3.665	1.325	1.960	3.775	3.036
Jarque-Bera	903.903	335.969	36.135	91.622	306.377	180.971
Sharpe ratio	0.137	0.160	0.324	0.241	0.023	0.034
Max. drawdown	49.887	59.811	15.764	12.035	48.397	73.680
Min	−32.711	−24.677	−7.824	−7.600	−20.050	−21.887
1 Quartile	−1.474	−1.694	−0.585	−0.922	−1.794	−2.668
Median	1.176	1.242	0.843	0.497	0.151	−0.161
3 Quartile	3.559	3.265	2.151	1.853	1.998	2.899
Max	12.523	14.612	8.851	12.660	13.384	26.336

From: '*Portfolio Allocation under Asymmetric Dependence in Asset Returns using Local Gaussian Correlations*', to appear in '*Finance Research Letters*'.

matrix calculated with the moving-grid approach. The naive $1/p$ weighted portfolio strategy is used as the benchmark model in the analysis, and we perform the study with sampling windows of $M = 120$ and $M = 240$ months.

Table 6.9 Portfolio strategies.

Strategy	Description
EW	$1/N$ without re-balancing
MVS	Mean-variance with short sales
MVSC	Mean-variance with short sales constraint
MIN	Minimum variance
MINC	Minimum variance with short sales constraint

The $1/p$ model distributes weights equally across the portfolio at the start of the sampling period and is left unadjusted for the rest of the investment horizon. The MVS strategy is the classic approach where historical mean returns and the covariance matrix are used to determine the weights for each out-of-sample period, where no consideration is given within the optimization rule to adjust for estimation error in any form. MVSC is the constrained version, where only positive weights are allowed. The MIN strategy aims to minimize portfolio risk measured as variance of portfolio returns. Finally, MINC is the constrained version, where only positive weights are allowed. All strategies allowing short sales have a lower limit on portfolio weights equal to -50%.

When implemented with the local covariance matrix, the strategies are presented as MVS-L, MVSC-L, MIN-L, and MINC-L. The local covariance matrices have been constructed by pairwise correlations with the moving-grid approach, where a simple moving average of length 3 is used to predict gridpoints for the next month. In the event that the resulting covariance matrix is not positive definite, it is adjusted with the method described by Higham (2002).

Inspired by the procedure of Low et al. (2013), we continue with a descriptive analysis of out-of-sample results, followed by an evaluation of portfolio re-balancing and terminal wealth.

Descriptive statistics of the portfolio strategies out-of-sample returns are shown in Table 6.10. We report mean, standard deviation, skewness, kurtosis, minimum value, maximum value, and the maximum portfolio drawdown, which is the maximum observed loss from a peak to a trough of the portfolio, before a new peak is attained, for window size $M = 120$ (top) and $M = 240$ (bottom).

The mean return tends to increase with the local Gaussian approach, and all portfolios achieve moderately higher average returns. In the case $M = 120$, MVS-L reach the highest mean, followed by MVSC-L, MIN-L, MINC-L, MVS, MVSC, MIN, MVSC, and EW. For the window size $M = 240$, the average return ranking is MIN-L, MINC-L, MVS-L, MVSC-L/MINC, MIN, MVS, MVSC, and EW. These findings indicate that the local Gaussian approach may be able to capture asymmetries and outperform the corresponding benchmark models.

The lowest standard deviation for $M = 120$ is achieved by MINC-L. This is however an exception, as all other strategies have slightly higher values when the local Gaussian method is applied. For $M = 240$, all local Gaussian portfolios have moderately higher standard deviations, with the exception for MINC-L. As noted by Low et al. (2013), this can be due to a larger upside variation, which is desirable for investors.

Table 6.10 Descriptive statistics portfolio strategies.

	Mean	Std. Dev.	Skewness	Kurtosis	Min	Max	Max. draw-down
Window size $M = 120$							
EW	0.423	1.999	−0.714	4.052	−11.916	7.342	22.857
MVS	0.455	1.492	−0.209	1.645	−5.451	5.778	9.479
MVSC	0.444	1.486	−0.256	1.644	−5.451	5.688	9.479
MIN	0.435	1.426	−0.190	1.211	−5.108	5.382	9.404
MINC	0.427	1.430	−0.195	1.181	−5.108	5.382	9.404
MVS-L	0.491	1.539	−0.214	1.693	−5.701	6.177	8.959
MVSC-L	0.484	1.494	−0.156	1.592	−5.020	6.079	8.881
MIN-L	0.462	1.459	−0.218	1.182	−5.194	5.429	8.577
MINC-L	0.460	1.401	−0.080	1.222	−4.620	5.743	8.065
Window size $M = 240$							
EW	0.376	2.158	−0.750	4.356	−11.916	7.342	22.857
MVS	0.447	1.671	−0.672	3.012	−8.294	5.061	15.677
MVSC	0.440	1.670	−0.703	3.047	−8.294	5.122	15.677
MIN	0.468	1.619	−0.564	2.316	−7.493	5.053	13.530
MINC	0.470	1.624	−0.558	2.272	−7.476	5.053	13.524
MVS-L	0.488	1.765	−0.243	3.461	−8.522	7.516	15.354
MVSC-L	0.470	1.737	−0.348	3.434	−8.522	7.182	15.364
MIN-L	0.503	1.673	0.805	7.357	−6.023	11.198	10.458
MINC-L	0.495	1.604	0.012	1.981	−5.926	7.142	11.036

All strategy returns exhibit small negative skewness, with the exception of MIN-L and MINC-L for the window $M = 240$, with values of 0.805 and 0.012, respectively. Disregarding the EW strategies, the largest negative skewness of −0.703 can be found in MVSC for $M = 240$. Hence the strategies are all moderately skewed or approximately symmetric.

The MIN-L for $M = 240$ holds the largest kurtosis value in the analysis. When examining the minimum and maximum returns for this strategy, we observe larger values for both. The MIN-L also achieves the lowest drawdown for $M = 240$. The smallest maximum drawdown for $M = 120$ is produced by MINC-L. Overall, the local Gaussian strategies all have lower maximum drawdowns in both windows when compared to their benchmarks.

The primary goal of a re-balancing strategy is minimizing the risk relative to a target asset allocation, rather than to maximizing returns. Yet over time, the asset classes will produce different returns, and the portfolio asset allocation changes. Then the portfolio will likely drift away from its primary target asset allocation, acquiring a risk-and-return characteristics that may be inconsistent with an investor's goals and preferences. Therefore, to re-capture the portfolio original risk-and-return characteristics, the portfolio should be re-balanced. As part of the portfolio-construction process, an optimal investment strategy involves two key issues: (1) frequency of re-balancing and (2) re-balancing fully toward the target allocation or an intermediate allocation. The only clear advantage for any of these strategies, as far as maintaining a portfolio risk-and-return characteristics, and without factoring in re-balancing costs, is that a re-balanced portfolio more closely aligns with the characteristics of the target asset allocation than a portfolio that is never re-balanced. If one is unable to re-balance fully toward the target portfolio weights as required by the portfolio strategy, then this results in sub-optimal diversification. Therefore, all other things equal, a strategy that leads to greater stability in target portfolio weights is desirable as it is easier for a practitioner to implement; see DeMiguel et al. (2009). As such, in addition to risk-adjusted performance, assessing the average standard deviation in target weights is a criterion that a practitioner uses in the selection of a portfolio strategy

The primary goal of a re-balancing strategy is to minimize risk relative to the target asset allocation produced by the trading strategy. According to Tokat and Wicas (2007), the asset manager needs to consider 1) frequency of re-balancing, 2) how large deviations to accept before triggering re-balancing, and 3) whether to restore a portfolio to its target or to some intermediate allocation. Inability to fully re-balance toward the target portfolio weights will lead to sub-optimal diversification. A decision maker facing practical limitations such as regulatory requirements and periods with weak market liquidity will find strategies with stable target portfolio weights easier to implement relative to those who require more trading; see DeMiguel et al. (2009). In our study, portfolios are fully re-balanced to target weights on a monthly basis. We evaluate differences in required trading activity and including transaction costs.

Table 6.11 provides a summary of the portfolio re-balancing analysis and the terminal wealth reached by each of the strategies. It shows the average standard deviation within target portfolio weights, maximum positive and maximum negative adjustments of weights, average turnover, and terminal wealth of a hypothetical investment at the starting time of \$ 1 for each strategy. The average standard deviation within target portfolio weights across the entire out-of-sample time period is calculated as follows:

$$\bar{\sigma}(\hat{w}_{k,M}) = \frac{\sum_{t=1}^{n-M} \sigma(\hat{w}_{k,t,M})}{n-M} \tag{6.6}$$

with

$$\sigma(\hat{w}_{k,t,M}) = \sqrt{\frac{1}{p}\sum_{i=1}^{p}(\hat{w}_{k,t,M,i} - \bar{w}_{k,t,M})^2}, \tag{6.7}$$

where $\hat{w}_{k,t,M,i}$ is the portfolio weight for asset i in a portfolio of p assets for strategy k based upon a window sampling of M months, and $\bar{w}_{k,t,M}$ is the average portfolio weight across the p assets in the portfolio. The maximum values for positive and negative weight adjustments are selected by identifying the largest positive and negative changes in weights on the asset level. Following DeMiguel et al. (2009), we also report the average turnover, which is calculated as the average sum of the absolute value of the transactions over the p assets with

$$\text{Average turnover} = \frac{1}{n-M}\sum_{t=1}^{n-M}\sum_{j=1}^{p}(|w_{k,j,t+1} - w_{k,j,t}|), \tag{6.8}$$

where p is the number of assets in the portfolio, n is the full length of the returns series, M is the window size, $w_{k,j,t+1}$ is the target weight for asset j at time $t+1$ for strategy k, and $w_{k,j,t}$ is the corresponding asset weight before re-balancing. The terminal wealth is calculated assuming no transaction costs and with a transaction cost of 1 basis point in Table 6.11.

The variability of portfolio weights reported in Table 6.11 shows the large values for the MIN-L strategy, both for $M = 120$ and $M = 240$. Results for the remaining strategies are mixed. The local Gaussian models does not seem to systematically achieve either higher or lower average standard deviation in target portfolio weights compared to their benchmarks. However, looking at the maximum and minimum adjustments of portfolio weights, there are clear differences. The local Gaussian strategies require adjustments of larger magnitude in both directions. This is particularly the case for the unconstrained models allowing short sales. For example, during a period of large market moves, the MIN-L strategy exploits nearly its full mandate with a maximum negative weight adjustment of −147% for one of the assets in the 120 window. This is a significant adjustment, which does generate additional costs. Viewing across all strategies, we see larger and

Table 6.11 Portfolio re-balancing and terminal wealth.

	$\bar{\sigma}(\hat{w}_{k,M})$	**Max. adj.**	**Min. adj.**	**Avg. turnover**	**Wealth**	**Wealth incl. tcost**
Window size M = 120						
EW	0	0	0	0	4.052	4.052
MVS	20.671	18.759	−14.112	8.402	4.680	4.548
MVSC	17.944	18.737	−17.349	7.117	4.506	4.399
MIN	19.332	6.966	−8.769	4.135	4.376	4.315
MINC	18.536	6.966	−8.769	3.533	4.254	4.203
MVS-L	20.760	122.681	−132.874	32.084	5.283	4.736
MVSC-L	16.521	29.529	−30.509	17.045	5.166	4.875
MIN-L	21.174	117.820	−147.244	38.222	4.775	4.192
MINC-L	17.710	45.461	−46.261	18.301	4.747	4.460
Window size M = 240						
EW	0	0	0	0	2.231	2.231
MVS	16.663	9.228	−6.741	6.325	2.605	2.569
MVSC	15.813	9.228	−7.426	5.622	2.571	2.539
MIN	16.249	5.036	−4.434	3.090	2.729	2.711
MINC	15.952	5.039	−4.428	2.793	2.742	2.725
MVS-L	15.660	73.184	−89.316	16.967	2.855	2.750
MVSC-L	14.253	18.096	−26.245	12.105	2.745	2.672
MIN-L	17.014	53.636	−79.931	21.617	2.953	2.815
MINC-L	15.243	19.646	−26.028	13.762	2.910	2.823

more frequent adjustments, resulting in an average turnover 2.7–9.2 times higher than the classical MV portfolios when the lowest negative weight allowed is set to −50%. For the long only portfolios, the differences are smaller but still significant. The average turnover is increased by a factor of 2.2–5.2.

The increase in traded volume translate into lower terminal wealth when transaction costs are included in the analysis. Whereas all local Gaussian strategies achieve larger terminal wealth when disregarding costs of trade, the MIN-L for $M = 120$ shows weakest performance when 1 basis point is added as transaction fee. The remaining local Gaussian strategies still reach a larger terminal wealth. Top ranked strategies without costs are MVS-L ($M = 120$) and MIN-L ($M = 240$). When costs are included, these are replaced by the long only portfolios MVSC-L and MINC-L. These two achieve a final wealth, which is 10.8% and 10.4% larger compared to their classical MV benchmarks.

Fig. 6.11 shows wealth accumulation and drawdowns for the hypothetical investment of \$ 1 in each of the nine strategies included in the analysis when a sampling window of $M = 120$ is used. As seen in the upper part of the figure, the local Gaussian MVS-L produces the largest final wealth when

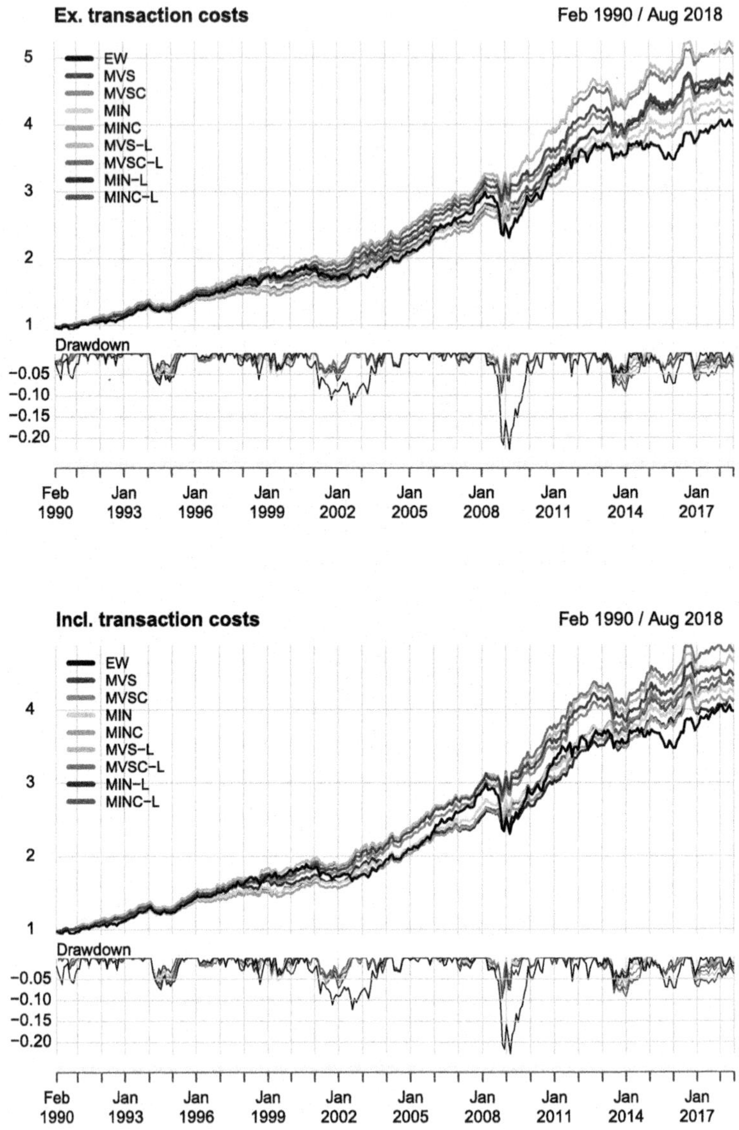

Figure 6.11 Wealth accumulation $M = 120$.

disregarding costs of trade. It remains top-ranked during most months in the sample and suffers from smaller drawdowns in volatile periods such as the 2008 financial crisis. When transaction costs are considered, the strategy still performs well but is pushed down from top position by the constrained

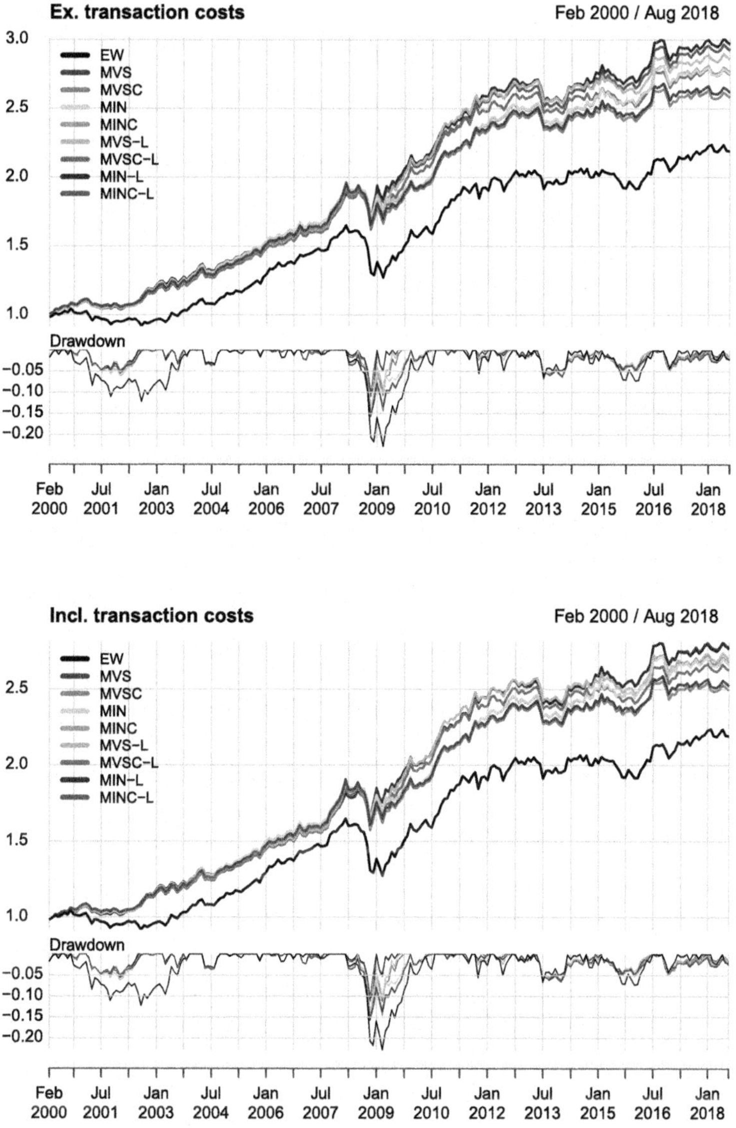

Figure 6.12 Wealth accumulation $M = 240$. (From: *'Portfolio Allocation under Asymmetric Dependence in Asset Returns using Local Gaussian Correlations'*, to appear in *'Finance Research Letters'*.)

MVSC-L, which has lower turnover. A similar illustration for $M = 240$ can be found in Fig. 6.12.

To conclude, the results in this section indicate that by taking account for the asymmetric dependence structures between asset returns, improved portfolio performance can be achieved, even when including transaction costs. We thus confirm earlier results (cf. the references in the beginning of Section 6.4) that have modeled this asymmetry by copula-based methods. However, further studies are needed to confirm to what extent the LGC approach to portfolio allocation does provide added value. In particular, it is of interest to examine the effect of other procedures for selecting the "most likely" local covariance matrix.

6.5 Financial contagion

In the past decades, the international financial markets have become ever more interlinked. Of particular interest is the spread of crises in these markets, that is, large falls in asset values in one country are quickly followed by falls in other countries. The existence of such an effect is called contagion if these falls cannot be explained by interdependence in trade or common macroeconomic factors. However, there exist other definitions of contagion in the literature; see, for instance, Pericoli and Sbracia (2003) and Billio and Caporin (2010). Regardless, this contagion effect is important for risk management and the performance of international portfolios. An increased interdependence in financial markets during a crisis period implies that the diversification effect can be less than anticipated.

Now there exist several methods for testing for contagion. Some of the first studies on testing for contagion focused on the cross-market correlations before a shock (that is, in a "stable period") and after the shock (in a "turmoil period"); see, for instance, Bertero and Mayer (1989) and King and Wadhwani (1990). Attention has often been focused on correlation of certain segments of returns (e.g., exceedance correlation). As already mentioned, the appellation conditional correlation has been used for these correlations, since they are computed conditionally on returns belonging to selected segments of the returns. However, the bias effect in these correlations makes interpretation difficult. Thus these "correlation breakdowns" can be generated by data whose correlation coefficient is constant. See also Sections 6.2 and 6.2.1. Further, as also noted by Boyer et al. (1999) and Forbes and Rigobon (2002), since the market volatility usually increases in unstable time periods, these correlations will be larger than in stable periods, and conclusions of contagion may thus be considered incorrect if synchronization in volatility is not considered a contagion effect. Forbes and Rigobon (2002) explicitly adjust for the increase in correlation due to increase in volatility and conclude that no contagion had occurred during the 1987 crash, the Mexican devaluation in 1994, and the East Asian crisis in 1997. However, they noted that there was a high degree of interdependence in all the periods studied.

Other alternative methods of testing for contagion include Longin and Solnik (2001), who have used extreme value theory models, whereas Ramchand and Susmel (1998), Ang and Bekaert (2002), and Gallo and Otranto (2008) have based themselves on Markov switching models. Rodriguez (2007) has proposed to use copula models with switching parameters to study contagion effects and suggested that contagion may be a nonlinear phenomenon. Especially, since the author notes that "patterns of change in tail behavior differ widely across markets, with tail dependence being more prevalent in times of financial turmoil." Thus the correlation coefficient is not appropriate in such cases, because it is designed to only measure the linear association between two markets.

A recent approach for studying financial contagion is network models. It examines how financial crises propagate through such networks; see, for example, Glasserman and Young (2015) and Cabrales et al. (2017). Further, models of financial contagion using mutually exciting jump processes were developed by Aït-Sahalia et al. (2015).

In the following sections, we present a bootstrap test for contagion introduced by Støve et al. (2014), based on the local Gaussian correlation, and as an example, we will apply it on the 1987 U.S. stock market crash. Contagion is also discussed by Lacal and Tjøstheim (2019) and briefly mentioned in Chapter 7.4.6.

The main reason for introducing such a test is that the local Gaussian correlation does not suffer from the bias problem of the ordinary correlation described above and in Sections 6.2 and 6.2.1. Note also that the traditional global correlation analysis implicitly assumes a Gaussian distribution for financial returns, which is just a local assumption in our approach. Another advantage of using local Gaussian correlation is that this approach is able to detect more complex, nonlinear changes in the dependence structure, which the global correlation may mask. It thus makes it possible to get a better understanding of the dependence between markets in the tails of the distribution, as well as in other segments. This is in contrast to the most common tests for contagion. Note that the copula method can also reveal nonlinear dependence and tail-dependence, but then we use one or more parameters that have a rather indirect interpretation as a measure of dependence. In this respect, our procedure has a more natural basis and retains a correlation interpretation based on local Gaussian approximation. In the next section, we present a review of different tests for contagion and their connection to our local correlation measure and test, primarily based on Støve et al. (2014).

6.5.1 A review of measures of interdependence and contagion

As outlined in the previous subsection, there have been a number of approaches to the problem of measuring interdependence and contagion. Hence there is a need for clarifying under what conditions the local Gaussian correlation can be used to measure and test for contagion. Moreover, we need to address the link between the local Gaussian correlation and contagion by explaining the similarities and differences between this nonlinear measure and other (nonlinear) measures of dependence presented in the literature.

A fact that makes such a comparison difficult is that there is no agreed upon definition of contagion. In fact, some researchers even take the stand that the whole concept of contagion is ill conceived, and that we should just study interrelationships between financial time series without more ado. We do not subscribe to such a view. We think that contagion is a useful concept in the description of crises and their spreading from one country to another. Under such circumstances, the relationships between markets are not exclusively described by economic "fundamentals", but there exist shocks that may propagate through several markets in terms of panic reactions, say. Such shocks typically appear in one country (or a group of countries) and then spread to other countries, having as a consequence that markets move together in a much stronger fashion than before the crisis started. However, there is no agreement as to how such an effect should be precisely described in mathematical and statistical terms. To illustrate, Pericoli and Sbracia (2003) give the following five definitions.

1. Contagion is a significant increase in the probability of a crisis in one country, conditional on a crisis occurring in another country.
2. Contagion occurs when volatility of asset prices spills over from the crisis country to other countries.
3. Contagion occurs when cross-country comovement of asset prices cannot be explained by fundamentals.
4. Contagion is a significant increase in comovement of prices and quantities across markets, conditional on a crisis occurring in one market or a group of markets.
5. (Shift-)contagion occurs when the transmission channel intensifies or, more generally, changes after a shock in one market.

These definitions themselves are not very precise, but they are starting points for more precise definitions, which can actually be used in estimating and testing for contagion. They have to various degrees served this purpose in some of the papers mentioned in the previous section, and in the remaining part of this section, we will compare them in more detail with the local Gaussian correlation.

Correlation methods

In the fundamental paper by Forbes and Rigobon (2002), contagion is defined as "a significant increase in cross-market linkages after a shock to one country (or a group of countries)." In practice, in that paper, cross-market linkages are measured by correlation. However, and this is the main contribution of the paper, it is shown how bias due to increase of volatility in the crisis period can be eliminated. The main result of the empirical study of Forbes and Rigobon is that once bias is removed, there is very little contagion left, only interdependence. Two main criticisms have been leveled against this approach. The sample size for the crisis period is small, leading to large errors in the correlation estimate, but more importantly, all the modeling is linear, which may not be realistic.

The local Gaussian correlation is based on the correlation concept, but it is localized and nonlinear. In principle it gives a much more complete description of dependence relationships. We follow Forbes and Rigobon (2002) in removing effects due to heteroskedasticity. This is done by fitting a GARCH model and then looking at the residuals. The local Gaussian correlation coincides with the ordinary correlation (and thus the measure of Forbes and Rigobon) if the residuals are Gaussian, but this as a rule is not the case, as will be demonstrated by our empirical example.

Extreme value methods

Contagion is supposed to occur when one market crashes and this spreads to other markets. It is therefore natural to try to apply the theory of multivariate tail behavior and extremes. Longin and Solnik (2001) pioneered this approach. There are several issues involved. It may be tempting to use conditional correlation and in the bivariate case to compute the correlation for values of X and Y larger than a threshold, but as mentioned, this is not a good way since it leads to serious bias. Longin and Solnik use asymptotic theory and identify asymptotic dependence by a parameter in the asymptotic tail index dependence function. For a multivariate Gaussian, it is well known that the asymptotic tail index dependence is zero; see, for example, McNeil et al. (2005), which is one of the reasons why

Gaussian distributions should not be used. Longin and Solnik demonstrate on monthly equity return index data that there is increasing asymptotic tail dependence in a bearish market (falling price trend) but not when the market is bullish (rising price trend). They do not apply this to contagion, but rather study general interrelationships. However, there are later applications to contagion, as we will further see.

Asymptotic tail behavior for local Gaussian correlation is briefly examined by Tjøstheim and Hufthammer (2013); see also Chapter 5.2.1. It is shown there that for bivariate distributions having heavier tail than the Gaussian, the local Gaussian correlation $\rho(x, x)$ tends to 1 as $x \to -\infty$, that is, when there is a complete market crash (very large negative returns), then the correlation tends to one for these extreme events. This is confirmed, again theoretically, for several copula models by Berentsen et al. (2014) and in Chapter 5.3. This phenomenon is also documented in a study of monthly data by Støve and Tjøstheim (2014), who found that the local Gaussian correlation increases in a bear market and decreases in a bull market, in complete agreement with Longin and Solnik (2001) and our analysis of financial returns earlier in this chapter.

The study of Longin and Solnik (2001) has been followed up among others by Bae et al. (2003), Baur and Schulze (2005), and Baur (2013). Bae et al. (2003) look at the number and probability of coexceedances over a given threshold. This probability can be studied in terms of explanatory variables in a logistic regression model. The probability of coexceedance of a given threshold (x, y) can be approximated in the local Gaussian case by computing the tail probability $\int_{-\infty}^{x} \int_{-\infty}^{y} \phi_{x,y}(y_1, y_2) \mathrm{d}y_1 \mathrm{d}y_2$, where $\phi_{x,y}$ is a Gaussian distribution having local parameters $\mu_i(x, y)$, $\sigma_i^2(x, y)$, and $\rho(x, y)$. Once these local parameters are estimated, the tail probability can be estimated (it is an approximation since the series of Gaussians in the tail is replaced by one Gaussian with local parameters at (x, y)). Such an approach was in fact used by Gourieroux and Jasiak (2010) to evaluate value-at-risk.

Baur and Schulze (2005) and Baur (2013) focus, instead, on the thresholds themselves or rather on the quantiles. Comparing the quantile regression approach in Baur and Schulze (2005) to the local Gaussian correlation (cf. also Chapter 12 in this book), we see that both approaches allow non-Gaussian distributions and do not depend on a single number like the global correlation or conditional correlation over a region. The local Gaussian correlation measures and quantifies potential contagion everywhere along the diagonal, whereas Baur and Schulze (2005) seem to put more emphasis on the tails. A recent approach, also based on quantile regressions, is Caporin et al. (2018). In this study, the authors compare the coefficient of the propagation of shocks between two countries that show values belonging to, respectively, the lowest quantiles (easily associated with turbulent times) and the middle ones (belonging to normal times). When the coefficients are stable over quantiles (i.e., they are not statistically different), the so-called shift-contagion hypothesis is rejected.

Regime models

These models have been used both in describing regimes, say bear or bull regimes, in dependence models and to describe crisis-like regimes with contagion; see, for example, Ang and Bekaert (2002), Gallo and Otranto (2008), Rodriguez (2007), and Akay et al. (2013). The regimes are described by a hidden Markov chain. Such a process is stationary under weak regularity conditions on the regime parameters and is approximated by a bivariate stationary process in each regime. In the simplest case the bivariate distribution in each regime is Gaussian, and in more general cases, as in Rodriguez (2007), more general distributions with dependence described by a copula are used. Then the Gaussian regimes can be described by a local Gaussian correlation whose parameters, including the local correlation, are constants within the regimes. An example of such a stepwise local Gaussian model, but without the hidden Markov mechanism, is given by Tjøstheim and Hufthammer (2013) (their equation (5)). In case the dependence in a regime is described by a copula, we refer to Berentsen et al. (2014). In that paper the local Gaussian correlation is computed analytically along the diagonal $x = y$ for exchangable Archimedean copulas; see also Chapter 5. Presumably, such results can be used in estimating and testing the dependence relation in each regime including tail behavior.

Local dependence models

The local Gaussian correlation is a local dependence measure. Bradley and Taqqu (2004), Bradley and Taqqu (2005a), Bradley and Taqqu (2005b), and Inci et al. (2011) have proposed another local dependence measure based on the so-called correlation curve introduced in Bjerve and Doksum (1993) and which is described in Chapter 4.2.2. This local dependence concept is based on localizing a first-order regression relation. In a regression of Y on X the regression parameters and the residual variance are allowed to depend on X. This is transformed into a correlation (depending on X) by using the relationship between correlation and regression parameters in an ordinary linear first-order regression. This means that (i) Y and X play different roles as output and input variables, (ii) only first-order regression is allowed in the definition, and (iii) unlike the case for local Gaussian correlation, where X and Y are treated as variables on the same basis, their correlation curve is local only as a function of X.

In the contagion analysis, we use the local correlation essentially in the same way as Forbes and Rigobon do for the ordinary correlation. Bradley and Taqqu use a rather different approach, where they declare that there is contagion from X to Y if $\rho_L(x) > \rho_M(x)$, where $\rho_M(x)$ is the correlation curve for $X = M$, the median, and $\rho_L(x)$ is the correlation curve for $X = L$, a quantile in the left tail (e.g., 5% quantile). The idea is that if there is contagion, then we expect larger correlation in the left-hand tail.

However, as demonstrated by Støve and Tjøstheim (2014), it is generally true for financial data of this sort that there is stronger dependence in the left-hand tail. Therefore $\rho_L(x) > \rho_M(x)$ might be an indication of a heavy tail and possibly asymmetry rather than an indication of contagion.

6.5.2 A bootstrap test for contagion based on the LGC

In this section, as mentioned, we adopt the definition of Forbes and Rigobon (2002) that contagion means "a significant increase in cross-market linkages after a shock to one country (or a group of countries)." In the following, we present a test for contagion and we use the measure of local Gaussian correlation to study whether cross-market linkages have increased. The test consists in a bootstrap procedure, and similar tests are often used in a nonparametric setting, for example, for testing difference between quantities in nonparametric regressions; see, for example, Hall and Hart (1990) and Vilar-Fernández et al. (2007).

Let Y_t, $t = 1, \ldots, n$, be the (log-)return (e.g., an index return) in the crisis country, and let X_t, $t = 1, \ldots, n$, be the (log-)return in another market. A filtration of the data is performed to remove dependence over time and to remove volatility effects as is done by Forbes and Rigobon (2002). In the example below, we will use a simple GARCH(1, 1) filtration, as in Section 6.3, but any filtration method can in principle be used, for example, a more general AR(k)-GARCH(p, q) process. These resulting standardized returns X_t' and Y_t' are denoted $\boldsymbol{d}_t = (X_t', Y_t')$. The data are then split up in a stable period (NC) and a turmoil period (C) (note that such a predefined split of observations may naturally impact the outcome; see Dungey et al. (2005), and thus the test can be performed on a number of splits to ensure robustness of the results). Contagion is present if the local correlation function for the turmoil period is significantly above the local correlation function for the stable period. We use fixed gridpoints (x_i, y_i) for

$i = 1, \ldots, m$, where the local correlations are estimated. Thus the test is

$$H_0 : \rho_{NC}(x_i, y_i) = \rho_C(x_i, y_i) \ \text{ for } i = 1, \ldots, m \ \text{ (no contagion)};$$

$$H_1 : \sum_{i=1}^{m} \left(\rho_C(x_i, y_i) - \rho_{NC}(x_i, y_i)\right) > 0 \ \text{ (contagion)}.$$

The bootstrap method works as follows: From the observations $\{\boldsymbol{d}_1, \ldots, \boldsymbol{d}_n\}$ draw a resample $\{\boldsymbol{d}_1^*, \ldots, \boldsymbol{d}_n^*\}$ at random and with replacement. Divide this resample into time periods NC and C and compute $\hat{\rho}_{NC}^*(x_i, y_i)$ and $\hat{\rho}_C^*(x_i, y_i)$ on the grid (x_i, y_i) for $i = 1, \ldots, m$. We suggest to use a diagonal grid, that is, $x_i = y_i$, to minimize the computational time. Next, calculate the test variable

$$D_1^* = \frac{1}{m} \sum_{i=1}^{m} [\hat{\rho}_C^*(x_i, x_i) - \hat{\rho}_{NC}^*(x_i, x_i)] w(x_i, x_i),$$

where w_i is a weight function to screen off parts of the local correlation or to concentrate on a certain region. Note that this does not imply disregarding any of the observations, but we choose the weight function such that the distance between the gridpoints and observations is not too large, that is, we avoid using an estimated local correlation in a gridpoint far away from any observations. By repeated resampling, D_1^* is computed for these resamples, and its distribution is constructed (i.e., the distribution under H_0). Finally, from the real filtered observations $\{\boldsymbol{d}_1, \ldots, \boldsymbol{d}_n\}$ calculate $\hat{\rho}_{NC}(x_i, x_i)$, $\hat{\rho}_C(x_i, x_i)$, and the test statistic $D_1 = \frac{1}{m} \sum_{i=1}^{m} [\hat{\rho}_C(x_i, x_i) - \hat{\rho}_{NC}(x_i, x_i)] w(x_i, x_i)$. The p-value in terms of the D_1^* distribution is found and implies a rejection of H_0 if it is below a chosen significant level α. Unlike some of the tests mentioned in the last subsection, this test focuses not only on possible changes in the tail, but overall differences in the correlation structure. Note that in the ordinary bootstrap resampling scheme suggested, we are in fact ignoring possible pairwise time-dependence between the univariate GARCH residuals. This potential problem can be alleviated by using the stationary or moving block bootstrap, as discussed by Lacal and Tjøstheim (2019). See also Chapter 7.4 and, in particular, Chapter 7.4.6 in this book, where the local Gaussian cross-correlation and accompanying tests are presented. For the validity of the moving block bootstrap, see also the supplemental material to Lacal and Tjøstheim (2019).

The finite sample performance of a test was examined by Støve et al. (2014), and it shows good level and power properties. As before, the local

Gaussian correlation estimator $\hat{\rho}(x, y)$ depends on two smoothing devices, the bandwidths $\boldsymbol{b} = (b_1, b_2)$ and, to a lesser degree, on the kernel used. In the empirical example below, we use the Gaussian kernel and choose the bandwidths using a simple rule of thumb, the global standard deviation times a constant close to one (usually chosen to be 1.1). We also prefer to oversmooth rather than undersmooth in the contagion setting, that is, we smooth slightly toward a constant local correlation (equal to the global correlation). However, any of the bandwidth selectors mentioned in Chapter 4.8.2 can be applied, and in practice, one should do several sensitivity studies by varying the bandwidth to ensure that the results are not an artifact of poorly chosen bandwidths.

This test procedure was used, among others, by Bampinas and Panagiotidis (2017), who study the effect of financial shocks on the cross-market linkages between oil prices and stock markets, and by Nguyen et al. (2020), who study the phenomenon of financialization amongst commodities markets, that is, through which commodity prices became more correlated with prices of financial assets and with each other.

6.5.3 Example: Testing for contagion in the 1987 US stock market crash

In this example, we follow Forbes and Rigobon (2002) and test for contagion caused by the 1987 US stock market crash to UK, Germany, and Japan. The data are daily prices from the S&P 500, FTSE 100, DAX 30, and TOPIX indices from January 2, 1985, through April 29, 1988. The price indices, where we normalize the indices to 100 on January 2, 1985 (by dividing later index values by the values at this start date), and the daily log returns are shown in Figs. 6.13 and 6.14, respectively.

The stable period is defined from January 2, 1985, to October 16, 1987, which imply 727 observations in this period. The crisis period is thus starting on Monday, October 19, 1987 (the day noted as the "Black Monday", since the leading indices in the US fell almost 23%). We set the end period to April 29, 1988, which imply 141 observations in the crisis period. We might dispute this long crisis period, but to ensure enough observations when estimating the local correlations, we chose to use a longer crisis period than Forbes and Rigobon (2002). The stable period is increased for the same reason.

In general, if a crisis has been short-lived, theoretically, there is no problem performing the proposed test. However, the estimated local correlations in the crisis period may be subject to great uncertainty, which

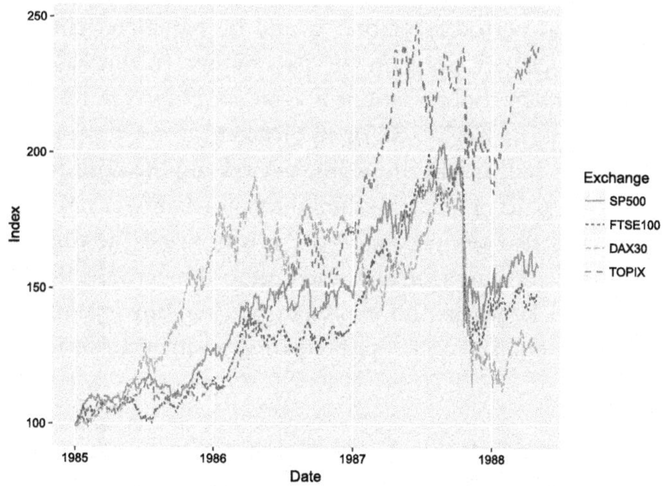

Figure 6.13 Market indices for the US, UK, Germany, and Japan normalized to 100 at the start date.

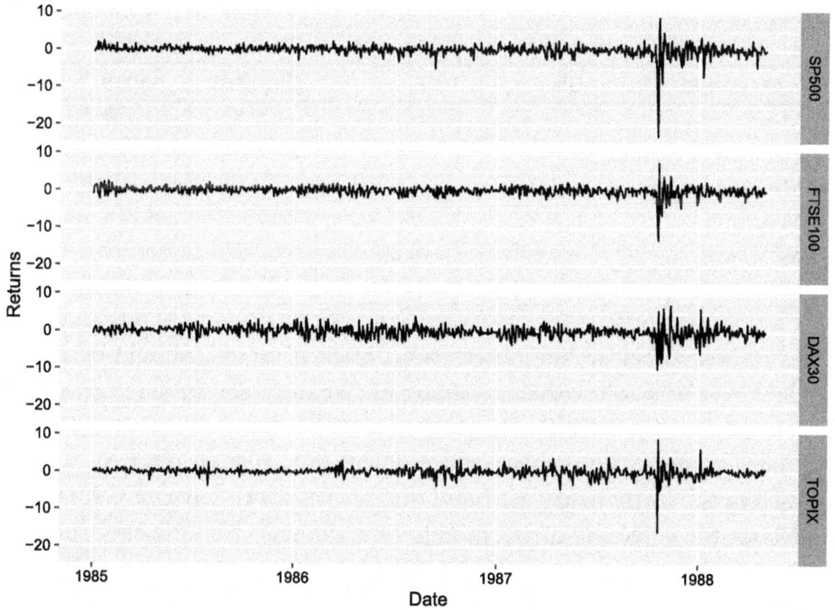

Figure 6.14 Returns for the market indices for the US, UK, Germany, and Japan (in this order, from top to bottom).

may affect the conclusion of the test. Another possible solution, instead of increasing the crisis period as before, would be parameterizing the LGC and looking for a change point in the parameters. In this case the problem of a small number of observations is avoided. However, finding a good parameterization of the LGC is an open problem.

The descriptive statistics for the stable period and the crisis period series are shown in Table 6.12. The data exhibit non-normality, as is seen from the skewness and kurtosis coefficients. In the crisis period the minimum and maximum returns are much smaller and larger, respectively. The standard deviations are also larger in the crisis period, and the mean is negative for all markets except Japan, as opposed to a positive mean in the stable period.

Table 6.12 Descriptive statistics for the different market returns.

Stable period	**US**	**UK**	**Germany**	**Japan**
Mean	0.074	0.087	0.077	0.118
Standard deviation	0.881	0.827	1.145	0.915
Minimum	−5.298	−2.446	−3.523	−4.531
Maximum	2.844	2.312	4.004	4.144
Skewness	−0.764	−0.255	−0.146	−0.277
Kurtosis	6.893	2.857	3.448	6.917
Crisis period	**US**	**UK**	**Germany**	**Japan**
Mean	−0.055	−0.174	−0.232	0.020
Standard deviation	2.748	2.222	2.430	2.039
Minimum	−22.900	−13.029	−9.859	−15.810
Maximum	8.709	7.597	7.170	8.978
Skewness	−4.158	−2.268	−0.587	−2.632
Kurtosis	36.519	15.364	6.254	30.293

As remarked before, the observations of each variable should be independent over time to use the bootstrap test. We thus filter each return series by a univariate GARCH(1, 1) model with a Student t error distribution and then compute the standardized residuals (i.e., filtered returns), which are used in the further analysis. Note that we do not fit separate GARCH-models for the stable and the turmoil period; doing so has little effect on the results. We then also remove possible effects due to synchrony in volatility. That is, for each series, we have the following model for log-return r_t:

$$r_t = \mu + a_t,$$
$$a_t = \sigma_t \epsilon_t,$$

$$\sigma_t^2 = \omega + \alpha a_{t-1}^2 + \beta\sigma_{t-1}^2,$$

where the notation is self-explanatory. The standardized residuals are calculated as $\hat{a}_t = (r_t - \hat{\mu})/\hat{\sigma}_t$. Note that $\hat{\mu}$ is just the mean of the observed log-returns r_t. We do not report the fitted GARCH-models. More sophisticated filtrations can naturally also be applied.

As the global correlations may mask more complex, nonlinear changes in the dependence structure, which the local Gaussian correlation may be able to detect, we estimate the local Gaussian correlations for the three country pairs involving the US based on the standardized residuals. The estimated local Gaussian correlations, where we resort to the full five-parameter estimation procedure (cf. the last paragraph of Section 6.1), between the standardized returns from US and the three other countries for both the stable and crisis period are shown in Fig. 6.15. The bandwidths used are 1.5 times the standard deviations of the standardized returns, that is, slightly oversmoothing when compared to the bandwidth selector based on cross-validation. The local Gaussian correlations between US and UK is shifted substantially upward from the stable to the crisis period, indicating contagion. The local correlations between US and Germany show an increased left-tail dependence in the crisis period, whereas the local correlations between US and Japan indicate increased dependence in both tails, in the crisis period.

To formally test for contagion, we use the proposed bootstrap test introduced before. We apply a diagonal grid ($x_i = y_i$) with a weight function equal to one from −3 to 2.5 and zero elsewhere, as most standardized residuals fall into this interval. Further, the number of bootstrap realizations B is set equal to 1000. The p-values from the bootstrap tests are as follows; 0.017 (US–UK), 0.017 (US–Germany), and 0.033 (US–Japan). We thus reject the null hypothesis and claim contagion in all cases at 5% significance level.

This is in contrast to Forbes and Rigobon (2002), who only find contagion from the US to UK. The explanation for our findings is that looking at the LGC curves, we observe increased tail-dependence between US–Germany and US–Japan in the crisis period. This effect will be missed by the global correlation. Thus this application is an example of the importance of taking into account the existence of non-linear dependence structures between asset returns when testing for financial contagion.

For possible contagion effects of the financial crisis of 2009, we refer to Chapter 7.4.6.

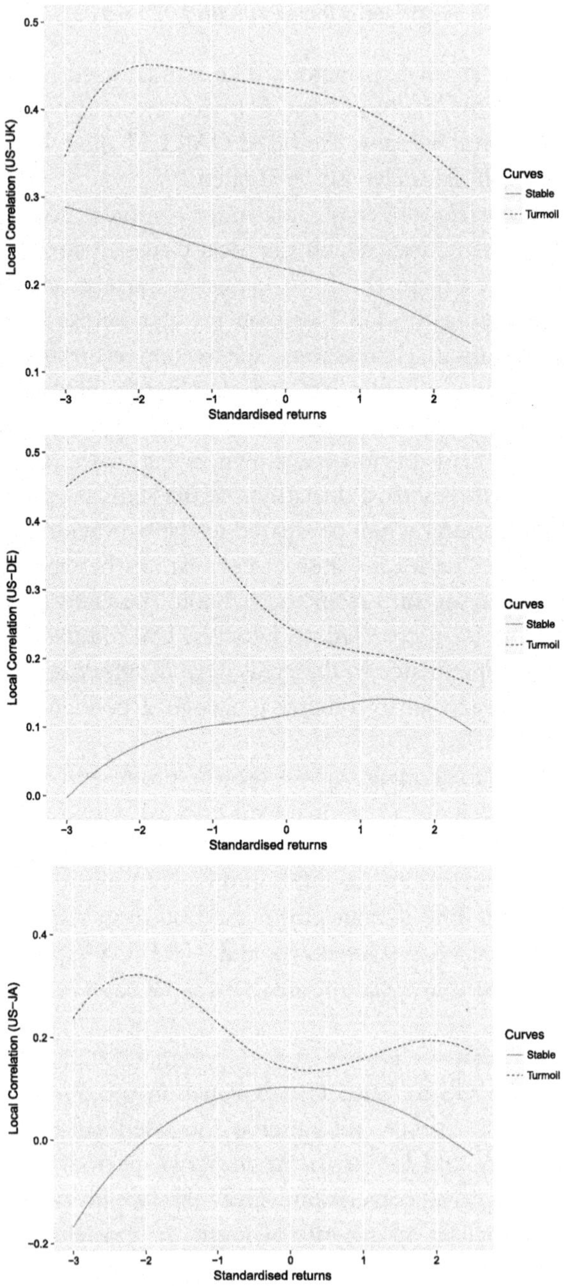

Figure 6.15 Local Gaussian correlation curves estimated from the market indices in the stable and crisis period.

References

Aas, K., Czado, C., Frigessi, A., Bakken, H., 2009. Pair-copula constructions of multiple dependence. Insurance: Mathematics and Economics 44 (2), 182–198.

Aït-Sahalia, Y., Cacho-Diaz, J., Laeven, R.J., 2015. Modeling financial contagion using mutually exciting jump processes. Journal of Financial Economics 117 (3), 585–606.

Akay, O.O., Senyuz, Z., Yoldas, E., 2013. Hedge fund contagion and risk-adjusted returns: a Markov-switching dynamic factor approach. Journal of Empirical Finance 22, 16–29.

Ang, A., Bekaert, G., 2002. International asset allocation with regime shifts. Review of Financial Studies 15 (4), 1137–1187.

Ang, A., Chen, J., 2002. Asymmetric correlations of equity portfolios. Journal of Financial Economics 63 (3), 443–494.

Bae, K., Karolyi, G., Stulz, R., 2003. A new approach to measuring financial contagion. Review of Financial Studies 16, 717–763.

Bampinas, G., Panagiotidis, T., 2017. Oil and stock markets before and after financial crises: a local Gaussian correlation approach. Journal of Futures Markets 37 (12), 1179–1204.

Baur, D., Schulze, N., 2005. Coexceedances in financial markets – a quantile regression analysis of contagion. Emerging Markets Review 6, 21–43.

Baur, D.G., 2013. The structure and degree of dependence: a quantile regression approach. Journal of Banking & Finance 37 (3), 786–798.

Bekiros, S., Hernandez, J.A., Hammoudeh, S., Nguyen, D.K., 2015. Multivariate dependence risk and portfolio optimization: an application to mining stock portfolios. Resources Policy 46, 1–11.

BenSaïda, A., Boubaker, S., Nguyen, D.K., 2018. The shifting dependence dynamics between the G7 stock markets. Quantitative Finance 18 (5), 801–812.

Berentsen, G.D., Støve, B., Tjøstheim, D., Nordbø, T., 2014. Recognizing and visualizing copulas: an approach using local Gaussian approximation. Insurance: Mathematics and Economics 57, 90–103.

Bertero, E., Mayer, C., 1989. Structure and performance: global interdependence of stock markets around the crash of October 1987. CEPR Discussion Papers.

Billio, M., Caporin, M., 2010. Market linkages, variance spillovers, and correlation stability: empirical evidence of financial contagion. Computational Statistics & Data Analysis 54 (11), 2443–2458.

Bjerve, S., Doksum, K., 1993. Correlation curves: measures of association as function of covariate values. Annals of Statistics 21 (2hol), 890–902.

Black, F., Scholes, M., 1973. The pricing of options and corporate liabilities. Journal of Political Economy 81 (3), 637–654.

Bouri, E., Gupta, R., Wang, S., 2020. Nonlinear contagion between stock and real estate markets: international evidence from a local Gaussian correlation approach. International Journal of Finance & Economics.

Boyer, B.H., Gibson, M.S., Loretan, M., 1999. Pitfalls in tests for changes in correlation. Discussion Paper 597. Federal Reserve Government Papers.

Bradley, B., Taqqu, M., 2004. Framework for analyzing spatial contagion between financial markets. Finance Letters 2 (6), 8–15.

Bradley, B., Taqqu, M., 2005a. Empirical evidence on spatial contagion between financial markets. Finance Letters 3 (1), 77–86.

Bradley, B., Taqqu, M., 2005b. How to estimate spatial contagion between financial markets. Finance Letters 3 (1), 64–76.

Cabrales, A., Gottardi, P., Vega-Redondo, F., 2017. Risk sharing and contagion in networks. The Review of Financial Studies 30 (9), 3086–3127.

Campbell, R., Koedijk, K., Kofman, P., 2002. Increased correlation in bear markets. Financial Analysts Journal 58 (1), 87–94.

Campbell, R.A., Forbes, C.S., Koedijk, K.G., Kofman, P., 2008. Increasing correlations or just fat tails? Journal of Empirical Finance 15 (2), 287–309.
Caporin, M., Pelizzon, L., Ravazzolo, F., Rigobon, R., 2018. Measuring sovereign contagion in Europe. Journal of Financial Stability 34, 150–181.
Chollete, L., Heinen, A., Valdesogo, A., 2009. Modeling international financial returns with a multivariate regime switching copula. Journal of Financial Econometrics 7, 437–480.
Chong, J., Miffre, J., 2010. Conditional return correlations between commodity futures and traditional assets. Journal of Alternative Investments 12 (3), 61–75.
Christoffersen, P., Errunza, V., Jacobs, K., Langlois, H., 2012. Is the potential for international diversification disappearing? a dynamic copula approach. The Review of Financial Studies 25 (12), 3711–3751.
Connolly, R., Stivers, C., Sun, L., 2005. Stock market uncertainty and the stock–bond return relation. Journal of Financial and Quantitative Analysis 40 (1), 161–194.
Creti, A., Joëts, M., Mignon, V., 2013. On the links between stock and commodity markets' volatility. Energy Economics 37, 16–28.
Dajcman, S., 2012. Comovement between stock and bond markets and the 'flight-to-quality' during financial market turmoil – a case of the Eurozone countries most affected by the sovereign debt crisis of 2010–2011. Applied Economics Letters 19 (17), 1655–1662.
DeMiguel, V., Garlappi, L., Uppal, R., 2009. Optimal versus naive diversification: how inefficient is the $1/n$ portfolio strategy? The Review of Financial Studies 22 (5), 1915–1953.
Dungey, M., Fry, R., González-Hermosillo, B., Martin, V.L., 2005. Empirical modelling of contagion: a review of methodologies. Quantitative Finance 5 (1), 9–24.
Engle, R., 2002. Dynamic conditional correlation: a simple class of multivariate generalized autoregressive conditional heteroskedasticity models. Journal of Business & Economic Statistics 20 (3), 339–350.
Engle, R.F., Bollerslev, T., 1986. Modelling the persistence of conditional variances. Econometric Reviews 5 (1), 1–50.
Fan, J., Yao, Q., 2015. The Elements of Financial Econometrics. Cambridge University Press.
Forbes, K.J., Rigobon, R., 2002. No contagion, only interdependence: measuring stock market comovements. The Journal of Finance 57 (5), 2223–2261.
Francis, J.C., Kim, D., 2013. Modern Portfolio Theory: Foundations, Analysis, and New Developments. John Wiley & Sons.
Gallo, G.M., Otranto, E., 2008. Volatility spillovers, interdependence and comovements: a Markov switching approach. Computational Statistics & Data Analysis 52, 3011–3026.
Glasserman, P., Young, H.P., 2015. How likely is contagion in financial networks? Journal of Banking & Finance 50, 383–399.
Gourieroux, C., Jasiak, J., 2010. Local likelihood density estimation and value-at-risk. Journal of Probability and Statistics 26, 1–26.
Hall, P., Hart, J.D., 1990. Bootstrap test for difference between means in nonparametric regression. Journal of the American Statistical Association 85 (412), 1039–1049.
Han, Y., Li, P., Xia, Y., 2017. Dynamic robust portfolio selection with copulas. Finance Research Letters 21, 190–200.
Hatherley, A., Alcock, J., 2007. Portfolio construction incorporating asymmetric dependence structures: a user's guide. Accounting & Finance 47 (3), 447–472.
Higham, N.J., 2002. Computing the nearest correlation matrix a problem from finance. IMA Journal of Numerical Analysis 22 (3), 329–343.
Hong, Y., Tu, J., Zhou, G., 2007. Asymmetries in stock returns: statistical tests and economic evaluation. Review of Financial Studies 20 (5), 1547–1581.
Ilmanen, A., 2003. Stock–bond correlations. The Journal of Fixed Income 13 (2), 55–66.
Inci, A., Li, H.C., McCarthy, J., 2011. Financial contagion: a local correlation analysis. Research in International Business and Finance 25, 11–25.

Jammazi, R., Tiwari, A.K., Ferrer, R., Moya, P., 2015. Time-varying dependence between stock and government bond returns: international evidence with dynamic copulas. The North American Journal of Economics and Finance 33, 74–93.

Jorion, P., 2006. Value at risk.

Kakouris, I., Rustem, B., 2014. Robust portfolio optimization with copulas. European Journal of Operational Research 235 (1), 28–37.

King, M., Wadhwani, S., 1990. Transmission of volatility between stock markets. Review of Financial Studies 3, 5–33.

Lacal, V., Tjøstheim, D., 2019. Estimating and testing nonlinear local dependence between two time series. Journal of Business and Economic Statistics 37 (4), 648–660.

Lintner, J., 1965. The valuation of risk assets and the selection of risky investments in stock portfolios and capital budgets. The Review of Economics and Statistics 47 (1), 13–37.

Longin, F., Solnik, B., 2001. Extreme correlation of international equity markets. The Journal of Finance 56 (2), 649–676.

Low, R.K.Y., Alcock, J., Faff, R., Brailsford, T., 2013. Canonical vine copulas in the context of modern portfolio management: are they worth it? Journal of Banking and Finance 37 (8), 3085–3099.

Low, R.K.Y., Faff, R., Aas, K., 2016. Enhancing mean–variance portfolio selection by modeling distributional asymmetries. Journal of Economics and Business 85, 49–72.

Markowitz, H., 1952. Portfolio selection. Journal of Finance 7 (1), 77–91.

McNeil, A.J., Frey, R., Embrechts, P., 2005. Quantitative Risk Management: Concepts, Techniques and Tools. Princeton University Press, Princeton.

Merton, R.C., 1973. Theory of rational option pricing. The Bell Journal of Economics and Management Science 4 (1), 141–183.

Mossin, J., 1966. Equilibrium in a capital asset market. Econometrica: Journal of the Econometric Society, 768–783.

Nguyen, Q.N., Aboura, S., Chevallier, J., Lyuyuan, Z., Zhu, B., 2020. Local Gaussian correlations in financial and commodity markets. European Journal of Operational Research.

Nikoloulopoulos, A., Joe, H., Li, H., 2012. Vine copulas with asymmetric tail dependence and applications to financial return data. Computational Statistics and Data Analysis 56, 3659–3673.

Oh, D.H., Patton, A.J., 2017. Modeling dependence in high dimensions with factor copulas. Journal of Business & Economic Statistics 35 (1), 139–154.

Okimoto, T., 2008. New evidence of asymmetric dependence structures in international equity markets. Journal of Financial and Quantitative Analysis 43, 787–816.

Patton, A.J., 2004. On the out-of-sample importance of skewness and asymmetric dependence for asset allocation. Journal of Financial Econometrics 2 (1), 130–168.

Pericoli, M., Sbracia, M., 2003. A primer on financial contagion. Journal of Economic Surveys 17 (4), 571–608.

Pukthuanthong, K., Roll, R., 2014. Internationally correlated jumps. The Review of Asset Pricing Studies 5 (1), 92–111.

Ramchand, L., Susmel, R., 1998. Volatility and cross correlation across major stock markets. Journal of Empirical Finance 5 (4), 397–416.

Rodriguez, J.C., 2007. Measuring financial contagion: a copula approach. Journal of Empirical Finance 14 (3), 401–423.

Rydberg, T.H., Shephard, N., 2000. A modelling framework for the prices and times of trades made on the New York stock exchange. Nonlinear and Nonstationary Signal Processing, 217–246.

Sharpe, W.F., 1964. Capital asset prices: a theory of market equilibrium under conditions of risk. The Journal of Finance 19 (3), 425–442.

Silvapulle, P., Granger, C.W., 2001. Large returns, conditional correlation and portfolio diversification. A value-at-risk approach. Quantitative Finance 1 (5), 542–551.

Silvennoinen, A., Thorp, S., 2013. Financialization, crisis and commodity correlation dynamics. Journal of International Financial Markets, Institutions and Money 24, 42–65.

Sleire, A., Støve, B., Otneim, H., Berentsen, G.D., Tjøstheim, D., Haugen, S.H., 2021. Portfolio allocation under asymmetric dependence in asset returns using local Gaussian correlations. To appear, Finance Research Letters.

Solnik, B., Watewai, T., 2016. International correlation asymmetries: frequent-but-small and infrequent-but-large equity returns. The Review of Asset Pricing Studies 6 (2), 221–260.

Støve, B., Tjøstheim, D., 2014. Measuring asymmetries in financial returns: an empirical investigation using local Gaussian correlation. In: Haldrup, N., Meitz, M., Saikkonen, P. (Eds.), Essays in Nonlinear Time Series Econometrics. Oxford University Press, Oxford, pp. 307–329.

Støve, B., Tjøstheim, D., Hufthammer, K., 2014. Using local Gaussian correlation in a nonlinear re-examination of financial contagion. Journal of Empirical Finance 25, 785–801.

Tang, K., Xiong, W., 2012. Index investment and the financialization of commodities. Financial Analysts Journal 68 (6), 54–74.

Tjøstheim, D., Hufthammer, K.O., 2013. Local Gaussian correlation: a new measure of dependence. Journal of Econometrics 172 (1), 33–48.

Tokat, Y., Wicas, N.W., 2007. Portfolio rebalancing in theory and practice. The Journal of Investing 16 (2), 52–59.

Tu, J., Zhou, G., 2011. Markowitz meets Talmud: a combination of sophisticated and naive diversification strategies. Journal of Financial Economics 99 (1), 204–215.

Vilar-Fernández, J.M., Vilar-Fernández, J.A., González-Manteiga, W., 2007. Bootstrap tests for nonparametric comparison of regression curves with dependent errors. Test 16 (1), 123–144.

Zimmer, D.M., 2012. The role of copulas in the housing crisis. Review of Economics and Statistics 94 (2), 607–620.

CHAPTER 7

Measuring dependence and testing for independence

Contents

7.1. Introduction 213
7.2. Testing of independence in iid pairs of variables using local correlation functionals 214
7.2.1 Bootstrap test of independence 217
7.2.2 Local independence testing 219
7.2.3 Example: Bivariate t-distribution 220
7.2.4 Example: Aircraft data 222
7.3. Testing for serial independence in time series 224
7.3.1 The bootstrap 228
7.3.2 Example: GARCH(1, 1) 229
7.3.3 Example: Exchange rates 231
7.3.4 Validity of the bootstrap 231
7.4. Describing nonlinear dependence and tests of independence for two time series 235
7.4.1 Local Gaussian cross-correlation 236
7.4.2 Asymptotic theory of the parameter estimates 238
7.4.3 Test of independence 240
7.4.4 The bootstrap and its validity 243
7.4.5 Example: Bivariate GARCH(1, 1) 245
7.4.6 Example: Financial returns 249
7.5. Proofs 253
7.5.1 Proof of Theorems 7.9 and 7.10 253
7.5.2 Proof of Theorems 7.11 and 7.12 and Corollary 7.1 256
References 259

7.1 Introduction

Independence is a fundamental concept in statistics, and there is much literature on measuring dependence and constructing tests of independence, as surveyed in Chapter 3. In this chapter, we present three types of tests using the theory of the local Gaussian correlation. The first test is a test for independence between independent and identically distributed (iid) pairs of variables introduced by Berentsen and Tjøstheim (2014). The second is a test for serial independence for a time series, and in this chapter, we also define the local Gaussian autocorrelation. This test was introduced by Lacal

https://doi.org/10.1016/B978-0-12-815861-6.00014-6

and Tjøstheim (2017). Finally, the third test is for independence between two time series, and we also define the local Gaussian cross-correlation. The last test was introduced by Lacal and Tjøstheim (2019).

All tests will be explained in detail, and their use will be illustrated through several examples. Theoretical results concerning their behavior will be presented, and a few selected accompanying proofs are given at the end of the chapter. Remaining proofs can be found in the above cited three references. However, the asymptotic theory for the test statistics examined in this chapter is not accurate unless the number of observations is exceedingly large, and thus we resort to using bootstrap procedures in practice and in particular block bootstrap for the time series case. The validity of the bootstrap procedures is demonstrated in the supplementary material of Lacal and Tjøstheim (2017) and Lacal and Tjøstheim (2019).

In the development of these tests, we will to a large degree work with variables on their original scales, but in many cases, transforming the variables to standard Gaussians, as described in Chapter 4.7, can be an advantage. As will become clear, all asymptotic results hold for the transformed variables as well, and some results will also be stated for that case.

As was already mentioned several times in this book, the traditional Pearson correlation in many cases fails to capture nonlinear dependence structures in bivariate data. Thus, intuitively, using the local Gaussian correlation as a basis for independence testing should lead to improved tests. Other scalar measures capable of capturing nonlinear dependence exist, and we will compare to the dcov test of Chapter 3.4.3. Similarly, the most used measure for serial dependence in a time series (or between time series) is the autocorrelation function (or cross-correlation function). However, again, this measure fails to capture the dependence in several nonlinear time series models, for instance, the GARCH-model (see, e.g., Chapter 2.4), and a local Gaussian auto- (or cross-)correlation-based test is expected to perform better.

7.2 Testing of independence in iid pairs of variables using local correlation functionals

Let X_1 and X_2 be stochastic variables with distribution functions F_1 and F_2 and joint distribution F, and let $\mathbf{X} = (X_1, X_2)$. We denote the observed values $(X_{1i}, X_{2i}), i = 1, ..., n$. In the first part of this section, we focus on testing the hypothesis

$$H_0 : X_1, X_2 \quad \text{independent} \quad \text{vs} \quad H_1 : X_1, X_2 \quad \text{not independent}. \tag{7.1}$$

To construct a global measure of dependence based on the local Gaussian correlation $\rho(\boldsymbol{x})$, it must in some way be aggregated on $\mathbb{R}^2$. When doing this, we should be aware that when the dependence structure of the data is non-linear, local Gaussian correlation can have different signs in different points. To avoid that the local correlation in different points cancels out, we follow earlier constructions of functionals for measuring dependence (see, e.g., Delicado and Smrekar, 2009) and look at the expectation of $\rho^2(\boldsymbol{X})$. Let τ denote the resulting measure of dependence:

$$\tau = \left(\mathrm{E}\rho^2(\boldsymbol{X})\right)^{1/2} = \left(\int \rho^2(\boldsymbol{x})\mathrm{d}F(\boldsymbol{x})\right)^{1/2}, \tag{7.2}$$

where F is the joint distribution function of $\boldsymbol{X}$. Clearly, this measure cannot discriminate between positive and negative dependence, but it will be refined later.

For estimating τ, we replace $\rho(\boldsymbol{x})$ by the local likelihood estimate $\widehat{\rho}_{\boldsymbol{b}}(\boldsymbol{x})$, obtained by maximizing the local log likelihood in (4.8) with respect to $\rho_{\boldsymbol{b}}$. Then the integral is approximated by taking the empirical average of $\widehat{\rho}_{\boldsymbol{b}}(X_i)$ $i = 1, \ldots, n$, that is, by replacing $\mathrm{d}F(\boldsymbol{x})$ with $\mathrm{d}F_n(\boldsymbol{x})$, where F_n is the joint empirical distribution function of the sample. Thus the sample version of τ is defined by

$$\tau_{n,\boldsymbol{b}} = \left(\int \widehat{\rho}_{\boldsymbol{b}}^2(\boldsymbol{x})\mathrm{d}F_n(\boldsymbol{x})\right)^{1/2}, \tag{7.3}$$

where

$$F_n(\boldsymbol{x}) = F_n(x_1, x_2) = n^{-1}\sum_{i=1}^{n} I(X_{1i} \leq x_1, X_{2i} \leq x_2) \tag{7.4}$$

with I denoting the indicator function. In practice, to screen outliers outside some subset S of $\mathbb{R}^2$, we can use the following version of $\tau_{n,\boldsymbol{b}}$, where I_S is the indicator function of the set S:

$$\tau_{n,\boldsymbol{b}}(S) = \left(\int \widehat{\rho}_b^2(\boldsymbol{x})I_S(\boldsymbol{x})\mathrm{d}F_n(\boldsymbol{x})\right)^{1/2}.$$

A generalized version of (7.2) for a functional T is obtained by defining

$$T \stackrel{\text{def}}{=} \int_S h(\rho(\boldsymbol{x}))\mathrm{d}F(\boldsymbol{x}), \tag{7.5}$$

where h may be an arbitrary function. This will give an opportunity to distinguish between positive and negative dependence on the set S. The test statistic is

$$T_{n,\boldsymbol{b}} \stackrel{\text{def}}{=} \int_S h(\widehat{\rho}_{\boldsymbol{b}}(\boldsymbol{x}))\mathrm{d}F_n(\boldsymbol{x}) \tag{7.6}$$

with the sample counterparts defined as before.

In the following, we will give some asymptotic properties of the test statistic $T_{n,\boldsymbol{b}}$, partly based on the limit theory of Chapter 4.4, and we will impose some conditions on the function h and other regularity conditions. However, since the asymptotic theory for the functional $T_{n,b}$ is not very accurate unless n is very large, in practice, one use the bootstrap or permutations for the actual use of the test. In Section 7.2.1, we will explain this in detail and give some practical examples of the use of the test, in particular, related to the choice of the region S. We will also return with suggestions on how to choose the bandwidths.

Note that we may also use the local normalized correlation function $\rho_{\boldsymbol{Z}}(\boldsymbol{z})$ and its estimated counterpart, as explained in Chapter 4.7, in the test functional $T_{n,\boldsymbol{b}}$. In the examples, we will resort the test statistic on both the original and transformed scale. The asymptotic theory will be stated in terms of the original scale. However, the results will also hold for the transformed scale, and references will be provided.

We focus our attention on the test statistic $T_{n,\boldsymbol{b}}$ estimating the functional T or in the case of fixed $\boldsymbol{b}$, estimating $T_{\boldsymbol{b}} \stackrel{\text{def}}{=} \int_S h(\rho_{\boldsymbol{b}}(\boldsymbol{x}))\mathrm{d}F(\boldsymbol{x})$. Here S is taken to be a compact subset of $\mathbb{R}^2$. A much more general situation as $\boldsymbol{b} \to \boldsymbol{0}$ and with time series $\{X_1(t)\}$ and $\{X_2(t)\}$ is considered in Section 7.3.

The first theorem considers the consistency of the test statistic. We will further assume that the density f of $\boldsymbol{X}$ exists.

Theorem 7.1. *Assume that the conditions of Theorem 4.1 hold and that:*

(i) *h is continuous differentiable with* $\sup_{\boldsymbol{x}\in S} \left|h'(\rho(\boldsymbol{x}))\right| \le C$ *for some constant* C.

(ii) *The density f is bounded on S.*

Then

$$T_{n,\boldsymbol{b}} \xrightarrow{a.s.} T.$$

Assumption (i) is fulfilled when $h(x) = x^2$ and $h(x) = x$, which is the case for the functionals used in the examples to follow. Assumption (ii) simply ensures that T is finite. In many cases, when the tails of the density

f are not too heavy, S can be chosen so that $\int_S h(\rho(\boldsymbol{x}))\mathrm{d}F(\boldsymbol{x})$ is arbitrarily close to $\int h(\rho(\boldsymbol{x}))\mathrm{d}F(\boldsymbol{x})$.

The asymptotic distribution of $T_{n,\boldsymbol{b}}$ is rather more difficult to obtain and generally depends on the distribution of $\boldsymbol{X}$ in a non-trivial way. Following Hjort and Jones (1996) and Berentsen and Tjøstheim (2014), in this subsection, we will only state the asymptotic distribution for fixed $\boldsymbol{b}$. In Sections 7.3 and 7.4, we will present extensions to an n-dependent $\boldsymbol{b} = \boldsymbol{b}_n$ in a more general setting.

Theorem 7.2. *Let $(X_{1i}, X_{2i}), \ldots, (X_{1n}, X_{2n})$ be iid random variables with distribution function F and density f. Assume that the conditions of Theorem 4.1 hold and that*

(i) *h has continuous second order derivatives,*
(ii) *the density f is bounded on S, and*
(iii) *the kernel K is symmetric.*

Then

$$n^{1/2}\left(T_{n,\boldsymbol{b}} - T_{\boldsymbol{b}}\right) \xrightarrow{d} N\left(0, \int A_{\boldsymbol{b}}^2(\boldsymbol{x})dF(\boldsymbol{x}) - \int\int A_{\boldsymbol{b}}(\boldsymbol{x})A_{\boldsymbol{b}}(\boldsymbol{y})dF(\boldsymbol{x})dF(\boldsymbol{y})\right), \tag{7.7}$$

where

$$A_{\boldsymbol{b}}(\boldsymbol{x}) = \int_S h'(\rho_{\boldsymbol{b}}(\boldsymbol{v}))\sum_{j=1}^{5} d_{\boldsymbol{b}}^j(\boldsymbol{v})K_{\boldsymbol{b}}(\boldsymbol{x}-\boldsymbol{v})u_j(\boldsymbol{x}, \rho_{\boldsymbol{b}}(\boldsymbol{v}))dF(\boldsymbol{v}) + h\left(\rho_{\boldsymbol{b}}(\boldsymbol{x})\right)I_S(\boldsymbol{x}). \tag{7.8}$$

Here $d_{\boldsymbol{b}}^j(\boldsymbol{x})$, $j = 1, \ldots, 5$, are the elements in the fifth row of $\boldsymbol{J}_{\boldsymbol{b}}^{-1}$ with $\boldsymbol{J}_{\boldsymbol{b}}$ defined by (4.13)*, and $u_j(\boldsymbol{x}, \theta(\boldsymbol{x}))$ is defined in* (4.9)*. Further, it is assumed that*

$$\int A_{\boldsymbol{b}}^2(\boldsymbol{x})dF(\boldsymbol{x}) - \int\int A_{\boldsymbol{b}}(\boldsymbol{x})A_{\boldsymbol{b}}(\boldsymbol{y})dF(\boldsymbol{x})dF(\boldsymbol{y}) \neq 0.$$

Here $K_{\boldsymbol{b}}$ is the kernel function defined in Chapter 2.5. The proofs of these theorems can be found in Berentsen and Tjøstheim (2014).

7.2.1 Bootstrap test of independence

It is well known that the asymptotic theory for functionals of type $T_{n,\boldsymbol{b}}$, as given in Theorem 7.2, is not accurate (see, e.g., Teräsvirta et al. (2010), Section 7.2.5) unless n is exceedingly large, and in practice, we resort to the bootstrap or to permutations. We will now consider the bootstrap; see Berentsen and Tjøstheim (2014). Let $T_{n,\boldsymbol{b}}$ be a statistic of the type

$\int_S h(\widehat{\rho}_{\boldsymbol{b}}(\boldsymbol{x}))\mathrm{d}F_n(\boldsymbol{x})$ and suppose we want to test the hypothesis

$$H_0 : X_1, X_2 \quad \text{independent} \quad \text{vs} \quad H_1 : X_1, X_2 \quad \text{not independent.} \tag{7.9}$$

Instead of relying on the asymptotic distribution of $T_{n,\boldsymbol{b}}$, we use a bootstrap test assuming that the pairs (X_{1i}, X_{2i}), $i = 1, ..., n$, are iid. The main idea is to compare the observed statistic $t_{n,\boldsymbol{b}}$ to R independent values of $T_{n,\boldsymbol{b}}$ computed from samples simulated under the null hypothesis. Let $F_{0,n}$ be the resampling distribution defined by

$$F_{0,n}(x_1, x_2) = F_{1,n}(x_1)F_{2,n}(x_2), \quad \text{where} \quad F_{j,n}(x_j) = \frac{1}{n}\sum_{i=1}^{n} I(X_{ji} \leq x_j). \tag{7.10}$$

Clearly, a pair of variables (X_1, X_2) sampled from $F_{0,n}$ satisfies H_0. Let $T^*_{n,\boldsymbol{b}}$ denote the test statistic calculated from a sample of size n simulated from $F_{0,n}$. Then (assuming large values of $T_{n,\boldsymbol{b}}$ is evidence against H_0) the P-value is given by

$$p_{\text{boot}} = P^*(T^*_{n,\boldsymbol{b}} \geq T_{n,\boldsymbol{b}} | F_{0,n}),$$

which we approximate by

$$p_{n,\text{boot}} = \frac{1 + \sum_r I(t^*_r \geq t_{n,\boldsymbol{b}})}{R+1}, \tag{7.11}$$

where $t^*_1, \ldots, t^*_R$ are the result from R bootstrap samples (i.e., realizations of $T^*_{n,\boldsymbol{b}}$).

The validity of the bootstrap was shown for the time series case by Lacal and Tjøstheim (2017) (see also Section 7.3) and naturally carries over to the present situation of independent and identically distributed variables.

The choice of bandwidth $\boldsymbol{b} = (b_1, b_2)$ is of course important in the testing procedures, and we have used the cross-validation bandwidth selector introduced in Chapter 4.8.2.

Berentsen and Tjøstheim (2014) performed an extensive simulation study, comparing the local Gaussian correlation-based independence test with other tests, in particular, the one based on distance covariance (see Chapter 3.4.3) but also the lag 1 version of the Ljung–Box statistic and the lag 1 version of the so-called BDS statistic. The power of the LGC-based test is comparable to alternative tests. Further, an advantage of using the local Gaussian correlation as a basis for independence testing is that if we are willing to assume symmetry patterns under the alternative hypothesis, then this can be exploited to increase the power, as shown by Berentsen and Tjøstheim (2014). This can also be used to focus the test on particular regions. Such enhancement of power can also work under much cruder symmetry patterns. For financial data, for instance, there is usually positive (local) correlation under both increasing (first quadrant) and decreasing returns (third quadrant), as shown in several examples in Chapter 6. For reflection symmetry, there is a pattern of positive and negative values of $\rho(\boldsymbol{x})$ such that typically $\rho(\boldsymbol{x})$ is positive in the interiors of the first and third quadrants and negative in the interiors of the second and fourth quadrants. A GARCH density is an example of the latter. In the next subsections, we will look at several examples illustrating these remarks.

7.2.2 Local independence testing

Formally, to test the hypothesis H_0 that X_1 and X_2 are independent, we would have to check that $\rho(\boldsymbol{x}) = 0$ for all $\boldsymbol{x} \in \mathbb{R}^2$. In practice, however, we can only investigate this property in a finite set of points. One possibility is estimating $\rho(\boldsymbol{x})$ at each observation (X_{1i}, X_{2i}), $i = 1, ..., n$. Alternatively, the selection of these points can be done using the methodology of Jones and Koch (2003). First, a regular grid is placed across the area of interest; we typically can use a 15×15 grid, but this may be increased or decreased depending on the data at hand. Then the regular grid can be screened by selecting the grid points $\boldsymbol{x}_1, \ldots, \boldsymbol{x}_k$ satisfying $\hat{f}(\boldsymbol{x}_j) \geq C$ for some constant C and a density estimator $\hat{f}$.

Next, consider the issue of testing the hypothesis that $\rho(\boldsymbol{x}_j) = 0$ at a grid point $\boldsymbol{x}_j$ against the alternative hypothesis that the variables X_1 and X_2 are dependent and $\rho(\boldsymbol{x}_j) \neq 0$. For the given data, we first obtain estimates $\widehat{\rho}_{\boldsymbol{b}}(\boldsymbol{x}_j)$ using the local likelihood method described in Chapter 4. Assuming that the pairs (X_{1i}, X_{2i}), $i = 1, \ldots, n$, are iid, we construct the distribution of $\widehat{\rho}_{\boldsymbol{b}}(\boldsymbol{x}_j)$ under the null hypothesis of independence of X_1 and X_2 by a bootstrap procedure similar to that described in the previous section. Then R bootstrap realization of size n is generated by sampling from $F_{0,n}$ given by (7.10). By property (iv) in Chapter 4.5 independence implies $\rho(\boldsymbol{x}_j) = 0$. Let $\widehat{\rho}_{\boldsymbol{b}}^{*,k}(\boldsymbol{x}_j)$ denote the local correlation estimated at $\boldsymbol{x}_j$ based on bootstrap realization number k. For a given significance level α, we reject the hypothesis that $\rho(\boldsymbol{x}_j) = 0$ if $\widehat{\rho}_{\boldsymbol{b}}(\boldsymbol{x}_j)$ is respectively smaller or larger than the $(\alpha/2)$ or $(1 - \alpha/2)$ quantile of $\widehat{\rho}_{\boldsymbol{b}}^{*,1}(\boldsymbol{x}_j), \ldots, \widehat{\rho}_{\boldsymbol{b}}^{*,R}(\boldsymbol{x}_j)$. Exactly the same bootstrap samples can be used to evaluate the local correlation in the other grid points, drastically reducing the computational cost. In practice, we typically can use $R = 1000$ bootstrap realizations.

One possible way to present such test results is adopting the idea used by Jones and Koch (2003) to construct so-called "dependence maps": If $\widehat{\rho}_b(\boldsymbol{x}_j)$ is significantly positive, $\boldsymbol{x}_j$ is assigned the color magenta; if significantly negative, the color cyan; if the null hypothesis is not rejected, the color white (see Berentsen and Tjøstheim (2014), Section 5 for an example). As pointed out by Jones and Koch (2003), a dependence map is a compromise between the very fine details given by the local measure of dependence itself and a scalar measure of dependence. It gives an overview of regions with significant positive or negative dependence. However, before investigating such details, we can perform a (perhaps less costly) global test of independence with power against non-linear alternatives.

7.2.3 Example: Bivariate t-distribution

Let (X_1', X_2') be Gaussian with standard normal marginals, and let V have a χ_ν^2 distribution independent of (X_1', X_2'). Then

$$(X_1, X_2) = (X_1'\sqrt{\nu/V}, X_2'\sqrt{\nu/V}) \tag{7.12}$$

has a bivariate t-distribution with ν degrees of freedom. When X_1' and X_2' are independent, the two variables X_1 and X_2 are uncorrelated but not independent; There is a positive dependence in the first and third quadrants and a negative dependence in the second and fourth. A plot of the estimated local Gaussian correlation, displaying this dependence structure, can be found in Chapter 4, Fig. 4.1.

In this example, we illustrate how the local Gaussian correlation can be used to construct test statistics with increased power against more specific alternative hypotheses to H_0 than just "dependence". Toward defining the alternative hypotheses, let

$$\begin{aligned}
S_1 &= [-5, 5]^2, \\
S_2 &= [1, 5]^2, \\
S_3 &= [1, 5]^2 \cup [-5, -1]^2, \\
S_4 &= [1, 5] \times [-5, -1] \cup [-5, -1] \times [1, 5].
\end{aligned}$$

Then we know that there is both positive and negative dependence in S_1, positive dependence in S_2 and S_3, and negative dependence in S_4. Consider the following hypothesis test of independence:

$$H_0 : X_1, X_2 \text{ independent} \quad \text{vs} \quad H_1, H_2, H_3, H_4,$$

where the alternative hypotheses are specified as

$$
\begin{aligned}
H_1 &: T_1 = \tau(S_1) = \left(\int \rho^2(\boldsymbol{x}) I_{S_1}(\boldsymbol{x}) \mathrm{d}F(\boldsymbol{x})\right)^{1/2} > 0 \text{ (dependence in } S_1\text{)},\\
H_2 &: T_2 = \int \rho(\boldsymbol{x}) I_{S_2}(\boldsymbol{x}) \mathrm{d}F(\boldsymbol{x}) > 0 \text{ (pos. dependence in } S_2\text{)},\\
H_3 &: T_3 = \int \rho(\boldsymbol{x}) I_{S_3}(\boldsymbol{x}) \mathrm{d}F(\boldsymbol{x}) > 0 \text{ (pos. dependence in } S_3\text{)},\\
H_4 &: T_4 = T_3 - \int \rho(\boldsymbol{x}) I_{S_4}(\boldsymbol{x}) \mathrm{d}F(\boldsymbol{x}) > 0\\
&\qquad \text{(pos. dependence in } S_3 \text{ and neg. dependence in } S_4\text{)}.
\end{aligned}
$$

An obvious objection to these choices of regions and corresponding alternative hypotheses is that we exploit the properties of the local Gaussian correlation for the t-distribution with $\rho = 0$. However, recall from Chapter 4.5.4 that if we would like to assume certain symmetry properties for the bivariate density $f(\boldsymbol{x})$, then there is a corresponding hierarchy of symmetry structures for the accompanying local correlation $\rho(\boldsymbol{x})$, and this can be exploited in choosing an alternative hypothesis. Moreover, for economic data, say, we often have an assumption about increasing (local) dependence as X_1 and X_2 decrease (market going down) or increase, in which case it is reasonable to use H_3 to test such assumptions. For other types of variables, there may be other assumptions we would want to test. For the test functional T, the corresponding test statistics are obtained by replacing $\rho(\boldsymbol{x})$ and $F(\boldsymbol{x})$ with $\widehat{\rho}_{\boldsymbol{b}}(\boldsymbol{x})$ and $F_n(\boldsymbol{x})$, respectively. Moreover, in the simulation example below, $\widehat{\rho}_{\boldsymbol{b}}(\boldsymbol{x})$ is estimated at each of the observations contained in the specified region.

Berentsen and Tjøstheim (2014) performed a simulation experiment for examining this setup. That experiment shows that the size of the tests corresponds reasonably well to all the significance levels examined (1%, 5%, and 10%) and for all sample sizes ($n = 250, 500, 750, 1000$); see Table 1 in their paper. Further, the empirical power of the proposed tests against zero correlated but dependent t(4)-distributed variables is reported in Table 7.1. The dcov test, here denoted by BDC (Brownian distance covariance) (see Chapter 3.4.3), is used as a benchmark. The study shows that the test based on T_1 is inferior to the BDC test. On the other hand, the power of the test based on T_2 is comparable to that of BDC, whereas the tests based on T_3 and T_4 are more powerful than BDC, confirming that power increase is possible if we want to use a more specific alternative hypothesis. Possibly similar power increases could be obtained for the BDC test, but it would require a localized version and analysis of positive and negative dependence for that measure. Also, note that the power of all the tests based on local Gaussian correlation increases with sample size.

Table 7.1 Power study when X_1 and X_2 are uncorrelated bivariate $t(4)$-distributed.

Test statistic	Level %	$n = 250$	$n = 500$	$n = 750$	$n = 1000$
T_1	1	4.2	12.6	15.8	28.4
	5	19.4	39.2	47.0	65.2
	10	35.2	59.2	67.4	81.4
T_2	1	16.8	40.0	54.6	70.6
	5	37.4	59.6	74.6	87.8
	10	47.6	71.0	83.8	92.0
T_3	1	30.6	67.8	82.2	93.6
	5	57.2	83.2	92.6	98.0
	10	68.0	90.2	96.4	98.6
T_4	1	65.4	93.6	99.2	100.0
	5	87.0	98.4	100.0	100.0
	10	89.8	99.6	100.0	100.0
BDC	1	11.2	24.4	38.6	57.8
	5	34.4	64.2	79.4	92.4
	10	50.6	82.2	91.6	98.4

7.2.4 Example: Aircraft data

The aircraft data of Bowman and Azzalini (1997) contain six variables describing aircrafts built between 1914 and 1984. Similarly to Bowman and Azzalini (1997), Székely and Rizzo (2009), and Jones and Koch (2003), consider the logged values of wing span (in meters) and maximum speed (in km/h) for aircrafts built in the last part of this period (1956–1984). A scatter plot of the $n = 230$ data points is displayed in Fig. 7.1. These variables are interesting from an independence-testing point of view: the (global) correlation between the variables is 0.0168, and the corresponding Pearson correlation test is not significant (p-value $= 0.8001$). Nevertheless, a closer look at the scatter plot does indicate a non-linear dependence structure.

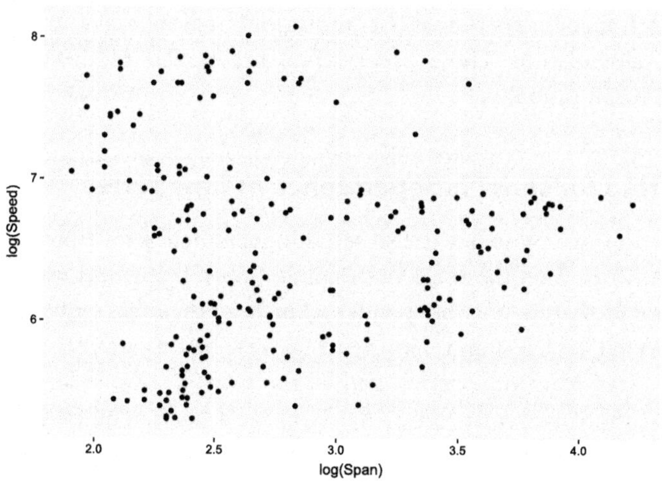

Figure 7.1 Savotti aircraft data.

The independence test described above, with the cross-validated bandwidth selector and the area S consisting of all observations, was significant (p-value ≈ 0). The estimated $\widehat{\rho}_b(\boldsymbol{x})$ is given in Fig. 7.2.

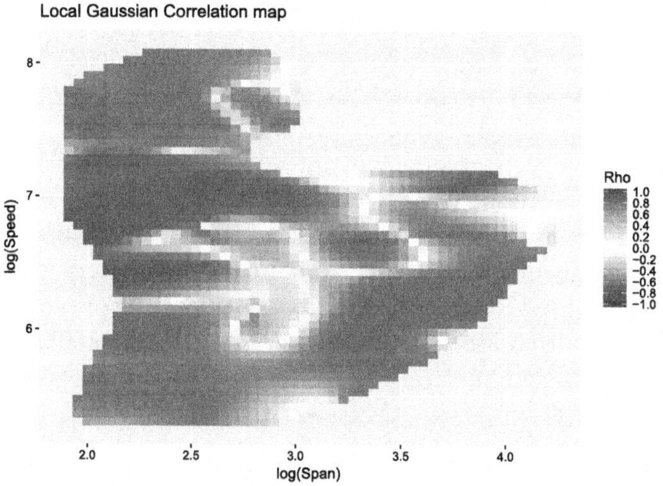

Figure 7.2 Local Gaussian correlation for the Savotti aircraft data.

Further, inspecting Fig. 7.2, we see that (log) speed increase with (log) span for aircrafts with small to large spans and small to moderate speeds, whereas the relationship is opposite for aircrafts with small spans and moderate to high speeds. There is also a "transition" region, where the variables behave independently. These observations are similar to those made by Jones and Koch (2003).

7.3 Testing for serial independence in time series

In this section, we present a test of serial independence for univariate time series that is based on the local Gaussian autocorrelation and uses a similar test statistic as the test for independence in the previous section. This test was developed by Lacal and Tjøstheim (2017). In this section, let $\{X_t\}$ be an ergodic stationary time series, and let the pair (X_1, X_2) described in the previous sections be replaced by (X_t, X_{t-k}) for a lag k. The pair (X_t, X_{t-k}) is assumed to have a bivariate density $f^{(k)}$ for all k.

For a bandwidth $\boldsymbol{b}$, we can then define a local parameter $\boldsymbol{\theta}_{\boldsymbol{b},k}(\boldsymbol{x}) = \boldsymbol{\theta}_{\boldsymbol{b}}(\boldsymbol{x}) = (\mu_{\boldsymbol{b},1}(\boldsymbol{x}), \mu_{\boldsymbol{b},2}(\boldsymbol{x}), \sigma^2_{\boldsymbol{b},1}(\boldsymbol{x}), \sigma^2_{\boldsymbol{b},2}(\boldsymbol{x}), \rho_{\boldsymbol{b},k}(\boldsymbol{x}))$, where $\boldsymbol{x} = (x_1, x_2)$, and in particular we can define a local Gaussian autocorrelation function at lag k as $\rho_{\boldsymbol{b},k}(\boldsymbol{x})$, the fifth element of the parameter vector $\boldsymbol{\theta}_{\boldsymbol{b},k}(\boldsymbol{x})$; see also Chapter 4.3. As in Tjøstheim and Hufthammer (2013), we can let $\boldsymbol{b} \to \boldsymbol{0}$ to obtain a bandwidth-independent quantity $\rho_k(\boldsymbol{x})$, which reduces to the ordinary global autocorrelation ρ_k in the Gaussian case. Then $\rho_k(\boldsymbol{x})$ for a fixed k is an appropriate local, and in general nonlinear, dependence measure between X_t and X_{t-k}. It should be noted that in contradistinction to the ordinary autocorrelation, $\rho_k(\boldsymbol{x})$ may be not positive definite. Nevertheless, it has a number of properties that are useful for our purposes.

In fact, we may be even more interested in the normalized local autocorrelation function. This is obtained by transforming each X_t to $Z_t = \Phi^{-1}(F(X_t))$, where F is the marginal cumulative distribution function of X_t, and Φ is the cumulative distribution function of the standard normal. The normalized local Gaussian autocorrelation $\rho'_k(\boldsymbol{z})$ is now defined as the local autocorrelation $\rho'_k(\boldsymbol{z})$ for the pair (Z_t, Z_{t-k}), where $\boldsymbol{z} = (z_1, z_2)$. Again, for a Gaussian time series $\{X_t\}$, $\rho'_k(\boldsymbol{z}) \equiv \rho_k(\boldsymbol{x}) \equiv \rho_k$, the global autocorrelation at lag k.

Ideally, we are interested in testing the null hypothesis H_0 that $\{X_t\}$ consists of independent and identically distributed (iid) random variables against the alternative hypothesis H_1 that $\{X_t\}$ is not iid. Of course, this is not feasible in practice since it would imply that we have to look at all joint distribution functions of $\{X_{t_1}, \ldots, X_{t_m}, t_1 < \cdots < t_m, m \text{ an integer}\}$. Instead, in our test functional, we will test for pairwise independence in the pair $\{X_t, X_{t-k}\}$, where, again, in principle, k could be taken to be an arbitrary lag, but where for illustration purposes, we have mainly settled for $k = 1, \ldots, 4$ in our examples to follow. We refer to Fig. 8.4 in Chapter 8 for a time series example where $k = 1, \ldots, 200$.

We can, in fact, construct a statistic composed of sums of local autocorrelations of various lags k, like it is done for the Box–Ljung statistic for the ordinary autocorrelation. However, the emphasis in this section is on studying the pairwise dependence and demonstrating that the use of local autocorrelations can lead to dramatic increase of power in tests of independence compared to the earlier linear and nonlinear dependence measures. However, Lacal and Tjøstheim (2019) contains examples of such sums of local correlations.

Then the main idea is defining a global measure of dependence as a function of the local parameters, similarly to the test for independence in the last section, such as the test statistic

$$T_{n,\boldsymbol{b}} = \int_S h\left(\widehat{\theta}_{n,\boldsymbol{b}}(\boldsymbol{x})\right) \mathrm{d}F_n^{(k)}(\boldsymbol{x}), \tag{7.13}$$

where $F_n^{(k)}$ is the empirical distribution function defined as

$$F_n^{(k)}(\boldsymbol{x}) = \frac{1}{n-k} \sum_{t=k+1}^{n} I\left(X_t \leq x_1,\ X_{t-k} \leq x_2\right), \quad \boldsymbol{x} = (x_1, x_2) \in \mathbb{R}^2,\ k \geq 1.$$

For fixed $\boldsymbol{b}$, it estimates the functional

$$T_{\boldsymbol{b}} = \int_S h\left(\boldsymbol{\theta}_{\boldsymbol{b}}(\boldsymbol{x})\right) \mathrm{d}F^{(k)}(\boldsymbol{x}), \tag{7.14}$$

where $F^{(k)}$ is the cumulative distribution function of (X_t, X_{t-k}), and $F_n^{(k)}$ can be used as an estimator. We can let h take on specific functional forms to test against specified types of dependence, as seen for the independence test in the last section. The set S is used to put a restriction on the data as before. Clearly, the functional in (7.13) may be ill-defined in practice without such a restriction because of sparsity of data close to the boundary of the data set. A typical choice of the set S for a zero-mean process $\{X_t\}$ could be $S = \left\{(x_1, x_2) \in \mathbb{R}^2 : x_i \leq c \cdot \mathrm{sd}(X_t)\right\}$ for some constant c, where $\mathrm{sd}(X_t)$ is the standard deviation of X_t, which has to be estimated in practice. The set S puts a restriction on our analysis in that we can only test for independence inside the set S, but, in practice, such a restriction should be imposed on any nonparametric dependence measure and test. In the asymptotic theory,

S will just be taken to be a compact set. This again is a common assumption in the literature on asymptotic theory of nonparametric test functionals.

Next, we will state the asymptotic normality of the test statistic $T_{n,\boldsymbol{b}}$ for fixed $\boldsymbol{b}$ under some regularity conditions: first, under the assumption that $\{X_t\}$ is not iid (Theorem 7.3), and then considering the case in which $\{X_t\}$ is iid as a particular case (Theorem 7.4). Note that consistency is established in Theorem 7.5, part **A**, and Theorem 7.6, part **A**. The proofs of Theorems 7.3 and 7.4 are given by Lacal and Tjøstheim (2017). Note also that the proofs of these theorems are similar to those of Theorems 7.11 and 7.12 (Section 7.5). Although a density function $f^{(k)}$ is assumed to exist, we phrase our results in terms of the cumulative distribution function $F^{(k)}$, because this makes it notationally simpler when the empirical distribution function is introduced in the bootstrap version of the tests.

A strictly stationary series of stochastic variables $\{X_t\}$, $t = 1, 2, \ldots$, is said to be α-mixing if $\alpha(m) \to 0$, where

$$\alpha(m) = \sup_{A \in \mathcal{F}_{-\infty}^{0}, B \in \mathcal{F}_{m}^{\infty}} |P(A)P(B) - P(A \cap B)|, \tag{7.15}$$

and where $\mathcal{F}_i^j$ is the σ-algebra generated in $\{X_t, i \le t \le j\}$; see Fan and Yao (2003, p. 68) for details.

Theorem 7.3. *Let $\{X_t\}$ be a univariate time series such that (X_t, X_{t-k}) has a bivariate density $f^{(k)}$ having support on all of $\mathbb{R}^2$, with $k \ge 1$. Assume that:*

- **(i)** *$\{X_t\}$ is stationary and α-mixing with $\alpha_n = O(\alpha^n)$, $\alpha \in (0, 1)$, and such that $E(X_t^{2+\delta}) < \infty$ for some $\delta > 0$;*
- **(ii)** *the kernel K is symmetric;*
- **(iii)** *$f^{(k)}$ is bounded on S, where S is defined in (7.13);*
- **(iv)** *h has continuous second-order derivatives.*

Then, as $n \to \infty$ with $\boldsymbol{b}$ fixed,

$$\sqrt{n}\left[C_{k,n}(A_{\boldsymbol{b}})\right]^{-\frac{1}{2}} \left(T_{n,\boldsymbol{b}} - T_{\boldsymbol{b}}\right) \xrightarrow{d} \mathcal{N}(0, 1),$$

where, for $\boldsymbol{x} = (x_1, x_2) \in \mathbb{R}^2$ and $\boldsymbol{v} = (v_1, v_2) \in \mathbb{R}^2$,

$$\begin{aligned} C_{k,n}(A_{\boldsymbol{b}}) = &\int A_{\boldsymbol{b}}^2(\boldsymbol{x}) dF^{(k)}(\boldsymbol{x}) - \int A_{\boldsymbol{b}}(\boldsymbol{x}) A_{\boldsymbol{b}}(\boldsymbol{v}) dF^{(k)}(\boldsymbol{x}) dF^{(k)}(\boldsymbol{v}) \\ &+ \int A_{\boldsymbol{b}}(\boldsymbol{x}) A_{\boldsymbol{b}}(\boldsymbol{v}) \sum_{j=1}^{n} \frac{n-j}{n} \left[dF^{(k,j)}(\boldsymbol{x}, \boldsymbol{v}) - dF^{(k)}(\boldsymbol{x}) dF^{(k)}(\boldsymbol{v}) \right] \end{aligned}$$

$$+\int A_b(\boldsymbol{x})A_b(\boldsymbol{v})\sum_{j=1}^{n}\frac{n-j}{n}\left[dF^{(k,-j)}(\boldsymbol{x},\boldsymbol{v})-dF^{(k)}(\boldsymbol{x})dF^{(k)}(\boldsymbol{v})\right],$$

where the sum converges as $n\to\infty$, and where (T is the transpose)

$$A_b(\boldsymbol{x})=\int_S \nabla h\left(\theta_b(\boldsymbol{v})\right)^T \boldsymbol{J}_b^{-1}(\boldsymbol{v})K_b\left(\boldsymbol{x}-\boldsymbol{v}\right)u\left(\boldsymbol{x},\theta_b(\boldsymbol{v})\right)dF^{(k)}(\boldsymbol{v})+h\left(\theta_b(\boldsymbol{x})\right)I_S(\boldsymbol{x}),$$

$$\boldsymbol{J}_b(\boldsymbol{x})=\int K_b\left(\boldsymbol{v}-\boldsymbol{x}\right)\boldsymbol{u}\left(\boldsymbol{v},\theta_b(\boldsymbol{x})\right)\boldsymbol{u}\left(\boldsymbol{v},\theta_b(\boldsymbol{x})\right)^T\psi\left(\boldsymbol{v},\theta_b(\boldsymbol{x})\right)d\boldsymbol{v} \qquad (7.16)$$
$$-\int K_b\left(\boldsymbol{v}-\boldsymbol{x}\right)\nabla\boldsymbol{u}\left(\boldsymbol{v},\theta_b(\boldsymbol{x})\right)\left[f(\boldsymbol{v})-\psi\left(\boldsymbol{v},\theta_b(\boldsymbol{x})\right)\right]d\boldsymbol{v}$$

with $\boldsymbol{u}(\boldsymbol{x},\boldsymbol{\theta})=\nabla\log(\psi(\boldsymbol{x},\boldsymbol{\theta}))$, ∇ the gradient vector with respect to $\boldsymbol{\theta}$, and $F^{(k,t-s)}$ the distribution function of $(X_t,X_{t-k},X_s,X_{s-k})$. Further, it is assumed that $C_{k,n}(A_b)\neq 0$ and that $|A_b|_p=(E(|A_b|^p))^{\frac{1}{p}}<\infty$ for some $p>1$.

The following theorem is similar to Theorem 7.2, in that it considers the situation under H_0 where $\{X_t\}$ consists of independent identically distributed variables. However, unlike the iid setting, in the present time series case, consecutive pairs (X_{t+1},X_t) and (X_t,X_{t-1}) are dependent.

Theorem 7.4. *Let $\{X_t\}$ be a univariate time series with density f having support on all of $\mathbb{R}$. Assume that:*

(i) *$\{X_t\}$ consists of iid variables;*
(ii) *the kernel K is symmetric.*
(iii) *f is bounded on S, where S is defined in (7.13);*
(iv) *h has continuous second-order derivatives.*

Then letting F be the cumulative distribution function of f

$$\sqrt{n}\left(T_{n,b}-T_b\right)\xrightarrow{d}\mathcal{N}\left(0,C_k\left(A_b\right)\right)$$

for $k\geq 1$, where, for $\boldsymbol{x}=(x_1,x_2)$ and $\boldsymbol{v}=(v_1,v_2)$,

$$C_k\left(A_b\right)=\int A_b^2(\boldsymbol{x})dF(x_1)dF(x_2)$$
$$-3\int A_b(\boldsymbol{x})A_b(\boldsymbol{v})dF(x_1)dF(x_2)dF(v_1)dF(v_2)$$
$$+2\int A_b\left((y_1,y_2)\right)A_b\left((z,y_1)\right)dF(y_1)dF(y_2)dF(z),$$
$$x_1,x_2,v_1,v_2,y_1,y_2,z\in\mathbb{R}.$$

Further, it is assumed that $C_k(A_b)\neq 0$ and that $A_b(\boldsymbol{x})$ is integrable.

Lacal and Tjøstheim (2017) and Lacal and Tjøstheim (2019) treated the case of normalized data set; that is, if we have a time series $\{(X_t, X_{t-k})\}$, then its normalized version is $\left\{(\hat{Z}_t, \hat{Z}_{t-k})\right\}$, where $\hat{Z}_t = \Phi^{-1}(F_n(X_t))$, and Φ^{-1} is the inverse of the cumulative distribution function of the standard normal density. Further, as $\boldsymbol{b} \to \mathbf{0}$, it is possible to show results analogous to Theorems 7.3 and 7.4. In fact, we have to use analogs of the proof of Theorem 4.5.

7.3.1 The bootstrap

In this section, we consider the null situation where $\{X_t\}$ consists of iid variables that are not normalized. The situation with a normalized series $\{\hat{Z}_t\}$ and $\boldsymbol{b} \to \mathbf{0}$ can be treated in essentially the same way with the difference between $\{\hat{Z}_t\}$ and $\{Z_t\}$ treated in Theorem 4.5. Let $(\Omega, \mathcal{F}, P)$ be the probability space where $\{X_t\}$ is defined, and let $(\Lambda, \mathcal{G}, P^*)$ be the probability space where the bootstrap $\left\{X_t^*\right\}$ is defined. Further,let $\left\{X_t^*\right\}$ be the ordinary nonparametric bootstrap of $\{X_t\}$ obtained by drawings from the empirical distribution function $F_n(x) = \frac{1}{n}\sum_{t=1}^{n} I(X_t \le x)$.

Let $\widehat{\boldsymbol{\theta}}^*_{n,\boldsymbol{b}}$ be the five-dimensional estimated vector of parameters obtained with the bootstrap. Based on the bootstrap estimates $\widehat{\boldsymbol{\theta}}^*_{n,\boldsymbol{b}}$, we can construct a new test statistic

$$T^*_{n,\boldsymbol{b}} = \int_S h\left(\widehat{\boldsymbol{\theta}}^*_{n,\boldsymbol{b}}(\boldsymbol{x})\right) dF_n^{*(k)}(\boldsymbol{x}), \tag{7.17}$$

where $F_n^{*(k)}$ is the empirical cumulative distribution function after the bootstrap:

$$F_n^{*(k)}(\boldsymbol{x}) = \frac{1}{n-k}\sum_{t=k+1}^{n} I\left(X_t^* \le x_1,\ X_{t-k}^* \le x_2\right),\ \boldsymbol{x} = (x_1, x_2) \in \mathbb{R}^2,\ k \ge 1.$$

To test the hypothesis that the time series $\{X_t\}$ is iid (or rather that X_t and X_{t-k} are independent) against the hypothesis that $\{X_t\}$ is not iid (or rather that X_t and X_{t-k} are not independent), we will compare $t_{n,\boldsymbol{b}}$, the value of the test statistic $T_{n,\boldsymbol{b}}$, with $t_1^*, \ldots, t_R^*$, that is, the R realizations of the bootstrapped test statistic $T^*_{n,\boldsymbol{b}}$. Indeed, for this test, we will use the p-value $p = P^*_\omega\left(T^*_{n,\boldsymbol{b}} \ge T_{n,\boldsymbol{b}}\right)$, which can be approximated by

$$p_n = \frac{1}{1+R}\left(1 + \sum_{r=1}^{R} I(t_r^* \ge t_{n,\boldsymbol{b}})\right). \tag{7.18}$$

The null hypothesis will be rejected if small values of p_n are observed. The choice of bandwidth $\boldsymbol{b} = (b_1, b_2)$ is of course important in the testing procedures, and we have used the cross-validation bandwidth selector introduced in Chapter 4.8.2, also in this case. The validity of the bootstrap procedure is considered in Section 7.3.4, whereas the proofs for the validity are available in the supplementary material of Lacal and Tjøstheim (2017).

Lacal and Tjøstheim (2017) performed a simulation study and compared the local Gaussian (LGC) test for serial independence using the proposed bootstrap procedure with the Brownian distance covariance (BDC) and the Pearson covariance test for time series. Overall, the performance of the LGC-based test is better or just as good as the BDC test for those simulation experiments. More specifically, for GARCH and ARCH models, the test based on the local Gaussian correlation is considerably better than the other two tests. The Pearson correlation is optimal for a Gaussian autoregressive model, but there is not much loss of power for the local correlation and the BDC test, in particular, for the latter (very similar results were obtained for a moving-average model). For the exponential autoregressive model, the local Gaussian correlation test and the BDC test are almost the same, whereas the Pearson test fails miserably. In the next subsection, we examine some specific power results for the GARCH(1, 1) model, as introduced in Chapter 2.4, and for a real data example.

7.3.2 Example: GARCH(1, 1)

In this example, we consider the following GARCH(1, 1) model:

$$X_t = \varepsilon_t \sqrt{h_t},\ h_1 = 1,\ h_t = 1 + 0.1 X_{t-1}^2 + 0.8 h_{t-1}, t \geq 0, \tag{7.19}$$

where the innovations $\{\varepsilon_t\} \sim \mathcal{N}(0, 1)$. We will consider this model both for non-normalized $\{X_t\}$ and normalized $\left\{\hat{Z}_t\right\}$ with $\hat{Z}_t = \Phi^{-1}(\hat{F}(X_t))$. The reason for analyzing this model is its dependence structure. Indeed, for the time series in (7.19), the local correlation is positive in the first and third quadrants, whereas it is negative in the second and fourth quadrants. Therefore in this example, we consider the functionals $T_1 = \left[\int \left(\hat{\rho}(x_1, x_2)\right)^2 I_{S_1}(x_1, x_2)\, \mathrm{d}F_n^{(k)}(x_1, x_2)\right]^{\frac{1}{2}}$, where $S_1 = [-8, 8]^2$ and $S_1 = [-3, 3]^2$ in the case of non-normalization and normalization, respectively, and $T_2 = \int \hat{\rho}(x_1, x_2) I_{S_2}(x_1, x_2)\, \mathrm{d}F_n^{(k)}(x_1, x_2)$, where $S_2 = [3, 8]^2 \cup [-8, -3]^2$ and $S_2 = [1, 3]^2 \cup [-3, -1]^2$. The functional T_2 is designed to capture for (X_t, X_{t-k}) the often occurring phenomenon of increased positive dependence in the tail of bivariate financial series. Further, we are now testing for serial independence for lags $k = 1, \ldots, 4$ and also a combination of lags ($\bar{k}_4$), that is, the case in which the test statistic is the average of the test statistic for lags $k = 1, 2, 3, 4$. The bandwidths are in all cases determined by cross-validation.

Lacal and Tjøstheim (2017) performed a power study using this setup with 300 realizations, the number of observations equal to 1000, and the number of bootstrap replications $R = 500$. The results for this study are reported in Tables 7.2 and 7.3 for the non-normalized and normalized cases, respectively. The distance covariance, BDC, test is included as a benchmark.

Table 7.2 Power of the serial independence test in a GARCH(1, 1) model.

Test Statistic	Level %	$k=1$	$k=2$	$k=3$	$k=4$	$\bar{k}_4$
T_1	1	38.7	32.0	30.7	27.0	78.7
	5	63.0	54.3	54.3	44.7	90.7
	10	74.3	68.7	69.3	59.3	95.0
T_2	1	51.7	44.7	38.3	36.3	72.3
	5	65.3	61.3	52.3	48.3	86.7
	10	72.7	69.3	61.7	58.3	91.0
BDC	1	3.3	2.7	2.3	2.3	13.7
	5	14.7	9.7	13.3	8.7	30.7
	10	28.7	23.7	26.0	18.7	44.7

Table 7.3 Power of a serial independence test for a normalized GARCH(1, 1) model.

Test Statistic	Level %	$k=1$	$k=2$	$k=3$	$k=4$	$\bar{k}_4$
T_1	1	47.7	37.3	37.0	24.7	75.0
	5	65.7	60.7	51.7	40.3	86.7
	10	76.0	70.0	61.7	54.0	91.3
T_2	1	62.3	59.0	48.7	46.0	95.0
	5	84.3	80.0	69.3	66.7	98.7
	10	91.3	87.0	81.3	75.0	99.3
BDC	1	2.3	2.0	2.3	2.7	8.7
	5	12.0	8.0	10.3	6.7	23.7
	10	23.7	18.7	20.7	14.7	37.0

The power for the original data set is generally lower than that after normalization. Moreover, the best results are given by T_2, and this is reasonable because of the symmetry properties of the GARCH(1, 1) model (7.19) (in fact, the power can even be improved further by designing a functional that takes into account negative local correlations in the second and fourth quadrants). For both functionals, the values of the power obtained using the distance covariance are substantially lower than those given by the local Gaussian correlation. We also note that the power, except for a few cases, decreases as the lag k increases. Finally, for the average of the test functionals, the power is significantly higher. This is to be expected since $\bar{k}_4$ picks up independent power from each of the lags $k = 1, \dots, 4$, so that $\bar{k}_4$ is a kind of playing the role of the Ljung–Box test statistic. The level of the tests, as reported in Lacal and Tjøstheim (2017), is approximately correct.

7.3.3 Example: Exchange rates

In this example, we study the changes in the log-daily spot Exchange Rate of the US dollar to the British pound from March 8, 2007, to February 25, 2011, in total 1001 observations. The global correlation between X_t and X_{t-1} is 0.0125, and the corresponding Pearson correlation p-value is 0.6911. Instead, the independence test based on the normalized local Gaussian correlation with the functional T_1 given above, gives a p-value (for the definition, see (7.18)) equal to 0.01 (100 bootstrap resamples), very much lower than that obtained with the Pearson correlation.

In Fig. 7.3 the upper left plot shows the observations. The upper right plot shows the estimated local Gaussian autocorrelation at lag 1. As can be seen from the plot, the dominating feature of this plot is its essential symmetry. Indeed, it has positive dependence and is increasing in the first and third quadrants and negative dependence in the second and fourth quadrants. This dependence behavior explains why the local Gaussian test for serial independence delivers a much lower p-value (in fact, rejection of serial independence at the 0.01 level) than the ordinary Pearson correlation p-value. Fig. 7.3, lower panel, shows the plots of the local Gaussian correlation for $\{(X_t, X_{t-k})\}$ with $k = 2$ and $k = 10$, showing much the same dependence tendency. In Chapter 8.3, we examine another example with much higher lags, in fact, showing long-range dependence in the local autocorrelation.

7.3.4 Validity of the bootstrap

To demonstrate the validity of the bootstrap in Section 7.3.1, that is, that the distribution of the test statistic under the bootstrap measure mimics

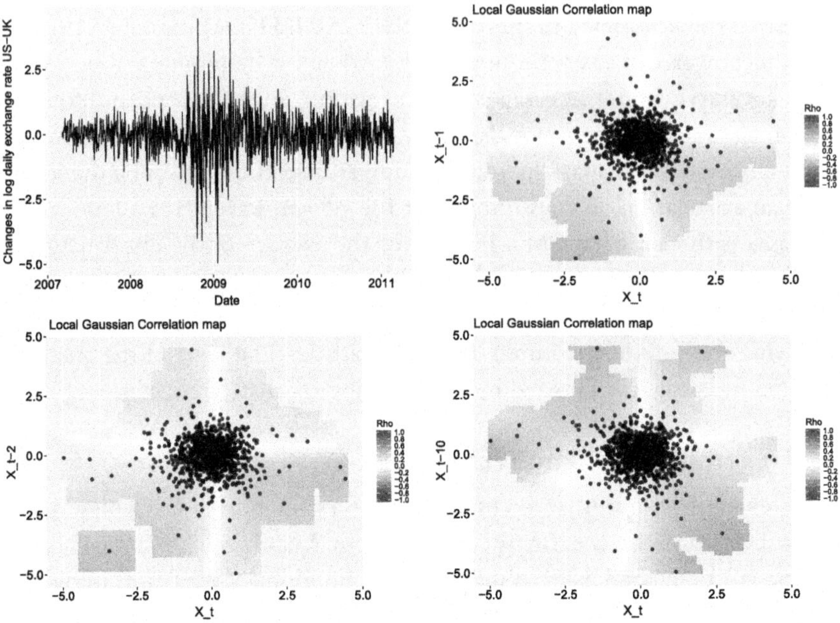

Figure 7.3 The changes in log-daily exchange rate (upper left), and local Gaussian autocorrelation maps for lag $k = 1$ (upper right), $k = 2$ (lower left), and $k = 10$ (lower right).

well the distribution of the statistics under the true measure as the number of observations grows to infinity, we need to check the consistency and asymptotic normality of $T^*_{n,\boldsymbol{b}}$. To simplify, we state these two properties, first, for the parameter estimates and then for the test statistic.

We assume that the bandwidth $\boldsymbol{b}$ and the point $\boldsymbol{x}$ at which the local-likelihood is estimated are fixed. Let $\boldsymbol{\theta}_0 = \boldsymbol{\theta}_b(\boldsymbol{x})$ and $\widehat{\boldsymbol{\theta}}_n = \widehat{\boldsymbol{\theta}}_{n,b}(\boldsymbol{x})$. Note that the local likelihood L_n of (4.8) can be written as

$$L_n(\boldsymbol{\theta}) = L_n(\boldsymbol{X}_n, \boldsymbol{\theta}) = \frac{1}{n}\sum_{t=1}^{n} L(X_t, \boldsymbol{\theta}), \tag{7.20}$$

where $L(X_t, \boldsymbol{\theta}) = K_b(X_t - \boldsymbol{x}) \log(\psi(X_t, \boldsymbol{\theta})) - \int K_b(\boldsymbol{v} - \boldsymbol{x})\psi(\boldsymbol{v}, \boldsymbol{\theta}) d\boldsymbol{v}$, $\boldsymbol{X}_n = (X_1, \ldots, X_n)$, n being the number of observations.

We start by stating the needed assumptions, also allowing for a somewhat more general situation. The assumptions are essentially taken from Gonçalves and White (2002) and Gonçalves and White (2004) but simplified and adapted to our situation, since we consider the ordinary bootstrap, whereas they considered the block bootstrap. We assume that the kernel function has a compact support.

A process $\{g(X_t, \boldsymbol{\theta})\}$ is defined to be r-dominated on $\boldsymbol{\Theta}$ uniformly in t, n for all $t = 1, \ldots, n$ if there exists $D_t : \mathbb{R} \longrightarrow \mathbb{R}$ such that $| g(X_t, \boldsymbol{\theta}) | \leq D_t$ for all $\boldsymbol{\theta} \in \boldsymbol{\Theta}$ and $t = 1, \ldots, n$, and D_t is $\mathcal{B}$-measurable ($\mathcal{B}$ is the Borel σ-field) such that, for some $\Delta > 0$, $|D_t|_r = \left(\int | D_t |^r \, dt\right)^{\frac{1}{r}} \leq \Delta < \infty$ for all $t = 1, \ldots, n$.

A1. $(\Omega, \mathcal{F}, P)$ is a complete probability space, $\boldsymbol{\Theta}$ is a compact subset of $\mathbb{R}^5$, $\{L_n : \Omega \times \boldsymbol{\Theta} \longrightarrow \bar{\mathbb{R}}\}$ is a sequence of random functions such that X_t is $\mathcal{F}$-measurable for all t, and $\bar{\mathbb{R}}$ is the extended real line.

A2. $\boldsymbol{\theta}_0$ is the unique maximizer of $\mathrm{E}\left(L_n(\boldsymbol{\theta})\right) : \boldsymbol{\Theta} \longrightarrow \bar{\mathbb{R}}$.

A3. $\{\boldsymbol{M}_{n,\boldsymbol{b}}\}$ is $O(1)$ and uniformly positive definite, where, using Var to denote the covariance matrix,

$$\boldsymbol{M}_{n,\boldsymbol{b}} = \mathrm{Var}\left(\sqrt{nb_1b_2}\nabla L_n(\boldsymbol{\theta}_0)\right).$$

$\{\boldsymbol{J}_{n,\boldsymbol{b}}\}$ is continuous on Θ uniformly in n, $O(1)$, and uniformly nonsingular, where

$$\boldsymbol{J}_{n,\boldsymbol{b}} = \mathrm{E}\left(-\nabla^2 L_n(\boldsymbol{\theta}_0)\right),$$

and ∇^2 is the Hessian matrix with respect to $\boldsymbol{\theta}$.

A4. $\{L(X_t, \boldsymbol{\theta})\}$ is 2-dominated on Θ uniformly in $t = 1, \ldots, n$.

A5. $(\Lambda, \mathcal{G})$ is a measurable space, $\left(\Lambda, \mathcal{G}, P^*_\omega\right)$ is a complete probability space for all $\omega \in \Omega$, and $\{L^*_n : \Lambda \times \Omega \times \boldsymbol{\Theta} \longrightarrow \bar{\mathbb{R}}\}$ is a sequence of random functions such that $L^*_n(\boldsymbol{\theta}) = L_n(\boldsymbol{X}^*_n(\lambda, \omega), \boldsymbol{\theta})$, where $X^*_t(\lambda, \omega) = X_{\tau_t(\lambda)}(\omega)$, $\tau_t : \Lambda \longrightarrow \mathbb{N}$, $\omega \in \Omega$, $\lambda \in \Lambda$, and τ_t is a vector of random indices representing the bootstrap operation.

A6. $\{L(X_t, \boldsymbol{\theta})\}$ is Lipschitz continuous on $\boldsymbol{\Theta}$, that is,

$$| L(X_t, \boldsymbol{\theta}) - L(X_t, \boldsymbol{\theta}') | \leq C_t \,| \boldsymbol{\theta} - \boldsymbol{\theta}' | \; P\text{-}a.s., \; \forall \boldsymbol{\theta}, \boldsymbol{\theta}' \in \boldsymbol{\Theta},$$

with a sufficiently large constant M such that $C_t \leq M$.

Assumption **A1** defines the probability space of $\{X_t\}$. The compactness assumption is an often used regularity condition. Here it is needed to use the theory of Gonçalves and White (2004). Assumption **A2** is needed only to apply Lemmas 3.2 and 3.3 of Gonçalves and White (2004), and assumption **A3** is used in the proof of the asymptotic normality of the parameter estimates. They are essentially the same as assumptions (ii) (**A3**) and (iii) (**A2**) of Theorem 1 in Tjøstheim and Hufthammer (2013), Theorem 4.1 in this book. Further, assumption **A4** is fulfilled, because the kernel function has a compact support and the continuous term $\log(\psi(X_t, \boldsymbol{\theta}))$ has a maximum in the compact $\boldsymbol{\Theta}$, so $\{L(X_t, \boldsymbol{\theta})\}$ is bounded by a constant. This implies that $\{L(X_t, \boldsymbol{\theta})\}$ is 2-dominated. Moreover, assumption **A5** is crucial for proving the validity of the bootstrap, because it defines the probability space of the bootstrapped sample $\{X_t^*\}$. Finally, assumption **A6** is also fulfilled, because the kernel function has a compact support and the term $\log(\psi(X_t, \boldsymbol{\theta}))$ is differentiable and therefore Lipschitz continuous.

We will use the following notations, taken from Gonçalves and White (2002) and Gonçalves and White (2004), for the convergence of variables in the probability space $(\Lambda, \mathcal{G}, P_\omega^*)$. First, we write $Y_n^* \xrightarrow{P_\omega^*, P} 0$ if for any $\epsilon, \delta > 0$,

$$\lim_{n\to\infty} P\left(\omega : P_\omega^*\left(\lambda : \mid Y_n^*(\lambda, \omega) \mid > \epsilon\right) > \delta\right) = 0.$$

Further, we write $Y_n^* \xrightarrow{d_{P_\omega^*}} \mathcal{N}(0, 1)$ prob-P if for every subsequence $\{n'\}$, there exists a further subsequence $\{n''\}$ such that $Y_{n''}^* \xrightarrow{d_{P_\omega^*}} \mathcal{N}(0, 1)$ a.s. (see Gonçalves and White (2004), p. 210). This definition is based on the fact that convergence in probability implies almost sure convergence for such kinds of subsequences (see Theorem 20.5 of Billingsley (2012)).

The proofs of the following results, Theorems 7.5–7.8, are given in Appendices B and C in the supplementary material of Lacal and Tjøstheim (2017).

First, we need to state the consistency of the parameter estimates, and then we can establish the same property for the test statistic, all with a fixed $\boldsymbol{b}$.

Theorem 7.5. *Let assumptions **A1**, **A2**, **A4**, **A5**, **A6** hold. Then:*

(A) $\boldsymbol{\theta}_n - \boldsymbol{\theta}_0 \xrightarrow{P} 0$;

(B) $\boldsymbol{\theta}_n^* - \boldsymbol{\theta}_n \xrightarrow{P_\omega^*, P} 0$.

The following theorem establishes the consistency of the test statistic.

Theorem 7.6. *Under the assumptions of Theorem 7.5 and assuming that h is continuous, it follows that:*

(A) $T_{n,\boldsymbol{b}} - T_{\boldsymbol{b}} \xrightarrow{P} 0$;

(B) $T_{n,\boldsymbol{b}}^* - T_{n,\boldsymbol{b}} \xrightarrow{P_\omega^*, P} 0$.

Even if we do not need the following theorem to prove the asymptotic normality of the test statistic, we think that it is of interest to establish this property also for the parameter estimates.

Theorem 7.7. *Let the assumptions of Theorem 4.1 and* ***A1–A6*** *hold, and let* $\{\nabla^2 L(X_t, \boldsymbol{\theta})\}$ *be Lipschitz continuous on* $\boldsymbol{\Theta}$ *and 2-dominated on* $\boldsymbol{\Theta}$ *uniformly in* t, n *for all* $t = 1, \ldots, n$. *Then:*

(A) $\sqrt{b_1 b_2}\boldsymbol{M}_{n,\boldsymbol{b}}^{-\frac{1}{2}}\boldsymbol{J}_{n,\boldsymbol{b}}\sqrt{n}\,(\boldsymbol{\theta}_n - \boldsymbol{\theta}_0) \xrightarrow{d} \mathcal{N}(0, \boldsymbol{I}_5)$, *where* $\boldsymbol{I}_5$ *is the five-dimensional identity matrix;*

(B) $\sqrt{b_1 b_2}\boldsymbol{M}_{n,\boldsymbol{b}}^{-\frac{1}{2}}\boldsymbol{J}_{n,\boldsymbol{b}}\sqrt{n}\left(\boldsymbol{\theta}_n^* - \boldsymbol{\theta}_n\right) \xrightarrow{d_{P_\omega^*}} N(0, \boldsymbol{I}_5)$ *prob-P.*

This result, together with consistency, shows that the bootstrap for the parameter estimation works. The assumptions on $\{\nabla^2 L(X_t, \boldsymbol{\theta})\}$ can be verified as for $\{L(X_t, \boldsymbol{\theta})\}$. The following theorem establishes the asymptotic normality of the test statistic.

Theorem 7.8. *Under the assumptions of Theorems 7.4 and 7.5, it follows that:*

(A) $\sqrt{n}\,[C_k(A_{\boldsymbol{b}})]^{-\frac{1}{2}}\left(T_{n,\boldsymbol{b}} - T_{\boldsymbol{b}}\right) \xrightarrow{d} \mathcal{N}(0, 1)$;

(B) $\sqrt{n}\,[C_k(A_{\boldsymbol{b}})]^{-\frac{1}{2}}\left(T_{n,\boldsymbol{b}}^* - T_{n,\boldsymbol{b}}\right) \xrightarrow{d_{\mathbb{P}_\omega^*}} \mathcal{N}(0, 1)$ *prob-P.*

Theorems analogous to Theorems 7.7 and 7.8 can also be established for normalized variables $\{\hat{Z}_t\}$ and for $\boldsymbol{b} \to 0$ using essentially the same techniques and Theorem 4.5.

7.4 Describing nonlinear dependence and tests of independence for two time series

Estimation of dependence between two time series is an important problem in many scientific disciplines, for instance, dependence between financial time series in a stock market, between geophysical and climate time series, between biological and environmental time series. Often it is of particular interest to investigate whether one series leads the other one, which means that we have to evaluate the dependence as a function of lag for the two time series. Traditionally, the ordinary Pearson cross-correlation has been used as a measure of dependence, but this is primarily a measure that has been developed for linear and Gaussian models. It is not difficult to find examples of nonlinear models where it fails completely, for example GARCH-type models. There are two main theoretical differences between the present subsection and two preceding subsections. First, we now consider the general situation of two stationary time series and with *both* estimation and testing. Second, the serial dependence of each component series makes it necessary to introduce the block bootstrap to construct confidence intervals and to do testing in practice. The asymptotic distributions of local parameter estimates and of test of independence are derived in the general case where the bandwidth $\boldsymbol{b} \to \mathbf{0}$, but they are too complicated and inaccurate to use in a finite sample situation, at least for a moderately sized sample.

In this subsection, we first define and estimate the local Gaussian cross-correlation and then present accompanying independence tests developed by Lacal and Tjøstheim (2019).

7.4.1 Local Gaussian cross-correlation

Let $\{X_t\}$ and $\{Y_t\}$ be two continuous valued strictly stationary, α-mixing (cf. (7.15)) with $\alpha(m) = \alpha^m$, time series defined on the probability space $(\Omega, \mathcal{F}, P)$. We denote by $f^{(k)}(x, y) = f_{\{X_t, Y_{t-k}\}}(x, y)$ the density function of $\{X_t, Y_{t-k}\}$ for $k = 0, \pm 1, \pm 2, \ldots$. Formula (4.4) in Chapter 4 can be written as

$$\begin{aligned}\psi((v, w), \boldsymbol{\theta}^{(k)}(x, y)) &= \frac{1}{2\pi\sigma_1^{(k)}(x, y)\sigma_2^{(k)}(x, y)\sqrt{1 - \rho^{(k)}(x, y)^2}} \\ &\times \exp\left[-\frac{1}{2(1 - \rho^{(k)}(x, y)^2)}\left(\frac{(v - \mu_1^{(k)}(x, y))^2}{\sigma_1^{(k)}(x, y)^2}\right.\right. \\ &\left.\left.-2\rho^{(k)}(x, y)\frac{(v - \mu_1^{(k)}(x, y))(w - \mu_2^{(k)}(x, y))}{\sigma_1^{(k)}(x, y)\sigma_2^{(k)}(x, y)} + \frac{(w - \mu_2^{(k)}(x, y))^2}{\sigma_2^{(k)}(x, y)^2}\right)\right]\end{aligned} \tag{7.21}$$

with an obvious interpretation for the superscript k. In the following, for notational ease, we will often omit k and ignore that sums extend from 1 to $n - |k|$ instead of n.

To estimate the local parameter $\boldsymbol{\theta}(x, y)$, we will use the local log-likelihood as before. Also as before, the local neighborhood is determined by a kernel function K and a bandwidth parameter $\boldsymbol{b}$ such that

$$\begin{aligned}L_{n,\boldsymbol{b}}\left((\boldsymbol{X}_n, \boldsymbol{Y}_n), \boldsymbol{\theta}_{\boldsymbol{b}}(x, y)\right) &= \frac{1}{n}\sum_{t=1}^{n} K_{\boldsymbol{b}}(X_t - x, Y_t - y)\log\left(\psi\left((X_t, Y_t), \boldsymbol{\theta}_{\boldsymbol{b}}(x, y)\right)\right) \\ &- \int K_{\boldsymbol{b}}(v - x, w - y)\psi\left((v, w), \boldsymbol{\theta}_{\boldsymbol{b}}(x, y)\right) \mathrm{d}v\,\mathrm{d}w,\end{aligned} \tag{7.22}$$

where $\boldsymbol{X}_n = (X_1, \ldots, X_n)$, $\boldsymbol{Y}_n = (Y_1, \ldots, Y_n)$, n being the number of observations, $x, y, v, w \in \mathbb{R}$, $\boldsymbol{\theta}_{\boldsymbol{b}}(x, y) = (\mu_{1,\boldsymbol{b}}(x, y), \mu_{2,\boldsymbol{b}}(x, y), \sigma^2_{1,\boldsymbol{b}}(x, y), \sigma^2_{2,\boldsymbol{b}}(x, y), \rho_{\boldsymbol{b}}(x, y))$ is the vector of parameters, $K_{\boldsymbol{b}}(v - x, w - y) = (b_1 b_2)^{-1} K\left(\frac{v-x}{b_1}\right) \times K\left(\frac{w-y}{b_2}\right)$ is a product kernel with bandwidth $\boldsymbol{b} = \boldsymbol{b}_n = (b_1, b_2) = (b_{1n}, b_{2n})$, and K is a non-negative kernel function with compact support such that $\int K(v, w)\, dv\, dw = 1$. Define $\boldsymbol{\theta}_{0,\boldsymbol{b}}(x, y)$ as the true bandwidth-dependent vector of local parameters, that is, the minimizer of the penalty function

$$\int K_{\boldsymbol{b}}(v-x, w-y)\left[\psi\left((v, w), \boldsymbol{\theta}(x, y)\right) - \log\left(\psi\left((v, w), \boldsymbol{\theta}(x, y)\right)\right) f(v, w)\right] dv\, dw. \tag{7.23}$$

In particular, we have that $\boldsymbol{\theta}_{0,\boldsymbol{b}} \to \boldsymbol{\theta}_0$ as $\boldsymbol{b} \to 0$, which is the true bandwidth-independent vector of parameters (see Chapter 4.3 and Tjøstheim and Hufthammer (2013) for more detail and regularity conditions). The corresponding estimates $\widehat{\boldsymbol{\theta}}_{n,\boldsymbol{b}}(x, y)$ are obtained maximizing the local log-likelihood (7.22). Note that $L_{n,\boldsymbol{b}}$ can be written as

$$L_{n,\boldsymbol{b}}(\boldsymbol{\theta}) = L_{n,\boldsymbol{b}}\left((\boldsymbol{X}_n, \boldsymbol{Y}_n, \boldsymbol{\theta}\right) = \frac{1}{n}\sum_{t=1}^{n} L^{(\boldsymbol{b})}((X_t, Y_t), \boldsymbol{\theta}), \tag{7.24}$$

where $L^{(\boldsymbol{b})}((X_t, Y_t), \boldsymbol{\theta}) = K_{\boldsymbol{b}}(X_t - x, Y_t - y)\log(\psi((X_t, Y_t), \boldsymbol{\theta})) - \int K_{\boldsymbol{b}}(v - x, w - y)\psi((v, w), \boldsymbol{\theta})dvdw$, and $L_{n,\boldsymbol{b}}$, $\boldsymbol{X}_n$, and $\boldsymbol{Y}_n$ are defined in (7.22).

In this section, we are mainly interested in $\rho(x, y) = \rho^{(k)}(x, y)$. The local parameters μ and σ are in a sense nuisance parameters, also in the alternative setup of a normalized time series with standard normal variables. In fact, in the alternative normalized case, we are interested in studying the situation in which X_t and Y_t are transformed into the standard normal variables $X'_t = \Phi^{-1}(F_X(X_t))$ and $Y'_t = \Phi^{-1}(F_Y(Y_t))$, where F_X and F_Y are the marginal cumulative distribution functions of, respectively, X_t and Y_t, and Φ is the standard normal cumulative distribution function. The normalized local Gaussian correlation $\rho'_b(x, y)$ is defined as the local correlation for the normalized pair (X'_t, Y'_t). In practice, we do not know the marginal distributions F_X and F_Y, and, in analogy with the copula usage of uniform pseudo-variables $U^X_{n,t} = \frac{n}{n+1}F^X_n(X_t)$ and $U^Y_{n,t} = \frac{n}{n+1}F^Y_n(Y_t)$, where F^X_n and F^Y_n are the empirical distribution functions, $F^X_n(x) = \frac{1}{n}\sum_{s=1}^{n} I(X_s \leq x)$ and $F^Y_n(y) = \frac{1}{n}\sum_{s=1}^{n} I\left(Y_s \leq y\right)$, we have the standard normal pseudo-variables $\hat{X}'_t = \Phi^{-1}(U^X_{n,t})$ and $\hat{Y}'_t = \Phi^{-1}(U^Y_{n,t})$. As $n \to \infty$, we have that $\hat{X}'_t \xrightarrow{a.s.} X'_t$ and $\hat{Y}'_t \xrightarrow{a.s.} Y'_t$. It is shown in Theorem 4.5 that under weak regularity conditions, the difference between F_n and F is a smaller-order effect and can be ignored in the asymptotic analysis of $\widehat{\boldsymbol{\theta}}_{n,\boldsymbol{b}}$. It is interesting to note that X_t and Y_t are independent if and only if so are X'_t and Y'_t. Finally, as $\boldsymbol{b} \to \infty$, $\rho_{\boldsymbol{b}}(x, y)$ converges to the Pearson global cross-correlation, whereas $\rho'_{\boldsymbol{b}}(x, y)$ converges to the global cross-correlation in the Gaussian case.

We further assume that the point (x, y) at which the local log-likelihood is estimated is fixed, so that we can write $\boldsymbol{\theta}_{0,\boldsymbol{b}} = \boldsymbol{\theta}_{0,\boldsymbol{b}}(x, y)$ and $\widehat{\boldsymbol{\theta}}_{n,\boldsymbol{b}} = \widehat{\boldsymbol{\theta}}_{n,\boldsymbol{b}}(x, y)$.

7.4.2 Asymptotic theory of the parameter estimates

For a given function g, the process $\{g((X_t, Y_t), \boldsymbol{\theta})\}$ is said to be r-dominated on $\boldsymbol{\Theta}$ uniformly in t, n for all $t = 1, \ldots, n$ if there exists $D_t : \mathbb{R} \longrightarrow \mathbb{R}$ such that $| g((X_t, Y_t), \theta) | \leq D_t$ for all $\boldsymbol{\theta} \in \boldsymbol{\Theta}$, $t = 1, \ldots, n$, D_t is $\mathcal{B}$-measurable ($\mathcal{B}$ is the Borel σ-field) such that $|D_t|_r = \left(\int | D_t |^r \, dt\right)^{\frac{1}{r}} \leq \Delta < \infty$ for all $t = 1, \ldots, n$ and some $\Delta > 0$. Moreover, the process $\{g((X_t, Y_t), \boldsymbol{\theta})\}$ is defined to be Lipschitz continuous on $\boldsymbol{\Theta}$ if, P being the probability for the probability space on which $\{X_t, Y_t\}$ is defined,

$$| g((X_t, Y_t), \boldsymbol{\theta}) - g((X_t, Y_t), \boldsymbol{\theta}') | \leq C_t \, | \boldsymbol{\theta} - \boldsymbol{\theta}' | \;\; P\text{-}a.s.$$

for all $\boldsymbol{\theta}, \boldsymbol{\theta}' \in \boldsymbol{\Theta}$ and a sufficiently large constant M such that $C_t \leq M$.

Before stating the asymptotic theory, we need the following assumptions:

B1. $(\Omega, \mathcal{F}, P)$ is a complete probability space, $\boldsymbol{\Theta}$ is a compact subset of $\mathbb{R}^5$, $\{L_{n,\boldsymbol{b}} : \Omega \times \boldsymbol{\Theta} \longrightarrow \bar{\mathbb{R}}\}$ is a sequence of random functions such that (X_t, Y_t) is $\mathcal{F}$-measurable, stationary, and α-mixing, as defined in (7.15), with $\alpha_k = O(\alpha^k)$, $\alpha \in (0, 1)$, for all t, $\bar{\mathbb{R}}$ is the extended real line, and the bivariate density f has support on all of $\mathbb{R}^2$.

B2. $\boldsymbol{\theta}_{0,b}$ is the unique maximizer of $\mathrm{E}\left(L_{n,\boldsymbol{b}}(\boldsymbol{\theta})\right) : \boldsymbol{\Theta} \longrightarrow \bar{\mathbb{R}}$, $L_{n,\boldsymbol{b}}(\boldsymbol{\theta})$ as in (7.22).

B3. For a fixed $\boldsymbol{b}$, using stationarity, the 5×5 matrix

$$\boldsymbol{J}_{n,\boldsymbol{b}} = \mathrm{E}\left(-\nabla^2 L_{n,\boldsymbol{b}}(\boldsymbol{\theta}_{0,\boldsymbol{b}})\right) = \boldsymbol{J}_b = \mathrm{E}\left(-\nabla^2 L^{(\boldsymbol{b})}((X_t, Y_t), \boldsymbol{\theta}_{0,\boldsymbol{b}})\right),$$

is continuous on $\boldsymbol{\Theta}$ uniformly in n, $O(1)$, and uniformly non-singular. Using Var to denote the covariance matrix, the 5×5 matrix

$$\boldsymbol{M}_{n,\boldsymbol{b}} = \mathrm{Var}\left(\sqrt{n b_1 b_2} \nabla L_{n,\boldsymbol{b}}(\boldsymbol{\theta}_{0,\boldsymbol{b}})\right)$$

is $O(1)$ and uniformly positive definite. Here ∇ is the gradient vector with respect to $\boldsymbol{\theta}$. Note that, due to stationarity,

$$\boldsymbol{M}_{n,\boldsymbol{b}} = b_1 b_2 \boldsymbol{M}_{\boldsymbol{b}} + \frac{b_1 b_2}{n} \sum_{t \neq s} \mathrm{Cov}\left(\nabla L^{(\boldsymbol{b})}((X_t, Y_t), \boldsymbol{\theta}_{0,\boldsymbol{b}}), \nabla L^{\boldsymbol{b})}((X_s, Y_s), \boldsymbol{\theta}_{0,\boldsymbol{b}})\right),$$

where

$$\boldsymbol{M}_{\boldsymbol{b}} = \mathrm{Var}\left(\nabla L^{(\boldsymbol{b})}((X_t, Y_t), \boldsymbol{\theta}_{0,\boldsymbol{b}})\right).$$

Assumption **B1** defines the probability space of $\{X_t\}$ and $\{Y_t\}$. Moreover, **B2** is needed to prove the consistency of the estimators, and **B3** is used in the proof of the asymptotic normality. They are essentially the same as, respectively, assumptions (ii) (**B3**) and (iii) (**B2**) of Theorem 4.1; see also Theorem 1 in Tjøstheim and Hufthammer (2013). We refer to that paper and to Chapter 4 for more detail and discussion. In all the proofs for the asymptotic theory, we first let the bandwidth be a fixed parameter, and then we let $\boldsymbol{b} \to \boldsymbol{0}$, like it is done in Joe (1989). This is justified by, for example, Proposition 6.3.9 of Brockwell and Davis (2006), where conditions (i)–(iii) of that proposition are implicitly verified in the course of our asymptotic analysis.

In parts of what we do, it is necessary to find two non-singular matrices that can approximate $\boldsymbol{J}_{n,\boldsymbol{b}}$ and $\boldsymbol{M}_{n,\boldsymbol{b}}$ as $\boldsymbol{b} \to \boldsymbol{0}$, as a natural extension of assumption **B3**. For details of this, we refer to Appendix A in the supplementary material of Lacal and Tjøstheim (2019). See also Chapter 4.4.2.

Theorem 7.9. *Let assumptions* **B1** *and* **B2** *hold, and let* $\left\{L^{(\boldsymbol{b})}((X_t, Y_t), \boldsymbol{\theta})\right\}$, $\boldsymbol{\theta} \in \boldsymbol{\Theta}$, *be Lipschitz continuous on* $\boldsymbol{\Theta}$ *and* 4*-dominated on* Θ *uniformly in* t, n. *Moreover, assume that, as* $\boldsymbol{b} = \boldsymbol{b}_n \to 0$, $\sigma_{\boldsymbol{b}}^2 \stackrel{def}{=} Var(L^{(\boldsymbol{b})}(X_t, Y_t), \boldsymbol{\theta}) \to \sigma^2 < \infty$ *and* $\mu_{\boldsymbol{b}} \stackrel{def}{=} E(L^{(\boldsymbol{b})}(X_t, Y_t), \boldsymbol{\theta})) \to \mu < \infty$ *for all* $t = 1, \ldots, n$ *and* $\boldsymbol{\theta} \in \Theta$. *Then* $\widehat{\boldsymbol{\theta}}_{n,\boldsymbol{b}} - \boldsymbol{\theta}_{0,\boldsymbol{b}} \stackrel{P}{\to} 0$ *and* $\widehat{\boldsymbol{\theta}}_{n,\boldsymbol{b}} - \boldsymbol{\theta}_0 \stackrel{P}{\to} 0$.

Remark: We need that $\sigma_{\boldsymbol{b}}^2 \to \sigma^2 < \infty$ and $\mu_{\boldsymbol{b}} \to \mu < \infty$ to avoid problems when we let the bandwidth go to 0. This is reasonable because by definition $\boldsymbol{\theta}_{0,\boldsymbol{b}} \to \boldsymbol{\theta}_0$.

The same arguments (see Section 7.5) of Theorem 7.9 can be repeated for the case in which the variables are normalized with the aid of Theorem 4.5.

Theorem 7.10. *Assume that:*

(i) *The kernel K is symmetric and Lipschitz;*

(ii) *The density f of (X_t, Y_t) is bounded on all of $\mathbb{R}^2$ and is such that in each fixed point (x, y), there exists a non-degenerate local Gaussian approximation $\psi((v, w), \boldsymbol{\theta}(x, y))$ such that*

$$E\left(\mid K_{\boldsymbol{b}}(X_t - x, Y_t - y)\frac{\partial}{\partial \theta_j}\log\left(\psi\left((X_t, Y_t), \boldsymbol{\theta}(x, y)\right)\right) \mid^{\gamma}\right) < \infty,$$

$j = 1, \ldots, 5$, *for some* $\gamma > 2$;

(iii) $n \to \infty$ *and* $b_1, b_2 \to 0$ *so that* $\dfrac{\log n}{n(b_1 b_2)^3} \to 0$;

(iv) *Assumptions* **B1** *and* **B2** *hold.*

Then $\sqrt{b_1 b_2}\boldsymbol{M}_{n,b}^{-\frac{1}{2}}\boldsymbol{J}_{n,b}\sqrt{n}\left(\widehat{\boldsymbol{\theta}}_{n,b} - \boldsymbol{\theta}_{0,b}\right) \xrightarrow{d} \mathcal{N}(\mathbf{0}, \boldsymbol{I}_5)$, *where* $\boldsymbol{I}_5$ *is the five-dimensional identity matrix, and* $\boldsymbol{M}_{n,b}$ *and* $\boldsymbol{J}_{n,b}$ *are defined in* **B3**.

Theorems 7.9 and 7.10 still hold for the case of $\{(X_t, Y_{t-k})\}$ instead of $\{(X_t, Y_t)\}$, because, to study this case, it is sufficient to substitute $\boldsymbol{\theta}$ and f with, respectively, $\boldsymbol{\theta}^{(k)}$ and $f^{(k)}$. Then the matrices $\boldsymbol{M}_{n,b}$ and $\boldsymbol{J}_{n,b}$ will depend on the lag k. Assumptions (i)–(iv) correspond to the assumptions of Theorem 4.2 and Theorem 2 of Tjøstheim and Hufthammer (2013).

Again, the same arguments can be used in the case where X_t and Y_t are transformed into normalized variables $\hat{X}_t'$ and $\hat{Y}_t'$ using Theorem 4.5.

The proofs of the above two theorems are given in Section 7.5. See also Lacal and Tjøstheim (2019).

7.4.3 Test of independence

In this section, we test the null hypothesis H_0 that in the pair $\{X_t, Y_{t-k}\}$, X_t and Y_{t-k} are independent against the alternative hypothesis H_1 that they are not, where k is an arbitrary lag. In the following, we consider the case of $\{X_t, Y_t\}$, but the results still hold when Y_t is replaced by Y_{t-k}. As before, we define a global measure of dependence as a function of the local parameters such that the test statistic

$$T_{n,b} = \int_S h\left(\widehat{\boldsymbol{\theta}}_{n,b}(x, y)\right) \mathrm{d}F_n(x, y) \tag{7.25}$$

estimates the global functionals

$$T_b = \int_S h\left(\boldsymbol{\theta}_{0,b}(x, y)\right) \mathrm{d}F(x, y) \tag{7.26}$$

and

$$T = \int_S h\left(\boldsymbol{\theta}_0(x, y)\right) \mathrm{d}F(x, y), \tag{7.27}$$

where F is the bivariate cumulative distribution function of $\{(X_t, Y_t)\}$, and F_n is the empirical distribution function. The function h takes on specific forms to test against specified types of dependence, for example, in the tails. For the asymptotic theory, S will be a compact subset of $\mathbb{R}^2$. In practice, the set S will be used to restrict the data. This is done, for example, to make the test more robust to outliers in the non-normalized case.

We now state the main results concerning the test functional above.

Theorem 7.11. *Under the assumptions of Theorem 7.9 and assuming that h is continuous,* $T_{n,\boldsymbol{b}} - T_{\boldsymbol{b}} \stackrel{P}{\to} 0$ *and* $T_{n,\boldsymbol{b}} - T \stackrel{P}{\to} 0$.

Theorem 7.12. *Let* $\{(X_t, Y_t)\}$ *be a bivariate time series with bivariate density* f *having support on all of* $\mathbb{R}^2$. *Moreover, let assumptions (i), (ii), and (iv) of Theorem 7.10 hold and assume that h has continuous second-order derivatives. Then, as* $n \to \infty$,

$$\sqrt{n}\left[C_n(A_{\boldsymbol{b}})\right]^{-\frac{1}{2}} \left(T_{n,\boldsymbol{b}} - T_{\boldsymbol{b}}\right) \stackrel{d}{\to} \mathcal{N}(0,1)$$

with

$$\begin{aligned} C_n(A_{\boldsymbol{b}}) &= \int A_{\boldsymbol{b}}^2(x,y)dF(x,y) - \int A_{\boldsymbol{b}}(x,y)A_{\boldsymbol{b}}(v,w)dF(x,y)dF(v,w) \\ &+ \int A_{\boldsymbol{b}}(x,y)A_{\boldsymbol{b}}(v,w)\sum_{k=1}^{n}\frac{n-k}{n}\left[dF^{(k)}(x,y,v,w) - dF(x,y)dF(v,w)\right] \\ &+ \int A_{\boldsymbol{b}}(x,y)A_{\boldsymbol{b}}(v,w)\sum_{k=1}^{n}\frac{n-k}{n}\left[dF^{(-k)}(x,y,v,w) - dF(x,y)dF(v,w)\right] \end{aligned}$$

where the sum converges as $n \to \infty$, *and with* $\boldsymbol{u}(x,y) = \nabla \log\left(\psi\left((x,y),\boldsymbol{\theta}\right)\right)$ *and* $K_{\boldsymbol{b}}$ *being a kernel function as defined in Chapter 2.5,*

$$\begin{aligned} A_{\boldsymbol{b}}(x,y) = \int_S & \nabla h\left(\boldsymbol{\theta}_{0,\boldsymbol{b}}(v,w)\right)^T \boldsymbol{J}_b^{-1}(v,w)K_{\boldsymbol{b}}\left(v-x, w-y\right) \\ & \times \boldsymbol{u}\left((x,y),\boldsymbol{\theta}_{0,\boldsymbol{b}}(v,w)\right)dF(v,w) \\ & + h\left(\boldsymbol{\theta}_{0,\boldsymbol{b}}(x,y)\right)I_S(x,y), \end{aligned}$$

$F^{(k)}$ *is the distribution function of* (X_t, Y_t, X_s, Y_s) *with* $k = t - s$, *and* $\boldsymbol{J}_{\boldsymbol{b}}$ *is defined in condition* ***B3***. *Further, assume that* $C_{k,n}(A_{\boldsymbol{b}}) \neq 0$ *and* $|A_{\boldsymbol{b}}|_p = (E(|A_b|^p))^{\frac{1}{p}} < \infty$ *for some* $p > 2$. *For the result to be true as* $n \to \infty$ *and* $\boldsymbol{b} \to \boldsymbol{0}$, *we must require in addition condition (iii) of Theorem 7.10. Then* $T_{\boldsymbol{b}}$ *can be replaced by* T.

Remark: Using the expression for $C_n(A_{\boldsymbol{b}})$ and $A_{\boldsymbol{b}}(x,y)$, a Taylor expansion of $A_{\boldsymbol{b}}(x,y)$ and the fact that $\boldsymbol{J}_{\boldsymbol{b}}(x,y) \sim b_1^2 b_2^2$ show that the convergence rate to standard normality is of the order $(\sqrt{n}b_1b_2)^{-1}$ as $\boldsymbol{b} \to \boldsymbol{0}$ and $n \to \infty$, which is faster than the convergence rate $(\sqrt{n}(b_1b_2)^{\frac{3}{2}})^{-1}$ of the local parameter estimates. This is consistent with similar results for test functionals for independence in Joe (1989). More details are given by Lacal and Tjøstheim (2019).

Corollary 7.1. *Let the assumptions of Theorem 7.12 hold. If* $\{X_t\}$ *and* $\{Y_t\}$ *are independent, then, as* $n \to \infty$,

$$\sqrt{n}\,[C_n(A_{\boldsymbol{b}})]^{-\frac{1}{2}}\left(T_{n,\boldsymbol{b}} - T_{\boldsymbol{b}}\right) \xrightarrow{d} \mathcal{N}(0,1)$$

where

$$\begin{aligned}
C_n(A_{\boldsymbol{b}}) = &\int A_{\boldsymbol{b}}^2(x,y)\,dF_X(x)\,dF_Y(y)\\
&- \int A_{\boldsymbol{b}}(x,y)A_b(v,w)\,dF_X(x)\,dF_Y(y)\,dF_X(v)\,dF_Y(w)\\
&+ \int A_{\boldsymbol{b}}(x,y)A_{\boldsymbol{b}}(v,w)\sum_{k=1}^{n}\frac{n-k}{n}\Big[dF_X^{(k)}(x,v)\,dF_Y^{(k)}(y,w)\\
&\qquad - dF_X(x)\,dF_Y(y)\,dF_X(v)\,dF_Y(w)\Big]\\
&+ \int A_{\boldsymbol{b}}(x,y)A_{\boldsymbol{b}}(v,w)\sum_{k=1}^{n}\frac{n-k}{n}\Big[dF_X^{(-k)}(x,v)\,dF_Y^{(-k)}(y,w)\\
&\qquad - dF_X(x)\,dF_Y(y)\,dF_X(v)\,dF_Y(w)\Big],
\end{aligned}$$

and F_X, F_Y, $F_X^{(k)}$, *and* $F_Y^{(k)}$ *are the cumulative distribution functions of* $\{X_t\}$, $\{Y_t\}$, $\{(X_t, X_{t-k}),\}$ *and* $\{(Y_t, Y_{t-k})\}$, *respectively. Moreover, if* $\{X_t\}$ *and* $\{Y_t\}$ *are also serially independent, then the last two terms of* C_n *disappear. The same result holds if* $T_{\boldsymbol{b}}$ *is replaced by* T, *as* $\boldsymbol{b} \to \boldsymbol{0}$, *if in addition condition (iii) of Theorem 7.10 holds.*

The same theorems can be shown to be valid for the case where the data set is normalized to $\left\{\hat{X}_t', \hat{Y}_t'\right\}$ by including arguments similar to those of the proof of Theorem 4.5.

Remark: Let $T_{n,\boldsymbol{b}}^{(k)} = \int_S h\left(\boldsymbol{\theta}_{n,\boldsymbol{b}}^{(k)}(x,y)\right) \mathrm{d}F_n^{(k)}(x,y)$. In Section 7.4.5, we will also use the test functionals

$$T_{n,\boldsymbol{b}}^{(\mathrm{sum})} = \sum_{k=k_1}^{k_2} T_{n,\boldsymbol{b}}^{(k)},$$

whose asymptotic distribution can be derived using the Wold device. For reasons of space, we omit the details. Moreover, we will also consider test functionals of the form

$$T_{n,\boldsymbol{b}}^{(\max)} = \max_{k_1 \le k \le k_2} | T_{n,\boldsymbol{b}}^{(k)} | .$$

Finding the distribution of the maximum of jointly normal variables is a hard problem (see Nadarajah and Kotz (2008) in the bivariate case). We suggest evaluating the distribution of $T_{n,\boldsymbol{b}}^{(\max)}$ using block bootstrapping, as we will discuss in the next subsection.

The proofs of the theorems and corollary are sketched in Section 7.5.

7.4.4 The bootstrap and its validity

As for the previous tests, the asymptotic expressions for the distributions of the local parameter estimates are complicated and may not be accurate for samples of moderate size. We therefore need to apply bootstrap procedures in practice. A bootstrap version of $T_{n,b}$ in (7.25) is given by the test statistic

$$T_{n,\boldsymbol{b}}^{*} = \int_S h\left(\boldsymbol{\theta}_{n,\boldsymbol{b}}^{*}(x, y)\right) \mathrm{d}F_n^{*}(x, y), \tag{7.28}$$

where $F_n^* = \frac{1}{n}\sum_t I\left(X_t^* \le x,\ Y_t^* \le y\right)$ is the empirical cumulative distribution function after the bootstrap, and $\{X_t\}$ and $\{Y_t\}$ are block bootstrapped separately to create the bootstrap distribution under H_0. Then the p-value is calculated as before; see Section 7.3.1.

Two kinds of block bootstrap have been used, the stationary bootstrap and the moving block bootstrap. As is well known (Künsch, 1989), the block bootstrap is a sampling technique that resamples blocks of consecutive observations. Indeed, if n is the length of the data and l_n is the length of the block, then the bootstrap resample is obtained by sampling $[\frac{n}{l_n}]$ blocks randomly with replacement and then putting them back together. This is done to capture the dependence of the neighboring observations. Lacal and Tjøstheim (2017) used the standard bootstrap ($l_n = 1$) because of the interest in testing the null hypothesis of a univariate time series consisting of iid random variables. The main difference between the moving-block bootstrap and the stationary bootstrap is the choice of the length of the blocks. For the first one, the length of the blocks is fixed at a value l_n, whereas for the second one, the length of the blocks is a geometric random variable with parameter $\frac{1}{l_n}$, so that the expected length is l_n; see Politis and Romano (1994), Künsch (1989), and Liu and Singh (1992).

In practical test situations, the following LGC test statistics are typically be used: $T_1 = T_{1,n,\boldsymbol{b}} = \int_S \rho_n(x, y)\mathrm{d}F_n(x, y)$ and $T_2 = T_{2,n,\boldsymbol{b}} =$

$\int_S |\rho_n(x, y)| dF_n(x, y)$, with $S = \mathbb{R}^2$. These two test statistics have been thoroughly examined by Lacal and Tjøstheim (2019) and compared with ordinary Pearson correlation and the distance covariance (see Chapter 3.4.3); see also Székely and Rizzo (2009) and Fokianos and Pitsillou (2017). Overall, the LGC-based tests perform on par or even better than the distance covariance test, in particular, if we want to choose the region S to focus on a more restricted alternative, as already mentioned for the independence tests in Sections 7.2 and 7.3. In summary, when it comes to the local Gaussian functionals, we recommend using T_2 on the normalized data. In the next section, several examples of the use of the test are included.

We now provide the results ensuring the validity of the stationary and moving-block bootstrap, both in the estimation and testing situation. The proofs of the following theorems are available in the supplementary material (section D) of Lacal and Tjøstheim (2019).

To show that the bootstrap is valid, we need to prove the consistency (Theorem 7.13) and asymptotic normality (Theorem 7.14) of the parameter estimates after the bootstrap. We are first considering the estimation situation. We need two additional assumptions using the likelihood function notation of Section 7.4.1:

B4. $(\Lambda, \mathcal{G})$ is a measurable space, $\left(\Lambda, \mathcal{G}, P^*_\omega\right)$ is a complete probability space for all $\omega \in \Omega$, with $(\Omega, \mathcal{F}, P)$ being the probability space of $\{X_t, Y_t\}$, and $\left\{L^*_{n,\boldsymbol{b}} : \Lambda \times \Omega \times \boldsymbol{\Theta} \longrightarrow \bar{\mathbb{R}}\right\}$ is a sequence of random functions such that $L^*_{n,\boldsymbol{b}}(\boldsymbol{\theta}) = L_{n,\boldsymbol{b}}((\mathbf{X}^*_n(\lambda, \omega), \mathbf{Y}^*_n(\lambda, \omega)), \boldsymbol{\theta})$, where $X^*_t(\lambda, \omega) = X_{\tau_t^X(\lambda)}(\omega)$, $Y^*_t(\lambda, \omega) = Y_{\tau_t^Y(\lambda)}(\omega)$, $\tau_t^X, \tau_t^Y : \Lambda \longrightarrow \mathbb{N}$, $\omega \in \Omega$, $\lambda \in \Lambda$, and τ_t^X and τ_t^Y are vectors of random blocks of indices representing the bootstrap operation. If the two time series are bootstrapped together, then $\tau_t^X = \tau_t^Y$. Moreover, the block lengths l_n are such that $l_n = o(\sqrt{n})$ as $n \to \infty$.

B5. For $\boldsymbol{\theta} \in \boldsymbol{\Theta}$ and every $t = 1, \ldots, n$, $\left\{L^{(\boldsymbol{b})}((X_t, Y_t), \boldsymbol{\theta})\right\}$ is Lipschitz continuous on Θ, $\left\{\nabla L^{(\boldsymbol{b})}((X_t, Y_t), \boldsymbol{\theta})\right\}$ is 6-dominated on $\boldsymbol{\Theta}$ uniformly in t, n, and $\left\{\nabla^2 L^{(\boldsymbol{b})}((X_t, Y_t), \boldsymbol{\theta})\right\}$ is Lipschitz continuous on Θ and 2-dominated on $\boldsymbol{\Theta}$ uniformly in t, n.

Assumption **B4** sets the stage for proving the validity of the bootstrap. It defines the probability space of the bootstrapped samples $\left\{X^*_t\right\}$ and $\left\{Y^*_t\right\}$. Assumption **B5** is needed in Theorem 7.14 and is fulfilled in the situation we consider.

Theorem 7.13. *Let assumptions **B1**, **B2**, and **B4** hold, and let* $\left\{L^{(\boldsymbol{b})}((X_t, Y_t), \boldsymbol{\theta})\right\}$, $\boldsymbol{\theta} \in \boldsymbol{\Theta}$, *be Lipschitz continuous on* $\boldsymbol{\Theta}$ *and 4-dominated on* $\boldsymbol{\Theta}$ *uniformly in*

t, n. Moreover, assume that, as $\boldsymbol{b} = \boldsymbol{b}_n \to \mathbf{0}$, $\sigma_{\boldsymbol{b}}^2 = Var(L^{(\boldsymbol{b})}(X_t, Y_t), \boldsymbol{\theta}) \to \sigma^2 < \infty$ and $\mu_{\boldsymbol{b}} = E(L^{(b)}(X_t, Y_t), \boldsymbol{\theta})) \to \mu < \infty$ for all $t = 1, \ldots, n$ and $\boldsymbol{\theta} \in \boldsymbol{\Theta}$. Then $\boldsymbol{\theta}^*_{n,\boldsymbol{b}} - \widehat{\boldsymbol{\theta}}_{n,\boldsymbol{b}} \xrightarrow{P^*_\omega, P} 0$.

Theorem 7.14. *Let the assumptions of Theorem 7.10 and **B1–B5** hold. Then $\sqrt{b_1 b_2} \boldsymbol{M}_{n,\boldsymbol{b}}^{-\frac{1}{2}} \boldsymbol{J}_{n,\boldsymbol{b}} \sqrt{n} \left(\boldsymbol{\theta}^*_{n,\boldsymbol{b}} - \widehat{\boldsymbol{\theta}}_{n,\boldsymbol{b}}\right) \xrightarrow{d_{P^*_\omega}} \mathcal{N}(\mathbf{0}, \boldsymbol{I}_5)$ prob-P.*

As before, Theorems 7.13 and 7.14 still hold if we consider the case of $\{(X_t, Y_{t-k})\}$ instead of $\{(X_t, Y_t)\}$, because to prove them, it is just sufficient to substitute $\boldsymbol{\theta}$ with $\boldsymbol{\theta}^{(k)}$. Also, in this case, the matrices $\boldsymbol{M}_{n,\boldsymbol{b}}$ and $\boldsymbol{J}_{n,\boldsymbol{b}}$ will depend on the lag k. Moreover, the same asymptotic results hold with essentially proofs modified according to the proof of Theorem 4.5 for the bootstrapped time series $\hat{X}_t'^*$ and $\hat{Y}_t'^*$, where $\hat{X}_t'^*$ and $\hat{Y}_t'^*$ originate from the transformed series $\left\{\hat{X}_t', \hat{Y}_t'\right\}$.

For the testing situation, to ensure the validity of the bootstrap, we need to provide the consistency (see Theorem 7.15) and asymptotic normality (see Theorem 7.16) of the test statistic $T^*_{n,\boldsymbol{b}}$. The theorems hold for both stationary and moving-block bootstraps. Again, proofs can be found in the supplementary material of Lacal and Tjøstheim (2019).

Theorem 7.15. *Under the assumptions of Theorem 7.13 and assuming that h is continuous in (7.28), we have that $T^*_{n,\boldsymbol{b}} - T_{n,\boldsymbol{b}} \xrightarrow{P^*_\omega, P} 0$.*

Theorem 7.16. *Under the assumptions of Corollary 7.1 and Theorem 7.14 and **B4**, with independent blocks of sampling for the $\{X_t\}$ and $\{Y_t\}$ processes, we have that*

$$\sqrt{n}\,[C_n(A_{\boldsymbol{b}})]^{-\frac{1}{2}} \left(T^*_{n,\boldsymbol{b}} - T_{n,\boldsymbol{b}}\right) \xrightarrow{d_{P^*_\omega}} \mathcal{N}(0, 1) \text{ prob-}P.$$

The situation with a normalized series $\left\{(\hat{X}_t', \hat{Y}_t')\right\}$ can be treated in essentially the same way using in addition the same technique as in the proof of Theorem 4.5.

7.4.5 Example: Bivariate GARCH(1, 1)

In this example, we consider a bivariate GARCH-type model with quite weak interdependence; see Table 7.4.

We will compare $T_1 = T_{1,n,\boldsymbol{b}} = \int_S \widehat{\rho}_n(x, y) \mathrm{d}F_n(x, y)$ and $T_2 = T_{2,n,\boldsymbol{b}} = \int_S |\widehat{\rho}_n(x, y)| \mathrm{d}F_n(x, y)$ with $S = \mathbb{R}^2$, based on the local Gaussian correlation, with the ordinary Pearson correlation and with the (Brownian) distance

Table 7.4 Bivariate GARCH(1, 1) model.

DEP-GARCH	$\begin{pmatrix} Z_t \\ W_t \end{pmatrix} \sim N\left(\begin{pmatrix} 0 \\ 0 \end{pmatrix}, \begin{pmatrix} 1 & 0 \\ 0 & 1 \end{pmatrix}\right),$ $X_t = h_X(t)Z_t,\ Y_t = h_Y(t)W_t,$ $h_X(1) = 1,\ h_X^2(t) = 1 + 0.5h_X^2(t-1) + 0.3X_{t-1}^2 + 0.1Y_{t-1}^2,$ $h_Y(1) = 1,\ h_Y^2(t) = 1 + 0.5h_Y^2(t-1) + 0.3Y_{t-1}^2 + 0.1X_{t-1}^2.$

covariance. Since the Pearson correlation and T_1 can take negative values, for these two cases, we performed a two-sided test, whereas we used a one-sided test for T_2 and the distance covariance, rejecting independence for large values. Further, we denote the (Brownian) distance covariance by BDC and the ordinary correlation by P.

In the experiments, we set the significance level to 1%, 5%, and 10%, and consider $N = 300$ or $N = 600$ replicates of $n = 1000$ observations,and for each realization, $R = 500$ bootstraps. For each model, we consider the case where the data set is not transformed (**NOSN**) and the case in which the marginals are transformed into a standard normal variable (**SN**). In this case, we used the stationary bootstrap, calculated the bandwidth using cross-validation for the original realization, and then used this value for all the bootstrap replicates.

In Table 7.5, we report the results from this power simulation experiment conducted by Lacal and Tjøstheim (2019) for lag $k = 0$ and 1. We see that the Pearson correlation and the test statistic T_1 fail, whereas the other two tests, in many cases are quite good. The failure of T_1 is because the local correlation $\rho(x, y)$ for the GARCH cases is predominantly negative in the second and fourth quadrants, to a large degree canceling out the positive values in the first and third quadrants. The distance covariance gives higher values of the power when the data set is not transformed, whereas the test statistic T_2 for the transformed case gives the overall best results. Moreover, note that in Table 7.5 the power for $k = 1$ is a bit higher than that for $k = 0$. Because $\rho(x, y)$ is a local quantity, the tests based on it can be focussed against a more restricted alternative hypothesis by appropriately choosing S, as was done by Berentsen and Tjøstheim (2014) and Lacal and Tjøstheim (2017) and in Sections 7.2 and 7.3. Using such a focussing, it is possible to obtain a power exceeding 0.9 even in the 1% significance level case. The stationary bootstrap and the moving-block bootstrap perform almost in the same way for this example.

Table 7.5 Power of GARCH model of Table 7.4.

Test	%	DEP-GARCH with $k=0$				DEP-GARCH with $k=1$			
		NOSN		SN		NOSN		SN	
		$N=300$	$N=600$	$N=300$	$N=600$	$N=300$	$N=600$	$N=300$	$N=600$
T_1	1	2.7	3.0	3.0	3.7	6.7	6.8	7.0	7.2
	5	8.3	8.3	10.0	10.2	12.7	12.8	15.3	14.3
	10	15.7	16.2	18.0	17.7	18.7	18.8	22.0	22.5
T_2	1	3.3	3.0	29.3	28.8	8.7	9.0	64.0	63.7
	5	11.7	12.5	57.0	57.0	23.0	23.3	87.7	87.5
	10	21.0	21.7	70.7	70.3	38.7	39.3	92.7	92.8
BDC	1	15.3	16.5	5.3	5.3	37.0	37.2	16.0	15.2
	5	41.3	41.7	22.7	22.5	71.0	70.5	47.3	46.5
	10	56.0	56.3	38.0	37.8	82.7	82.5	67.7	67.5
P	1	8.3	8.0	2.3	2.8	10.3	10.7	4.0	3.8
	5	16.3	16.0	10.0	10.3	19.3	19.5	11.3	11.5
	10	20.7	20.5	15.7	15.2	26.3	26.8	17.3	18.3

Table 7.6 Power for max and sum statistics.

Test	%	DEP-GARCH	
		MAX	SUM
T_1	1	10.0	5.5
	5	17.5	14.5
	10	24.0	20.5
T_2	1	59.5	94.0
	5	79.5	97.0
	10	89.0	97.5
BDC	1	6.5	50.5
	5	16.0	68.0
	10	27.5	75.5
P	1	5.0	5.5
	5	13.5	9.5
	10	20.0	16.5

A level study was also performed by Lacal and Tjøstheim (2019) for this setup. The level for the local Gaussian correlation tests T_1 and T_2 is good, as it is for the other two tests. They also did level experiments for other nonlinear models, for example, two independent exponential autoregressive models, with quite similar results, albeit with an overestimation of the level in some cases.

Finally, the power of the DEP-GARCH model in Table 7.4, for the test statistics $T^{(\text{sum})}$ and $T^{(\text{max})}$ defined at the end of Subsection 7.4.3 with similar definitions for $BDC^{(\text{sum})}$ and $P^{(\text{sum})}$ were studied. The bounds $k_1 = -5$ and $k_2 = 5$ were used, and further, a one-sided test for $T_2^{(\text{sum})}$ and $BDC^{(\text{sum})}$, two-sided test for $T_1^{(\text{sum})}$ and $P^{(\text{sum})}$, and one-sided tests for all statistics involving max were used. Moreover, $N = 200$ replicates of $n = 500$ observations are chosen, and for each realization, $R = 300$ bootstraps. To save computational time, the plug-in bandwidth $b_n = 1.75n^{-\frac{1}{6}}$ has been applied. Moreover, only the case in which the data is transformed into standard normal variables (**SN**) and only the stationary bootstrap were considered. As we can see from Table 7.6, again taken from Lacal and Tjøstheim (2019), the results for the power or the local Gaussian correlation are better than the other two tests. More simulation experiments are given by Lacal and Tjøstheim (2019).

7.4.6 Example: Financial returns

In this example, we analyze log-returns of stock market indices for the UK (FTSE 100) and the US (S&P 500) in the period starting from January 1, 2005, to November 15, 2016. Since the financial crisis emerged on August 9, 2007 (see Støve et al., 2014), the data set is divided into three parts: the period from January 1, 2005 to August 8, 2007 is called "Before Crisis", from August 9, 2007 to August 7, 2009 "During Crisis", and from August 8, 2009 to November 15, 2016 "After Crisis". Thus this example relates to the test for financial contagion introduced in Section 6.5.2. However, with the methods developed in this chapter, we can extend this procedure by formally examining whether there are any lead-lag effects using the local Gaussian cross-correlation between different markets.

The dependence between the two series of returns, FTSE100 and S&P 500, is very strong, and, not surprisingly, tests of independence based on the local correlation lead to clear rejection of independence for the pair of indices with $k = 0$. It is more interesting to look at the shape of the local correlation curves with accompanying confidence intervals.

In Figs. 7.4, 7.5, and 7.6, there are, respectively, the plots of the local Gaussian correlation $\hat{\rho}(x, x)$, along the diagonal $x = y$ for the X_t = FTSE 100 and the Y_{t-k} = S&P 500 indices for $k = 0, 1, -1$ when the data set is not transformed, when it is transformed into standard normal variables using the empirical distribution function, and when the component series are GARCH(1, 1)-filtered but not normalized. This is done for the data sets before and during the financial crisis. The GARCH-filter is used because it should remove marginal auto-dependence over time and volatilities effects, as done in Chapter 6. In this way, it is easier to analyze causality and also to see whether, and to what degree, one of the two time series is leading the other.

Note that GARCH filtered data and the use of the ordinary bootstrap when computing, say, confidence intervals implicitly assume that individual GARCH filtering for each component time series $\{X_t\}$ and $\{Y_t\}$ also should result in serially independent and identically distributed observations for the bivariate series $\{(X_t, Y_t)\}$. However, we see that this does not really hold for the $\{(\text{FTSE}_t, \text{SP}_t)\}$ series (see, e.g., Fig. 7.6c). This means that also the GARCH filtered data should be examined by the stationary or the moving-block bootstrap, and the stationary bootstrap was used in this example to obtain 95% pointwise confidence intervals. Hence, in the test for financial contagion introduced in Chapter 6.5.2, before using the ordinary bootstrap

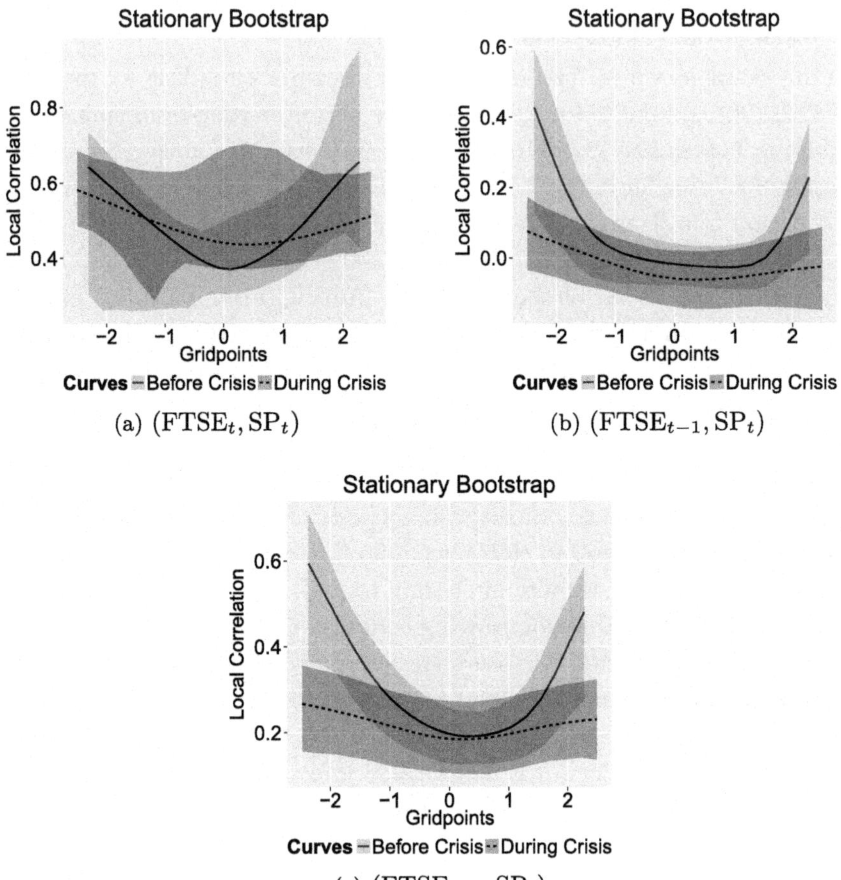

(a) $(\mathrm{FTSE}_t, \mathrm{SP}_t)$ (b) $(\mathrm{FTSE}_{t-1}, \mathrm{SP}_t)$ (c) $(\mathrm{FTSE}_{t+1}, \mathrm{SP}_t)$

Figure 7.4 Local Gaussian correlation for FTSE versus S&P with no transformation.

proposed in that test, we need to confirm that GARCH filtered data indeed are iid.

Looking closer at the results for the FTSE_t and SP_t time series, Figs. 7.4a and 7.6a demonstrate that both before and during the crisis, the local correlation is increasing both when the market is going down (negative log returns x) and up (positive log returns x). The increase is close to being monotonous and slightly stronger for a falling market. Figs. 7.5a and 7.6a show clear increase of the local correlation during crisis, again most in the falling market case.

In Figs. 7.4b & 7.6b and 7.4c & 7.6c, we try to investigate if there are any (nonlinear) lead-lag effects for the series $\{\mathrm{FTSE}_t\}$ and $\{\mathrm{SP}_t\}$. In ordi-

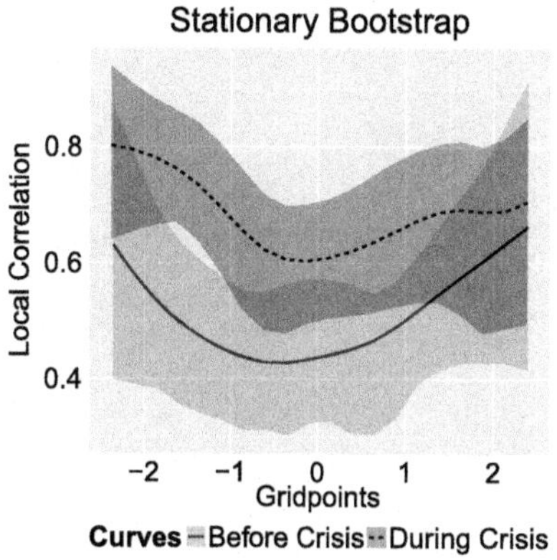

(a) $(\mathrm{FTSE}_t, \mathrm{SP}_t)$

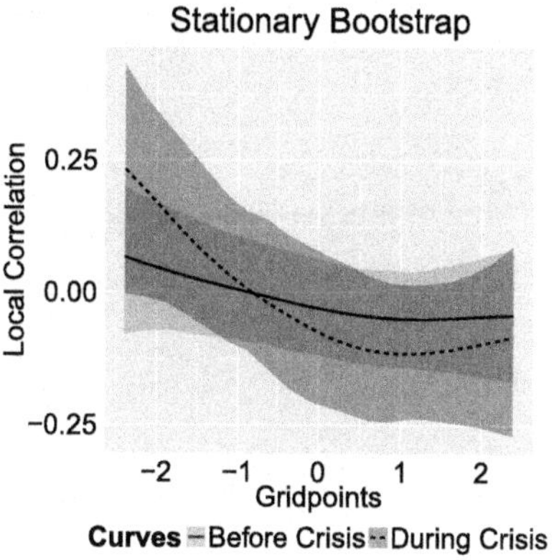

(b) $(\mathrm{FTSE}_{t-1}, \mathrm{SP}_t)$

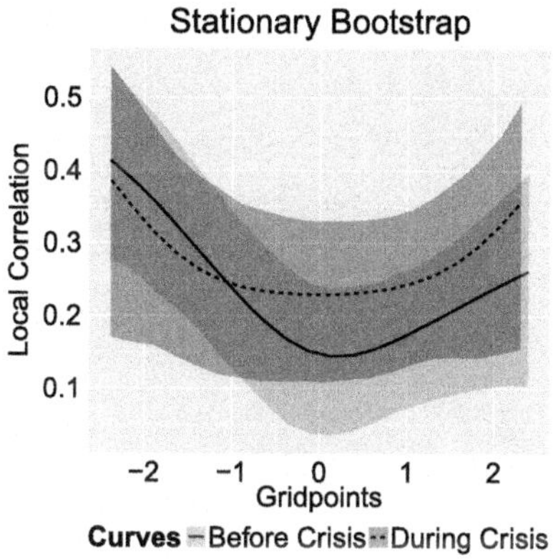

(c) $(\mathrm{FTSE}_{t+1}, \mathrm{SP}_t)$

Figure 7.5 Local Gaussian correlation for FTSE versus S&P with marginals transformed into standard normal variables.

nary linear time series analysis, it is well known that lead-lag effects can be masked by autocorrelation, and this is usually tried removing by prewhitening the series. By GARCH(1, 1) filtering with a Student-t distribution on the residuals, the individual GARCH residuals pass a test of iid residuals. This means that the local cross-correlation plot of Figs. 7.6b and 7.6c should be best suited to conduct a lead-lag investigation. From this figure we see that the $(\mathrm{FTSE})_t$ series is influenced by the $(\mathrm{SP})_t$ series, not only in the same day, but also from the day before. It seems to be no such clear effect going on in the other direction, which is perhaps slightly surprising

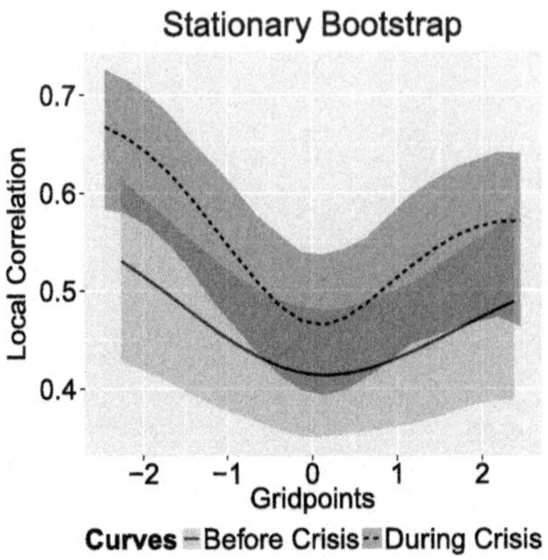

(a) $(\mathrm{FTSE}_t, \mathrm{SP}_t)$

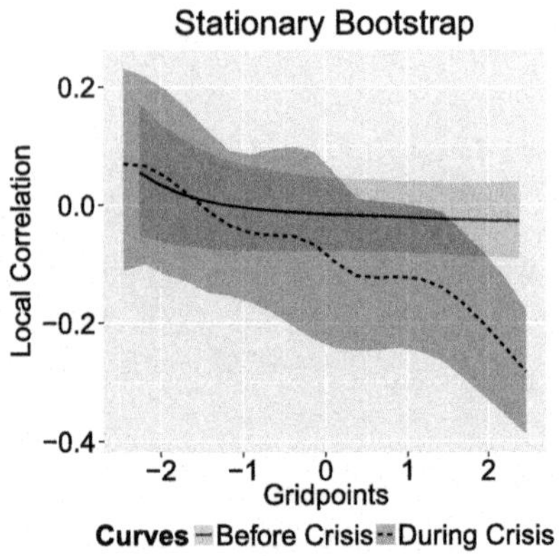

(b) $(\mathrm{FTSE}_{t-1}, \mathrm{SP}_t)$

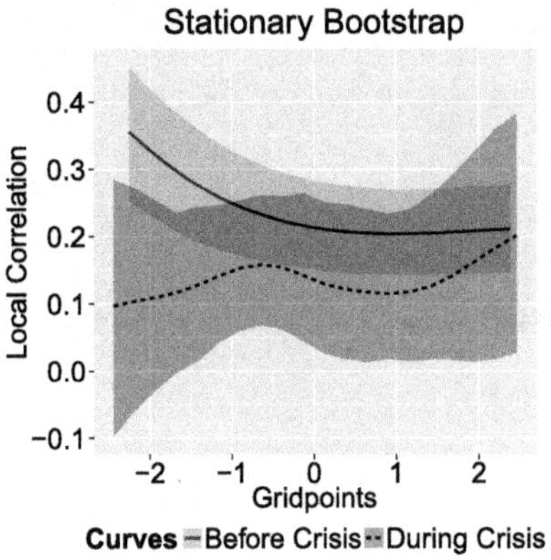

(c) $(\mathrm{FTSE}_{t+1}, \mathrm{SP}_t)$

Figure 7.6 Local Gaussian correlation for FTSE versus S&P GARCH-filtered.

when the time difference between the FTSE- and SP-markets is taken into account. In contrast to the zero-lag results, there is now a very clear difference between a market upturn and downturn, the lag 1 effect being much stronger in the downturn case (Fig. 7.6c). Contrasting the zero-lag effects, the before crisis lag 1 effect is consistently higher than the lag 1 effect during crisis. It appears that the crisis has led to a more concentrated zero-lag effect.

We also computed the local correlation for higher lags (2, 3, 4, 5, 10, 15). No clear effects in either direction were found. For similar studies between other market indices, we refer to Lacal and Tjøstheim (2019).

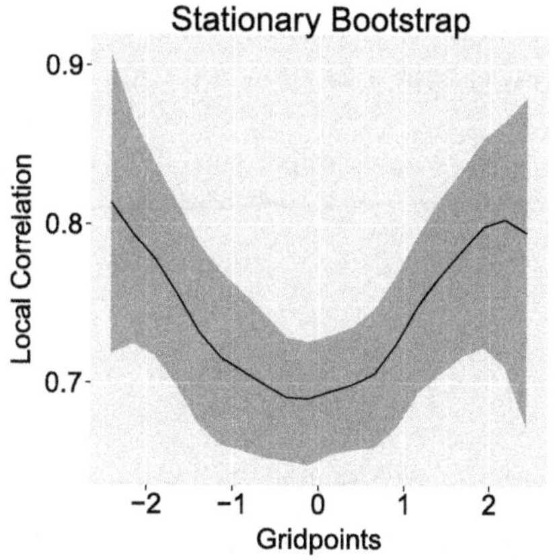

Figure 7.7 Local Gaussian correlation for FTSE versus S&P with marginals transformed into standard normal variables for the period 2009–2016.

As already mentioned, Figs. 7.5a and 7.6a show clear increase of the local correlation during crisis, which is in line with the findings of Chapter 6.5 and Støve et al. (2014). Indeed, the plots in Figs. 7.4–7.6 give a nonlinear *distributional* based measure of dependence between the indices, with much more detailed information than the ordinary correlation.

In addition, Lacal and Tjøstheim (2019) also looked at the period from August 7, 2009 to November 15, 2016 for the indices when the data is transformed into standard normal variables. The corresponding plot is given in Fig. 7.7 (note that the scale is different from that of Fig. 7.5a). As we can be notice, the plot in Fig. 7.7 shows the same pattern as the plot in Fig. 7.5a, that is, also for the period 2009–2016, there is a stronger local correlation for downturns and upturns than for a stable market. Moreover, the curves are essentially of the same level as during the financial crisis, in this respect, demonstrating a lasting effect of this crisis. Note that this is consistent with a study by Aastveit et al. (2017) of other economic variables using a linear VAR model, where they identified a structural break in 2008 in a data set extending to 2015.

7.5 Proofs

7.5.1 Proof of Theorems 7.9 and 7.10

Proof of Theorem 7.9. Let $M < \infty$ and $\Delta < \infty$ be such that $|L^{(\boldsymbol{b})}((X_t, Y_t), \boldsymbol{\theta}) - L^{(\boldsymbol{b})}((X_t, Y_t), \boldsymbol{\theta}')| \leq C_t|\boldsymbol{\theta} - \boldsymbol{\theta}'|$, $C_t \leq M$, and, using 4-dominance,

$|L^{(\boldsymbol{b})}((X_t, Y_t), \boldsymbol{\theta})|_4 \leq \Delta$. For $\delta > 0$, let $\{\eta(\boldsymbol{\theta}_i, \delta) : i = 1, \ldots, B\}$ be a finite subcover of $\boldsymbol{\Theta}$, where $\eta(\boldsymbol{\theta}_i, \delta) = \{\boldsymbol{\theta} \in \boldsymbol{\Theta} : |\boldsymbol{\theta} - \boldsymbol{\theta}_i| < \delta\}$. Then

$$\sup_{\boldsymbol{\theta}\in\boldsymbol{\Theta}} |L_{n,\boldsymbol{b}}(\boldsymbol{\theta}) - \mu_{\boldsymbol{b}}| = \max_i \sup_{\boldsymbol{\theta}\in\eta(\boldsymbol{\theta}_i,\delta)} |L_{n,\boldsymbol{b}}(\boldsymbol{\theta}) - \mu_{\boldsymbol{b}}|. \tag{7.29}$$

Hence we can write

$$P\left(\sup_{\boldsymbol{\theta}\in\boldsymbol{\Theta}} |L_{n,\boldsymbol{b}}(\boldsymbol{\theta}) - \mu_{\boldsymbol{b}}| > \epsilon\right) \leq \sum_{i=1}^{B} P\left(\sup_{\boldsymbol{\theta}\in\eta(\boldsymbol{\theta}_i,\delta)} |L_{n,\boldsymbol{b}}(\boldsymbol{\theta}) - \mu_{\boldsymbol{b}}| > \epsilon\right). \tag{7.30}$$

By the Lipschitz continuity of $\left\{L^{(\boldsymbol{b})}((X_t, Y_t), \boldsymbol{\theta})\right\}$, if $\boldsymbol{\theta} \in \eta(\boldsymbol{\theta}_i, \delta)$, then

$$\begin{aligned}|L_{n,\boldsymbol{b}}(\boldsymbol{\theta}) - \mu_{\boldsymbol{b}}| &\leq |L_{n,\boldsymbol{b}}(\boldsymbol{\theta}) - L_{n,\boldsymbol{b}}(\boldsymbol{\theta}_i)| + |L_{n,\boldsymbol{b}}(\boldsymbol{\theta}_i) - \mu_{\boldsymbol{b}}| \\ &\leq \frac{\delta}{n}\sum_{t=1}^{n} C_t + |L_{n,\boldsymbol{b}}(\boldsymbol{\theta}_i) - \mu_{\boldsymbol{b}}|.\end{aligned}$$

By the Markov inequality,

$$\begin{aligned}P\left(\sup_{\boldsymbol{\theta}\in\eta(\boldsymbol{\theta}_i,\delta)} |L_{n,\boldsymbol{b}}(\boldsymbol{\theta}) - \mu_{\boldsymbol{b}}| > \epsilon\right) &\leq P\left(\frac{\delta}{n}\sum_{t=1}^{n} C_t > \frac{\epsilon}{2}\right) + P\left(|L_{n,\boldsymbol{b}}(\boldsymbol{\theta}_i) - \mu_b| > \frac{\epsilon}{2}\right) \\ &\leq \frac{2\delta}{n\epsilon}\mathrm{E}\left(\sum_{t=1}^{n} C_t\right) + \frac{4}{\epsilon^2}\mathrm{Var}\left(L_{n,\boldsymbol{b}}(\boldsymbol{\theta}_i)\right) \\ &\leq \frac{2\delta M}{\epsilon} + \frac{4}{\epsilon^2}\mathrm{Var}\left(L_{n,\boldsymbol{b}}(\boldsymbol{\theta}_i)\right).\end{aligned}$$

Using the α-mixing assumption for $\{X_t, Y_t\}$, by the mixing inequality (Corollary A.2, Hall and Heyde (1980)) and the 4-dominance of $\left\{L^{(\boldsymbol{b})}((X_t, Y_t), \boldsymbol{\theta})\right\}$,

$$\begin{aligned}\mathrm{Var}\left(L_{n,\boldsymbol{b}}(\boldsymbol{\theta}_i)\right) &= \frac{1}{n^2}\mathrm{Var}\left(\sum_{t=1}^{n} L^{(\boldsymbol{b})}((X_t, Y_t), \boldsymbol{\theta}_i)\right) \\ &= \frac{1}{n^2}\sum_{t=1}^{n}\sum_{s=1}^{n}\mathrm{Cov}\left(L^{(\boldsymbol{b})}((X_t, Y_t), \theta_i), L^{(\boldsymbol{b})}((X_s, Y_s), \boldsymbol{\theta}_i)\right) \\ &\leq \frac{8}{n^2}\sum_{t=1}^{n}\sum_{s=1}^{n}|L^{(\boldsymbol{b})}((X_t, Y_t), \boldsymbol{\theta}_i)|_4 |L^{(\boldsymbol{b})}((X_s, Y_s), \boldsymbol{\theta}_i)|_4 \alpha^{\frac{|t-s|}{2}} \\ &\leq \frac{8\Delta^2}{n^2}\sum_{t=1}^{n}\sum_{s=1}^{n}\alpha^{\frac{|t-s|}{2}} = \frac{8\Delta^2}{n^2}\left(n + 2\sum_{j=1}^{n-1}(n-j)\alpha^{\frac{j}{2}}\right)\end{aligned}$$

$$\leq \frac{8\Delta^2}{n^2}\left(n+2(n-1)\sum_{j=1}^{n-1}\alpha^{\frac{j}{2}}\right)$$
$$= \frac{8\Delta^2}{n^2}\left(n+2(n-1)\frac{\alpha^{\frac{1}{2}}-\alpha^{\frac{n}{2}}}{1-\alpha^{\frac{1}{2}}}\right).$$

Therefore

$$P\left(\sup_{\theta\in\eta(\theta_i,\delta)}|L_{n,b}(\boldsymbol{\theta})-\mu_b|>\epsilon\right)\leq\frac{2\delta M}{\epsilon}+\frac{32\Delta^2}{n^2}\left(n+2(n-1)\frac{\alpha^{\frac{1}{2}}-\alpha^{\frac{n}{2}}}{1-\alpha^{\frac{1}{2}}}\right)$$
$$<\zeta+\frac{32\Delta^2}{n^2}\left(n+2(n-1)\frac{\alpha^{\frac{1}{2}}-\alpha^{\frac{n}{2}}}{1-\alpha^{\frac{1}{2}}}\right)$$

for all n sufficiently large, $\zeta>0$, and $\delta<\frac{\epsilon\zeta}{2M}$. From this it follows that, as $n\to\infty$,

$$P\left(\sup_{\theta\in\Theta}|L_{n,b}(\boldsymbol{\theta})-\mu_b|>\epsilon\right)<B\zeta,\ \forall\zeta>0,\ B<\infty,$$

and therefore

$$\lim_{n\to\infty}P\left(\sup_{\theta\in\Theta}|\,L_{n,b}(\boldsymbol{\theta})-\mu_b\,|>\epsilon\right)=0,\ \forall\epsilon>0.$$

This means that

$$L_{n,b}(\boldsymbol{\theta})-\mathrm{E}\left(L_{n,b}(\boldsymbol{\theta})\right)\xrightarrow{P}0 \text{ uniformly on } \boldsymbol{\Theta}. \tag{7.31}$$

Note that from the stationarity of the process $\{(X_t,Y_t)\}$ it follows that $\mathrm{E}\left(L_{n,b}(\boldsymbol{\theta})\right)=\mathrm{E}(L^{(b)}((X_t,Y_t),\boldsymbol{\theta}))$. Since $L_{n,b}$ is continuous on $\boldsymbol{\Theta}$ P-a.s. with maximizer $\widehat{\boldsymbol{\theta}}_{n,b}$, from assumption **B2** and (7.31) it follows that $L_{n,b}(\boldsymbol{\theta}_{0,b})-\mathrm{E}\left(L_{n,b}(\boldsymbol{\theta}_{0,b})\right)\xrightarrow{P}0$. Moreover, using (7.31) and the definition of $\widehat{\boldsymbol{\theta}}_{n,b}$ and $\boldsymbol{\theta}_{0,b}$ (that is, assumption **B2**), we have that $L_{n,b}(\widehat{\boldsymbol{\theta}}_{n,b})-\mathrm{E}\left(L^{(b)}((X_t,Y_t),\boldsymbol{\theta}_{0,b})\right)=\sup_{\theta\in\Theta}L_{n,b}(\boldsymbol{\theta})-\sup_{\theta\in\Theta}\mathrm{E}\left(L^{(b)}((X_t,Y_t),\boldsymbol{\theta})\right)\xrightarrow{P}0$. This means that $L_{n,b}(\widehat{\boldsymbol{\theta}}_{n,b})-L_{n,b}(\boldsymbol{\theta}_{0,b})\xrightarrow{P}0$. By the assumption that $\widehat{\boldsymbol{\theta}}_{n,b}$ is a maximizer of $L_{n,b}$, for every $\epsilon>0$, there exists $\eta>0$ such that $|\,L_{n,b}(\widehat{\boldsymbol{\theta}}_{n,b})-L_{n,b}(\boldsymbol{\theta})\,|>\eta$ for every $\boldsymbol{\theta}$ with $|\,\boldsymbol{\theta}_{n,b}-\boldsymbol{\theta}\,|>\epsilon$. Therefore, if we take $\boldsymbol{\theta}=\boldsymbol{\theta}_{0,b}$, then the event $\left\{|\,\widehat{\boldsymbol{\theta}}_{n,b}-\boldsymbol{\theta}_{0,b}\,|>\epsilon\right\}$ is contained in the event $\left\{|\,L_{n,b}(\widehat{\boldsymbol{\theta}}_{n,b})-L_{n,b}(\boldsymbol{\theta}_{0,b})\,|>\eta\right\}$, meaning that for every $\epsilon>0$, there exists $\eta>0$ such that

$$P\left(|\,\widehat{\boldsymbol{\theta}}_{n,b}-\boldsymbol{\theta}_{0,b}\,|>\epsilon\right)\leq P\left(|\,L_{n,b}(\widehat{\boldsymbol{\theta}}_{n,b})-L_{n,b}(\boldsymbol{\theta}_{0,b})\,|>\eta\right)\xrightarrow{P}0.$$

The last statement of the theorem follows since $\boldsymbol{\theta}_{0,\boldsymbol{b}} \to \boldsymbol{\theta}_0$ by definition. □

Proof of Theorem 7.10. It is a generalization of Theorem 3 of Tjøstheim and Hufthammer (2013) and of the proof of Theorem 4.2. Define $Q_n(\boldsymbol{\theta}) = -\frac{n}{(b_1 b_2)^2} L_{n,\boldsymbol{b}}(\boldsymbol{\theta})$ and consider the Taylor expansion of $\nabla Q_n(\boldsymbol{\theta})$:

$$0 = \frac{1}{\sqrt{n}} \nabla Q_n(\widehat{\boldsymbol{\theta}}_{n,\boldsymbol{b}}) = \frac{1}{\sqrt{n}} \nabla Q_n(\boldsymbol{\theta}_{0,\boldsymbol{b}}) + \frac{1}{n} \nabla^2 Q_n(\tilde{\boldsymbol{\theta}}) \sqrt{n}(\widehat{\boldsymbol{\theta}}_{n,\boldsymbol{b}} - \boldsymbol{\theta}_{0,\boldsymbol{b}}),$$

where $\tilde{\boldsymbol{\theta}}$ is determined by the mean value theorem. Therefore

$$\begin{aligned} -\frac{(b_1 b_2)^{\frac{3}{2}}}{\sqrt{n}} \nabla Q_n(\boldsymbol{\theta}_{0,\boldsymbol{b}}) &= \frac{(b_1 b_2)^{\frac{3}{2}}}{n} \nabla^2 Q_n(\tilde{\boldsymbol{\theta}}) \sqrt{n}(\widehat{\boldsymbol{\theta}}_{n,\boldsymbol{b}} - \boldsymbol{\theta}_{0,\boldsymbol{b}}) \\ &= \frac{(b_1 b_2)^{\frac{3}{2}}}{n} \left[\nabla^2 Q_n(\boldsymbol{\theta}_{0,\boldsymbol{b}}) + \left(\nabla^2 Q_n(\tilde{\boldsymbol{\theta}}) - \nabla^2 Q_n(\boldsymbol{\theta}_{0,\boldsymbol{b}}) \right) \right] \sqrt{n}(\widehat{\boldsymbol{\theta}}_{n,\boldsymbol{b}} - \boldsymbol{\theta}_{0,\boldsymbol{b}}). \end{aligned}$$

Suppose we can prove that

(i) $\frac{1}{n} \nabla Q_n(\boldsymbol{\theta}_{0,\boldsymbol{b}}) \to 0$ a.s.;

(ii) $\frac{1}{n} \nabla^2 Q_n(\boldsymbol{\theta}_{0,\boldsymbol{b}}) \to \tilde{\boldsymbol{J}}$ a.s., where $\tilde{\boldsymbol{J}}$ is a 5×5 positive definite matrix that can be identified with the limit of $\frac{1}{(b_1 b_2)^2} \boldsymbol{J}_{n,\boldsymbol{b}}$ as $n \to \infty$ and $\boldsymbol{b} \to 0$;

(iii) $\lim_{n\to\infty} \limsup_{\delta \to 0} \frac{1}{n\delta} \mid \nabla^2 Q_n(\tilde{\boldsymbol{\theta}}) - \nabla^2 Q_n(\boldsymbol{\theta}_{0,\boldsymbol{b}}) \mid < \infty$;

(iv) $\mathrm{Var}\left(-\frac{(b_1 b_2)^{\frac{3}{2}}}{\sqrt{n}} \nabla Q_n(\boldsymbol{\theta}_{0,\boldsymbol{b}}) \right) = \frac{1}{(b_1 b_2)^2} \boldsymbol{M}_{n,\boldsymbol{b}}$.

Then, using Theorem 4.4 of Masry and Tjøstheim (1995) and Theorem 2.2 of Klimko and Nelson (1978), we have the result.

The proof of (i)–(iii) is essentially the same as that of Theorem 4.2.

Finally, item (iv) is a straightforward consequence of the definition of $\nabla Q_n(\boldsymbol{\theta}_{0,\boldsymbol{b}})$. □

7.5.2 Proof of Theorems 7.11 and 7.12 and Corollary 7.1

Proof of Theorem 7.11. The proof is just an application of the continuous mapping theorem. □

Proof of Theorem 7.12. The proof is essentially the same as that of Theorem 3.1 in Lacal and Tjøstheim (2017). We refer to that proof for further details. The asymptotic normality for fixed $\boldsymbol{b}$ is proved as in that theorem.

We need to evaluate the variance of $\int A_{\boldsymbol{b}}(x, y) \mathrm{d}G_n(x, y)$, where $G_n(x, y) = \sqrt{n}(F_n(x, y) - F(x, y))$. Since $\mathrm{E}\left(\int A_{\boldsymbol{b}}(x, y) \mathrm{d}G_n(x, y)\right) = 0$,

$$\mathrm{Var}\left(\int A_{\boldsymbol{b}}(x, y) \mathrm{d}G_n(x, y) \right) = \mathrm{E}\left(\int A_{\boldsymbol{b}}(x, y) A_{\boldsymbol{b}}(v, w) \mathrm{d}G_n(x, y) \mathrm{d}G_n(v, w) \right)$$

$$
\begin{aligned}
&= \frac{1}{n} \sum_r \sum_s \mathrm{E}\left(A_b\left(X_r, Y_r\right) A_b\left(X_s, Y_s\right)\right) \\
&- \sum_r \mathrm{E}\left(\int A_b\left(X_r, Y_r\right) A_b(v, w) \mathrm{d}F(v, w)\right) \\
&- \sum_s \mathrm{E}\left(\int A_b(x, y) A_b\left(X_s, Y_s\right) \mathrm{d}F(x, y)\right) \\
&+ n \int A_b(x, y) A_b(v, w) \mathrm{d}F(x, y) \mathrm{d}F(v, w) \\
&= D_1 + D_2 + D_3 + D_4 .
\end{aligned}
$$

The contribution of terms with $r \neq s$ to D_1 is

$$
\begin{aligned}
&\frac{1}{n} \sum_{r \neq s} \int A_b(x, y) A_b(v, w) \mathrm{d}F^{(r-s)}(x, y, v, w) \\
&\quad = \sum_{k=1}^{n} \frac{n-k}{n} \int A_b(x, y) A_b(v, w) \left[\mathrm{d}F^{(k)}(x, y, v, w) + \mathrm{d}F^{(-k)}(x, y, v, w)\right],
\end{aligned}
$$

whereas the terms with $r = s$ contribute with $\int A_b(x, y) A_b(x, y) \mathrm{d}F(x, y)$. Moreover, $D_2 = D_3 = -D_4$, so that

$$
\begin{aligned}
\operatorname{Var}&\left(\int A_b(x, y) \mathrm{d}G_n(x, y)\right) = \int A_b^2(x, y) \mathrm{d}F(x, y) \\
&- n \int A_b(x, y) A_b(v, y) \mathrm{d}F(x, y) \mathrm{d}F(v, w) \\
&+ \int A_b(x, y) A_b(v, w) \sum_{k=1}^{n} \frac{n-k}{n} \left[\mathrm{d}F^{(k)}(x, y, v, w) + \mathrm{d}F^{(-k)}(x, y, v, w)\right] \\
&+ \int A_b(x, y) A_b(v, w) \mathrm{d}F(x, y) \mathrm{d}F(v, w) \\
&- \int A_b(x, y) A_b(v, w) \mathrm{d}F(x, y) \mathrm{d}F(v, w) \\
&= \int A_b^2(x, y) \mathrm{d}F(x, y) \\
&- \int A_b(x, y) A_b(v, w) \mathrm{d}F(x, y) \mathrm{d}F(v, w) \\
&+ \int A_b(x, y) A_b(v, w) \sum_{k=1}^{n} \frac{n-k}{n} \left[\mathrm{d}F^{(k)}(x, y, v, w) + \mathrm{d}F^{(-k)}(x, y, v, w)\right]
\end{aligned}
$$

$$+\int A_b(x,y)A_b(v,w)\sum_{k=1}^{n}\frac{1-n}{n}\mathrm{d}F(x,y)\mathrm{d}F(v,w).$$

Focusing on the last two terms, adding and subtracting $\sum_{k=1}^{n}\frac{2(n-k)}{n}\mathrm{d}F(x,y)\cdot\mathrm{d}F(v,w)$, we have:

$$\begin{aligned}&\int A_b(x,y)A_b(v,w)\sum_{k=1}^{n}\left[\frac{n-k}{n}\left(\mathrm{d}F^{(k)}(x,y,v,w)+\mathrm{d}F^{(-k)}(x,y,v,w)\right)\right.\\&\quad\left.+\frac{1-n}{n}\mathrm{d}F(x,y)\mathrm{d}F(v,w)\right]\\&=\int A_b(x,y)A_b(v,w)\sum_{k=1}^{n}\frac{n-k}{n}\left[\mathrm{d}F^{(k)}(x,y,v,w)-\mathrm{d}F(x,y)\mathrm{d}F(v,w)\right]\\&\quad+\int A_b(x,y)A_b(v,w)\sum_{k=1}^{n}\frac{n-k}{n}\left[\mathrm{d}F^{(-k)}(x,y,v,w)-\mathrm{d}F(x,y)\mathrm{d}F(v,w)\right].\end{aligned}$$

Therefore

$$\begin{aligned}\mathrm{Var}\left(\int A_b(x,y)\mathrm{d}G_n(x,y)\right)&=\int A_b^2(x,y)\mathrm{d}F(x,y)\\&\quad-\int A_b(x,y)A_b(v,w)\mathrm{d}F(x,y)\mathrm{d}F(v,w)\\&\quad+\int A_b(x,y)A_b(v,w)\sum_{k=1}^{n}\frac{n-k}{n}\left[\mathrm{d}F^{(k)}(x,y,v,w)-\mathrm{d}F(x,y)dF(v,w)\right]\\&\quad+\int A_b(x,y)A_b(v,w)\sum_{k=1}^{n}\frac{n-k}{n}\left[\mathrm{d}F^{(-k)}(x,y,v,w)-\mathrm{d}F(x,y)\mathrm{d}F(v,w)\right].\end{aligned}$$

To check whether the variance converges, we need to prove the convergence of the sum in the last two integrals. Using Assumption **B1** and Corollary A.2 of Hall and Heyde (1980) and choosing arbitrary $1<q<p$ such that $\frac{1}{p}+\frac{1}{q}<1$, we have

$$\begin{aligned}&\left|\sum_{k=1}^{n}\frac{n-k}{n}\int A_b(x,y)A_b(v,w)\left[f^{(k)}(x,y,v,w)-f(x,y)f(v,w)\right]\mathrm{d}x\mathrm{d}y\mathrm{d}v\mathrm{d}w\right|\\&\leq\sum_{k=1}^{n}\frac{n-k}{n}\left|\mathrm{E}\left(A_b(X_s,Y_s)A_b(X_{s-k},Y_{s-k})\right)\right.\\&\qquad\left.-\mathrm{E}\left(A_b(X_s,Y_s)\right)\mathrm{E}\left(A_b(X_{s-k},Y_{s-k})\right)\right|\end{aligned}$$

$$\leq 8\sum_{k=1}^{n}\frac{n-k}{n}|A_{\boldsymbol{b}}|_p|A_{\boldsymbol{b}}|_q\alpha_k^{1-\frac{1}{p}-\frac{1}{q}} = 8|A_{\boldsymbol{b}}|_p|A_{\boldsymbol{b}}|_q\ O\left(\frac{(n-1)}{n}\sum_{k=1}^{n}\left(\alpha^{1-\frac{1}{p}-\frac{1}{q}}\right)^k\right)$$

$$\xrightarrow{n\to\infty} 8\frac{\alpha^{1-\frac{1}{p}-\frac{1}{q}}}{1-\alpha^{1-\frac{1}{p}-\frac{1}{q}}}|A_{\boldsymbol{b}}|_p|A_{\boldsymbol{b}}|_q < \infty,$$

where $f^{(k)}$ is the density function of (X_t, Y_t, X_s, Y_s) with $k = t - s$. The same is true for $k = s - t$. For $n \to \infty$ and $\boldsymbol{b} \to \mathbf{0}$, we need assumption (iii) of Theorem 7.10 and use the approach of Joe (1989) and let $\boldsymbol{b} \to \mathbf{0}$ in the expressions for fixed $\boldsymbol{b}$. Finally, the asymptotic normality of $\int A_{\boldsymbol{b}}(x, y)\mathrm{d}G_n(x, y)$ follows from Francq and Zakoïan (2005) since $p > 2$, assumption **B1** holds, and

$$\lim_{n\to\infty} \mathrm{Var}\left(\int A_{\boldsymbol{b}}(x, y)\mathrm{d}G_n(x, y)\right) < \infty.$$

The last part of the theorem follows from the above proof and Proposition 6.3.9 of Brockwell and Davis (2006). □

Proof of Corollary 7.1. It follows in a straightforward fashion from the method of the proof of Theorem 7.12. □

References

Aastveit, K.A., Carriero, A., Clark, T.E., Marcellino, M., 2017. Have standard VARs remained stable since the crisis? Journal of Applied Econometrics 32 (5), 931–951.

Berentsen, G.D., Tjøstheim, D., 2014. Recognizing and visualizing departures from independence in bivariate data using local Gaussian correlation. Statistics and Computing 24 (5), 785–801.

Billingsley, P., 2012. Probability and Measure. John Wiley & Sons.

Bowman, A., Azzalini, A., 1997. Applied Smoothing Techniques for Data Analysis: The Kernel Approach With S-Plus Illustrations. Oxford Science Publications. Clarendon Press.

Brockwell, P., Davis, R.A., 2006. Time Series: Theory and Methods. Springer.

Delicado, P., Smrekar, M., 2009. Measuring non-linear dependence for two random variables distributed along a curve. Statistics and Computing 19, 255–269. https://doi.org/10.1007/s11222-008-9090-y.

Fan, J., Yao, Q., 2003. Nonlinear Time Series. Nonparametric and Parametric Methods. Springer.

Fokianos, K., Pitsillou, M., 2017. Consistent testing for pairwise dependence in time series. Technometrics 59 (2), 262–270.

Francq, C., Zakoïan, J.-M., 2005. A central limit theorem for mixing triangular arrays of variables whose dependence is allowed to grow with the sample size. Econometric Theory 21 (6), 1165–1171.

Gonçalves, S., White, H., 2002. The bootstrap of the mean for dependent heterogeneous arrays. Econometric Theory 18 (6), 1367–1384.

Gonçalves, S., White, H., 2004. Maximum likelihood and the bootstrap for nonlinear dynamic models. Journal of Econometrics 119 (1), 199–219.

Hall, P., Heyde, C.C., 1980. Martingale Limit Theory and Its Application. Academic Press, New York.

Hjort, N., Jones, M., 1996. Locally parametric nonparametric density estimation. Annals of Statistics 24 (4), 1619–1647.

Joe, H., 1989. Estimation of entropy and other functionals of a multivariate density. Annals of the Institute of Statistical Mathematics 41 (4), 683–697.

Jones, M.C., Koch, I., 2003. Dependence maps: local dependence in practice. Statistics and Computing 13 (3), 241–255.

Klimko, L.A., Nelson, P.I., 1978. On conditional least squares estimation for stochastic processes. Annals of Statistics 6 (3), 629–642.

Künsch, H.R., 1989. The jackknife and the bootstrap for general stationary observations. Annals of Statistics, 1217–1241.

Lacal, V., Tjøstheim, D., 2017. Local Gaussian autocorrelation and tests of serial dependence. Journal of Time Series Analysis 38 (1), 51–71.

Lacal, V., Tjøstheim, D., 2019. Estimating and testing nonlinear local dependence between two time series. Journal of Business and Economic Statistics 37 (4), 648–660.

Liu, R.Y., Singh, K., 1992. Moving blocks jackknife and bootstrap capture weak dependence. Exploring the Limits of Bootstrap 225, 248.

Masry, E., Tjøstheim, D., 1995. Nonparametric estimation and identification of ARCH non-linear time series: strong convergence and asymptotic normality. Econometric Theory 11 (2), 258–289.

Nadarajah, S., Kotz, S., 2008. Estimation methods for the multivariate t distribution, Acta Applicandae Mathematicae 102 (1), 99–118.

Politis, D.N., Romano, J.P., 1994. The stationary bootstrap. Journal of the American Statistical Association 89 (428), 1303–1313.

Støve, B., Tjøstheim, D., Hufthammer, K., 2014. Using local Gaussian correlation in a nonlinear re-examination of financial contagion. Journal of Empirical Finance 25, 785–801.

Székely, G.J., Rizzo, M.L., 2009. Brownian distance covariance. Annals of Applied Statistics 3 (4), 1236–1265.

Teräsvirta, T., Tjøstheim, D., Granger, C.W., 2010. Modelling Nonlinear Economic Time Series. Oxford University Press.

Tjøstheim, D., Hufthammer, K.O., 2013. Local Gaussian correlation: a new measure of dependence. Journal of Econometrics 172 (1), 33–48.

CHAPTER 8

Time series dependence and spectral analysis

Contents

8.1. Introduction 261
8.2. Local Gaussian spectral densities 265
8.2.1 The local Gaussian correlations 265
8.2.2 The local Gaussian spectral densities 270
8.2.3 Estimation 272
8.2.4 Asymptotic theory for $\widehat{f_{\boldsymbol{x}}^m}(\omega)$ and $\widehat{f_{\boldsymbol{z}}^m}(\omega)$ 275
8.2.5 Convergence theorems for $\widehat{f_{\boldsymbol{x}}^m}(\omega)$ 279
8.3. Visualizations and interpretations 280
8.3.1 The input parameters and some other technical details 281
8.3.2 Estimation aspects for the given parameter configuration 283
8.3.3 Sanity testing the implemented estimation algorithm 285
8.3.4 Real data and a fitted GARCH-type model 292
References 297

8.1 Introduction

Spectral analysis is an important tool in time series analysis. In its classical form the spectral density function of a stationary times series $\{X_t\}_{t\in\mathbb{Z}}$ is the Fourier transform of the autocovariances $\gamma_k = \mathrm{Cov}(X_{t+k}, X_t)$, assuming $\sum|\gamma_k| < \infty$. Furthermore, since $\gamma_k = \mathrm{Var}(X_t)\rho_k$ with autocorrelations ρ_k, this can be expressed as

$$f(\omega) \stackrel{\text{def}}{=} \sum_{k=-\infty}^{\infty} \gamma_k e^{-2\pi i\omega k} = \mathrm{Var}(X_t) \sum_{k=-\infty}^{\infty} \rho_k e^{-2\pi i\omega k}. \tag{8.1}$$

The relationship $\mathrm{Var}(X_t) = \int_{-1/2}^{1/2} f(\omega)d\omega$ follows from the inverse Fourier transformation, and this reveals how $f(\omega)$ represents a decomposition of the variance over different frequencies. In particular, the spectral density function $f(\omega)$ captures the components of a periodic linear structure decomposed over frequency for $\{X_t\}$, and the peaks and troughs of $f(\omega)$ can thus reveal important features of the time series under investigation.

However, nonlinear dependencies between the terms of a time series $\{X_t\}$ are not in general reflected in the spectral density $f(\omega)$, since the lin-

Statistical Modeling using Local Gaussian Approximation
https://doi.org/10.1016/B978-0-12-815861-6.00015-8

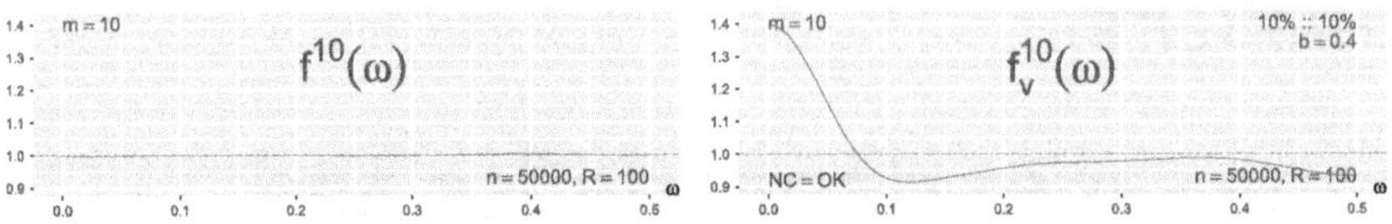

Figure 8.1 Left: Estimated ordinary (variance-rescaled) spectral density based on a GARCH(1, 1)-example. Right: Estimated local Gaussian spectral density at a point in the lower tail. See Appendix G:2 of **JTSu** for details regarding the underlying data.

ear dependencies t are detected by the autocovariance functions γ_k; see, for example, Chapter 3.2.3. The most obvious example, repeatedly used in this book, is the GARCH model; see Chapter 2.4 for a definition. The GARCH model is much used in econometrics, and it is well known that this model in general exhibits dependence over many lags (long-range dependence). However, this dependence is not captured by the autocovariance function, since γ_k is zero for lags $|k| \geq 1$. This again implies that the spectral density is flat for a GARCH model.

An estimate of $f(\omega)$ based on samples from, for example, a GARCH(1, 1)-model will, as seen in the left panel of Fig. 8.1, not reveal any information at all. An investigation based on the method presented in this chapter can however detect the nonlinear structure, as seen in the right panel of Fig. 8.1, where a point in the lower tail was inspected.

Note that the present chapter is based on Jordanger and Tjøstheim (2020), but the notation is changed to be consistent with the rest of the book. In this chapter, we also refer extensively to the Supplement of Jordanger and Tjøstheim (2020) for technical details. The notation in that supplement is of course consistent with that of Jordanger and Tjøstheim (2020). Because of its frequent use, it will be further referred to as **JTSu**.

We may ask whether there exist classes of processes for which the spectral density gives complete information about the probabilistic dependence structure. The answer is simple: If $\{X_t\}$ is a stationary Gaussian process, then its complete distributional dependence structure (assuming a zero-mean process) can be set up in terms of its spectral density. This is in fact a starting point for the Whittle-type likelihood in time series analysis.

This chapter is concerned with finding a generalization of (8.1) that enables the investigation of nonlinear structures in general non-Gaussian stationary processes. This is based on the local approach using Gaussian approximations, which is advocated in this book. It ensures the desirable property that the ordinary spectral density is returned for a Gaussian process since it is the linear dependence that is detected.

A number of attempts have been made in the literature to extend the standard spectral density $f(\omega)$, and these can roughly be divided into three categories.

Perhaps the best known, and probably the procedure going most far back in time, is represented by the higher-order spectra; see Brillinger (1984, 1991) and Tukey (1959). Then the formula for the ordinary spectral density $f(\omega)$ from (8.1) is supplemented by considering the Fourier transformations of the higher-order moments (or cumulants), such as $E(X_r X_s X_t)$ resulting in the bi-spectrum depending on a double set of frequencies and $E(X_r X_s X_t X_u)$ producing the tri-spectrum dependent on a triple of frequencies. These cumulant-based higher-order spectra are identical to zero for Gaussian processes. The multi-frequency dependence of the bi-spectrum and tri-spectrum is not always easy to interpret, and we may also question the existence of higher-order moments; in econometrics, thick tails often make this an issue.

Another approach is to replace γ_k in (8.1) by another measure of dependence as a function of k. Recently, there has been much activity in constructing an alternative to (8.1) by considering covariances of a stationary process obtained by describing quantile crossings; see Hagemann (2011) for a well-written introduction and many references. This is a local spectrum in the sense that it varies with the chosen quantile. It is not always possible to give a local periodic frequency interpretation as in (8.1), but Li (2012c) emphasizes a local sinusoidal construction by analogy with quantile regression models. See also Linton and Whang (2007); Han et al. (2016); Li (2008, 2010c, 2014, 2012a, 2010a,b, 2012b). These approaches usually do not recover the ordinary spectrum for a Gaussian process. This loss of recovery is also the case if a local spectrum is constructed on the basis of the so-called conditional correlation function (Silvapulle and Granger, 2001). Still another viewpoint is obtained in a spectral analysis of the distance covariance function of Székely and Rizzo (2009).

A third alternative is constituted by Hong's generalized spectrum (see Hong, 1999, 2000), which is obtained by replacing the covariance function γ_k in (8.1) by the bivariate covariance function $\sigma_k(u, v)$ constructed by taking the covariances between the characteristic function expressions $\exp(iuX_{t+k})$ and $\exp(ivX_t)$. Again, this gives a complete distributional characterization of dependence properties, but so far not much attention has been given to concrete data analytic interpretation of this frequency representation. Rather, it has been used to test for independence, conditional independence, and predictability; see Li et al. (2016) and Wang and Hong (2018). It is briefly mentioned in Chapter 3.4.2.

In the new approach presented in this chapter, we follow the strategy where the γ_k of (8.1) is replaced by the local Gaussian autocorrelation that was used quite extensively in Chapters 7.3 and 7.4. The gist of this idea in the present context is that the joint distribution of (X_{t+k}, X_t) is approximated locally at a point $\boldsymbol{x} = (x_1, x_2)$, say, by a Gaussian bivariate distribution, and the correlation parameter from this approximating Gaussian distribution is then taken as the local Gaussian autocorrelation $\rho_k(\boldsymbol{x})$ at the point $\boldsymbol{x}$. If $\sum |\rho_k(\boldsymbol{x})| < \infty$, then the *local Gaussian spectral density* at the point $\boldsymbol{x}$ can be defined as follows:

$$f_{\boldsymbol{x}}(\omega) = \sum_{k=-\infty}^{\infty} \rho_k(\boldsymbol{x}) e^{-2\pi i\omega k}. \tag{8.2}$$

This enables a local frequency decomposition with different frequency representations at different points $\boldsymbol{x}$, for example, different oscillatory behavior at extremes (cf. also the extremogram of Davis and Mikosch, 2009) as compared to oscillatory behavior in the center of the process. The point $\boldsymbol{x}$ could naturally correspond to a pair of quantiles, but this concept is distinctly different from the quantile spectra referred to above in that it considers a neighborhood of $\boldsymbol{x}$ and not $\boldsymbol{x}$ as a threshold. Moreover, this approach returns a scaled version of the ordinary spectrum when a Gaussian process is investigated, with equality when $\text{Var}(X_t) = 1$.

Due to issues related to numerical convergence, the estimates presented in this chapter, as in much of the material in the other chapters, will be based on an initial normalization Z_t introduced in this book in Chapter 4.7 and subsequently used in a number of chapters. In the context of the present chapter, it is considered in Subsection 8.2.1.2. For the normalized processes, the correlation ρ_k will always equal the covariance γ_k. All references to $f(\omega)$ will henceforth refer to the spectral density of a normalized process, that is, $f(\omega)$ will now refer to the following rescaled version instead of the one given in (8.1):

$$f_{\boldsymbol{z}}(\omega) \stackrel{\text{def}}{=} \sum_{k=-\infty}^{\infty} \rho_k(\boldsymbol{z}) e^{-2\pi i\omega}. \tag{8.3}$$

For the normalized processes, $f(\omega)$ and $f_{\boldsymbol{z}}(\omega)$ will by construction be identical for Gaussian time series, and a comparison of the ordinary spectrum

$f(\omega)$ and the local Gaussian spectrum $f_{\mathbf{z}}(\omega)$ can thus be used to investigate at a local level how a non-Gaussian time series deviates from being Gaussian.

Much more details of this framework are given in Section 8.2. That section also contains the asymptotic theory with detailed proofs in **JTSu**. The real and simulated examples of Section 8.3, which can be read independently of the details of **JTSu**, show that local spectral estimates can detect local periodic phenomena and detect nonlinearities in a non-Gaussian white noise. Note that the scripts needed for the reproduction of these examples are contained in the R-package `localgaussSpec`,[1] where in addition it is possible to use an interactive tool to see how adjustments of the input parameters (used in the estimation algorithms) influence the estimates of $f_{\mathbf{z}}(\omega)$.

The theory developed in this chapter can be extended to the multivariate case.

8.2 Local Gaussian spectral densities

The local Gaussian correlation (LGC) was introduced in Chapter 4 with theory and applications that showed how it could be used to estimate the local Gaussian autocorrelations for a time series in Chapters 6 and 7.

In this section, we give a brief summary of the local Gaussian autocorrelations, use them to define the local Gaussian spectral density for strictly stationary univariate time series $\{X_t\}$ and $\{Z_t\}$, and give estimators with a corresponding asymptotic theory. Strict stationarity is necessary in order for the machinery of the local Gaussian approximations to be feasible, since Gaussian probability density functions (pdfs) will be used to locally approximate the pdfs corresponding to the bivariate pairs (X_{t+k}, X_t). Details related to the estimation regime and asymptotic properties can be found in Appendix B.1.2 of **JTSu**.

8.2.1 The local Gaussian correlations

8.2.1.1 Local Gaussian correlation, general version

Consider a bivariate random variable $\mathbf{X} = (X_1, X_2)$ with joint cdf $G(\mathbf{x})$ and joint pdf $g(\mathbf{x})$. (Note that in this chapter, we use g and G for probability density function (pdf) and cumulative distribution function (cdf) because f is reserved for the spectral density). For a specified point $\mathbf{x} = (x_1, x_2)$,

[1] See `https://github.com/LAJordanger/localgaussSpec` for details.

the main idea is finding the bivariate Gaussian distribution whose density function best approximates $g(\boldsymbol{x})$ in a neighborhood of the point of interest. Then the LGC will be defined to be the correlation of this local Gaussian approximation.

As elsewhere in the book, the vector containing the five local parameters $\mu_1(\boldsymbol{x})$, $\mu_2(\boldsymbol{x})$, $\sigma_1(\boldsymbol{x})$, $\sigma_2(\boldsymbol{x})$, and $\rho(\boldsymbol{x})$ is denoted $\boldsymbol{\theta} = \boldsymbol{\theta}(\boldsymbol{x})$, and the approximating bivariate Gaussian density function at the point $\boldsymbol{x}$ is denoted $\psi(\boldsymbol{v}; \boldsymbol{\theta}(\boldsymbol{x}))$, that is,

$$\begin{aligned}\psi(\boldsymbol{v}; \boldsymbol{\theta}(\boldsymbol{x})) &= \frac{1}{2\pi\sigma_1(\boldsymbol{x})\sigma_2(\boldsymbol{x})\sqrt{1-\rho^2(\boldsymbol{x})}} \\ &\times \exp\left\{ -\frac{1}{2}\frac{1}{1-\rho^2(\boldsymbol{x})}\left(\frac{(v_1-\mu_1(\boldsymbol{x}))^2}{\sigma_1^2(\boldsymbol{x})}\right.\right. \\ &\left.\left. - 2\rho(\boldsymbol{x})\frac{(v_1-\mu_1(\boldsymbol{x}))(v_2-\mu_2(\boldsymbol{x}))}{\sigma_1(\boldsymbol{x})\sigma_2(\boldsymbol{x})} + \frac{(v_2-\mu_2(\boldsymbol{x}))^2}{\sigma_2^2(\boldsymbol{x})}\right)\right\}\end{aligned} \tag{8.4}$$

In the following, we will often suppress the $\boldsymbol{x}$-dependence of $\boldsymbol{\theta}(\boldsymbol{x})$, writing simply $\boldsymbol{\theta}$.

In order for $\psi(\boldsymbol{v}, \boldsymbol{\theta})$ to be considered a good approximation of $g(\boldsymbol{v})$ in a neighborhood of the point $\boldsymbol{x}$, it should at least coincide with $g(\boldsymbol{v})$ at $\boldsymbol{x}$, and it should be close to $g(\boldsymbol{v})$ in a neighborhood of $\boldsymbol{x}$ as described in Chapter 4, where a neighborhood is defined by a bandwidth parameter $\boldsymbol{b}$.

Applying the approach used in Chapter 4 based on the local likelihood estimation procedure of Hjort and Jones (1996), we can consider the limit as $\boldsymbol{b} \to \boldsymbol{0}$ of the parameters $\boldsymbol{\theta}_{\boldsymbol{b}} = \boldsymbol{\theta}_{\boldsymbol{b}}(\boldsymbol{x})$ that minimizes the penalty function (cf. (4.5))

$$q_{\boldsymbol{b}} = \int K_{\boldsymbol{b}}(\boldsymbol{v}-\boldsymbol{x})\left[\psi(\boldsymbol{v}, \boldsymbol{\theta}(\boldsymbol{x})) - g(\boldsymbol{v})\log(\psi(\boldsymbol{v}, \boldsymbol{\theta}(\boldsymbol{x})))\right]d\boldsymbol{v}, \tag{8.5}$$

where $K_{\boldsymbol{b}}(\boldsymbol{v}-\boldsymbol{x})$ is a kernel function with bandwidth $\boldsymbol{b}$. As explained by Hjort and Jones (1996, Section 2.1), this can be interpreted as a locally weighted Kullback–Leibler distance between the targeted density $g(\boldsymbol{v})$ and the approximating density $\psi(\boldsymbol{v}, \boldsymbol{\theta})$. An optimal parameter configuration $\boldsymbol{\theta}_{\boldsymbol{b}}(\boldsymbol{x})$ for expression (8.5) should solve the vector equation

$$\int K_{\boldsymbol{b}}(\boldsymbol{v}-\boldsymbol{x})\boldsymbol{u}(\boldsymbol{v}, \boldsymbol{\theta}(\boldsymbol{x}))\left[\psi(\boldsymbol{v}, \boldsymbol{\theta}(\boldsymbol{x})) - g(\boldsymbol{v})\right]d\boldsymbol{v} = \boldsymbol{0}. \tag{8.6}$$

Under suitable assumptions (see Hjort and Jones (1996), Tjøstheim and Hufthammer (2013), or Chapter 4), there will be a unique limiting solution of Eq. (8.6), that is,

$$\boldsymbol{\theta}_0 = \boldsymbol{\theta}_0(\boldsymbol{x}) = \lim_{\boldsymbol{b}\to\boldsymbol{0}} \boldsymbol{\theta}_{\boldsymbol{b}}(\boldsymbol{x}) \tag{8.7}$$

will be well-defined, and the ρ-part of the $\boldsymbol{\theta}_0$-vector can be used to define an LGC at the point $\boldsymbol{x}$.

In the particular case where g is a bivariate normal, for $\boldsymbol{X} = (X_1, X_2)$,

$$\boldsymbol{X} \sim \mathcal{N}\left(\begin{pmatrix}\mu_1\\ \mu_2\end{pmatrix}, \begin{pmatrix}\sigma_1^2 & \sigma_1\sigma_2\rho\\ \sigma_1\sigma_2\rho & \sigma_2^2\end{pmatrix}\right), \tag{8.8}$$

and for any point $\boldsymbol{x}$ and any bandwidth $\boldsymbol{b}$, the parameter $\boldsymbol{\theta}_{\boldsymbol{b}}$ that gives the optimal solution of Eq. (8.6) will be the parameters given in (8.8). Thus the limit $\boldsymbol{\theta}_0$ in (8.7) will also be these parameters, which implies that the LGC coincides with the global parameter ρ at all points in the Gaussian case. See Chapter 4 for further details and remarks that motivate the use of the LGC.

An estimate of the local Gaussian parameters $\boldsymbol{\theta}_0(\boldsymbol{x})$ in (8.7) can, for a given bivariate sample $\{\boldsymbol{X}_t\}_{t=1}^n$ and some reasonable bandwidth $\boldsymbol{b}$, be found as the parameter vector $\widehat{\boldsymbol{\theta}}_{\boldsymbol{b}}(\boldsymbol{x})$ that maximizes the local log-likelihood

$$L_n(\boldsymbol{\theta}) = n^{-1}\sum_{t=1}^{n} K_b(\boldsymbol{X}_t - \boldsymbol{x}) \log \psi(\boldsymbol{X}_t, \boldsymbol{\theta}) - \int_{\mathbb{R}^2} K_{\boldsymbol{b}}(\boldsymbol{v} - \boldsymbol{x})\psi(\boldsymbol{v}, \boldsymbol{\theta})d\boldsymbol{v}. \tag{8.9}$$

The asymptotic behavior of $\widehat{\boldsymbol{\theta}}_{\boldsymbol{b}}(\boldsymbol{x})$ (as $n \to \infty$ and $\boldsymbol{b} \to \boldsymbol{0}$) is in Chapter 4 investigated by entities derived from a local penalty function $Q_n(\boldsymbol{\theta})$ defined as $-nL_n(\boldsymbol{\theta})$, that is,

$$Q_n(\boldsymbol{\theta}) = -\sum_{t=1}^{n} K_b(\boldsymbol{X}_t - \boldsymbol{x}) \log \psi(\boldsymbol{X}_t, \boldsymbol{\theta}) + n\int_{\mathbb{R}^2} K_{\boldsymbol{b}}(\boldsymbol{v} - \boldsymbol{x})\psi(\boldsymbol{v}, \boldsymbol{\theta})d\boldsymbol{v}. \tag{8.10}$$

The key ingredient in the analysis is the corresponding vector of partial derivatives,

$$\nabla Q_n(\boldsymbol{\theta}) = -\sum_{t=1}^{n}\left[K_{\boldsymbol{b}}(\boldsymbol{X}_t - \boldsymbol{x})\boldsymbol{u}(\boldsymbol{X}_t, \boldsymbol{\theta}) - \int_{\mathbb{R}^2} K_{\boldsymbol{b}}(\boldsymbol{v} - \boldsymbol{x})\boldsymbol{u}(\boldsymbol{v}, \boldsymbol{\theta})\psi(\boldsymbol{v}, \boldsymbol{\theta})d\boldsymbol{v}\right], \tag{8.11}$$

and, as we will see later, the asymptotic investigation of the local Gaussian spectral density $f_{\boldsymbol{x}}(\omega)$ introduced in this chapter is also built on this entity.

Note that the bias-variance balance of the estimate $\widehat{\boldsymbol{\theta}}_{\boldsymbol{b}}(\boldsymbol{x})$ depends on the bandwidth vector $\boldsymbol{b}$, and thus an estimate based on $\boldsymbol{b}$ too close to $\boldsymbol{0}$ may be dubious. However, it can still be of interest (for a given sample) to compare estimates $\widehat{\boldsymbol{\theta}}_{\boldsymbol{b}}(\boldsymbol{x})$ for different scales of $\boldsymbol{b}$ to see how they behave.

Since the goal is estimating $\boldsymbol{\theta}_0(\boldsymbol{x})$, it is of course important to find $\widehat{\boldsymbol{\theta}}_{\boldsymbol{b}}(\boldsymbol{x})$ for not too large bandwidth vectors $\boldsymbol{b}$, but it may still be of interest to point out how (8.9) behaves in the "global" limit as $\boldsymbol{b} \to \infty = (\infty, \infty)$. In this case the second term loses its $\boldsymbol{x}$-dependence, and the parameter vector $\widehat{\boldsymbol{\theta}}_{\infty}(\boldsymbol{x})$ that maximizes the first term becomes the ordinary (global) least squares estimate of a global parameter vector $\boldsymbol{\theta}$, which contains the ordinary means, variances, and correlation.

8.2.1.2 Local Gaussian correlation, normalized version

The algorithm that estimates the LGC (see Berentsen et al. (2014) and the more recent Otneim (2019) for R-implementations) can run into problems if the data under investigation contain outliers, that is, the numerical convergence may not succeed for points $\boldsymbol{x}$ in the periphery of the data. It is possible to counter this problem by removing the most extreme outliers, but an alternative approach based on the normalization strategy, also presented and used in other chapters of this book, will be applied; see, in particular, Chapter 4.7.

A key observation is that the numerical estimation problem does not occur when the marginal distributions are standard normal. It can also be motivated as an adjusted strategy similar to the copula-concept; see Chapters 3.3 and 5. Sklar's theorem gives the existence of a copula $C(u_1, u_2)$ such that the joint cdf $G(\boldsymbol{v})$ can be expressed as $C(G_1(v_1), G_2(v_2))$. This copula C contains all the interdependence information between the two marginal random variables V_1 and V_2; it will be unique when the two margins are continuous, and it will then be invariant under strictly increasing transformations of the margins. Under this continuity assumption, the random variable $\boldsymbol{X}_t = (X_{1t}, X_{2t}) = (X_1, X_2)$ will have the same copula as the transformed random variable $\boldsymbol{Z} = (\Phi^{-1}(G_1(X_1)), \Phi^{-1}(G_2(X_2)))$, where Φ is the cdf of the standard normal distribution, whose corresponding pdf as usual will be denoted by ϕ. This transformed version of $\boldsymbol{X}$ has standard normal margins, so the LGC-estimation algorithm will not run into numerical problems. This motivates the alternative approach to the definition of LGC used in this chapter and in other chapters of this book. Instead of finding a Gaussian approximation of the pdf g (of the original random variable $\boldsymbol{X}$ at a point $\boldsymbol{x}$), find a Gaussian approximation of the pdf $g_{\boldsymbol{Z}}(\boldsymbol{z})$

of the transformed random variable $\boldsymbol{Z}$ at a transformed point $\boldsymbol{z}$. Expressed relative to the pdf c of the copula C, this means that the setup in (8.12b) below will be used instead of the setup in (8.12a):

$$g(\boldsymbol{x}) = c(G_1(x_1), G_2(x_2))g_1(x_1)g_2(x_2) \text{ at } \boldsymbol{x} = (x_1, x_2), \tag{8.12a}$$

$$g_{\boldsymbol{Z}}(\boldsymbol{z}) = c(\Phi(z_1), \Phi(z_2))\phi(z_1)\phi(z_2) \text{ at } \boldsymbol{z} = (\Phi^{-1}(G_1(x_1)), \Phi^{-1}(G_2(x_2))). \tag{8.12b}$$

The normalized version of the LGC will return values that differ from those obtained from the general LGC-version introduced in Section 8.2.1.1, but the two versions coincide when the random variable $\boldsymbol{X}$ is bivariate Gaussian. Then the transformed random variable $\boldsymbol{Z}$ corresponding to $\boldsymbol{X}$ from (8.8) is $\boldsymbol{Z} = ((X_1 - \mu_1)/\sigma_1, (X_2 - \mu_2)/\sigma_2)$, which implies

$$\boldsymbol{Z} \sim \mathcal{N}\left(\begin{pmatrix} 0 \\ 0 \end{pmatrix}, \begin{pmatrix} 1 & \rho \\ \rho & 1 \end{pmatrix}\right), \tag{8.13}$$

and thus the normalized LGC coincides with the global parameter ρ at all points.

The convergence rate for the estimates is rather slow for the LGC cases discussed above. It is $1/\sqrt{n(b_1 b_2)^3}$, as was seen in Chapter 4. This is true both for the $\boldsymbol{x}$-representation and the general 5-parameter $\boldsymbol{z}$-representation. Briefly summarizing, the 5×5 covariance matrix of the estimate $\widehat{\boldsymbol{\theta}}_{\boldsymbol{b}}$ will have the form $J_{\boldsymbol{b}}^{-1} M_{\boldsymbol{b}} J_{\boldsymbol{b}}^{-1}$. The presence of the kernel $K_{\boldsymbol{b}}$ means that the matrices $J_{\boldsymbol{b}}$ and $M_{\boldsymbol{b}}$ have rank one in the limit as $\boldsymbol{b} \to \boldsymbol{0}$, and this slows down the convergence rate; cf. Tjøstheim and Hufthammer (2013, Th. 3) or Chapter 4.4.2 for the details.

The property that the limiting matrices have rank one does not pose a problem if only one parameter is estimated with the other parameters fixed, and the convergence rate would then be much faster (i.e., $1/\sqrt{nb_1 b_2}$). Inspired by the fact that the transformed random variable $\boldsymbol{Z}$ has standard normal margins, there was introduced a simplified normalized version of the LGC, where only the ρ-parameter should be estimated when using the approximation approach from (8.12b), that is, the values of $\mu_1(\boldsymbol{z})$ and $\mu_2(\boldsymbol{z})$ are taken to be identically zero, whereas $\sigma_1^2(\boldsymbol{z})$ and $\sigma_2^2(\boldsymbol{z})$ are taken to be 1. This simplified approach has been applied successfully with regard to density estimation by Otneim and Tjøstheim (2017, 2018), or see Chapters 9 and 10, but for the local spectrum analysis considered in this chapter, it gave inferior results. Therefore in this chapter, we do not include any plots based on the normalized one-parameter version, but we estimate $\mu_i(\boldsymbol{z})$, $\sigma_i^2(\boldsymbol{z})$, $i = 1, 2$, in addition to the estimates of $\rho_k(\boldsymbol{z})$. The thesis of Jordanger (2017) contains a discussion with regard to why an approach based on the normalized one-free-parameter approach may fail to produce decent results.

8.2.2 The local Gaussian spectral densities

An extension of the spectral density $f(\omega)$ from (8.3) can be based on any of the three LGC-versions mentioned in Sections 8.2.1.1 and 8.2.1.2. The one presented below is based on the normalized five-parameter local Gaussian autocorrelation, since that ensures that the estimation algorithm avoids the aforementioned numerical convergence problems, but the theory developed in the **JTSu** does also cover the general situation.

Definition 1. The local Gaussian spectral density (LGSD) at a point $\boldsymbol{z} = (z_1, z_2)$ for a strictly stationary univariate time series $\{X_t\}$ is constructed as follows.

(a) With G the univariate *marginal* cumulative distribution of $\{X_t\}$, and Φ the cumulative distribution of the standard normal distribution, define a normalized version $\{Z_t\}$ of $\{X_t\}$ by

$$\{Z_t = \Phi^{-1}(G(X_t))\}. \tag{8.14}$$

(b) For a given point $\boldsymbol{z} = (z_1, z_2)$ and for each *bivariate pair* (Z_{t+k}, Z_t), a *local Gaussian autocorrelation* $\rho_k(\boldsymbol{z})$ can be computed. The convention $\rho_0(\boldsymbol{z}) \equiv 1$ is used when $k = 0$.

(c) When $\sum |\rho_k(\boldsymbol{z})| < \infty$, the *local Gaussian spectral density* at the point $\boldsymbol{z}$ is defined as

$$f_{\boldsymbol{z}}(\omega) = \sum_{k=-\infty}^{\infty} \rho_k(\boldsymbol{z}) e^{-2\pi i \omega k}. \tag{8.15}$$

Note that the requirement $\sum |\rho_k(\boldsymbol{z})| < \infty$ implies that the concept of local Gaussian spectral density in general may not be well defined for all stationary time series $\{X_t\}_{t \in \mathbb{Z}}$ and all points $\boldsymbol{z} \in \mathbb{R}^2$.

The normalization in (8.14) preserves the copula structure of the original time series, but a standard normal marginal will be used instead of its original marginal distribution. This implies that the transformed time series has all moments, even though that may be not the case for a thick-tailed original time series $\{X_t\}$. A local Gaussian investigation of the normalized time series can detect non-Gaussian dependency structures in the original time series, but an investigation of the original marginal may also be of interest in many situations, for example, with regard to discriminant analysis.

Finally, note that the normalization in (8.14) can be compared to but is very different from the normalization in Klüppelberg and Mikosch (1994).

The following definition of time reversible time series from Tong (1990, Def. 4.6) is needed in Lemma 8.1 and Theorem 8.2.

Definition 2. A stationary time series $\{X_t\}_{t\in\mathbb{Z}}$ is time reversible if for every positive integer n and every $t_1, t_2, \ldots, t_n$, the vectors $\left(X_{t_1}, X_{t_2}, \ldots, X_{t_n}\right)$ and $\left(X_{-t_1}, X_{-t_2}, \ldots, X_{-t_n}\right)$ have the same distribution.

Lemma 8.1. *The following properties hold for $f_{\boldsymbol{z}}(\omega)$.*

(a) *$f_{\boldsymbol{z}}(\omega)$ coincides with $f(\omega)$ for all $\boldsymbol{z} \in \mathbb{R}^2$ when $\{X_t\}$ is a Gaussian time series, or when $\{X_t\}$ consists of iid observations.*

(b) *The following holds when $\breve{\boldsymbol{z}} \stackrel{def}{=} (z_2, z_1)$ is the diagonal reflection of $\boldsymbol{z} = (z_1, z_2)$:*

$$f_{\boldsymbol{z}}(\omega) = 1 + \sum_{k=1}^{\infty} \rho_k(\breve{\boldsymbol{z}}) e^{2\pi i \omega k} + \sum_{k=1}^{\infty} \rho_k(\boldsymbol{z}) e^{-2\pi i \omega k}, \tag{8.16a}$$

$$f_{\breve{\boldsymbol{z}}}(\omega) = \overline{f_{\boldsymbol{z}}(\omega)}. \tag{8.16b}$$

(c) *When $\{X_t\}_{t\in\mathbb{Z}}$ is time reversible, then $f_{\boldsymbol{z}}(\omega)$ is real-valued for all $\boldsymbol{z} \in \mathbb{R}^2$, that is,*

$$f_{\boldsymbol{z}}(\omega) = 1 + 2\sum_{k=1}^{\infty} \rho_k(\boldsymbol{z}) \cos(2\pi \omega k). \tag{8.17}$$

(d) *$f_{\boldsymbol{z}}(\omega)$ is in general complex-valued, but it is always real-valued when the point $\boldsymbol{z}$ lies on the diagonal $z_1 = z_2$. Eq. (8.17) holds in this diagonal case too.*

This is not difficult to prove. Point (a) follows for the Gaussian case since the local Gaussian autocorrelations $\rho_k(\boldsymbol{z})$ by construction coincide with the ordinary (global) autocorrelations ρ_k in the Gaussian case. Similarly, when $\{X_t\}$ consists of iid observations, both local and global autocorrelations will be 0 when $k \neq 0$, and the local and global spectra both become the constant function 1.

(b)–(d) are trivial consequences of the diagonal folding property from Lemma C.1 of **JTSu**, that is, $\rho_{-k}(\boldsymbol{z}) = \rho_k(\breve{\boldsymbol{z}})$, and the definition of time reversibility; see Appendices C.1 and C.2 of **JTSu** for details.

For general points $\boldsymbol{z} = (z_1, z_2)$, the complex-valued $f_{\boldsymbol{z}}(\omega)$ might be hard to investigate and interpret, but due to Lemma 8.1, the investigation becomes simpler for points on the diagonal. This might also be the situation of most practical interest, since it corresponds to estimating the local spectrum at (or around) a given value of $\{X_t\}$, such as a certain quantile for the distribution of X_t. The real-valued results $f_{\boldsymbol{z}}(\omega)$ for $\boldsymbol{z}$ along the diagonal can be compared with the result of the ordinary (global) spectral density $f(\omega)$, as given in (8.3), and this might detect cases where the times series $\{X_t\}$ deviates from *being Gaussian*. Furthermore, if the global spectrum $f(\omega)$ is flat, then any peaks and troughs of $f_{\boldsymbol{z}}(\omega)$ may be interpreted as indicators of, for example, *periodicities at a local level.* This implies that estimates of $f_{\boldsymbol{z}}(\omega)$ may be useful as an exploratory tool, an idea that will be pursued in Section 8.3.

Note that for a fixed $\boldsymbol{z}$, the collection of local Gaussian autocorrelations $\{\rho_k(\boldsymbol{z})\}$ may not be non-negative definite, which implies that both theoretical and estimated local Gaussian spectral densities may become negative. However, as the artificial process investigated in Fig. 8.7 will show, the peaks of $f_k(\boldsymbol{z})$ still occur at the expected frequencies for the investigated points, which implies that the lack of non-negativity does not prevent this tool from detecting nonlinear and periodic structures in non-Gaussian white noise.

We need the following definition when the discussion later on refers to m-truncated versions of different spectra.

Definition 3. The m-truncated versions $f_{\boldsymbol{z}}^m(\omega)$ and $f^m(\omega)$ of $f_{\boldsymbol{z}}(\omega)$ and $f(\omega)$ for some lag-window function $\lambda_m(k)$ are defined as

$$f_{\boldsymbol{z}}^m(\omega) \stackrel{\text{def}}{=} 1 + \sum_{k=1}^{m} \lambda_m(k)\rho_k(\boldsymbol{z})e^{2\pi i\omega k} + \sum_{k=1}^{m} \lambda_m(k)\rho_k(\boldsymbol{z})e^{-2\pi i\omega k}, \tag{8.18a}$$

$$f^m(\omega) \stackrel{\text{def}}{=} \sum_{k=-m}^{m} \lambda_m(k)\rho_k e^{-2\pi i\omega}. \tag{8.18b}$$

8.2.3 Estimation

Theoretical and numerical estimates of the ordinary spectral density $f(\omega)$ is typically investigated by means of the fast Fourier transform (FFT) and techniques related to the periodogram. The FFT approach cannot be used in the local case since there is no natural factorization of terms making up a local estimated covariance, but there does exist a pre-FFT approach for the estimation of $f(\omega)$, where the Fourier transform is taken of the estimated autocorrelations after they have been smoothed and truncated by means of some lag-window function, and the pre-FFT approach can be adapted to deal with the estimates of the local Gaussian spectral densities.

Algorithm 1. For a sample $\{X_t\}_{t=1}^n$ of size n, an m-truncated estimate $\widehat{f_{\boldsymbol{z}}^m}(\omega)$ of $f_{\boldsymbol{z}}(\omega)$ is constructed by means of the following procedure.

(a) Find an estimate $\widehat{G}_n$ of the marginal cumulative distribution function, and compute the *pseudo-normalized observations* $\left\{\widehat{Z}_t \stackrel{\text{def}}{=} \Phi^{-1}(\widehat{G}_n(X_t))\right\}_{t=1}^n$ that correspond to $\{X_t\}_{t=1}^n$.

(b) Create the lag-k pseudo-normalized pairs $\{(\widehat{Z}_{t+k}, \widehat{Z}_t)\}_{t=1}^{n-k}$ for $k = 1, 2, \ldots, m$, and estimate, both for the point $\boldsymbol{z} = (z_1, z_2)$ and its diagonal reflection $\breve{\boldsymbol{z}} = (z_2, z_1)$, the local Gaussian autocorrelations $\{\widehat{\rho}_k(\boldsymbol{z}|\boldsymbol{b}_k)\}_{k=1}^m$ and $\{\widehat{\rho}_k(\breve{\boldsymbol{z}}|\boldsymbol{b})\}_{k=1}^m$, where the $\{\boldsymbol{b}_k\}_{k=1}^m$ are the bandwidths used during the estimation of the local Gaussian autocorrelation for the different lags.

(c) Adjust Eq. (8.16a) from Lemma 8.1b with some lag-window function $\lambda_m(k)$ to get the estimate

$$\widehat{f_{\boldsymbol{z}}^m}(\omega) = 1 + \sum_{k=1}^{m} \lambda_m(k)\widehat{\rho}_k(\breve{\boldsymbol{z}}|\boldsymbol{b}_k)e^{2\pi i\omega k} + \sum_{k=1}^{m} \lambda_m(k)\widehat{\rho}_k(\boldsymbol{z}|\boldsymbol{b}_k)e^{-2\pi i\omega k}. \tag{8.19}$$

The presence of the kernel $K_{\boldsymbol{b}}(\boldsymbol{v} - \boldsymbol{z})$ in the analogue of (8.5) at $\boldsymbol{z}$-level implies that small sample effects can occur when the local Gaussian spectrum $f_{\boldsymbol{z}}(\omega)$ is estimated for some combinations of points $\boldsymbol{z}$ and bandwidths $\boldsymbol{b}$, and this can in particular be an issue if the points lie in the low-density regions corresponding to the tails of our distribution. Roughly speaking: When the bandwidth $\boldsymbol{b}$ becomes "too small", the estimated local Gaussian autocorrelations will have a tendency to approach either -1 or $+1$ (cf. Appendix D.3 of **JTSu**), and then these estimates will in general only reflect the random configuration of those lag-k pairs that happened to lie closest to the point $\boldsymbol{z}$. Section 8.3.1 presents strategies that can be used to detect/avoid this issue, and additional details are presented in **JTSu**.

The following result is an analogue to Eq. (8.17) of Lemma 8.1.

Lemma 8.2. *When it is assumed that the sample* $\{X_t\}_{t=1}^n$ *comes from a time reversible stochastic process* $\{X_t\}$, *the m-truncated estimate* $\widehat{f_{\boldsymbol{z}}^m}(\omega)$ *can for all points*

$z \in \mathbb{R}^2$ be written as

$$\widehat{f}_{z}^{m}(\omega) = 1 + 2\sum_{k=1}^{m} \lambda_m(k)\widehat{\rho}_k(z|b_k)\cos(2\pi\omega k). \tag{8.20}$$

Moreover, (8.20) always holds when the point z lies on the diagonal $z_1 = z_2$.

This result follows immediately from (c) and (d) of Lemma 8.1.

The estimated $\widehat{G}_n$ in Algorithm 1 can, for example, be the rescaled empirical cumulative distribution function created from the sample $\{X_t\}_{t=1}^{n}$, which transforms original data into ranks divided by n or $n+1$, or it could be based on some logspline technique like that implemented by Otneim and Tjøstheim (2017) and elaborated on in Chapters 9 and 10.

The bandwidths $b_k = (b_{1k}, b_{2k})$ in Algorithm 1 do not need to be equal for all the lags k when an estimate $\widehat{f}_{z}^{m}(\omega)$ is computed. For the asymptotic investigation, it is sufficient to require that b_{1k} and b_{2k} approach zero at the same rate, that is, that there exists $b = (b_1, b_2)$ such that $b_{ik} \asymp b_i$ for $i = 1, 2$ and for all k (that is, $\lim b_{ik}/b_i = 1$).

The asymptotic theory for $\widehat{\rho}_k(z|b_k)$, given that the required regularity conditions are satisfied, follows along the original argument from Chapter 4. The analysis in Chapter 4 considered the general case where the original observations $\{X_t\}_{t=1}^{n}$ were used instead of the normalized observations $\{Z_t = \Phi^{-1}(G(X_t))\}_{t=1}^{n}$. Since the cumulative distribution function G in general is unknown, the present asymptotic analysis must work with the pseudo-normalized observations $\{\widehat{Z}_t\}_{t=1}^{n}$, which makes it necessary to take into account the difference between the true normalized values Z_t and the estimated pseudo-normalized values $\widehat{Z}_t$. This has been done in Theorem 4.5 and its proof. The analysis of this theorem implies that $\widehat{G}_n(X_t)$ approaches $G(X_t)$ at a faster rate than the rate of convergence for the estimated local Gaussian correlation, and thus (under some regularity conditions stated there) the convergence rate of $\widehat{\rho}_k(z|b_k)$ will not be affected by the distinction between Z_t and $\widehat{Z}_t$.

The bias-variance balance for the estimates $\widehat{f}_{z}^{m}(\omega)$ must consider the size of m relative to both n and the bandwidths $\{b_k\}_{k=1}^{m}$, that is, the kernel function reduces the number of observations that effectively contributes to the computations of the estimates, and the number of effective contributors can also depend on the location of the point z, that is, whether the point z lies at the center or in the periphery of the pseudo-normalized observations $\{(\widehat{Z}_{t+k}, \widehat{Z}_t)\}_{t=1}^{n-k}$; see Section 8.3.2 for further details.

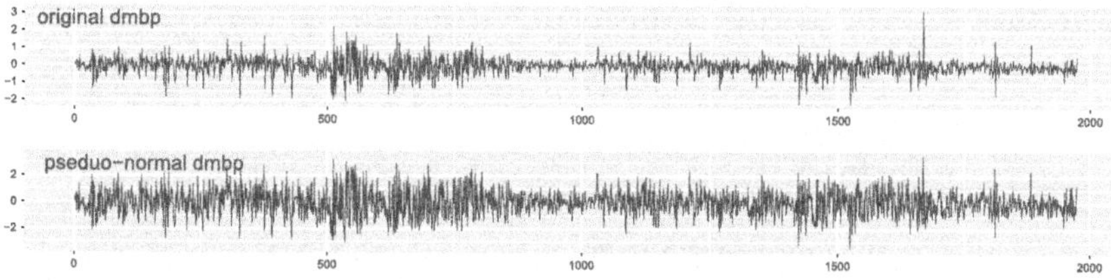

Figure 8.2 dmbp, original version and pseudo normalized version.

Fig. 8.2 shows the effect of the pseudo-normalization on the dmbp example, which is the Bollerslev–Ghysel benchmark data set (JBES Data Archive: ftp://www.amstat.org/jbes/View) on the exchange rate of Deutsche mark versus British pound, which will be discussed in Section 8.3.4. The uppermost part shows the original dmbp-series (of length 1974), whereas the lowermost part shows the pseudo-normalized transformation of it, and it is clear that the shape of the pseudo-normalized version resembles the shape of the original version.

8.2.4 Asymptotic theory for $\widehat{f_{\boldsymbol{x}}^m}(\omega)$ and $\widehat{f_{\boldsymbol{z}}^m}(\omega)$

In this section, we present asymptotic results for the cases where $\widehat{f_{\boldsymbol{x}}}(\omega)$ and $\widehat{f_{\boldsymbol{z}}^m}(\omega)$ are real-valued functions. Note that both assumptions and results are stated relative to the original observations instead of the pseudo-normalized observations. This simplification does not affect the final convergence rates. Given that the replacement of $\{Z_t\}$ by $\{\widehat{Z}_t\}$ is a higher-order effect, the asymptotic analysis for the five-parameter $\boldsymbol{\theta}$ becomes the same for the cases of $\widehat{f_{\boldsymbol{x}}^m}(\omega)$ and $\widehat{f_{\boldsymbol{z}}^m}(\omega)$. Since we choose in this section to state conditions in terms of the original time series $\{X_t\}$, it is deemed best to explicitly state asymptotic results in terms of $\widehat{f_{\boldsymbol{x}}^m}(\omega)$. It could equivalently, but with a bit more cumbersome notation, be stated in terms of $\widehat{f_{\boldsymbol{z}}^m}(\omega)$. As remarked in Section 8.2.1.2, the normalization to $\boldsymbol{z}$-level is primarily for computational purposes (although it also generates invariance for marginal transformations), and we will return to the $\boldsymbol{z}$-representation in Section 8.3 when we treat simulations and real data.

The assumption to be imposed on the univariate time series $\{X_t\}$ is given in terms of components related to the bivariate lag-k pairs that can be constructed from it. The theoretical analysis of $\widehat{f_{\boldsymbol{x}}^m}(\omega)$ also requires $(m+1)$-variate pairs to be considered. Note that Algorithm 1c implies that it is sufficient to only consider positive values for k.

Definition 4. For a strictly stationary univariate time series $\{X_t\}$ with $k \geq 1$ and $m \geq 2$, we define bivariate and $(m+1)$-variate time series as follows:

$$\boldsymbol{X}_{k:t} \stackrel{\text{def}}{=} [X_{t+k}, X_t]^T, \qquad \boldsymbol{X}_{\bar{m}:t} \stackrel{\text{def}}{=} [X_{t+m}, \ldots, X_t]^T, \tag{8.21}$$

and let $g_k(\boldsymbol{x}_k)$ and $g_{\bar{m}}(\boldsymbol{x}_{\bar{m}})$ denote the respective probability density functions.

The bivariate densities g_k can all be obtained from the $(m+1)$-variate density $g_{\bar{m}}$ by integrating out the $m-1$ redundant marginals, which in particular implies that if an $(m+1)$-variate function $\tilde{\eta}_k(\boldsymbol{X}_{\bar{m}}) : \mathbb{R}^{m+1} \to \mathbb{R}^1$ is the *obvious extension* of a bivariate function $\eta_k(\boldsymbol{X}_k) : \mathbb{R}^2 \to \mathbb{R}^1$, then

$$E[\eta_k(\boldsymbol{X}_{k:t})] = E[\tilde{\eta}_k(\boldsymbol{X}_{\bar{m}:t})] \qquad \text{for } k \in \{1, \ldots, m\}. \tag{8.22}$$

With the notation from Definition 4, Assumption 1 stated below can now be imposed on $\{X_t\}$. Note that (e)–(g) of Assumption 1 contain references to definitions that are explicitly given in Appendix B in **JTSu**. These definitions are related to an $(m+1)$-variate penalty function for the time series $\{\boldsymbol{X}_{\bar{m}:t}\}$, and they are quite technical, so it would impede the flow of this chapter to include all the details here. For the present section, it is sufficient to know that the new $(m+1)$-variate function can be expressed as a sum of m bivariate penalty functions of the form given in (8.10).

The key idea is that $\boldsymbol{X}_t$ and $g(\boldsymbol{x})$ in Eqs. (8.10)–(8.11) are replaced with $\boldsymbol{X}_{k:t}$ and $g_k(\boldsymbol{x}_k)$ with an additional index k to take care of the bookkeeping. In particular, an inspection of (8.11) motivates the introduction of a random vector variable $\boldsymbol{Y}_{k:t} = K_{\boldsymbol{b}}(\boldsymbol{X}_{k:t} - \boldsymbol{x})\boldsymbol{u}(\boldsymbol{X}_{k:t}, \boldsymbol{\theta})$, and the corresponding variables $\boldsymbol{Y}^n_{kq:i}$ that will occur in Assumption 1g below are the components of $\sqrt{b_1 b_2}\boldsymbol{Y}_{k:t}$ with $q, r = 1, \ldots, 5$ keeping track of the appropriate derivatives of the five-dimensional parameter $\boldsymbol{\theta}$. Further, note that different combinations of the indices k, i, l, and j in the product $\boldsymbol{Y}^n_{kq:i} \cdot \boldsymbol{Y}^n_{lr:j}$ imply that it can contain from two to four different terms of the time series $\{X_t\}$, so the corresponding density function can thus be either bi-, tri-, or tetravariate. See Definitions B.7 and B.11 in **JTSu** for details.

Assumption 1. The univariate process $\{X_t\}$ satisfies the following properties with $\boldsymbol{x} = (x_1, x_2)$ in item (d) below being the point at which the estimate $\widehat{f^m_{\boldsymbol{x}}}(\omega)$ of $f_{\boldsymbol{x}}(\omega)$ is to be computed.

(a) $\{X_t\}$ is strictly stationary.

(b) $\{X_t\}$ is strongly mixing (see (7.15)) with mixing coefficient $\alpha(j)$ satisfying

$$\sum_{j=1}^{\infty} j^a[\alpha(j)]^{1-2/\nu} < \infty \quad \text{for some } \nu > 2 \text{ and } a > 1 - 2/\nu. \tag{8.23}$$

(c) $\mathrm{Var}(X_t) < \infty$.

The bivariate density functions $g_k(\boldsymbol{x}_k)$ of the lag-k pairs $\boldsymbol{X}_{k:t}$ of the univariate time series $\{X_t\}$ satisfy the following requirements for a given point $\boldsymbol{x} = (x_1, x_2)$.

(d) $g_k(\boldsymbol{x}_k)$ is differentiable at $\boldsymbol{x}$, so that Taylor's theorem can be used to write $g_k(\boldsymbol{x}_k)$ as

$$g_k(\boldsymbol{x}_k) = g_k(\boldsymbol{x}) + \nabla g_k(\boldsymbol{x}) \cdot (\boldsymbol{x}_k - \boldsymbol{x}) + \boldsymbol{R}_k(\boldsymbol{x}_k) \cdot (\boldsymbol{x}_k - x), \tag{8.24}$$

where

$$\nabla g_k(\boldsymbol{x}) = \left[\frac{\partial}{\partial \boldsymbol{x}_k} g_k(\boldsymbol{x}_k)|_{\boldsymbol{x}_k=\boldsymbol{x}}, \frac{\partial}{\partial \boldsymbol{x}_0} g_k(\boldsymbol{x}_k)|_{\boldsymbol{x}_k=\boldsymbol{x}}\right] \text{ and } \lim_{\boldsymbol{x}_k \to \boldsymbol{x}} \boldsymbol{R}_k(\boldsymbol{x}_k) = \boldsymbol{0}, \tag{8.25}$$

and the same requirement also holds for the diagonally reflected point $\breve{\boldsymbol{x}} = (x_2, x_1)$.

(e) There exists a bandwidth $\boldsymbol{b}_{k0}$ such that for every $\boldsymbol{0} < \boldsymbol{b} < \boldsymbol{b}_{k0}$, there is a unique minimizer $\boldsymbol{\theta}_{k:\boldsymbol{b}}$ of the penalty function $q_{k:\boldsymbol{b}}$ defined in equation (B.4) of **JTSu**, which is obtained from (8.5) by putting $\boldsymbol{x} = \boldsymbol{x}_k$.

(f) The collection of bandwidths $\{\boldsymbol{b}_{k0}\}_{k\in\mathbb{Z}}$ has a positive infimum, that is, there exists $\boldsymbol{b}_0$ such that $\boldsymbol{0} < \boldsymbol{b}_0 \overset{\text{def}}{=} \inf_{k\in\mathbb{Z}} \boldsymbol{b}_{k0}$, which implies that this $\boldsymbol{b}_0$ can be used simultaneously for all the lags.

(g) For $\mathbf{Y}^n_{kq:i}$, the bivariate, trivariate, and tetravariate density functions (see Definition B.11 in **JTSu**) must be such that the expectations $E[\mathbf{Y}^n_{kq:i}]$, $E[|\mathbf{Y}^n_{kq:i}|^\nu]$, and $E[\mathbf{Y}^n_{kq:i} \cdot \mathbf{Y}^n_{jr:l}]$ all are finite

These assumptions on $\{X_t\}$ are extensions of those used for the LGC-case in Chapter 4. Assumption 1b is a bit more general than the geometric ergodicity used in Chapter 4, but this is not a problem since the arguments given there trivially extend to the present case.

The α-mixing requirement in (b) ensures that X_{t+k} and X_t are asymptotically independent as $k \to \infty$, that is, the bivariate density functions $g_k(\boldsymbol{x}_k)$

for large lags k approach the product of the marginal densities, and the situation will thus stabilize when k is large enough. This is in particular of importance for item (f) above since it implies that it is possible to find a nonzero $\boldsymbol{b}_0$ that works for all k.

We do not consider the α-mixing condition to be very strong. In particular, note that GARCH-type models, which are frequently used in econometrics and also in the present chapter (see Section 8.3.4.3), are β-mixing under weak conditions (see, e.g., Carrasco and Chen, 2002), and β-mixing implies α-mixing.

The finiteness requirements in Assumption 1g are trivially satisfied if the densities are bounded, that is, then they are consequences of properties of the kernel function $K_{\boldsymbol{b}}$ and the function $\boldsymbol{u}(\boldsymbol{v}, \boldsymbol{\theta}(\boldsymbol{x}))$; see Lemma C.6 of **JTSu** for details.

8.2.4.1 An assumption for X_t and the function $\boldsymbol{u}(\boldsymbol{v}, \boldsymbol{\theta}(\boldsymbol{x}))$

The function $\boldsymbol{u}$ in (8.6), $\boldsymbol{u}(\boldsymbol{v}, \boldsymbol{\theta}(\boldsymbol{x})) = \frac{\partial}{\partial \boldsymbol{\theta}} \log(\psi(\boldsymbol{v}, \boldsymbol{\theta}(\boldsymbol{x})))$, plays a central role in the local density estimation approach of Hjort and Jones (1996), and it also plays a pivotal role in the local Gaussian correlation theory developed in Chapter 4.

In particular, the convergence rate that in Chapter 4 is given for $\widehat{\boldsymbol{\theta}}(\boldsymbol{x}) - \boldsymbol{\theta}(\boldsymbol{x})$ does implicitly require that $\boldsymbol{u}(\boldsymbol{x}, \boldsymbol{\theta}(\boldsymbol{x})) \neq \boldsymbol{0}$ in order for the corresponding asymptotic covariance matrix to be well defined. The investigation of $(\widehat{f_{\boldsymbol{x}}^{m}}(\omega) - f_{\boldsymbol{x}}^{m}(\omega))$ (or $\widehat{f_{\boldsymbol{z}}^{m}}(\omega) - f_{\boldsymbol{z}}^{m}(\omega)$) in this chapter is built on the asymptotic results from Chapter 4, and the following assumption must be satisfied in order for the given convergence rates and asymptotic variances to be valid.

Assumption 2. The collection of local Gaussian parameters $\{\boldsymbol{\theta}_k(\boldsymbol{x})\}$ at the point $\boldsymbol{x}$ for the bivariate probability density functions $g_k(\boldsymbol{x}_k)$ is such that

(a) $\boldsymbol{u}(\boldsymbol{x}, \boldsymbol{\theta}_k(\boldsymbol{x})) \neq \boldsymbol{0}$ for all finite k;

(b) $\lim_k \boldsymbol{u}(\boldsymbol{x}, \boldsymbol{\theta}_k(\boldsymbol{x})) \neq \boldsymbol{0}$.

It is, for a given time series $\{X_t\}$ and a given point $\boldsymbol{x}$, possible to inspect the five equations in $\boldsymbol{u}(\boldsymbol{v}, \boldsymbol{\theta}(\boldsymbol{x})) = 0$ to see when (a) and (b) of Assumption 2 might fail.

8.2.4.2 Assumptions for n, m, and $\boldsymbol{b}$

For simplicity, in the present analysis, we will use the $\boldsymbol{b} = (b_1, b_2)$ introduced in the second paragraph after Lemma 8.2, that is, we will assume that the individual bandwidths $\boldsymbol{b}_k$ for the different lags k approach zero at the same rate and that for the asymptotic investigation, we can thus assume that the same bandwidth is used for all the lags.

Assumption 3. Let $m = m_n \to \infty$ be a sequence of integers denoting the number of lags to include, and let $\boldsymbol{b} = \boldsymbol{b}_n \to \boldsymbol{0}$ be the bandwidths used when estimating the local Gaussian correlations for the lags $k = 1, \ldots, m$ (based on n observations). Let b_1 and b_2 refer to the two components of $\boldsymbol{b}$, and let α, ν, and a be as introduced in Assumption 1b. Let $s = s_n \to \infty$ be a sequence of integers such that $s = o(\sqrt{nb_1b_2/m})$, and let τ be a positive constant. The following requirements must be satisfied for these entities:

(a) $\log n/n(b_1b_2)^3 \to 0$,
(b) $nb_1b_2/m \to \infty$,
(c) $m^\delta \max(b_1, b_2) \to 0$, where $\delta = \max(2, \frac{\nu(a+1)}{\nu(a-1)-2})$,
(d) $\sqrt{nm/b_1b_2}s^\tau\alpha(s-m-1) \to \infty$,
(e) $m = o((nb_1b_2)^{\tau/(2+5\tau)-\lambda})$ for some $\lambda \in (0, \tau/(2+5\tau))$,
(f) $m = o(s)$.

Assumption 3a is needed in order for the asymptotic theory from Chapter 4 to be valid for the estimates $\widehat{\rho}_k(\boldsymbol{x})$. See Lemma C.3 of **JTSu** for a verification of the internal consistency of the requirements given in Assumption 3.

The expected number of observations near $\boldsymbol{x}$ will for large n and small b_1 and b_2 be of order $nb_1b_2g_k(\boldsymbol{x})$, and this will, when $g_k(\boldsymbol{x}) > 0$, go to infinity as $n \to \infty$ and $\boldsymbol{b} \to \boldsymbol{0}$. See the end of Appendix C.3 of **JTSu** for further details.

8.2.5 Convergence theorems for $\widehat{f_{\boldsymbol{x}}^m}(\omega)$

Note that an identical theorem holds for $\widehat{f_{\boldsymbol{z}}^m}(\omega)$.

Theorem 8.1. *Let $\boldsymbol{x} = (x_1, x_2)$ with $x_1 = x_2$. The local Gaussian spectral density $\widehat{f_{\boldsymbol{x}}}(\omega)$ is a real-valued function when the point $\boldsymbol{x}$ lies on the diagonal. Furthermore, when the univariate time series $\{X_t\}$ satisfies Assumptions 1 and 2, and n, m, and $\boldsymbol{b} = (b_1, b_2)$ are as given in Assumption 3, then the following asymptotic results holds for the m-truncated estimate $\widehat{f_{\boldsymbol{x}}^m}(\omega)$:*

$$\sqrt{n(b_1b_2)^3/m}\left(\widehat{f_{\boldsymbol{x}}^m}(\omega) - f_{\boldsymbol{x}}(\omega)\right) \xrightarrow{d} \mathcal{N}(\boldsymbol{0}, \sigma_{\boldsymbol{x}}^2(\omega)), \tag{8.26}$$

where the formula

$$\sigma_{\boldsymbol{x}}^2(\omega) = 4 \lim_{m\to\infty} \frac{1}{m} \sum_{k=1}^{m} \lambda_m^2(k) \cos^2(2\pi\omega k)\tilde{\sigma}_k^2(\boldsymbol{x}) \tag{8.27}$$

relates the variance $\sigma_{\boldsymbol{x}}^2(\omega)$ *to the asymptotic variances* $\tilde{\sigma}_k^2(\boldsymbol{x})$ *of* $\sqrt{n(b_1 b_2)^3}(\widehat{\rho}_k(\boldsymbol{x}|\boldsymbol{b}_k) - \rho_k(\boldsymbol{x}))$.

The proof is given in Appendix A.1 of **JTSu**.

The variance $\sigma_{\boldsymbol{x}}^2(\omega)$ depends on all the bivariate density functions through the variances $\tilde{\sigma}_k^2(\boldsymbol{x})$. Moreover, it is clear from (8.27) that $\sigma_k^2(\boldsymbol{x})$ as a function of the frequency ω is symmetric around $\omega = \frac{1}{4}$ with its highest values when $\omega \in \{0, \frac{1}{2}\}$. The same symmetry is not present for the variance of the m-truncated spectral estimates $\widehat{f_{\boldsymbol{x}}^m}(\omega)$, and the variance of $\widehat{f_{\boldsymbol{x}}^m}(\omega)$ has its highest value when $\omega = 0$; see Appendix A.3 of **JTSu**.

A similar result to Theorem 8.1 can be stated for time-reversible stochastic processes.

Theorem 8.2 ($\{X_t\}$ time reversible). *The local Gaussian spectral density* $f_{\boldsymbol{x}}(\omega)$ *is a real-valued function for all points* $\boldsymbol{x}$ *when* $\{X_t\}$ *is time reversible (see Definition 2). Furthermore, under Assumptions 1–3, the same asymptotic results as stated in Theorem 8.1 hold for the m-truncated estimate* $\widehat{f_{\boldsymbol{x}}^m}(\omega)$.

Lemma 8.1c states that $f_{\boldsymbol{x}}(\omega)$ is a real-valued function, and then the proof of Theorem 8.1 (see Appendix A.1 of **JTSu**) can be repeated without any modifications.

The asymptotic normality results in Theorems 8.1 and 8.2 do not easily enable a practical computation of pointwise confidence intervals for the estimated LGSD. Thus the pointwise confidence intervals later on will either be estimated based on suitable quantiles obtained by repeated sampling from a known distribution, or they will be based on bootstrapping techniques for those cases where real data have been investigated; see Teräsvirta et al. (2010, Chs. 7.2.5 and 7.2.6) for further details with regard to the need for bootstrapping in such situations. See also Lacal and Tjøstheim (2017, 2019) and Chapter 7 for analytic results on validity of the bootstrap and block bootstrap in the case of estimation of the local Gaussian auto- and cross-correlation functions.

The asymptotic result for complex-valued $\widehat{f_{\boldsymbol{x}}^m}(\omega)$ is given in Appendix A.2 of **JTSu**, where we can see that $\sqrt{n(b_1 b_2)^3/m}\left(\widehat{f_{\boldsymbol{x}}^m}(\omega) - f_{\boldsymbol{x}}(\omega)\right)$ asymptotically approaches a complex-valued normal distribution.

8.3 Visualizations and interpretations

As explained in Section 8.2.1.2 and the beginning of Section 8.2.4, we now return to the $\boldsymbol{z}$-level and the estimate $\widehat{f_{\boldsymbol{z}}^m}(\omega)$. This section shows how different visualizations of the m-truncated normalized estimates $\widehat{f_{z}^{m}}(\omega)$ can be used to detect nonlinear dependency and frequency structures in a time series. Similar graphical methods can also be found in Li (2019), Birr et al. (2019), and the heatmap plot presented in this section is in particular inspired by that encountered in Li (2019).

Technical details and the description of the selected tuning parameters of $\widehat{f_{z}^{m}}(\omega)$ are given in Section 8.3.1. In Section 8.3.2, we use the aforementioned `dmbp`-data introduced in Section 8.2.3 to highlight how the different tuning parameters of the estimation algorithm are interconnected.

A sanity test of the implemented estimation algorithm is presented in Section 8.3.3, and we see there that $\widehat{f_{z}^{m}}(\omega)$ can detect local periodic structures in an example where a heuristic argument enables the prediction of the anticipated result.

In Section 8.3.4, we apply the local Gaussian machinery to the `dmbp`-data, and it also contains the results from a GARCH-type model fitted to the `dmbp`-data. A comparison of the results from the original data and the fitted model can reveal to what extent the internal dependency structure of the fitted model actually reflects the dependency structure of the original sample, and this may be of interest with regard to model selection.

A few extreme examples have been included in **JTSu** to investigate the limitations of the local spectral method. Appendix G.4.3 of **JTSu** examines the detection of a periodic component located far out in the tail of a large sample, and *Appendix G.4.4* considers a situation based on a deterministic function perturbed by very weak random fluctuations.

8.3.1 The input parameters and some other technical details

Several tuning parameters must be selected to compute the m-truncated local Gaussian spectral density estimates $\widehat{f_{z}^{m}}(\omega)$, and the tuning values used for the plots in this section are given below. Note that these parameters were selected to provide a *proof of concept* for the fact that nonlinear dependency and frequency structures can be detected by this approach, and the quest for "optimal parameters" is a topic for further work. The interested reader can consult Appendix D of **JTSu** for a sensitivity analysis of the different tuning parameters.

The pseudo-normalization: The initial step of the computation of $\widehat{f_{z}}(\omega)$ is replacing the observations $\{X_t\}_{t=1}^{n}$ with the corresponding pseudo-normalized observations $\{\widehat{Z}_t\}_{t=1}^{n}$ (see Algorithm 1), that is, an estimate of the marginal cumulative density function G is needed. The present analysis has used the rescaled empirical distribution function $\widehat{G}_n$ for this purpose, but the computations could also be based on a logspline estimate of G. A preliminary test revealed that the two normalization procedures created strikingly similar estimates $\widehat{f_{\boldsymbol{z}}^{m}}(\omega)$, so the computationally faster approach based on the empirical distribution function was applied for the present investigation.

The length n of the samples: All samples have the same length as the `dmbp`-data, $n = 1974$. The estimation machinery produces similar results for shorter samples, but it is important to keep in mind that too short samples might not reveal the dependency structure of interest, which in particular may be an issue for the tails of the distribution.

The points $\boldsymbol{z}$ of investigation: Three diagonal points, with coordinates corresponding to the 10%, 50%, and 90% percentiles of the standard normal distribution, are used in the basic plots in this section. These points will often be referred to as *lower tail*, *center*, and *upper tail* when discussed in the text; see Appendix D.3 in **JTSu** for further details related to the selection of $\boldsymbol{z}$, and see Fig. 8.8 for a heatmap-based plot.

The lag-window function $\lambda_m(k)$: The smoothing of the estimated local Gaussian autocorrelations (see Algorithm 1c) was done by the Tukey–Hanning lag-window kernel $\lambda_m(k) = \frac{1}{2}(1 + \cos(\pi \frac{k}{m}))$ for $|k| \leq m$, $\lambda_m(k) = 0$ for $|k| > m$.

The bandwidth $\boldsymbol{b}$: The estimation of the local Gaussian autocorrelations requires the selection of a bandwidth vector $\boldsymbol{b} = (b_1, b_2)$, and the majority of the plots in this section have used $\boldsymbol{b} = (0.5, 0.5)$. Note that it is natural to require $b_1 = b_2$ since both components in the lag-k pseudo-normalized pairs come from the same univariate time series. Further discussion of choice of bandwidth is given in Appendix E of **JTSu**.

The truncation level m: The value $m = 10$ was used for the truncation level, since it was possible to detect nonlinear dependency structures even for that low truncation level.

The number of replicates R: The estimated values (means and 90% pointwise confidence intervals) were based on $R = 100$ bootstrap replicates. Simulations were used for the cases with known parametric models, whereas a block bootstrap-based resampling strategy was used for the real-data example (see Appendix F of **JTSu** for the technical details).

Numerical convergence: The R-package localgauss (see Berentsen et al., 2014) estimates the local Gaussian autocorrelations $\rho_k(\boldsymbol{z})$ and returns them together with an attribute that reveals whether or not the estimation algorithm converged numerically. The m-truncated estimates $\widehat{f_{z}^{m}}(\omega)$ inherit the convergence attributes from the estimates $\{\widehat{\rho}_k(z)\}$, and either "NC = OK" or "NC = FAIL" will be added to the plot depending on the convergence status. Note that convergence problems hardly occur when the computations are based on pseudo-normalized observations.

Reproducibility and interactive investigations: All the examples in this chapter can be reproduced by the scripts (see Appendix J of **JTSu**) contained in the R-package `localgaussSpec`. Note that the computations of $\widehat{f_{z}^{m}}(\omega)$ can be performed for a wide range of tuning parameters, which allows an integrated interactive investigation of the results by means of the application `shiny`. See Chang et al. (2017) for details about `shiny`.

8.3.2 Estimation aspects for the given parameter configuration

The estimation of $\widehat{f_{z}^{m}}(\omega)$ for a point $z = (z_1, z_2)$ that lies on the diagonal $z_1 = z_2$ is based on the estimates of $\widehat{\rho}_k(z)$ for $k = 1, \ldots, m$, and it is thus of interest to first investigate how these estimates depend on the configuration of the tuning parameters given in Section 8.3.1. This is most easily done in terms of an example, and the pseudo-normalized `dmbp`-data (of length 1974) are used for this purpose.

First of all, note that the combination of a point z and a bandwidth b influence how many of the k-lagged pairs effectively contribute to the computation of $\widehat{\rho}_k(z)$. This is shown in Fig. 8.3 for the pseudo-normalized `dmbp`-data. In the plot of the pseudo-normalized time series (top panel) the three horizontal dashed lines represent the "levels", which correspond to the coordinates of the three points z, whereas the horizontal strips centered at those lines show which observations lie within a distance of $b = 0.5$ from the respective lines. The three plots at the bottom show the corresponding 1-lagged pairs, each with a *bandwidth-square* (of width $2b$) centered at one of the selected points z.

The estimates of $\rho_k(z)$ are based on the k-lagged pairs seen in the lower part of Fig. 8.3 for $k = 1$, and these and similar estimates for lags up to 200 (based on $b = (0.5, 0.5)$) are shown in Fig. 8.4. An investigation of Fig. 8.4 shows how $\widehat{\rho}_k(z)$ varies for the three points of interest, and there is a clear distinction between the center and two tails. Note that the bias-variance balance of the estimates $\widehat{\rho}_k(z)$ depends on the number of k-lagged pairs that effectively contribute during the computation, and it is thus clear that

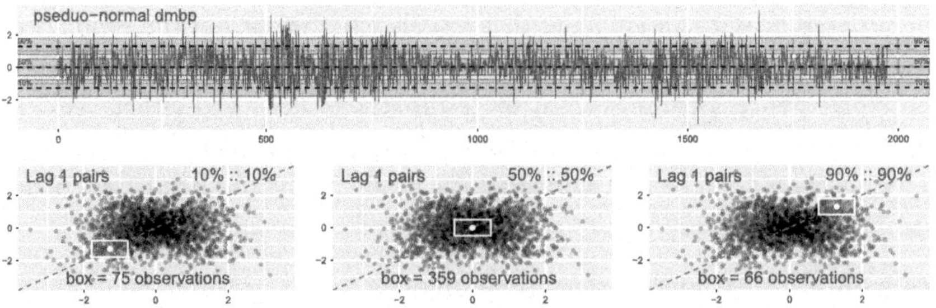

Figure 8.3 `dmbp` (pseudo-normalized version), *levels*, and *bandwidth-bands* (top) and *lag 1 bandwidth-squares* (bottom). Further details in the main text.

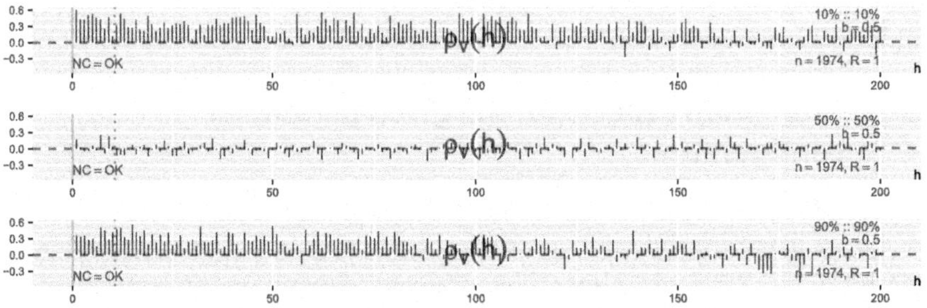

Figure 8.4 `dmbp`-data, $\widehat{\rho}_k(\boldsymbol{z})$ estimated for $k = 1, \ldots, 200$ in the three points of interest. The estimates for $k = 1, \ldots, 10$ will be used for producing $\widehat{f_{\boldsymbol{z}}^m}(\omega)$; cf. Fig. 8.9.

the variance increases for points $\boldsymbol{z}$ that lie farther out in the tails. Selecting the tail-points to investigate, we must take into account the number of available observations for the lags to be included.

The $\widehat{\rho}_k(\boldsymbol{z})$ tends to fluctuate around 0 at the center, which implies that the corresponding estimated spectral density $\widehat{f_{\boldsymbol{z}}^m}(\omega)$ most likely will be rather flat and close to 1; cf. Fig. 8.9. For the two tails, it seems natural to assume that some long-range dependency must be present, and we may also suspect that there is an asymmetry between the two tails. A further investigation of this is easy when the `shiny`-application in the R-package `localgaussSpec` is used, since then it is possible to immediately switch to an investigation of the corresponding spectra.

Based on the impression from Fig. 8.4, there may be a connection between the global long-range dependence in the `dmbp`-data and the local dependency structure in the tails, but note that the estimates in Fig. 8.4 are based on the pseudo-normalized data, so the information from the marginal distribution is not directly present here. However, the same kind of behavior was observed for pseudo-normalized samples from different GARCH-type models, so the dependency structure of the tails can be a significant contributor to the global long-range dependency seen in time series models like ARCH and GARCH.

8.3.3 Sanity testing the implemented estimation algorithm

The purpose of this section is checking whether or not the implemented estimation algorithm returns reasonable results for some simulated examples. Basically, only for the Gaussian case, the true values of the local Gaussian spectral densities $f_{\boldsymbol{z}}(\omega)$ are known, and thus it is important to specifically construct an example where heuristic arguments enable the prediction of the anticipated results.

The strategy to create the plots for the simulated data works as follows: First, draw a given number of independent replicates from the specified model and compute $\widehat{f_{\boldsymbol{z}}^m}(\omega)$ and $\widehat{f^m}(\omega)$ (an estimate of the m-truncated global spectrum) for each replicate. Then extract the mean of these estimates to get estimates of the true values of $f_{\boldsymbol{z}}^m(\omega)$ and $f^m(\omega)$, and select suitable upper and lower percentiles of the estimates to produce an estimate of the pointwise confidence intervals.

Note that the plots were annotated with the following information: The numerical convergence status $\{\text{NC}\}$ in the lower left corner; the truncation level m in the upper left corner; the percentiles of the point $\boldsymbol{z}$ of investigation and the bandwidth $\boldsymbol{b}$ in the upper right corner; the length n and the number of replicates R in the lower right corner.

8.3.3.1 Gaussian white noise

The sanity testing of the implemented estimation algorithm starts with the trivial case. Fig. 8.5 shows the result when the estimation procedure is used on 100 independent samples of length 1974 from the standard normal distribution $\mathcal{N}(0,1)$. The computations are based on the bandwidth $\boldsymbol{b} = (0.5, 0.5)$, and the points (on the diagonal) correspond to the 0.1, 0.5, and 0.9 quantiles of the standard normal distribution. The top left panel shows the pseudo-normalized version of the first time series sampled from the model with dashed lines at the levels that correspond to the above-mentioned points. The three other panels contain information about the m-truncated ordinary spectral density $f^m(\omega)$ (red part, the same for all plots) and the m-truncated local Gaussian spectral densities $f_{\boldsymbol{z}}^m(\omega)$ for the three points under investigation (blue part).

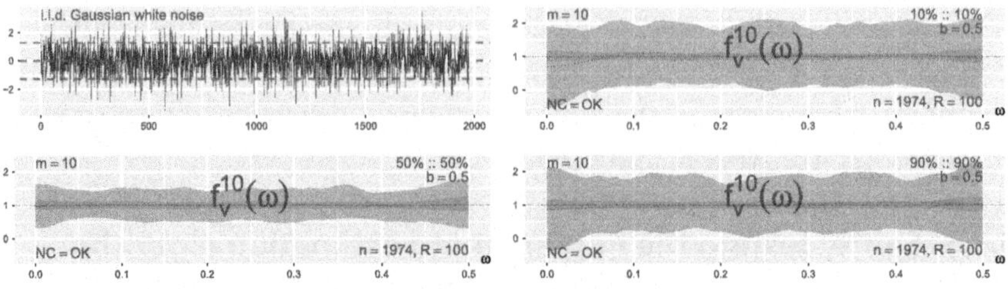

Figure 8.5 iid Gaussian white noise with global and local spectra for three points.

We can see from Fig. 8.5 that the means of the estimates (the dashed lines at the center of the regions) are good estimates of $f(\omega)$ and $f_{\mathbf{z}}(\omega)$, that is, it is known that the true values are identical to 1 for both local and global cases. Observe that the estimated 90% pointwise confidence intervals are wider for the local Gaussian spectral densities, which is as expected since the bandwidth used in the estimation of the local Gaussian autocorrelations reduces the number of observations, which effectively contributes to the estimated values and thus makes the estimates more prone to small-sample variation. Note also that the pointwise confidence intervals are wider in the tails, which is a natural consequence of the reduced number of points in those regions; see the discussion related to Fig. 8.3. The width of these pointwise confidence intervals decreases as the bandwidth increases; see the plots and the discussion related to Fig. 8.6.

The estimation procedure gave good estimates of the true values $f(\omega)$ and $f_{\mathbf{z}}(\omega)$ in the simple example of Fig. 8.5, but it is important to keep in mind that these plots actually show estimates of $f^m(\omega)$ and $f_{\mathbf{z}}^m(\omega)$. In other situations, it may be necessary to apply a (much) higher truncation level m before $f^m(\omega)$ and $f_{\mathbf{z}}^m(\omega)$ give good approximations of the true values $f(\omega)$ and $f_{\mathbf{z}}(\omega)$.

However, for the task of interest in Section 8.3, it is actually not a problem if the selected truncation level does not give "optimal estimates" of $f(\omega)$ and $f_{\mathbf{z}}(\omega)$, since the detection of nonlinear dependence and frequency structures can be seen for a wide range of different truncation levels. The recommended approach is computing the estimate $\widehat{f_{\mathbf{z}}^m}(\omega)$ for a range of possible truncation levels m and then checking if the shapes of the estimates for different truncations share the same properties with regard to the position of any peaks and troughs. The R-package `localgaussSpec` is designed in such a way that this is trivial to do.

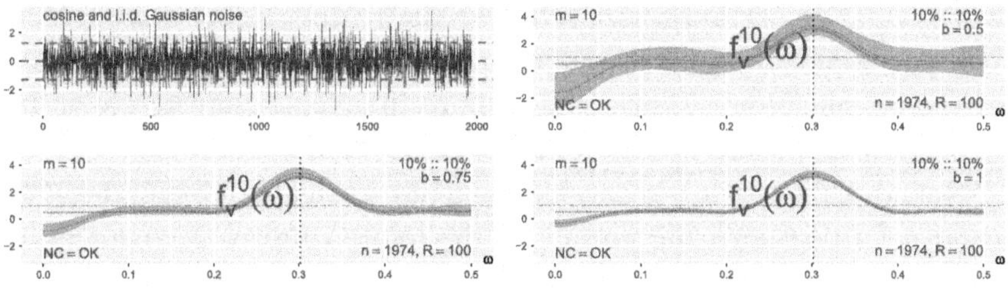

Figure 8.6 Single cosine and iid white noise, same point, bandwidths 0.5, 0.75, and 1.

8.3.3.2 Some trigonometric examples

Beyond the realm of Gaussian time series, it is basically not known what the true value for the local Gaussian spectral density actually should be. In this subsection, we test the sanity of the implemented estimation algorithm by means of an artificially constructed *local trigonometric* time series, for which it at least can be reasonably argued what the expected outcome should be for some specially designated points $\boldsymbol{z}$ (given a suitable bandwidth $\boldsymbol{b}$). These artificial time series do not satisfy the requirements needed for the asymptotic theory to hold (as is also the case for standard global spectral analysis), but they can still be used to show how an exploratory tool based on the local Gaussian spectral density can detect local periodic properties that the ordinary spectral density fails to detect.

As a prerequisite (and a reference) for the investigation of the local trigonometric time series, it is prudent to first investigate the result based on independent samples from a time series of the form $X_t = \cos(2\pi\alpha t + \varphi) + w_t$, where w_t is Gaussian white noise with mean zero and standard deviation σ, and in addition α is fixed for all the replicates, whereas the phase-adjustment φ is randomly generated for each individual replicate. A realization with $\alpha = 0.302$ and $\sigma = 0.75$ is shown in Fig. 8.6, where the frequency α is indicated with a vertical line to show that both local and global approaches in this case have a peak at the expected position. The plots are based on 100 samples of length 1974 and show 90% pointwise confidence intervals. Some useful remarks can be based on Fig. 8.6 before *the local trigonometric* case is defined and investigated.

All the plots in Fig. 8.6 show the same point (corresponding to the 10% quantile) in the lower tail, but they differ with regard to the bandwidths used. In particular, the upper right plot is based on the bandwidth $\boldsymbol{b} = (0.5, 0.5)$ (the bandwidth used in all the other examples), whereas the two plots at the bottom show the situation for the bandwidths $\boldsymbol{b} = (0.75, 0.75)$

and $\boldsymbol{b} = (1, 1)$, respectively, at the left and right. In this case the widths of the pointwise confidence intervals are influenced by the selected bandwidths, but the overall shape is similar and close to the global estimate shown in red. This feature is also present for the other investigated examples.

Note that the cosine is recovered using just a neighborhood of the 10% quantile. Furthermore, the portion of the local Gaussian spectral density that is negative decreases with increasing bandwidth, which is in accordance with the remark at the end of Section 8.2.1.1. Using the notation from Algorithm 1, for the estimates of the local Gaussian autocorrelations, we can state that $\widehat{\rho}_k(\boldsymbol{z}|\boldsymbol{b}) \to \widehat{\rho}_k$ as $\boldsymbol{b} \to \infty$, which implies that the estimate $\widehat{f_{\boldsymbol{z}}^m}(\omega)$ converges toward the global non-negative estimate $\widehat{f^m}(\omega)$. Thus it is possible to reduce the amount of negative values for the estimates $\widehat{f_{\boldsymbol{z}}^m}(\omega)$ by increasing the bandwidth $\boldsymbol{b}$, but we should keep in mind that the limits as $\boldsymbol{b} \to \boldsymbol{0}$ and $m \to \infty$ should be considered to actually estimate the local Gaussian spectral density $f_{\boldsymbol{z}}(\omega)$.

The truncation level used in Fig. 8.6 is rather low, $m = 10$, but we can see that the peak is observed at the correct frequency. The peak grows taller and narrower when a higher truncation level is used, but it stays at the same frequency. This indicates that these plots (even for low truncation values) can detect properties of the underlying structure. Again, this feature is shared with the other investigated examples.

The local Gaussian spectral densities in Fig. 8.6 goes below zero for low frequencies, a feature that is not entirely unexpected as $\{\rho_k(\boldsymbol{z})\}_{k\in\mathbb{Z}}$, the collection of local Gaussian autocorrelations, may not be a non-negative definite function. In fact, based on the observation that the estimates of $\widehat{f_{\boldsymbol{z}}^m}(\omega)$ have peaks that are taller and wider than those of $\widehat{f^m}(\omega)$, as expected, these estimates may need to have negative values somewhere. The reason for this is that all the spectral densities (global, local, and m-truncated) by construction necessarily must integrate to one over the interval $(-\frac{1}{2}, \frac{1}{2}]$. Thus higher and wider peaks of the estimates $\widehat{f_{\boldsymbol{z}}^m}(\omega)$ require that it has to lie below the estimates $\widehat{f^m}(\omega)$ in some other region, and if necessary, it must attain negative values somewhere. Thus the interesting details in the plots are the positions of the peaks of $\widehat{f_{\boldsymbol{z}}}(\omega)$, and regions with negative values should not in general be considered a too troublesome feature.

Note that, under certain circumstances, $\widehat{f_{\boldsymbol{z}}^m}(\omega)$ may contain spurious artifacts when it is computed for time series having a non-flat ordinary spectrum; see Appendix G.4.4 of **JTSu** for a discussion related to a case based on a deterministic function in very weak noise.

The local trigonometric case: The key idea in this example is that an artificial time series $\{X_t\}_{t\in\mathbb{Z}}$ can be constructed by the following scheme:

1. Select r time series $\{C_i(t)\}_{i=1}^r$.
2. Select a random variable J with values in the set $\{1,\dots,r\}$ and use this to sample a collection of indices $\{J_t\}_{t\in\mathbb{Z}}$ (i.e., for each t, an independent realization of J is taken). Let $p_i = P(J_t = i)$ denote the probabilities for the different outcomes.
3. Define

$$X_t = \sum_{i=1}^{r} I\{J_t = i\} C_i(t). \tag{8.28}$$

The indicator function I ensures that only one of the $C_i(t)$ contributes for a given value t, that is, it is also possible to write $X_t = C_{J_t}(t)$.

The *local trigonometric* time series (needed for the sanity testing of the implemented estimation algorithm) is constructed by selecting r cosine functions so that it oscillates around different horizontal baselines L_i:

$$C_i(t) = L_i + A_i(t)\cos(2\pi\alpha_i t + \varphi_i), \qquad i = 1,\dots,r, \tag{8.29}$$

where α_i and φ_i, respectively, represent the frequency and phase-adjustment occurring in the cosine function, and the amplitudes $A_i(t)$ are uniformly distributed in some interval $[a_i, b_i]$. Note that we assume that the phases φ_i are uniformly drawn (one time for each realization) from the interval $[0, 2\pi]$ and, moreover, that the stochastic processes φ_i, $A_i(t)$, and J_t are independent of each other.

The autocorrelation ρ_k of the time series $\{X_t\}$ with $C_i(t)$ as given in (8.29) is computed in equation (G.5) in Appendix G.4 in **JTSu**. For the present subsection, it is sufficient to know that it is possible to find parameter configurations for which the global spectrum is rather flat (at least when truncated at $m = 10$), which implies that it cannot detect the frequencies α_i of the underlying structure.

Strictly speaking, neither $f(\omega)$ nor $f_{\boldsymbol{z}}(\omega)$ are well defined for the *local trigonometric* times series, but this is not important since it is still possible to predict (see Appendix G.4 of **JTSu** for details) that the m-truncated estimates $\widehat{f_{\boldsymbol{z}}^m}(\omega)$ for some points $\boldsymbol{z}$ should resemble Fig. 8.6, and this can be used (see Fig. 8.7) to test the sanity of the implemented estimation algorithm.

The explicit expression for the *local trigonometric* example depicted in Fig. 8.7 is given by $r = 4$ components $C_i(t)$ of the form (8.29), where the

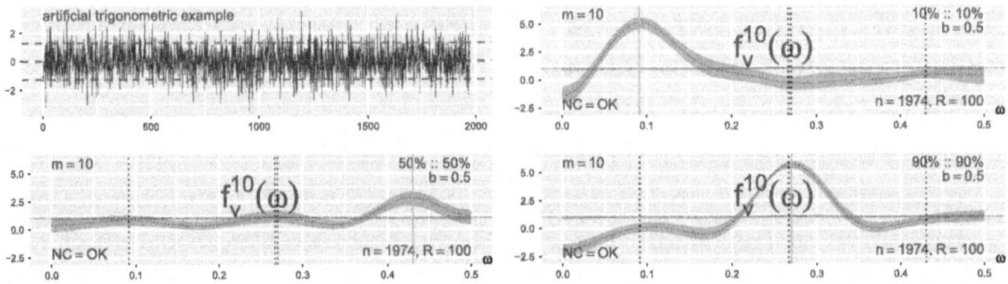

Figure 8.7 Artificial example, *local trigonometric components*. Global and local spectra for the three points $\boldsymbol{z}$ on the diagonal: lower tail, center, and upper tail.

probabilities p_i are given by $(0.05, 1/3 - 0.05, 1/3, 1/3)$, the frequencies α_i are given by $(0.267, 0.091, 0.431, 0.270)$, the base-lines L_i are given by the values $(-2, -1, 0, 1)$, and the lower and upper ranges for the uniform sampling of the amplitudes $A_i(t)$ are respectively given by $\{(0.5, 0.2, 0.2, 0.5)\}$ and $\{(1.0, 0.5, 0.3, 0.6)\}$. Note that L_i and $A_i(t)$ should be selected to give a minimal amount of overlap between the different components; see Appendix G.4 in **JTSu**.

Fig. 8.7 shows $\widehat{f^m}(\omega)$ and $\widehat{f_{\boldsymbol{z}}^m}(\omega)$ for the *local trigonometric* example. The ordinary spectrum does not detect the frequencies α_i (indicated by vertical lines), whereas the local Gaussian spectra do have clear peaks at the frequencies from $C_2(t)$, $C_3(t)$, and $C_4(t)$. Moreover, a comparison with Fig. 8.6 shows that $\widehat{f_{\boldsymbol{z}}^m}(\omega)$ indeed looks like predicted, which verifies the sanity of the implemented estimation algorithm.

The selected probabilities $\{p_i\}_{i=1}^4$ imply that observations from the $C_3(t)$ component after pseudo-normalization should lie between $\Phi^{-1}(1/3) = -0.43$ and $\Phi^{-1}(2/3) = 0.43$. The estimation of $\widehat{f_{\boldsymbol{z}}^m}(\omega)$ is based on the bandwidth $\boldsymbol{b} = (0.5, 0.5)$, which implies that the estimate at the center will be "contaminated" by observations from the neighboring components, and this explains the lower amplitude seen for this point.

The three points $\boldsymbol{z}$ in Fig. 8.7 correspond roughly to the base-lines L_2, L_3, and L_4, and the corresponding frequencies α_2, α_3, and α_4 are detected by $\widehat{f_{\boldsymbol{z}}^m}(\omega)$. But what about the base-line L_1 and the α_1-frequency?

The low probability at which the $C_1(t)$ component is selected implies that the point $\boldsymbol{z}$ corresponding to the baseline L_1 must lie far out in the lower tail, and for the present sample size ($n = 1974$), the scarcity of observations in this region implies that it is not possible to obtain decent estimates of the required local Gaussian autocorrelations $\rho_k(\boldsymbol{z})$. A countermeasure to this problem would be to use a larger bandwidth $\boldsymbol{b}$, but then the result would be "contaminated" by the observations from the $C_2(t)$ component, and the peak of $\widehat{f_{\boldsymbol{z}}}(\omega)$ would be at the frequency α_2 instead of α_1. This implies that misleading results can occur when the bandwidth $\boldsymbol{b}$ is too large.

However, note that for a large enough sample, it is possible to detect the frequency α_1 that belongs to the $C_1(t)$-component; see Appendix G.4.3 in **JTSu**.

The $C_1(t)$-component was included in this example to emphasize that extra care is needed when investigating the far out tails of a sample. This of course begs the question: For a given sample $\{X_t\}_{t=1}^{n}$, how can an investigator figure out whether or not the estimate of $f_{\boldsymbol{z}}^{m}(\omega)$, for a given combination of point $\boldsymbol{z}$ and bandwidth $\boldsymbol{b}$, seems trustworthy or not? Another important question for an investigator is deciding if some points $\boldsymbol{z}$ may be more interesting than others. Both these questions can be investigated by means of the two plots seen in Fig. 8.8, which (for a single sample from the aforementioned *local trigonometric* construction) investigates the $m = 10$ truncated local Gaussian spectra $\widehat{f_{\boldsymbol{z}}^{m}}(\omega)$ for points along the diagonal. Note that the points $\boldsymbol{z}$ are represented by their respective percentiles, and the range goes from the 5% to the 95%.

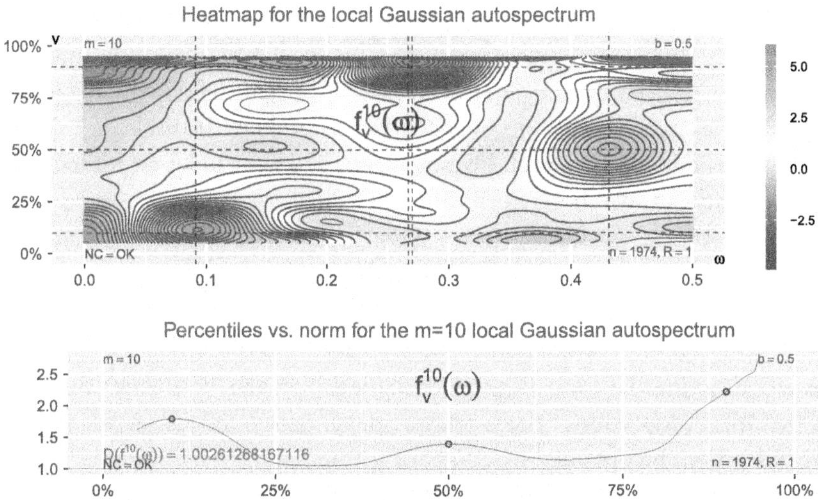

Figure 8.8 Heatmap plot with corresponding distance-plot, based on the local trigonometric case, showing how $\widehat{f_{\boldsymbol{z}}^{10}}(\omega)$ varies with the percentiles for the diagonal points $\boldsymbol{z}$. The percentiles and frequencies used in Fig. 8.7 are indicated with lines/points.

The upper part of Fig. 8.8 is a heatmap plot for $\widehat{f}_{\mathbf{z}}^{m}(\omega)$ (inspired by plots in Li, 2019), which in this case is based on one sample of length $n = 1974$. The contour lines in this plot clearly reveal that the highest peaks occur approximately at the points investigated in Fig. 8.7. In fact, looking at the heatmap, the peak at the 90th percentile of Fig. 8.8, may have its maximum closer to the 95th percentile, but we have to be a little careful here since the estimates of $\rho_k(\mathbf{z})$ may degenerate toward $+1$ (or -1) in the far out part of the tail.

The lower part of Fig. 8.8 shows the corresponding distance plot $D(\widehat{f}_{\mathbf{z}}^{m}(\omega))$, where the norms of the m-truncated spectra (realized as elements of the complex Hilbert space of Fourier series; see Appendix D.1 of **JTSu** for details) are plotted against the diagonal points. Note that distance-based plots do not contain any information about the frequencies, and completely different spectral densities can have the same distance value. It is thus important to always combine a distance-based plot with a plot that reveals the frequency component.

The horizontal line at the bottom of the distance plot gives the norm of the ordinary spectrum, and we can see that this line is very close to the white-noise value 1. It is interesting and reassuring that $D(\widehat{f}_{\mathbf{z}}^{m}(\omega))$ picks up the peaks at the 10th and 50th percentiles. However, it does not indicate a peak close to the 95th percentile, but this is also the least clear peak of the heatmap.

This discussion shows that it is important to include a wide range of points when performing an investigation based on local Gaussian spectral densities, since it is necessary to check how $\widehat{f}_{\mathbf{z}}^{m}(\omega)$ changes as the diagonal point $\mathbf{z}$ varies from the lower tail to the upper tail. The R-package `localgaussSpec` is designed for such investigations, and it includes an interactive interface that can switch between different visualizations. Note that `localgaussSpec` also can deal with points $\mathbf{z}$ that lie outside the diagonal, and it can also handle multivariate time series.

8.3.4 Real data and a fitted GARCH-type model

We will now use the local Gaussian machinery on the `dmbp`-data. We will see that local properties of the nonlinear dependency and frequency structure indeed can be obtained by comparing $\widehat{f}^{m}(\omega)$ and $\widehat{f}_{\mathbf{z}}^{m}(\omega)$, and this works even for low values of the truncation level m.

Another topic that it is natural to consider is the comparison of $\widehat{f}_{\mathbf{z}}^{m}(\omega)$ based on the data and $\widehat{f}_{\mathbf{z}}^{m}(\omega)$ based on simulations from a model fitted to the data, and this will in particular be investigated for a GARCH-type model that was fitted to the `dmbp`-data by the R-package `rugarch`; see Ghalanos (2020).

8.3.4.1 The real data example

We will now investigate the `dmbp`-data (length 1974), whose original and pseudo-normalized versions can be seen in Fig. 8.2, by the m-truncated local Gaussian spectral densities $\widehat{f_{\boldsymbol{z}}^m}(\omega)$. These estimates are based on the bandwidth $\boldsymbol{b} = (0.5, 0.5)$ and will be computed for the three diagonal points corresponding to the 10th, 50th, and 90th percentiles of the standard normal distribution. The estimated local Gaussian autocorrelations $\widehat{\rho_k}(\boldsymbol{z})$ is used in the computation of $\widehat{f_{\boldsymbol{z}}^m}(\omega)$ can be seen in Fig. 8.4, and the estimated values $\widehat{f^m}(\omega)$ and $\widehat{f_{\boldsymbol{z}}^m}(\omega)$ (for the $m = 10$ case) are shown as the red and blue solid lines in Fig. 8.9. The pointwise confidence intervals are based on the resampling strategy discussed at the end of this sub-section.

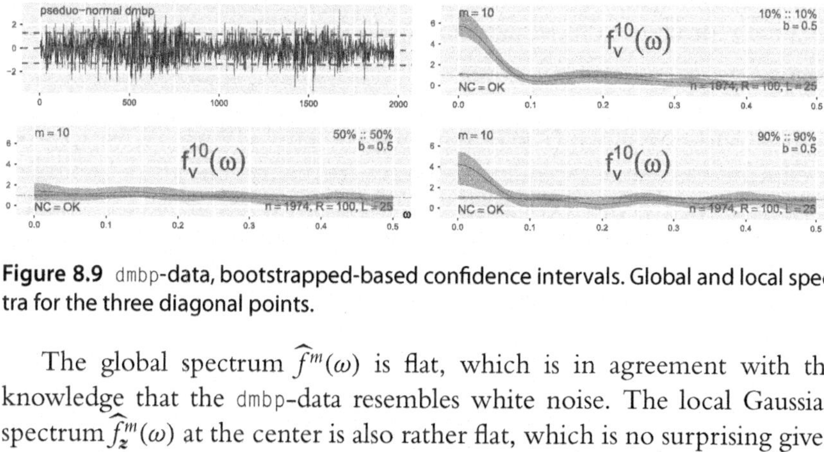

Figure 8.9 `dmbp`-data, bootstrapped-based confidence intervals. Global and local spectra for the three diagonal points.

The global spectrum $\widehat{f^m}(\omega)$ is flat, which is in agreement with the knowledge that the `dmbp`-data resembles white noise. The local Gaussian spectrum $\widehat{f_{\boldsymbol{z}}^m}(\omega)$ at the center is also rather flat, which is no surprising given the values $\widehat{\rho_k}(\boldsymbol{z})$ seen in the middle panel of Fig. 8.4. The estimates $\widehat{f_{\boldsymbol{z}}^m}(\omega)$ in the tails are obviously not flat, and the clear peaks at the frequency $\omega = 0$ are again in agreement with the corresponding values $\widehat{\rho_k}(\boldsymbol{z})$ from Fig. 8.4.

The difference between the (solid lines in the) lower and upper tails can indicate the presence of an asymmetry, that is, the peak is more prominent for the lower tail. It would be premature to draw a firm conclusion regarding asymmetry based on a single plot using the low truncation level $m = 10$, but the asymmetry can also be seen for higher truncation levels (investigated up to $m = 200$) with an increasing difference between the height of these peaks. Such an asymmetry, with a higher peak at the lower tail, would be in agreement with the asymmetry between a *bear market* (going down) and a *bull market* (going up); see Chapter 6.

A comparison solely based on the solid lines in Fig. 8.9 is not sufficient, since an observed difference could be due to the variability of the estimator used to find $\widehat{f_{\boldsymbol{z}}^{m}}(\omega)$. Thus it is necessary to decide on a reasonable resampling strategy (described below) that can provide pointwise confidence intervals like those shown in Fig. 8.9. Based on the pointwise confidence intervals, it is clear that the truncated local and global spectra indeed show that the `dmbp`-data contain local non-linear dependency structures in the tails. Note that the width of the pointwise confidence interval is a function of the frequency (see Appendix A.3 of **JTSu**), and this can in some cases give it a wide "trumpet shape" near $\omega = 0$, as seen in the lower and upper tails in Fig. 8.9 (and which is even more prominent in Fig. 8.11).

The pointwise confidence intervals in Fig. 8.9 require a resampling strategy that takes into account that the local Gaussian autocorrelations $\rho_1(\boldsymbol{z}), \ldots, \rho_m(\boldsymbol{z})$ are estimated by a local likelihood approach. The asymptotic properties of these estimates were developed in the present chapter using the procedure from Klimko and Nelson (1978); see Appendix B.1 in **JTSu**.

The block bootstrap can be used for a variety of estimators and can, in particular (see Künsch (1989), Example 2.4, pp. 1219–1920), be applied for estimators based on the Klimko–Nelson procedure. The block bootstrap was indeed used as the resampling strategy in an earlier draft of Jordanger and Tjøstheim (2020), and the results were similar to Fig. 8.9 when a block length of $L = 100$ was used. The selected block length L seemed reasonable based on the $\widehat{\rho}_k(\boldsymbol{z})$-values seen in Fig. 8.4. See Appendix F.6 in **JTSu** for further details.

Some comments related to the block bootstrap were received during the review process of Jordanger and Tjøstheim (2020), and they motivated the investigation presented in Appendix F in the **JTSu**, which led to the adjusted resampling strategy given in Algorithm F.4 in **JTSu**. The adjusted resampling method uses a two step procedure, where the first step uses the block bootstrap on the *indices of the observations*, and the next step uses those resampled indices to identify the k-lagged pairs (X_{t+k}, X_t) that should be used when estimating $\rho_k(\boldsymbol{z})$ for the resampled data.

In contradistinction to the block bootstrap, the adjusted procedure is especially designed to handle the situation of k-lagged pairs. This means that it is far more robust with respect to choice of block length, and it also reduces the edge-effect noise, which occurs when the components of a resampled pair belong to different blocks. A sensitivity analysis related to the selection of the block length L is presented in Appendix F.5 of **JTSu**.

8.3.4.2 A heatmap/distance plot for the `dmbp`-data

It is of interest to know how $\widehat{f_z^m}(\omega)$ behaves for other diagonal points, and this can be seen in Fig. 8.10 constructed in the same manner as Fig. 8.8. Keep in mind that these plots are based on pseudo-normalized data, that is, the information in the marginal distribution is not directly present, and thus Fig. 8.10 primarily reveals information about the copula structure of the time series under investigation; see Appendix D.2 of **JTSu**.

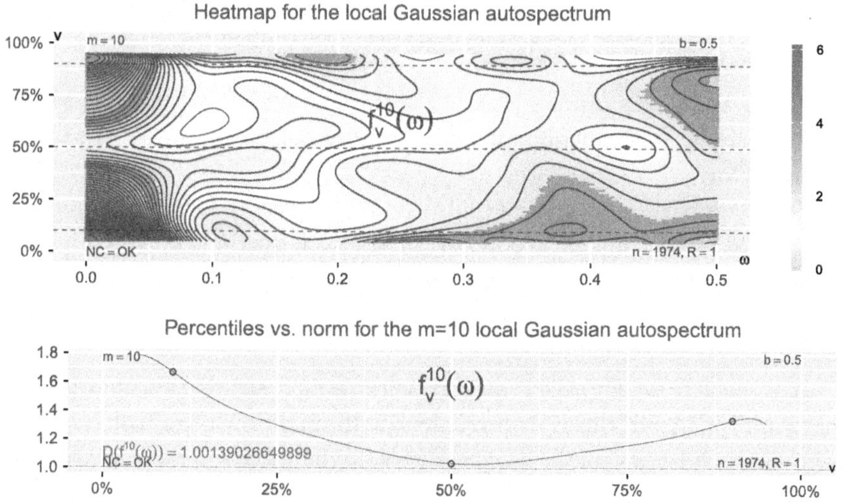

Figure 8.10 Heatmap and corresponding distance-based plots based on the `dmbp`-`data`, showing how $f_z^{10}(\omega)$ varies with the percentiles for the diagonal-points z. The percentiles used in Fig. 8.9, 10%, 50%, and 90%, are highlighted with lines/points.

Fig. 8.10 supports the impression that there is an asymmetry between the lower and upper tails, and we can also see that the local dependency structure is weak near the center. Note that these plots go from the 5th to 95th percentiles to show that it may be perilous to go too far out in the tail for the present sample size ($n = 1974$). This is discussed in more detail in Appendix D.2 of **JTSu**, where heatmap-based plots of the estimated underlying local Gaussian autocorrelations can be found; see Figs. D.2–D.4 of **JTSu**.

8.3.4.3 A GARCH-type model

In this section, we consider an *asymmetric power ARCH-model* (apARCH) of order $(2, 3)$ with parameters based on a fitting to the `dmbp`-data. Techni-

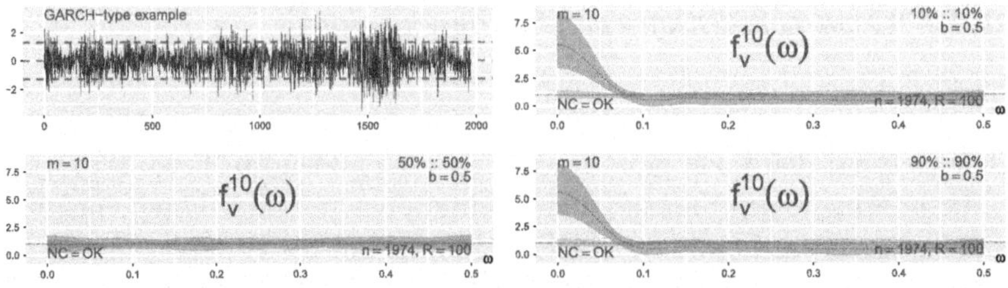

Figure 8.11 GARCH-type model, based on `dmbp`. Global and local spectra for three points.

cal details about this model, together with comments regarding the script needed for the reproduction of this example, can be found in Appendix G.3 in **JTSu**.

For a comparison with the results based on the `dmbp`-data, it is natural to consider $R = 100$ samples of length $n = 1974$ from the fitted apARCH(2, 3) model, and the estimates $\widehat{f}^m_{\boldsymbol{z}}(\omega)$ should be computed for the same points $\boldsymbol{z}$ and with the same tuning parameters $\boldsymbol{b}$ and m. The result of such an investigation can be seen in Fig. 8.11.

It is clear from Fig. 8.11 that the estimate of the m-truncated global spectrum is flat, and this is in agreement with the knowledge that $f(\omega) = 1$ for a GARCH-type model (since $\rho(k) = 0$ when $k \neq 0$). We can also see that the estimates $\widehat{f}^m_{\mathbf{z}}(\omega)$ based on the fitted model have the same overall structure as those in Fig. 8.9. In particular, there is a flat spectrum at the center, and the tails show the presence of nonlinear structures with peaks at $\omega = 0$. However, Fig. 8.11 does not pick up the apparent and intuitively reasonable asymmetry seen in the solid lines in Fig. 8.9, which are also supported by the plots in Fig. 8.10.

8.3.4.4 Local testing of fitted models

A comparison of plots like those in Figs. 8.9 and 8.11 can be used to perform a "local sanity check" of whether or not the dependency structure of the fitted model properly matches the dependency structure of the data, and it is also possible to perform "local comparisons" of different models fitted to the same data. The interested reader can find similar local investigations of data and fitted models in, for example, Li (2019) and Birr et al. (2019).

Note that for such comparisons, it is also of interest to include points $\mathbf{z}$ outside the diagonal. The plots needed for off-diagonal points must take into account that $\hat{f}_{\mathbf{z}}^{m}(\omega)$ will be complex-valued outside the diagonal, but this has already been taken care of in the R-package `localgaussSpec`, where the implemented solution simply mimics the co-spectra, quadrature-spectra, phase-spectra, and amplitude spectra, which are used for the ordinary complex-valued cross-spectra. A bivariate local Gaussian spectral analysis is contained in preliminary form as part of the doctoral thesis of Jordanger (2017).

An alternative strategy to the comparison of two sets of plots, like those in Figs. 8.9 and 8.11, is to superimpose the $\hat{f}_{\mathbf{z}}^{m}(\omega)$ from the `dmbp`-data on the top of the corresponding plots based on the fitted model. A plot based on this superposition principle (inspired by a similar plot from Birr et al., 2019) is given in Figure F.1 in **JTSu**. Note that this plot also contains visualizations of complex-valued spectra.

References

Berentsen, G.D., Kleppe, T., Tjøstheim, D., 2014. Introducing localgauss, an R package for estimating and visualizing local Gaussian correlation. Journal of Statistical Software 56 (12), 1–18.

Birr, S., Kley, T., Volgushev, S., 2019. Model assessment for time series dynamics using copula spectral densities: a graphical tool. In: Dependence Models. Journal of Multivariate Analysis 172, 122–146.

Brillinger, D.R. (Ed.), 1984. The Collected Works of John W. Tukey. Volume I. Time Series: 1949–1964. Wadsworth Statistics/Probability Series. Wadsworth, Pacific Grove, CA, USA. With introductory material by William S. Cleveland and Frederick Mosteller.

Brillinger, D.R., 1991. Some history of the study of higher-order moments and spectra. Statistica Sinica 1 (465–476), 24.

Carrasco, M., Chen, X., 2002. Mixing and moment properties of various GARCH and stochastic volatility models. Econometric Theory 18 (1), 17–39.

Chang, W., Cheng, J., Allaire, J., Xie, Y., McPherson, J., 2017. shiny: web application framework for R. R package version 1.0.3.

Davis, R.A., Mikosch, T., 2009. The extremogram: a correlogram for extreme events. Bernoulli 15 (4), 977–1009.

Ghalanos, A., 2020. Introduction to the rugarch package (Version 1.4-2).

Hagemann, A., 2011. Robust spectral analysis.

Han, H., Linton, O., Oka, T., Whang, Y.-J., 2016. The cross-quantilogram: measuring quantile dependence and testing directional predictability between time series. Journal of Econometrics 193 (1), 251–270.

Hjort, N., Jones, M., 1996. Locally parametric nonparametric density estimation. Annals of Statistics 24 (4), 1619–1647.

Hong, Y., 1999. Hypothesis testing in time series via the empirical characteristic function: a generalized spectral density approach. Journal of the American Statistical Association 94 (448), 1201–1220.

Hong, Y., 2000. Generalized spectral tests for serial dependence. Journal of the Royal Statistical Society Series B 62 (3), 557–574.

Jordanger, L.A., 2017. Nonlinear spectral analysis via the local Gaussian correlation and model selection for copulas.

Jordanger, L.A., Tjøstheim, D., 2020. Nonlinear spectral analysis: A local Gaussian approach. Journal of the American Statistical Association, 1–55.

Klimko, L.A., Nelson, P.I., 1978. On conditional least squares estimation for stochastic processes. Annals of Statistics 6 (3), 629–642.

Klüppelberg, C., Mikosch, T., 1994. Some limit theory for the self-normalised periodogram of stable processes. Scandinavian Journal of Statistics 21 (4), 485–491.

Künsch, H.R., 1989. The jackknife and the bootstrap for general stationary observations. Annals of Statistics 17 (3), 1217–1241.

Lacal, V., Tjøstheim, D., 2017. Local Gaussian autocorrelation and tests of serial dependence. Journal of Time Series Analysis 38 (1), 51–71.

Lacal, V., Tjøstheim, D., 2019. Estimating and testing nonlinear local dependence between two time series. Journal of Business and Economic Statistics 37 (4), 648–660.

Li, H., Zhong, W., Park, S.Y., 2016. Generalized cross-spectral test for nonlinear Granger causality with applications to money–output and price–volume relations. Economic Modelling 52 (Part B), 661–671.

Li, T.-H., 2008. Laplace periodogram for time series analysis. Journal of the American Statistical Association 103 (482), 757–768.

Li, T.-H., 2010a. A nonlinear method for robust spectral analysis. IEEE Transactions on Signal Processing 58 (5), 2466–2474.

Li, T.-H., 2010b. Robust coherence analysis in the frequency domain. In: 2010 18th European Signal Processing Conference. IEEE, pp. 368–371.

Li, T.-H., 2010c. A robust periodogram for high-resolution spectral analysis. Signal Processing 90 (7), 2133–2140.

Li, T.-H., 2012a. Detection and estimation of hidden periodicity in asymmetric noise by using quantile periodogram. In: 2012 IEEE International Conference on Acoustics, Speech and Signal Processing (ICASSP), pp. 3969–3972.

Li, T.-H., 2012b. On robust spectral analysis by least absolute deviations. Journal of Time Series Analysis 33 (2), 298–303.

Li, T.-H., 2012c. Quantile periodograms. Journal of the American Statistical Association 107 (498), 765–776.

Li, T.-H., 2014. Quantile periodogram and time-dependent variance. Journal of Time Series Analysis 35 (4), 322–340.

Li, T.-H., 2019. Quantile-frequency analysis and spectral divergence metrics for diagnostic checks of time series with nonlinear dynamics. arXiv.org.

Linton, O., Whang, Y.-J., 2007. The quantilogram: with an application to evaluating directional predictability. In: Semiparametric Methods in Econometrics. Journal of Econometrics 141 (1), 250–282.

Otneim, H., 2019. Package 'lg'. R package version 0.4, p. 1.

Otneim, H., Tjøstheim, D., 2017. The locally Gaussian density estimator for multivariate data. Statistics and Computing 27 (6), 1595–1616.

Otneim, H., Tjøstheim, D., 2018. Conditional density estimation using the local Gaussian correlation. Statistics and Computing 28 (2), 303–321.

Silvapulle, P., Granger, C.W., 2001. Large returns, conditional correlation and portfolio diversification. A value-at-risk approach. Quantitative Finance 1 (5), 542–551.

Székely, G.J., Rizzo, M.L., 2009. Brownian distance covariance. Annals of Applied Statistics 3 (4), 1236–1265.

Teräsvirta, T., Tjøstheim, D., Granger, C.W., 2010. Modelling Nonlinear Economic Time Series. Oxford University Press.

Tjøstheim, D., Hufthammer, K.O., 2013. Local Gaussian correlation: a new measure of dependence. Journal of Econometrics 172 (1), 33–48.

Tong, H., 1990. Non-Linear Time Series: A Dynamical System Approach. Oxford University Press, Oxford.

Tukey, J.W., 1959. An introduction to the measurement of spectra. In: Grenander, U. (Ed.), Probability and Statistics, The Harald Cramér Volume. Almqvist and Wiksell, Stockholm, Sweden, pp. 300–330.

Wang, X., Hong, Y., 2018. Characteristic function based testing for conditional independence: a nonparametric regression approach. Econometric Theory 34 (4), 815–849.

CHAPTER 9

Multivariate density estimation

Contents

9.1. Introduction 301
9.2. Description of the estimator 304
 9.2.1 Estimation of the marginals 305
 9.2.2 Estimation of the joint dependence function 306
9.3. Asymptotic theory 308
9.4. Bandwidth selection 313
9.5. An example 316
9.6. Investigating performance in the multivariate case 318
9.7. A more flexible version of the LGDE 323
9.8. Proofs 327
 9.8.1 Proof of Theorem 9.1 327
 9.8.2 Proof of Theorems 9.2 and 9.3 328
 9.8.3 Proof of Theorem 9.4 332
References 333

9.1 Introduction

Thus far, we have defined the local Gaussian correlation chiefly as a measure of statistical dependence by taking the work by Hjort and Jones (1996) as an initial inspiration. The purpose of Hjort and Jones (1996) is rather different though. They estimate an unknown probability density function $f(\boldsymbol{x})$ by fitting a general parametric family of densities *locally* to $f(\boldsymbol{x})$, the Gaussian family being one possible choice, which, as we argue in this book, has many powerful properties and applications that stretch far beyond the particular task of estimating a density function. However, in this chapter, we return to this fundamental task and see that exploiting the properties of the normal distribution as a local approximant leads to a density estimator that is particularly well suited to handle multivariate problems as indicated in Section 4.9. See Otneim and Tjøstheim (2017) for the original proposal of the estimator described in this chapter. We only treat the case of iid multivariate observations, but an extension to time series is not too hard, and time series are in fact treated in Chapter 10 on conditional density estimation.

The *curse of dimensionality* precludes the use of many common statistical methods in higher dimensions. The problem is a consequence of the geom-

Statistical Modeling using Local Gaussian Approximation
https://doi.org/10.1016/B978-0-12-815861-6.00016-X

etry of Euclidean spaces and will not be solved when the next generation of computing power arrives; it will potentially get worse, as the amount and complexity of data increase. There exist techniques for multivariate data analysis that relieve the effects of the curse of dimensionality in various ways. This is especially true for nonparametric regression analysis but to a much smaller extent in density estimation. In this chapter, we present the *locally Gaussian density estimator* (LGDE) for probability density functions. It is especially designed to be flexible, yet robust, when fitted to increasingly higher-dimensional data of unknown parametric origin.

Suppose that observations $\boldsymbol{X}_1, \ldots, \boldsymbol{X}_n$ are independent and identically distributed with an unknown density function $f(\boldsymbol{x})$, which we wish to estimate. Classical statistics provides two fundamentally different approaches to the problem. If we know the functional form of the unknown density up to a set of parameters, then they can be efficiently estimated by maximum likelihood. If a parametric assumption cannot be supported by the data, or prior knowledge, then a nonparametric method such as the kernel estimator is the natural alternative. However, it is well known that the kernel estimator breaks down quickly as the dimension of our data increases. Silverman (1986) shows that we need close to a million ten-dimensional observations to produce a kernel density estimate with the same accuracy as would be with only four observations in one dimension.

Techniques for dimensionality reduction exist, including the widely used principal component analysis. The reduced observation vector may still have too many dimensions to produce a fully nonparametric estimate, possibly forcing the experimenter to choose a parametric model far from the true distribution. In many cases, that means fitting the multivariate normal distribution, because the parameter estimates are quick to calculate and easy to interpret.

We travel a middle road in this book, which can be labeled broadly as semiparametric estimation or, more specifically, for this particular chapter, semiparametric density estimation. Methods include the aforementioned local likelihood estimator by Hjort and Jones (1996) and the contemporary work by Loader (1996), who fits local polynomials to the unknown density function. Another option is the combination of nonparametric and parametric estimates provided by Hjort and Glad (1995). A semiparametric model can be considered as a trade-off between nonparametric flexibility and parametric performance, making them very attractive in practical use. The density estimator described in this chapter explicitly trades variance for bias by limiting the analysis to pairwise nonlinear dependencies between the variables.

There are two important steps that define the LGDE:

- **The transformation step.** It has been noted and exploited by many developers and practitioners of statistical methods that certain pre-transformations of raw data sets may increase performance, precision and overall quality of their analysis. This is also the case within the realm of density estimation. For example, nonparametric estimates of densities having bounded support may be hampered by severe bias near the boundaries if not properly handled. Geenens (2014) and Geenens et al. (2017) attack this problem by transforming the data to unbounded scales. The latter paper presents an algorithm for applying a local likelihood density estimator to pseudo-normal observations produced by applying an empirical transformation to the data. This idea will be developed further below and implemented as an important step toward estimating a general multivariate density. Although our motivation for working with Gaussian pseudo-observations is rather to conform with our local Gaussian analysis, this transformation technique carries several advantages with it besides. The transformed multivariate density to be estimated has short tails, and all its variables are on the same scale. Furthermore, several authors have noted that densities become easier to estimate when they are transformed toward normality; see, for example, Wand et al. (1991) and Ruppert and Cline (1994).
- **The pairwise estimation step.** A large number of dimensions does not necessarily mean trouble when we face the problem of density estimation. If we know that the observations are Gaussian, then the means, variances, and covariances are estimated based on the first and second empirical moments only; each correlation coefficient, for example, is estimated by its corresponding empirical counterpart, which in turn is calculated using only the corresponding *pair* of observation vectors. The second main step in the implementation of the LGDE is creating an equivalent of this basic procedure in the local case. Simply put, in the p-variate case the local correlation between variables X_i and X_j will be estimated in a simplified form, also using only its corresponding pair of observation vectors, leading to estimates on the form

$$\widehat{\rho}_{ij}(x_1, \ldots, x_p) = \widehat{\rho}_{ij}(x_i, x_j),$$

which in turn serve as elements in the $p \times p$ local correlation matrix leading to p-variate probability density estimates.

The details of these crucial steps and other important elements of the LGDE, will be laid out in the next section.

9.2 Description of the estimator

Let $\boldsymbol{X}_1, \ldots, \boldsymbol{X}_n$ be a random sample from the p-variate distribution with density function $f(\boldsymbol{x})$. The observations and the variable $\boldsymbol{x} = (x_1, \ldots, x_p)^T$ are column vectors of length p, so that $\boldsymbol{X}_j = (X_{1j}, \ldots, X_{pj})^T$. Denote by $F(\boldsymbol{x})$ the cumulative distribution function (cdf) corresponding to f, and further, let $f_i(x_i)$ and $F_i(x_i)$ denote the marginal densities and cdfs, respectively, for $i = 1, \ldots, p$. The univariate standard normal density and distribution function are identified by ϕ and Φ:

$$\phi(z) = (2\pi)^{-1/2} \exp\{-z^2/2\}, \qquad \Phi(z) = \int_{-\infty}^{z} \phi(y)\, \mathrm{d}y.$$

We transform each observation vector to standard normality using the marginal cdfs (assuming that these are known at the present stage) and the Gaussian quantile function, so that observation number j becomes

$$\boldsymbol{Z}_j = \left(\Phi^{-1}\left(F_1(X_{1j})\right), \ldots, \Phi^{-1}\left(F_p(X_{pj})\right)\right)^T. \tag{9.1}$$

The marginal distributions of the transformed data are now standard normal, and the joint density function $f_{\boldsymbol{Z}}(\boldsymbol{z})$ is given by

$$f_{\boldsymbol{Z}}(\boldsymbol{z}) = f\left(F_1^{-1}\left(\Phi(z_1)\right), \ldots, F_p^{-1}\left(\Phi(z_p)\right)\right) \prod_{i=1}^{p} q_i(\Phi(z_i))\phi(z_i),$$

where $q_i(z_i) = \mathrm{d}/\mathrm{d}z\, F_i^{-1}(z_i)$, $i = 1, \ldots, p$, are the marginal quantile density functions. By a change of variables we express the original density in terms of $f_{\boldsymbol{Z}}$ and the marginal distributions as

$$f(\boldsymbol{x}) = f_{\boldsymbol{Z}}\left(\Phi^{-1}\left(F_1(x_1)\right), \ldots, \Phi^{-1}\left(F_p(x_p)\right)\right) \prod_{i=1}^{p} \frac{f_i(x_i)}{\phi\left(\Phi^{-1}\left(F_i(x_i)\right)\right)}. \tag{9.2}$$

The decomposition of the density in (9.2) is parallel to what we find in the copula framework of analysis. Sklar's (1959) theorem states that any multivariate cdf can be expressed by a unique copula function of its marginals, enabling us to model dependence between variables separately from their individual marginal distributions; see Chapters 3.3 and 5.

The copula function is simply a cdf with standard uniform margins; the transformed density $f_{\boldsymbol{Z}}$ in (9.2) has standard normal margins but contains complete information on the dependence between the variables constituting our data, and its estimation is the main task in this chapter.

In fact, we believe that analyzing the Gaussian observations $\boldsymbol{Z}_1, \ldots, \boldsymbol{Z}_n$, which in practice must be estimated from data making them into Gaussian pseudo-observations instead of uniform ones, is advantageous in many situations, because distributions of real data are usually closer to being Gaussian than uniform, with less tail distortions in the former case. This is illustrated by Berentsen et al. (2014) and in Chapter 5 in identification of copula structures.

9.2.1 Estimation of the marginals

We need estimates $\widehat{F}_i(x_i)$ of the marginal distribution functions $F_i(x_i)$ for two distinct purposes. First, we need an empirical version of the transformation step (9.1), and we must have estimates of the marginal distribution and density functions to use the back-transformation (9.2). The logspline estimator is very handy in this respect, because it is smooth and differentiable; see Kooperberg and Stone (1991) for an introduction to the topic and Stone et al. (1997) for an updated version and further discussion. In short, the logspline method fits a cubic spline to the logarithm of a univariate density function by maximum likelihood. The model complexity is determined automatically by the AIC-criterion, We choose this method in the practical implementation of the LGDE for producing pseudo-observations both through (9.1) and in the back-transformation (9.2). Stone et al. (1997) point out several advantages of the logspline density estimates compared to traditional nonparametric methods, which are especially beneficial in our particular setting. The estimates are non-negative, and they always integrate to one. They are twice differentiable functions, also in the tails, so that we evade practical problems in transformation of data and the change of variables in (9.2). Further, the logspline density estimates are easy to integrate, so the estimated cdfs are readily available.

As an alternative, we may, as we have done in several instances in this book, produce the pseudo-observations (9.1) by applying the marginal empirical distribution functions to the observation vectors:

$$F_{i,n}(x_i) = \frac{1}{n}\sum_{j=1}^{n} I\{X_{ij} < x_i\}, \;\; i = 1, \ldots, p,$$

where I is the indicator function, and where sometimes $1/n$ is replaced by $1/(n+1)$ to obtain better stability for smaller samples.

9.2.2 Estimation of the joint dependence function

Let $\psi(\cdot, \boldsymbol{\theta})$ be a parametric family of p-variate density functions. Below ψ is taken to be the multinormal. We recall from Chapter 4 that Hjort and Jones (1996) estimate the unknown density f using the sample $\boldsymbol{X}_1, \ldots, \boldsymbol{X}_n$ by fitting ψ locally. The local parameter estimate $\widehat{\boldsymbol{\theta}} = \widehat{\boldsymbol{\theta}}(\boldsymbol{x})$ maximizes the *local likelihood function*

$$L(\boldsymbol{X}_1, \ldots, \boldsymbol{X}_n, \boldsymbol{\theta}) = L_n(\boldsymbol{\theta}, \boldsymbol{x}) = n^{-1} \sum_{i=1}^{n} K_{\boldsymbol{B}}(\boldsymbol{X}_i - \boldsymbol{x}) \log \psi\,(\boldsymbol{X}_i, \boldsymbol{\theta}) - \int K_{\boldsymbol{B}}(\boldsymbol{y} - \boldsymbol{x}) \psi(\boldsymbol{y}, \boldsymbol{\theta})\, \mathrm{d}\boldsymbol{y}, \tag{9.3}$$

where K is a kernel function that integrates to one and is symmetric about the origin, $\boldsymbol{B}$ is a positive definite matrix of bandwidths, and $K_{\boldsymbol{B}}(x) = |\boldsymbol{B}|^{-1} K(\boldsymbol{B}^{-1}\boldsymbol{x})$, $|\cdot|$ being the determinant. For small bandwidths, the local estimate $\widehat{f}(\boldsymbol{x}) = \psi\left(\boldsymbol{x}, \widehat{\boldsymbol{\theta}}_n(\boldsymbol{x})\right)$ is close to $f(\boldsymbol{x})$ in the limit, because if the bandwidth matrix $\boldsymbol{B}$ is held fixed and $u_j(\cdot, \boldsymbol{\theta}) = \partial/\partial\theta_j \log \psi(\cdot, \boldsymbol{\theta})$, we have

$$0 = \frac{\partial L_n(\widehat{\boldsymbol{\theta}}_n, \boldsymbol{x})}{\partial \theta_j} \xrightarrow{P} \int K_B(\boldsymbol{y} - \boldsymbol{x}) u_j(\boldsymbol{y}, \boldsymbol{\theta}_{\boldsymbol{B},K}(\boldsymbol{y})) \left\{f(\boldsymbol{y}) - \psi(\boldsymbol{y}, \boldsymbol{\theta}_{\boldsymbol{B},K}(\boldsymbol{y}))\right\} \mathrm{d}\boldsymbol{y} \tag{9.4}$$

for some value of the parameter $\boldsymbol{\theta}_{\boldsymbol{B},K}(\boldsymbol{x})$ toward which $\widehat{\boldsymbol{\theta}}_n(\boldsymbol{x})$ converges in probability. However, for finite sample sizes, the curse of dimensionality comes into play. The number of coordinates in $\boldsymbol{\theta} = \boldsymbol{\theta}(\boldsymbol{x})$ typically grows with the dimension of $\boldsymbol{x}$, making the local estimates difficult to obtain at every point in the sample space. One solution might be increasing the bandwidths so that the estimation becomes almost parametric. However, here we propose a different path around the *Curse* directly exploiting decomposition (9.2). The first step might be choosing a standardized multivariate normal distribution as parametric family in (9.3) for modeling $f_{\boldsymbol{Z}}$ in (9.2) locally:

$$\psi(\boldsymbol{z}, \boldsymbol{\theta}) = \psi(\boldsymbol{z}, \boldsymbol{R}) = (2\pi)^{-p/2} |\boldsymbol{R}|^{-1/2} \exp\left\{-\frac{1}{2}\boldsymbol{z}^T \boldsymbol{R}^{-1} \boldsymbol{z}\right\}, \tag{9.5}$$

where $\boldsymbol{R}$ denotes the local correlation matrix. Using a univariate local fit, the local Gaussian expectations and variances in (9.5) are constant and equal to zero and one, respectively, reflecting our knowledge that the margins of the unknown density function f_Z are standard normal. However, as $\boldsymbol{B} \to \boldsymbol{0}$ in the p-variate case, as briefly described in Chapter 4.9, the local mean $\boldsymbol{\mu}$ and variance $\boldsymbol{\sigma}$ in general depend on $\boldsymbol{z}$. In this chapter, we make the additional assumption in our p-dimensional local Gaussian approximation that $\boldsymbol{\mu}(\boldsymbol{z}) \equiv \boldsymbol{0}$ and $\boldsymbol{\sigma}^2(\boldsymbol{z}) = \boldsymbol{1}$. This is more restrictive than in Chapters 7 and 8, where it was assumed that $\boldsymbol{\mu} = \boldsymbol{\mu}(\boldsymbol{z}) = \boldsymbol{\mu}(z_1, z_2)$ and $\boldsymbol{\sigma} \equiv \boldsymbol{\sigma}(\boldsymbol{z}) = \boldsymbol{\sigma}(z_1, z_2)$ in the bivariate case, and this more general assumption was crucial in obtaining the local spectral results in Chapter 8.

With this more restrictive assumption that $\boldsymbol{\mu}(\boldsymbol{z}) \equiv \boldsymbol{0}$ and $\boldsymbol{\sigma}^2(\boldsymbol{z}) \equiv \boldsymbol{1}$, we are left with the problem of estimating the pairwise correlations ρ_{ij}, $1 \leq i < j \leq p$, in (9.5). Fitting the Gaussian distribution according to the scheme described above results in a local correlation matrix at each point. Specifically, the estimated local correlations are written as $\widehat{\rho}_{ij} = \widehat{\rho}_{ij}(z_1, \ldots, z_p)$, $i, j = 1, \ldots, p$, indicating that each parameter depends on all variables. The dependence between variables is captured in the variation of the parameter estimates in the p-dimensional Euclidean space, and its estimate maximizes the local likelihood function (9.3). However, as mentioned, the quality of the estimate deteriorates quickly with the dimension.

If the data were jointly normally distributed, there would be no dimensionality problem, since the entire distribution would be characterized by the global correlation coefficients between pairs of variables, and their empirical counterparts are easily computed from the data. A local Gaussian fit would then coincide with a global fit and result in estimates of the form $\widehat{\rho}_{ij} = \widehat{\rho}_{ij}(Z_i, Z_j)$, where the arguments indicate which of the transformed observation variables were used to obtain the estimate. This points to a natural simplification, which we may use to estimate the density f_Z, analogous to the additive regression model in Chapter 2.7.1. We allow the local correlations to depend on their own variables only:

$$\widehat{\rho}_{ij}(z_1, \ldots, z_p) = \widehat{\rho}_{ij}(z_i, z_j). \tag{9.6}$$

We could also simplify the estimation problem by estimating the local means and variances as functions of "their own" coordinate only: $\mu_i(\boldsymbol{z}) = \mu_i(z_i)$ and $\sigma_i^2(\boldsymbol{z}) = \sigma_i^2(z_i)$, but, as mentioned before, here we have chosen the stricter approximation

$$\boldsymbol{\mu}(\boldsymbol{z}) = \boldsymbol{0} \ \text{ and } \ \boldsymbol{\sigma}^2(\boldsymbol{z}) = \boldsymbol{1}. \tag{9.7}$$

We refer to Section 9.7 for a further discussion of this point.

The resulting estimation is carried out in four steps:

1. Estimate the marginal distributions using the logspline method (or the empirical distribution function) and transform each observation vector to pseudo-standard normality as described in the previous subsection.
2. Estimate the joint density of the transformed data using the Hjort and Jones (1996) local likelihood function (9.3), the standardized normal parametric family (9.5), and simplifications (9.6) and (9.7). In practice, this means fitting the bivariate version of (9.5) to each pair of the transformed variables (Z_i, Z_j). Put the estimated local correlations into the estimated local correlation matrix: $\widehat{\boldsymbol{R}}(\boldsymbol{z}) = \{\widehat{\rho}_{ij}(z_i, z_j)\}_{i,j=1,\dots,p}$.
3. Let $\widehat{f}_{\boldsymbol{Z}}(\boldsymbol{z}) = \psi\left(\boldsymbol{z}, \widehat{\boldsymbol{R}}(\boldsymbol{z})\right)$ and obtain the final estimate of $f(\boldsymbol{x})$ by replacing $f_{\boldsymbol{Z}}$ with $\widehat{f}_{\boldsymbol{Z}}$, and the marginal distribution and density functions with their logspline estimates in (9.2):

$$\widehat{f}(\boldsymbol{x}) = \widehat{f}_{\boldsymbol{Z}}\left(\Phi^{-1}\left(\widehat{F}_1(x_1)\right), \dots, \Phi^{-1}\left(\widehat{F}_p(x_p)\right)\right) \prod_{i=1}^{p} \frac{\widehat{f}_i(x_i)}{\phi\left(\Phi^{-1}\left(\widehat{F}_i(x_i)\right)\right)}. \tag{9.8}$$

4. Normalize the density estimate so that it integrates to one.

The existence of population values corresponding to the estimated local correlations is discussed in the following section. It is clear that assumptions (9.6) and (9.7) represent an approximation to most multivariate distributions. The authors are aware of no other distributions than those possessing the Gaussian copula or step functions thereof as in Tjøstheim and Hufthammer (2013) or Chapter 4.3, for which (9.6) and (9.7) are exact properties of the true local correlations. In that case the local correlations are constant or stepwise constant in *all* its variables. The quality of the LGDE thus depends to a large degree on the severity of assumptions (9.6) and (9.7) on the underlying density. The pairwise assumption is hard to interpret except in general statements about "pairwise dependence structures", and so we proceed in this chapter to explore the impact of (9.6) and (9.7) in practice in Section 9.6 and the subsequent discussion in Section 9.7. Before we do that, we take a closer look at the theoretical foundations of the LGDE.

9.3 Asymptotic theory

Let us establish some notation and then state theorems regarding the asymptotic behavior of the LGDE. Product kernels will be used both in theory and in practice, so the matrix of bandwidths $\boldsymbol{B} = \text{diag}(\boldsymbol{b})$ is diagonal, and $\boldsymbol{b} \to \boldsymbol{0}$ means that each element of $\boldsymbol{b}$ tends to zero at the same rate.

For each pair of variables, we maximize the local likelihood function $L_n(\rho_{ij}, z_i, z_j)$ to obtain the estimated local correlation for that pair. Indeed, simplifications (9.6) and (9.7) mean that we can develop most of the asymptotic theory by looking only at the bivariate case. Therefore we keep the pair of indices (i, j) fixed for the time being, so that $\boldsymbol{z} = (z_i, z_j)^T$, $\boldsymbol{b} = (b_i, b_j)$, and for simplicity, we write $\rho_{ij}(z_i, z_j) = \rho(\boldsymbol{z})$. The marginally standardized Gaussian family $\psi(\boldsymbol{z}, \rho)$ represents the bivariate version of (9.5) in the following.

Denote by I the integral in (9.4). As the sample size increases to infinity, $\partial L_n(\rho, \boldsymbol{z})/\partial\rho$ satisfies the equation

$$I = \int K_{\boldsymbol{b}}(\boldsymbol{y} - \boldsymbol{z}) u(\boldsymbol{y}, \rho)\{f_{ij}(\boldsymbol{y}) - \psi(\boldsymbol{y}, \rho)\}\, \mathrm{d}\boldsymbol{y} = 0, \tag{9.9}$$

where $f_{ij}(\boldsymbol{z})$ is the joint density of (Z_i, Z_j), and $u(\cdot, \rho) = \partial/\partial\rho \log\psi(\cdot, \rho)$. Thus, as mentioned before, the estimate $\widehat{\rho}_n(\boldsymbol{z})$ aims at the solution of (9.9), which, ignoring the dependence on K in our notation, we denote by $\rho_{\boldsymbol{b}}(\boldsymbol{z})$. However, there are two problems in perceiving $\rho_{\boldsymbol{b}}(\boldsymbol{z})$ as the "true" parameter function. First, it is hard to do any general analysis on the existence and uniqueness based on the integral in (9.9) considering that $\rho = \rho(\boldsymbol{z})$ is an unknown function of $\boldsymbol{z}$. Second, $\rho_{\boldsymbol{b}}(\boldsymbol{z})$ depends on the bandwidths and kernel function K, whereas the true local correlation function for a given pair of variables should ideally be a property of their unknown bivariate density f_{ij} only.

By letting the bandwidth tend to zero as the sample size increases we solve the second problem and make the first easier. To see this, we reproduce the Taylor expansions of (9.9) in powers of $\boldsymbol{b} = (b_i, b_j)$ as provided by Hjort and Jones (1996). Let the index $\boldsymbol{b}$ to functions $\psi(\boldsymbol{z})$ and $u(\boldsymbol{z})$ mean that we insert the parameter value $\rho_{\boldsymbol{b}}$. It follows that

$$\begin{aligned} &u_{\boldsymbol{b}}(\boldsymbol{z})\{f_{ij}(\boldsymbol{z}) - \psi_{\boldsymbol{b}}(\boldsymbol{z})\} \\ &\quad = \frac{1}{2}\sum_{k=i,j} \sigma_k^2 b_k^2 \{u_{\boldsymbol{b}}(\psi_{\boldsymbol{b}} - f_{ij})\}''(\boldsymbol{z}) + O((b_i^2 + b_j^2)^2), \end{aligned} \tag{9.10}$$

where $\sigma_i = \sigma_{K_i}^2 = \int y^2 K_i(y)\, \mathrm{d}y$, and the cross-term is zero because of the symmetry of K. The differentiation on the right-hand side is taken with respect to z_k. There is only one such equation for each local correlation, and it follows readily that the limit $\rho_0(\boldsymbol{z}) = \lim_{\boldsymbol{b}\to\boldsymbol{0}} \rho_{\boldsymbol{b}}(\boldsymbol{z})$ must satisfy $\psi(\boldsymbol{z}, \rho) = f_{ij}(\boldsymbol{z})$. However, this is not sufficient to ensure the uniqueness of ρ_0. It is essential that $\rho_0(\boldsymbol{z})$ is the result of a limiting process as $\boldsymbol{b} \to \boldsymbol{0}$ in

(9.9). Said in another way, this means that the local fit is done in a neighborhood of $\boldsymbol{z}$, which shrinks to zero with $\boldsymbol{b}$. Such a process eliminates fits of Gaussians that just pass through the point $\boldsymbol{z}$.

For a fixed $\boldsymbol{b}$, we can obtain the local parameter $\rho_{\boldsymbol{b}}$ (cf. Eq. (4.5) in Chapter 4.3) by minimizing the penalty function

$$\mathrm{E}(L_n(\rho, \boldsymbol{Z})) = \int K_{\boldsymbol{b}}(\boldsymbol{y} - \boldsymbol{z})\{\psi(\boldsymbol{y}, \rho) - \log \psi(\boldsymbol{y}, \rho) f_{ij}(\boldsymbol{y})\} \, \mathrm{d}\boldsymbol{y}. \tag{9.11}$$

As seen in Hjort and Jones (1996), this can be interpreted as a locally weighted Kullback–Leibler distance from f to $\psi(\cdot, \rho(\cdot))$.

Let $\boldsymbol{b}_n$ be a sequence of bandwidths tending to zero as $n \to \infty$. If $\{\rho_{\boldsymbol{b}_n}(\boldsymbol{z})\}$ converges toward the value $\rho_0(\boldsymbol{z})$, then we take this to be the population parameter. Then this essentially requires (see Hjort and Jones (1996), Tjøstheim and Hufthammer (2013), and Chapter 4.3) that there is a unique maximum of the local likelihood function once $\boldsymbol{b}$ is small enough. This is akin to the assumption of a unique maximum in global maximum likelihood estimation. The continuity of ψ as a function of ρ ensures that the population parameter defined above automatically satisfies $\psi(\boldsymbol{z}, \rho_0) = f_{ij}(\boldsymbol{z})$ (even if a unique maximum should not exist, this approach could still, as a purely data algorithmic tool, produce a good approximation to the theoretical density $f(\boldsymbol{x})$).

The following theorems provide conditions for the consistency and asymptotic normality of the local correlation estimate $\widehat{\rho}_n(\boldsymbol{z})$, provided that the marginals of the observations are standard normally distributed and simplification (9.7) holds.

Theorem 9.1. *Let $\{\boldsymbol{Z}_j, 1 \leq j \leq n\}$ be a sequence of bivariate iid random variables with standard normal marginals such that (9.7) holds. Assume that*

(i) *for a sequence $\boldsymbol{b}_n$, $n = 1, 2, \ldots$, converging to zero as n tends to infinity, there exists a unique minimizer ρ_0 of $\mathrm{E}(L_n(\rho, \boldsymbol{Z}))$ such that $\rho_{\boldsymbol{b}_n}(\boldsymbol{z}) \to \rho_0(\boldsymbol{z})$,*

(ii) *the parameter space Θ for ρ is a compact subset of $(-1, 1)$.*

Then, for each $\boldsymbol{z}$ at which ρ_0 exists, $\widehat{\rho}_n(\boldsymbol{z}) \xrightarrow{P} \rho_0(\boldsymbol{z})$ as $n \to \infty$.

See Section 9.8.1 for a proof of this result. The local correlation estimate is asymptotically normal according to the following theorem.

Theorem 9.2. *Denote by $f_{12}(\boldsymbol{z})$ the common joint density function of the bivariate iid random variables $\{\boldsymbol{Z}_j, 1 \leq j \leq n\}$. Assume that the conditions of Theorem 9.1 are satisfied, and further that*

(iii) *the sequence of bandwidths $\boldsymbol{b}_n$ satisfies $\boldsymbol{b}_n \to \boldsymbol{0}$, $\lim_n nb_{1n}b_{2n} = \infty$, and*

(iv) *the kernel function satisfies* $\sup_{\boldsymbol{z}} |K(\boldsymbol{z})| < \infty$, $\int |K(\boldsymbol{y})| d\boldsymbol{y} < \infty$, $|\partial/\partial z_k K(\boldsymbol{z})| < \infty$, *and* $\lim_{z_k \to \infty} |z_k K(z_k)| = 0$ *for* $k = 1, 2$.

Then

$$\sqrt{nb_{1n}b_{2n}}\,(\widehat{\rho}_n - \rho_0) \xrightarrow{d} \mathcal{N}(0, M/J^2),$$

where

$$M = f_{12}(\boldsymbol{z})\left(\int K^2(\boldsymbol{y})\, d\boldsymbol{y}\right),\quad J = u(\boldsymbol{z}, \rho_0(\boldsymbol{z}))\psi(\boldsymbol{z}, \rho_0(\boldsymbol{z})),$$

The preceding result is contained in the following and more general Theorem 9.3 regarding the joint asymptotic normality of the local correlations $\{\widehat{\rho}_{ij,n}\}_{i<j}$. Assume now that the observations $\{\boldsymbol{Z}_j, 1 \le j \le n\}$ are p-variate with standard normal marginals and that we calculate one local correlation for each pair of variables. There are $m = p(p-1)/2$ pairs. Denote by $\boldsymbol{\rho} = \{\rho_k\}_{k=1,\ldots,m}$ the vector of local correlations and by $\widehat{\boldsymbol{\rho}}_n$ its estimate. To stress that $\boldsymbol{\rho}$ is a vector and not a matrix, we use the single index k to identify the individual components. The matrix of bandwidths is defined as before by $\boldsymbol{B} = \text{diag}(\boldsymbol{b}) = \text{diag}(b_1, \ldots, b_p)$, but the symbol b^2 now means the product of any two bandwidths, which we do not need to specify in the asymptotic analysis, because we assume that they all tend to zero at the same rate.

Theorem 9.3. *Let* $\{\boldsymbol{Z}_j, 1 \le j \le n\}$ *be a sequence of p-variate iid marginally standard normal random variables such that* (9.6) *and* (9.7) *hold. Enumerate each pair of variables by* $k = 1, \ldots, m$, *and for each pair, calculate the local Gaussian correlation. Assume that conditions* (i)–(iv) *of Theorems 9.1 and 9.2 are satisfied.*

Then the estimated local Gaussian correlations are jointly asymptotically normal with

$$\sqrt{nb_n^2}(\widehat{\boldsymbol{\rho}}_n - \boldsymbol{\rho}_0) \xrightarrow{d} \mathcal{N}(0, \boldsymbol{\Sigma}),$$

where $\boldsymbol{\Sigma}$ *is the diagonal matrix in which the element* (k, k) *is the corresponding asymptotic variance* M/J^2 *defined in Theorem 9.2:*

$$\Sigma^{(k,k)} = \frac{f_k(\boldsymbol{z}_k) \int K^2(\boldsymbol{y}_k)\, d\boldsymbol{y}_k}{u^2(\boldsymbol{z}_k, \rho_{0,k}(\boldsymbol{z}_k))\psi^2(\boldsymbol{z}_k, \rho_{0,k}(\boldsymbol{z}_k))}. \tag{9.12}$$

See Section 9.8.2 for a proof.

Note that thus far we assume that the sequence of stochastic variables $\{\boldsymbol{Z}_j\}$ have exactly standard normally distributed marginals, or, in other words, if we observe the not marginally normal sequence $\{\boldsymbol{X}_j\}$, then we know the true marginal distribution functions $F_1, \ldots, F_p$ needed to produce $\{\boldsymbol{Z}_j\}$ through transformation (9.1). This is not a realistic assumption, and wet we will eliminate it in Theorem 9.5. First, we still assume that we know how to produce a sequence of variables $\{\boldsymbol{Z}_j\}$ having exactly normally distributed margins as above, but we estimate the marginal distributions and densities from the data to produce the final probability density estimate $\widehat{f}(\boldsymbol{x})$ by means of the final back transformation (9.8). Then we can prove the following result.

Theorem 9.4. *Assume that we fit the LGDE to a sequence of p-variate iid random variables $\{\mathbf{X}_j\}$ with density function $f(\boldsymbol{x})$. Assume that each pair of the (exactly) transformed observation vectors $\{\mathbf{Z}_j\}$ satisfies conditions* (i)–(iv) *of Theorems 9.1 to 9.3. Assume further that*

(v) *the estimates of the marginal densities and quantile functions used for back-transformations* (9.2) *are asymptotically normal with convergence rates faster than $(nb^2)^{-1/2}$.*

Let $f_0(\boldsymbol{x})$ be the LGDE density function obtained by replacing $f_{\mathbf{Z}}$ with $\psi(\cdot, \mathbf{R}_0)$ in (9.2)*. Then, for all $\boldsymbol{x}$ such that $F_i(x_i) \in (0,1)$, $i = 1, \ldots, p$, with $\widehat{f}(\boldsymbol{x})$ estimated by the LGDE,*

$$\sqrt{nb_n^2}\left(\widehat{f}(\boldsymbol{x}) - f_0(\boldsymbol{x})\right) \xrightarrow{d} \mathcal{N}(0, \psi(\boldsymbol{z}, \mathbf{R}_0(\boldsymbol{z}))^2 g(\boldsymbol{x})^2 \boldsymbol{u}^T(\boldsymbol{z}, R_0(\boldsymbol{z}))\boldsymbol{\Sigma}\, \boldsymbol{u}(\boldsymbol{z}, R_0(\boldsymbol{z}))),$$

where $\boldsymbol{u}(\cdot, \mathbf{R})$ is the gradient of $\log \psi(\cdot, \mathbf{R})$ with respect to the vector of local correlations,

$$g(\boldsymbol{x}) = \prod_{i=1}^{p} f_i(x_i)/\phi(\Phi^{-1}(F_i(x_i))),$$

and

$$\boldsymbol{z} = \left\{\Phi^{-1}(F_i(x_i))\right\}_{i=1\ldots,p}.$$

We give a proof of this result in Section 9.8.3. The next step is stating a fundamental result regarding empirical transformations. This result follows directly from Theorem 4.5, and it allows $\boldsymbol{Z}_j$ to be replaced by $\widehat{\boldsymbol{Z}}_j$ using the empirical distribution function F_n.

Theorem 9.5. *Suppose*

(i) *we produce marginally Gaussian pseudo observations $\{\widehat{\mathbf{Z}}_j\}$ using transformation* (9.1) *by means of the marginal empirical distribution functions*

$$F_{i,n}(x_i) = \widehat{F}_i(x_i) = \frac{1}{n}\sum_{j=1}^{n} I\{X_{ij} \le x_i\},$$

and

(ii) *the kernel function K has bounded support.*
Then Theorems 9.1–9.4 still hold when replacing $\{Z_j\}$ with $\{\widehat{Z}_j\}$.

9.4 Bandwidth selection

The general local likelihood density estimator by Hjort and Jones (1996) requires three distinct modeling choices to be made by a practitioner. She must pick (i) a parametric family $\psi(\cdot, \boldsymbol{\theta})$ for local approximation, (ii) a kernel function K, and (iii) a smoothing matrix $\boldsymbol{B}$.

We have already settled the first point. Transforming the marginals to standard normality leaves the marginally standardized multivariate normal family (9.5) as the logical choice for the parametric family with the additional restrictions (9.6) and (9.7) to open up for high-dimensional applications. Items (ii) and (iii) are traditional nonparametric problems, but we argue that they have natural solutions when using the LGDE as well.

We use the bivariate Gaussian product kernel function $K(\boldsymbol{z}) = (2\pi)^{-1} \times \exp\left(-\boldsymbol{z}^T\boldsymbol{z}/2\right)$ for two reasons. First, K and ψ both being Gaussian functions means that the integral in the likelihood function (9.3) has a closed-form expression, which greatly simplifies its numerical optimization. Second, we will see below that the Gaussian kernel works very well in conjunction with our bandwidth selector. Previous developments in this chapter imply that it is suffices to look at the bivariate case.

There is a subtle difference between smoothing local likelihood and kernel density estimates. As the bandwidth goes to infinity, the kernel estimate loses its structure and approaches zero at every point. On the other hand, the local likelihood estimate is smoothed toward a global maximum likelihood fit by the parametric family. We can thus interpret bandwidth selection in the latter case as determining to which degree we believe the parametric family to be the true underlying distribution of the data.

However, in most practical situations, we need a data-driven bandwidth selection routine, and to this end, we adapt to our needs general, already existing schemes for model selection. The principle of cross-validation has been applied in many statistical methods. Stone (1974) provides a thorough treatment on the topic, Stone (1984) treats bandwidth selection for kernel density estimates by cross-validation, and Berentsen and Tjøstheim (2014) use cross-validation to select bandwidths for bivariate local likelihood density estimates (see also Chapter 4.8.2). However, the latter authors note that the procedure is sensitive to outliers, so raw data must be screened in advance. Hall (1987) investigates this phenomenon and shows that the kernel function and the true density must have approximately the same tail thickness for cross-validation to work properly. This is the second reason why the Gaussian kernel is such a natural choice for the LGDE; the density and kernel both having Gaussian tails means that no screening of the data is needed, in particular, if the margins are transformed to pseudo-normals.

The Kullback–Leibler divergence between the true density and its estimate is defined by

$$\begin{aligned}\mathrm{KL}\left(f,\widehat{f}\right) &= \int f(\boldsymbol{z})\log\left\{f(\boldsymbol{z})/\widehat{f}(\boldsymbol{z})\right\}\,\mathrm{d}\boldsymbol{z}\\ &= \int f(\boldsymbol{z})\log f(\boldsymbol{z})\,\mathrm{d}\boldsymbol{z} - \int f(\boldsymbol{z})\log\widehat{f}(\boldsymbol{z})\,\mathrm{d}\boldsymbol{z},\end{aligned}$$

where the last term depends on the bandwidth. It can be estimated by cross-validation, and so for each pair of variables, we choose the bandwidth $\boldsymbol{b} = (b_1, b_2)$ that maximizes

$$CV(\boldsymbol{b}) = n^{-1}\sum_{i=1}^{n}\log\widehat{f}_{\boldsymbol{b}}^{(-i)}(\boldsymbol{Z}_i),$$

where $\widehat{f}_{\boldsymbol{b}}^{(-i)}$ is the bivariate local Gaussian density estimate calculated using the bandwidth $\boldsymbol{b}$ without the observation with index i. In practice the normal observations $\boldsymbol{Z}_i$ are replaced by the pseudo-normal observations $\widehat{\boldsymbol{Z}}_i$.

We also obtain adaptive bandwidths using the k-nearest-neighbor strategy, for which the bandwidth used in a particular point $\boldsymbol{z}$ is taken to be the Euclidean distance to the kth nearest observation measured from $\boldsymbol{z}$. That way, we allow more details to appear in areas with much data while keeping a fairly large bandwidth in the tails of the distribution. We choose k using cross-validation as before, as the maximizer of

$$CV(k) = n^{-1}\sum_{i=1}^{n}\log\widehat{f}_{k}^{(-i)}(\boldsymbol{Z}_i),$$

where $\widehat{f}_{k}^{(-i)}$ as before denotes the cross-validated density estimate calculated using as bandwidth the distance to the kth nearest neighbor of $\boldsymbol{Z}_i$.

To avoid overfitting, we must keep k from becoming too small. In practice, we may do this by requiring k to be at least 20, which seems to be a reasonable number for moderate sample sizes.

Finally, we must acknowledge that cross-validation is computationally demanding, especially in our case for which each evaluation of the objective function CV requires $np(p-1)/2$ numerical optimizations. For $p = 2$

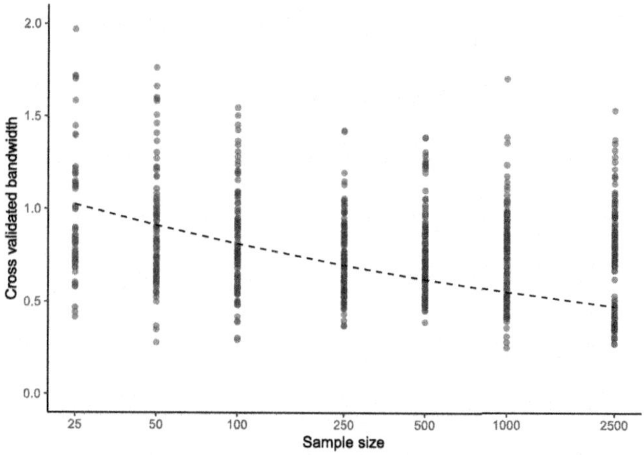

Figure 9.1 Dots show cross validated bandwidths for various sample sizes and a variety of data-generating processes; the dashed line represents the curve $b = 1.75 \cdot n^{-1/6}$.

and $n = 1000$, one of the authors typically produces a set of cross-validated bandwidths in less than a minute on his laptop, which is perfectly acceptable in many practical situations, for example, if a single probability density function is the target of estimation. In other cases, such as when implementing resampling techniques as we do repeatedly in this book, we may require thousands of bandwidths at the same time, which for practical purposes points to the need of a quicker (but admittedly less precise) method for selecting the smoothing parameter.

Silverman (1986) derives a plug-in bandwidth for use with the kernel density estimator. In particular, he shows that the bandwidth that minimizes the mean integrated squared error is given by $b = c \cdot n^{-1/5}$ in the univariate case, where the constant c depends on the kernel function and unknown density function $f(\boldsymbol{x})$ (through its second derivative f''). Under the additional assumption that the data are normal, we can calculate the coefficient c, resulting in the simple formula

$$b = 1.06 \cdot sd(X) n^{-1/5}, \tag{9.13}$$

and we can calculate the corresponding formula in the bivariate case by changing the exponent from $-1/5$ to $-1/6$. For non-normal data, (9.13) serves as an approximation, but the coefficient may be more finely tuned, for example, by choosing a smaller coefficient for less smooth densities (i.e., densities that have larger values of $\int f''(x)\,\mathrm{d}x$).

It is possible to produce a corresponding formula for choosing the amount of smoothing of local Gaussian correlations. Formulas like (9.13) exist for local likelihood estimates as well; see Hjort and Jones (1996). However, we cannot choose the normal as a reference distribution in our case, because that would always lead to infinite bandwidths. We have, instead, calculated the cross-validated bandwidths in a number of different simulated cases to locate a reasonable value for c so that the approximation $b_{CV} \approx cn^{-1/6}$ generally holds. Keep in mind that $sd(Z) \approx 1$ in all our applications, because we apply all our statistical analysis in this chapter on approximately standard normal variables $\widehat{\boldsymbol{Z}}$.

See Fig. 9.1 for the results of this experiment. For reference, we have added the curve $b = 1.75 \cdot n^{-1/6}$, which, from visual inspection, seems to be an overall sound choice, although a bit small for large sample sizes.

9.5 An example

Otneim and Tjøstheim (2017) analyze the multivariate performance of the LGDE by simulation experiments. In this section, we rather present an example using some real data. Simulation experiments are presented in Section 9.6.

We have observed monthly prices on the US and Norwegian total market values[1] and the monthly prices of oil and gold from January 1, 2000, until June 1, 2018, a total of 222 months. From these price series we construct individual monthly log-returns on the form

$$R_{it} = 100 \log \left(\frac{P_{it}}{P_{i,t-1}} \right),$$

which we collect, along with the lagged values R_{t-1}, in an 8-variate data set comprising observations on the stochastic vector

$$\boldsymbol{R}_t = (R_{\text{US},t}, R_{\text{NO},t}, R_{\text{Oil},t}, R_{\text{Gold},t}, R_{\text{US},t-1}, R_{\text{NO},t-1}, R_{\text{Oil},t-1}, R_{\text{Gold},t-1})^T.$$

We wish to estimate the joint density of $\boldsymbol{R}_t$ using the LGDE and compare the results with the corresponding kernel density estimates. To visualize the results, we choose to project the density estimates on two variables, namely the US and Norwegian total market returns, $R_{\text{US, t}}$ and

[1] Total market indices representing all the stocks trading in a country's stock market. Data collected from Datastream: https://libguides.princeton.edu/datastream/Datastream5.

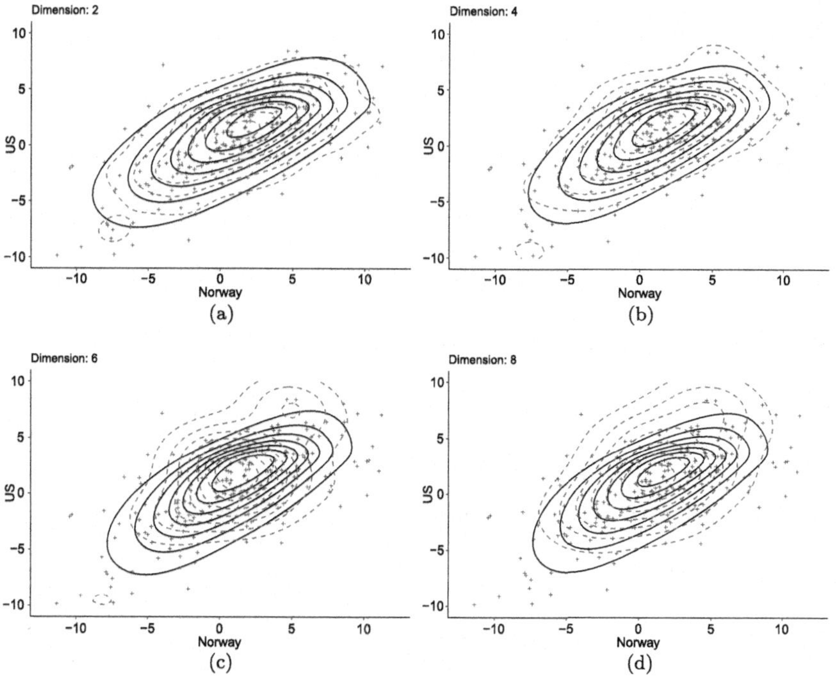

Figure 9.2 Projections of locally Gaussian density estimates (solid level curves) and kernel density estimates (dashed level curves) of increasing dimension on a fixed pair $(R_{US,t}, R_{NO,t})$ of variables.

$R_{\text{NO},\,t}$, while keeping the other variables fixed at their respective sample means. This choice of presentation also demonstrates the robustness of the LGDE against an increasing number of variables, which is not at all surprising given its foundation on bivariate analysis.

Fig. 9.2 shows the estimated densities. In the upper left panel, we see the estimated bivariate joint density of $R_{\text{US,t}}$ and $R_{\text{NO,t}}$ calculated using the LGDE (solid level curves) and the kernel density estimate (dashed curve), with bandwidths chosen using the cross-validation method by Duong and Hazelton (2005). For the LGDE, we have used plug-in bandwidths on the form $b = 2.5 \cdot n^{-1/6}$. In the two-dimensional case of Fig. 9.2a, both estimates perform comparably.

In the remaining panels, we have added an increasing number of variables to the density estimation problem; first, the returns on the oil and gold price in the upper right panel, then the lagged values of the US and Norwegian total market return in the lower left panel, and finally, the two remaining variables, the lagged values of the oil and gold returns. For all variables apart from $R_{\mathrm{US,t}}$ and $R_{\mathrm{NO,t}}$, we have evaluated the density estimates in their respective sample means.

The LGDE is, not surprisingly, very similar across all panels, which points to its main feature as well as to its main weakness. First of all, a practitioner can be quite certain that the addition of variables to his or her density estimation task will not completely ruin the estimate, because the new variable does not change the dependence structure between the original variables. This also means, however, that any higher-order dependencies, or "interactions" if you wish, that exist jointly between more than two variables cannot be captured by the pairwise LGDE. Again, it is tempting to make a comparison with additive regression modeling.

9.6 Investigating performance in the multivariate case

The large sample properties in Section 9.3 clearly show that we trade asymptotic unbiasedness for faster convergence if we choose the LGDE instead of the kernel density estimator for multivariate data. We proceed to investigate the practical consequences of doing so in a series of controlled experiments using simulated data. They are taken from Otneim and Tjøstheim (2017).

There are many ways to evaluate the performance of a density estimator. When introducing a new estimator, we seek a presentation that emphasizes the advantageous aspects and the fallacies we may encounter in practical applications. We believe that the LGDE enjoys two particularly beneficial properties that we wish to confirm:

- It approximates the unknown density by simplifying the dependence structure in a way that is true for distributions having the Gaussian copula ($\boldsymbol{R}(\boldsymbol{z}) = \boldsymbol{R}$); see Berentsen and Tjøstheim (2014) and Chapter 5.3.2. Therefore the LGDE should work particularly well for distributions for which the joint structure is not too far from normal. This is confirmed in our simulations, but it also works well for many non-Gaussian joint structures.
- In the tail of the distribution, where there is little or no data, the LGDE does what is perhaps most natural. It fits a Gaussian tail based on the general direction toward the main body of the data. The influence from the data will change neither much from point to point in the tail nor the local parameter estimates. The kernel estimator, on the other hand, assigns density estimates in the tail by adding up values far out

Table 9.1 Test distributions.

1.	χ_3^2 marginals, Gaussian copula with all parameters equal to 0.5
2.	$t(10)$ marginals, Clayton copula with parameter 0.9
3.	Log-normal marginals, t-copula with 10 degrees of freedom
4.	Uniform marginals with observations taken directly from the Clayton copula with parameter 0.9
5.	Mixture of two Gaussians centered at $(0, \ldots)^T$ and $(4, \ldots)^T$
6.	Multivariate $t(4)$ distribution

in the tail of the kernels, which may well be zeroes if the kernel is compactly supported. This effect becomes increasingly troublesome as the number of variables increases and is indeed a demonstration of the curse of dimensionality (see, e.g., Hastie et al. (2009), Section 2.5).

We calculate density estimates for data from a selection of distributions (listed in Table 9.1), which can be generalized to higher dimensions in a natural way. These include various copula models, the multivariate t-distribution, and mixtures of two Gaussians. We use the integrated *relative* squared error (IRSE) as a measure of discrepancy between the estimate and the true density because it is more natural to compare this measure across dimensions than the more common ISE. Further, the relative error emphasizes the performance in the tails. We also report the Hellinger distance (H) from the density estimate to the true density, so that

$$IRSE(\widehat{f}) = \int \frac{\left(\widehat{f}(\boldsymbol{x}) - f(\boldsymbol{x})\right)^2}{f(\boldsymbol{x})} \, \mathrm{d}\boldsymbol{x}, \qquad H^2(\widehat{f}) = 1 - \int \sqrt{f(\boldsymbol{x})\widehat{f}(\boldsymbol{x})} \, \mathrm{d}\boldsymbol{x}.$$

For each distribution listed in Table 9.1, we generate data sets comprising $n = 500$ and $n = 2000$ observations and estimate their densities using the LGDE with the cross-validated bandwidths at $m = 4000$ grid points $\{\boldsymbol{y}_j, j = 1, \ldots, m\}$, which we generate from the same distribution, but independently from the data. We repeat the procedure $2^7 = 128$ times and report the median of the estimated IRSE and Hellinger error, which we obtain by Monte Carlo integration;

$$IRSE(\widehat{f}) \approx m^{-1} \sum_{j=1}^{m} \frac{\left(\widehat{f}(\boldsymbol{y}_j) - f(\boldsymbol{y}_j)\right)^2}{f(\boldsymbol{y}_j)^2}, \qquad H(\widehat{f}) \approx \sqrt{1 - m^{-1} \sum_{j=1}^{m} \sqrt{\widehat{f}(\boldsymbol{y}_j)/f(\boldsymbol{y}_j)}}.$$

We do the same for three other density estimation algorithms, namely, the kernel estimator using the commonly used plug-in bandwidth selector by

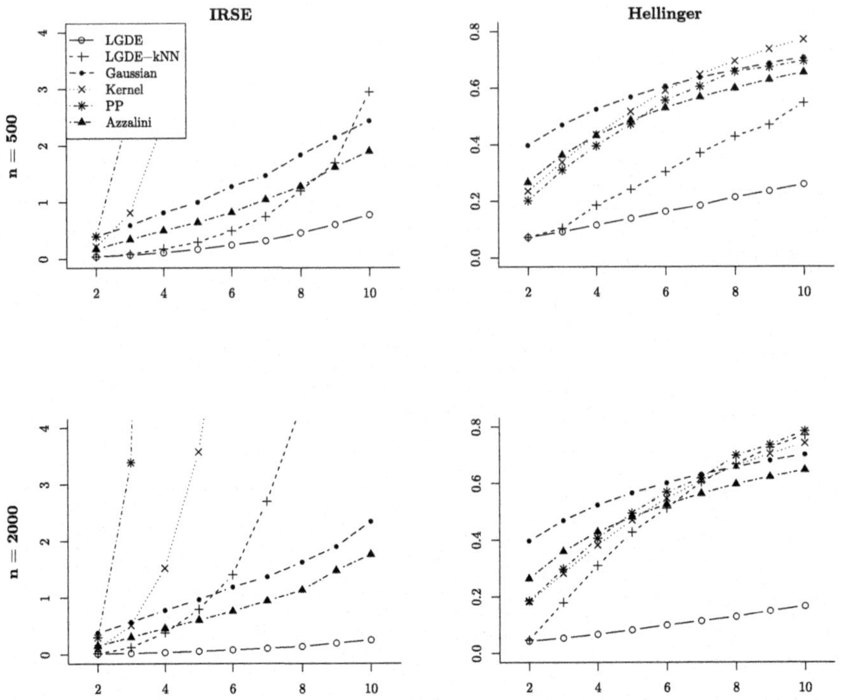

Figure 9.3 χ^2-distributed marginals with 3 degrees of freedom, Gaussian copula with all correlations equal to 0.5.

Wand and Jones (1994), the flexible but parametric skewed *t*-distribution by Azzalini (2005), and the projection pursuit (PP) algorithm by Friedman et al. (1984). PP estimates the univariate densities of a small number of highly non-Gaussian linear projections of the data and uses these to build a multivariate density estimate. The latter is included for completeness and reference only, and we do point out that PP cannot be expected to fare well in our simulation study. First, Friedman et al. (1984) state clearly that PP is inaccurate in the tails, which will be greatly emphasized by the IRSE. Second, PP seems to be very good at recovering sharp structures in high-dimensional data, but all but one of our test distributions are unimodal and do not have dramatic features. At last, we compute the error of the *global* Gaussian fit and compare it to the *local* Gaussian fit to quantify the severity of parametric miss-specification side by side with the curse of dimensionality.

Figs. 9.3–9.8 display the results from our simulations. Each figure represents one distribution. The upper panels report results for the sample size

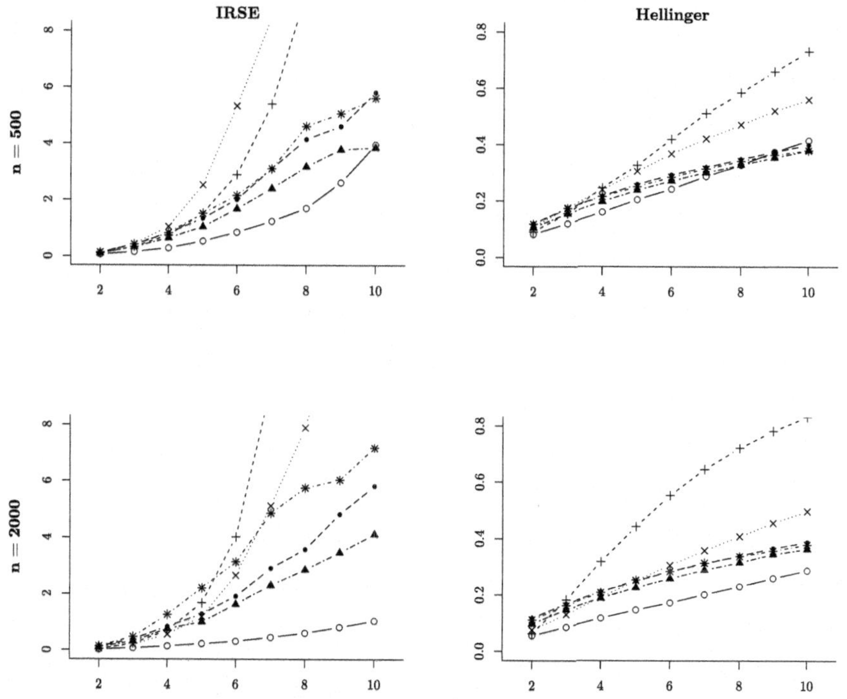

Figure 9.4 Shows the estimated IRSE (left) and Hellinger error (right) for estimates of a density with *t*-distributed marginals with 10 degrees of freedom, Clayton copula with parameter equal to 0.9.

$n = 500$, and the lower panels show results for $n = 2000$. The panels on the left-hand side report IRSE, whereas the right-hand panels display the Hellinger error. The horizontal axis represents the number of variables. Fur a further legend of the figures, see Fig. 9.3, upper left panel.

Let us briefly comment on the individual figures.

Fig. 9.3. The marginals are χ^2-distributed with 3 degrees of freedom, and the dependence is governed by the Gaussian copula. In this situation the pairwise simplification is theoretically true, so the LGDE naturally outperforms all its competitors.

Fig. 9.4. The marginals are t-distributed with 10 degrees of freedom, but the distribution is asymmetric after the initial transformation due to the Clayton copula; see Chapter 5.3.1. The LGDE with a global choice of bandwidths is clearly the best estimator if evaluated using IRSE or the Hellinger distance. Note that the

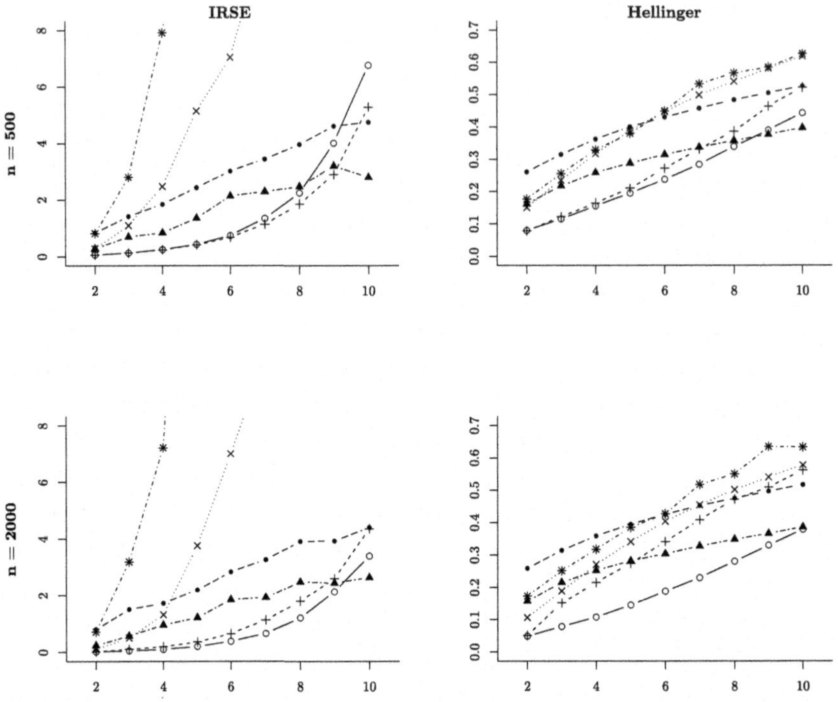

Figure 9.5 Log-normally distributed marginals with $\mu = 0$ and $\sigma = 0.4$, *t*-copula with all correlations equal to 0.7 and 10 degrees of freedom.

parametric skewed *t*-distribution beats all other nonparametric competitors.

Fig. 9.5. We introduce asymmetrical marginals and choose a *t*-copula with 10 degrees of freedom. The LGDE is the overall best performer.

Fig. 9.6. In this case, we generate observations directly from the Clayton copula, meaning that the marginals are uniformly distributed, and nonparametric methods can be expected to exhibit boundary issues. We clearly see that the LGDE with the global bandwidth selector is the best alternative here.

Fig. 9.7. Mixtures of distributions are not easy to recover under the pairwise restriction, but the LGDE performs reasonably well in this case. The PP has been shown to estimate the main body of mixture distributions very well (Hwang et al., 1994). This is the only example for which the kNN bandwidth selector performs acceptably.

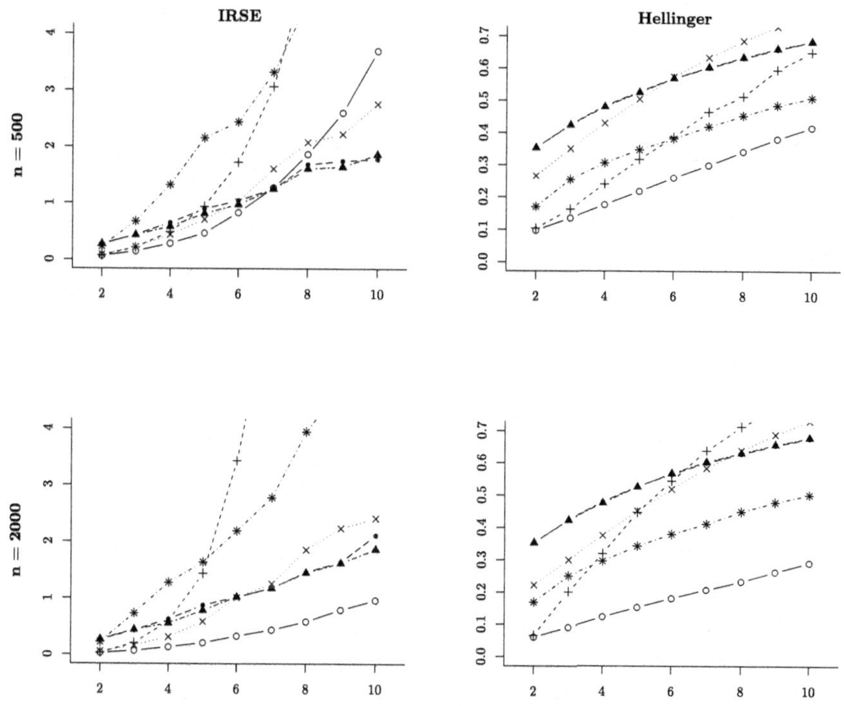

Figure 9.6 Uniform marginals with observations drawn directly from the Clayton copula in Fig. 9.4.

Fig. 9.8. The LGDE does not seem to cope very well with the $t(4)$-distribution in higher dimensions. When weighing up the tail error, we see that fitting the Gaussian distribution globally is actually better than a local Gaussian fit, suggesting that the cross-validation bandwidth is too small in this case. The skewed t-distribution is naturally the best estimator here, because it contains the true distribution as a particular case.

9.7 A more flexible version of the LGDE

By accepting a somewhat simplified historical view we may derive the following chronology: Hjort and Jones (1996) provide a general framework for fitting a parametric family of density functions $\psi(\boldsymbol{x}, \theta)$ to an unknown density $f(\boldsymbol{x})$ by means of the local likelihood function (9.3). Then Tjøstheim and Hufthammer (2013) take ψ to be the bivariate normal, and

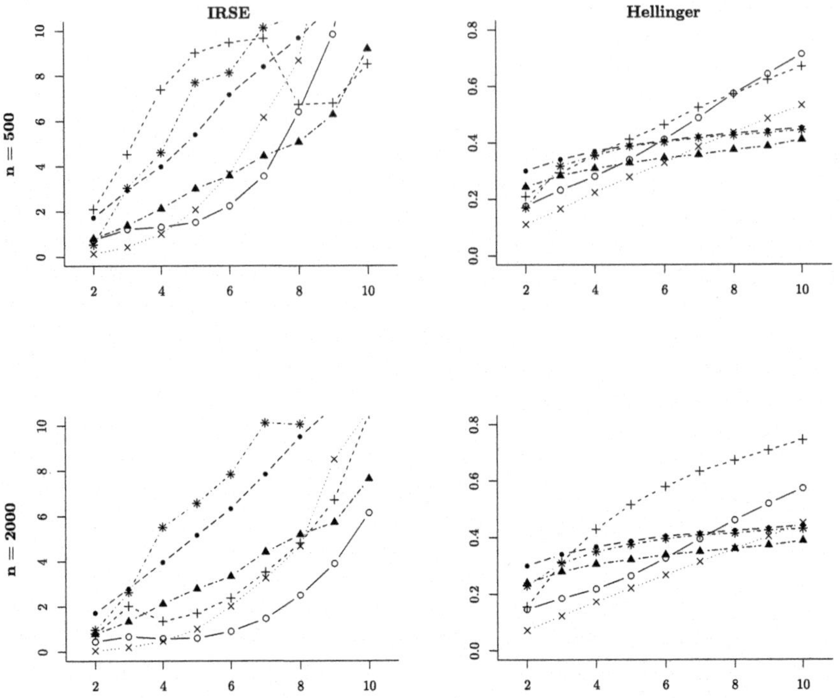

Figure 9.7 Mixture of two Gaussians; $0.7N\ (\mu = 0, \sigma = 1, \rho = 0.5) + 0.3N\ (\mu = 4, \sigma = 1, \rho = 0.1)$.

thus $\theta = \theta(\boldsymbol{x}) = (\mu_1(\boldsymbol{x}), \mu_2(\boldsymbol{x}), \sigma_1(\boldsymbol{x}), \sigma_2(\boldsymbol{x}), \rho(\boldsymbol{x}))$, and use the estimated local correlation $\widehat{\rho}(\boldsymbol{x})$ as a local measure of statistical dependence, as explicitly laid out in Chapter 4.

The topic of the present chapter is constructing a multivariate density estimator along these lines by making some structural simplifications facilitated in part by the transformation from the original $\boldsymbol{x}$-scale to the marginally normal $\boldsymbol{z}$-scale. In particular, we recognize that a "full" locally Gaussian approximation of a p-variate density function would require nonparametric estimates of the p-variate functions

$$\boldsymbol{\mu}(\boldsymbol{x}) = \begin{pmatrix} \mu_1(x_1, \ldots, x_p) \\ \vdots \\ \mu_p(x_1, \ldots, x_p) \end{pmatrix}, \qquad \boldsymbol{\sigma}(\boldsymbol{x}) = \begin{pmatrix} \sigma_1(x_1, \ldots, x_p) \\ \vdots \\ \sigma_p(x_1, \ldots, x_p) \end{pmatrix},$$

and

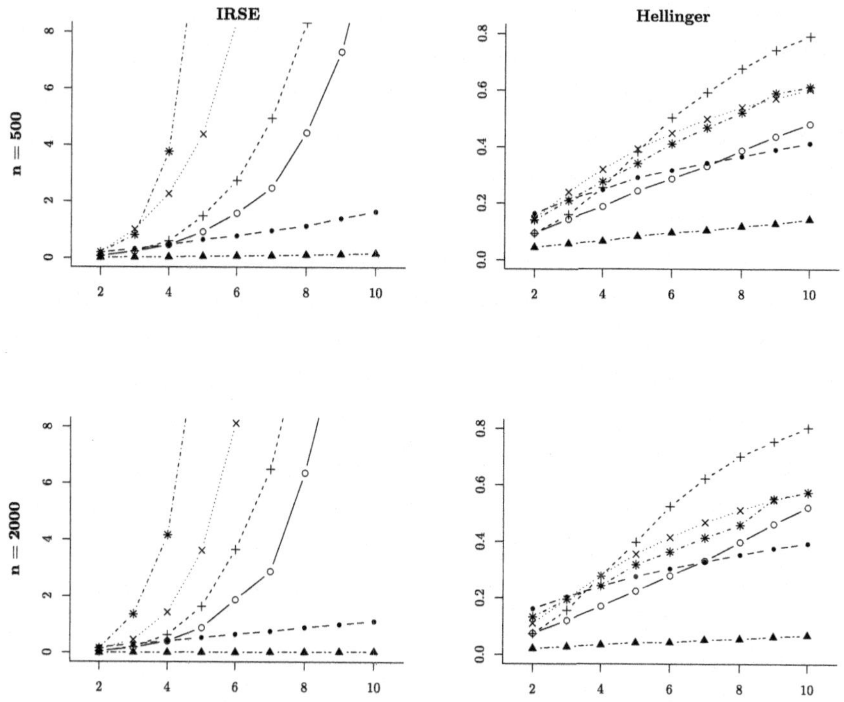

Figure 9.8 Multivariate *t*-distribution with 4 degrees of freedom.

$$\boldsymbol{\rho}(\boldsymbol{x}) = \begin{pmatrix} 1 & \rho_{12}(x_1, \ldots, x_p) & \cdots & \rho_{1p}(x_1, \ldots, x_p) \\ \rho_{21}(x_1, \ldots, x_p) & 1 & \cdots & \rho_{2p}(x_1, \ldots, x_p) \\ \vdots & \vdots & \ddots & \vdots \\ \rho_{p1}(x_1, \ldots, x_p) & \rho_{p2}(x_1, \ldots, x_p) & \cdots & 1 \end{pmatrix},$$

which is practically impossible to obtain because of the curse of dimensionality. We therefore reduce the estimation of $\rho_{ij}(x_1, \ldots, x_p)$ to a bivariate problem by fitting the normal distribution locally to the marginal density $f_{ij}(x_1, x_j)$ of X_i, X_j, from which we obtain the simplified estimate of $\rho_{ij}(x_1, \ldots, x_p)$ of the form $\widehat{\rho}_{ij}(x_i, x_j)$.

Furthermore, having the knowledge that the marginal distributions of our transformed data are all standard normal, we succumb to the temptation of letting $\mu_i(x_1, \ldots, x_p) \equiv 0$ and $\sigma_i(x_1, \ldots, x_p) \equiv 1$, $i = 1, \ldots, p$, resulting in a fairly simple density estimator, based on (9.7), which has a transparent theoretical foundation and produces good estimates in a range of problems.

Upon closer inspection, we may realize that the fixation of local means and standard deviations lacks analytical justification. Indeed, we must point out that this is a *modeling choice* and does not result from, for example, limiting arguments or from looking for a solution to the equation

$$\psi(\boldsymbol{z}, \boldsymbol{\mu}(\boldsymbol{z}), \boldsymbol{\sigma}(\boldsymbol{z}), \boldsymbol{\rho}(\boldsymbol{z})) = f_{\boldsymbol{Z}}(\boldsymbol{z}).$$

Even under the assumption of $f_{\boldsymbol{Z}}$ having standard normal marginals, we can not in general conclude from the equation above that $\boldsymbol{\mu}(\boldsymbol{z}) \equiv 0$ and $\boldsymbol{\sigma}(\boldsymbol{z}) \equiv 1$, except, of course, when $f_{\boldsymbol{Z}}$ is itself the multivariate normal density.

We can therefore construct a slightly more flexible version of the LGDE by adding a new step, say "1⋆", to the algorithm concluding Section 9.2.2 to be carried out between steps 1 and 2:

1⋆. Estimate each marginal density f_i of the unknown joint density f using univariate locally Gaussian fits resulting in estimates of the local means and standard deviations of the form $\widehat{\mu}_i(z_i)$ and $\widehat{\sigma}_i(z_i)$. Keep these local parameter functions fixed in the next step when estimating the pairwise local correlations. Alternatively, and probably better, $\mu_i(z_i)$ and $\sigma_i(z_i)$ can be estimated in a full local likelihood algorithm also including $\rho_{ij}(z_i, z_j)$.

Under the (unrealistic) assumption that the marginals of our unknown density are *exactly* standard normal, this additional step would be superfluous and only add unnecessary uncertainty to our final density estimate, since we would know the *exact* representation of the marginals: $f_i \equiv \psi(\cdot, \mu_i(\cdot), \sigma_i(\cdot))$ with $\mu_i \equiv 0$ and $\sigma_i \equiv 1$. However, the procedure including step 1⋆ does carry some merit for at least two reasons:

1. In practice the empirical version of our transformation (9.1) produces pseudo-observations that in any case are merely *approximately* standard normal. Adding step 1⋆ to the LGDE algorithm is a way to also take this discrepancy into account and improve results in certain situations. We do not notice big differences when applying this modification to density estimation, but Jordanger and Tjøstheim (2020) experience dramatic improvements in their locally Gaussian spectrum analysis (see Chapter 8) when creating estimates of the local means and standard deviations in a bivariate local analysis with $\boldsymbol{\mu}$ and $\boldsymbol{\sigma}$ depending on two coordinates, even for transformed pseudo-observations.
2. If we, for some reason, do not wish to apply the transformation from the original x-scale to the standard normal z-scale, then we may actually replace step 1 with step 1⋆ in the LGDE algorithm. Many argu-

ments for making this transformation remain valid though, to which we have provided references in the beginning of this chapter.

9.8 Proofs

9.8.1 Proof of Theorem 9.1

The method of proof is the same as that of Severini (2000, pp. 105–107) for ordinary maximum likelihood estimates. The proof requires the additional assumption of uniform convergence in probability of the local likelihood function toward the function $\mathrm{E}(L_{\boldsymbol{b}_n,K}(\rho,\boldsymbol{Z}))$, which is the quantity defined in (9.11) inserted $\boldsymbol{b}_n$ and K:

$$\sup_{\rho\in\Theta}\left|L_n(\rho,Z)-\mathrm{E}(L_{\boldsymbol{b}_n,K}(\rho,\boldsymbol{Z}))\right|\xrightarrow{P}0 \quad \text{as} \quad n\to\infty. \tag{9.14}$$

The bivariate version of (9.3) satisfies condition (9.14), provided that condition (ii) is fulfilled. To see this, consider $\psi(\cdot,\rho)$ as a function of the parameter ρ; it is bounded and differentiable to any order on the compact set Θ, and so is its logarithm. Thus $g(\rho)=\log\psi(\cdot,\rho)f(\cdot)-\psi(\cdot;\rho)$ is uniformly continuous there, so for every $\epsilon>0$, there exists $\delta>0$ such that if $|\rho_1-\rho_2|<\delta$, then $|g(\rho_1)-g(\rho_2)|<\epsilon$. Multiplying by a kernel and integrating over another variable $\boldsymbol{y}$ conserve this property, because if $|\rho_1-\rho_2|<\delta$, then

$$\begin{aligned}
&\left|\int K_{\boldsymbol{b}_n}(\boldsymbol{y}-\boldsymbol{z})g(\rho_1)\,\mathrm{d}\boldsymbol{y}-\int K_{\boldsymbol{b}_n}(\boldsymbol{y}-\boldsymbol{z})g(\rho_2)\,\mathrm{d}\boldsymbol{y}\right|\\
&\quad\le\int K_{\boldsymbol{b}_n}(\boldsymbol{y}-\boldsymbol{z})|g(\rho_1)-g(\rho_2)|\,\mathrm{d}\boldsymbol{y}\\
&\quad<\epsilon\int K_{\boldsymbol{b}_n}(\boldsymbol{y}-\boldsymbol{z})\,\mathrm{d}\boldsymbol{y}=\epsilon.
\end{aligned}$$

The ϵ and δ depend neither on $\boldsymbol{b}$ nor on n, so $\{\mathrm{E}(L_{\boldsymbol{b}_n,K}(\rho,\boldsymbol{Z}))\}$ form an equicontinuous family of functions. Further, and again exploiting the smoothness of $\psi(\cdot,\rho)$ on a compact set Θ, the local likelihood functions are Lipschitz continuous there by the mean value theorem. The conditions in Corollary 2.2 by Newey (1991) are thus satisfied, and (9.14) follows thereof. It follows from the uniform convergence that

$$\sup_{\rho\in\Theta}L_n(\rho,\boldsymbol{Z})=L_n(\widehat{\rho},\boldsymbol{Z})\xrightarrow{P}\sup_{\rho\in\Theta}\mathrm{E}(L_n(\rho,\boldsymbol{Z}))=\mathrm{E}(L(\rho_0,\boldsymbol{Z})).$$

The rest of the argument follows exactly that of Severini (2000, pp. 105–107) for ordinary maximum likelihood estimates. □

9.8.2 Proof of Theorems 9.2 and 9.3

We establish joint asymptotic normality of the local correlation vector by first following the standard argument for ordinary maximum likelihood estimates in the bivariate and thus one-parameter cases, and then apply a central limit argument, which amounts to a proof of Theorem 9.2. Then we use the Cramér–Wold device to include the multi-parameter case. In the end, we show that the off-diagonal elements in the covariance matrix asymptotically vanish. In the bivariate case, we must verify the following conditions to use Theorem 7.63 of Schervish (1995) and Theorem 1A of Parzen (1962):

I. The parametric family $\psi(z, \rho)$ is continuously differentiable with respect to ρ;

II. $\int |u(z, \rho_0) f(z)| \, dz < \infty$;

III. There exists a function $T_r(z, \rho)$ such that for each $\rho_0 \in \text{int}(\Theta)$,

$$\sup_{|\rho-\rho_0|\le r} \left|\partial^2 L_n(\rho_0, z)/\partial\rho^2 - \partial^2 L_n(\rho, z)/\partial\rho^2\right| \le T_r(z, \rho_0)$$

with $\lim_{r\to 0} \mathrm{E}(T_r(\boldsymbol{Z}, \rho_0)) = 0$ (stochastic equicontinuity).

The parametric family is Gaussian, so condition I is obviously true. The function $u(z, \rho) = \partial \log \psi(z, \rho)/\partial\rho$ in the bivariate Gaussian case is given by

$$u(z_1, z_2, \rho) = \frac{\rho^3 - z_1 z_2(1+\rho^2) + (z_1^2 + z_2^2 - 1)\rho}{(1-\rho^2)^2}, \tag{9.15}$$

and the stochastic variable $\boldsymbol{Z} = (Z_1, Z_2)$, having density $f_{\boldsymbol{Z}}$, has moments of all orders since the marginals are standard normal. Therefore, $\mathrm{E}|u(\boldsymbol{Z}, \rho)| < \infty$, so II is satisfied. Further, Andrews (1992) shows that the uniform continuity of $\partial^2 L_n(\rho)/\partial\rho^2$ and Lipschitz continuity of $|\partial^2 L_n(\rho, z)/\partial\rho^2 - \partial^2 L(\rho_0, z)/\partial\rho^2|$ suffice for the stochastic equicontinuity as required in condition III. The argument in Section 9.8.1 here also goes through.

Using a one-term Taylor expansion of the function $\partial L_n(\widehat{\rho}, z)/\partial\rho$ and following Schervish (1995, p. 422), we get

$$\partial L_n(\rho_0, z)/\partial\rho + B_{n,b}(\widehat{\rho}_n - \rho_0) = o_P\left((nb_n^2)^{-1/2}\right),$$

where $B_{n,b} = \partial^2 L_n(\rho^*, z)/\partial\rho^2$, and ρ^* lies between ρ_0 and $\widehat{\rho}$. As $n \to \infty$, $B_{n,b}$ tends to its expectation

$$J_b = \int K_b(y - z)u^2(y, \rho^*(z))\psi(y, \rho^*(z))\,dy - \int K_b(y - z)u'(y, \rho^*(z))[f(y) - \psi(y, \rho^*(z))]\,dy. \qquad (9.16)$$

The arguments of Hjort and Jones (1996) and the consistency of $\widehat{\rho}_n$ can be used to see that

$$J = \lim_{b\to 0} J_b = u^2(z, \rho_{0,k})\psi(z, \rho_{0,k}).$$

Further, the variance of $\sqrt{nb^2}\partial L_n(\rho_0, z)/\partial\rho$ approaches M_b as $n \to \infty$, where

$$M_b = b_1 b_2 \int (b_1 b_2)^{-2} K^2(b^{-1}(y - z))u^2(y, \rho_{k,0}(z))f(y)\,dy - b_1 b_2 \left(\int K_b(y - z)u(y, \rho_0(z))f(y)\,dy\right)^2.$$

The second term vanishes as $b \to 0$, so we have in the limit that

$$M = \lim_{b\to 0} M_b = u^2(z, \rho_0(z))f(z)\int K^2(y)\,dy.$$

Following the details of Theorem 7.63 in Schervish (1995), it follows that

$$\sqrt{nb_n^2}\,(\widehat{\rho}_n - \rho_0) \xrightarrow{d} \mathcal{N}(0, M/J^2),$$

provided that the quantity

$$Y_n(z) = \frac{1}{n}\sum_{i=1}^{n} K_{b_n}(z_i - z)u(z_i, \rho_0) \stackrel{\text{def}}{=} \frac{1}{n}\sum_{i=1}^{n} V_{ni}, \qquad (9.17)$$

is asymptotically normal, and this follows along the lines of Parzen (1962), which we now proceed to establish.

Only the first term of the two comprising the local likelihood function (9.3) depends on data. It follows readily from Theorem 1A of Parzen (1962) that the variance of the summands in (9.17), all identically distributed as $V_{ni} = K_{b_n}(z_i - z)u(z_i, \rho_0)$, satisfies

$$b_n^2\mathrm{Var}(V_{ni}) \to f_Z(z)u^2(z, \rho_0)\int_{-\infty}^{\infty} K^2(y)\,dy. \qquad (9.18)$$

Further, a simple Taylor expansion reveals that

$$\begin{aligned}\mathrm{E}|V_{ni}|^{2+\delta} &= \int_{-\infty}^{\infty} \left|K_{\boldsymbol{b}_n}(\boldsymbol{y}-\boldsymbol{z})\, u(\boldsymbol{y},\rho_0)\right|^{2+\delta} f(\boldsymbol{y})\,\mathrm{d}\boldsymbol{y} \\ &= \frac{1}{(b_{1n}b_{2n})^{1+\delta}} f\boldsymbol{z}(\boldsymbol{z})|u(\boldsymbol{z},\rho_0)|^{2+\delta} \int_{-\infty}^{\infty} |K(\boldsymbol{y})|^{2+\delta}\,\mathrm{d}\boldsymbol{y} \\ &\quad + \text{higher-order terms.}\end{aligned} \tag{9.19}$$

The quantity in (9.18) is finite because of assumption (iv) in Theorem 9.2. Here and in what follows, we use the notation $\sigma(X) = \mathrm{sd}(X)$ and $\sigma^a(X) = (\sigma(X))^a$. Further,

$$\frac{\mathrm{E}\,|V_{ni} - \mathrm{E}(V_{ni})|^{2+\delta}}{n^{\delta/2}\sigma^{2+\delta}(V_{ni})} = \frac{(b_{1n}b_{2n})^{1+\delta}\mathrm{E}|V_{ni} - \mathrm{E}(V_{ni})|^{2+\delta}}{(nb_{1n}b_{2n})^{\delta/2}(b_{1n}b_{2n})^{1+\delta/2}\sigma^{2+\delta}(V_{ni})}, \tag{9.20}$$

which tends to zero as $n \to \infty$ because of (9.18), (9.19), and the second part of assumption (iv). The summands comprising $Y_n(\boldsymbol{z})$ therefore satisfy the Lyapunov and thus the Lindeberg conditions, so $Y_n(\boldsymbol{z})$ is asymptotically normal.

Having established the asymptotic normality for each $\widehat{\rho}_k$ (and thus proven Theorem 9.2), we extend the argument above to the p-variate and thus $m = p(p-1)/2$-parameter, case; let $\boldsymbol{\rho} = (\rho_1, \ldots, \rho_m)$ be the vector of local correlations, let $\boldsymbol{u}(\boldsymbol{z}, \boldsymbol{\rho}_0) = (u_1(\boldsymbol{z}, \boldsymbol{\rho}_0), \ldots, u_m(\boldsymbol{z}, \boldsymbol{\rho}_0))$ be the vector of functions defined before as $u_k(\boldsymbol{z}, \boldsymbol{\rho}) = \partial \log \psi(\boldsymbol{z}, \boldsymbol{\rho})/\partial \rho_k$, and, finally, note that $\boldsymbol{Y}_n(\boldsymbol{z}) = n^{-1}\sum_{i=1}^n \boldsymbol{V}_{ni}$ is now a stochastic vector, so that $\boldsymbol{Y}_n(\boldsymbol{z}) = \{Y_{nk}(\boldsymbol{z})\}_{k=1}^m$ and $\boldsymbol{V}_{ni} = \{V_{nik}\}_{k=1}^m$.

We proceed to show that

$$\sum_{k=1}^{m} t_k Y_{nk}(\boldsymbol{z}) \xrightarrow{d} \sum_{k=1}^{m} t_k Z_k^*, \tag{9.21}$$

where $\boldsymbol{t} = (t_1, \ldots, t_m)$ is an arbitrary vector of constants, and $\boldsymbol{Z}^* = (Z_1^*, \ldots, Z_m^*)$ is jointly normally distributed. Then the asymptotic normality of the vector $\boldsymbol{Y}_n(\boldsymbol{z})$ follows from the Cramér–Wold device (Billingsley, 2008, p. 383). The asymptotic normality of $\boldsymbol{t}^T\boldsymbol{Y}_n(z)$ follows immediately from the one-dimensional case by writing $W_{ni} = \sum_{k=1}^m t_k V_{nik}$ so that $\sum_{k=1}^m t_k Y_{nk}(\boldsymbol{z}) = \sum_{i=1}^n W_{ni}$, where all summands are identically distributed as $W_n = \sum_{k=1}^m t_k K_{\boldsymbol{b}_n}(\boldsymbol{z}_i - \boldsymbol{z}) u_k(\boldsymbol{z}, \rho_0) = \sum_{k=1}^m t_k V_{nk}$. Jensen's inequality implies

$|\sum_{k=1}^{m} Z_k|^{2+\delta} \le m^{1+\delta} \sum_{k=1}^{m} |Z_k|^{2+\delta}$, and so

$$\frac{\mathrm{E}\,|W_n - \mathrm{E}(W_n)|^{2+\delta}}{n^{\delta/2}\sigma^{2+\delta}(W_n)} = \frac{\mathrm{E}\left|\sum t_k V_{nk} - \mathrm{E}(\sum t_k V_{nk})\right|^{2+\delta}}{n^{\delta/2}\sigma^{2+\delta}(\sum t_k V_{nk})}$$
$$\le m^{1+\delta} \sum_{k=1}^{m} \frac{|t_k|^{2+\delta}(b_{1n}b_{2n})^{1+\delta}\mathrm{E}|\,V_{nk} - \mathrm{E}(V_{nk})|^{2+\delta}}{(nb_{1n}b_{2n})^{\delta/2}(b_{1n}b_{2n})^{1+\delta/2}\sigma^{2+\delta}(\sum t_k V_{nk})}. \tag{9.22}$$

Recall that all variables are on the same Gaussian scale and that all bandwidths tend to zero at the same rate. Therefore it does not matter which bandwidths we use in the above expression. Further, the variance in the denominator of (9.22) stays away from zero because of (9.18). Following the same reasoning as in the univariate case (9.20), the Lyapunov condition is satisfied for the W_n, implying (9.21), and so the vector $\mathbf{Y}_n(x)$ is jointly asymptotically normal.

It remains to show that the asymptotic covariance matrix is diagonal. Indeed, we will see below that the covariance between two local correlation estimates *with no common index* goes to zero as n^{-1}. If they share a common index, then we can go through the arguments below once again and see that their covariance $\mathrm{Cov}(\widehat{\rho}_{ij}, \widehat{\rho}_{jk})$ tends to zero as $(nb_n)^{-1}$. Both rates are negligible compared to $(nb_n^2)^{-1}$.

Assume without loss of generality that we have four variables $Z_1, \ldots, Z_4$ with joint density $f_{\mathbf{Z}}(\mathbf{z})$, and we estimate the local correlations $\widehat{\rho}_{12}$ and $\widehat{\rho}_{34}$ according to the scheme described in Section 9.2. Again, we identify the parameters with single indices, so that in this case, we have $\boldsymbol{\rho} = (\rho_1, \rho_2)$. They are estimated independently from each other by maximizing the local likelihood functions $L_{1,n}(\rho_1, Z_1, Z_2)$ and $L_{2,n}(\rho_2, Z_3, Z_4)$, as defined by Eq. (9.3). Taylor expansion of the estimation equations $L_{1,n} = 0$ and $L_{2,n} = 0$ about the population values $\rho_{1,0}$ and $\rho_{2,0}$, respectively, yields

$$0 = \begin{pmatrix} \partial L_{1,n}(\widehat{\rho}_1)/\partial\rho_1 \\ \partial L_{2,n}(\widehat{\rho}_2)/\partial\rho_2 \end{pmatrix} \stackrel{\text{def}}{=} \begin{pmatrix} S_1(\widehat{\rho}_1) \\ S_2(\widehat{\rho}_2) \end{pmatrix}$$
$$= \begin{pmatrix} S_1(\rho_{1,0}) \\ S_2(\rho_{2,0}) \end{pmatrix} + \begin{pmatrix} \partial S_1(\rho_1^*)/\partial\rho_1 & 0 \\ 0 & \partial S_2(\rho_2^*)/\partial\rho_2 \end{pmatrix} \begin{pmatrix} \widehat{\rho}_1 - \rho_{1,0} \\ \widehat{\rho}_2 - \rho_{2,0} \end{pmatrix},$$

where ρ_k^* again lies between $\widehat{\rho}_k$ and $\rho_{k,0}$. More compactly, we write ($b_{1n} = b_{2n} = b_n$)

$$(nb_n^2)^{1/2}(\widehat{\boldsymbol{\rho}} - \boldsymbol{\rho}_0) = -\boldsymbol{U}^{-1}(\boldsymbol{\rho}^*)(nb_n^2)^{1/2}\boldsymbol{S}(\boldsymbol{\rho}_0),$$

where $\boldsymbol{U}$ is the diagonal matrix of derivatives. The non-zero elements in $\boldsymbol{U}$ converge as $n \to \infty$ and $b_n \to 0$ to the quantities J_1 and J_2, which we have seen to be

$$J_k = u_k^2(\boldsymbol{z}_k, \rho_{0,k})\psi(\boldsymbol{z}_k, \rho_{0,k}), \qquad k = 1, 2.$$

Denote by $\boldsymbol{M_b}$ the covariance matrix of $\sqrt{nb^2}\boldsymbol{S}(\boldsymbol{\rho}_0)$. The diagonal elements of $\boldsymbol{M_b}$ are given by

$$M_k = u_k^2(\boldsymbol{z}_k, \rho_{k.0}(\boldsymbol{z}_k))f_k(\boldsymbol{z}_k)\int K^2(\boldsymbol{y}_k)\,\mathrm{d}\boldsymbol{y}_k.$$

The off-diagonal element in $\boldsymbol{M}_b$ is $O(b^2)$, because

$$\begin{aligned} M_{\boldsymbol{b}}^{(1,2)} &= M_{\boldsymbol{b}}^{(2,1)} \\ &= b^2 \int K_b(y_1 - z_1)K_b(y_2 - z_2)u_1(y_1, \rho_{1,0}(z_1))u_2(y_2, \rho_{2,0}(z_2))f_Z(y)\,\mathrm{d}y \\ &\quad + \text{a higher-order term.} \end{aligned}$$

Writing $\boldsymbol{J}_b = \operatorname{diag}(J_{1,b}, J_{2,b})$, where $J_{k,b}$ was defined in (9.16), we collect these results and write the covariance matrix of $\sqrt{nb^2}(\widehat{\rho}_1, \widehat{\rho}_2)^T$ in terms of its asymptotic order:

$$\begin{aligned} \boldsymbol{J}_{\boldsymbol{b}}^{-1}\boldsymbol{M}_b(\boldsymbol{J}_{\boldsymbol{b}}^{-1})^T &\sim \begin{pmatrix} J_{1,\boldsymbol{b}}^{-1} & 0 \\ 0 & J_{1,\boldsymbol{b}}^{-1} \end{pmatrix} \begin{pmatrix} M_{1,\boldsymbol{b}} & b^2 \\ b^2 & M_{2,\boldsymbol{b}} \end{pmatrix} \begin{pmatrix} J_{1,\boldsymbol{b}}^{-1} & 0 \\ 0 & J_{2,\boldsymbol{b}}^{-1} \end{pmatrix} \\ &\to \begin{pmatrix} M_1/J_1^2 & 0 \\ 0 & M_2/J_2^2 \end{pmatrix} \end{aligned}$$

as $\boldsymbol{b} \to \boldsymbol{0}$, indicating that the asymptotic covariance between $\widehat{\rho}_1$ and $\widehat{\rho}_2$ tends to zero as n^{-1}. The same procedure must be repeated to establish $\mathrm{Cov}(\widehat{\rho}_{ij}, \widehat{\rho}_{jk}) = O((nb)^{-1})$. □

9.8.3 Proof of Theorem 9.4

It follows from the delta method that $\widehat{f_Z}(\boldsymbol{z})$ is asymptotically normal. It remains to show that the asymptotic normality still holds after the final back-transformation (9.8) with suitable estimates for the marginal density and distribution functions. Under assumption (v) of Theorem 9.4, the normalized estimates $\sqrt{nb^2}\left(\widehat{f_i}(x_i) - f_i(x_i)\right)$ and $\sqrt{nb^2}\left(\widehat{F}_i(x_i) - F_i(x_i)\right)$ both converge in distribution to the constant 0, which again implies

$\widehat{f}_i(x_i) - f_i(x_i) = o_P((nb^2)^{-1/2})$ and $\widehat{F}_i(x_i) - F_i(x_i) = o_P((nb^2)^{-1/2})$. It follows that

$$\begin{aligned}\phi\left(\Phi^{-1}(\widehat{F}_i(x_i))\right) = &\phi\left(\Phi^{-1}(F_i(x_i))\right)\\ &+\phi'\left(\Phi^{-1}(F_i(x_i))\right)\left[\Phi^{-1}\right]'(F_i(x_i))(\widehat{F}_i(x_i) - F_i(x_i))\\ &+\text{higher-order terms,}\end{aligned}$$

where the second term is $o_P(1)$ in all $\boldsymbol{x}$ such that $F(\boldsymbol{x}) \in (0,1)$. Then we can write

$$\frac{\widehat{f}_i(x_i)}{\phi\left(\Phi^{-1}(\widehat{F}_i(x_i))\right)} = \frac{f_i(x_i)}{\phi\left(\Phi^{-1}(F_i(x_i))\right)} + o_P(1),$$

from which it follows that

$$\prod_{i=1}^{p}\frac{\widehat{f}_i(x_i)}{\phi\left(\Phi^{-1}(\widehat{F}_i(x_i))\right)} = \prod_{i=1}^{p}\frac{f_i(x_i)}{\phi\left(\Phi^{-1}(F_i(x_i))\right)} + o_P(1).$$

By Slutsky's theorem we have that $\widehat{f}(\boldsymbol{x})$ as defined by Eq. (9.8) is asymptotically normal. The expression for the asymptotic variance of the density estimate follows from Theorem 9.3 and the delta method applied to the asymptotic covariance matrix of the local correlations (9.12) using function (9.2). □

References

Andrews, D.W., 1992. Generic uniform convergence. Econometric Theory 8 (2), 241–257.

Azzalini, A., 2005. The skew-normal distribution and related multivariate families. Scandinavian Journal of Statistics, 159–188.

Berentsen, G.D., Støve, B., Tjøstheim, D., Nordbø, T., 2014. Recognizing and visualizing copulas: an approach using local Gaussian approximation. Insurance: Mathematics and Economics 57, 90–103.

Berentsen, G.D., Tjøstheim, D., 2014. Recognizing and visualizing departures from independence in bivariate data using local Gaussian correlation. Statistics and Computing 24 (5), 785–801.

Billingsley, P., 2008. Probability and Measure. John Wiley & Sons.

Duong, T., Hazelton, M.L., 2005. Cross-validation bandwidth matrices for multivariate kernel density estimation. Scandinavian Journal of Statistics 32 (3), 485–506.

Friedman, J.H., Stuetsle, W., Schroeder, A., 1984. Projection pursuit density estimation. Journal of the American Statistical Association 79, 599–608.

Geenens, G., 2014. Probit transformation for kernel density estimation on the unit interval. Journal of the American Statistical Association 109 (505), 346–358.

Geenens, G., Charpentier, A., Paindaveine, D., 2017. Probit transformation for nonparametric kernel estimation of the copula density. Bernoulli 23 (3), 1848–1873.

Hall, P., 1987. On Kullback–Leibler loss and density estimation. Annals of Statistics 15 (4), 1491–1519.
Hastie, T., Tibshirani, R., Friedman, J., 2009. The Elements of Statistical Learning. Data Mining, Inference, and Prediction, 2nd edition. Springer, New York.
Hjort, N., Jones, M., 1996. Locally parametric nonparametric density estimation. Annals of Statistics 24 (4), 1619–1647.
Hjort, N.L., Glad, I.K., 1995. Nonparametric density estimation with a parametric start. Annals of Statistics 23 (3), 882–904.
Hwang, J.-N., Lay, S.-R., Lippman, A., 1994. Nonparametric multivariate density estimation: a comparative study. Signal Processing, IEEE Transactions on 42 (10), 2795–2810.
Jordanger, L.A., Tjøstheim, D., 2020. Nonlinear spectral analysis: a local Gaussian approach. Journal of the American Statistical Association, 1–55.
Kooperberg, C., Stone, C.J., 1991. A study of logspline density estimation. Computational Statistics & Data Analysis 12 (3), 327–347.
Loader, C.R., 1996. Local likelihood density estimation. Annals of Statistics 24 (4), 1602–1618.
Newey, W.K., 1991. Uniform convergence in probability and stochastic equicontinuity. Econometrica 59 (4), 1161–1167.
Otneim, H., Tjøstheim, D., 2017. The locally Gaussian density estimator for multivariate data. Statistics and Computing 27 (6), 1595–1616.
Parzen, E., 1962. On estimation of a probability density function and mode. Annals of Mathematical Statistics 33 (3), 1065–1076.
Ruppert, D., Cline, D.B., 1994. Bias reduction in kernel density estimation by smoothed empirical transformations. Annals of Statistics 22 (1), 185–210.
Schervish, M.J., 1995. Theory of Statistics. Springer.
Severini, T.A., 2000. Likelihood Methods in Statistics. Oxford Science Publications. Oxford University Press.
Silverman, B.W., 1986. Density Estimation for Statistics and Data Analysis. Chapman and Hall, London.
Sklar, A., 1959. Fonctions de répartition à *n* dimensions et leurs marges. Université Paris 8.
Stone, C.J., 1984. An asymptotically optimal window selection rule for kernel density estimates. Annals of Statistics 12 (4), 1285–1297.
Stone, C.J., Hansen, M.H., Kooperberg, C., Truong, Y.K., 1997. Polynomial splines and their tensor products in extended linear modeling: 1994 Wald Memorial Lecture. Annals of Statistics 25 (4), 1371–1470.
Stone, M., 1974. Cross-validatory choice and assessment of statistical predictions. Journal of the Royal Statistical Society Series B 36 (2), 111–147.
Tjøstheim, D., Hufthammer, K.O., 2013. Local Gaussian correlation: a new measure of dependence. Journal of Econometrics 172 (1), 33–48.
Wand, M., Jones, M., 1994. Multivariate plug-in bandwidth selection. Computational Statistics 9 (2), 97–116.
Wand, M.P., Marron, J.S., Ruppert, D., 1991. Transformations in density estimation. Journal of the American Statistical Association 86 (414), 343–353.

CHAPTER 10

Conditional density estimation

Contents

10.1. Introduction 335
10.2. Estimating the conditional density 337
10.3. Asymptotic theory for dependent data 339
10.4. Examples 342
    10.4.1 Stock data 342
    10.4.2 Simulations 345
    10.4.3 Simulated data from a heavy-tailed distribution 346
    10.4.4 Simulated data with irrelevant variables 347
10.5. Proof of theorems 348
    10.5.1 Proof of Theorem 10.1 348
    10.5.2 Proof of Theorem 10.2 349
References 352

10.1 Introduction

The need for expressing statistical inference in terms of conditional quantities is ubiquitous in most natural and social sciences. The obvious example is the estimation of the mean of some set of response variables conditioned on sets of explanatory variables taking specified values. Other common tasks are the forecasting of volatilities or quantiles of financial time series conditioned on past history. Problems of this kind often call for some sort of regression analysis, of which the literature provides an abundance of choices.

Conditional means, variances, and quantiles are all properties of the conditional distribution or density in case the variables are (and we assume that they are) continuous. So are all other probabilistic statements that we might ever want to make about the response variables given the explanatory variables. It is therefore clearly of interest to obtain good estimates of the entire conditional distribution to make use of all the evidence contained in the data and to provide the user with a wide variety of options in analyzing and visualizing the relationships of the variables under study.

We now continue the study initialized in the preceding chapter concerning local Gaussian approximations of multivariate densities and show that we can produce robust estimates of conditional densities with little

Statistical Modeling using Local Gaussian Approximation
https://doi.org/10.1016/B978-0-12-815861-6.00017-1

effort. Let $\boldsymbol{X} = (X_1, \ldots, X_p)^T$ be a stochastic vector, and, assuming the existence, denote by $f_{\mathbf{X}}$ its joint density function. Further, let $(\boldsymbol{X}_1; \boldsymbol{X}_2) = (X_1, \ldots, X_k; X_{k+1}, \ldots, X_p)$ be a partitioning of $\boldsymbol{X}$. Then the conditional density of $\boldsymbol{X}_1$ given $\boldsymbol{X}_2 = \boldsymbol{x}_2$ is defined by

$$f_{\mathbf{X}_1|\mathbf{X}_2}(\boldsymbol{x}_1|\boldsymbol{X}_2 = \boldsymbol{x}_2) = \frac{f_{\mathbf{X}}(\boldsymbol{x}_1, \boldsymbol{x}_2)}{f_{\mathbf{X}_2}(\boldsymbol{x}_2)}, \tag{10.1}$$

where $f_{\mathbf{X}_2}$ is the marginal density of $\boldsymbol{X}_2 = (X_{k+1}, \ldots, X_p)^T$.

The problem of estimating (10.1) is not trivial. We do not observe data directly from the density that we wish to estimate, so we need a set of tools different from those used in the unconditional case. A natural course of action is to follow Rosenblatt (1969) in obtaining good estimates of the numerator and denominator of (10.1) separately using the kernel estimator and then use this to compute the ratio in (10.1). Chen and Linton (2001) provide a discussion of choosing the bandwidths when using the kernel estimator to estimate the components, as do Bashtannyk and Hyndman (2001). Hall et al. (2004) give a unified approach to estimating conditional densities using the kernel estimator, which allows a mix of continuous and discrete variables, and automatically smooths out the irrelevant ones.

However, unless we have a very good estimate of the marginal density, it may be less than ideal to put a kernel estimate into the denominator of (10.1). This is remedied by Faugeras (2009), who writes the conditional density as a product of the marginal and copula density functions in the bivariate case:

$$f_{\mathbf{X}_1|\mathbf{X}_2}(\boldsymbol{x}_1|\boldsymbol{X}_2 = \boldsymbol{x}_2) = f_{\mathbf{X}_1}(\boldsymbol{x}_1)c\{F_1(\boldsymbol{x}_1), F_2(\boldsymbol{x}_2)\}, \tag{10.2}$$

where $f_{\mathbf{X}_1}$ is the marginal density of $\boldsymbol{X}_1$, F_1 and F_2 are the marginal distribution functions, c is the copula density of $(\boldsymbol{X}_1, \boldsymbol{X}_2)$, and those are estimated separately using the kernel estimator. Formula (10.2) can be generalized to the case of several covariates, but its practical use in higher dimensions is questionable because of boundary and dimensionality issues, unless we obtain better estimates of the multivariate copula density than those provided by the kernel estimator, such as the local likelihood approach by Geenens et al. (2017).

Hyndman et al. (1996) starts to move away from the kernel estimator by adjusting the conditional mean to match a better performing regression technique, such as local polynomials, whereas Fan et al. (1996) estimate the conditional density directly using locally linear and locally quadratic fits, a method that Hyndman and Yao (2002) refine by constraining it to always be non-negative. The latter authors propose in the same paper a local likelihood approach based on some of the same machinery we will employ in this chapter, and Fan and Yim (2004) provide a cross-validation rule for bandwidth selection in the locally parametric models. However, these methods are to date implemented in the bivariate case only, where the response and explanatory variables are both scalars.

Indeed, the main motivation behind the method presented in this chapter is providing an estimator that can handle a greater number of variables without the requirement that either response or explanatory variables are scalar. In the next section, we show how the locally Gaussian density estimator (LGDE) can be modified to produce conditional density estimates.

10.2 Estimating the conditional density

Conditional density estimates are in principle available from any non-parametric estimate of the unconditional density of all variables. Let us return to the problem in Section 10.1 and suppose that we obtain an estimate $\tilde{f}_{\mathbf{X}}$ of $f_{\mathbf{X}}$ in the process of estimating the right-hand side of (10.1). The corresponding marginal density $\tilde{f}_{\mathbf{X}_2}$ that ideally we should put into the denominator of (10.1) is given by

$$\tilde{f}_{\mathbf{X}_2} = \int \tilde{f}_{\mathbf{X}}\, \mathrm{d}\boldsymbol{x}_1,$$

but we must usually turn to numerical methods to obtain this integral, which can be a costly affair in terms of computing power, especially, when there are many variables over which to integrate. Thus estimating the marginal density directly from the data is often quicker but introduces a new source of uncertainty, which, again, will be difficult to handle in case of several explanatory variables.

We proceed to show that this problem is completely circumvented if we use the LGDE strategy for estimation. As is well known for a multivariate Gaussian distribution, every conditional density that can be formed by partitioning the Gaussian vector and computing fraction (10.1) is again Gaussian, and the (conditional) mean and (conditional) covariance matrix in that Gaussian can be easily computed; see, for example, Johnson and Wichern (2007, Ch. 4). This is of course also the case for the fraction of Gaussians that are local approximations, and we can obtain estimates by using these formulas. In more detail, starting from the p-variate density in

Eq. (9.2),

$$f_{\mathbf{X}_1|\mathbf{X}_2}(\boldsymbol{x}_1|\mathbf{X}_2=\boldsymbol{x}_2) = \frac{f_{\mathbf{X}}(\boldsymbol{x})}{f_{\mathbf{X}_2}(\boldsymbol{x}_2)}$$
$$= \frac{f_{\mathbf{Z}}(z_1,\ldots,z_p)}{f_{\mathbf{Z}_2}(z_{k+1},\ldots,z_p)}\prod_{i=1}^{k}\frac{f_i(x_i)}{\phi(z_i)}, \qquad (10.3)$$

where the variables $\boldsymbol{Z}=(Z_1,\ldots,Z_p)^T$ are obtained as $Z_i=\Phi^{-1}(F_{X_i}(X_i))$ as described in Chapter 9.2, and we assume that the simplifying assumptions of Eqs. (9.6) and (9.7) are fulfilled so that $\boldsymbol{\mu}(\boldsymbol{z})=\mathbf{0}$, $\boldsymbol{\sigma}(\boldsymbol{z})=\mathbf{1}$, and $\rho_{Z_i,Z_j}(\boldsymbol{z})=\rho_{Z_i,Z_j}(z_i,z_j)$. Let $\boldsymbol{R}(\boldsymbol{z})$ be the corresponding local correlation matrix of $\boldsymbol{Z}$ and partition $\boldsymbol{R}(\boldsymbol{z})$ into four blocks, of which the lower right block is $\boldsymbol{R}_{22}(\boldsymbol{z})$:

$$\boldsymbol{R}(\boldsymbol{z})=\begin{pmatrix}\boldsymbol{R}_{11} & \boldsymbol{R}_{12}\\ \boldsymbol{R}_{21} & \boldsymbol{R}_{22}\end{pmatrix}.$$

We can use the basic result for the multivariate normal distribution mentioned above locally to rewrite the fraction in (10.3) as

$$f_{\mathbf{Z}}/f_{\mathbf{Z}_2}=\Psi^*(z_1,\ldots,z_k;\boldsymbol{\mu}^*,\boldsymbol{\Sigma}^*), \qquad (10.4)$$

where Ψ^* is the general k-variate Gaussian density with expectation vector and covariance matrix given by

$$\boldsymbol{\mu}^*=\boldsymbol{R}_{12}\boldsymbol{R}_{22}^{-1}\boldsymbol{z}_2, \qquad (10.5)$$
$$\boldsymbol{\Sigma}^*=\boldsymbol{R}_{11}-\boldsymbol{R}_{12}\boldsymbol{R}_{22}^{-1}\boldsymbol{R}_{21}, \qquad (10.6)$$

where $\boldsymbol{z}_2=(z_{k+1},\ldots,z_p)$. Note that we may use correlation and covariance matrices interchangeably, because all standard deviations are equal to one in $f_{\mathbf{Z}}$ and $f_{\mathbf{Z}_2}$ in that we are using the simplified representations (9.6) and (9.7).

We can now obtain an estimate of $f_{\mathbf{X}_1|\mathbf{X}_2=\boldsymbol{x}_2}$ by plugging in local estimates of $\boldsymbol{R}(\boldsymbol{z})=\{\rho_{ij}(z_i,z_j)\}$, resulting in

$$\widehat{f}_{\mathbf{X}_1|\mathbf{X}_2}(\boldsymbol{x}_1|\mathbf{X}_2=\boldsymbol{x}_2)=\Psi^*\left(\boldsymbol{z};\widehat{\boldsymbol{\mu}^*}(\boldsymbol{z}),\widehat{\boldsymbol{\Sigma}^*}(\boldsymbol{z})\right)\prod_{i=1}^{k}\frac{f_i(x_i)}{\phi(z_i)}, \qquad (10.7)$$

where $\widehat{\boldsymbol{\mu}^*}(\boldsymbol{z})$ and $\widehat{\boldsymbol{\Sigma}^*}(\boldsymbol{z})$ are obtained by substituting local correlation estimates into Eqs. (10.5) and (10.6), and where we write $z_i=\Phi^{-1}(F_i(x_i))$. Moreover, the second factor in (10.7) requires estimates $\widehat{f_i}(x_i)$ of the marginal densities $f_i(x_i)$, $i = 1, \ldots, k$. As in Chapter 9, this can be any smooth estimate and will not affect the asymptotic results as long as they converge faster than $(nb^2)^{-1/2}$. To this end, we continue to use the logspline method for estimating cumulative distribution functions in this chapter as well.

According to the discussion above, we estimate conditional densities by following these steps:

1. Transform each marginal observation to standard normality as in Eq. (9.1) and produce marginally standard normal pseudo-observations $\widehat{Z}_i = \Phi^{-1}\left(\widehat{F}_i(X_i)\right)$.
2. Estimate the local correlation matrix of the transformed data by following the recipe in Chapter 9. See Eq. (9.6).
3. Calculate the local mean and covariance matrix of $\widehat{f_{\mathbf{Z}}}/\widehat{f_{\mathbf{Z}_2}}$ using formulas (10.5) and (10.6), so that the conditional density estimate becomes as given in (10.7).
4. Normalize the density estimate so that it integrates to one.

We proceed in the next section to discuss regularity conditions and to explore the large-sample properties of this method.

10.3 Asymptotic theory for dependent data

Here we state similar results as those found in Chapter 9 but prove them under a new set of regularity conditions, which include dependence between observations opening up their use in time series applications. Let us recapitulate some central notational elements, which, for the time being, revolve around the locally Gaussian approximation to a bivariate density $f_{ij}(z_i, z_j)$ of the marginally standard normal variables (Z_i, Z_j). We recall two population values $\rho_{\boldsymbol{b}}(\boldsymbol{z})$ and $\rho_0(\boldsymbol{z})$ of the local correlation, the former being defined for a fixed set of bandwidths $\boldsymbol{b} = (b_1, b_2)$ as the solution to

$$\frac{\partial L_n(\rho; \boldsymbol{z})}{\partial \rho} \xrightarrow{P} \int K_{\boldsymbol{b}}(\boldsymbol{y} - \boldsymbol{z}) u(\boldsymbol{y}, \rho_{\boldsymbol{b}}) \left\{f_{ij}(\boldsymbol{y}) - \psi(\boldsymbol{y}, \rho_{\boldsymbol{b}})\right\} \mathrm{d}\boldsymbol{y} = 0, \qquad (10.8)$$

where $u(\cdot, \rho) = \partial/\partial\rho \log \psi(\cdot, \rho)$ as in (9.4), and the latter as the limiting value $\rho_0(\boldsymbol{z}) = \lim_{\boldsymbol{b}\to 0} \rho_{\boldsymbol{b}}(\boldsymbol{z})$ satisfying $\psi(\boldsymbol{z}, \rho_0(\boldsymbol{z})) = f_{ij}(\boldsymbol{z})$. All statements about the vector of bandwidths $\boldsymbol{b}$ are made element-wise.

We allow serial dependence of the observations through the concepts of strict stationarity and α-mixing; see Eq. (7.15). We require the mixing coefficients (7.15) of our observations to tend to zero at an appropriate rate, which means that we can turn to standard theorems to establish the asymptotic properties of the conditional density estimator.

We are now ready to state results corresponding to Theorems 9.1–9.3 under a milder set of conditions, and we start by stating conditions for consistency of each of the local correlations (we use the simplifying assumption (9.7) as well as in the following theorems).

Theorem 10.1. *Let* $\{(Z_{it}, Z_{jt})\}$ *be identically distributed bivariate stochastic vectors with standard normal margins. Denote by* $\rho_0(\boldsymbol{z})$ *the local Gaussian correlation between* Z_i *and* Z_j*, and by* $\widehat{\rho}_n(\boldsymbol{z})$ *its local likelihood estimate. We make the following assumptions:*

- **(i)** *For any sequence of bandwidths matrices* $\boldsymbol{B}_n = diag(\boldsymbol{b}_n)$ *tending to the zero matrix as* $n \to \infty$ *and for the bivariate marginally standard Gaussian vector* (Z_i, Z_j)*, there exist a unique* $\rho_{\boldsymbol{b}_n}(\boldsymbol{z})$ *that satisfies* (10.8) *and* $\rho_0(\boldsymbol{z})$ *such that* $\rho_{\boldsymbol{b}_n}(\boldsymbol{z}) \to \rho_0(\boldsymbol{z})$.
- **(ii)** $\{(Z_{it}, Z_{jt})\}$ *is* α*-mixing with the mixing coefficients satisfying* $\sum_{s\geq 1} s^{\lambda}\alpha(s)^{1-2/\delta} < \infty$ *for some* $\lambda > 1 - 2/\delta$ *and* $\delta > 2$.
- **(iii)** *Each component bandwidth* b *in* $\boldsymbol{B}_n$ *tends to zero so that* $nb^{\frac{\lambda+2-2/\delta}{\lambda+2/\delta}} = O(n^{\epsilon_0})$ *as* $n \to \infty$ *for some constant* $\epsilon_0 > 0$.
- **(iv)** *The parameter space* Θ *for* ρ *is a compact subset of* $(-1, 1)$.
- **(v)** *The kernel function satisfies* $\sup_{\boldsymbol{z}} |K(\boldsymbol{z})| < \infty$, $\int |K(\boldsymbol{y})|\, d\boldsymbol{y} < \infty$, $|\partial/\partial z_i K(z)| < \infty$*, and* $\lim_{z_i \to \infty} |z_i K(z_i)| = 0$ *for* $i = 1, 2$.

Then

$$\widehat{\rho}_n(\boldsymbol{z}) \xrightarrow{P} \rho_0(\boldsymbol{z}) \quad as \quad n \to \infty.$$

This theorem is stated for the bivariate process $\{(Z_{it}, Z_{jt})\}_n$ with standard normal margins, but it is readily pairwise valid also for the general p-variate process $\{\boldsymbol{X}_t\}$. In Theorem 10.1, Assumption (ii) means that the general p-variate observations $\{\boldsymbol{X}_t\}$ are α-mixing with the specified convergence rate for the mixing coefficients. This distinction has no practical importance when transforming back and forth between these two scales, because the mixing properties of a process are conserved under any measurable transformation; see Fan and Yao (2003, p. 69).

Fan and Yao (2003, pp. 76–77) provide a general central limit theorem for non-parametric regression. It is applicable to the local correlations, with obvious adaptations to achieve consistent notation. Assume now that $\{\boldsymbol{Z}_t\}$ is a sequence of p-variate observations having standard normal margins, and denote by $\boldsymbol{\rho} = (\rho_1, \ldots, \rho_{p(p-1)/2})$ the vector of local correlations, which has one component for each pair of variables. The local correlations are estimated one by one using the scheme described above, and we denote by $\widehat{\rho}$ the estimate of ρ. Further, as all bandwidths are assumed to tend to zero at the same rate, notations like b^2 are taken to mean the product of any two bandwidths b_i and b_j.

Theorem 10.2. *Under assumptions* (i)–(v) *of Theorem 10.1,*

$$\sqrt{nb_n^2}\left(\widehat{\rho}_n - \rho_0\right) \xrightarrow{d} \mathcal{N}(\mathbf{0}, \boldsymbol{\Sigma}),$$

where $\boldsymbol{\Sigma}$ *is a diagonal matrix with components*

$$\boldsymbol{\Sigma}^{(k,k)} = \frac{f_k(z_k) \int K^2(y_k)\, dy_k}{u^2(z_k, \rho_{0,k}(z_k))\psi^2(z_k, \rho_{0,k}(z_k))},$$

where $k = 1, \ldots, p(p-1)/2$ *runs over all pairs of variables,* f_k *is the corresponding bivariate marginal density of the pair* $\mathbf{Z}_k = (Z_i, Z_j)$, ψ *is defined in Eq.* (9.5), *and* u *is defined immediately after Eq.* (10.8).

Proceeding as in Chapter 9, we may apply the δ-method to obtain an expression for the asymptotic variance of the conditional density estimate.

Theorem 10.3. *Let* $\{\mathbf{X}_t\}$ *be a strictly stationary process with density function* $f_{\mathbf{X}}(\mathbf{x})$. *Partition* $\mathbf{X}$ *into* $\mathbf{X}_1 = (X_1, \ldots, X_k)^T$ *and* $\mathbf{X}_2 = (X_{k+1}, \ldots, X_p)^T$, *and let* $\widehat{f}_{\mathbf{X}_1|\mathbf{X}_2}(\mathbf{x}_1|\mathbf{X}_2 = \mathbf{x}_2)$ *be the estimate of the conditional density* $f_{\mathbf{X}_1|\mathbf{X}_2}$ *obtained using the procedure in Section 10.2 in the particular case where transformation* (9.1) *to marginally standard normal variables is exactly known. Then, under assumptions* (i)–(v) *of Theorem 10.1 and assumption*

(vi) *the estimates of the marginal densities and quantile functions that are used for the back-transformations in* (10.7) *are asymptotically normal with convergence rates faster than* $(nb^2)^{-1}$,

$$\sqrt{nb_n^2}\left(\widehat{f}_{\mathbf{X}_1|\mathbf{X}_2}(\mathbf{x}_1|\mathbf{X}_2 = \mathbf{x}_2) - f_0(\mathbf{x}_1|\mathbf{X}_2 = \mathbf{x}_2)\right)$$
$$\xrightarrow{d} \mathcal{N}\left(0, \psi^*(\mathbf{z}; \boldsymbol{\mu}_0^*, \boldsymbol{\Sigma}_0^*)^2 g(\mathbf{x}_1)^2 \mathbf{u}^T(\mathbf{z}; \boldsymbol{\mu}_0^*, \boldsymbol{\Sigma}_0^*)\, \boldsymbol{\Sigma}\, \mathbf{u}(\mathbf{z}; \boldsymbol{\mu}_0^*, \boldsymbol{\Sigma}_0^*)\right),$$

where

$$g(\mathbf{x}_1) = \prod_{i=1}^{k} f_i(x_i)/\phi(z_i),$$
$$\mathbf{z} = \{z_i\}_{i=1,\ldots,p} = \{\Phi^{-1}(F_i(x_i))\}_{i=1,\ldots,p},$$

and $\mathbf{u}(\mathbf{z}) = \nabla \log \psi^*(\mathbf{z}, \boldsymbol{\mu}_0^*, \boldsymbol{\Sigma}_0^*)$ *with the gradient taken with respect to the vector of local correlations.*

This result follows directly from the δ-method and the proof of Theorem 9.4. We will analyze some key factors in the expression for the above asymptotic variance when we introduce the local *partial* Gaussian correlation in the next chapter.

Finally, we state Theorem 9.5 in the context of conditional density estimation, which again follows directly from Theorem 4.5.

Theorem 10.4. *Suppose that*

(i) *we produce marginally Gaussian pseudo observations* $\widehat{\mathbf{Z}}_t = \{\Phi^{-1}(\widehat{F}_{it}(X_{it}))\}_{i=1}^p$ *using transformation* (9.1) *by means of the marginal empirical distribution functions*

$$\widehat{F}_i(x_i) = \frac{1}{n}\sum_{j=1}^{n} I\{X_{ij} \le x_i\}$$

(where $1/n$ *may be replaced by* $1/(n+1)$ *for* n *small or moderate), and*

(ii) *the kernel function* K *has bounded support.*

Then Theorems 10.1–10.3 still hold when replacing $\{\mathbf{Z}_t\}$ *with* $\{\widehat{\mathbf{Z}}_t\}$.

10.4 Examples

10.4.1 Stock data

Let us continue to analyze the time series data considered in Section 9.5 that record the monthly total market return in the US and Norwegian stock markets, as well as returns on the prices of North Sea oil and gold, but this time from a prediction perspective. We delete the final observation in the data set (made on June 1, 2018) and rather try to make predictions about the return in the Norwegian stock market, R_{NO}, in the next month (observed on June 1) based on observations made at or before May 1, 2018.

Tools of every flavor for predicting moments and quantiles in predictive distributions exist in abundance in the time series literature. However, the conditional density estimator derived in the present chapter produces estimates of the full conditional density, from which all such quantities may be subsequently derived. Although several non-parametric and semiparametric density estimators have been developed over the last couple of decades (see Section 10.1 for references), to our knowledge, only one is readily available to the R-user who does not accept the restriction that either $\mathbf{X}_1$ or $\mathbf{X}_2$ are scalar, namely, the cross-validated kernel approach by Hall et al. (2004), which is available in R through the `np`-package (Hayfield and Racine, 2008). This method also accepts discrete variables.

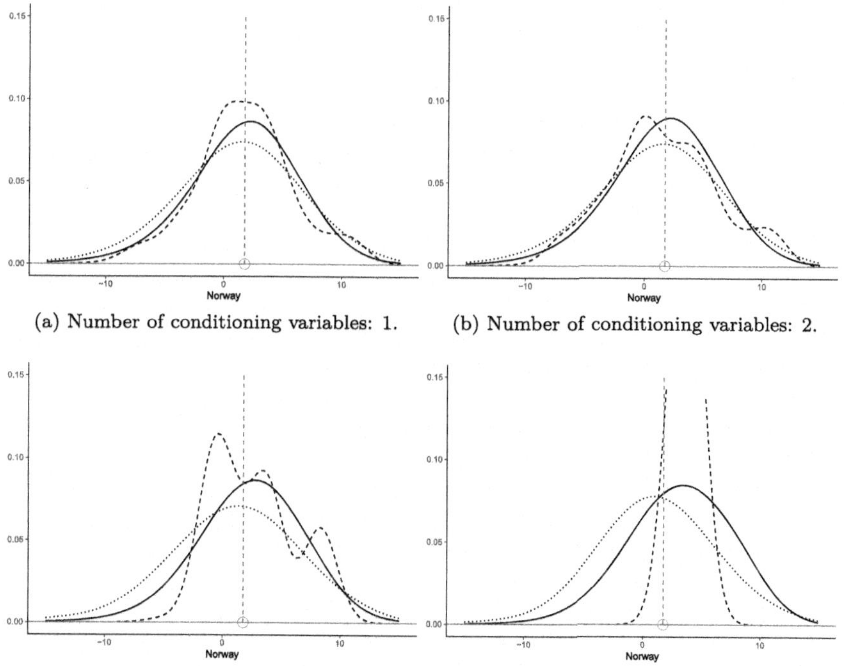

(a) Number of conditioning variables: 1.

(b) Number of conditioning variables: 2.

(c) Number of conditioning variables: 4.

(d) Number of conditioning variables: 8.

Figure 10.1 Conditional density estimates of $R_{NO,\text{ JUNE 2018}}$ for various sets of conditioning variables. The solid line is the locally Gaussian conditional density estimator, the dashed line is a naive kernel density estimator, and the dotted line is the Hall et al. (2004) estimator.

Consider first the simplest case where we use the data to estimate the predictive density of $R_{NO,\text{ JUNE 2018}}$ given $R_{NO,\text{ MAY 2018}} = 6.23\%$. For this application, we use the plugin bandwidths $b = 2.5 \cdot n^{-1/6}$ for the locally Gaussian estimator. See Fig. 10.1a for a plot of the estimate along with the Hall et al. (2004) estimate. The blue circle and vertical dotted line indicate the value that was actually observed, $R_{NO,\text{ JUNE 2018}} = 1.76\%$.

To demonstrate some potential disastrous effects of careless applications of the kernel estimator in multivariate problems, we include the case where we replace the numerator and denominator of (10.1) with all bandwidth matrices, somewhat arbitrarily, chosen to have the value 2 on its diagonal and zero elsewhere. In Figs. 10.1b–d, we increase the set of conditioning variables and fix each to the values observed on May 1, 2018, as detailed in Table 10.1. We see that the cross-validated Hall et al. (2004) estimator

Table 10.1 Conditioning sets.

	$R_{\text{NO},t-1}$	$R_{\text{NO},t-2}$	$R_{\text{US},t-1}$	$R_{\text{US},t-2}$	$R_{\text{Oil},t-1}$	$R_{\text{Oil},t-2}$	$R_{\text{Gold},t-1}$	$R_{\text{Gold},t-2}$
Fig. 10.1a	6.23%	—	—	—	—	—	—	—
Fig. 10.1b	6.23%	—	2.74%	—	—	—	—	—
Fig. 10.1c	6.23%	—	2.74%	—	8.12%	—	−2.63%	—
Fig. 10.1d	6.23%	0.13%	2.74%	−3.48%	8.12%	7.18%	−2.63%	2.53%

and the local Gaussian approximation provide reasonable predictive distributions, also in the high-dimensional cases. The "naive" kernel estimator, on the other hand, struggles when the number of covariates increases to 4 and even more so when we have 8 conditioning variables, in particular, in the tails.

10.4.2 Simulations

10.4.2.1 Simulated data with relevant variables

In this section, we investigate the sensitivity of various methods with respect to the number of explanatory variables in the problem and begin by presenting some simulation experiments in which we generate data from test distributions, measure the integrated squared error (ISE) of our conditional density estimate, and compare it with the two natural competitors, which are readily available for implementation: the naïve approach, where the numerator and denominator of (10.1) are estimated separately using the multivariate kernel estimator with the plugin bandwidth selector of Wand and Jones (1994) and the specialized kernel method by Hall et al. (2004), which we denote by the name of the software package written in the R programming language by which it can be calculated, `np` (Hayfield and Racine, 2008).

The first test distribution has standard exponentially distributed margins, and the dependence structure is defined by the Joe copula (see, e.g., Nelsen, 1999, p. 116, distribution 6) with parameter $\theta = 3.83$, which corresponds to a Kendall's tau of 0.6 between all pairs of variables. For each dimension p ranging from 2 to 6, we generate $2^7 = 128$ data sets and estimate the conditional density of $X_1|X_2 = \cdots = X_p = c$, with c being equal to 1, 2, and 3 in this example. We calculate the ISE of the density estimates numerically over 2000 equally spaced grid points and graph the mean of the estimated errors as a function of the dimension for two different sample sizes ($n = 250$ and $n = 1000$); see Fig. 10.2.

The basic kernel estimator performs well in the center of the distribution, especially, in the example with sample size 1000. However, when we condition on values that are farther out in tail, it quickly deteriorates as the dimension increases. This behavior is of course expected because of the curse of dimensionality. The `np`-estimator is clearly a major improvement to naïve kernel estimation of conditional densities, but in this example, we see that the LGDE approach is the overall best performer. It matches the purely non-parametric methods in lower-dimensional cases but also boasts

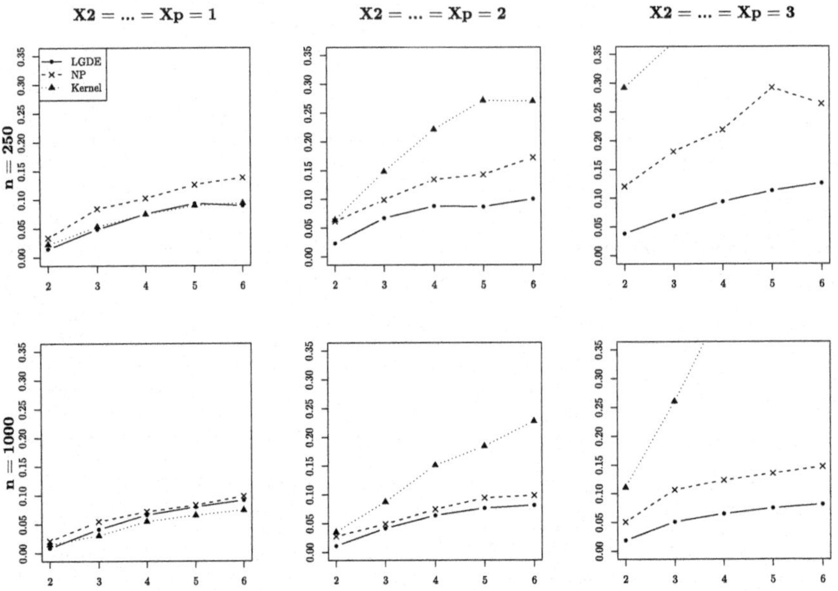

Figure 10.2 The integrated squared error of conditional density estimates of $f_{X_1|X_2,\ldots,X_p}$ as a function of p, generated from a density with exponential margins and a Joe copula with Kendall's tau equal to 0.6.

a greater robustness against increasing dimensionality than its competitors. The tail behavior of the LGDE is much better than that of the other two methods. It is governed by a Gaussian distribution, which again is determined locally by the behavior of $f_{X_1|X_2,\ldots,X_p}$ in the tail.

10.4.3 Simulated data from a heavy-tailed distribution

Otneim and Tjøstheim (2017) show that the unconditional version of the LGDE does not work very well when fitted to the heavy-tailed $t(4)$-distribution. The reason for this is not entirely clear, but one explanation is that the cross-validated bandwidths are too small. The conditional version of the LGDE also starts to struggle when presented with data from this distribution, as can be seen in Fig. 10.3. We expect that using the t-distribution in the same pairwise and local manner as we use the Gaussian distribution here will improve this fit. The conditional density estimator by Hall et al. (2004) is the best alternative in this case if the explanatory variables are not in the center of the distribution.

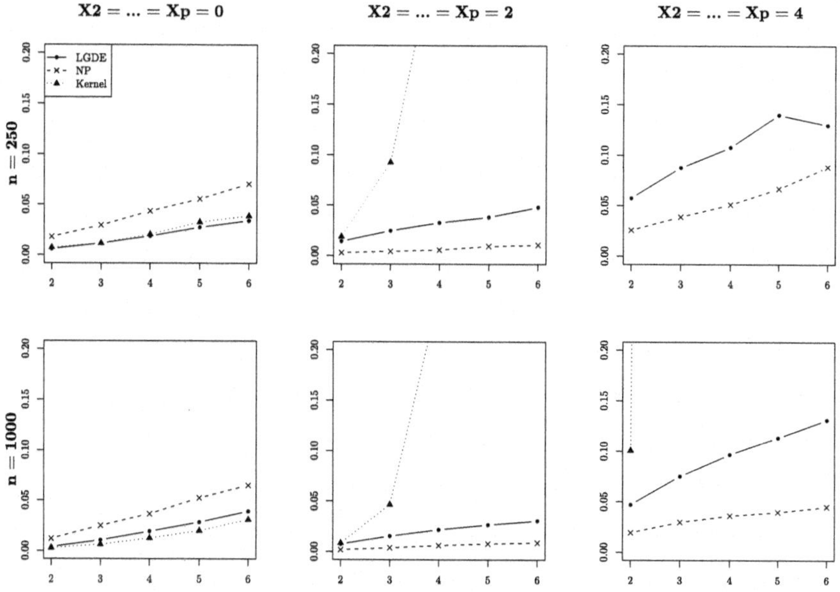

Figure 10.3 The integrated squared error of conditional density estimates of $f_{X_1|X_2,\dots,X_p}$ as a function of p, generated from the multivariate t-distribution with 4 degrees of freedom.

10.4.4 Simulated data with irrelevant variables

One challenge in estimating conditional densities is to discover, and take account of, independence between variables. We have not addressed this problem explicitly in the derivation of our estimator, contrary to the np-estimator by Hall et al. (2004), which automatically smooths irrelevant variables away. However, in our next example, most of the explanatory variables are independent from the response variable, but they are mutually dependent themselves. In the two-dimensional case with $\boldsymbol{X} = (X_1, X_2)$, we generate data from a bivariate distribution with log-normal margins assembled using the t-copula with 10 degrees of freedom. For all dimensions greater than two, the remaining variables $X_3, \dots, X_p$ are drawn from a multivariate t-distribution with 5 degrees of freedom, but independent from (X_1, X_2).

It turns out that our approach handles this case very well, see Fig. 10.4. None of the methods has errors that grow sharply with the dimension, which indicates that they more or less ignore the extra noise that the extra dimensions contain. However, the LGDE-method is clearly the best according to this particular choice of error measure. The explanation for this

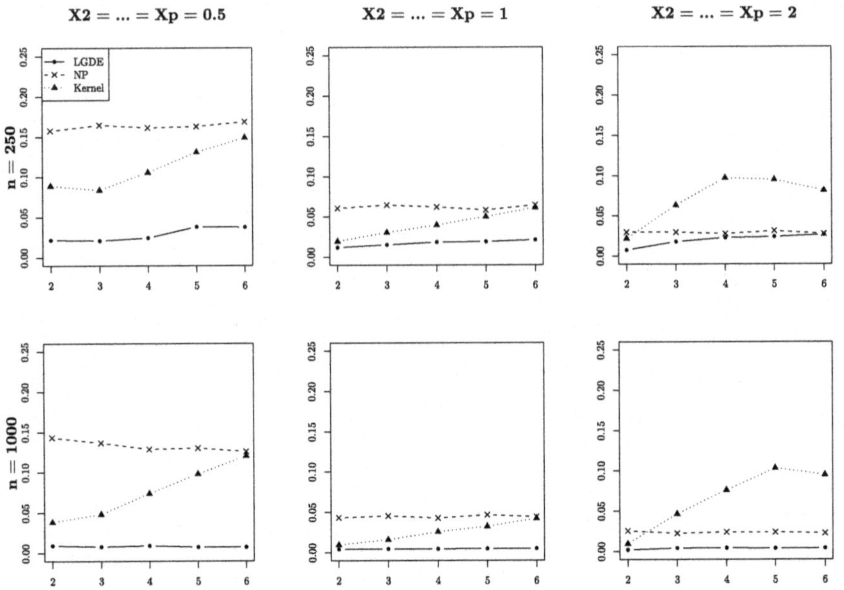

Figure 10.4 The integrated squared error of conditional density estimates of $f_{X_1|X_2,\ldots,X_p}$ as a function of p, generated from a density in which the first two variables are marginally log-normal with a $t(10)$-copula, and the rest of the variables are multivariate $t(5)$-distributed, independently from (X_1, X_2).

is the equivalence between the independence and the zero local correlation between marginally Gaussian Z-variables, which in turn means that, by construction, variables that are independent from the response variable will have very little influence in the final conditional density estimate.

10.5 Proof of theorems

10.5.1 Proof of Theorem 10.1

Except a slight modification that accounts for the replacement of independence with α-mixing, the proof of Theorem 10.1 is identical to the corresponding proof of Theorem 9.1, which again is based on the global maximum likelihood case covered by Severini (2000). For each location $\boldsymbol{z}$, which we suppress from notation for simplicity, denote by $\mathrm{E}(L_{\boldsymbol{b}_n,K}(\rho))$ the expectation of the local likelihood function $L_n(\rho, \boldsymbol{Z})$. The consistency follows from the uniform convergence in probability of $L_n(\rho, \boldsymbol{Z})$ toward $\mathrm{E}(L\boldsymbol{b}_n, K(\rho))$, conditions for which are provided in Corollary 2.2 by Newey (1991).

The result requires a compact support of the parameter space, the equicontinuity, and Lipschitz continuity of the family of functions $\{\mathrm{E}(L_{\boldsymbol{b}_n,K}(\rho))\}$ as well as the pointwise convergence of the local likelihood functions. The compactness is covered by assumption (iv), and the demonstration of equicontinuity and Lipschitz continuity in the proof of Theorem 9.1 does not rely on the independent data assumption. The pointwise convergence follows from a standard non-parametric law of large numbers in the independent case. However, our assumption (ii) about α-mixing data ensures that pointwise convergence still holds; see, for example, Theorem 1 by Irle (1997), conditions for which are straightforward to verify in our local likelihood setting. □

10.5.2 Proof of Theorem 10.2

Consider first the bivariate case, in which there is only one local correlation to estimate. The first part of the proof goes through exactly as in the iid case in Theorem 9.2 of Chapter 9. We follow the argument for global maximum likelihood estimators as presented in Theorem 7.63 by Schervish (1995). The statement of Theorem 10.2 follows provided that

$$Y_n(\boldsymbol{z}) = \sum_{t=1}^{n} K_{\boldsymbol{b}_n}(\boldsymbol{z}_t - \boldsymbol{z})\, u(\boldsymbol{z}_t, \rho_0) \stackrel{\text{def}}{=} \sum_{t=1}^{n} V_{nt} \tag{10.9}$$

is asymptotically normal, and this follows from a standard Taylor expansion. In the iid case, the limiting distribution of (10.9) is derived using the same technique as when demonstrating the asymptotic normality for the standard kernel estimator, for example, as in the proof of Theorem 1A by Parzen (1962). We establish the asymptotic normality of (10.9) in the case of α-mixing data by going through the steps used in proving Theorem 2.22 in Fan and Yao (2003). Let $W_t = b_n^{-1} V_{nt}$, where b_n is the component bandwidth in $\boldsymbol{B}_n = \mathrm{diag}(\boldsymbol{b}_n)$. Then

$$\begin{aligned}\frac{1}{nb_n^2}\mathrm{Var}(Y_n(\boldsymbol{z})) &= \frac{1}{nb_n^2}\left\{\sum_{t=1}^{n}\mathrm{Var}(V_{nt}) + 2\sum\sum\nolimits_{1\le t<s\le n}\mathrm{Cov}(V_{nt}, V_{ns})\right\}\\ &= \mathrm{Var}(W_1) + 2\sum_{s=1}^{n}(1 - s/n)\mathrm{Cov}(W_1, W_{s+1}),\end{aligned}$$

where

$$\mathrm{Var}(W_1) = \mathrm{E}(W_1^2) - (\mathrm{E}(W_1))^2$$

$$= \int b_n^{-2} u^2(\boldsymbol{z}, \rho_0) K^2(b_n^{-1}(\boldsymbol{y} - \boldsymbol{z})) f(\boldsymbol{y})\, \mathrm{d}\boldsymbol{y} + O(b_n^2)$$
$$= \int u^2(\boldsymbol{z} + b_n \boldsymbol{v}, \rho_0) K^2(\boldsymbol{v}) f(\boldsymbol{z} + b_n \boldsymbol{v})\, \mathrm{d}\boldsymbol{v} + O(b_n^2)$$
$$\to u^2(\boldsymbol{z}, \rho_0) f(\boldsymbol{z}) \int K^2(\boldsymbol{v})\, \mathrm{d}\boldsymbol{v} \stackrel{\text{def}}{=} M(\boldsymbol{z}) \text{ as } b_n \to 0,$$

and

$$|\mathrm{Cov}(W_1, W_{s+1})| = |\mathrm{E}(W_1 W_{s+1}) - \mathrm{E}(W_1)\mathrm{E}(W_{s+1})| = O(b_n^2)$$

using the same argument. Therefore

$$\left| \sum_{s=1}^{m_n} \mathrm{Cov}(W_1, W_{s+1}) \right| = O(m_n b_n^2).$$

Fan and Yao (2003) require that

$$\mathrm{E}(u(\boldsymbol{Z}_t, \rho_0(\boldsymbol{z}))^{\delta}) < \infty \tag{10.10}$$

for some $\delta > 2$, and this is of course true for our transformed data, because it is marginally normal. In Proposition 2.5(i) by Fan and Yao (2003), we can therefore use $p = q = \delta > 2$ to obtain, for some constant C,

$$|\mathrm{Cov}(W_1, W_{s+1})| \leq C\alpha(s)^{1-2/\delta} b_n^{4/\delta - 2}.$$

Let $m_n = (b_n^2 |\log b_n^2|)^{-1}$. Then $m_n \to \infty$, $m_n b_n^2 \to 0$, and

$$\sum_{s=m_n+1}^{n-1} |\mathrm{Cov}(W_1, W_{s+1})| \leq C \frac{b_n^{4/\delta-2}}{m_n^{\lambda}} \sum_{s=m_n+1}^{n} s^{\lambda} \alpha(s)^{1-2/\delta} \to 0,$$

which follows from assumption (ii). Thus

$$\sum_{s=1}^{n-1} \mathrm{Cov}(W_1, W_{s+1}) \to 0,$$

and it follows that

$$\frac{1}{n b_n^2} \mathrm{Var}(Y_n(\boldsymbol{z})) = M(\boldsymbol{z})(1 + o(1)).$$

The proof now continues exactly as in Fan and Yao (2003) using the "big block–small block" technique, but with the obvious replacement of b_n by b_n^2 to accommodate the bivariate case.

We expand the argument to the multivariate case using the Cramér–Wold device. Let $\boldsymbol{\rho} = (\rho_1, \ldots, \rho_m)^T$ be the vector of local correlations, where $m = p(p-1)/2$, write $\boldsymbol{u}(\boldsymbol{z}, \boldsymbol{\rho}_0) = (u_1(\boldsymbol{z}, \boldsymbol{\rho}_0), \ldots, u_m(\boldsymbol{z}, \boldsymbol{\rho}_0))$, and let $\boldsymbol{S}_n(\boldsymbol{z}) = \{S_{ni}(z)\}_{i=1}^m$, where

$$S_{ni} = \sum_{t=1}^{n} u_i(\boldsymbol{Z}_t, \boldsymbol{\rho}_{0,i}) K_{\boldsymbol{b}_n}(\boldsymbol{Z}_t - \boldsymbol{z}).$$

We must show that

$$\sum_{k=1}^{m} a_k S_{nk} \xrightarrow{d} \sum_{k=1}^{m} a_k Z_k^*, \tag{10.11}$$

where $\boldsymbol{a} = (a_1, \ldots, a_m)^T$ is an arbitrary vector of constants, and $\boldsymbol{Z}^* = (Z_1^*, \ldots, Z_m^*)$ is a jointly normally distributed random vector. It suffices to show that the left-hand side of (10.11) is asymptotically normal, and this follows from observing that it is of the same form as the original sequence comprising S_n with

$$\sum_k a_k S_{nk} = \sum_t \boldsymbol{u}^*(Z_t, \boldsymbol{\rho}_0) K_{\boldsymbol{b}_n}(\boldsymbol{Z}_t - \boldsymbol{z}),$$

where $\boldsymbol{u}^*(\boldsymbol{Z}_t, \boldsymbol{\rho}_0) = \sum_k a_k u_k(\boldsymbol{Z}_t, \boldsymbol{\rho}_0)$. It is well known that any measurable mapping of a mixing sequence of random variables inherit the mixing properties of the original series, so condition (ii) is therefore satisfied by the linear combination. The new sequence of observations satisfies (10.10) because it follows from Jensen's inequality that for any even integer $\delta > 2$ (making the function $f(x) = x^\delta$ convex),

$$\left[\frac{\boldsymbol{u}^*(\boldsymbol{Z}_t, \boldsymbol{\rho}_0)}{\sum_k a_k}\right]^\delta = \left[\frac{\sum_k a_k u_k(\boldsymbol{Z}_t, \boldsymbol{\rho}_0)}{\sum_k a_k}\right]^\delta \leq \frac{\sum_k a_k [u_k(\boldsymbol{Z}_t, \boldsymbol{\rho}_0)]^\delta}{\sum_k a_k},$$

so that

$$\mathrm{E}[u^*(\boldsymbol{Z}_t, \boldsymbol{\rho}_0)]^\delta \leq \sum_k a_k \mathrm{E}[u_k(\boldsymbol{Z}_t, \boldsymbol{\rho}_0)]^\delta \left[\sum_k a_k\right]^{\delta-1} < \infty.$$

Hence condition (10.10) is fulfilled, and the results follow from Theorem 2.22 in Fan and Yao (2003).

The off-diagonal elements in the asymptotic covariance matrix are asymptotically zero by the same arguments as in the proof of Theorem 9.3 in Chapter 9. □

References

Bashtannyk, D.M., Hyndman, R.J., 2001. Bandwidth selection for kernel conditional density estimation. Computational Statistics & Data Analysis 36 (3), 279–298.

Chen, X., Linton, O.B., 2001. The estimation of conditional densities. LSE STICERD Research Paper No. EM415.

Fan, J., Yao, Q., 2003. Nonlinear Time Series. Nonparametric and Parametric Methods. Springer.

Fan, J., Yao, Q., Tong, H., 1996. Estimation of conditional densities and sensitivity measures in nonlinear dynamical systems. Biometrika 83 (1), 189–206.

Fan, J., Yim, T.H., 2004. A crossvalidation method for estimating conditional densities. Biometrika 91 (4), 819–834.

Faugeras, O.P., 2009. A quantile-copula approach to conditional density estimation. Journal of Multivariate Analysis 100 (9), 2083–2099.

Geenens, G., Charpentier, A., Paindaveine, D., 2017. Probit transformation for nonparametric kernel estimation of the copula density. Bernoulli 23 (3), 1848–1873.

Hall, P., Racine, J.S., Li, Q., 2004. Cross-validation and the estimation of conditional probability densities. Journal of the American Statistical Association 99 (468), 1015–1026.

Hayfield, T., Racine, J.S., 2008. Nonparametric econometrics: the np package. Journal of Statistical Software 27, 1–32.

Hyndman, R.J., Bashtannyk, D.M., Grunwald, G.K., 1996. Estimating and visualizing conditional densities. Journal of Computational and Graphical Statistics 5 (4), 315–336.

Hyndman, R.J., Yao, Q., 2002. Nonparametric estimation and symmetry tests for conditional density functions. Journal of Nonparametric Statistics 14 (3), 259–278.

Irle, A., 1997. On consistency in nonparametric estimation under mixing conditions. Journal of Multivariate Analysis 60 (1), 123–147.

Johnson, R.A., Wichern, D.W., 2007. Applied Multivariate Statistical Analysis. Pearson Education.

Nelsen, R.B., 1999. An Introduction to Copulas. Springer, New York.

Newey, W.K., 1991. Uniform convergence in probability and stochastic equicontinuity. Econometrica 59 (4), 1161–1167.

Otneim, H., Tjøstheim, D., 2017. The locally Gaussian density estimator for multivariate data. Statistics and Computing 27 (6), 1595–1616.

Parzen, E., 1962. On estimation of a probability density function and mode. Annals of Mathematical Statistics 33 (3), 1065–1076.

Rosenblatt, M., 1969. Conditional probability density and regression estimators. Multivariate Analysis II 25, 31.

Schervish, M.J., 1995. Theory of Statistics. Springer.

Severini, T.A., 2000. Likelihood Methods in Statistics. Oxford Science Publications. Oxford University Press.

Wand, M., Jones, M., 1994. Multivariate plug-in bandwidth selection. Computational Statistics 9 (2), 97–116.

CHAPTER 11

The local Gaussian partial correlation

Contents

11.1. Introduction 353
11.2. The local Gaussian partial correlation 354
  11.2.1 Definition 355
11.3. Properties 358
11.4. Estimation of the LGPC by local likelihood 360
  11.4.1 Estimation of $\boldsymbol{R}(\boldsymbol{z})$ when $p = 3$ and $\boldsymbol{X}^{(2)}$ is a scalar 361
  11.4.2 Estimation of $\boldsymbol{R}(\boldsymbol{z})$ when $\boldsymbol{X}^{(2)}$ is a vector 361
11.5. Asymptotic theory 362
11.6. Examples 365
11.7. Testing for conditional independence 370
  11.7.1 The recent fauna of nonparametric tests 370
  11.7.2 A test for conditional independence 372
  11.7.3 Comparing with other tests 373
11.8. The multivariate LGPC 376
  11.8.1 Definition 376
  11.8.2 Some particular cases 378
References 382

11.1 Introduction

Estimation of *conditional* dependence and testing for *conditional* independence are important topics in classical and modern statistics. In the last two decades, for instance, there have been intense developments in using conditional dependence for probabilistic networks, multivariate time series analysis, and copula analysis. In this chapter, we extend the ideas from Chapters 4 and 7 regarding the measurement of dependence and testing for independence to their conditional counterparts, using a parallel motivation. For jointly Gaussian variables $\boldsymbol{X} = (X_1, \ldots, X_p)^T$, the conditional dependence between some subset of variables $\boldsymbol{X}_1$ and a second subset $\boldsymbol{X}_2$ given a third subset $\boldsymbol{X}_3$ is fully described by the *partial* correlation matrix. In general, for non-Gaussian populations, this will not suffice for the same reasons we have discussed before, and we will therefore introduce the *local* Gaussian partial correlation (LGPC), which serves as a general measure of

Statistical Modeling using Local Gaussian Approximation
https://doi.org/10.1016/B978-0-12-815861-6.00018-3

conditional dependence and subsequently as a basis for a test for conditional independence.

The LGPC retains all the properties of the ordinary partial correlation in the Gaussian case but seeks to avoid the weaknesses of this measure in the non-Gaussian case. This is again done by fitting a family of Gaussian distributions to a given continuous multivariate distribution and exploiting simple conditioning rules of the Gaussian distribution locally in the same way as in Chapter 10.2. The LGPC, being directly related to the ordinary partial correlation, is easy to interpret and reduces to the very same ordinary partial correlation in the Gaussian case. Moreover, it distinguishes between positive and negative conditional dependence, whereas competing non-linear measures report only the *strength* of the conditional dependence on some non-negative scale. The local view again gives much more flexibility. It allows the conditional dependence to be stronger or weaker in certain regions of a multivariate distribution than in the others. This is of particular interest in finance, where description of tail behavior is important, and we will see practical examples of this. The bulk of this chapter is based on Otneim and Tjøstheim (2021), most of the technical details of which are presented in an online supplement of that paper.

11.2 The local Gaussian partial correlation

Let $\boldsymbol{X} = (X_1, \ldots, X_p)^T$ be a random vector. Denote by $(\boldsymbol{X}_1, \boldsymbol{X}_2, \boldsymbol{X}_3)$ a partition of $\boldsymbol{X}$ into vectors of dimensions p_1, p_2, and p_3, respectively, such that $\boldsymbol{X}^{(1)} = (\boldsymbol{X}_1, \boldsymbol{X}_2) = (X_1, \ldots, X_{p_1+p_2})^T$ consists of the first $p_1 + p_2$ components in $\boldsymbol{X}$, and $\boldsymbol{X}^{(2)} = \boldsymbol{X}_3 = (X_{p_1+p_2+1}, \ldots, X_{p_1+p_2+p_3})^T$ contains the remaining p_3 variables, where $p = p_1 + p_2 + p_3$. We assume that the mean vector $\boldsymbol{\mu}$ and covariance matrix $\boldsymbol{\Sigma}$ of $\boldsymbol{X}$ exist and partition them correspondingly writing

$$\boldsymbol{\mu} = \begin{pmatrix} \boldsymbol{\mu}_1 \\ \boldsymbol{\mu}_2 \\ \boldsymbol{\mu}_3 \end{pmatrix} \quad \text{and} \quad \boldsymbol{\Sigma} = \begin{pmatrix} \boldsymbol{\Sigma}_{11} & \boldsymbol{\Sigma}_{12} & \boldsymbol{\Sigma}_{13} \\ \boldsymbol{\Sigma}_{21} & \boldsymbol{\Sigma}_{22} & \boldsymbol{\Sigma}_{23} \\ \boldsymbol{\Sigma}_{31} & \boldsymbol{\Sigma}_{32} & \boldsymbol{\Sigma}_{33} \end{pmatrix}, \tag{11.1}$$

where $\boldsymbol{\Sigma}_{ij}$ is the covariance matrices of $(\boldsymbol{X}_i, \boldsymbol{X}_j)$, $i, j = 1, 2, 3$. There are two main concepts of correlation when $\boldsymbol{X}^{(2)} = \boldsymbol{X}_3$ is given, the *partial* and *conditional* correlations, which coincide in several joint distributions, among them, the Gaussian. See, for example, Baba et al. (2004) for details. We will use the partial correlation as a starting point when defining the LGPC. The partial variance–covariance matrix of $\boldsymbol{X}^{(1)} = (\boldsymbol{X}_1, \boldsymbol{X}_2)$ given $\boldsymbol{X}^{(2)} = \boldsymbol{X}_3$ is

$$\boldsymbol{\Sigma}_{12|3} = \boldsymbol{\Sigma}^{11} - \boldsymbol{\Sigma}^{12}\left(\boldsymbol{\Sigma}^{22}\right)^{-1}\boldsymbol{\Sigma}^{21}, \tag{11.2}$$

where

$$\boldsymbol{\Sigma}^{11} = \begin{pmatrix} \boldsymbol{\Sigma}_{11} & \boldsymbol{\Sigma}_{12} \\ \boldsymbol{\Sigma}_{21} & \boldsymbol{\Sigma}_{22} \end{pmatrix}, \quad \boldsymbol{\Sigma}^{12} = \begin{pmatrix} \boldsymbol{\Sigma}_{13} \\ \boldsymbol{\Sigma}_{23} \end{pmatrix}, \quad \boldsymbol{\Sigma}^{21} = \begin{pmatrix} \boldsymbol{\Sigma}_{31} & \boldsymbol{\Sigma}_{32} \end{pmatrix}, \quad \text{and } \boldsymbol{\Sigma}^{22} = \boldsymbol{\Sigma}_{33},$$

and $\boldsymbol{\Sigma}_{12|3}$ is the covariance matrix in the conditional (Gaussian) distribution of $\boldsymbol{X}^{(1)}$ given $\boldsymbol{X}_3$ if $\boldsymbol{X}$ is jointly normal. The partial correlation matrix between $\boldsymbol{X}_1$ and $\boldsymbol{X}_2$ given $\boldsymbol{X}_3$ is naturally defined as

$$\boldsymbol{R}_{12|3} = \boldsymbol{D}^{-1/2}\boldsymbol{\Sigma}_{12|3}\boldsymbol{D}^{-1/2}, \tag{11.3}$$

where $\boldsymbol{D} = \text{diag}(\boldsymbol{\Sigma}_{12|3})$. We identify in the same way the partial correlation matrix (11.3) with the correlation matrix in the conditional (Gaussian) distribution of $\boldsymbol{X}^{(1)}$ given $\boldsymbol{X}^{(2)}$ if $\boldsymbol{X}$ is jointly normal. Eqs. (11.2) and (11.3) will serve as the starting point for our definition of the *local* partial correlation.

11.2.1 Definition

We further assume that the components of $\boldsymbol{X}$ are continuous with joint density function $f_{\boldsymbol{X}}$, and we again set up a local likelihood framework for obtaining local estimates of the parameters in the multivariate normal distribution. Given a point $\boldsymbol{x}$, we approximate $f_{\boldsymbol{X}}$ in a neighborhood of $\boldsymbol{x}$ by a multivariate Gaussian density

$$\psi(\boldsymbol{x}, \boldsymbol{v}) = \frac{1}{(2\pi)^{p/2}|\boldsymbol{\Sigma}(\boldsymbol{x})|^{1/2}} \exp\left\{-\frac{1}{2}(\boldsymbol{v} - \boldsymbol{\mu}(\boldsymbol{x}))^T\boldsymbol{\Sigma}^{-1}(\boldsymbol{x})(\boldsymbol{v} - \boldsymbol{\mu}(\boldsymbol{x}))\right\}, \tag{11.4}$$

where $\boldsymbol{x} = (x_1 \ldots, x_p)^T$, $\boldsymbol{\mu}(\boldsymbol{x}) = \{\mu_j(\boldsymbol{x})\}$, and $\boldsymbol{\Sigma}(\boldsymbol{x}) = \{\sigma_{jk}(\boldsymbol{x})\}$ for $j, k = 1, \ldots, p$. Moving to another point $\boldsymbol{y}$, there is another (generally, different) Gaussian approximation $\psi(\boldsymbol{y}, \boldsymbol{v})$. In this way, we approximate $f_{\boldsymbol{X}}$ by a family of multivariate Gaussian densities defined by a set of smooth parameter functions $\{\boldsymbol{\mu}(\boldsymbol{x}), \boldsymbol{\Sigma}(\boldsymbol{x})\}$, and if $f_{\boldsymbol{X}}$ is itself a Gaussian density, then the parameter functions collapse to constants corresponding to the true parameter values, and $\psi(\boldsymbol{x}) \equiv f_{\boldsymbol{X}}(\boldsymbol{x})$. Hjort and Jones (1996) provide a general framework for estimating such parameter functions non-parametrically from a given data set using a local likelihood procedure, and the basic idea in the following treatment is replacing the components in the partial covariance matrix (11.2) by their locally estimated counterparts to obtain a local measure of conditional dependence.

In this chapter, we use the same transformation technique as that introduced already in Chapter 4.7 and subsequently used in the following chapters. This improves and simplifies the estimation of the LGPC. It is shown that the estimation of the local parameter functions $\{\boldsymbol{\mu}(\boldsymbol{x}), \boldsymbol{\Sigma}(\boldsymbol{x})\}$ becomes easier by transforming each X_j to a standard normal variable $Z_j = \Phi^{-1}(U_j)$, where U_j is a uniform variable, $U_j = F_j(X_j)$ with F_j being the cumulative distribution function of X_j. Define the random vector $\boldsymbol{Z}$ by this transformation of $\boldsymbol{X} = (\boldsymbol{X}^{(1)}, \boldsymbol{X}^{(2)}) = (\boldsymbol{X}_1, \boldsymbol{X}_2, \boldsymbol{X}_3) = (X_1, X_2, \ldots, X_p)^T$ to marginal standard normality:

$$\boldsymbol{Z} = \left(\Phi^{-1}\left(F_1(X_1)\right), \Phi^{-1}\left(F_2(X_2)\right), \ldots, \Phi^{-1}\left(F_p(X_p)\right)\right)^T. \tag{11.5}$$

The transformation enables us to simplify the local Gaussian approximation (11.4) by writing the density $f_{\boldsymbol{Z}}$ of $\boldsymbol{Z}$ at the point $\boldsymbol{v} = \boldsymbol{z}$ as

$$f_{\boldsymbol{Z}}(\boldsymbol{z}) = \psi(\boldsymbol{z}, R(\boldsymbol{z})) = \frac{1}{|2\pi \boldsymbol{R}(\boldsymbol{z})|^{1/2}} \exp\left\{-\frac{1}{2}\boldsymbol{z}^T \boldsymbol{R}^{-1}(\boldsymbol{z})\boldsymbol{z}\right\}, \tag{11.6}$$

where, as in Otneim and Tjøstheim (2017, 2018) and in Eqs. (9.6) and (9.7) in Chapter 9, in a further simplified approximation, we have fixed local means and standard deviations $\mu_j(\boldsymbol{z}) \equiv 0$ and $\sigma_j^2(\boldsymbol{z}) \equiv 1$, $j = 1, \ldots, p$, and where $\boldsymbol{R}(\boldsymbol{z}) = \{\rho_{jk}(\boldsymbol{z})\}$ is the *local correlation matrix*.

In practice, we do not know F_j, but we can instead use the empirical distribution function

$$\widehat{F}_j(x) = \frac{1}{n}\sum_{i=1}^{n} I\left(X_{ji} \leq x\right),$$

where I is the indicator function, n is the number of observations, and X_{ji} is the ith observation of X_j, and where $1/n$ can be replaced by $1/(n+1)$ for small or moderate sample sizes. This results in pseudo-standard normal variables $\widehat{Z}_j = \Phi^{-1}(\widehat{F}_j(X_j))$.

In the following, we will not always distinguish between Z_j and $\widehat{Z}_j$. In fact, by using the technique of proof of Theorem 4.5 under the regularity conditions of that theorem, the error made by estimating $\boldsymbol{R}(\boldsymbol{z})$ using the empirically transformed variables $\widehat{Z}_j$ instead of Z_j is smaller in the limit than the estimation error made when estimating the local correlations themselves.

In this chapter, we refer to $\boldsymbol{X}$ and its probability density function $f_{\boldsymbol{X}}$ as being on the $\boldsymbol{x}$-scale and to $\boldsymbol{Z}$ and its probability density function $f_{\boldsymbol{Z}}$ as being on the $\boldsymbol{z}$-scale. For further discussion of the simplified $\boldsymbol{z}$-approximation, we refer to Chapters 9.2.2 and 9.7.

Denote by $(\boldsymbol{Z}^{(1)}, \boldsymbol{Z}^{(2)}) = (\boldsymbol{Z}_1, \boldsymbol{Z}_2, \boldsymbol{Z}_3)$ the partitioning of $\boldsymbol{Z}$ corresponding to the partitioning $(\boldsymbol{X}^{(1)}, \boldsymbol{X}^{(2)}) = (\boldsymbol{X}_1, \boldsymbol{X}_2, \boldsymbol{X}_3)$ of $\boldsymbol{X}$. A natural definition of the *local* partial covariance matrix of $\boldsymbol{Z}^{(1)}|\boldsymbol{Z}^{(2)}$ is the local version of Eq. (11.2):

$$\boldsymbol{\Sigma}_{12|3}(\boldsymbol{z}) = \boldsymbol{R}^{11}(\boldsymbol{z}^{(1)}) - \boldsymbol{R}^{12}(\boldsymbol{z}) \left(\boldsymbol{R}^{22}(\boldsymbol{z}^{(2)})\right)^{-1} \boldsymbol{R}^{21}(\boldsymbol{z}). \tag{11.7}$$

If $p_1 = p_2 = 1$, then $\boldsymbol{\Sigma}_{12|3}(\boldsymbol{z})$ is a 2×2 matrix, and we define the local Gaussian partial correlation $\alpha(\boldsymbol{z})$ between the two variables in $\boldsymbol{Z}^{(1)} = (Z_1, Z_2)$ given $\boldsymbol{Z}^{(2)} = \boldsymbol{Z}_3$ in accordance with the ordinary (global) partial correlation provided by Eq. (11.3):

$$\alpha(\boldsymbol{z}) = R_{12|3}(\boldsymbol{z}) = \frac{\left\{\boldsymbol{\Sigma}_{12|3}(\boldsymbol{z})\right\}_{12}}{\left\{\boldsymbol{\Sigma}_{12|3}(\boldsymbol{z})\right\}_{11}^{1/2}\left\{\boldsymbol{\Sigma}_{12|3}(\boldsymbol{z})\right\}_{22}^{1/2}}, \tag{11.8}$$

which, when $\boldsymbol{Z}^{(2)} = Z_3$ is scalar, reduces to

$$\alpha(\boldsymbol{z}) = \rho_{12|3}(z_1, z_2|z_3) = \frac{\rho_{12}(z_1, z_2) - \rho_{13}(z_1, z_3)\rho_{23}(z_2, z_3)}{\sqrt{1 - \rho_{13}^2(z_1, z_3)}\sqrt{1 - \rho_{23}^2(z_2, z_3)}}. \tag{11.9}$$

This is easily recognizable as a local version of the standard global partial correlation coefficient. It is of course possible to introduce an LGPC $\alpha(\boldsymbol{x})$ directly on the $\boldsymbol{x}$-scale, but that representation is in many ways harder to handle both computationally and asymptotically. For a multivariate Gaussian distribution, we have that $\alpha_{\boldsymbol{X}}(\boldsymbol{x}) = \alpha_{\boldsymbol{Z}}(\boldsymbol{z}) = \alpha$. In the remainder of this chapter, we write mainly in terms of the $\boldsymbol{z}$-representation using the LGPC $\alpha(\boldsymbol{z}) = \alpha_{\boldsymbol{Z}}(\boldsymbol{z})$, but when we write the local partial correlation between X_1 and X_2 given $\boldsymbol{X}_3 = \boldsymbol{x}_3$ at the point $(x_1, x_2, \boldsymbol{x}_3)$, this is simply $\alpha(\boldsymbol{z})$ with inserted $z_j = \Phi^{-1}(F_j(x_j)), j = 1, \ldots, p$.

In the more general case where $p_1 > 1$ and/or $p_2 > 1$, $\boldsymbol{\Sigma}_{12|3}(\boldsymbol{z})$ is a $(p_1 + p_2) \times (p_1 + p_2)$ matrix that describes the non-linear conditional dependence among the variables in $\boldsymbol{Z}^{(1)} = (\boldsymbol{Z}_1, \boldsymbol{Z}_2)$ given $\boldsymbol{Z}^{(2)} = \boldsymbol{Z}_3$ (or, alternatively, $\boldsymbol{X}^{(1)} = (\boldsymbol{X}_1, \boldsymbol{X}_2)$ given $\boldsymbol{X}^{(2)} = \boldsymbol{X}_3$), which in particular can be used to analyze the conditional dependence between two *sets* of random variables of dimensions p_1 and p_2, respectively, given a third set of variables of dimension p_3. This case poses no conceptual challenges to our approach, but it requires a rather large investment in new notation and does not lead to simple formulas like Eq. (11.9). We will therefore, for the most part, focus on the local Gaussian partial correlation between two stochastic scalar variables in the remainder of this chapter. A complete description of the general multivariate case can be found in the online supplement of Otneim and Tjøstheim (2021) and, somewhat briefly, in Section 11.8.

11.3 Properties

The local Gaussian partial correlation is closely related to the partial correlation between jointly normally distributed variables. We see this also from the following properties, valid under the simplification in Eq. (11.6):

1. The LGPC $\alpha(\boldsymbol{z})$ satisfies $-1 \leq \alpha(\boldsymbol{z}) \leq 1$.
2. If $\boldsymbol{X}$ is jointly normally distributed, then the LGPC coincides with the ordinary (global) partial correlation.
3. For stochastic vectors having joint density function on $\boldsymbol{z}$-scale of the form (11.6), the LGPC $\alpha(\boldsymbol{z})$ is identically equal to zero if and only if X_1 and X_2 are conditionally independent given $\boldsymbol{X}_3$. Note that $\alpha(\boldsymbol{z}) \equiv 0$ if and only if $\alpha(\boldsymbol{x}) \equiv 0$.
4. The LGPC $\alpha(\boldsymbol{z})$ is invariant with regard to a set of monotone transformations $\boldsymbol{Y} = \boldsymbol{h}(\boldsymbol{X}) = (h_1(X_1), \ldots, h_p(X_p))$.

Property 1 is trivially true if $\boldsymbol{R}(\boldsymbol{z})$ is a valid correlation matrix. By removing the $\boldsymbol{z}$-dependence in the local correlations it follows immediately from Eq. (11.6) and from the results referred to in Section 11.2.1 that property 2 holds.

To see that conditional independence between X_1 and X_2 given $\boldsymbol{X}_3$ is equivalent to $\alpha(\boldsymbol{z}) \equiv 0$ or, equivalently, to $\alpha(\boldsymbol{x}) \equiv 0$, we need to follow a few simple steps that would also work in the global Gaussian case. Working on the standard normal $\boldsymbol{z}$-scale and assuming that $(Z_1, Z_2, \boldsymbol{Z}_3)$ has a density function $f_Z(\boldsymbol{z})$ as in (11.6), it follows from Otneim and Tjøstheim (2018) (or see Chapter 10.2) that we can calculate conditional distributions in the same way as in the global Gaussian case. For example, the conditional density of $Z_1|\boldsymbol{Z}_3$ at the point $(z_1, \boldsymbol{z}_3)$ is given by

$$f_{Z_1|\boldsymbol{Z}_3}(z_1|\boldsymbol{z}_3) = \frac{1}{(2\pi)^{1/2}\sigma_{1|3}(z_1)} \times \exp\left\{-\frac{1}{2}\left(\frac{z_1 - \mu_{1|3}(z_1)}{\sigma_{1|3}(z_1)}\right)^2\right\},$$

where

$$\mu_{1|3}(z_1) = \boldsymbol{R}_{12}(z_1, \boldsymbol{z}_3)\boldsymbol{R}_{22}(\boldsymbol{z}_3)^{-1}\boldsymbol{z}_3 \text{ and } \sigma_{1|3}^2(z_1) = \boldsymbol{\Sigma}_{Z_1|\boldsymbol{Z}_3}, \tag{11.10}$$

and where the latter expression is defined analogously to (11.7). The conditional density $f_{Z_2|\boldsymbol{Z}_3}(z_2|\boldsymbol{z}_3)$ is defined in the same way. If Z_1 and Z_2 are conditionally independent given $\boldsymbol{Z}_3$, then

$$\begin{aligned} f_{Z_1,Z_2|\boldsymbol{Z}_3}(z_1, z_2|\boldsymbol{z}_3) &= f_{Z_1|\boldsymbol{Z}_3}(z_1|\boldsymbol{z}_3) f_{Z_2|\boldsymbol{Z}_3}(z_2|\boldsymbol{z}_3) \\ &= \frac{1}{2\pi\sigma_{1|3}(z_1)\sigma_{2|3}(z_2)} \\ &\qquad \times \exp\left\{-\frac{1}{2}\left(\frac{z_1 - \mu_{1|3}(z_1)}{\sigma_{1|3}(z_1)}\right)^2\right\} \\ &\qquad\qquad \times \exp\left\{-\frac{1}{2}\left(\frac{z_2 - \mu_{2|3}(z_2)}{\sigma_{2|3}(z_2)}\right)^2\right\}, \end{aligned}$$

and we at once identify the conditional density of $(Z_1, Z_2)|\boldsymbol{Z}_3$ as another Gaussian distribution but without any cross-term involving $z_1 z_2$, which then implies that the off-diagonal element in the partial covariance matrix (11.7) is identically equal to zero. We see immediately from our definition (11.8) that the LGPC is also identically equal to zero.

The converse statement follows straightforwardly by considering the conditional density of $(Z_1, Z_2|\boldsymbol{Z}_3)$.

Let the transformation $\boldsymbol{Y} = \boldsymbol{h}(\boldsymbol{X})$ define the $\boldsymbol{y}$-scale in the same way as transformation (11.5) defines the $\boldsymbol{z}$-scale. We define the LGPC in terms of the marginally standard normal $\boldsymbol{Z}$-variables, which for the $\boldsymbol{Y}$-variables can be calculated as

$$\boldsymbol{Z} = \left(\Phi^{-1}\left(F_{Y_1}(Y_1)\right), \ldots, \Phi^{-1}\left(F_{Y_p}(Y_p)\right)\right)^T,$$

but if h_j are monotone for all $j = 1, \ldots, p$, then

$$F_{Y_j}(y_j) = P(h_j(X_j) \leq y_j) = P(X_j \leq h_j^{-1}(y_j)) = P(X_j \leq x_j) = F_{X_j}(x_j),$$

where x_j is the point on the $\boldsymbol{x}$-scale corresponding to the point y_j on the $\boldsymbol{y}$-scale. The $\boldsymbol{Z}$-variables are the same for the stochastic variables $\boldsymbol{X}$ and $\boldsymbol{Y} = \boldsymbol{h}(\boldsymbol{X})$. Their LGPC-function $\alpha(\boldsymbol{z})$ must therefore be the same as well according to our definition in the preceding section. Entirely analogous arguments for properties 1–4 in the general multivariate case can be constructed from the arguments in the online supplement of Otneim and Tjøstheim (2021). See also Section 11.8.

11.4 Estimation of the LGPC by local likelihood

From the defining equations (11.7) and (11.8) we see that the basic building blocks for the *local Gaussian partial correlation* are the *local Gaussian correlation functions* that populate the local correlation matrix $\boldsymbol{R}(\boldsymbol{z})$ in the density function $f_{\boldsymbol{Z}}$ in (11.6), which we have defined, discussed, estimated, and explored throughout this book. Consider the random vector $\boldsymbol{X} = (X_1, X_2, \ldots, X_p)^T$ having a joint probability density function (pdf) $f_{\boldsymbol{X}}(\boldsymbol{x})$ and its transformed counterpart $\boldsymbol{Z} = \left(\Phi^{-1}(F_1(X_1)), \ldots, \Phi^{-1}(F_p(X_p))\right)^T$ on the marginally standard normal z-scale. The relation between the pdfs of $\boldsymbol{X}$ and $\boldsymbol{Z}$ was expressed in Eq. (9.2) in Chapter 9.2, which we repeat here:

$$f_{\boldsymbol{X}}(\boldsymbol{x}) = f_{\boldsymbol{Z}}\left(\Phi^{-1}\left(F_1(x_1)\right), \ldots, \Phi^{-1}\left(F_p(x_p)\right)\right) \prod_{j=1}^{p} \frac{f_j(x_j)}{\phi\left(\Phi^{-1}\left(F_j(x_j)\right)\right)}, \qquad (11.11)$$

where f_j, $j = 1, \ldots, p$, are the marginal density functions of $\boldsymbol{X}$, and ϕ is the standard normal density function. Let $\boldsymbol{X}_1, \ldots, \boldsymbol{X}_n$ be a random sample identically distributed as $\boldsymbol{X}$ and construct the pseudo-standard normal observations $\widehat{\boldsymbol{Z}}_1, \ldots, \widehat{\boldsymbol{Z}}_n$ as

$$\widehat{\boldsymbol{Z}}_t = \left(\Phi^{-1}\left(\widehat{F}_1(X_{1t})\right), \ldots, \Phi^{-1}\left(\widehat{F}_p(X_{pt})\right)\right)^T, \qquad (11.12)$$

where $\boldsymbol{X}_t = (X_{1t}, X_{2t}, \ldots, X_{pt})$, and $\widehat{F}_j$ is an estimate of the marginal distribution function of X_j, for example, the empirical distribution function. Next, we must produce an estimate $\widehat{\boldsymbol{R}}(\boldsymbol{z})$ of the local correlation matrix, and we will in this chapter consider two variations of this task in Subsections 11.4.1 and 11.4.2. Then, following (11.7), it is natural to estimate the local Gaussian partial covariance matrix as

$$\widehat{\boldsymbol{\Sigma}}_{12|3}(\boldsymbol{z}) = \widehat{\boldsymbol{R}}^{11}(\boldsymbol{z}) - \widehat{\boldsymbol{R}}^{12}(\boldsymbol{z})\left(\widehat{\boldsymbol{R}}^{22}(\boldsymbol{z})\right)^{-1}\widehat{\boldsymbol{R}}^{21}(\boldsymbol{z}), \qquad (11.13)$$

and if we assume that X_1 and X_2 constitute the two first elements in $\boldsymbol{X}$, then, following (11.8), the local Gaussian partial correlation between X_1 and X_2 given $\boldsymbol{X}^{(2)} = \boldsymbol{X}_3$ on the z-scale is estimated by

$$\widehat{\alpha}(\boldsymbol{z}) = \frac{\left\{\widehat{\boldsymbol{\Sigma}}_{12|3}(\boldsymbol{z})\right\}_{12}}{\left\{\widehat{\boldsymbol{\Sigma}}_{12|3}(\boldsymbol{z})\right\}_{11}^{1/2}\left\{\widehat{\boldsymbol{\Sigma}}_{12|3}(\boldsymbol{z})\right\}_{22}^{1/2}}. \qquad (11.14)$$

A corresponding value of $\widehat{\alpha}(\boldsymbol{x})$ at the point $\boldsymbol{x} = \widehat{F}^{-1}(\Phi(\boldsymbol{z}))$ is obtained by inserting $\boldsymbol{z} = \Phi^{-1}(\widehat{F}(\boldsymbol{x}))$ into (11.14).

11.4.1 Estimation of $\boldsymbol{R}(\boldsymbol{z})$ when $p = 3$ and $\boldsymbol{X}^{(2)}$ is a scalar

If $\dim(\boldsymbol{X}) = 3$, then $\dim(\boldsymbol{X}^{(2)}) = 1$, and $\boldsymbol{R}(\boldsymbol{z})$ is a 3×3 symmetric matrix of local correlation functions having arguments $\boldsymbol{z} = (z_1, z_2, z_3)$,

$$\boldsymbol{R}(\boldsymbol{z}) = \begin{pmatrix} 1 & \rho_{12}(\boldsymbol{z}) & \rho_{13}(\boldsymbol{z}) \\ \rho_{12}(\boldsymbol{z}) & 1 & \rho_{23}(\boldsymbol{z}) \\ \rho_{13}(\boldsymbol{z}) & \rho_{23}(\boldsymbol{z}) & 1 \end{pmatrix}, \tag{11.15}$$

containing three parameter functions that must be estimated from data. Note that here we deviate from the pairwise scheme found earlier in this book where $\rho_{ij}(\boldsymbol{z}) = \rho_{ij}(z_i, z_j)$. In Eq. (11.15), $\boldsymbol{z} = (z_1, z_2, z_3)$. Based on the sample (11.12), $\boldsymbol{R}(\boldsymbol{z})$ is estimated by fitting the parametric family $\psi(\boldsymbol{z}, \boldsymbol{R})$, defined in (11.6), locally to the density $f_{\boldsymbol{Z}}(\boldsymbol{z})$ by maximizing the local likelihood function (cf. Hjort and Jones (1996) and Eq. (9.3)), so that

$$\widehat{\boldsymbol{R}}(\boldsymbol{z}) = \arg\max_{\boldsymbol{R}} n^{-1} \sum_{t=1}^{n} K_{\boldsymbol{B}}(\widehat{\boldsymbol{Z}}_t - \boldsymbol{z}) \log \psi(\widehat{\boldsymbol{Z}}_t, \boldsymbol{R}) - \int K_{\boldsymbol{B}}(\boldsymbol{y} - \boldsymbol{z})\psi(\boldsymbol{y}, \boldsymbol{R})\,\mathrm{d}\boldsymbol{y} \tag{11.16}$$

in each point $\boldsymbol{z}$, where $K_{\boldsymbol{B}}(\boldsymbol{x}) = |\boldsymbol{B}|^{-1}K(\boldsymbol{B}^{-1}\boldsymbol{x})$, K is a non-negative and radially symmetric kernel function that satisfies $\int K(\boldsymbol{x})\,\mathrm{d}\boldsymbol{x} = 1$, and $\boldsymbol{B}$ is a diagonal 3×3 matrix of bandwidths that serve as smoothing parameters. The estimate $\widehat{f_{\boldsymbol{Z}}}(\boldsymbol{z}) = \psi(\boldsymbol{z}, \widehat{\boldsymbol{R}}(\boldsymbol{z}))$ again aims at minimizing a locally weighted Kullback–Leibler distance to $f_{\boldsymbol{Z}}(\boldsymbol{z})$, and we refer to Chapters 4, 9, and 10 for much more details about this construction and to Section 11.5 for the relevant asymptotic estimation theory.

Finally, we obtain the estimated LGPC $\widehat{\alpha}(\boldsymbol{z})$ by plugging the estimated local correlations $\widehat{\boldsymbol{R}}(\boldsymbol{z})$ into Eqs. (11.13) and (11.14) and the corresponding value of $\widehat{\alpha}(\boldsymbol{x})$ at the point $\boldsymbol{x} = \widehat{F}^{-1}(\Phi(\boldsymbol{z}))$ by inserting $\boldsymbol{z} = \Phi^{-1}(\widehat{F}(\boldsymbol{x}))$.

11.4.2 Estimation of $\boldsymbol{R}(\boldsymbol{z})$ when $\boldsymbol{X}^{(2)}$ is a vector

The complexity of the estimation problem (11.16) increases sharply with the number of variables involved. The basic idea in Chapters 9 and 10 to avoid the curse of dimensionality is modeling local correlations in $\boldsymbol{R}(\boldsymbol{z})$ as functions of their corresponding *pair* of variables only:

$$\boldsymbol{R}(\boldsymbol{z}) = \left\{\rho_{jk}(z_j, z_k)\right\}, \qquad j, k = 1, 2, \ldots, p, \tag{11.17}$$

which reduces the estimation of the p-variate correlation functions $\rho_{jk}(\boldsymbol{z})$ to a series of bivariate estimation problems. We suggest to use this approach when modeling local dependence if, in the present chapter, the number of variables in $\boldsymbol{X}$ is larger than three. This allows nonlinear dependence between variables to be approximated by the pairwise structure (11.17) while still being computationally tractable. An analogue to the pairwise approximation is the additive approximation in nonparametric regression.

We transform the observations to the $\boldsymbol{z}$-scale as in (11.12), but now we estimate the individual components in $\boldsymbol{R}(\boldsymbol{z})$ one by one, taking only into consideration the pair of variables in question:

$$\widehat{\rho}_{jk}(z_j, z_k) = \arg\max_{\rho_{jk}} n^{-1} \sum_{t=1}^{n} K_{\boldsymbol{B}}(\widehat{\boldsymbol{Z}}_t - \boldsymbol{z}) \log \psi(\widehat{\boldsymbol{Z}}_t, \rho_{jk}) - \int K_{\boldsymbol{B}}(\boldsymbol{y} - \boldsymbol{z}) \psi(\boldsymbol{y}, \rho_{jk}) \, \mathrm{d}\boldsymbol{y}, \tag{11.18}$$

where all running variables and samples are bivariate subsets corresponding to the indices (j, k), $\psi(\cdot, \rho)$ is the bivariate version of (11.6), and $\boldsymbol{B}$ now is a 2×2 diagonal matrix of bandwidths. After estimating all local correlations in this way, we proceed to calculate the LGPC using Eqs. (11.13) and (11.14) as before.

11.5 Asymptotic theory

Eqs. (11.7) and (11.8) and their empirical counterparts (11.13) and (11.14) demonstrate clearly that the LGPC is nothing more than a deterministic function of the local correlation matrix, in the same way as the ordinary partial correlation is a function of the ordinary correlation matrix. The asymptotic behavior of $\widehat{\alpha}(\boldsymbol{z})$ can thus be derived directly from the asymptotic behavior of $\widehat{\boldsymbol{R}}(\boldsymbol{z})$, which we established for the pairwise simplification in Theorems 10.1 and 10.2 under a mixing condition. Some additional results that are relevant for the LGPC follow below, and we refer to the supplementary material of Otneim and Tjøstheim (2021) for proofs and discussions of more general situations.

Consider first the full trivariate fit $\widehat{R}(\boldsymbol{z})$ with $\boldsymbol{z} = (z_1, z_2, z_3)$, which we described for the first time in Section 11.4.1. We estimate the local correlation matrix $\boldsymbol{R}(\boldsymbol{z})$ by maximizing the local likelihood function in (11.16), which we denote by $L_n(\boldsymbol{R}(\boldsymbol{z}), \boldsymbol{z})$, with the only exception that for the sake of this particular argument, we assume the true transformation between the $\boldsymbol{x}$- and the $\boldsymbol{z}$-scale to be known. We know from Theorem 4.5 in Chapter 4.7 that the asymptotic results regarding the local Gaussian correlation also hold when the marginal transformations are estimated from data. For a fixed diagonal matrix $\boldsymbol{B}$ with bandwidths $\boldsymbol{b}$ along the diagonal, denote by $\boldsymbol{R}_b(\boldsymbol{z})$ the local correlation that satisfies, as $n \to \infty$,

$$\nabla L_n(\boldsymbol{R}_b, \boldsymbol{z}) \to \int K_b(\boldsymbol{y} - \boldsymbol{z})\boldsymbol{u}(\boldsymbol{y}, \boldsymbol{R}_b(\boldsymbol{z}))\{f_{\boldsymbol{Z}}(\boldsymbol{y}) - \psi(\boldsymbol{y}, \boldsymbol{R}_b)\}\, d\boldsymbol{y} = 0, \quad (11.19)$$

where $f_{\boldsymbol{Z}}(\boldsymbol{z}) = f_{Z_1,Z_2,Z_3}(z_1, z_2, z_3)$ is the density function of $\boldsymbol{Z}$ (at the point $\boldsymbol{z}$), $\boldsymbol{u}(\cdot, \boldsymbol{\rho}_b)$ is the column vector of functions $\nabla \log \psi(\cdot, \boldsymbol{\rho}_b)$, and the gradient is taken with respect to the parameters $\rho_{12}(\boldsymbol{z})$, $\rho_{13}(\boldsymbol{z})$, and $\rho_{23}(\boldsymbol{z})$, with $\boldsymbol{\rho} = \boldsymbol{\rho}(\boldsymbol{z}) = \{\rho_{12}(\boldsymbol{z}), \rho_{13}(\boldsymbol{z}), \rho_{23}(\boldsymbol{z})\}$ the vector of local correlations. The joint limiting distribution of $\widehat{\boldsymbol{\rho}}$ (for convenience only stated on the $\boldsymbol{z}$-scale below) is given by the following result as $n \to \infty$ and $\boldsymbol{b} \to \boldsymbol{0}$.

Theorem 11.1. *Let $\{\boldsymbol{Z}_t\}_{t=1}^n$ be observations on the marginally standard normally distributed random vector $\boldsymbol{Z}$ having joint density $f_{\boldsymbol{Z}}(\boldsymbol{z})$. Assume that the following conditions hold:*

- **(i)** *For any sequence of bandwidth matrices $\boldsymbol{b}_n$ tending to zero element-wise and for the trivariate marginally standard Gaussian vector $\boldsymbol{Z}$, there exists a unique set of local correlations $\boldsymbol{\rho}_b(\boldsymbol{z})$ that satisfies (11.19), and there exists $\boldsymbol{\rho}_0(\boldsymbol{z})$ such that $\boldsymbol{\rho}_b(\boldsymbol{z}) \to \boldsymbol{\rho}_0(\boldsymbol{z})$.*
- **(ii)** *The process generating $\{\boldsymbol{Z}_t\}_{t=1}^n$ is α-mixing as defined in Eq. (7.15) with mixing coefficients $\alpha(m)$ satisfying $\sum_{m\geq 1} m^{\lambda}\alpha(m)^{1-2/\delta} < \infty$ for some $\lambda > 1 - 2/\delta$ and $\delta > 2$.*
- **(iii)** *each bandwidth $b = b_n$ tends to zero as $n \to \infty$ so that $nb^{\frac{\lambda+2-2/\delta}{\lambda+2/\delta}} = O(n^{\epsilon_0})$ for some constant $\epsilon_0 > 0$.*
- **(iv)** *In a given point $\boldsymbol{z}$ the parameter space Θ for each local correlation $\rho(\boldsymbol{z})$ is a compact subset of $(-1, 1)$.*
- **(v)** *The non-negative kernel function K satisfies $\sup_{\boldsymbol{z}} K(\boldsymbol{z}) < \infty$, $\int K(\boldsymbol{y})\, d\boldsymbol{y} < \infty$, $|\partial/\partial z_i K(\boldsymbol{z})| < \infty$, and $\lim_{z_i\to\infty} |z_i K(\boldsymbol{z})| = 0$ for $i = 1, 2, 3$.*

Then, by writing $b_{n1} = b_{n2} = b_{n3} = b \to 0$ and assuming that they all converge to zero at the same rate,

$$\sqrt{nb^3}\boldsymbol{M}_b^{-1/2}\boldsymbol{J}_b\left(\widehat{\boldsymbol{\rho}}_n - \boldsymbol{\rho}_0\right) \xrightarrow{d} \mathcal{N}(\boldsymbol{0}, \boldsymbol{I}), \quad (11.20)$$

where $\boldsymbol{I}$ is the 3×3 identity matrix,

$$\boldsymbol{J}_b = \int K_b(\boldsymbol{y} - \boldsymbol{z})\boldsymbol{u}(\boldsymbol{y}, \boldsymbol{\rho}_b(\boldsymbol{z}))\boldsymbol{u}^T(\boldsymbol{y}, \boldsymbol{\rho}_b(\boldsymbol{z}))\psi(\boldsymbol{y}, \boldsymbol{\rho}_b(\boldsymbol{z}))\, d\boldsymbol{y}$$

$$- \int K_b(y - z)\nabla u(y, \rho_b(z))\Big\{f_Z(y) - \psi(y, \rho_b(z))\Big\}\, dy,$$

and

$$M_b = b^3 \int K_b^2(y - z)u(y, \rho_b(z))u^T(y, \rho_b(z))f_Z(y)\, dy$$
$$- b^3 \int K_b(y - z)u(y, \rho_b(z))f_Z(y)\, dy \int K_b(y - z)u^T(y, \rho_b(z))f_Z(y)\, dy.$$

It is a straightforward exercise to modify the proof of Theorem 4.2 to suit this particular situation, which demonstrates that the three local correlations converge jointly in distribution at the rate $1/(nb^3)^{1/2}$. See the online supplement of Otneim and Tjøstheim (2021) for details.

The limiting distribution of the local Gaussian correlations estimated under the pairwise simplification described in Section 11.4.2 is given in Theorem 10.2.

We can now calculate the limiting distribution of the LGPC by means of the delta method. Denote by $g : \mathbb{R}^{p(p-1)/2} \to \mathbb{R}$ translation (11.8) from the vector of local correlations between the components in $\boldsymbol{Z}$ (or, equivalently, $\boldsymbol{X}$) to the local partial correlation $\alpha(z)$ between Z_1 and Z_2 given $Z_3, \ldots, Z_p$. From the expression of our estimate (11.14) we have that $\widehat{\alpha}(z) = g(\widehat{\rho}(z))$, so we use the delta method to see that

$$\sqrt{nb^m}\left(\widehat{\alpha}(z) - \alpha(z)\right) \xrightarrow{d} \mathcal{N}\left(0, \nabla g(\rho)^T \boldsymbol{\Lambda} \nabla g(\rho)\right), \qquad (11.21)$$

where m is equal to 2 or 5, and $\boldsymbol{\Lambda}$ is either equal to the leading term of $\boldsymbol{J}_b^{-1}\boldsymbol{M}_b(\boldsymbol{J}_b^{-1})^T$ or to $\boldsymbol{\Sigma}$ in Theorem 10.2, depending on whether we use the full trivariate locally Gaussian fit described in Section 11.4.1 or the sequentially pairwise simplification described in Section 11.4.2. In any case, it is only a matter of basic differentiation to work out an expression for ∇g, the details of which can be found in the online supplement of Otneim and Tjøstheim (2021) in the case $p_1 = p_2 = 1$.

Finally, we present the limiting distribution of the LGPC between Z_1 and Z_2 given $Z_3, \ldots, Z_p$ when the components in $\boldsymbol{Z} = (Z_1, \ldots, Z_p)$ are replaced by marginally standard normal *pseudo-observations* as defined in Eq. (11.12). The following result follows directly from Theorem 4.5.

Theorem 11.2. *Under the conditions in Theorem 11.1, assume further that the kernel function K has a bounded support. Replacing the marginally standard normal vector $\boldsymbol{Z}$ with the approximately marginally standard normal vector $\widehat{\boldsymbol{Z}}$ does not change the conclusions in this theorem.*

11.6 Examples

In this section, we demonstrate how the estimated LGPC can be used to reveal nonlinear departures from conditional independence and to measure conditional dependence. All plots are presented on the $\boldsymbol{x}$-scale.

First, we provide some reference pictures from the simplest situation imaginable. Let X_1, X_2, and X_3 be independent standard (and thus also jointly) normal variables. Since X_1 is conditionally independent from X_2 given X_3 (written $X_1 \perp X_2|X_3$) in this particular case, we also know from property 3 in Section 11.3 that the LGPC between X_1 and X_2 is zero everywhere.

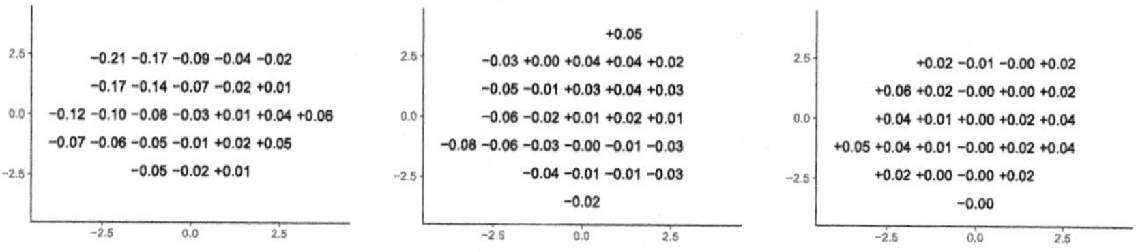

(a) $n = 100$ (b) $n = 500$ (c) $n = 2000$

Figure 11.1 Estimated local Gaussian partial correlation between X_1 and X_2 given $X_3 = 0$, where (X_1, X_2, X_3) is a jointly standard normally distributed vector. The fully trivariate model of Section 11.4.1 is used.

In Fig. 11.1, we see the estimated LGPC between X_1 and X_2 given $X_3 = 0$ for three samples, having sample sizes 100, 500, and 2000, respectively, mapped out on a grid. In this and all other examples, we select bandwidths based on the simple plug-in formula, which follows naturally from classical asymptotic arguments and which we have encountered several times in this book: $b = cn^{-1/9}$ for the full trivariate fit and $b = cn^{-1/6}$ for the bivariate simplification, where the constant c controls the amount of smoothing and must be chosen appropriately based on the task at hand. In Chapter 9, we settled on $c = 1.75$ for multivariate density estimation. We will later in this chapter see that we obtain good power in our test for conditional independence if c is somewhat smaller than that. However, for the visual display of conditional dependence maps, we tend to prefer a fair amount of smoothing, and in Fig. 11.1, we have used $c = 4$. A theory of efficient and accurate bandwidth selection for local likelihood estimation remains a topic for future research. Cross-validation has been used in other chapters of this book, but here a rigorous theory is also not available.

As expected, $\widehat{\alpha}(\boldsymbol{x}) = \widehat{\alpha}(\boldsymbol{z})$ is close to zero in all three plots in Fig. 11.1, and a significance test carried out as in Section 11.7 does not reject conditional independence at any reasonable significance level.

In the next simulated example, we demonstrate an important feature of the LGPC: It is able to *distinguish between positive and negative conditional relationships*, which, to our knowledge, has until now not been possible beyond the linear and jointly Gaussian setting using the ordinary partial correlation. Our approach also allows exploration of conditionally different dependence patterns across different levels of the conditioning variable.

Generate $X_3 \stackrel{\text{def}}{=} \rho \sim U(-1, 1)$, and then generate (X_1, X_2) from the bivariate Gaussian distribution having standard normal marginals and correlation coefficient equal to ρ. We observe $\mathbf{X} = (X_1, X_2, \rho)$ and seek to visualize the dependence between X_1 and X_2 conditional on ρ.

We see the results in Fig. 11.2. In panel (a), we display $n = 1000$ simulated pairs (X_1, X_2) from this model. In panels (b)–(d), we see the estimated LGPC plotted over suitable grids, where the conditioning variable $X_3 = \rho$ was fixed at the respective values -0.9, 0, and 0.9, and we clearly see how the dependence between X_1 and X_2 dramatically changes in an intuitively reasonable way. All this is completely missed by the ordinary partial correlation, since by a conditioning argument we can see that X_1 and X_2 are uncorrelated and that the ordinary partial correlation between X_1 and X_2 given X_3 is equal to zero. Furthermore, we note that the pairwise simplification defined in Section 11.4.2 would also not be able to measure the *conditional* relationship between X_1 and X_2 given X_3 in this case, as we clearly see from Eq. (11.9), because X_1 and X_2 are both marginally independent from X_3. This means that the two pairwise correlations $\rho_{13}(z_1, z_3)$ and $\rho_{23}(z_2, z_3)$ are equal to zero.

We conclude this section by using the LGPC to analyze real data in an example regarding Granger causality between financial time series. Again, we have used the full trivariate fit presented in Section 11.4.1. Granger causality has been a central concept in economics and econometrics ever since its inception by Granger (1969). In layman's terms the time series $\{X_t\}$ Granger causes $\{Y_t\}$ if past values of $\{X_t\}$ are helpful when predicting future values of $\{Y_t\}$. Formally, $\{X_t\}$ Granger causes $\{Y_t\}$ if (Granger, 1980)

$$Y_t \not\perp \mathcal{I}^*(t-1) \mid \mathcal{I}^*_{-X}(t-1), \tag{11.22}$$

where $\perp$ denotes independence, $\not\perp$ denotes dependence, where $\mathcal{I}^*(t-1)$ is all information available at time $t-1$, and $\mathcal{I}^*_{-X}(t-1)$ is the same information

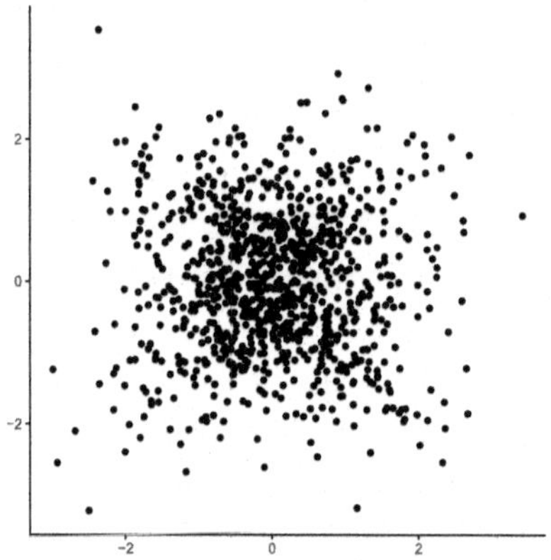

(a) Observed pairs (X_1, X_2) from the conditionally Gaussian model.

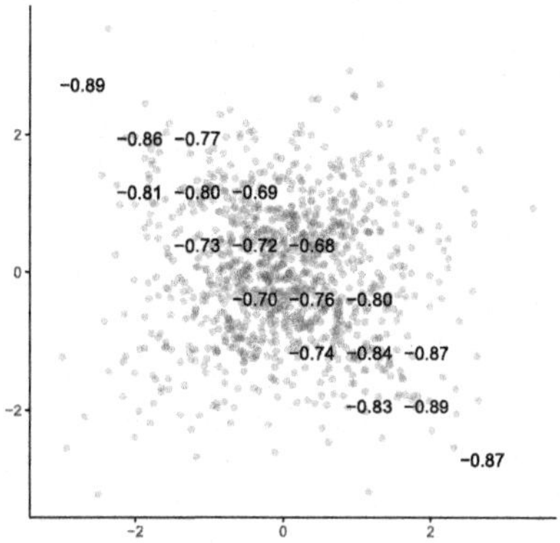

(b) The estimated LGPC between X_1 and X_2 given $\rho = -0.9$.

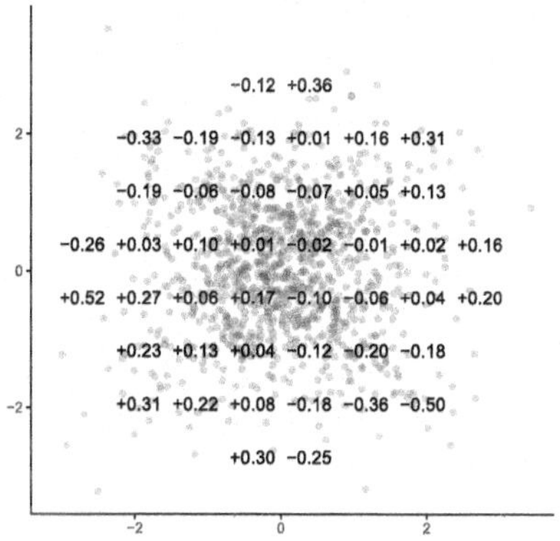

(c) The estimated LGPC between X_1 and X_2 given $\rho = 0$

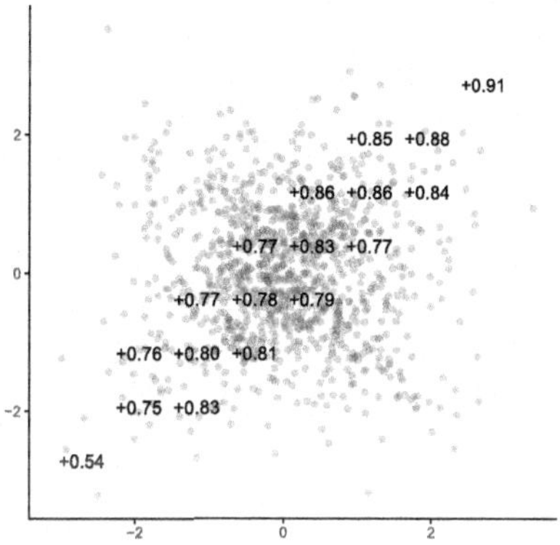

(d) The estimated LGPC between X_1 and X_2 given $\rho = 0.9$

Figure 11.2 The conditionally Gaussian model. The full trivariate fit of Section 11.4.1 is used.

with the exception of the values of $\{X_t\}$ up to, but not including, time t. Of course, hypothesis (11.22) cannot be tested in practice in its full generality. By taking only effects up to the first lag into account we may formulate a sufficient (but not necessary) condition for (11.22): $Y_t \not\perp X_{t-1} \mid Y_{t-1}$, the converse of which constitutes a testable null hypothesis of Granger non-causality:

$$H_0 : Y_t \perp X_{t-1} \mid Y_{t-1}. \tag{11.23}$$

There are many ways to carry out this test. The simplest and original one is based on the further restriction of linear relationships between $\{X_t\}$ and $\{Y_t\}$ and is thus a test for *conditional uncorrelatedness* rather than conditional independence. Nonparametric tests that have power against many nonlinear types of conditional dependence have also been developed, and we refer to Section 11.7 for further references to this literature and a new test for conditional independence based on the LGPC.

Francis et al. (2010) investigate how stock returns of large firms may Granger cause the stock returns of small firms and vice versa from a nonlinear standpoint. They point to earlier evidence that such nonlinear lead-lag relationships have been found and investigate this further using the test for Granger non-causality by Baek and Brock (1992). Utilizing a long series of US data, they find evidence that there is a bi-directional causal link between the stock prices of the firms in the most valuable quintile (20 percent) and the firms in the least valuable quintile. We will repeat this exercise for stocks traded on the Oslo Stock Exchange in Norway, but this time from a point of view using the estimated LGPC.

Denote by $R_{1,t}$ the log-returns on a value-weighted portfolio consisting of the most valuable quintile of firms listed on the Oslo Stock Exchange as of April 27, 2020 (the big firms), and denote by $R_{2,t}$ the corresponding log-returns for the least valuable companies (the small firms). We will investigate the possibility of Granger causality from the small to the big firms, the hypothesis being that smaller firms are more market sensitive and quickly react to changes in the economy, leading the larger firms that more slowly adapt to small variations. The null hypothesis of non-causality of the first order (11.23) in this particular case means that

$$R_{1,t} \perp R_{2,t-1} \mid R_{1,t-1}, \tag{11.24}$$

which we may test formally using the approaches described in the following section or the references therein. Let us rather concentrate on *describing* this conditional dependence relationship by estimating the local Gaussian partial correlation between $R_{1,t}$ and $R_{2,t-1}$ given a few different values of $R_{1,t-1}$, which gives considerable more information than a single p-value of a test. We collect daily observations on Oslo Stock Exchange[1] from January 1, 2018, until December 31, 2019. In Fig. 11.3, we see the estimated LGPC

[1] Thanks to *Børsprosjektet (The Stock Exchange Project)* at the Norwegian School of Economics for providing the data.

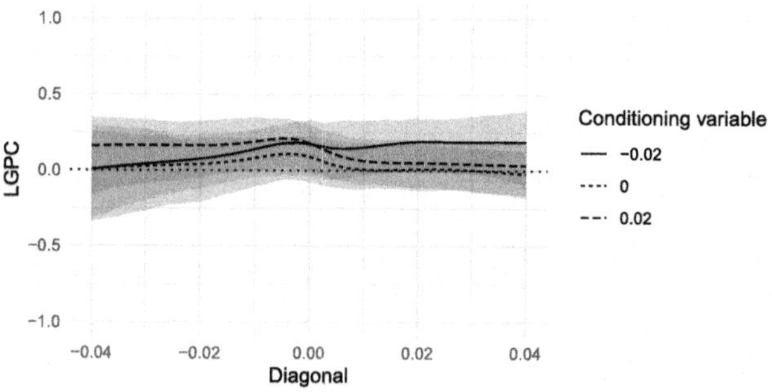

Figure 11.3 The estimated LGPC between $R_{1,t}$ and $R_{2,t-1}$ given $R_{1,t-1}$ along the diagonal of the sample space for three values of the conditioning variable.

along the diagonal $R_{1,t} = R_{2,t-1}$ for three different values $R_{1,t-1} = -0.02, 0,$ and 0.02, along with their block-bootstrapped 95% confidence intervals. The constant $\alpha(\boldsymbol{z}) = 0$ is indicated as a dotted line.

We could perhaps make the argument that $R_{1,t}$ and $R_{2,t-1}$ seem to be somewhat positively dependent in the right half of the graph for *small* values of the conditioning variable $R_{1,t-1}$. Roughly translated to this particular situation, this means that if the large-firm portfolio gives a negative return on day $t-1$, then its value on day t depend on the performance of small-firm portfolio on day $t-1$ in a nonlinear and non-Gaussian way that is characterized by positive dependence in the first quadrant. However, the evidence displayed in Fig. 11.3 is quite weak, because the confidence intervals include zero in most of the sample space.

Francis et al. (2010) go on to analyze if there is Granger causality from small to big firms in the US data if another lag is taken into account, which in general means finding evidence against the hypothesis

$$R_{1,t} \perp (R_{2,t-1}, R_{2,t-2}) \,|\, (R_{1,t-1}, R_{1,t-2}), \tag{11.25}$$

departures from which can be quantified and tested for in a linear fashion using multiple regressions or tested for directly by means of a nonlinear test, as we discuss in the following section. Let us here, on the other hand, use the LGPC to quantify the conditional dependence relationship (11.25) nonlinearly for the Norwegian returns data to obtain a more detailed information. This means estimating a 3×3 partial correlation matrix $\widehat{\boldsymbol{\alpha}}(\boldsymbol{z})$, which we again do along the diagonal $R_{1,t} = R_{2,t-1} = R_{2,t-2}$ in this particular case.

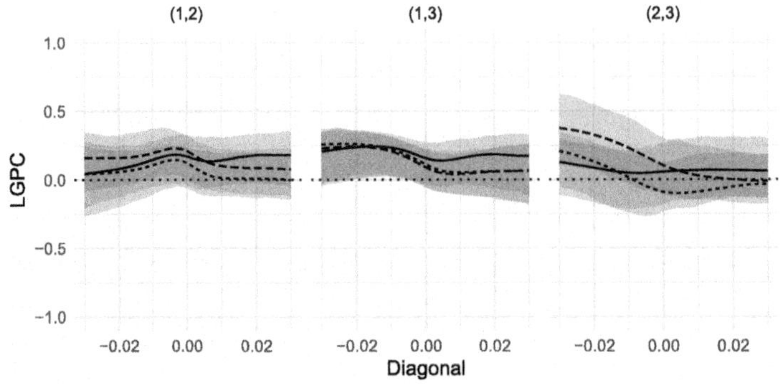

Figure 11.4 The estimated local Gaussian partial correlations for the three variable pairs in $(R_{1,t}, R_{2,t-1}, R_{2,t-2})$ given $(R_{1,t-1}, R_{1,t-2})$ estimated along the diagonal in the sample space. The first two plots represent the pairs $(R_{1,t}, R_{2,t-1})$ and $(R_{1,t}, R_{2,t-2})$, which are of particular interest when analyzing the conditional dependence relationship (11.25). The legend in Fig. 11.3 is still valid, except that the solid line now represents the LGPC conditional on *both* $R_{1,t-1}$ and $R_{1,t-2}$ being equal to −0.02.

Including another lag (see Fig. 11.4) does not change much the estimated conditional relationship between $R_{1,t}$ and $R_{2,t-1}$ compared to the first-order estimate displayed in Fig. 11.3. There does, however, seem to be a clearer picture when considering the LGPC between $R_{1,t}$ and $R_{2,t-2}$, which seems to be positive in the third quadrant for all values of the conditioning variables. In this particular problem, this means that conditioning on the log return of the small-firm portfolio on days $t-1$ and $t-2$, the large-firm log-return on day t depends on the small-firm log-return on day $t-2$ in a nonlinear way and more specifically; this conditional relationship can be described using the LGPC as stronger dependence in the lower left tail of the relevant conditional distribution.

11.7 Testing for conditional independence

11.7.1 The recent fauna of nonparametric tests

Property 3 in Section 11.3 states that the LGPC characterizes conditional dependence within a quite large class of distributions: Two stochastic variables X_1 and X_2 are independent given $\boldsymbol{X}_3$ if and only if the locally Gaussian partial correlation between them is identically equal to zero everywhere on the sample space of $(X_1, X_2, \boldsymbol{X}_3)$. The road is therefore short to a test for conditional independence that may have power against a great deal of nonlinear alternatives compared to a test based on the ordinary partial correlation coefficient.

The last decade or so has seen the publication of many new tests for conditional independence. Su and White have published a series of such tests: Su and White (2007) is based on detecting differences between estimated characteristic functions (which is also the method used by Wang and Hong, 2018). Su and White (2008) is based on estimating the Hellinger distance between conditional density estimates, Su and White (2012) use local polynomial quantile regression to test for conditional independence, and Su and White (2014) present a test based on empirical likelihood. Huang (2010) introduces the maximal nonlinear conditional correlation, which is used in a test for conditional independence, in turn extended to dependent data by Cheng and Huang (2012). Song (2009) constructs a test via Rosenblatt transformations, whereas Bergsma (2010) and Bouezmarni et al. (2012) present new tests for conditional independence based on copula constructions. Bouezmarni and Taamouti (2014) test for conditional independence by measuring the L_2 distance between estimated conditional distribution functions, and Patra et al. (2016) use empirical transformations to translate conditional independence to joint independence, tests for which exist in abundance. Wang et al. (2015) introduce the *conditional distance correlation*, which they use to construct a test for conditional independence. Linton and Gozalo (1997, 2014) formulate conditional independence in terms of probability statements, which then forms the basis of a test. Also, Delgado and Manteiga (2001) develop a test for conditional independence in a nonparametric regression framework. Finally, we mention testing by way of characterizing conditional independence via reproducing kernel Hilbert spaces (RKHS); see, for example, Zhang et al. (2012) and references therein.

A test based on the LGPC is quite different from the methods quoted above. It is semiparametric and does not rely on traditional estimates of density, distribution, or characteristic functions. Furthermore, due to our transformation of the data (11.5) to marginal standard normality, we do not necessarily have to specify weight functions in our test functional to lessen the impact of outliers, unless of course we wish to test for conditional independence in a specific portion of the sample space.

On the other hand, we have to pay a price when imposing structure on the dependence. Certain types of conditional dependence remain invisible to our test statistic, but simulation experiments show that our test performs on par with and sometimes better than existing fully nonparametric tests.

11.7.2 A test for conditional independence

We construct a test statistic for testing $\mathrm{H}_0 : X_1 \perp X_2 \mid \boldsymbol{X}_3$ or, equivalently, a test statistic in terms of the marginally Gaussian observations,

$$\mathrm{H}_0 : Z_1 \perp Z_2 \mid \boldsymbol{Z}_3, \tag{11.26}$$

by aggregating our local measure of dependence over the sample space of $\boldsymbol{X}$ (or $\boldsymbol{Z}$). A natural test statistic on the $\boldsymbol{z}$-scale is

$$T_{n,\boldsymbol{b}} = \int_S h\left(\widehat{\alpha}_{\boldsymbol{b}}(\boldsymbol{z})\right)\, \mathrm{d}F_n(\boldsymbol{z}), \tag{11.27}$$

where F_n is the empirical distribution function, h is a real-valued function, which is typically even and non-negative for most standard applications, and $S \subseteq \mathbb{R}^p$ is an integration area, which can be altered to focus the test on specific portions of the sample space. Standard laws of large numbers ensure that under regularity conditions, $T_{n,\boldsymbol{b}}$ converges in probability toward its population value

$$T = \int_S h\left(\alpha(\boldsymbol{z})\right)\, \mathrm{d}F(\boldsymbol{z});$$

see supplement of Otneim and Tjøstheim (2021).

Departures from conditional independence lead to large values of $T_{n,\boldsymbol{b}}$ that, if larger than a critical value, lead to the rejection of (11.26). Asymptotically, we might expect that approximate p-values for our test can be extracted from the limiting distribution of the test statistic $T_{n,\boldsymbol{b}}$, which is derived in the supplement of Otneim and Tjøstheim (2021) for the two modes of estimation that we discuss in Sections 11.4.1 and 11.4.2. However, several authors, for example, Teräsvirta et al. (2010), have noted that asymptotic analysis of nonparametric (or semiparametric) test statistics of the form (11.27) tends to be too crude for finite sample applications. Therefore we approximate the distribution of $T_{n,\boldsymbol{b}}$ using the bootstrap. The validity of the bootstrap in such contexts was examined by Lacal and Tjøstheim (2019).

In accordance with our treatment so far, let $\{Z_{1t}, Z_{2t}, \boldsymbol{Z}_{3t}\}$, $t = 1, \ldots, n$, be observations (in practice, pseudo-observations $\{\widehat{Z}_{1t}, \widehat{Z}_{2t}, \widehat{\boldsymbol{Z}}_{3t}\}$) of the p-variate stochastic vector $\boldsymbol{Z}$, $p \geq 3$, with Z_1 and Z_2 being scalar and $\boldsymbol{Z}_3$ being $(p-2)$-variate. To calculate the statistic $T_{n,\boldsymbol{b}}$ for testing the null hypothesis $Z_1 \perp Z_2 \mid \boldsymbol{Z}_3$, we must estimate the joint local correlation matrix $\boldsymbol{\Sigma}(\boldsymbol{z})$ of $\boldsymbol{Z} = (Z_1, Z_2, \boldsymbol{Z}_3)$. We exploit this in the following algorithm designed to produce approximate resampled versions of $T_{n,b}$ under the null hypothesis of conditional independence. This procedure is a variation of the so-called local bootstrap, which has been used by several authors when testing for conditional independence.

1. Use the local correlation estimates to estimate the conditional densities $f_{Z_1|\mathbf{Z}_3}$ and $f_{Z_2|\mathbf{Z}_3}$ by means of the method by Otneim and Tjøstheim (2018) outlined in Chapter 10.2. In practice, to reduce the computational load, we evaluate $\widehat{f}_{Z_1|\mathbf{Z}_3}$ and $\widehat{f}_{Z_2|\mathbf{Z}_3}$ on a fine grid on their support, over which a continuous representation of the estimates is produced using cubic splines.
2. Using the accept–reject algorithm, generate B samples, each of size n, from $\widehat{f}_{Z_1|\mathbf{Z}_3}$ and $\widehat{f}_{Z_2|\mathbf{Z}_3}$, leading to B replicates

$$Z_m^* = \left\{ \{Z_{1t}^*, Z_{2t}^*, \mathbf{Z}_{3t}^*\}_i \right\}_m, \qquad t = 1, \dots, n, \;\; m = 1, \dots, B,$$

of $\mathbf{Z}$ under the null hypothesis.
3. Calculate $\{T_{n,b}\}_m^*$, $m = 1, \dots, B$, for the replicated data sets and obtain the approximate p-value for the conditional independence test.

We refer to Otneim and Tjøstheim (2021) for more details.

11.7.3 Comparing with other tests

Su and White (2008) formulate a simulation experiment for evaluating their nonparametric test for conditional independence by generating data from 10 different data-generating processes (DGPs) and then check the power and level for their test. Many of the later works that were discussed in the preceding section contain very similar experiments, and some of them present simulation results for tests published prior to Su and White (2008). This allows us to present comprehensive comparisons between the new test presented above and many alternatives.

Let $(\epsilon_{1t}, \epsilon_{2t}, \epsilon_{3t})$ be iid observations from the $\mathcal{N}(0, I_3)$-distribution, where I_3 is the 3×3 identity matrix. We test $\mathrm{H}_0 : X_{1t} \perp X_{2t} \mid X_{3t}$ in 10 cases listed in Table 11.1 taken from Su and White (2008), which cover various types of linear and nonlinear time series dependence.

The null hypothesis of conditional independence between X_{1t} and X_{2t} given X_{3t} is true for DGPs 1–4, which will be used to check the level of the test, whereas for DGPs 5–10, we measure the power. By evaluating our test using the sample sizes $n = 100$ at the 5% level, we can harvest a great number of corresponding results from the literature, as presented below.

Table 11.1 Data generating processes in simulation experiment.

1.	$(X_{1t}, X_{2t}, X_{3t}) = (\epsilon_{1t}, \epsilon_{2t}, \epsilon_{3t})$.
2.	$X_{1t} = 0.5X_{1,t-1} + \epsilon_{1t}$, $X_{2t} = 0.5X_{2,t-1} + \epsilon_{2t}$, $X_{3t} = X_{1,t-1}$.
3.	$X_{1t} = \epsilon_{1t}\sqrt{0.01 + 0.5X^2_{1,t-1}}$, $X_{2t} = 0.5X_{2,t-1} + \epsilon_{2t}$, $X_{3t} = X_{1,t-1}$.
4.	$X_{1t} = \epsilon_{1t}\sqrt{h_{1t}}$, $X_{2t} = \epsilon_{2t}\sqrt{h_{2t}}$, $X_{3t} = X_{1,t-1}$, $h_{1t} = 0.01 + 0.9h_{1,t-1} + 0.05X^2_{1,t-1}$, $h_{2t} = 0.01 + 0.9h_{2,t-1} + 0.05X^2_{2,t-1}$.
5.	$X_{1t} = 0.5X_{1,t-1} + 0.5X_{2t} + \epsilon_{1t}$, $X_{2t} = 0.5X_{2,t-1} + \epsilon_{2t}$, $X_{3t} = X_{1,t-1}$.
6.	$X_{1t} = 0.5X_{1,t-1} + 0.5X^2_{2t} + \epsilon_{1t}$, $X_{2t} = 0.5X_{2,t-1} + \epsilon_{2t}$, $X_{3t} = X_{1,t-1}$.
7.	$X_{1t} = 0.5X_{1,t-1}0.5X_{2t} + \epsilon_{1t}$, $X_{2t} = 0.5X_{2,t-1} + \epsilon_{2t}$, $X_{3t} = X_{1,t-1}$.
8.	$X_{1t} = 0.5X_{1,t-1} + 0.5X_{2t}\epsilon_{1t}$, $X_{2t} = 0.5X_{2,t-1} + \epsilon_{2t}$, $X_{3t} = X_{1,t-1}$.
9.	$X_{1t} = \epsilon_{1t}\sqrt{0.01 + 0.5X^2_{1,t-1}} + 0.25X_{2t}$, $X_{2t} = X_{2,t-1} + \epsilon_{2t}$, $X_{3t} = X_{1,t-1}$.
10.	$X_{1t} = \epsilon_{1t}\sqrt{h_{1t}}$, $X_{2t} = \epsilon_{2t}\sqrt{h_{2t}}$, $X_{3t} = X_{1,t-1}$, $h_{1t} = 0.01 + 0.1h_{1,t-1} + 0.4X^2_{1,t-1} + 0.5X^2_{2t}$, $h_{2t} = 0.01 + 0.9h_{2,t-1} + 0.5X^2_{t-1}$.

The first set of simulation results are collected from Su and White (2008): In Table 11.2, LIN is a standard linear Granger causality test, SCM and SKS are tests by Linton and Gozalo (1997), which use statistics of the two versions of the nonparametric test developed by Delgado and Manteiga (2001), and HEL refers to the Hellinger distance test that Su and White (2008) present. Next, we move to Su and White (2014), who provide simulations for their test for conditional independence based on the empirical likelihood (SEL) and the test by Su and White (2007), which is based on properties of the conditional characteristic function (CHF). Cheng and Huang (2012) provide simulations for their tests based on the maximal conditional correlation (MCC).

Finally, we include the results from simulations using our new test based on the LGPC using the trivariate specification defined in Section 11.4.1 for two different levels of smoothing and include them in Table 11.2. We highlight the new results in gray to indicate that they, as opposed to all the other numbers, have not appeared in the literature before. Also, to the best of our knowledge, these results have not been compared simultaneously prior to Otneim and Tjøstheim (2021).

We see in Table 11.2 that our test has the approximate correct level and is quite powerful against all alternative specifications of conditional dependence in the additive models 5 and 6, as well as the remaining examples 7–10, which are more multiplicative in nature.

We refer to the supplement of Otneim and Tjøstheim (2021) for more power studies, which confirm that the conditional independence test presented in this section performs well also in higher dimensions.

Table 11.2 Level and power, $n = 100$.

	Level				Power					
↓ Test | DGP →	1	2	3	4	5	6	7	8	9	10
CHF	0.034	0.058	-	-	0.780	0.792	0.520	0.780	0.728	0.580
CM	0.054	0.058	0.060	0.048	0.920	0.548	0.504	0.412	0.384	0.188
HEL, $c=2$	0.072	0.036	0.072	0.048	0.952	<u>0.944</u>	0.576	0.940	<u>0.988</u>	<u>0.912</u>
KS	0.042	0.056	0.056	0.040	0.780	0.404	0.380	0.288	0.292	0.156
LGPC, $c=1.0$	0.054	0.048	0.046	0.046	0.910	0.722	0.559	<u>0.990</u>	0.968	0.866
LGPC, $c=1.4$	0.047	0.043	0.046	0.047	0.971	0.855	0.727	0.969	0.916	0.765
LIN	0.044	0.061	0.050	0.060	<u>0.999</u>	0.337	0.213	0.126	0.163	0.153
MCC, $c=2$	0.041	0.050	0.053	0.062	0.852	0.793	0.218	0.860	0.631	0.348
SCM	0.076	0.060	0.084	0.064	0.924	0.464	0.352	0.500	0.224	0.196
SEL	0.054	0.038	-	-	0.840	0.856	<u>0.760</u>	0.904	0.716	0.556
SKS	0.064	0.056	0.088	0.068	0.728	0.236	0.288	0.340	0.120	0.112

11.8 The multivariate LGPC

11.8.1 Definition

The literature on nonlinear conditional dependence modeling is mostly concerned with the simple case where the vector of conditionally dependent variables consists of two scalar random variables, $\boldsymbol{Z}^{(1)} = (Z_1, Z_2)$, and this case is therefore the focus of our treatment of the LGPC in this chapter. This means that we estimate a single local Gaussian partial correlation function $\widehat{\alpha}(\boldsymbol{z})$. However, one of the most attractive properties of the LGPC is a close parallel to the multivariate Gaussian distribution, and this is also the case when describing conditional dependence among more than two variables, which in our case leads to the estimation of a *matrix* of local Gaussian partial correlations. Besides needing a slightly more involved notation, this is a straightforward exercise in our framework as we will see further; much more details can be found in the supplement of Otneim and Tjøstheim (2021).

Let $\boldsymbol{Z}$ be a vector of continuous random variables, which we split into two components $\boldsymbol{Z} = (\boldsymbol{Z}^{(1)}, \boldsymbol{Z}^{(2)})$, but this time, $\boldsymbol{Z}^{(1)} = (Z_1, \ldots, Z_{p_1+p_2})^T$ is itself a vector of dimension $p_1 + p_2$, which is split into two groups, the p_1-dimensional vector $\boldsymbol{Z}_1$ and the p_2-dimensional vector $\boldsymbol{Z}_2$. The vector $\boldsymbol{Z}^{(2)} = \boldsymbol{Z}_3$ is a vector of p_3 random variables. Denote by $\boldsymbol{\mu}$ and $\boldsymbol{\Sigma}$ the expectation vector and covariance matrix of $\boldsymbol{Z}$, now partitioned according to our partition of $\boldsymbol{Z} = (\boldsymbol{Z}_1, \boldsymbol{Z}_2, \boldsymbol{Z}_3)$ as in Eq. (11.1):

$$\boldsymbol{\mu} = \begin{pmatrix} \boldsymbol{\mu}_1 \\ \boldsymbol{\mu}_2 \\ \boldsymbol{\mu}_3 \end{pmatrix}, \qquad \boldsymbol{\Sigma} = \begin{pmatrix} \boldsymbol{\Sigma}_{11} & \boldsymbol{\Sigma}_{12} & \boldsymbol{\Sigma}_{13} \\ \boldsymbol{\Sigma}_{21} & \boldsymbol{\Sigma}_{22} & \boldsymbol{\Sigma}_{23} \\ \boldsymbol{\Sigma}_{31} & \boldsymbol{\Sigma}_{32} & \boldsymbol{\Sigma}_{33} \end{pmatrix},$$

where $\boldsymbol{\Sigma}_{11}$ is the covariance matrix of $\boldsymbol{Z}_1$, $\boldsymbol{\Sigma}_{23}$ contains the covariances between $\boldsymbol{Z}_2$ and $\boldsymbol{Z}_3$, and so forth, and where naturally $\boldsymbol{\Sigma}^T = \boldsymbol{\Sigma}$, $\boldsymbol{\Sigma}_{12}^T = \boldsymbol{\Sigma}_{21}$, $\boldsymbol{\Sigma}_{13}^T = \boldsymbol{\Sigma}_{31}$, and $\boldsymbol{\Sigma}_{23}^T = \boldsymbol{\Sigma}_{32}$.

All of these parameters can be described and estimated locally in the exact same way as earlier in this chapter, resulting from the locally approximating Gaussian joint density $\psi(\boldsymbol{z}, \boldsymbol{v})$ at the point $\boldsymbol{v} = \boldsymbol{z}$

$$\psi(\boldsymbol{z}) = \frac{1}{(2\pi)^{(p_1+p_2+p_3)/2} |\boldsymbol{\Sigma}(\boldsymbol{z})|^{1/2}} \exp\left\{ -\frac{1}{2}(\boldsymbol{z} - \boldsymbol{\mu}(\boldsymbol{z}))^T \boldsymbol{\Sigma}^{-1}(\boldsymbol{z})(\boldsymbol{z} - \boldsymbol{\mu}(\boldsymbol{z})) \right\} \tag{11.28}$$

and the locally Gaussian *conditional* quantity

$$\psi(z_1, z_2|\boldsymbol{Z}_3 = z_3) = \frac{1}{(2\pi)^{(p_1+p_2)/2}|\boldsymbol{\Sigma}_{12|3}(z)|^{1/2}} \times \exp\left\{-\frac{1}{2}(z - \boldsymbol{\mu}_{12|3}(z))^T \boldsymbol{\Sigma}_{12|3}^{-1}(z)(z - \boldsymbol{\mu}_{12|3}(z))\right\}$$

with $z = (z_1, z_2)$. To simplify notation, in the following, we will drop the z-dependence in the parameters. To define $\boldsymbol{\mu}_{12|3}$ and $\boldsymbol{\Sigma}_{12|3}$, let $\boldsymbol{\Sigma}^{11}$, $\boldsymbol{\Sigma}^{12}$, $\boldsymbol{\Sigma}^{21}$, and $\boldsymbol{\Sigma}^{22}$ be matrices of dimensions $(p_1 + p_2) \times (p_1 + p_2)$, $(p_1 + p_2) \times p_3$, $p_3 \times (p_1 + p_2)$, and $p_3 \times p_3$, respectively, given by

$$\boldsymbol{\Sigma}^{11} = \begin{pmatrix} \boldsymbol{\Sigma}_{11} & \boldsymbol{\Sigma}_{12} \\ \boldsymbol{\Sigma}_{21} & \boldsymbol{\Sigma}_{22} \end{pmatrix}, \boldsymbol{\Sigma}^{12} = \begin{pmatrix} \boldsymbol{\Sigma}_{13} \\ \boldsymbol{\Sigma}_{23} \end{pmatrix}, \boldsymbol{\Sigma}^{21} = \begin{pmatrix} \boldsymbol{\Sigma}_{31} & \boldsymbol{\Sigma}_{32} \end{pmatrix}, \text{ and } \boldsymbol{\Sigma}^{22} = \boldsymbol{\Sigma}_{33}$$

such that

$$\boldsymbol{\Sigma} = \begin{pmatrix} \boldsymbol{\Sigma}^{11} & \boldsymbol{\Sigma}^{12} \\ \boldsymbol{\Sigma}^{21} & \boldsymbol{\Sigma}^{22} \end{pmatrix}.$$

It follows by standard arguments (cf. Otneim and Tjøstheim (2018), Chapter 10.2 or Section 11.2) that

$$\begin{aligned} \boldsymbol{\mu}_{12|3} &= \begin{pmatrix} \boldsymbol{\mu}_1 \\ \boldsymbol{\mu}_2 \end{pmatrix} + \boldsymbol{\Sigma}^{12}\left(\boldsymbol{\Sigma}^{22}\right)^{-1}\left(z^{(2)} - \boldsymbol{\mu}_3\right) \\ &= \begin{pmatrix} \boldsymbol{\mu}_1 \\ \boldsymbol{\mu}_2 \end{pmatrix} + \begin{pmatrix} \boldsymbol{\Sigma}_{13}\boldsymbol{\Sigma}_{33}^{-1}\left(z^{(2)} - \boldsymbol{\mu}_3\right) \\ \boldsymbol{\Sigma}_{23}\boldsymbol{\Sigma}_{33}^{-1}\left(z^{(2)} - \boldsymbol{\mu}_3\right) \end{pmatrix} \end{aligned} \tag{11.29}$$

and

$$\begin{aligned} \boldsymbol{\Sigma}_{12|3} &= \boldsymbol{\Sigma}^{11} - \boldsymbol{\Sigma}^{12}\left(\boldsymbol{\Sigma}^{22}\right)^{-1}\boldsymbol{\Sigma}^{21} = \boldsymbol{\Sigma}^{11} - \begin{pmatrix} \boldsymbol{\Sigma}_{13} \\ \boldsymbol{\Sigma}_{23} \end{pmatrix}\boldsymbol{\Sigma}_{33}^{-1}\begin{pmatrix} \boldsymbol{\Sigma}_{31} & \boldsymbol{\Sigma}_{32} \end{pmatrix} \\ &= \begin{pmatrix} \boldsymbol{\Sigma}_{11} - \boldsymbol{\Sigma}_{13}\boldsymbol{\Sigma}_{33}^{-1}\boldsymbol{\Sigma}_{31} & \boldsymbol{\Sigma}_{12} - \boldsymbol{\Sigma}_{13}\boldsymbol{\Sigma}_{33}^{-1}\boldsymbol{\Sigma}_{32} \\ \boldsymbol{\Sigma}_{21} - \boldsymbol{\Sigma}_{23}\boldsymbol{\Sigma}_{33}^{-1}\boldsymbol{\Sigma}_{31} & \boldsymbol{\Sigma}_{22} - \boldsymbol{\Sigma}_{23}\boldsymbol{\Sigma}_{33}^{-1}\boldsymbol{\Sigma}_{32} \end{pmatrix}. \end{aligned} \tag{11.30}$$

We proceed now to establish the notion of conditional independence between $\boldsymbol{Z}_1$ and $\boldsymbol{Z}_2$ using the LGPC in the multivariate case. The conditional densities of $\boldsymbol{Z}_1|\boldsymbol{Z}_3$ and $\boldsymbol{Z}_2|\boldsymbol{Z}_3$ in terms of the local Gaussian parameters at the point (z_1, z_2, z_3) are given by

$$f(z_1|z_3) = \frac{1}{(2\pi)^{p_1/2}|\boldsymbol{\Sigma}_{1|3}|^{1/2}} \exp\left\{-\frac{1}{2}(z_1 - \boldsymbol{\mu}_{1|3})^T \boldsymbol{\Sigma}_{1|3}^{-1}(z_1 - \boldsymbol{\mu}_{1|3})\right\},$$

$$f(z_2|z_3) = \frac{1}{(2\pi)^{p_2/2}|\boldsymbol{\Sigma}_{2|3}|^{1/2}} \exp\left\{-\frac{1}{2}(z_2 - \boldsymbol{\mu}_{2|3})^T \boldsymbol{\Sigma}_{2|3}^{-1}(z_2 - \boldsymbol{\mu}_{2|3})\right\},$$

where

$$\boldsymbol{\mu}_{1|3} = \boldsymbol{\mu}_1 + \boldsymbol{\Sigma}^{13}\left(\boldsymbol{\Sigma}^{33}\right)^{-1}\left(z_3 - \boldsymbol{\mu}_3\right), \ \boldsymbol{\mu}_{2|3} = \boldsymbol{\mu}_2 + \boldsymbol{\Sigma}^{23}\left(\boldsymbol{\Sigma}^{33}\right)^{-1}\left(z_3 - \boldsymbol{\mu}_3\right), \tag{11.31}$$

and

$$\boldsymbol{\Sigma}_{1|3} = \boldsymbol{\Sigma}_{11} - \boldsymbol{\Sigma}_{13}\boldsymbol{\Sigma}_{33}^{-1}\boldsymbol{\Sigma}_{31}, \ \boldsymbol{\Sigma}_{2|3} = \boldsymbol{\Sigma}_{22} - \boldsymbol{\Sigma}_{23}\boldsymbol{\Sigma}_{33}^{-1}\boldsymbol{\Sigma}_{32}. \tag{11.32}$$

Under conditional independence between $\boldsymbol{Z}_1$ and $\boldsymbol{Z}_2$ given $\boldsymbol{Z}_3$, the joint conditional density of $(\boldsymbol{Z}_1, \boldsymbol{Z}_2|\boldsymbol{Z}_3)$ at the point (z_1, z_2, z_3) is given by

$$\begin{aligned} f(z_1, z_2|z_3) &= f(z_1|z_3)f(z_2|z_3) \\ &= \frac{1}{(2\pi)^{(p_1+p_2)/2}|\boldsymbol{\Sigma}_{1|3}|^{1/2}|\boldsymbol{\Sigma}_{2|3}|^{1/2}} \\ &\quad \times \exp\left\{-\frac{1}{2}\left[(z_1 - \boldsymbol{\mu}_{1|3})^T \boldsymbol{\Sigma}_{1|3}^{-1}(z_1 - \boldsymbol{\mu}_{1|3})\right.\right. \\ &\qquad \left.\left. + (z_2 - \boldsymbol{\mu}_{2|3})^T \boldsymbol{\Sigma}_{2|3}^{-1}(z_2 - \boldsymbol{\mu}_{2|3})\right]\right\}. \end{aligned}$$

Comparing expressions (11.28)–(11.32), we see that we have conditional independence if and only if the matrix $\boldsymbol{\Sigma}_{12|3}$ in (11.30) is block diagonal, that is, if and only if

$$\boldsymbol{\Sigma}_{12} - \boldsymbol{\Sigma}_{13}\boldsymbol{\Sigma}_{33}^{-1}\boldsymbol{\Sigma}_{32} = \boldsymbol{\Sigma}_{21} - \boldsymbol{\Sigma}_{23}\boldsymbol{\Sigma}_{33}^{-1}\boldsymbol{\Sigma}_{31} = \mathbf{0}.$$

11.8.2 Some particular cases

Let $\boldsymbol{D} = \text{diag}\left\{\boldsymbol{\Sigma}_{12|3}\right\}$. The local Gaussian partial correlation matrix can be expressed as the lower left-hand block matrix of $\boldsymbol{D}^{-1/2}\boldsymbol{\Sigma}_{12|3}\boldsymbol{D}^{-1/2}$, and so the LGPC matrix is given as the lower left-hand block of the matrix

$$\boldsymbol{D}^{-1/2}\boldsymbol{\Sigma}_{12|3}\boldsymbol{D}^{-1/2} = \boldsymbol{D}^{-1/2}\begin{pmatrix} \boldsymbol{\Sigma}_{11} - \boldsymbol{\Sigma}_{13}\boldsymbol{\Sigma}_{33}^{-1}\boldsymbol{\Sigma}_{31} & \boldsymbol{\Sigma}_{12} - \boldsymbol{\Sigma}_{13}\boldsymbol{\Sigma}_{33}^{-1}\boldsymbol{\Sigma}_{32} \\ \boldsymbol{\Sigma}_{21} - \boldsymbol{\Sigma}_{23}\boldsymbol{\Sigma}_{33}^{-1}\boldsymbol{\Sigma}_{31} & \boldsymbol{\Sigma}_{22} - \boldsymbol{\Sigma}_{23}\boldsymbol{\Sigma}_{33}^{-1}\boldsymbol{\Sigma}_{32} \end{pmatrix}\boldsymbol{D}^{-1/2}. \tag{11.33}$$

Consider this expression for a few particular cases:

a) **Let** $p_1 = p_2 = p_3 = 1$. Consider the partial covariance matrix, where we again drop the z-dependence in all parameters:

$$\boldsymbol{\Sigma}_{12|3} = \boldsymbol{\Sigma}^{11} - \boldsymbol{\Sigma}^{12}\left(\boldsymbol{\Sigma}^{22}\right)^{-1}\boldsymbol{\Sigma}^{21}.$$

Here, since all variables are normalized with variance one, we have that

$$\mathbf{\Sigma} = \begin{pmatrix} 1 & \rho_{12} & \rho_{13} \\ \rho_{21} & 1 & \rho_{23} \\ \rho_{31} & \rho_{32} & 1 \end{pmatrix}$$

and

$$\mathbf{\Sigma}^{11} = \begin{pmatrix} 1 & \rho_{12} \\ \rho_{21} & 1 \end{pmatrix}, \ \mathbf{\Sigma}^{12} = \begin{pmatrix} \rho_{13} \\ \rho_{23} \end{pmatrix}, \ \left(\mathbf{\Sigma}^{22}\right)^{-1} = 1, \ \mathbf{\Sigma}^{21} = \begin{pmatrix} \rho_{31} & \rho_{32} \end{pmatrix}.$$

Hence

$$\begin{aligned} \mathbf{\Sigma}^{11} - \mathbf{\Sigma}^{12}\left(\mathbf{\Sigma}^{22}\right)^{-1}\mathbf{\Sigma}^{21} &= \begin{pmatrix} 1 & \rho_{12} \\ \rho_{21} & 1 \end{pmatrix} - \begin{pmatrix} \rho_{13} \\ \rho_{23} \end{pmatrix}\begin{pmatrix} \rho_{31} & \rho_{32} \end{pmatrix} \\ &= \begin{pmatrix} 1-\rho_{13}^2 & \rho_{12}-\rho_{13}\rho_{23} \\ \rho_{12}-\rho_{13}\rho_{23} & 1-\rho_{23}^2 \end{pmatrix}. \end{aligned}$$

This is a covariance matrix and not a correlation matrix, so normalizing with standard deviations results in the partial correlation matrix

$$\begin{pmatrix} 1 & \frac{\rho_{12}-\rho_{13}\rho_{23}}{\sqrt{1-\rho_{13}^2}\sqrt{1-\rho_{23}^2}} \\ \frac{\rho_{12}-\rho_{13}\rho_{23}}{\sqrt{1-\rho_{13}^2}\sqrt{1-\rho_{23}^2}} & 1 \end{pmatrix}, \tag{11.34}$$

which should be compared to (11.9). This result can also be obtained by a direct application of (11.33):

$$\begin{aligned} &\begin{pmatrix} 1-\rho_{13}^2 & 0 \\ 0 & 1-\rho_{23}^2 \end{pmatrix}^{-1/2} \begin{pmatrix} 1-\rho_{13}^2 & \rho_{12}-\rho_{13}\rho_{23} \\ \rho_{12}-\rho_{13}\rho_{23} & 1-\rho_{23}^2 \end{pmatrix} \\ &\qquad \times \begin{pmatrix} 1-\rho_{13}^2 & 0 \\ 0 & 1-\rho_{23}^2 \end{pmatrix}^{-1/2}. \end{aligned}$$

b) Let $p_3 = 1$, and let p_1 and p_2 be arbitrary. In this case,

$$\mathbf{\Sigma}^{11} = \begin{pmatrix} \mathbf{\Sigma}_{11} & \mathbf{\Sigma}_{12} \\ \mathbf{\Sigma}_{21} & \mathbf{\Sigma}_{22} \end{pmatrix},$$

where

$$\mathbf{\Sigma}_{11} = \left\{\rho_{ij}^{1,1}\right\}, i = 1, \ldots, p_1; j = 1, \ldots, p_1,$$

$$\boldsymbol{\Sigma}_{12} = \left\{\rho_{ij}^{1,2}\right\}, i = 1, \ldots, p_1; j = 1, \ldots, p_2,$$
$$\boldsymbol{\Sigma}_{21} = \left\{\rho_{ij}^{2,1}\right\}, i = 1, \ldots, p_2; j = 1, \ldots, p_1,$$
$$\boldsymbol{\Sigma}_{22} = \left\{\rho_{ij}^{2,2}\right\}, i = 1, \ldots, p_2; j = 1, \ldots, p_2.$$

Since $\boldsymbol{\Sigma}^{22} = \boldsymbol{\Sigma}_{33} = 1$,

$$\boldsymbol{\Sigma}^{12}\left(\boldsymbol{\Sigma}^{22}\right)^{-1}\boldsymbol{\Sigma}^{21} = \boldsymbol{\Sigma}^{12}\boldsymbol{\Sigma}^{21} = \begin{pmatrix}\boldsymbol{\Sigma}_{13}\\ \boldsymbol{\Sigma}_{23}\end{pmatrix}\left(\boldsymbol{\Sigma}_{31}\boldsymbol{\Sigma}_{32}\right),$$

where

$$\boldsymbol{\Sigma}_{13} = \left\{\rho_{i3}^{1,3}\right\}, i = 1, \ldots, p_1; \qquad \boldsymbol{\Sigma}_{23} = \left\{\rho_{j3}^{2,3}\right\}, j = 1, \ldots, p_2,$$
$$\boldsymbol{\Sigma}_{31} = \left\{\rho_{3i}^{3,1}\right\}, i = 1, \ldots, p_1; \qquad \boldsymbol{\Sigma}_{32} = \left\{\rho_{3j}^{3,2}\right\}, j = 1, \ldots, p_2.$$

Furthermore,

$$\boldsymbol{\Sigma}_{12|3} = \begin{pmatrix}\boldsymbol{\Sigma}_{11} & \boldsymbol{\Sigma}_{12}\\ \boldsymbol{\Sigma}_{21} & \boldsymbol{\Sigma}_{22}\end{pmatrix} - \begin{pmatrix}\boldsymbol{\Sigma}_{13}\\ \boldsymbol{\Sigma}_{23}\end{pmatrix}\begin{pmatrix}\boldsymbol{\Sigma}_{31} & \boldsymbol{\Sigma}_{32}\end{pmatrix}.$$

The diagonals of $\boldsymbol{\Sigma}_{11}$ and $\boldsymbol{\Sigma}_{22}$ are populated with ones, whereas, using symmetry of correlations, $\begin{pmatrix}\boldsymbol{\Sigma}_{13} & \boldsymbol{\Sigma}_{23}\end{pmatrix}^T\begin{pmatrix}\boldsymbol{\Sigma}_{31} & \boldsymbol{\Sigma}_{32}\end{pmatrix}$ has $\left(\rho_{i3}^{1,2}\right)^2$, $i = 1, \ldots, p_1$, and $\left(\rho_{3j}^{3,2}\right)^2$, $j = 1, \ldots, p_2$, along the diagonal, so that $\boldsymbol{D}$ is the $(p_1 + p_2) \times (p_1 + p_2)$ diagonal matrix with the concatenated sequence $1 - \left(\rho_{i3}^{1,2}\right)^2$, $i = 1, \ldots, p_1$, and $1 - \left(\rho_{3j}^{3,2}\right)^2$, $j = 1, \ldots, p_2$, along the diagonal.

Pre- and post-multiplying $\boldsymbol{\Sigma}_{12|3}$ by $\boldsymbol{D}^{-1/2}$ converts $\boldsymbol{\Sigma}_{12|3}$ into a correlation matrix. All the off-diagonal elements in this matrix have the same form as the off-diagonal elements in (11.34), so that

$$\rho(Z_{1,i}, Z_{1,j}|Z_3) = \frac{\rho(Z_{1,i}, Z_{1,j}) - \rho(Z_{1,i}, Z_3)\rho(Z_{1,j}, Z_3)}{\sqrt{1 - \rho^2(Z_{1,i}, Z_3)}\sqrt{1 - \rho^2(Z_{1,j}, Z_3)}}, \quad i, j = 1, \ldots, p_1, \tag{11.35}$$

$$\rho(Z_{2,i}, Z_{2,j}|Z_3) = \frac{\rho(Z_{2,i}, Z_{2,j}) - \rho(Z_{2,i}, Z_3)\rho(Z_{2,j}, Z_3)}{\sqrt{1 - \rho^2(Z_{2,i}, Z_3)}\sqrt{1 - \rho^2(Z_{2,j}, Z_3)}}, \quad i, j = 1, \ldots, p_2, \tag{11.36}$$

$$\rho(Z_{1,i}, Z_{2,j}|Z_3) = \frac{\rho(Z_{1,i}, Z_{2,j}) - \rho(Z_{1,i}, Z_3)\rho(Z_{2,j}, Z_3)}{\sqrt{1-\rho^2(Z_{1,i}, Z_3)}\sqrt{1-\rho^2(Z_{2,j}, Z_3)}},$$
$$i = 1, \ldots, p_1, j = 1, \ldots, p_2. \tag{11.37}$$

Testing for conditional independence between $\boldsymbol{Z}_1$ and $\boldsymbol{Z}_2$ given $\boldsymbol{Z}_3$ is in our context the same as testing for zero local partial correlation between all pairs of variables, a test presented in Section 11.7 and discussed in technical detail in the supplement of Otneim and Tjøstheim (2021). We can also, based on (11.35) and (11.36), test for conditional independence between combinations of components given $\boldsymbol{Z}_3$. Eqs. (11.35)–(11.37) give explicit expressions for the conditional correlation matrix of $\boldsymbol{Z}_1$ and $\boldsymbol{Z}_2$ given $\boldsymbol{Z}_3$, where estimated values give a measure of local conditional dependence between the components.

c) Let $p_1 = p_2 = 1$, and let p_3 be arbitrary. This is the case usually treated in the literature and also the focus of the discussions of this chapter. In this case,

$$\boldsymbol{\Sigma}^{11} = \begin{pmatrix} 1 & \rho_{12} \\ \rho_{21} & 1 \end{pmatrix}, \boldsymbol{\Sigma}_{13} = \left\{\rho_{1i}^{1,3}\right\}, i = 1, \ldots, p_3;$$
$$\boldsymbol{\Sigma}_{23} = \left\{\rho_{2i}^{2,3}\right\}, i = 1, \ldots, p_3,$$

and hence $\begin{pmatrix} \boldsymbol{\Sigma}_{13} & \boldsymbol{\Sigma}_{23} \end{pmatrix}^T$ is of dimension $2 \times p_3$, whereas $\begin{pmatrix} \boldsymbol{\Sigma}_{31} & \boldsymbol{\Sigma}_{32} \end{pmatrix}$ is of dimension $p_3 \times 2$, so that

$$\begin{pmatrix} \boldsymbol{\Sigma}_{13} \\ \boldsymbol{\Sigma}_{23} \end{pmatrix} \boldsymbol{\Sigma}_{33}^{-1} \begin{pmatrix} \boldsymbol{\Sigma}_{31} & \boldsymbol{\Sigma}_{32} \end{pmatrix}$$

is of dimension 2×2. However, as we immediately see, no formulas like (11.35)–(11.37) appear; they are much more complicated and include sums and products of various correlations.

d) Let p_1, p_2, and p_3 be arbitrary. This is the general case, and it seems impossible to obtain simple explicit formulas for the local Gaussian partial correlations, but, of course, the general fact still holds: The local partial correlation matrix of $\boldsymbol{Z}_1$ and $\boldsymbol{Z}_2$ given $\boldsymbol{Z}_3$ can be identified by the lower left-hand block matrix of $\boldsymbol{D}^{-1/2}\boldsymbol{\Sigma}_{12|3}\boldsymbol{D}^{-1/2}$ and can be estimated using pairwise local correlations in (11.33).

We refer to the supplement of Otneim and Tjøstheim (2021) for more details of relevant estimation theory in the general multivariate situation.

References

Baba, K., Shibata, R., Sibuya, M., 2004. Partial correlation and conditional correlation as measures of conditional independence. Australian & New Zealand Journal of Statistics 46 (4), 657–664.

Baek, E., Brock, W., 1992. A general test for nonlinear Granger causality: bivariate model. Iowa State University and University of Wisconsin at Madison Working Paper.

Bergsma, W., 2010. Nonparametric testing of conditional independence by means of the partial copula. Available at SSRN: https://ssrn.com/abstract=1702981 or https://doi.org/10.2139/ssrn.1702981.

Bouezmarni, T., Rombouts, J.V.K., Taamouti, A., 2012. Nonparametric copula-based test for conditional independence with applications to Granger causality. Journal of Business and Economic Statistics 30 (2), 275–287.

Bouezmarni, T., Taamouti, A., 2014. Nonparametric tests for conditional independence using conditional distributions. Journal of Nonparametric Statistics 26 (4), 697–719.

Cheng, Y.-H., Huang, T.-M., 2012. A conditional independence test for dependent data based on maximal conditional correlation. Journal of Multivariate Analysis 107, 210–226.

Delgado, M.A., Manteiga, W.G., 2001. Significance testing in nonparametric regression based on the bootstrap. Annals of Statistics 29 (5), 1469–1507.

Francis, B.B., Mougoue, M., Panchenko, V., 2010. Is there a symmetric nonlinear causal relationship between large and small firms? Journal of Empirical Finance 17 (1), 23–38.

Granger, C.W., 1969. Investigating causal relations by econometric models and cross-spectral methods. Econometrica, 424–438.

Granger, C.W., 1980. Testing for causality: a personal viewpoint. Journal of Economic Dynamics and control 2, 329–352.

Hjort, N., Jones, M., 1996. Locally parametric nonparametric density estimation. Annals of Statistics 24 (4), 1619–1647.

Huang, T.-M., 2010. Testing conditional independence using maximal nonlinear conditional correlation. Annals of Statistics 38 (4), 2047–2091.

Lacal, V., Tjøstheim, D., 2019. Estimating and testing nonlinear local dependence between two time series. Journal of Business and Economic Statistics 37 (4), 648–660.

Linton, O., Gozalo, P., 1997. Conditional independence restrictions: testing and estimation. Cowles Foundation Discussion Paper.

Linton, O., Gozalo, P., 2014. Testing conditional independence restrictions. Econometric Reviews 33 (5–6), 523–552.

Otneim, H., Tjøstheim, D., 2017. The locally Gaussian density estimator for multivariate data. Statistics and Computing 27 (6), 1595–1616.

Otneim, H., Tjøstheim, D., 2018. Conditional density estimation using the local Gaussian correlation. Statistics and Computing 28 (2), 303–321.

Otneim, H., Tjøstheim, D., 2021. The locally Gaussian partial correlation. Journal of Business & Economic Statistics, 1–33.

Patra, R.K., Sen, B., Székely, G.J., 2016. On a nonparametric notion of residual and its applications. Statistics and Probability Letters 109, 208–213.

Song, K., 2009. Testing conditional independence via Rosenblatt transforms. Annals of Statistics 37 (6B), 4011–4045.

Su, L., White, H., 2007. A consistent characteristic-function-based test for conditional independence. Journal of Econometrics 141 (2), 807–837.

Su, L., White, H., 2008. A nonparametric Hellinger metric test for conditional independence. Econometric Theory 24 (4), 829–864.

Su, L., White, H., 2014. Testing conditional independence via empirical likelihood. Journal of Econometrics 182 (1), 27–44.

Su, L., White, H.L., 2012. Conditional independence specification testing for dependent processes with local polynomial quantile regression. In: Essays in Honor of Jerry Hausman. Emerald Group Publishing Limited, pp. 355–434.

Teräsvirta, T., Tjøstheim, D., Granger, C.W., 2010. Modelling Nonlinear Economic Time Series. Oxford University Press.
Wang, X., Hong, Y., 2018. Characteristic function based testing for conditional independence: a nonparametric regression approach. Econometric Theory 34 (4), 815–849.
Wang, X., Pan, W., Hu, W., Tian, Y., Zhang, H., 2015. Conditional distance correlation. Journal of the American Statistical Association 110 (512), 1726–1734.
Zhang, K., Peters, J., Janzing, D., Schölkopf, B., 2012. Kernel-based conditional independence test and applications in causal discovery. In: Proceedings of the Uncertainty in Artificial Intelligence. AUAI Press, Corvallis, Oregon, pp. 804–813.

CHAPTER 12

Regression and conditional regression quantiles

Contents

12.1. Introduction 385
12.2. Comparison with additive regression modeling 387
12.3. Local Gaussian regression estimation 388
12.4. Asymptotic normality 390
12.5. Example 394
12.6. Conditional quantiles 396
12.6.1 Distribution of the conditional empirical distribution function 396
12.6.2 Convergence rate 396
12.6.3 Distribution of conditional quantiles 397
12.7. Proof 398
References 401

12.1 Introduction

Arguably, the most important nonparametric estimation technique is nonparametric regression estimation. In general, in nonlinear regression, we seek to model an output variable Y by means of a number of explanatory variables $(X_1, \ldots, X_p)$ such that, in the simplest case,

$$Y = g(X_1, \ldots, X_p) + \varepsilon,$$

where g is an unknown function to be estimated, and ε is a residual term. In the case that ε is independent from $(X_1, \ldots, X_p)$, the function g can be identified with the conditional mean so that $\mathrm{E}(Y|X_1, \ldots, X_p) = g(X_1, \ldots, X_p)$. The nonparametric estimation of such models was briefly discussed in Chapter 2.6 in the scalar case using the Nadaraya–Watson kernel estimator in Eq. (2.16) of that chapter. This formula can readily be extended to the vector case, where the explanatory variables form a vector $\mathbf{X} = (X_1, \ldots, X_p)^T$. With $\mathbf{x} = (x_1, \ldots, x_p)^T$, in principle, $g(\mathbf{x})$ can be estimated as in Eq. (2.16), so that for given observations $\{Y_j, \mathbf{X_j}\}$, $j = 1, \ldots, n$, the estimate is given by

$$\hat{g}(\mathbf{x}) = \frac{\sum_{j=1}^{n} Y_j K_{\mathbf{B}}(\mathbf{X}_j - \mathbf{x})}{\sum_{j=1}^{n} K_{\mathbf{B}}(\mathbf{X}_j - \mathbf{x})}. \tag{12.1}$$

Statistical Modeling using Local Gaussian Approximation
https://doi.org/10.1016/B978-0-12-815861-6.00019-5

Here $K_{\mathbf{B}}(\cdot) = |\mathbf{B}^{-1}|K(\mathbf{B}^{-1}\cdot)$, where $\mathbf{B}$ is a bandwidth matrix, usually taken to be diagonal with $\mathbf{B} = \text{diag}(\mathbf{b}) = \text{diag}(b_i)$, and K is a kernel function, usually taken to be a product of p kernel functions K_i, $i = 1, \ldots, p$, so that $K_{\mathbf{b}}(\mathbf{X}_j - \mathbf{x}) = \prod_{i=1}^{p} b_i^{-1} K(b_i^{-1}(X_{ij} - x_i))$, where X_{ij} is the jth observation of the component X_i of $\mathbf{X}$.

The problem with (12.1), as already indicated in Chapter 2, is the curse of dimensionality. As p increases, there will be fewer and fewer observations available in each data cell. Extremely large sample sizes are required to get reasonably accurate results for $p > 4$.

In Chapter 2, we outlined various ways of avoiding the curse: additive regression, semiparametric estimation, and partial linear models. How does the local Gaussian modeling enter into this setting? We have seen in several chapters, most recently in Chapters 9–11, how the curse can be at least partially circumvented using the pairwise simplification introduced already in Chapter 4.9. Can it be made useful for the regression case as well? How does the pairwise simplification compare with, for example, the additive approximation? We try to indicate an answer to these and related questions in the present chapter.

In a sense, this chapter is different from the other chapters based more directly on the concept of local Gaussian approximation. The route from a local distributional concept to a local regression concept is a little circuitous, and the results in the present chapter are a bit more preliminary. However, we believe they serve to demonstrate the potential of a local Gaussian approximation. This chapter is the only chapter on the local Gaussian approximation that is not based on a published paper. Nevertheless, in view of the importance of nonparametric regression, we have decided to include a brief chapter on this theme from the angle of local Gaussian approximation. In Section 12.2, we compare it with additive regression modeling. We formulate a local Gaussian regression (LGR) estimate in Section 12.3 and sketch an asymptotic theory in Section 12.4. A simple example is given in Section 12.5.

Another type of regression modeling mentioned briefly in Chapter 2 is the quantile regression. In standard nonparametric regression, we estimate the conditional mean and variance. In regression quantile modeling, we try to estimate the conditional quantiles. In Section 12.6, we cover quite briefly and quite schematically the conditional quantile estimation using a local Gaussian approximation. Here too there is a curse of dimensionality as the number of regressors increases.

12.2 Comparison with additive regression modeling

In the following, we use f as a symbol for a probability density function. The density function for all variables involved will be implicitly assumed to exist.

If an additive model is true, then

$$Y = \sum_{i=1}^{p} g_i(X_i) + \varepsilon,$$

and letting $f(y|\mathbf{x})$ be the conditional density of Y given $\mathbf{X}=\mathbf{x}$, we have

$$f(y|\mathbf{X}=\mathbf{x}) = f_\varepsilon(y - \sum_i g_i(x_i)),$$

where f_ε is the density of ε. If ε is Gaussian, then the distribution of $Y|\mathbf{X}=\mathbf{x}$ is Gaussian $\mathcal{N}(\sum_i g_i(x_i), \sigma_\varepsilon^2)$, and local pairwise conditional density estimation should be optimal, and we would think that $\int y\hat{f}(y|\mathbf{x})dy$ will be close to the "global" mean in this Gaussian distribution, that is, close to $E(Y|\mathbf{X}=\mathbf{x}) = \sum_i g_i(x_i)$. Heteroskedasticity with

$$Y = \sum_i g(X_i) + \sum_i h(X_i)\varepsilon$$

where

$$f(y|\mathbf{x}) = f_\varepsilon((y - \sum_i g(x_i))/\sum_i h_i(x_i))$$

is possible to treat in the same way. In fact, and in principle, exactly the same reasoning is valid for a Gaussian ε for the general case where

$$Y = g(X_1, \ldots, X_p) + h(X_1, \ldots, X_q)\varepsilon.$$

If ε is non-Gaussian, then the situation is more unclear. The pairwise model may or may not be a good approximation.

Our method should work also for models such as

$$Y = X_1X_2 + \varepsilon,$$

where $E(Y|\mathbf{X}=\mathbf{x}) = x_1x_2$ and $f(y|\mathbf{X}=\mathbf{x}) = f_\varepsilon(y - x_1x_2)$. Here an additive approximation via backfitting may not work, because $E(Y|X_1) = X_1E(X_2) = 0$ and $E(Y|X_2) = X_2E(X_1) = 0$ if X_1 and X_2 are independent and have zero mean. Note, however, that pairwise interaction additivity will get this right (cf. Chapter 2.7). Other and more complicated examples can be found with the degree of the product increased gradually. All this indicates that a pairwise density approximation of a conditional expectation is distinct from an additive approximation and can be made to work in some cases where the additive approximation does not work, but examples of the opposite situation can also be found.

12.3 Local Gaussian regression estimation

In Chapter 10, we treated conditional density estimates $\hat{f}(y|\mathbf{x})$. An estimate of $g(\mathbf{x}) = \mathrm{E}(Y|\mathbf{X} = \mathbf{x})$ can then formally be obtained by numerical integration:

$$\hat{g}(\mathbf{x}) = \int y\hat{f}(y|\mathbf{x})\,\mathrm{d}y. \tag{12.2}$$

Starting from (12.2) under regularity conditions, we have

$$E(\hat{g}(x)) = \int y\mathrm{E}(\hat{f}(y|\mathbf{x}))\,\mathrm{d}y, \quad \mathrm{Var}(\hat{g}(x)) = \int (y - \mathrm{E}(\hat{g}(x)))^2 f(y|\mathbf{x})\,\mathrm{d}y.$$

Alternatively, we can use the estimate

$$\hat{g}_w(\mathbf{x}) = \frac{1}{n}\sum_i \frac{Y_i\hat{f}(Y_i|\mathbf{X} = \mathbf{x})}{\hat{f}(Y_i)} w(Y_i), \tag{12.3}$$

where w is a weight function. This estimate perhaps illustrates the somewhat circuitous way of getting an estimate of the conditional mean using local Gaussian approximation, although the denominator in (12.3) can be compared to the denominator in the Nadaraya–Watson kernel estimator of the conditional expectation.

Intuitively, assuming ergodicity and using the ergodic theorem on (12.3), this should converge to

$$\int \frac{yf(y|\mathbf{x})}{f(y)} w(y) f(y)\,\mathrm{d}y = \int yf(y|\mathbf{x})w(y)\,\mathrm{d}y.$$

Here is an argument for this: We will take $w(Y_i) = I_A(Y_i)$, where A is a compact set, $I_A(y)$ is the indicator function with $I_A(y) = 1$ for $y \in A$ and zero else, and where $f(y)$ may be assumed to be positive on A. By taking A large enough we see that its introduction in (12.3) is not a strong restriction in practice, but it makes the mathematical analysis far easier.

In Chapter 9, we have proved that $\hat{f}(y) - f(y) = o_P(1)$ (i.e., the pointwise consistency) under weak regularity conditions. A standard argument involving a finite covering of A with suitable intervals shows that $[\hat{f}(y) - f(y)]I_A(y) = o_P(1)$ uniformly on A. Similarly, starting with pointwise consistency, as demonstrated by Otneim and Tjøstheim (2018), $[\hat{f}(y|\mathbf{x}) - f(y|\mathbf{x})]I_A(y) = o_P(1)$ uniformly on A.

Let $F(y) = F_Y(y)$ be the cumulative distribution function of Y, and let $F_n(y)$ be the corresponding empirical distribution function,

$$F_n(y) = \frac{1}{n}\sum_{i=1}^{n} I(Y_i \le y).$$

Note that

$$\frac{1}{n}\sum_{i=1}^{n} \frac{Y_i\hat{f}(Y_i|\mathbf{X}=\mathbf{x})}{\hat{f}(Y_i)} I_A(Y_i) = \int_A \frac{y\hat{f}(y|\mathbf{X}=\mathbf{x})}{\hat{f}(y)}\,\mathrm{d}F_n(y)$$

$$= \int_A \frac{yf(y|\mathbf{X}=\mathbf{x})}{f(y)}\,\mathrm{d}F_n(y) + \left(\int_A \frac{y\hat{f}(y|\mathbf{X}=\mathbf{x})}{\hat{f}(y)} - \int_A \frac{yf(y|\mathbf{X}=\mathbf{x})}{f(y)}\right)\mathrm{d}F(y)$$

$$+ \left(\int_A \frac{y\hat{f}(y|\mathbf{X}=\mathbf{x})}{\hat{f}(y)} - \int_A \frac{yf(y|\mathbf{X}=\mathbf{x})}{f(y)}\right)(\mathrm{d}F_n(y) - \mathrm{d}F(y)). \tag{12.4}$$

Assuming that $f(y) > 0$ for $y \in A$, here the first term in the second line of (12.4) by ergodicity converges in probability (and almost surely) to $g_A(\mathbf{x}) = \int_A yf(y|\mathbf{x})\,\mathrm{d}y$, which comes close to $g(\mathbf{x})$ for A large enough. The other terms approach zero in probability due to the convergence of the empirical distribution function to the cumulative distribution function and due to the above uniformity argument. Moreover, note that in the denominator of (12.3), $\hat{f}(Y_i)$ can be written as $f(Y_i)$ in theoretical arguments. This is because $\hat{f}(Y_i)$ can be written as

$$f(Y_i)\left(1 - \frac{f(Y_i) - \hat{f}(Y_i)}{f(Y_i)}\right),$$

the convergence on A is uniform, $f(y) > 0$, and the convergence rate for $\hat{f}(y)$ is faster than for $\hat{f}(y|\mathbf{X}=\mathbf{x})$.

12.4 Asymptotic normality

Before stating a theorem on asymptotic normality of the estimator

$$\hat{g}_A(x) = \frac{1}{n} \sum_i \frac{Y_i \hat{f}(Y_i | \mathbf{X} = \mathbf{x})}{\hat{f}(Y_i)} I_A(Y_i) \tag{12.5}$$

of the conditional mean, we need to introduce some additional notation and to do some preliminaries on the relation between results on the normalized $\boldsymbol{z}$-scale and the original $\boldsymbol{x}$-scale. The different status of the Y and $\mathbf{X}$-variables make this a non-trivial task. In the following, we use the shorthand notation $F(y)$ for $F_Y(y)$ and $F_i(x_i)$ for $F_{X_i}(x_i)$, and similarly for the density functions.

(i) We have already mentioned that $\hat{f}$ in the denominator of (12.5) has a faster rate than the numerator, so that $\hat{f}(Y_i)$ can be replaced by $f(Y_i)$ in an asymptotic analysis.

(ii) The standard normal variables $Z = Z_Y = \Phi^{-1}(F(Y))$ and $Z_i = \Phi^{-1}(F_i(X_i))$ play an important role in the following and in the simplified pairwise model of Otneim and Tjøstheim (2017, 2018) and Chapters 9–11; see, in particular, Eq. (9.6) for a precise definition. Here Φ is the cumulative distribution of the standard normal, and in the following, ϕ is the standard normal density. In practice, Z and Z_i are not observed and have to be replaced by the pseudo-standard normal observations $\hat{Z} = \Phi^{-1}(F_n(Y))$ and $\hat{Z}_i = \Phi^{-1}(F_{in}(X_i))$. It was shown in Chapter 4.7, the proof of Theorem 4.5, that in a derivation of asymptotic distributions involved in a pairwise approximation, the variables $\hat{Z}$ and $\hat{Z}_i$ can be replaced by Z and Z_i. The error caused by this replacement is smaller in order than the error involved in the conditional estimates, essentially because the latter contains a bandwidth parameter. Therefore, in the asymptotic analysis below, we will treat the variables Z and Z_i as known.

In Chapter 10.2, Eq. (10.3), we looked generally at $\hat{f}(\mathbf{X}_1 | \mathbf{X}_2 = \mathbf{x}_2)$ with $\mathbf{X} = (\mathbf{X}_1, \mathbf{X}_2)$. We will further take $\mathbf{X}_1 = Z$ such that $\dim(\boldsymbol{X}_1) = 1$ and $\mathbf{X}_2 = \mathbf{Z}_2 \stackrel{\text{def}}{=} (Z_1, \ldots, Z_p)$. It follows from Chapter 10.2, Eq. (10.3), that

$$f_{\mathbf{X}_1|\mathbf{X}_2}(\mathbf{x}_1 | \mathbf{X}_2 = \mathbf{x}_2) = \frac{f_{\mathbf{X}}(\mathbf{x})}{f_{\mathbf{X}_2}(\mathbf{x}_2)} = \frac{f_{Z,\mathbf{Z}}(z, z_1, \ldots, z_p)}{f_{\mathbf{Z}}(z_1, \ldots, z_p)} \frac{f(y)}{\phi(z)}. \tag{12.6}$$

Recall that $z = \Phi^{-1}(F(y))$, $z_i = \Phi^{-1}(F_i(x_i))$, so that the expression in (12.6) is in fact a function of $(y, x_1, \ldots, x_p)$. However, as just stated, neglecting the difference between the empirical and theoretical cumulative distribution functions, everything that we have to do with estimation is inherent in the $(Z, \mathbf{Z})$-representation. Then using the strongest form of approximation in Chapter 9, Eqs. (9.6) and (9.7), where the pairwise local Gaussian approximation of $(Z, \mathbf{Z})$ has $Z \sim \mathcal{N}(0,1)$ and $Z_i \sim \mathcal{N}(0,1)$ (i.e., $\mu(z) = \mu_i(z_i) = 0$ and $\sigma^2(z) = \sigma_i^2(z_i) = 1$), we only have to take into account the estimation of the local correlations $\rho(z_i, z_j)$ and $\rho(z, z_j)$.

(iii) Using the conditional representation in (10.3) of Chapter 10.2, we obtain

$$f(z|\mathbf{z}) = \Psi^\star(z; \mu^\star, (\sigma^*)^2),$$

where $\Psi^\star$ is the univariate Gaussian density with expectation and variance given by (see Eqs. (10.5) and (10.6))

$$\mu^\star|\mathbf{z} = \mathbf{R}_{12}\mathbf{R}_{22}^{-1}\mathbf{z},$$
$$(\sigma^\star)^2|\mathbf{z} = \mathbf{R}_{11} - \mathbf{R}_{12}\mathbf{R}_{22}^{-1}\mathbf{R}_{21},$$

where $\mathbf{R}_{11}$ is a scalar, and the $\mathbf{R}$-matrices are the appropriate block matrices of the full $\mathbf{R}$ matrix consisting of all of the local correlations $\{\rho(z, z_i)\}$ and $\{\rho(z_i, z_j)\}$ at $(z, \mathbf{z})$-level.

All this means that the estimate $\hat{f}(y|\mathbf{x})$ can be obtained by the pairwise method of Chapter 10, which in turn means that the estimate will be a function of the vector comprised by $\{\hat{\rho}(z, z_i); \hat{\rho}(z_i, z_j),\ i, j = 1, \dots, p, i \neq j\}$, with $z = \Phi^{-1}(F(y))$ and $z_i = \Phi^{-1}(F(x_i))$. We will denote by $\boldsymbol{\rho}(z, \mathbf{z})$ the corresponding parameter vector and by $\hat{\boldsymbol{\rho}} = \widehat{\boldsymbol{\rho}}_{n,b}(z, \mathbf{z})$ the estimated parameter vector.

The next task is writing $\hat{g}_A(\mathbf{x})$ in a format that can be recognized using the techniques of Lacal and Tjøstheim (2017, 2019) and of Chapters 9 and 10. In particular, using Eqs. (9.5) and (10.4), $f(y|\mathbf{x})$ can be expressed as a function of $(y, \mathbf{x})$ and an exponential function of the ρ-parameters on the $(z, \mathbf{z})$-level. Using the just defined notation of $\boldsymbol{\rho}(z, \mathbf{z})$, we can write $f(y|\mathbf{x})$ as a function $H(y, \mathbf{x}, \boldsymbol{\rho}(z, \mathbf{z}))$, which again can be transformed into a function in $(y, \mathbf{x})$ by the transformations $y = F^{-1}(\Phi(z))$ and $x_i = F_i^{-1}(\Phi(z_i))$.

For convenience, we use b for a common scalar bandwidth parameter, using that (z, z_i) and (z_i, z_j) are all on the same scale and hence assuming that $\mathbf{b} = (b_1, \dots, b_{p+1})$ and $b_i = b$. We have

$$\hat{g}_A(\mathbf{x}) = \int y \frac{H(y, \mathbf{x}, \hat{\boldsymbol{\rho}}_b(z, \mathbf{z}))}{\hat{f}(y)} I_A(y)\, \mathrm{d}F_n(y), \tag{12.7}$$

where $\hat{f}(y)$ can be replaced by $f(y)$. By a further simplification in notation this can be written as

$$\hat{g}_A(\mathbf{x}) = \int_A y G(y, \mathbf{x}, \hat{\boldsymbol{\rho}}_b(z, \mathbf{z}))\, \mathrm{d}F_n(y) \stackrel{\text{def}}{=} \int_A R(y, \mathbf{x}, \hat{\boldsymbol{\rho}}_b(z, \mathbf{z}))\, \mathrm{d}F_n(y) \quad (12.8)$$

with obvious definitions of the functions H, G, and R. We have now obtained a form of $\hat{g}_A(x)$ where the method of the proof of Theorem 3.1 of Lacal and Tjøstheim (2017) can be applied. (Note that at this stage the bandwidth parameter b is fixed.)

Following the notation of Lacal and Tjøstheim (2017) and Chapter 7, we write

$$G_n(y) = \sqrt{n}(F_n(y) - F(y)) \quad \text{and} \quad \mathbf{V}_n(z, \mathbf{z}) = \sqrt{n}(\widehat{\boldsymbol{\rho}}_{n,b}(z, \mathbf{z}) - \boldsymbol{\rho}_b(z, \mathbf{z})). \quad (12.9)$$

Then, again following Lacal and Tjøstheim (2017), the leading term of $\hat{g}_A(\mathbf{x}) - g_A(\mathbf{x})$ is given by

$$\hat{g}_A(\mathbf{x}) - g_A(\mathbf{x}) \sim \frac{1}{\sqrt{n}}\Big[\int_A R(y, \mathbf{x}, \boldsymbol{\rho}(z, \mathbf{z})\, \mathrm{d}G_n(y) + \int_A (\nabla_\rho R(y, \mathbf{x}, \boldsymbol{\rho}(z, \mathbf{z}))^T \mathbf{V}_n(z, \mathbf{z})\, \mathrm{d}F(y)\Big]. \quad (12.10)$$

Note that $\nabla_\rho R$ and $\mathbf{V}_n$ are $p + (p(p-1)/2$ dimensional vectors and that the inner product between them results in a sum containing $p + p(p-1)/2$ terms. From Lacal and Tjøstheim (2017) to obtain an integral expressed in terms of G_n only, we need to approximate and re-express $\mathbf{V}_n$. We do that by pairwise likelihood estimation as in Chapters 9 and 10. We first focus on the (z, z_i)-component of $\mathbf{V}_n(z, \mathbf{z})$.

We will neglect the bias (by an appropriate choice of b), as it was done by Lacal and Tjøstheim (2017, 2019) and Joe (1989), that much of our derivation here builds on. Our reasoning will be concentrated on demonstrating asymptotic normality and, in particular, on finding an expression for the asymptotic variance and the order of this variance in terms of n and b, this making it possible to compare with the rate in additive regression.

Before stating the asymptotic result, we need to define some expressions that will appear in the asymptotic expression. Further, since these results are valid for a stationary time series regression case, we use t as an index for Y, Z and X_i, Z_i, so that Z_{it} is the observation at time t of Z_i. We first look at the pair (Z, Z_i). Let

$$A_b^{(i)}(\mathbf{x}, v, w_i) = \int_A \frac{\partial}{\partial \rho(z, z_i)} R(y, \mathbf{x}, \boldsymbol{\rho}(z, \mathbf{z})) J_b(z, z_i) K_b(v - z, w_i - z_i) \times u(v, w_i, \rho_b(z, z_i))\, \mathrm{d}F(y), \quad (12.11)$$

where we recall that $z_i = \Phi^{-1}(F_i(x_i))$ and $z = \Phi^{-1}(F(y))$, and where

$$u(v, w_i, \rho) = \nabla_\rho \log \psi(v, w_i, \rho) \quad (12.12)$$

with $\psi(v, w_i, \rho)$ being a bivariate normal density with correlation $\rho = \rho(z, z_i)$, zero expectations, and unity standard deviations. Further,

$$J_b(z, z_i) = E[-\nabla_\rho^2 L^{(b)}(Z_t, Z_{it}, \rho(z, z_i))] \quad (12.13)$$

with

$$L^{(b)}(Z_t, Z_{it}, \rho) = K_b(Z_t - z, Z_{it} - z_i) \log \psi(Z_t, Z_{it}, \rho) - \int K_b(v - z, w_i - z_i) \psi(v, w_i, \rho)\, \mathrm{d}v\, \mathrm{d}w_i. \quad (12.14)$$

Moreover, we use the notation

$$F_n^{(z, z_i)}(v, w_i) = \frac{1}{n} \sum_{t=1}^{n} I(Z_t \le v, Z_{it} \le w_i)$$

and

$$G_n^{(z, z_i)}(v, w_i) = \sqrt{n}(F_n^{(z, z_i)}(v, w_i) - F^{(z, z_i)}(v, w_i)) \quad (12.15)$$

with similar definitions of $F_n^{(z_i, z_j)}(w_i, w_j)$ and $G_n^{(z_i, z_j)}(w_i, w_j)$.

Theorem 12.1. *Let $\{Y_t, \mathbf{X}_t\}$ be a stationary ergodic time series such that the marginally transformed series $\{Z_t, \mathbf{Z}_t\}$ has components with density $f(z, \mathbf{z})$. Assume that*

(i) *$\{Y_t, \mathbf{X}_t\}$ is α-mixing (cf. definition in Eq. (7.15)) with $\alpha_n = O(\alpha^n)$, $\alpha \in (0, 1)$, and such that for each component of $\{Y_t, \mathbf{X}_t\}$, the moment of order $2 + \delta$ is finite for some $\delta > 0$.*

(ii) *The kernel function K is symmetric (and otherwise is fulfilling the standard assumptions for a kernel function).*

(iii) *The density function $f(y, \mathbf{x})$ and hence $f(z, \mathbf{z})$ are bounded for $y \in A$.*

(iv) *The marginal density $f(y) > 0$ for $y \in A$, and $f(y, \mathbf{x})$ has continuous second-order derivatives.*

Then, as $n \to \infty$, $b \to 0$, *and* $nb \to \infty$,

$$\sqrt{n}[C_n(A_b)]^{-1/2}[\hat{g}_A(x) - g_A(\mathbf{x})] \xrightarrow{d} \mathcal{N}(0,1),$$

where for $(y, \mathbf{x}) \in \mathbb{R}^{p+1}$ *and* $(u, \mathbf{v}) \in \mathbb{R}^{p+1}$,

$$C_n(A_b) = \sum_{i=1}^{p} Var\Big(\int A_b^{(i)}(\mathbf{x}, v, w_i)\, dG_n^{(z,z_i)}(v, w_i)\Big)$$
$$+ \sum_{i \neq j} Cov\Big(\int A_b^{(i)}(\mathbf{x}, v, w_i)\, dG_n^{(z,z_i)}(v, w_i), \int A_b^{(j)}(\mathbf{x}, v, w_j)\Big)\, dG_n^{(z,z_j)}(v, w_j), \tag{12.16}$$

where $A_b^{(i)}(\mathbf{x}, v, w_i)$ *is given by* (12.11).

Moreover, $\hat{g}_A(\mathbf{x})$ *approaches* $g_A(\mathbf{x})$ *at a convergence rate of* $(nb)^{-1/2}$ *in probability, which is of the same order as in the ordinary additive modeling case.*

A proof for this result is sketched in Section 12.7.

Note that we can obtain a more explicit expression of (12.11) analogous to that given in the proof of Theorem 4.4 in the supplement of Lacal and Tjøstheim (2017). Convergence of these expressions is guaranteed by the mixing assumption.

In practice the terms of (12.16) are extremely difficult to evaluate analytically, and therefore the estimation error evaluation has been done by a type of block bootstrap; see Chapter 10. The validity of the block bootstrap in a related situation is established by Lacal and Tjøstheim (2017, 2019).

In the case of a sequence of independent observations $\{(Y_j, \mathbf{X}_j)\}, j = 1, \ldots, n$, it is easy to prove asymptotic normality using the classical central limit theorem.

12.5 Example

Let us briefly demonstrate the concept of local Gaussian regression estimation using a simulated example. Assume that we observe two stochastic variables X and Y that depend on each other through the regression relationship

$$Y = X^3 + \epsilon, \tag{12.17}$$

where ϵ is normally distributed with mean zero and standard deviation equal to two, and where we simulate X uniformly on the interval $[-2, 2]$.

In addition, we generate a number of extra noise variables $\boldsymbol{W}$ from a multivariate t-distribution with 10 degrees of freedom, resulting in observed samples $(X_i, Y_i, W_{i1}, \ldots, W_{ik})$, where $i = 1, \ldots, n$, $n = 500$, and $k \in \{0, 2, 5\}$.

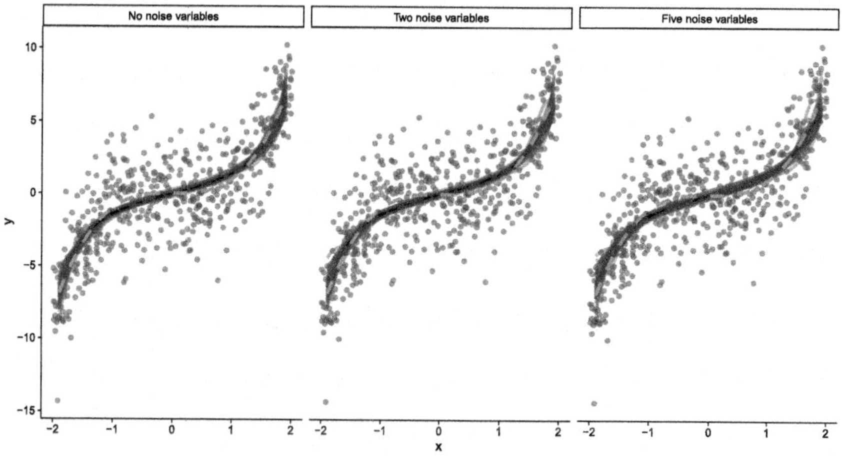

Figure 12.1 Nonlinear regression using local Gaussian approximations. Each black line represents one realization, and the red dashed line represents the true relationship between the explanatory and response variables. One sample from this model is displayed in the background as a scatter plot.

We seek to recover relationship (12.17) by estimating the joint density of the observations and then estimating the conditional mean $g(x) = \mathrm{E}(Y|X = x, W_1 = \cdots = W_k = 0)$ by applying formula (12.2):

$$\widehat{g}(x) = \int y\widehat{f}_{Y|X=x,W_1=\cdots=W_k=0}(y|x)\,\mathrm{d}y.$$

We estimate the conditional density function $f_{Y|X=x,W_1=\cdots=W_k=0}$ using the pairwise restriction described in Chapter 9 and choose the bandwidths by visual inspection of the smoothness of the regression curves in this small example. Data driven bandwidth selection along the lines of Li and Racine (2008) should be possible.

See Fig. 12.1 for the results of this experiment. We estimate (12.17) in the case where we only observe X and Y, as well as the multivariate cases where we also observe two and five noise variables.

The results indicate that local Gaussian approximations may be useful when estimating nonlinear relationships such as (12.17), in particular, in multivariate problems.

12.6 Conditional quantiles

There are a number of references to conditional quantile (or regression quantile) estimation. We have in particular found Samanta (1989), Cai (2002), Li and Racine (2008), and Racine and Li (2017) to be useful. These are all based on kernel estimation and are sensitive to the curse of dimensionality. One way of avoiding the curse is to use an additive approach as in Horowitz and Lee (2005) and Yu and Lu (2004).

Our idea is using a local Gaussian approach and pairwise modeling as introduced above to lessen the effect of the curse of dimensionality. We just sketch the approach. It is quite similar to that in Section 12.4 for the conditional mean.

12.6.1 Distribution of the conditional empirical distribution function

A regression p-quantile $q_p(\mathbf{x})$ is formally defined as

$$q_p(\mathbf{x}) = \inf\{y \in \mathbb{R} : F(y|\mathbf{x}) \geq p\} \equiv F^{-1}(p|\mathbf{x}),$$

where, as in Section 12.4, $F(y|\mathbf{x})$ is the conditional cumulative distribution function. Hence a key part of establishing asymptotic properties in the cited papers is first proving asymptotic properties of the conditional empirical distribution function and then examining the process of inversion. So we start by looking at the estimate (see Eq. (12.3))

$$\hat{F}(u|\mathbf{x}) = \frac{1}{n}\sum_i \frac{I(Y_i \leq u)\hat{f}(Y_i|\mathbf{X}=\mathbf{x})}{\hat{f}(Y_i)} \tag{12.18}$$

of the conditional cumulative distribution function. Using the ergodic theorem (see Section 12.3) we see that estimate (12.18) converges to $\int_{-\infty}^{u} f(y|\mathbf{x})\,dy$.

Estimator (12.18) has exactly the same structure as the conditional mean estimator (12.3), and we can in principle prove asymptotic normality with asymptotic mean and variance (again, we will ignore the asymptotic bias term). The only difference is in the definition of $R(y, \mathbf{x}, \boldsymbol{\rho})$ in (12.8), where y is replaced by $I_u(y) = I(y \leq u)$.

12.6.2 Convergence rate

The convergence rates for the local Gaussian estimates of the conditional mean and the conditional distribution function are the same. For the fixed

b-case, the convergence rate is $n^{-1/2}$. As $b \to 0$, the reasoning in Section 12.4 and the proof of Theorem 12.1 can be used. This, in turn, is based on the reasoning in Lacal and Tjøstheim (2017, 2019); see, in particular, Remark 3.1 of Lacal and Tjøstheim (2019).

In the simplified pairwise approximation of the $(Z, \mathbf{Z})$-case the rate is $(nb)^{-1/2}$, which is the same as in the regression additive case and in the scalar-x kernel estimate of the conditional mean and the conditional distribution (see Cai (2002) for the latter case). In the higher-dimensional $\mathbf{x}$-kernel case the rate is $(nb^p)^{-1/2}$ for both the conditional mean and the conditional distribution function, where p is the dimension of $\mathbf{x}$.

12.6.3 Distribution of conditional quantiles

The approach here is using Lemma 4 and Theorem 3 of Cai (2002). The key result is his Lemma 4, where, corresponding to that lemma, we must prove that for any $\delta_n \to 0$, $\hat{F}(y+\delta_n|\mathbf{x}) - \hat{F}(y|\mathbf{x}) = f(y|\mathbf{x})\delta_n + o_P(\delta_n) + o_P$ (convergence rate of $\hat{F}(y|\mathbf{x})$). Using the same notation as in Section 12.4, we have

$$\hat{F}(y|\mathbf{x}) = \int I(r \le y)\frac{\hat{f}(r|\mathbf{x})}{\hat{f}(r)}\,\mathrm{d}F_n(r) = \int I(r \le y)\frac{H(r, \mathbf{x}, \hat{\boldsymbol{\rho}}(z, \mathbf{z}))}{\hat{f}(r)}\,\mathrm{d}F_n(r).$$

Then

$$\hat{F}(y+\delta_n|\mathbf{x}) - \hat{F}(y|\mathbf{x}) = \int_y^{y+\delta_n} \frac{H(r, \mathbf{x}, \hat{\boldsymbol{\rho}}(z, \mathbf{z})}{\hat{f}(r)}\,\mathrm{d}F_n(r).$$

Similarly, we can write

$$F(y+\delta_n|\mathbf{x}) - F(y|\mathbf{x}) = \int_y^{y+\delta_n} \frac{H(r, \mathbf{x}, \boldsymbol{\rho}(z, \mathbf{z})}{f(r)}\,\mathrm{d}F(r).$$

We now put $\hat{f}(r) = f(r)$ in the denominator and use the analogue of equation (12.10) to write (identifying $g_A(\mathbf{x})$ with $F_A(y+\delta_n|\mathbf{x}) - F_A(y|\mathbf{x}) = \int_y^{y+\delta_n} \frac{H(r,\mathbf{x},\boldsymbol{\theta}(z,\mathbf{z})}{f(r)} I_A(r)\,\mathrm{d}F(r)$)

$$\begin{aligned}
&[\hat{F}_A(y+\delta_n|\mathbf{x}) - \hat{F}_A(y|\mathbf{x})] - [F_A(y+\delta_n|\mathbf{x}) - F_A(y|\mathbf{x})] \\
&\sim \frac{1}{\sqrt{n}}\Big[\int_{A_n} R'(r, \mathbf{x}, \boldsymbol{\rho}(z, \mathbf{z})I_A(r)\,\mathrm{d}G_n(r) \\
&+ \int_{A_n} \nabla_\rho R'(r, \mathbf{x}, \boldsymbol{\rho}(z, \mathbf{z}))^T \mathbf{V}_n(z, \mathbf{z}) I_A(r)\,\mathrm{d}F(r)\Big], \qquad (12.19)
\end{aligned}$$

where the integration region is given by $A_n = \{r : y \le r \le y + \delta_n\}$,

$$R'(r, \mathbf{x}, \boldsymbol{\rho}(z, \mathbf{z})) = \frac{f(r|\mathbf{x}, \boldsymbol{\rho}(z, \mathbf{z}))}{f(r)},$$

and G_n and $\mathbf{V}_n$ are defined in equation (12.9). We are now in a position to evaluate the terms of equation (12.19). A simple Taylor expansion reveals that

$$F(y + \delta_n|\mathbf{x}) - F(y|\mathbf{x}) \sim f(y|\mathbf{x})\delta_n + o(\delta_n)$$

(here $o(\delta_n)$ is changed to $o_P(\delta_n)$ if $\mathbf{x} = \mathbf{X}$ is stochastic). The terms on the right-hand side of (12.19) can be evaluated in exactly the same way as the evaluation of (12.10). For a fixed δ_n it is of order $O_P(nb)^{-1/2}$ in the case of a simplified $(Z, \mathbf{Z})$-representation. As $\delta_n \to 0$, this order changes into $o_P(nb)^{-1/2}$, and a result analogous to Lemma 4 of Cai (2002) is easily proved.

Having established this lemma, we can now proceed as in Cai (2002) to prove asymptotic normality of the quantile estimates $\widehat{q}_p(\mathbf{x})$ by inversion of the estimated conditional cumulative distribution function. The expression for the asymptotic variance is different, now being given by $\frac{\mathrm{Var}(\hat{F}_A(q_p(\mathbf{x}))|\mathbf{x})}{(f(q_p(\mathbf{x})|\mathbf{x}))^2}$, where the notation is as in Cai (2002), and the variance of the estimate of the conditional cumulative distribution function can be found using the analog of the earlier expressions for $A_b^{(i)}(y, \mathbf{x})$ in (12.11) of Section 12.4.

12.7 Proof

Proof of Theorem 12.1. We start with

$$\begin{aligned} V_n(z, z_i) &= \sqrt{n}(\widehat{\rho}_{n,b}(z, z_i) - \rho_b(z, z_i)) \\ &\sim J_b^{-1}(z, z_i) \int K_b(v - z, w_i - z_i) u(v, w_i, \rho_b(z, z_i))\, \mathrm{d}G_n^{(z,z_i)}(v, w_i), \end{aligned} \qquad (12.20)$$

where J_b and u are defined in (12.12) and (12.13), and $G_n^{(z,z_i)}(v, w_i) = \sqrt{n}(F_n^{(z,z_i)}(v, w_i) - F^{(z,z_i)}(v, w_i))$. Note that implicitly the integral expression is a function of (y, x_i). From Otneim and Tjøstheim (2017, Theorem 2) we have that in the limit as $b \to 0$, $J_b(z, z_i) \to J(z, z_i) = u(z, z_i, \rho(z, z_i))\psi(z, z_i, \rho(z, z_i))$. An identical reasoning can be carried out for $V_n(z_i, z_j)$:

$$V_n(z_i, z_j) = \sqrt{n}(\widehat{\rho}_{n,b}(z_i, z_j) - \rho_b(z_i, z_j))$$

$$\sim J_b^{-1}(z_i, z_j) \int K_b(w_i - z_i, w_j - z_j) u(w_i, w_j, \rho_b(z_i, z_j)) \, \mathrm{d}G_n^{(z_i,z_j)}(w_i, w_j). \tag{12.21}$$

The next step is expressing the second term in (12.10) as integrals over the differentials $\mathrm{d}G_n(z)$ and $\mathrm{d}G_n(z_i)$ using the technique of the proof of Theorem 3.1 of Lacal and Tjøstheim (2017); see also the proof of Theorem 7.2. To this end, consider

$$\int_A (\nabla_{\rho(z,z_i)} R(y, \mathbf{x}, \boldsymbol{\rho}(z, \mathbf{z}) V_n(z, z_i) \, \mathrm{d}F(y), \tag{12.22}$$

where the ∇ symbol is with respect to the component $\rho(z, z_i)$; it is the partial derivative $\partial/\partial\rho(z, z_i)$. By inserting from (12.20) expression (12.22) becomes

$$\int_A (\nabla_{\rho(z,z_i)} R(y, \mathbf{x}, \boldsymbol{\rho}(z, \mathbf{z})) J_b^{-1}(z, z_i) \int K_b(v - z, w_i - z_i) \\ \times u(v, w_i, \rho_b(z, z_i)) \, \mathrm{d}F(y) \, \mathrm{d}G_n^{(z,z_i)}(v, w_i), \tag{12.23}$$

which is indeed an implicit function of $\mathbf{x}$ only.

We have to make a similar computation for the pair (z_i, z_j) of variables. Corresponding to (12.22), we have

$$\int_A (\nabla_{\rho(z_i,z_j)} R(y, \mathbf{x}, \boldsymbol{\rho}(z, \mathbf{z}) V_n(z_i, z_j) \, \mathrm{d}F(y),$$

where the ∇ symbol is the derivative with respect to the component $\rho(z_i, z_j)$. By inserting from (12.21) this equals

$$\int_A (\nabla_{\rho(z_i,z_j)} R(y, \mathbf{x}, \boldsymbol{\rho}(z, \mathbf{z})) J_b^{-1}(z_i, z_j) \int K_b(w_i - z_i, w_j - z_j) \\ \times u(w_i, w_j, \rho_b(z_i, z_j) \, \mathrm{d}F(y) \, \mathrm{d}G_n^{(z_i,z_j)}(w_i, w_j), \tag{12.24}$$

which is a function of $\boldsymbol{x}$ and not of y.

Then there are three type of terms to consider in the evaluation of the asymptotic distribution of $\hat{g}_A(\mathbf{x}) - g_A(\mathbf{x})$ in (12.10). They are $\frac{1}{\sqrt{n}} \int_A R(y, \mathbf{x}, \boldsymbol{\rho}(z, \mathbf{z})) \, \mathrm{d}G_n(y)$ and the terms in equations (12.23) and (12.24). The first one can be written

$$\frac{1}{\sqrt{n}} \int_A R(y, \mathbf{x}, \boldsymbol{\rho}(z, \mathbf{z})) \, \mathrm{d}G_n(y) \stackrel{\text{def}}{=} \frac{1}{\sqrt{n}} \int_A C(y, \mathbf{x}) \, \mathrm{d}G_n(y). \tag{12.25}$$

Here $C(y, \mathbf{x})$ is a function of $(\mathbf{x}, y)$ since $z = \phi^{-1}(F(y))$ and $z_i = \phi^{-1}(F(x_i))$. This term is seen to be of order $O_P(n^{-1/2})$. The term coming from (12.23) gives rise to the term

$$\frac{1}{\sqrt{n}} \sum_{i=1}^{n} \int A_b^{(i)}(\mathbf{x}, v, w_i)\, \mathrm{d}G_n^{(z,z_i)}(v, w_i) \tag{12.26}$$

with $A_b^{(i)}(\mathbf{x}, v, w_i)$ defined in (12.11).

Note here that the integration over y in $A_b^{(i)}(\mathbf{x}, v, w_i)$ in (12.11) also involves terms containing $z = \Phi^{-1}(F(y))$. This means that if the kernel function in (12.11) is split into a product $K_b(v - z, w_i - z_i) = K_b(v - z)K_b(w_i - z_i)$, then the term with $K_b(v - z)$ is absorbed into this integration over $\mathrm{d}F(y)$ and only the kernel $K_b(w_i - z_i)$ is involved in the integration over $\mathrm{d}G_n^{(z,z_i)}(v, w_i)$, and using the reasoning in Remark 3.1 of Lacal and Tjøstheim (2019), we have that the term corresponding to equation (12.23) gets a reduction of one b, and the order is $O_P(bn)^{-1/2}$ as $n \to \infty$ and $b \to 0$.

Finally, the term corresponding to equation (12.24) can be written

$$\frac{1}{\sqrt{n}} \sum_{i \neq j} \int A_b^{(ij)}(\mathbf{x}, w_i, w_j)\, \mathrm{d}G_n^{(z_i,z_j)}(w_i, w_j)$$

with

$$A_b^{(ij)}(\mathbf{x}, w_i, w_j) = \int_A \frac{\partial}{\partial \rho(z_i, z_j)} R(y, \mathbf{x}, \boldsymbol{\rho}(z, \mathbf{z})) J_b^{-1}(z_i, z_j) K_b(w_i - z_i, w_j - z_j)$$
$$\times u(w_i, w_j, \rho_b(z_i, z_j))\, \mathrm{d}F(y).$$

In this case, there is no kernel function absorbed in the integration over $\mathrm{d}F(y)$, and this leads to a two-dimensional kernel left for the integration over $\mathrm{d}G_n^{(z_i,z_j)}(w_i, w_j)$, which in turn leads to a reduction of b^2 as $b \to 0$, which again means that the term coming from equation (12.24), is of order $O_p(n^{-1/2})$ as $n \to \infty$ and $b \to 0$. From this the variance expression in (12.16) and the claimed rate of $(nb)^{-1/2}$ follow.

It remains to prove asymptotic normality, but this follows by an easy mixing argument as in Lacal and Tjøstheim (2019). Letting $b \to 0$, we can use Proposition 3.6 of Brockwell and Davis (2006) to obtain normality as $n \to \infty$ and $b \to 0$.

Summing up this means that in the asymptotic analysis as $b \to 0$ and $n \to \infty$ the term originating from equation (12.23) is of order $O_p((nb)^{-1/2})$ and is dominating, and this is of the same order as in the ordinary additive modeling case. □

References

Brockwell, P., Davis, R.A., 2006. Time Series: Theory and Methods. Springer.

Cai, Z., 2002. Regression quantiles for time series. Econometric Theory 18 (1), 169–192.

Horowitz, J.L., Lee, S., 2005. Nonparametric estimation of an additive quantile regression model. Journal of the American Statistical Association 100 (472), 1238–1249.

Joe, H., 1989. Estimation of entropy and other functionals of a multivariate density. Annals of the Institute of Statistical Mathematics 41 (4), 683–697.

Lacal, V., Tjøstheim, D., 2017. Local Gaussian autocorrelation and tests of serial dependence. Journal of Time Series Analysis 38 (1), 51–71.

Lacal, V., Tjøstheim, D., 2019. Estimating and testing nonlinear local dependence between two time series. Journal of Business and Economic Statistics 37 (4), 648–660.

Li, Q., Racine, J.S., 2008. Nonparametric estimation of conditional CDF and quantile functions with mixed categorical and continuous data. Journal of Business and Economic Statistics 26 (4), 423–434.

Otneim, H., Tjøstheim, D., 2017. The locally Gaussian density estimator for multivariate data. Statistics and Computing 27 (6), 1595–1616.

Otneim, H., Tjøstheim, D., 2018. Conditional density estimation using the local Gaussian correlation. Statistics and Computing 28 (2), 303–321.

Racine, J., Li, K., 2017. Nonparametric conditional quantile estimation: a locally weighted quantile kernel approach. Journal of Econometrics 201, 72–94.

Samanta, M., 1989. Non-parametric estimation of conditional quantiles. Statistics and Probability Letters 7, 407–412.

Yu, K., Lu, Z., 2004. Local linear additive quantile regression. Scandinavian Journal of Statistics 31, 333–346.

CHAPTER 13

A local Gaussian Fisher discriminant

Contents

13.1. Introduction 403
 13.1.1 Background 404
 13.1.2 Estimating densities and discriminants 405
13.2. A local Gaussian Fisher discriminant 408
13.3. Some asymptotics of Bayes risk 413
13.4. Choice of bandwidth 417
13.5. Illustrations 420
 13.5.1 Simulations 420
 13.5.2 Illustration: Fraud detection 424
13.6. Summary remark 425
References 426

13.1 Introduction

The statistical classification problem consists of allocating observed data samples to one of several possible classes based on information obtained from a set of observations having a known class membership. A standard classifier is the Fisher discriminant; see Fisher (1936). It is easy to understand intuitively and apply and has been much used in practice. The Fisher discriminant requires continuous data, and its derivation, but not application, is based on each class being multivariate normally distributed.

Many discrimination problems involve discrete and categorical variables. This is not the topic of this chapter, but it is treated in numerous papers and books, among them Otneim et al. (2020), which includes both continuous and discrete variables and their combinations. Much of the material on the locally Gaussian Fisher discriminant is taken from the continuous part of that paper.

The normal distribution assumption of the Fisher discriminant leads to some obvious problems. It cannot separate classes that only differ in their dependence structure beyond second moments. In this chapter, we seek to rectify this by replacing the standard Fisher classifier by a local Gaussian Fisher discriminant, which uses locally normal approximations for the class distributions. The local approximation has a pairwise dependence structure

Statistical Modeling using Local Gaussian Approximation
https://doi.org/10.1016/B978-0-12-815861-6.00020-1

and is constructed such that, in the limit experiment, it coincides with the standard Fisher discriminant if, in fact, the class distributions are multinormal.

13.1.1 Background

Let us first provide some background for the classification[1] problem. The K-class discrimination problem consists in assigning the p-dimensional data vector $\mathbf{X} = (X_1, \ldots, X_p)^T$ to one of K classes. Examples range from fraud detection, authorship and text analysis, spam-email detection, credit rating, bankruptcy prediction, and even seismic discrimination (see, e.g., Phua et al. (2010), Jullum et al. (2020), Zheng et al. (2006), Aggarwal and Zhai (2012), Satabdi (2018), Min and Jeong (2009), Blanzieri and Bryl (2008), and Tjøstheim (1978)). Usually (in supervised learning), a training data set is available. Each training set consists of data $\mathbf{X}$ from a known class that we use to get an idea of the stochastic features within each class and that we describe by the class-wise probability distribution functions f_k, $k = 1, \ldots, K$, hereafter referred to as class distributions. In general, these distributions may be continuous, discrete or mixed, but in this chapter, they are densities reflecting the fact that we are only considering continuous data. We may also have available an (unconditional) prior probability $\pi_k = P(\text{class}(\mathbf{X}) = k)$ for each class. In some cases, such a probability can be estimated from training data.

Let D be a decision variable taking the values $1, \ldots, K$. Let us also write $\mathbf{f} = (f_1, \ldots, f_K)$ and $\boldsymbol{\pi} = (\pi_1, \ldots, \pi_K)$. On the basis of a new sample $\mathbf{X}$ and the available training data, we must determine the value of D in an optimal way. Optimality is usually defined by minimizing the so-called Bayes risk. Assuming that f_k and $\pi_k = P(D = k)$ are known for all k, we obtain the posterior probability of having $D = k$ using the Bayes theorem:

$$P_{\mathbf{f}}(D = k | \mathbf{X} = \mathbf{x}) = \frac{\pi_k f_k(\mathbf{x})}{\sum_{j=1}^{K} \pi_j f_j(\mathbf{x})}. \tag{13.1}$$

Now assign a loss function $L(k, j)$ that gives the loss of assigning $\mathbf{X}$ to k when in fact $D = j$. The Bayes risk is defined as the expected loss with

[1] We use the terms discrimination and classification interchangeably throughout this chapter, referring to the same concept.

respect to the posterior probabilities:

$$R_{\mathbf{f}}(k, \mathbf{x}, \pi) = \sum_{j} L(k, j) P_{\mathbf{f}}(D = j | \mathbf{X} = \mathbf{x}). \tag{13.2}$$

Then the classification rule D_B, which is Bayes optimal with respect to $R_{\mathbf{f}}$, follows by minimizing $R_{\mathbf{f}}$ over k; in other words, D_B is given by

$$D_B(\mathbf{x}, \boldsymbol{\pi}) = \underset{k=1,\ldots,K}{arg\,min}\, R_{\mathbf{f}}(k, \mathbf{x}, \boldsymbol{\pi}). \tag{13.3}$$

In the particular case of a 0–1 loss, that is, $L(k, j) = \mathrm{I}(k \neq j)$ where I is the indicator function, it is easy to compute the Bayes rule, since the decision rule takes the simple form

$$D_B(\mathbf{x}, \boldsymbol{\pi}) = \underset{k=1,\ldots,K}{arg\,max}\, P_{\mathbf{f}}(D = k | \mathbf{X} = \mathbf{x}) = \underset{k=1,\ldots,K}{arg\,max}\, \pi_k f_k(\mathbf{x}). \tag{13.4}$$

This is a small but vital part of Bayesian decision theory and Bayesian inference, whose foundations are explored, for example, in the classic text of Box and Tiao (1973). Expression (13.4) forms the "intuitive" solution to the classification problem, and we will rely on this decision rule throughout this chapter. Note, however, that the methodology we develop and the comparisons we perform are equally valid with decision rules originating from other loss functions. In the practical situation where f (and $\boldsymbol{\pi}$) are not known, these need to be estimated from data to reach a decision. When $\boldsymbol{\pi}$ is unknown, it may sometimes be estimated by the relative class-wise frequencies observed in the training data if this is randomly drawn from the complete data set under consideration, so that $\widehat{\pi}_k = n_k/n$, where n is the total number of observations, and n_k is the number of observations belonging to class k. The estimation of f_k, $k = 1, \ldots, K$, may typically be done in a number of different ways, and this choice of estimation method essentially distinguishes different classification methods from each other. Therefore the remaining part of the chapter will, to a large extent, be concerned with methods for estimating f_k, $k = 1, \ldots, K$, using the local Gaussian estimation approach in Chapter 9. In many situations, there are only two classes, $K = 2$. Although all presented methodology works for general K, we for simplicity concentrate on the $K = 2$ case in the illustrations considered here.

13.1.2 Estimating densities and discriminants

If f_k, $k = 1, \ldots, K$, are continuous, then we may assume that they belong to a particular parametric family of densities. Then the estimation problem consists in estimating the parameters of that parametric density. The classic Fisher discriminant originates from the work by Fisher (1936), who assumes that the p-variate data from each class k are normally distributed, written $\mathcal{N}(\boldsymbol{\mu}_k, \boldsymbol{\Sigma}_k)$, where $\boldsymbol{\mu}_k$ and $\boldsymbol{\Sigma}_k$ are the class-wise mean vectors and covariance matrices, respectively, that is,

$$f_k(\mathbf{x}) = \frac{1}{(2\pi)^{p/2}|\boldsymbol{\Sigma}_k|^{1/2}} \exp\left(-\frac{1}{2}(\mathbf{x}-\boldsymbol{\mu}_k)^T \boldsymbol{\Sigma}_k^{-1}(\mathbf{x}-\boldsymbol{\mu}_k)\right),$$

where $|\cdot|$ denotes the determinant, and T is the transpose. If we assume that $\boldsymbol{\Sigma}_k = \boldsymbol{\Sigma}$ for all k, then the Bayes rule (13.4) takes the form (Johnson and Wichern, 2007, Chapter 11.3)

$$\widehat{D}_{\text{LDA}}(\mathbf{x}) = \underset{k=1,\ldots,K}{arg\,max}\, \mathbf{x}^T \widehat{\boldsymbol{\Sigma}}^{-1}\widehat{\boldsymbol{\mu}}_k - \frac{1}{2}\widehat{\boldsymbol{\mu}}_k^T \widehat{\boldsymbol{\Sigma}}^{-1}\widehat{\boldsymbol{\mu}}_k + \log \widehat{\pi}_k,$$

where $\widehat{\boldsymbol{\mu}}_k$ are the class-wise empirical mean vectors, and $\widehat{\boldsymbol{\Sigma}}$ is the common empirical covariance matrix, which we calculate using the training data. This particular classification rule is called *linear discriminant analysis* (LDA) because the estimated decision boundaries between classes are linear in $\mathbf{x}$ and thus form hyper-planes in the p-dimensional Euclidean space. The general case, where we allow the covariance matrices $\boldsymbol{\Sigma}_k$ to be different within each class, leads to the classification rule

$$\begin{aligned}\widehat{D}_{\text{QDA}}(\mathbf{x}) = \underset{k=1,\ldots,K}{arg\,max} & -\frac{1}{2}\mathbf{x}^T \widehat{\boldsymbol{\Sigma}}_k^{-1}\mathbf{x} + \mathbf{x}^T \widehat{\boldsymbol{\Sigma}}_k^{-1}\widehat{\boldsymbol{\mu}}_k \\ & - \frac{1}{2}\widehat{\boldsymbol{\mu}}_k^T \widehat{\boldsymbol{\Sigma}}_k^{-1}\widehat{\boldsymbol{\mu}}_k - \frac{1}{2}\log|\widehat{\boldsymbol{\Sigma}}_k| + \log \widehat{\pi}_k, \end{aligned} \tag{13.5}$$

which is termed *quadratic discriminant analysis* (QDA) due to the quadratic term in (13.5), causing a second-order (quadratic) decision boundary.

One advantage of the Fisher discriminant is that f_k is easy to estimate also for quite a large p, since for each k, the estimation reduces to *marginal* estimates of means μ_{kj}, $j = 1, \ldots, p$, and *pairwise* estimates of covariances $\sigma_{k,jl}$, $j, l = 1, \ldots, p$. This corresponds to pairwise dependencies between components. A general p-dimensional density does not have this property, so that dependence between any two variables may not be so easily extracted from the joint distribution. Despite, or perhaps due to, their simplicity, QDA and LDA have a proven track record in many situations where the class distributions are clearly non-normal; cf. Chapter 4 in Hastie et al. (2009).

However, it is crucially important to note here that the QDA and LDA discriminants do not see any difference between populations having equal mean vectors and covariance matrices, even though the populations may be radically different in terms of nonlinear dependence. In that case, we would rather resort to a method that does allow for non-linear dependence or more flexibility in terms of the distributional form of $f_k(\mathbf{x})$. A very simple example is provided by the naive Bayes classifier. This is a well-known reference discriminant of this type, allowing for more flexibility for the marginal distributions but completely ignoring any dependence between the component variables X_j and X_l. Naive Bayes, which works both for discrete and continuous data, takes the form

$$P_{\mathbf{f}}(D=k|\mathbf{X}=\mathbf{x}) = \prod_{j=1}^{p} P_{f_{(j)}}(D=k|X_j=x_j), \tag{13.6}$$

where $f_{(j)}$ denotes the marginal distribution of X_j. This approximation may work surprisingly well even in situations where property (13.6) is not satisfied. The marginal distributions in (13.6) may be estimated parametrically, for instance, with a Gaussian distribution, or nonparametrically, for instance, with a kernel density estimator, in both cases avoiding the curse of dimensionality. Note that naive Bayes may actually work in cases where the means and covariances of the populations are identical, that is, in cases where the Fisher discriminant cannot work. This is because it is possible to have different non-Gaussian marginal distributions where variances and means are the same. A simple example is when class 1 has Uniform$[-3, 3]$ marginals, whereas class 2 has $\mathcal{N}(0, 3^2)$ marginals. These distributions have the same mean and variances, but the distributions are still very different.

In this chapter, we focus on constructing generalizations of the QDA using the local Gaussian approach, which is the unifying theme of this book. Let us first mention the obvious alternative to the local Gaussian approximations, namely, the pursuit of a fully nonparametric approach. Then f_k can be estimated, for example, using the kernel density estimator

$$\widehat{f}_{\text{kernel},\,k}(\mathbf{x}) = \frac{1}{n_k} \sum_{i=1}^{n_k} K_{\mathbf{B}_k}(\mathbf{X}_i^{(k)} - \mathbf{x}),$$

where $\{\mathbf{X}_i^{(k)}, i = 1, \ldots, n_k\}$ are observations in the training set of class k, and $K_{\mathbf{B}_k}(\cdot) = |\mathbf{B}_k^{-1}|K(\mathbf{B}_k^{-1}\cdot)$, with K being a kernel function, $\mathbf{B}_k$ is a non-singular bandwidth parameter (matrix) for class k, and $|\cdot|$ is the determinant. As $n_k \to \infty$, $\widehat{f}_k \xrightarrow{P} f_k$ under weak regularity conditions, but a considerable disadvantage is the curse of dimensionality. For p moderate or large, larger than 3 or 4, say, the kernel estimator may not work well; see, for example, Silverman (1986, Chapter 4.5). This limits the potential usefulness of the kernel estimator in discrimination problems, where p may be quite big. In these situations the problem may be alleviated to some extent by a judicious choice of bandwidth. See, in particular, Hall et al. (2004) and Li and Racine (2007). Other nonparametric approaches are nearest-neighbor classifiers; see, for example, Samworth (2012) and classification using data depth (Li et al., 2012), but the basic problem of the curse of dimensionality remains unless we accept the radical simplification provided by the naive Bayes with nonparametric margins.

The literature provides various other approaches to density estimation, such as the use of mixtures of a parametric and nonparametric approach, which may reduce the consequences of the curse of dimensionality; see, for example, Hjort and Glad (1995). To a lesser degree, this has also been the case in discrimination; see Chaudhuri et al. (2009), who basically choose a parametric approach but allow a nonparametric perturbation similar to that of Hjort and Glad (1995). Another such method is the local likelihood estimator proposed by Hjort and Jones (1996) and Loader (1996), who estimate $f_k(\boldsymbol{x})$ by fitting a whole family of parametric distributions such that the parameter vector $\boldsymbol{\theta} = \boldsymbol{\theta}(\mathbf{x})$ is allowed to vary locally with $\mathbf{x}$. We pursue this idea in this chapter by using the local Gaussian approximation. This makes it possible to replace the pairwise correlations used by the Fisher discriminant by pairwise locally Gaussian correlations. An alternative, non-equivalent option, which we will also visit, is performing classification by inserting the class distributions obtained with the local (Gaussian) likelihood approach into (13.4).

The rest of the chapter is organized as follows: In Section 13.2, we recapitulate some aspects of local Gaussian density estimation from Chapter 9. In Sections 13.3 and 13.4, we present asymptotics of the Bayes risk and bandwidth choice in the context of local Gaussian discrimination. In Section 13.5, we give a number of illustrations. Finally, in Section 13.6, we present some conclusions and a brief discussion.

13.2 A local Gaussian Fisher discriminant

We start by writing up the local Gaussian approximation for a class distribution of a single class k. Following the general idea of the local Gaussian approximation, $f_k(\mathbf{x})$ is approximated in a neighborhood $N_{\mathbf{x}}$ around $\mathbf{x}$ by a

Gaussian density

$$\psi\Big(\mathbf{v}, \boldsymbol{\mu}_k(\mathbf{x}), \boldsymbol{\Sigma}_k(\mathbf{x})\Big) = (2\pi)^{-p/2}|\boldsymbol{\Sigma}_k(\mathbf{x})|^{-1/2} \times \exp\Big\{-\frac{1}{2}(\mathbf{v}-\boldsymbol{\mu}_k(\mathbf{x}))^T\boldsymbol{\Sigma}_k^{-1}(\mathbf{x})(\mathbf{v}-\boldsymbol{\mu}_k(\mathbf{x}))\Big\}, \tag{13.7}$$

where $\mathbf{v}$ is the running variable. The size of $N_{\mathbf{x}}$ is determined by a bandwidth parameter (matrix). In the bivariate case ($p=2$) with $\mathbf{x}=(x_1, x_2)$ and parameters $\boldsymbol{\theta}_k(\mathbf{x}) = (\mu_{k1}(\mathbf{x}), \mu_{k2}(\mathbf{x}), \sigma_{k1}(\mathbf{x}), \sigma_{k2}(\mathbf{x}), \rho_k(\mathbf{x}))$, we write (13.7) as

$$\psi(\mathbf{v}, \mu_{k1}(\mathbf{x}), \mu_{k2}(\mathbf{x}), \sigma_{k1}(\mathbf{x}), \sigma_{k2}(\mathbf{x}), \rho_k(\mathbf{x})) = \frac{1}{2\pi\sigma_{k1}(\mathbf{x})\sigma_{k2}(\mathbf{x})\sqrt{1-\rho_k^2(\mathbf{x})}}$$
$$\times \exp\left[-\frac{1}{2(1-\rho_k^2(\mathbf{x}))}\left(\frac{(v_1-\mu_{k1}(\mathbf{x}))^2}{\sigma_{k1}^2(\mathbf{x})} - 2\rho_k(\mathbf{x})\frac{(v_1-\mu_{k1}(\mathbf{x}))(v_2-\mu_{k2}(\mathbf{x}))}{\sigma_{k1}(\mathbf{x})\sigma_{k2}(\mathbf{x})} + \frac{(v_2-\mu_{k2}(\mathbf{x}))^2}{\sigma_{k2}^2(\mathbf{x})}\right)\right].$$

Moving from $\mathbf{x}$ to another point $\mathbf{y}$, we use a possibly different Gaussian approximation $\psi(\mathbf{v}, \mu_k(\mathbf{y}), \Sigma_k(\mathbf{y}))$, $\mathbf{v} \in N_{\mathbf{y}}$. As has been stated throughout this book, the family of Gaussian distributions is especially attractive in practical use because of its exceptionally simple mathematical properties, which truly stand out in the theory of multivariate analysis. Our intention in this chapter, as elsewhere in the book, is exploiting these properties *locally*. Note that the multivariate normal $\mathcal{N}(\boldsymbol{\mu}_k, \boldsymbol{\Sigma}_k)$ is a particular case of the family of locally Gaussian distributions (13.7) with $\boldsymbol{\mu}_k(\mathbf{x}) \equiv \boldsymbol{\mu}_k$ and $\boldsymbol{\Sigma}_k(\mathbf{x}) \equiv \boldsymbol{\Sigma}_k$. Tjøstheim and Hufthammer (2013) and Chapter 4 discuss non-trivial questions of existence and uniqueness. As the local parameter functions $\boldsymbol{\mu}_k(\mathbf{x})$ and $\boldsymbol{\Sigma}_k(\mathbf{x})$ take the place of the fixed parameters $\boldsymbol{\mu}_k$ and $\boldsymbol{\Sigma}_k$ for each class distribution k in the Gaussian case, it is natural to extend the QDA of (13.5) by simply replacing $\boldsymbol{\mu}_k$ and $\boldsymbol{\Sigma}_k$ by $\boldsymbol{\mu}_k(x)$ and $\boldsymbol{\Sigma}_k(x)$ for $k=1,\ldots,K$. This gives the so-called *local Fisher discriminant*

$$\widehat{D}_{\text{Local Fisher}}(\mathbf{x}) = \underset{k=1,\ldots,K}{arg\,max} -\frac{1}{2}\mathbf{x}^T\widehat{\boldsymbol{\Sigma}}_k^{-1}(\mathbf{x})\mathbf{x} + \mathbf{x}^T\widehat{\boldsymbol{\Sigma}}_k^{-1}(\mathbf{x})\widehat{\boldsymbol{\mu}}_k(\mathbf{x}) - \frac{1}{2}\widehat{\boldsymbol{\mu}}_k(\mathbf{x})^T\widehat{\boldsymbol{\Sigma}}_k^{-1}(\mathbf{x})\widehat{\boldsymbol{\mu}}_k(\mathbf{x}) - \frac{1}{2}\log|\widehat{\boldsymbol{\Sigma}}_k(\mathbf{x})| + \log\widehat{\pi}_k. \tag{13.8}$$

To practically apply this procedure, we need estimates of the involved parameter functions for all class distributions $k=1,\ldots,K$. Following Hjort and Jones (1996) and Chapter 4, we estimate the parameters $\boldsymbol{\mu}_k(\mathbf{x})$ and $\boldsymbol{\Sigma}_k(\mathbf{x})$ given data $\mathbf{X}_1^{(k)}, \ldots, \mathbf{X}_{n_k}^{(k)}$ with class label k by maximizing the local log likelihood

$$L(\mathbf{X}_1^{(k)}, \ldots, \mathbf{X}_{n_k}^{(k)}, \boldsymbol{\theta}_k(\mathbf{x})) = n_k^{-1} \sum_{i=1}^{n_k} K_{\mathbf{B}_k}(\mathbf{X}_i^{(k)} - \mathbf{x}) \log \psi(\mathbf{X}_i^{(k)}, \boldsymbol{\theta}_k(\mathbf{x})) - \int K_{\mathbf{B}_k}(\mathbf{v} - \mathbf{x}) \psi(\mathbf{v}, \boldsymbol{\theta}_k(\mathbf{x}))\, \mathrm{d}\mathbf{v}, \quad (13.9)$$

where $K_{\mathbf{B}_k}$ is a kernel function depending on a bandwidth parameter matrix $\mathbf{B}_k$. We refer to Tjøstheim and Hufthammer (2013), Chapter 4, and Otneim and Tjøstheim (2017), Chapter 9, for details on parameter estimation.

From the description of the local Gaussian likelihood above, the two discriminants in (13.8) and in (13.12) below appear to be highly affected by the curse of dimensionality. Otneim and Tjøstheim (2017), as stated in Chapter 9, suggest a particular simplification to relieve this effect, which we will adopt throughout the chapter. The solution is to apply the following simplification:

$$\mu_{kj}(\mathbf{x}) = \mu_{kj}(x_j) \quad \text{and} \quad \sigma_{k,jl}(\mathbf{x}) = \sigma_{k,jl}(x_j, x_l) \qquad (13.10)$$

with $j, l = 1, \ldots, p$, leading to a pairwise local dependence structure. Examples can be found where this approximation is not at all valid, but the experience so far indicates that it covers a fairly wide set of circumstances as explained in Chapters 7 and 8; or see Lacal and Tjøstheim (2019), Jordanger and Tjøstheim (2021), and the references therein. With this simplification, it is possible to do a *pairwise* local dependence analysis in a multivariate non-Gaussian and nonlinear context, such as the local Fisher discriminant (13.8). This can be done such that, as $n_k \to \infty$, it reduces to the familiar pairwise correlation case if the true class distributions are indeed Gaussian. We illustrate this point graphically in Fig. 13.1.

In the left panel of Fig. 13.1, we have plotted 250 observations, each from two bivariate Gaussian populations, signified by "•" and "+", which have different mean vectors and covariance matrices. In this case the LDA, being derived from the assumption of equal covariance matrices, is not optimal, as we appreciate from the plot where we have drawn the linear decision boundary as a solid line. The QDA, on the other hand, is in fact optimal because the parametric assumption of binormal populations having unequal covariance matrices is correct. The quadratic decision boundary is indicated by a dashed line. Furthermore, in this particular case, we observe that the local Fisher discriminant (13.8) essentially reduces to the global QDA in (13.5), and we achieve precisely this by choosing a large bandwidth in the estimation of the local parameters in (13.10) using the local likelihood function in (13.9). The resulting decision boundary is displayed in the figure as a dotted line, which for the most part coincides with the QDA boundary. It is important to note that the bandwidth selection in this illustration is completely data driven by means of a cross-validation procedure that we describe in Section 13.4.

In the second panel of Fig. 13.1, we have a different situation. The two populations are clearly not normally distributed, but their covariance matrices are equal (indeed, they are diagonal). This means that the QDA in practice collapses to the LDA, producing a nearly straight line. In this constructed example, though, from the plot we immediately see that a linear decision boundary is sub-optimal. In this case, our bandwidth selection algorithm that we present in Section 13.4 produces a small smoothing parameter, allowing the local Fisher discriminant (13.8) to become very local, non-linear, and non-quadratic. This appears to work well for this discrimination problem.

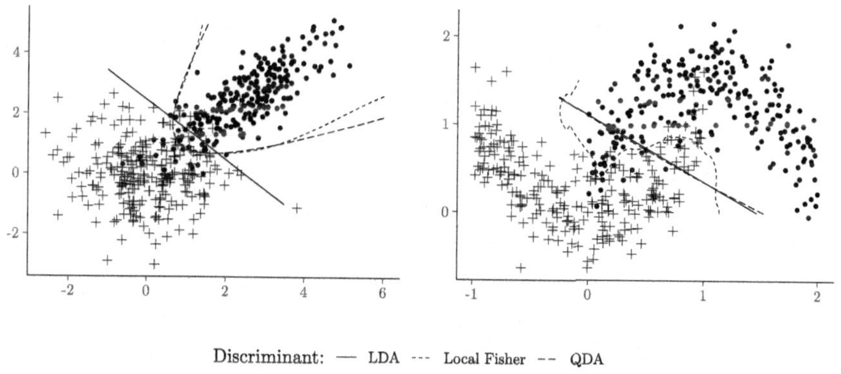

Figure 13.1 The two-class discrimination problem in two different cases.

As a by-product of the local likelihood set-up and estimation procedure in (13.9), we approximate $f_k(\mathbf{x})$ itself by a family $\{\psi(\mathbf{v}, \boldsymbol{\mu}_k(\mathbf{x}), \boldsymbol{\Sigma}_k(\mathbf{x}))\}$ of multivariate Gaussians with estimates of the parameter functions $\widehat{\boldsymbol{\mu}}_k(\mathbf{x})$ and $\widehat{\boldsymbol{\Sigma}}_k(\mathbf{x})$:

$$\widehat{f}_{\mathrm{LGDE},k}(x) = \psi(\mathbf{x}, \widehat{\boldsymbol{\mu}}_k(\mathbf{x}), \widehat{\boldsymbol{\Sigma}}_k(\mathbf{x})). \tag{13.11}$$

These *locally Gaussian density estimates (LGDE)* of the class distributions $f_k(\mathbf{x})$ give rise to a second option for utilizing the local Gaussian likelihood method in the discrimination setting. This option is using $f_k(\mathbf{x})$, $k = 1, \ldots, K$, directly to compute posterior probabilities and perform classification via (13.1) and (13.4), respectively. This gives the following discriminant:

$$\widehat{D}_{\text{LGDE}}(\mathbf{x}) = \underset{k=1,\ldots,K}{arg\,max}\, \pi_k \widehat{f}_{\text{LGDE},\,k}(\mathbf{x}). \tag{13.12}$$

With the pairwise simplification described above, the estimate $\widehat{f}_{\text{LGDE}}$, as used here, involves a further simplification resulting from transforming each variable to approximate standard normality, that is, we can use the transformation $\widehat{Z}_j^{(k)} = \Phi^{-1}\left(\widehat{F}_{n_k}(X_j^{(k)})\right)$, $j = 1, \ldots, n_k$, which we have used on a number of occasions in this book, of the marginals $X_j^{(k)}$ in each population, where $\widehat{F}_{n_k}$ is the empirical distribution function, and Φ the cumulative distribution function of the standard normal. Then, as a further simplification, we fix $\mu_{kj}(z_j) \equiv 0$ and $\sigma_{kj}(z_j) \equiv 1$, $j = 1, \ldots, p$; cf. Eqs. (9.6) and (9.7). Alternatively, we could estimate $\boldsymbol{\mu}_k(\mathbf{z})$ and $\boldsymbol{\sigma}_k(\mathbf{z})$ by local likelihood for each pair, as has been done by Lacal and Tjøstheim (2019) and Jordanger and Tjøstheim (2021) and as is described in Chapters 7 and 8. The latter option leads to larger flexibility and accuracy in the estimation but at the cost of more complicated asymptotic analysis. The transformation procedure is especially attractive if the data contain extreme outliers.

Transforming back, we obtain estimates $\widehat{f}_k(\mathbf{x})$. As it is not guaranteed that $\int \widehat{f}_k(\mathbf{x})d\mathbf{x} = 1$ for a fixed n_k and bandwidth matrix $\mathbf{B}_k$, the recipe also involves normalization of the f_k by a simple Monte Carlo procedure in the end. However, we do not normalize the locally Gaussian density estimates in this chapter. Our experience is that the factor by which the density estimate $\widehat{f}_{\text{LGDE}}$ departs from the unit integral mostly depends on the number of variables and thus will not significantly affect the ratio $\widehat{f}_{\text{LGDE},k}/\widehat{f}_{\text{LGDE},j}$ for two classes k and j. Furthermore, as noted in Section 13.4, we do not pursue precise density estimates as such in this chapter, but rather tune our bandwidths to optimize discrimination performance. This can, in principle and in practice, be done regardless of whether the class-wise probability density estimates exactly integrate to one. In both constructed examples shown in Fig. 13.1, the LGDE-based discriminant (13.12) is essentially identical to the local Fisher discriminant. This is not always the case though.

Asymptotic theory has been developed for the estimate $\widehat{f}_k(\mathbf{x}) = \psi(\mathbf{x}, \widehat{\boldsymbol{\mu}}_k(\mathbf{x}), \widehat{\boldsymbol{\Sigma}}_k(\mathbf{x}))$ as $n_k \to \infty$ and as the bandwidth matrix $\mathbf{B}_k \to \mathbf{0}$. Otneim and Tjøstheim (2017, Theorems 3 and 4), as outlined in Chapter 9, demonstrate asymptotic normality and consistency under certain regularity conditions. In particular, $\widehat{f_k}(\mathbf{x}) = \psi(\mathbf{x}, \widehat{\boldsymbol{\mu}}_k(\mathbf{x}), \widehat{\boldsymbol{\Sigma}}_k(\mathbf{x})) \xrightarrow{P} f_k(\mathbf{x})$ implies that $\int \widehat{f_k}(\mathbf{x})\,\mathrm{d}x \to 1$, which is relevant also for the asymptotic behavior of the Bayes risk.

13.3 Some asymptotics of Bayes risk

The Bayes risk in (13.2), as has already been seen, depends on density functions which may be estimated parametrically or nonparametrically. In the former case, assuming for simplicity that $n_k = n$, $k = 1, \ldots, K$, this typically gives an asymptotic standard error of order $n^{-1/2}$, where n is the size of the training set. In the latter case, using kernel density estimation, assume that the bandwidth matrix $\mathbf{B}_k$ is diagonal, $\mathbf{B}_k = \text{diag}\{b_{kj}\}$ with $b_{kj} = b_k$ for $j = 1, \ldots, p$. A kernel estimate of f_k has an asymptotic standard error of order $(nb_k^p)^{-1/2}$, which is large if p is large. Due to the reduction to a pairwise structure, the locally Gaussian parameters discussed above and thus the corresponding density estimate have errors of order $(nb_k^2)^{-1/2}$ irrespective of the dimension p. The full asymptotic distribution is given in Chapter 9 based on Theorem 4 of Otneim and Tjøstheim (2017).

In discrimination the asymptotics of the density estimates do not hold the main interest, but rather the asymptotics of the related Bayes risk. The purpose of the present section is showing that the local Gaussian discriminant has an asymptotic Bayes risk independent of p under weak regularity conditions. To do this, we base ourselves on Marron (1983), who shows that a broad class of nonparametric density estimates (not restricted to kernel density estimates) achieves a mean square convergence rate of n^{-r} for some $0 < r < 1$.

To indicate how these results can be applied to locally Gaussian estimation, assume first that the class densities $f_1, \ldots, f_K$ are known. Recall from (13.3) that the Bayes rule takes the form $D_B = \mathit{arg\,min}_{k\in(1,\ldots,K)} R_{\mathbf{f}}(k, \mathbf{x}, \boldsymbol{\pi})$ for all $\mathbf{x}$ and $\boldsymbol{\pi}$. However, in practice, $\mathbf{f}$ is unknown and has to be estimated. Estimating $\mathbf{f}$ by $\widehat{\mathbf{f}} = (\widehat{f_1}, \ldots, \widehat{f_K})$ leads to an estimate

$$\widehat{D}_n = \underset{k\in(1,\ldots,K)}{\mathit{arg\,min}}\; R_{\widehat{\mathbf{f}}}(k, \mathbf{x}, \boldsymbol{\pi})$$

of the Bayes rule, and we are interested in the asymptotic behavior of $\widehat{D}_n$ relative to D_B as n increases, in terms of consistency and its rate of convergence. To this end, we need some assumptions on the loss function L

introduced in (13.2) and the smoothness of $\mathbf{f}$. The loss function L must satisfy

$$\max_k L(k, k) \leq \min_{k \neq j} L(k, j). \tag{13.13}$$

To define the mode of convergence, let $C \subset \mathbb{R}^p$ be a compact set, and let S_K be the simplex defined by $\sum_i \pi_i = 1$. Marron (1983) studies the mode of convergence of

$$\int_{S_K} \int_C \left| R_{\mathbf{f}}(\widehat{D}_n, \mathbf{x}, \boldsymbol{\pi}) - R_{\mathbf{f}}(D_B, \mathbf{x}, \boldsymbol{\pi}) \right| \mathrm{d}\mathbf{x}\, \mathrm{d}\boldsymbol{\pi},$$

where we in fact do not need to take the absolute value of the integrand since by definition, for every $\mathbf{x} \in \mathbb{R}^p$, $k \in (1, \dots, K)$,

$$R_{\mathbf{f}}(k, \mathbf{x}, \pi) \geq R_{\mathbf{f}}(D_B, \mathbf{x}, \boldsymbol{\pi}).$$

Let further $\nabla_{\boldsymbol{\alpha}} = \partial^{|\boldsymbol{\alpha}|}/(\partial x_1^{\alpha_1} \cdots \partial x_p^{\alpha_p})$, $|\mathbf{x}| = (x_1^2 + \cdots + x_p^2)^{1/2}$, and $|\boldsymbol{\alpha}| = \sum_{j=1}^p \alpha_j$. Then the following boundedness and smoothness assumptions are imposed on f. Let $M_k > 1$ be a constant, let m be a non-negative integer, let $\beta \in (0, 1]$, and let $q = m + \beta$. We denote by $\mathcal{F}_k$ the class of probability densities f_k on $\mathbb{R}^p$ such that for all $k = 1, \dots, K$,

(i) $f_k \leq M_k$ on $\mathbb{R}^p$;
(ii) $f_k \geq M_k^{-1}$ on C;
(iii) for all $\mathbf{x}, \mathbf{y} \in \mathbb{R}^p$ and all $|\boldsymbol{\alpha}| = m$, we have

$$|\nabla_{\boldsymbol{\alpha}} f_k(\mathbf{x}) - \nabla_{\boldsymbol{\alpha}} f_k(\mathbf{y})| \leq M_k |\mathbf{x} - \mathbf{y}|^\beta.$$

As is well known, the smoothness of f_k determines the rate of convergence of $\widehat{f}_{n,k}$. More specifically, let $f_k \in \mathcal{F}_k$. Then, according to Marron (1983, Theorem 3), there are a constant $c > 0$ and a density estimator $\widehat{f}_{n,k}$ such that when $r = 2q/(2q + p)$,

$$\lim_{n \to \infty} \sup_{f_k \in \mathcal{F}_k} P_{\mathbf{f}} \left[\int_C \left(\widehat{f}_{n,k}(\mathbf{x}) - f_k(\mathbf{x}) \right)^2 \mathrm{d}\mathbf{x} > cn^{-r} \right] = 0. \tag{13.14}$$

Moreover, let $\mathcal{F}$ denote the K-fold Cartesian product of the $\mathcal{F}_k$, and let T^n be the set of training samples, each of size n. By Marron (1983, Theorem 1) there are a constant $c > 0$ and a classification rule $\widehat{D}_n(\mathbf{x}, \boldsymbol{\pi}, T^n)$ such that

$$\lim_{n \to \infty} \sup_{f \in \mathcal{F}} P_{\mathbf{f}} \left[\int_{S_k} \int_C \left[R_{\mathbf{f}} \left(\widehat{D}_n, \mathbf{x}, \boldsymbol{\pi} \right) - R_{\mathbf{f}}(D_B, \mathbf{x}, \boldsymbol{\pi}) \right] \mathrm{d}\mathbf{x}\, \mathrm{d}\boldsymbol{\pi} > cn^{-r} \right] = 0. \tag{13.15}$$

The rate r in (13.15) describes the rate at which $\widehat{D}_n$ approaches the Bayes rule D_B. The rate turns out to be the same as for the density estimation rate for the class of densities in $\mathcal{F}_k$. In Theorem 2 of Marron (1983), it is shown that this rate is optimal in the sense that no better rate can be obtained for any classification rule $\widehat{D}_n$ based on density estimates $\widehat{f}_{n,k}$ of densities in $\mathcal{F}_k$.

It is easy to find density estimates that satisfy (13.14). If $\mathbf{X}$ is p-dimensional, then assuming the existence of a bounded second derivative of f_k, the traditional kernel estimate has a variance of order $(nb_k^p)^{-1}$ and a bias of order b_k^2. Balancing the order of variance and bias squared, that is, putting $(nb_k^p)^{-1} = b_k^4$, leads to $r = 4/(4+p)$. Assuming the existence of a bounded qth order derivative of f_k and using higher-order kernels, as in, for example, Jones and Signorini (1997), leads to a bias of order b^q, whereas the order of the variance is unchanged. Again, equating the order of the variance and the bias squared leads to $r = 2q/(2q+p)$. By increasing q it may seem like we may in the limit obtain the parametric rate of n^{-1} for the mean square error, but this is illusory as extremely large sample sizes would be required for the higher-order asymptotics to kick in. In fact, as demonstrated by Jones and Signorini (1997), the practical usefulness of higher-order kernels is debatable, and a realistic mean square convergence rate in practice is $n^{-4/(4+p)}$, which is a slow rate for p greater than 4, say.

The key of Marron's paper is that the derivation of (13.15) only uses the general convergence property in (13.14), the definition of $R_{\mathbf{f}}$, and the general assumptions on L and f stated earlier in this section. This means that it is not limited to kernel estimation, but can be applied to any density estimate that satisfies these requirements and has a rate as determined by (13.14). In turn, this means that it can be applied to the locally Gaussian density estimator, LGDE, described in the preceding section, satisfying the regularity conditions of Theorem 4 of Otneim and Tjøstheim (2017); or see Chapter 9 and the additional mild conditions (13.13) and (i)–(iii) in this section. Note that the pairwise LGDE is operable irrespective of whether there actually is such a structure. In general, it can serve as a computational approximation in the same way as an additive computational model can serve such a purpose in nonlinear regression.

Under the regularity assumptions stated in Theorem 4 by Otneim and Tjøstheim (2017) (or see Theorem 9.4 in Chapter 9), it follows that the variance of the LGDE is of order $(nb^2)^{-1}$. From the log likelihood expression in (13.9) we see that by taking derivatives and using the weak law of large numbers a local likelihood estimate of $\boldsymbol{\theta}$ should satisfy (with a common scalar bandwidth b and omitting the class index k)

$$0 = \frac{\partial L_n(\widehat{\boldsymbol{\theta}}, \mathbf{x})}{\partial \theta_j} \xrightarrow{P} \int K_b(\mathbf{y}-\mathbf{x}) u_j(\mathbf{y}, \boldsymbol{\theta}_b) \Big\{ f(\mathbf{y}) - \psi(\mathbf{y}, \boldsymbol{\theta}_b(\mathbf{y})) \Big\} \, d\mathbf{y}, \quad (13.16)$$

where $u_j(\cdot, \boldsymbol{\theta}) = \partial/\partial\theta_j \log \psi(\cdot, \boldsymbol{\theta})$. By Taylor expanding this integral we see that the difference between $f(\mathbf{y})$ and $\psi(\mathbf{y}, \boldsymbol{\theta}_b)$ is of order b^2 as $b \to 0$. This means that $\psi(\boldsymbol{\theta}_b)$ approximates f at this rate, and it is in fact the reason for including the last term in the log likelihood in (13.9). Contemplating that we obtain the estimates $\widehat{\boldsymbol{\theta}}$ by setting the log likelihood equal to zero, it is not difficult to see that the bias of the LGDE is of order b^2; see also Hjort and Jones (1996). Combining this with the expression for the order of the variance of the LGDE and equating the bias squared and variance lead to $b = n^{-1/6}$ and $r = -2/3$, and this would lead to a rate of the mean square risk of $n^{-2/3}$, which is much better than the risk rate for the kernel estimator as p increases.

However, in Chapter 9, based on Otneim and Tjøstheim (2017), the log-spline approach is used in density estimation; see Stone (1990) and Stone et al. (1997). Its convergence rate as applied to local Gaussian density estimation is explained in detail in Appendix A1 in Otneim and Tjøstheim (2017). The density estimate requires the added restriction on the bandwidth that $n^{1/2+\epsilon} b^2 \to 0$, where $\epsilon \in (0, 1/2)$ is a design parameter having to do with the density of knots in the spline approximation (ϵ close to 0 means that new knots are added very fast, whereas ϵ close to 1/2 means a slower rate). If the limit theorem was valid over the entire ϵ-range, then this would imply the added condition $n^{1/2} b^2 \to 0$ (see condition (iv) of Theorem 4 in Otneim and Tjøstheim, 2017) or the corresponding result in Theorem 9.4 in Chapter 9, leading to a non-sharp convergence rate of the Bayes risk with $b = n^{-(1/2+\epsilon)}$, where $\epsilon \in (0, 1/2)$. However, by taking the design parameter, which is user-controlled, in the range $1/6 < \epsilon < 1/2$, we see that no extra restriction on the bandwidth is required, leading to the mean square convergence rate of $n^{-r} = n^{-2/3}$ irrespective of the dimension p. We also remark that condition (iii) of Theorem 2 in Otneim and Tjøstheim (2017) or the corresponding result in Theorem 9.2 in Chapter 9 implies a mild tail behavior condition on $\mathbf{f}$.

An alternative to the log-spline approach is obtained by taking as an estimate of the marginal cumulative distribution function F the integral of the kernel density estimate; see, for example, Nadaraya (1964) and Azzalini (1981). The problem of the design parameter ϵ is then avoided. The marginal density must be sufficiently smooth to guarantee the existence of the derivative of $F^{-1}(\boldsymbol{x})$, and again in the pairwise local Gaussian case, we obtain a mean square convergence rate of $n^{-2/3}$.

To summarize, all this means that using pairwise local Gaussian density estimation (with Bayes risk convergence rate $n^{-2/3}$) instead of kernel estimation (with Bayes risk convergence rate $n^{-4/(4+p)}$) leads to improvements as p increases. We confirm this in the simulation experiments in Section 13.5.1 with p in the range $2 \leq p \leq 8$.

It is not difficult to check that a higher-order kernel applied to (13.16) reduces the bias in the same way as for ordinary kernel estimation. Moreover, since no moments of the kernel function enter into the calculation of the variance of the local Gaussian density estimate, the convergence rate of the variance is not influenced by this, and higher-order kernels lead to a convergence rate of $n^{-\frac{2q}{2q+2}}$ of the Bayes risk. We remain relatively skeptical to the practical significance of this result, though.

In practical error estimation in discrimination the empirical error frequencies are inserted in the AUC and Brier measures; see Section 13.5.2. If the population densities were known, error estimates and upper bounds could be obtained by integrating over the tails of the densities. This is related to the evaluation of value-at-risk (VaR) in finance, and it is well known that it is sensitive to misspecification of densities. Especially, if Gaussians are used when true densities are thick-tailed, then very serious underestimation may occur. This is illustrated in Table 1 in Otneim and Tjøstheim (2018) in a comparison between Gaussian, kernel estimates, so-called np-estimates (Li and Racine, 2008), and local Gaussian estimates, the latter being a clear winner in that particular example.

13.4 Choice of bandwidth

The preceding section concerns asymptotic results as the size of the training sets grows to infinity. We proceed now to establish rules for selecting bandwidths in finite-sample situations, which is clearly a problem of greater practical interest.

Nonparametric and semiparametric density estimators must as a general rule be *tuned* in one way or the other, usually by fixing a set of hyperparameters. The development of optimal strategies has been a topic of great interest in nonparametric analysis over the last couple of decades. The kernel density estimator, in particular, is associated with many bandwidth selection algorithms, and results on optimal choice of bandwidth have been known for some time; see, for example, Hart and Vieu (1990) for a fairly general cross-validation case. See also Jiang et al. (2020) for the spatial density case. That paper also contains some new results for choice of bandwidth in the time series case. The locally Gaussian density estimator is recent, and there have been few results on bandwidth selection.

Berentsen and Tjøstheim (2014), as it was seen in Chapters 5 and 7, suggest cross-validation as a viable strategy. Based on Berentsen et al. (2014), Otneim and Tjøstheim (2017), and Otneim and Tjøstheim (2018), it is applied with reasonable results in Chapters 5, 7, and 9. It clearly works best on data that have been transformed toward marginal standard normality, which is a strategy mentioned at the end of Section 13.2. However, the method is time consuming, and the plug-in estimator $b_n = cn^{-1/6}$ has been used as well, for which the value of c may be determined empirically. To our knowledge, no optimality theory of bandwidth selection exists for local likelihood density estimation.

The purpose of most bandwidth routines is obtaining good estimates of a density function f. We must here ask the following basic question: Is it true that an optimal bandwidth algorithm developed for density estimation is still optimal in a discrimination context? In the discrimination problem, we are more concerned with the local properties of f_k, where these densities overlap, rather than the overall quality of the estimate of f_k. There are in fact several indications that a density-optimal bandwidth may not be discrimination-optimal.

This issue has been examined in some particular cases by Ghosh and Chaudhuri (2004). They examine the misclassification probability as a function of the bandwidth in the case of two multivariate Gaussian populations of dimensions 1–6, and they found that the density-optimal bandwidth performed much worse than a bandwidth optimized with respect to the discrimination error in the case of equal a priori probabilities $\pi_1 = \pi_2 = 0.5$. The latter bandwidth was much larger, and in fact the classification error was largely insensitive to the choice of the bandwidth when it exceeded a certain threshold, whereas the density-optimal bandwidth was far below this threshold. For unequal prior probabilities, $\pi_1 = 0.4$ and $\pi_2 = 0.6$, they reported less clear results.

We are interested in obtaining the best possible discriminant, rather than the best possible density estimators for the different classes. We therefore rely on a cross-validation scheme that optimizes the bandwidth parameter matrix in terms of discrimination performance (Ghosh and Hall, 2008).

The AUC (area under the receiver operating characteristic (ROC) curve) is a widely used *ranking-based* metric for measuring the quality of a probability-based discrimination procedure (Fawcett, 2006). The AUC is constructed for two-class classification, but generalizations to $K > 2$ classes exist (Fawcett, 2006, Section 10), and may replace the AUC in the description below when $K > 2$. A classifier that has an AUC value equal to 0.5 in a balanced classification problem is equivalent to pure guesswork, whereas if AUC $= 1$, then this enables perfect classification.

We have chosen to optimize the bandwidth parameter in terms of this metric in our cross-validation scheme. As a reasonable trade-off between stability and computational expense, we perform cross-validation with a single split into m separate sets, that is, m-fold cross-validation (Kohavi, 1995). To reduce the search space for the cross-validation procedure, we require the bandwidth matrix $\mathbf{B}_n$ to be diagonal, with all diagonal entries on the form $b_n = cn^{-1/6}$, as mentioned before. The precise metric we optimize over is the average of the AUCs computed for each fold separately. To summarize, we tune the c parameter in b_n for the locally Gaussian discriminants according to the following cross-validation procedure:

1. Divide the training set into m folds at random. We have used $m = 5$ in our experiments.

2. For each proportionality constant c on a specified grid:

   (a) For each fold $j = 1, \ldots, m$:

      (i) For each class $k = 1, \ldots, K$:

         A. Extract the variables corresponding to class k from all folds except fold j, and fit a local Gaussian density estimators with bandwidth matrix $\mathbf{B}_n = \mathrm{diag}(cn^{-1/6})$.

         B. Use the fitted density to compute the out-of-fold estimated posterior probabilities $P_f(D = k|\mathbf{X} = \mathbf{x})$ for all variable combinations $\mathbf{x}$ in fold j.

      (ii) Compute the AUC in fold j using all the out-of-fold estimated $P_f(D = k|\mathbf{X} = \mathbf{x})$ and corresponding true classes, and denote it by $\mathrm{AUC}_j(\mathbf{B}_n)$.

   (b) Compute the averaged AUC over all folds: $\overline{\mathrm{AUC}}(\mathbf{B}_n) = (1/5) \times \sum_{j=1}^{5} \mathrm{AUC}_j(\mathbf{B}_n)$

3. Choose the bandwidth matrix $\mathbf{B}_n$ with the largest $\overline{\mathrm{AUC}}(\mathbf{B}_n)$.

In our illustrations in the following sections, we also tune the nonparametric kernel estimators in the same way. Note further that if there is a high degree of class imbalance in the training set, then we may consider stratification when splitting the data into m folds.

13.5 Illustrations

13.5.1 Simulations

Let us demonstrate some properties of the local Fisher discriminant (13.8) from a two-class simulation perspective. We generate data in increasing dimension p from three different multivariate classification problems that pose increasingly difficult conditions for the traditional discriminants:

- **Problem 1:** Two multivariate normal distributions, both having all correlations equal to zero and all standard deviations equal to one (so their covariance matrices are equal), but the first population has the mean vector $(0, \ldots, 0)^T$, whereas the second population has the mean vector $(1, \ldots, 1)^T$.
- **Problem 2:** Two multivariate normal distributions having means and standard deviations equal to zero and one, respectively (so their marginal distributions are equal), but the first population has all correlations equal to 0.7, and the second population has all correlations equal to 0.2.
- **Problem 3:** The first population consists of observations on the stochastic vector $\mathbf{X}$ having $t(10)$-distributed marginals and a Clayton copula (Nelsen, 2007) with parameter $\theta = 2$. The second population consists of observations on $-\mathbf{X}$.

We have plotted realizations with $n = 500$ of the bivariate versions of these problems in Fig. 13.2.

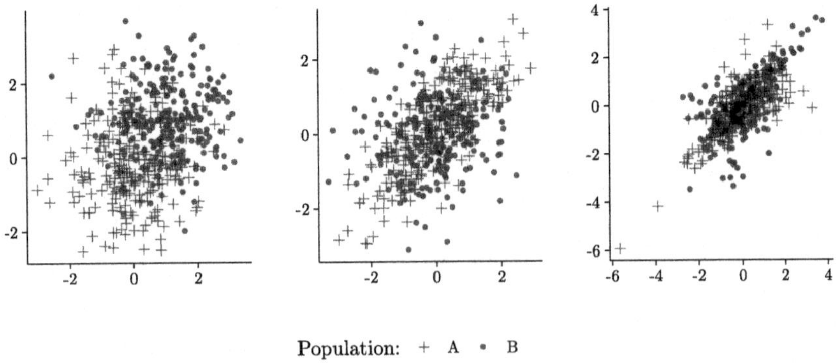

Figure 13.2 Data from the bivariate versions of the three simulated classification problems.

In all simulations, we let $\pi_1 = \pi_2 = 0.5$. We measure classification performance in two standard ways. First, we use the AUC, as briefly introduced in Section 13.4. In addition to the AUC, we also measure the *Brier score* of our predictions (Brier, 1950). The Brier score is essentially the mean squared error of a 0–1-loss classifier. For a test data set of size N in the two-class problem with class labels $D=0,1$, it takes the form

$$\text{Brier score} = \frac{1}{N}\sum_{i=1}^{N}\left(P_{\hat{f}}(D=1|\mathbf{X}=\mathbf{x}) - D\right)^2.$$

As such, *smaller* Brier scores translate to better classification.

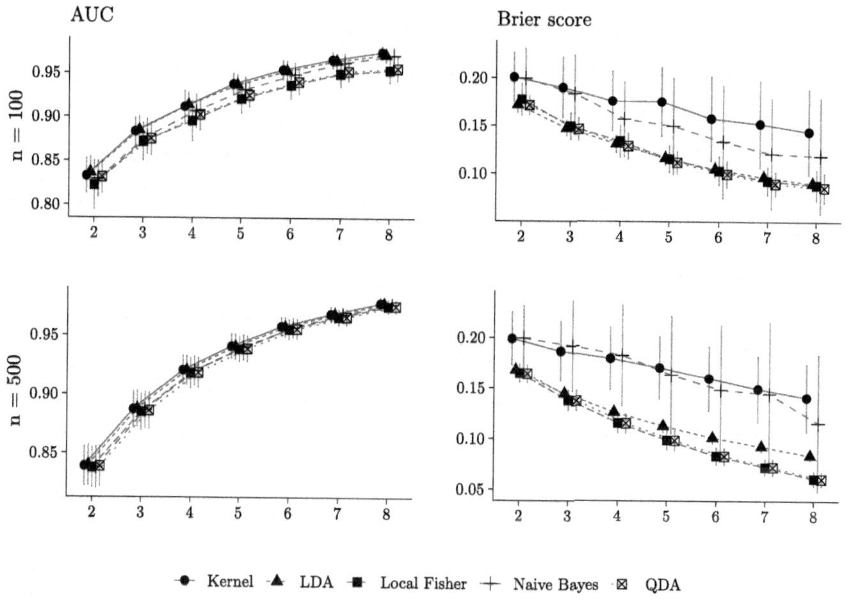

Figure 13.3 Simulation results for the first illustration: Two multinormal distributions with different means but equal covariance matrices. Error measured as a function of dimension.

In Fig. 13.3, we see results for the first illustration, where we try to classify previously unseen test data into one of two multinormal populations that differ only in their means. In particular, we generate training data of total sizes $n=100$ and $n=500$ (i.e., on average, 50 and 250 in each class) and try *five* separate discrimination methods: the parametric LDA and QDA, the multivariate kernel density estimator, the naive Bayes with marginal kernel density estimates, and the new local Fisher discriminant ($\widehat{D}_{\text{LGDE}}$ of Eq. (13.12) gives very similar results to the local Fisher discriminant in these illustrations). For the latter three discriminants, we choose one bandwidth for each population based on the cross-validation routine that seeks to maximize the AUC as described in the preceding section. We repeat the experiment 100 times for each combination of sample size and dimension. In each experiment, we evaluate the discrimination using a test data set of size $N = 500$. The plots report the average AUC and Brier scores for the various discriminants as functions of the number of variables, as well as the standard deviation over the 100 repetitions, which we plot as error bars.

In terms of AUC, all methods perform similarly in this case, but in terms of the Brier score, the correctly specified LDA and QDA are clearly better than the two non-parametric methods, and we also see that the local Fisher discriminant performs on par with the QDA, which comes as no surprise because the QDA-rate is attainable for the local Fisher discriminant by choosing large bandwidths.

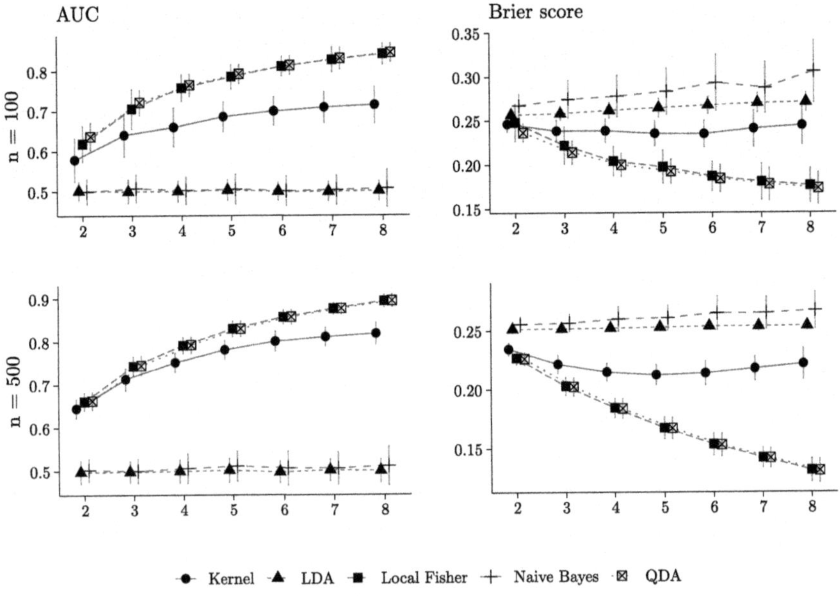

Figure 13.4 Simulation results for the second illustration: Two multinormal distributions with different covariance matrices. Error measured as a function of dimension.

The results from the second illustration are shown in Fig. 13.4, and we clearly see that the various discrimination methods are more separated in this case. The two populations, while both being Gaussian, differ only in their covariance matrices, which means that the LDA and the naive Bayes can simply not see any difference between them, and this clearly emerges in the plots. The kernel density estimator is able to discriminate in this case but seems to struggle with the curse of dimensionality, especially from the Brier perspective. The QDA represents a correct parametric specification and thus also the optimal discriminant in this case, but we also see that the local Fisher discriminant has no problems at all to match its performance. This is again due to our cross-validated choice of bandwidths, which seeks to maximize the AUC.

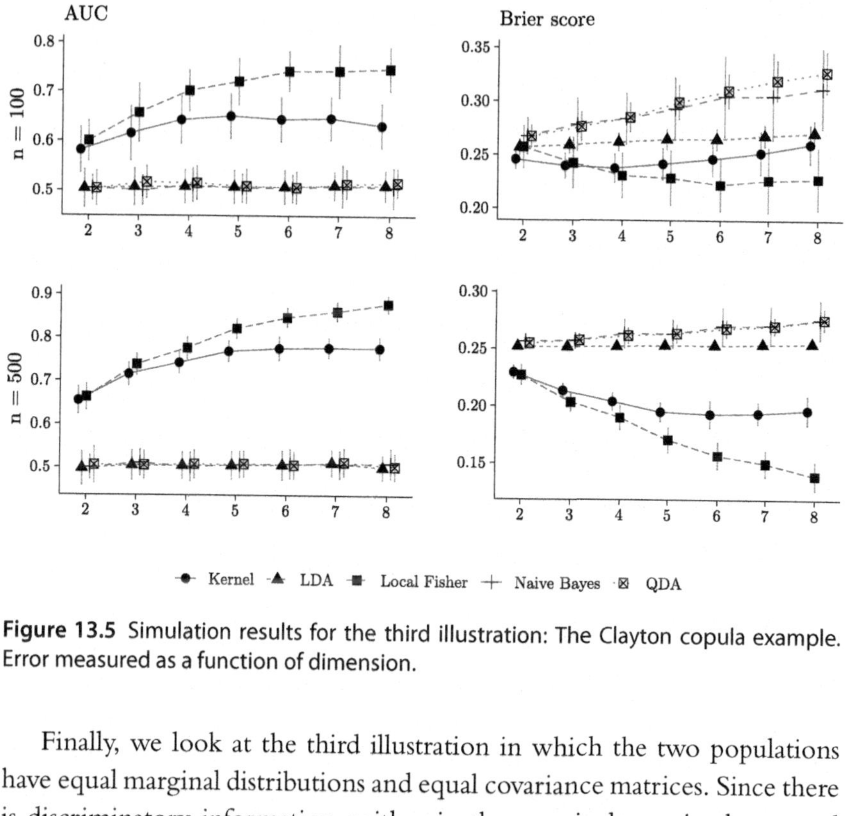

Figure 13.5 Simulation results for the third illustration: The Clayton copula example. Error measured as a function of dimension.

Finally, we look at the third illustration in which the two populations have equal marginal distributions and equal covariance matrices. Since there is discriminatory information neither in the marginals nor in the second moments, we see in Fig. 13.5 that also the QDA collapses. We are left with the purely nonparametric kernel estimator – which works but clearly feels the curse of dimensionality – and the local Fisher discriminant, which now must allow its bandwidths to shrink to reveal non-Gaussian structures. It does that very well, as we see in the plots, and the pairwise estimation structure for the local covariance matrices is seemingly able to detect clear differences between the two populations regardless of the number of variables.

13.5.2 Illustration: Fraud detection

Due to the enormous amounts involved, financial crimes such as money laundering is considered a serious threat to societies and economies across the world (Schott, 2006). It is therefore crucial that banks and other financial institutions report suspicious transactions and behavior to the authorities, such that thorough investigations and monitoring can be put into effect, ultimately leading to stopping the criminal activity and making the source legally liable. In a money laundering setting with a large Norwegian bank, Jullum et al. (2020) develop and train a machine learning model for filtering out suspicious transactions from the legitimate ones. Working with a simplified subset of their data, both in terms of the transactions used and the variables used for discrimination, the use of the local Fisher (and $\widehat{D}_{\text{LGDE}}$) discriminant is compared to the classical discriminants from the above simulation experiments.

We use a data set consisting of 1011 transactions, of which roughly 28% are marked as suspicious. To check how well the discriminants perform, we randomly split this full data into training and test sets, repeating this process 100 times. This is typically referred to as Monte Carlo cross-validation or repeated learning-testing validation (Burman, 1989). The reported results are thus mean AUC and Brier scores over the 100 sets, accompanied with 95% confidence intervals for the means using a central limit theorem-based normal distribution approximation. To simplify, we restricted the analysis to three continuous variables only. In Section 8.3 of Otneim et al. (2020), discrete variables were added to this illustration. Due to data restrictions, we cannot provide further details about the variables in the data set. The data are plotted in Fig. 13.6. As seen from the plot, the *combination* of the two first variables, seems to distinguish the two classes fairly well. The third variable may also improve slightly upon their contribution.

Table 13.1 shows the AUC and Brier scores obtained by the various methods, averaged over the 100 repeated training/test splits, with 95% confidence intervals. Generally speaking, all methods are able to distinguish between the two classes fairly well, as all methods have AUCs larger than 0.9. The LGDE model, however, is clearly the best model for this classification task, both in terms of the AUC and the Brier score, with narrow confidence intervals. The local Fisher model is the second best model, with QDA, kernel, and naive Bayes not too far behind. The LDA model appears to be the least appropriate of these models, with significantly smaller AUC and larger Brier score than the other methods.

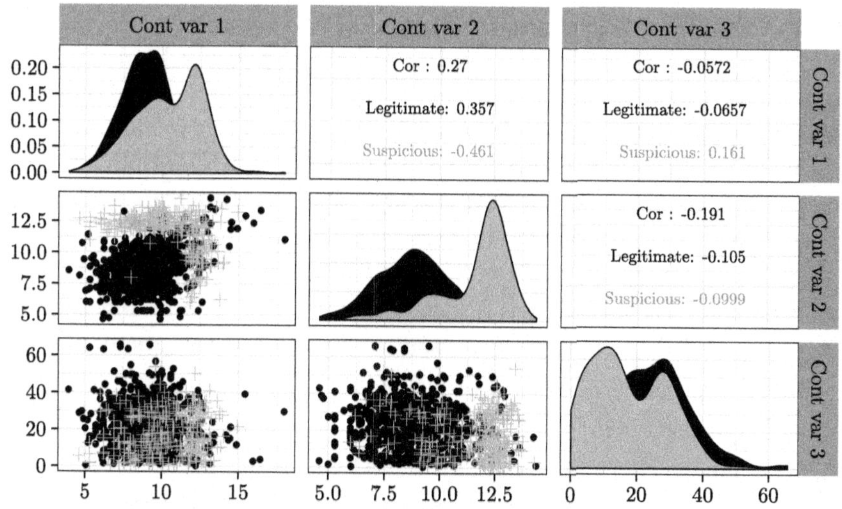

Figure 13.6 Summary plots for the three continuous variables in the fraud detection illustration. Grey (crosses) marks suspicious transactions, whereas black (dots) marks legitimate ones.

Table 13.1 Results using the three continuous variables in the fraud detection example. 95% confidence intervals are shown in brackets.

	LGDE	**LDA**	**QDA**
AUC	0.964 [0.962, 0.966]	0.904 [0.900, 0.908]	0.949 [0.946, 0.951]
Brier	0.0649 [0.0635, 0.0664]	0.116 [0.115, 0.118]	0.0807 [0.079, 0.0824]
	Naive Bayes	**Kernel**	**Local Fisher**
AUC	0.947 [0.944, 0.949]	0.944 [0.941, 0.946]	0.953 [0.950, 0.955]
Brier	0.0794 [0.0774, 0.0813]	0.0847 [0.0828, 0.0866]	0.0768 [0.0748, 0.0787]

13.6 Summary remark

It should be kept in mind, as mentioned in the introduction of this chapter, that in many classification problems, discrete and categorical variables play a very important role. This problem is touched on by Otneim et al. (2020), who introduce a new pairwise discrete naive Bayes discriminant and combine it with the local Gaussian Fisher discriminant. Clearly, there is room for further work here.

Finally, the purpose and motivation for this chapter is not inventing the ultimately best discriminant in every situation, but merely extending a classical discriminant (and another classical one in Otneim et al., 2020) in a coherent way. This is also the reason for comparing the local Gaussian method to the most natural statistically founded alternatives – as opposed to comparing to highly developed algorithmic methods in the machine learning literature, which often require specification of long lists of tuning parameters. It would, however, be interesting to see whether the local Fisher approach, being built on completely different grounds, can utilize the data differently than those methods and therefore bring a new tool to discriminatory methods. If this is indeed the case, then combining the different flavored discriminants, for instance, by an ensemble method from Ranjan and Gneiting (2010), seems like a promising approach.

References

Aggarwal, C.C., Zhai, C., 2012. A survey of text classification algorithms. In: Mining Text Data. Springer, pp. 163–222.
Azzalini, A., 1981. A note on the estimation of a distribution function and quantiles by a kernel method. Biometrika 68 (1), 326–328.
Berentsen, G.D., Støve, B., Tjøstheim, D., Nordbø, T., 2014. Recognizing and visualizing copulas: an approach using local Gaussian approximation. Insurance: Mathematics and Economics 57, 90–103.
Berentsen, G.D., Tjøstheim, D., 2014. Recognizing and visualizing departures from independence in bivariate data using local Gaussian correlation. Statistics and Computing 24 (5), 785–801.
Blanzieri, E., Bryl, A., 2008. A survey of learning-based techniques of email spam filtering. Artificial Intelligence Review 29 (1), 63–92.
Box, G.E.P., Tiao, G.C., 1973. Bayesian Inference in Statistical Analysis. John Wiley & Sons.
Brier, G.W., 1950. Verification of forecasts expressed in terms of probability. Monthly Weather Review 78 (1), 1–3.
Burman, P., 1989. A comparative study of ordinary cross-validation, v-fold cross-validation and the repeated learning-testing methods. Biometrika 76 (3), 503–514.
Chaudhuri, P., Ghosh, A.K., Oja, H., 2009. Classification based on hybridization of parametric and nonparametric classifiers. IEEE Transactions on Pattern Analysis and Machine Intelligence 31 (7), 1153–1164.
Fawcett, T., 2006. An introduction to ROC analysis. Pattern Recognition Letters 27 (8), 861–874.
Fisher, R., 1936. The use of multiple measurements in taxonomic problems. Annals of Eugenics 7 (2), 179–188.
Ghosh, A., Hall, P., 2008. On error rate estimation in nonparametric classification. Statistica Sinica 18, 1081–1100.
Ghosh, A.K., Chaudhuri, P., 2004. Optimal smoothing in kernel discriminant analysis. Statistica Sinica 14, 457–483.
Hall, P., Racine, J.S., Li, Q., 2004. Cross-validation and the estimation of conditional probability densities. Journal of the American Statistical Association 99 (468), 1015–1026.
Hart, J.D., Vieu, P., 1990. Data-driven bandwidth choice for density estimation based on dependent data. Annals of Statistics 18 (2), 873–890.
Hastie, T., Tibshirani, R., Friedman, J., 2009. The Elements of Statistical Learning. Data Mining, Inference, and Prediction, 2nd edition. Springer, New York.

Hjort, N., Jones, M., 1996. Locally parametric nonparametric density estimation. Annals of Statistics 24 (4), 1619–1647.

Hjort, N.L., Glad, I.K., 1995. Nonparametric density estimation with a parametric start. Annals of Statistics 23 (3), 882–904.

Jiang, Z., Ling, N., Lu, Z., Tjøstheim, D., Zhang, Q., 2020. On bandwidth choice for spatial data density estimation. Journal of the Royal Statistical Society: Series B (Statistical Methodology) 82 (3), 817–840.

Johnson, R.A., Wichern, D.W., 2007. Applied Multivariate Statistical Analysis. Pearson Education.

Jones, M.C., Signorini, D., 1997. A comparison of higher-order bias kernel density estimators. Journal of the American Statistical Association 92 (439), 1063–1073.

Jordanger, L.A., Tjøstheim, D., 2021. Nonlinear spectral analysis: a local Gaussian approach. Journal of the American Statistical Association. https://doi.org/10.1080/01621459.2020.1840991.

Jullum, M., Løland, A., Huseby, R.B., Ånonsen, G., Lorentzen, J.P., 2020. Detecting money laundering transactions which transactions should we learn from? Journal of Money Laundering Control 23, 173–186.

Kohavi, R., 1995. A study of cross-validation and bootstrap for accuracy estimation and model selection. In: International Joint Conference on Artificial Intelligence (IJCAI). Montreal, Canada, vol. 14, pp. 1137–1145.

Lacal, V., Tjøstheim, D., 2019. Estimating and testing nonlinear local dependence between two time series. Journal of Business and Economic Statistics 37 (4), 648–660.

Li, J., Cuesta-Albertos, J.A., Liu, R.Y., 2012. Dd-classifier: nonparametric classification procedure based dd-plot. Journal of the American Statistical Association 107 (498), 737–753.

Li, Q., Racine, J., 2008. Nonparametric estimation of conditional CDF and quantile functions with mixed categorical and continuous data. Journal of Business and Economic Statistics 26, 423–434.

Li, Q., Racine, J.S., 2007. Nonparametric Econometrics: Theory and Practice. Princeton University Press, Princeton.

Loader, C.R., 1996. Local likelihood density estimation. Annals of Statistics 24 (4), 1602–1618.

Marron, J.S., 1983. Optimal rates of convergence to Bayes risk in nonparametric discrimination. Annals of Statistics 11 (4), 1142–1155.

Min, J.H., Jeong, C., 2009. A binary classification method for bankruptcy prediction. Expert Systems with Applications 36 (3), 5256–5263.

Nadaraya, E.A., 1964. Some new estimates for distribution functions. Theory of Probability & Its Applications 9 (3), 497–500.

Nelsen, R.B., 2007. An Introduction to Copulas. Springer Science & Business Media.

Otneim, H., Jullum, M., Tjøstheim, D., 2020. Pairwise local Fisher and naive Bayes: improving two standard discriminants. Journal of Econometrics 216, 284–304.

Otneim, H., Tjøstheim, D., 2017. The locally Gaussian density estimator for multivariate data. Statistics and Computing 27 (6), 1595–1616.

Otneim, H., Tjøstheim, D., 2018. Conditional density estimation using the local Gaussian correlation. Statistics and Computing 28 (2), 303–321.

Phua, C., Lee, V., Smith, K., Gayler, R., 2010. A comprehensive survey of data mining-based fraud detection research. arXiv preprint. arXiv:1009.6119.

Ranjan, R., Gneiting, T., 2010. Combining probability forecasts. Journal of the Royal Statistical Society: Series B (Statistical Methodology) 72 (1), 71–91.

Samworth, R., 2012. Optimal weighted nearest neighbour classifiers. Annals of Statistics 40, 2733–2763.

Satabdi, P., 2018. A SVM approach for classification and prediction of credit rating in the Indian market. Working paper.

Schott, P.A., 2006. Reference Guide to Anti-Money Laundering and Combating the Financing of Terrorism. The World Bank.

Silverman, B.W., 1986. Density Estimation for Statistics and Data Analysis. Chapman and Hall, London.

Stone, C.J., 1990. Large-sample inference for log-spline models. The Annals of Statistics, 717–741.

Stone, C.J., Hansen, M.H., Kooperberg, C., Truong, Y.K., et al., 1997. Polynomial splines and their tensor products in extended linear modeling: 1994 Wald memorial lecture. The Annals of Statistics 25 (4), 1371–1470.

Tjøstheim, D., 1978. Improved seismic discrimination using pattern recognition. Physics of the Earth and Planetary Interiors 16, 85–108.

Tjøstheim, D., Hufthammer, K.O., 2013. Local Gaussian correlation: a new measure of dependence. Journal of Econometrics 172 (1), 33–48.

Zheng, R., Li, J., Chen, H., Huang, Z., 2006. A framework for authorship identification of online messages: writing style features and classification techniques. Journal of the American Society for Information Science and Technology 57 (3), 378–393.

Author index

Note: Page numbers followed by "*f*" indicate figures and "*t*" indicate tables.

A

Aas, K., 60, 162, 183, 185
Aastveit, K.A., 253
Aboura, S., 175, 180, 204
Abrahams, J., 64
Aggarwal, C.C., 404
Aït-Sahalia, Y., 163, 197
Akay, O.O., 201
Alcock, J., 60, 182, 183, 189, 190
Allaire, J., 283
Almeida, C., 61
An, H.Z., 40
Anderson, T.W., 9
Andrews, D.W., 328
Ang, A., 162, 165, 197, 201
Ånonsen, G., 404, 424
Aronszajn, N., 74
Atwal, G.S., 80
Auestad, B., 34, 35
Azari, A., 39
Azzalini, A., 222, 320, 416

B

Baba, K., 354
Bae, K., 200
Baek, E., 368
Bakirov, N.K., 66–69, 71
Bakken, H., 60, 162
Bampinas, G., 175, 204
Bartels, R., 53
Bashtannyk, D.M., 336
Bassett, G., 38
Battey, H., 15
Baur, D., 200
Beare, B.K., 61
Beaudoin, D., 149, 151–154, 156
Beering, C., 68
Bekaert, G., 162, 197, 201
Bekiros, S., 183
BenSaïda, A., 162
Berentsen, G.D., 6, 43, 96, 104, 105, 112, 135, 136, 152, 153, 156, 157, 159, 182, 200, 201, 213, 217, 218, 220, 221, 246, 268, 282, 305, 313, 318, 418
Berg, D., 152–154, 156
Bergsma, W., 371
Berlinet, A., 72
Berrett, T.B., 72, 77, 78
Bertero, E., 196
Bickel, P., 39, 78
Billingsley, P., 51, 234, 330
Billio, M., 196
Bilodeau, M., 77
Birr, S., 281, 296, 297
Bjerve, S., 92, 201
Black, F., 161
Blanzieri, E., 404
Blomqvist, N., 90
Blum, J.R., 65
Bollerslev, T., 21, 163
Böttcher, B., 77
Boubaker, S., 162
Bouezmarni, T., 371
Bouri, E., 175
Bousquet, O., 72, 74, 75
Bowman, A., 222
Box, G.E.P., 8, 21, 405
Boyer, B.H., 92, 164, 196
Bradley, B., 201
Brailsford, T., 60, 183, 189, 190
Breiman, L., 36, 37, 64
Brier, G.W., 421
Brillinger, D.R., 263
Brock, W., 368
Brockwell, P., 21, 239, 259, 400
Brychkov, A., 69
Bryl, A., 404
Bühlmann, P., 72, 77
Burman, P., 424

C

Cabrales, A., 197
Cacho-Diaz, J., 163, 197
Cai, Z., 38, 40, 396–398
Campbell, R.A., 164, 165, 168
Cao, R., 43, 96, 105
Caporin, M., 196, 200
Carrasco, M., 278
Carriero, A., 253
Casella, G., 15
Chang, W., 283
Charpentier, A., 303, 336
Chaudhuri, P., 408, 418
Chen, H., 404
Chen, J., 162, 165
Chen, R., 34, 40
Chen, X., 149, 278, 336
Cheng, J., 283
Cheng, Y.-H., 371, 374
Chevallier, J., 175, 180, 204
Chollete, L., 162
Chong, J., 180
Christoffersen, P., 162
Chwialkowski, K., 76
Clark, T.E., 253
Cleveland, W.S., 33
Cline, D.B., 303
Connolly, R., 179
Creti, A., 180
Csiszár, I., 78
Csörgö, S., 66, 67
Cuesta-Albertos, J.A., 408
Cybenko, G., 19
Czado, C., 28, 60, 61, 162
Czáki, P., 64

D

Dajcman, S., 179
Darsow, W.F., 61
Davis, R.A., 21, 68, 239, 259, 264, 400
De Gooijer, J.G., 22
de Micheaux, P.L., 66, 67, 77
Deheuvels, P., 66
Delgado, M.A., 371, 374
Delicado, P., 215
DeMiguel, V., 183, 185, 191, 192
Dey, D.K., 13
Doksum, K., 92, 201
Dong, C., 40
Douc, R., 22
Doukhan, P., 16, 22, 23
Draper, N.R., 8, 18
Dueck, J., 68
Dungey, M., 202
Duong, T., 317

E

Edelman, D., 68
Embrechts, P., 12–15, 140, 199
Engle, R.F., 21, 39, 55, 163
Errunza, V., 162
Escanciano, J.C., 67

F

Faff, R., 60, 183, 185, 189, 190
Fan, J., 22, 25–27, 31, 33, 40, 125, 131, 184, 226, 336, 337, 340, 349–351
Fan, Y., 66, 67, 149
Faugeras, O.P., 336
Fawcett, T., 419
Ferguson, T.S., 53, 54
Ferraty, F., 73
Ferrer, R., 180, 181
Finucane, H.K., 80
Fischer, J., 64
Fisher, R., 50, 403, 406
Fokianos, K., 16, 22, 23, 68, 244
Forbes, C.S., 164, 165, 168
Forbes, K.J., 92, 196, 199, 202, 204, 207
Francis, B.B., 368, 369
Francis, J.C., 184
Francisco-Fernández, M., 43, 96, 105
Francq, C., 22, 259
Frey, R., 12–15, 140, 199
Friedman, J.H., 19, 28, 36, 37, 40, 64, 319, 320, 406
Frigessi, A., 60, 162
Fry, R., 202
Fukumizu, K., 72, 76

G

Gabr, M.M., 56
Gallo, G.M., 197, 201
Galton, F., 50

Gao, J., 19, 23, 39, 40, 151
Garlappi, L., 183, 185, 191, 192
Gayler, R., 404
Gebelein, H., 63
Geenens, G., 303, 336
Genest, C., 53, 54, 57, 61, 81, 149, 151–154, 156
Ghalanos, A., 293
Ghosh, A.K., 408, 418
Ghoudi, K., 66, 81
Gibson, M.S., 92, 164, 196
Gijbels, I., 26, 27, 31, 33, 131
Giles, D., 50
Glad, I.K., 302, 408
Glasserman, P., 197
Gneiting, T., 68, 426
Gómez, E., 52
Gómez-Villegas, M.A., 52
Gonçalves, S., 232–234
González-Hermosillo, B., 202
González-Manteiga, W., 202
Gorfine, M., 80, 93
Gottardi, P., 197
Gourieroux, C., 200
Gozalo, P., 371, 374
Granger, C.W., 21–23, 39, 56, 77, 92, 151, 162, 217, 263, 280, 366, 372
Grassberger, P., 79
Greene, W.H., 18
Grenander, U., 263
Gretton, A., 72, 74–77
Grossman, S.R., 80
Grunwald, G.K., 336
Gupta, R., 94, 175
Györfi, L., 72

H

Hagemann, A., 263
Haldrup, N., 105, 162, 175, 200, 202
Hall, P., 40, 80, 202, 254, 258, 313, 336, 342, 343, 343*f*, 345–347, 408, 418
Hallin, M., 53, 54
Hamilton, J.D., 23
Hammoudeh, S., 183
Han, H., 263
Han, Y., 183
Hansen, B.E., 105
Hansen, M.H., 305, 416
Härdle, W., 20, 24, 26, 27, 150, 151
Harrell, F.E., 18
Hart, J.D., 27, 202, 417
Hastie, T., 19, 32, 35–37, 40, 64, 319, 406
Hatherley, A., 182
Haugen, S.H., 182
Hayfield, T., 27, 28, 342, 345
Hazelton, M.L., 317
Heinen, A., 162
Heller, R., 80, 93
Heller, Y., 80, 93
Herbrich, R., 72
Hernandez, J.A., 183
Heyde, C.C., 254, 258
Higham, N.J., 189
Hinich, M.J., 56
Hjort, N., 2, 3, 5, 8, 41–43, 95, 96, 98–100, 217, 266, 267, 278, 301, 302, 306, 308–310, 313, 316, 323, 329, 355, 361, 408, 409, 416
Hoeffding, W., 57, 65, 67, 75, 90
Holland, P.W., 93
Hong, Y., 65–67, 77, 80, 162, 165, 263, 264, 371
Horowitz, J.L., 38, 396
Hu, W., 371
Hualde, J., 67
Huang, T.-M., 64, 371, 374
Huang, Z., 404
Hufthammer, K.O., 41, 88, 94, 96, 100, 104, 105, 120, 121, 132, 140, 197, 198, 200, 201, 203, 224, 233, 237, 239, 240, 249, 253 256, 267, 269, 308, 310, 323, 409, 410
Huseby, R.B., 404, 424
Hwang, J.-N., 322
Hyndman, R.J., 336, 337

I

Ibragimov, R., 61
Ilmanen, A., 179
Inci, A., 94, 201
Irle, A., 349

J

Jacobs, K., 162

Jain, S., 72, 74, 75
Jammazi, R., 180, 181
Janzing, D., 76, 371
Jasiak, J., 200
Jenkins, G.M., 21
Jentsch, C., 68
Jeong, C., 404
Jiang, Z., 27, 418
Joe, H., 57, 58, 149, 162, 239, 242, 259, 392
Joëts, M., 180
Johnson, R.A., 9, 337, 406
Jones, M., 2, 3, 5, 8, 24, 41–43, 94–96, 98–100, 104, 217, 219, 220, 222, 224, 266, 267, 278, 301, 302, 306, 308–310, 313, 316, 320, 323, 329, 345, 355, 361, 408, 409, 415, 416
Jordanger, L.A., 105, 262, 270, 294, 297, 326, 410, 412
Jorion, P., 162
Jullum, M., 403, 404, 424–426

K

Kakizawa, Y., 123–125
Kakouris, I., 183
Karlis, D., 16
Karlsen, H.A., 31
Karolyi, G., 200
Kauermann, G., 32
Keller-Ressel, M., 77
Kendall, M.G., 54
Kiefer, J., 65
Kim, D., 184
King, M., 50, 151, 196
Kinney, J.B., 80
Klaassen, C.A., 39, 57, 58
Kleppe, T., 6, 105, 268, 282
Kley, T., 281, 296, 297
Klimko, L.A., 19, 102, 123–125, 127, 256, 294
Klüppelberg, C., 271
Knoke, J.D., 53
Koch, I., 94, 219, 220, 222, 224
Koedijk, K.G., 164, 165, 168
Koenker, R., 38
Kofman, P., 164, 165, 168
Kohavi, R., 419
Kooperberg, C., 305, 416
Kotz, S., 14, 243
Koyak, R., 64
Kraskov, A., 79
Kreiss, J.-P., 17
Künsch, H.R., 243, 294

L

Lacal, V., 105, 175, 197, 203, 213, 214, 218, 224–226, 228–231, 234, 236, 239, 240, 242–246, 248, 252, 253, 256, 280, 372, 391, 392, 394, 397, 399, 400, 410, 412
Laeven, R.J., 163, 197
Lancaster, H.O., 63
Lander, E.S., 80
Landsman, Z.M., 12, 52
Langlois, H., 162
Lay, S.-R., 322
Lee, S., 38, 396
Lee, T.-H., 67
Lee, V., 404
Lehmann, E.L., 15, 88, 90, 107
Leipnik, R., 14
Leontief, W., 34
Leucht, A., 68
Li, D., 19, 23
Li, H., 162, 264
Li, H.C., 94, 201
Li, J., 404, 408
Li, K., 396
Li, P., 183
Li, Q., 336, 342, 343, 343*f*, 345–347, 395, 396, 408, 417
Li, T.-H., 263, 281, 292, 296
Li, W.K., 56
Ling, N., 27, 418
Lintner, J., 161
Linton, O., 15, 32, 34, 35, 263, 336, 371, 374
Lippman, A., 322
Liu, C., 14, 15
Liu, R.Y., 243, 408
Loader, C.R., 8, 41, 43, 95, 302, 408
Løland, A., 404, 424
Longin, F., 162, 165, 174, 197, 199, 200

Lorentzen, J.P., 404, 424
Loretan, M., 92, 164, 196
Low, R.K.Y., 60, 183, 185, 189, 190
Lu, Z., 27, 34, 36, 38–40, 151, 396, 418
Lundervold, A., 34, 36
Lyons, R., 76
Lyuyuan, Z., 175, 180, 204

M

Maasoumi, E., 77
Mammen, E., 20, 32, 34, 35, 150, 151
Mangold, B., 61
Manteiga, W.G., 151, 371, 374
Marcellino, M., 253
Marichev, O., 69
Mari'in, J., 52
Markowitz, H., 92, 161, 182
Marron, J.S., 303, 413–415
Martin, V.L., 202
Masry, E., 30, 31, 125, 127, 256
Matsui, M., 68
Mayer, C., 196
McCarthy, J., 94, 201
McFadden, D., 39
McLeod, A.I., 56
McNeil, A.J., 12–15, 140, 149, 157, 199
McPherson, J., 283
McVean, G., 80
Meitz, M., 105, 162, 175, 200, 202
Mélard, G., 53
Merton, R.C., 161
Meucci, A., 60
Meyer, M., 68
Meyn, S.P., 23, 101
Miffre, J., 180
Mignon, V., 180
Mikosch, T., 68, 264, 271
Min, A., 61
Min, J.H., 404
Mitzenmacher, M., 80
Mossin, J., 161
Mougoue, M., 368, 369
Moulines, E., 22
Moya, P., 180, 181
Muscat, J., 72
Myklebust, T., 31

N

Nadarajah, S., 13, 14, 243
Nadaraya, E.A., 416
Nagler, T., 28
Nangue, A.G., 77
Nelsen, R.B., 57, 58, 139, 143, 345, 420
Nelson, P.I., 19, 102, 123–125, 127, 256, 294
Nešlehová, J., 57
Newbold, P., 21
Newey, W.K., 34, 327, 348
Nguyen, B., 61
Nguyen, D.K., 162, 183
Nguyen, Q.N., 175, 180, 204
Nielsen, J.P., 32, 34, 35
Nikoloulopoulos, A., 162
Nordbø, T., 104, 105, 135, 136, 152, 153, 156, 157, 159, 200, 201, 305, 418

O

Oh, D.H., 61, 162
Oja, H., 408
Oka, T., 263
Okimoto, T., 162
Olsen, E.T., 61
Olshen, R.A., 37
Opsomer, J., 32
Opsomer, J.D., 35
Otneim, H., 6, 28, 49, 65, 105, 116, 127, 131, 182, 268, 269, 274, 301, 316, 318, 346, 354, 356, 358, 360, 362, 364, 372–374, 376, 377, 381, 389, 390, 398, 403, 410, 412, 413, 415–418, 424–426
Otranto, E., 197, 201
Owen, J., 12

P

Paindaveine, D., 303, 336
Pan, W., 371
Panagiotidis, T., 175, 204
Panchenko, V., 368, 369
Park, J.Y., 19, 23
Park, S.Y., 264
Parzen, E., 24, 328, 329, 349
Patra, R.K., 371
Patton, A.J., 61, 162, 182

Pawitan, Y., 39
Pearson, K., 50
Pelizzon, L., 200
Penev, S., 66, 67
Pericoli, M., 196, 198
Peters, J., 72, 75–77, 371
Pfister, N., 72, 75, 77
Phillips, P.C.B., 19, 23
Phua, C., 404
Pinkse, J., 66, 67
Pitsillou, M., 68, 244
Politis, D.N., 243
Powell, J.L., 39
Prudnikov, A., 69
Pukthuanthong, K., 163

Q

Quindimil, M.P., 151

R

Rabinovitch, R., 12
Racine, J.S., 27, 28, 77, 336, 342, 343, 343*f*, 345–347, 395, 396, 408, 417
Rahbek, A., 22
Ramchand, L., 197
Ranjan, R., 426
Rao, T.S., 71, 75, 77
Ravazzolo, F., 200
Rémillard, B., 54, 61, 66, 81, 149, 151–154, 156
Rényi, A., 62, 64, 71, 74, 77, 95
Reshef, D., 80
Reshef, Y., 80
Rice, J., 39
Richards, D., 68
Rigobon, R., 92, 196, 199, 200, 202, 204, 207
Ripley, B.D., 19
Ritov, Y., 39
Rizzo, M.L., 64, 66–69, 71, 72, 76, 222, 244, 263
Robinson, P.M., 30, 31, 64, 77, 79, 80
Rodriguez, J.C., 162, 197, 201
Roll, R., 163
Romano, C., 149
Romano, J.P., 243
Rombouts, J.V.K., 371
Rosenblatt, M., 24, 64, 65, 77–80, 136, 137, 336
Rubin, D.B., 14, 15
Ruppert, D., 35, 303
Rustem, B., 183
Rydberg, T.H., 22, 162

S

Sabeti, P., 80
Sabeti, P.C., 80
Saikkonen, P., 105, 162, 175, 200, 202
Samanta, M., 396
Samworth, R.J., 72, 77, 78, 408
Sankaran, P., 94
Sapolek, D., 66, 67
Satabdi, P., 404
Sbracia, M., 196, 198
Schervish, M.J., 328, 329, 349
Schilling, R.L., 77
Schmidhuber, J., 37
Scholes, M., 161
Schölkopf, B., 72, 74–77, 371
Schott, P.A., 424
Schroeder, A., 28, 320
Schulze, N., 200
Sejdinovic, D., 72, 76
Sen, B., 371
Senyuz, Z., 201
Severini, T.A., 327, 328, 348
Shao, X., 68, 71
Sharpe, W.F., 161
Shephard, N., 22, 162
Shibata, R., 354
Shumway, R., 21, 39
Sibuya, M., 354
Signorini, D., 415
Silvapulle, P., 92, 162, 263
Silvennoinen, A., 180
Silverman, B.W., 24–27, 33, 122, 302, 315, 408
Simon, U., 72, 74, 75
Singh, K., 243
Skaug, H.J., 64–66, 71, 75, 77, 79, 80
Sklar, A., 56, 57, 138, 304
Sleire, A., 182
Smith, H., 18
Smith, K., 404

Smith, M., 61
Smola, A., 72, 74, 75
Smrekar, M., 215
Solnik, B., 162, 163, 165, 174, 197, 199, 200
Song, K., 371
Spearman, C., 53
Sperlich, S., 36
Sriperumbudur, B., 72, 76
Stander, J., 38
Stanton, J.M., 50
Stein, M.L., 52
Stigler, S.M., 50
Stivers, C., 179
Stoffer, D., 21, 22
Stögbauer, H., 79
Stone, C.J., 37, 305, 313, 416
Stone, M., 122, 313
Støve, B., 16, 22, 23, 49, 65, 104, 105, 135, 136, 152, 153, 156, 157, 159, 162, 175, 182, 197, 198, 200–203, 249, 253, 305, 418
Stuetzle, W., 28, 40, 320
Stulz, R., 200
Stute, W., 151
Su, L., 66, 77, 371, 373, 374
Subba Rao, T., 56
Sun, L., 179
Susmel, R., 197
Székely, G.J., 64, 66–69, 71, 72, 76, 90, 222, 244, 263, 371

T

Taamouti, A., 371
Taleb, N.N., 2, 8, 91, 105
Tang, K., 180
Tanggaard, C., 32
Taniguchi, M., 123–125
Taqqu, M., 201
Teräsvirta, T., 22, 23, 56, 77, 151, 217, 280, 372
Thomas, J.B., 64
Thomas-Agnan, C., 72
Thorp, S., 180
Tian, Y., 371
Tiao, G.C., 405
Tibshirani, R., 18, 19, 32, 35–37, 40, 64, 319, 406
Tiwari, A.K., 180, 181
Tjøstheim, D., 6, 16, 19, 22, 23, 27, 28, 30, 31, 34–36, 39–41, 43, 49, 54–56, 64–66, 71, 75, 77, 79, 80, 88, 94, 96, 100, 104, 105, 112, 116, 120, 123, 125, 127, 131, 132, 135, 136, 140, 151–153, 156, 157, 159, 162, 175, 182, 197, 198, 200–203, 213, 214, 217, 218, 220, 221, 224–226, 228–231, 233, 234, 236, 237, 239, 240, 242–246, 248, 249, 252, 253, 256, 262, 267–269, 274, 280, 282, 294, 301, 305, 308, 310, 313, 316, 318, 323, 326, 346, 354, 356, 358, 360, 362, 364, 372–374, 376, 377, 381, 389–392, 394, 397–400, 403, 404, 409, 410, 412, 413, 415–418, 424–426
Tokat, Y., 191
Tomita, E., 72, 74, 75
Tong, H., 22, 271, 336
Truong, Y.K., 305, 416
Tsay, R.S., 34, 40
Tsukahara, H., 149
Tsyrennikov, V., 149
Tu, J., 162, 165, 185
Tukey, J.W., 91, 263
Turnbaugh, P.J., 80
Tweedie, R.L., 23, 101

U

Uppal, R., 183, 185, 191, 192

V

Valdesogo, A., 162
Valdez, E.A., 12, 52
van der Waerden, B.L., 54, 115
Vega-Redondo, F., 197
Velasco, C., 67
Vieu, P., 27, 73, 417
Vilar-Fernández, J.A., 202
Vilar-Fernández, J.M., 202
Volgushev, S., 281, 296, 297
von Neumann, J., 50

W

Wadhwani, S., 196
Wan, P., 68

Wand, M., 24, 303, 320, 345
Wang, S., 175
Wang, X., 264, 371
Wang, Y.J., 93
Watewai, T., 163
Weiss, A., 39
Wellner, J.A., 39, 57, 58
Whang, Y.-J., 263
White, H., 66, 77, 80, 232–234, 371, 373, 374
Wicas, N.W., 191
Wichern, D.W., 9, 337, 406
Wilcox, R.R., 93

X

Xia, X., 40
Xia, Y., 183
Xie, Y., 283
Xiong, W., 180

Y

Yang, L., 36
Yao, Q., 22, 25, 34, 36, 40, 125, 184, 226, 336, 337, 340, 349–351
Yao, S., 68, 71
Yenigün, C.D., 64
Yim, T.H., 337
Yoldas, E., 201
Young, H.P., 197
Yu, K., 38, 396

Z

Zakoian, J.-M., 22, 259
Zhai, C., 404
Zhang, H., 371
Zhang, K., 76, 371
Zhang, Q., 27, 418
Zhang, X., 68, 71
Zheng, R., 404
Zhong, W., 264
Zhou, G., 162, 165, 185
Zhou, Z., 68
Zhu, B., 175, 180, 204
Zimmer, D.M., 162
Zou, H., 18

Subject index

A

Accept–reject algorithm, 373
Additive models, 34, 36, 374, 387
Aircraft data, 222, 223
Akaike information criteria (AIC), 157
Almost surely, 97, 98, 104, 105, 108, 118, 119, 126, 130, 389
α-mixing, 125, 226, 238, 277, 278, 339, 340, 348, 349, 363, 393
Alternating conditional expectations (ACE), 36
Applications in finance, 12, 161
ARCH model, 55, 229, 285, 295
Archimedean copula, 58, 143
Asymmetric power ARCH-model, 295
Asymmetry, 13, 162, 165, 166, 183, 196, 202, 284, 293, 295, 296
Asymptotic results, 89, 123, 214, 245, 275, 278–280, 339, 363, 417
- for conditional density estimation, 342
- for local Gaussian correlation estimates, 280, 363
- for local Gaussian partial correlation, 360
- for local Gaussian regression, 388
- for multivariate density estimation, 324
- for spectral estimation, 272, 275

Asymptotic theory, 19, 43, 65, 79, 99, 102, 116, 117, 151, 199, 214, 216, 217, 225, 238, 265, 275, 308, 339, 362, 412
- for ***b*** fixed, 99

Asymptotically normal, 66, 104, 118, 119, 310–312, 329–333, 341, 349, 351
Asymptotics of Bayes risk, 413
AUC, 417, 419–424
Auto-dependence, 61, 249
Autocorrelation, 3, 5, 9, 21, 51, 55, 89, 99, 116, 214, 224, 225, 231, 251, 289
Autoregressive (AR), 20

B

Bandwidth, 2, 26, 32, 33, 79, 95, 122, 126, 136, 152, 236, 266, 282, 313, 323, 390–392, 407, 409, 410, 418, 419
Bandwidth in regression, 32
Bandwidth matrix, 306, 311, 343, 361, 363, 386, 412, 413, 419
Bandwidth selection, 26–28, 122, 313, 365, 395, 411, 417, 418
Bayes optimal, 405
Bayes risk, 404, 408, 413, 416, 417
Bayes theorem, 404
BDS statistic, 218
BDS test, 81
Bear market, 162, 171, 175, 187, 200, 293
Bi-spectrum, 56, 263
Bivariate GARCH, 245
Bivariate standard normal, 112
Bivariate t-distribution, 220
Block bootstrap, 121, 203, 214, 233, 235, 243, 280, 294, 394
Block length, 294
Bonds, 178–181
Bootstrap, 65, 80, 120, 152, 174, 202, 203, 214, 216, 217, 219, 228, 229, 233, 235, 243, 244, 280
Bootstrap test, 197, 202, 206, 207, 218
- of independence, 217

Brier score, 421, 422, 424
Bull market, 162, 177, 200, 293

C

Causality from small to big firms, 369
Central limit theorem, 9, 51, 340, 394, 424
Characteristic functional, 68
Characteristic generator, 12–15
Choice of bandwidth, 27, 32, 103, 122, 152, 218, 229, 282, 321, 408, 417, 418, 423
Clayton copula, 58, 60, 112, 114, 119, 141, 143–145, 158, 159, 182, 321, 322, 420
Cointegration, 23

Commodities, 178–180, 187
Comparing with other tests for conditional independence, 373
Condition for independence, 106
Conditional correlation, 92, 95, 164–166, 199, 200, 263, 354, 371, 381
Conditional density, 2, 5, 28, 29, 60, 91, 336, 337, 341, 358, 359, 371, 387
Conditional density estimation, 5, 6, 27, 41, 89, 116, 123, 301, 337, 339, 341, 342, 388
Conditional empirical distribution function, 396
Conditional Gaussian distribution, 355
Conditional mean, 20, 36–38, 335, 336, 385, 386, 396, 397
Conditional quantiles, 386, 396, 397
Conditional value at risk, 183
Conditional variance, 36, 38, 163, 386
Conditional variance matrix, 30, 37
Confidence intervals, 109, 114, 119, 120, 165, 174, 178, 235, 249, 369, 424
Convergence rate, 8, 25, 34, 75, 104, 136, 152, 241, 269, 274, 275, 278, 340, 389, 394, 396, 397, 413, 415–417
Convergence theorem, 279
Copula, 4, 54, 56–58, 61, 89, 96, 116, 135, 136, 140–145, 149, 154, 157, 162, 183, 197, 201, 237, 269, 305
Copula-GARCH, 183
Covariance operator, 74
Cramér–von Mises distance, 65
Cramér–Wold device, 328, 330, 351
Crisis period, 196, 199, 204, 206, 207
Cross-market linkage, 199, 202, 204
Cross-product ratio, 94
Cross-validation, 26, 33, 122, 166, 207, 230, 246, 313, 314, 317, 323, 365
Cumulative distribution function, 56, 62, 106, 115, 116, 136, 137, 224–228, 237, 242, 243, 265, 273, 274, 304, 356, 389, 391, 396, 398, 412, 416
Curse of dimensionality, 2, 3, 8, 9, 23, 24, 28, 29, 33, 35, 38, 43, 56, 62, 71, 78, 301, 302, 306, 319, 320, 325, 345, 386, 396, 407, 408, 410, 423

D

Daily stock index returns, 168
Danish fire insurance claims, 157
DAX, 168, 175, 204
Decision variable, 404
Density-based tests of independence, 77
Dependence, 3, 4, 49, 50, 55, 56, 61, 62, 64, 67, 87, 88, 90, 91, 93, 94, 114, 136, 161, 163, 178–180, 215, 220, 225, 231, 235, 240, 243, 249, 262, 263, 304, 305, 307, 321, 371, 406
Dependence measure, 4, 49, 52, 54, 62, 88, 106, 163, 165, 224
Diagonal bandwidth matrix, 362, 363
Diagonal local Gaussian correlation, 115, 121, 172–174, 177, 178
Distance covariance, 66, 67, 74, 76, 77, 218, 221, 230, 231, 244, 246
Distribution of conditional quantiles, 397
`dmbp`-data, 281, 282, 284, 292–297
Dynamic conditional correlation, 163

E

Edgeworth expansion, 79, 80
Elliptical copula, 60, 146
Elliptical distribution, 11, 12, 14, 52, 53, 56, 108, 111, 112, 146
Empirical copula process, 153
Empirical distribution function, 67, 71, 116, 130, 149, 225, 226, 228, 240, 249, 282, 308, 312, 356, 360, 372, 389, 412
Ensemble method, 426
Equicontinuous family of functions, 327
Exceedance correlation, 164, 165, 196
Exchange rate, 231, 275
Exchange symmetry, 108, 110, 111
Exponential family, 15–17
Extreme value, 157, 162, 178, 197
Extreme value methods, 199

F

f-divergence, 78
Fast Fourier transform, 272
Filtering, 114, 163, 164, 249, 251, 424
Financial contagion, 4, 6, 163, 196, 197, 207, 249

Financial crises, 8, 197
Financial returns, 59, 61, 98, 100, 120, 162, 167, 175, 182, 200, 249
Fisher discriminant, 5, 403, 404, 406–412, 420–423
Flexible version of the LGDE, 323, 326
Fourier transform, 56, 66, 261, 273
Frank copula, 4, 58, 145
Fraud detection, 404, 424
FTSE 100, 59, 114, 115, 121, 168, 170, 171, 173–175, 204
Full investment constraint, 184

G

GARCH model, 21, 108–111, 113, 199, 262, 295
GARCH(1, 1) filtration, 167, 178, 202
GARCH(1, 1) model, 55, 109, 164, 173, 206, 229–231, 246
Gaussian copula, 58, 60, 89, 107, 146, 147, 153, 154, 156, 157, 308, 318, 321
Gaussian distribution, 1, 2, 4, 8–10, 12, 16, 51, 62, 89, 92, 105, 140, 161, 162, 165, 168, 175, 178, 197, 200, 307, 323, 346, 354, 359, 387, 407, 409
Gaussian pseudo observations, 116, 142, 149–151, 154, 156–158, 303, 305
Gaussian white noise, 285, 287
Generalized additive model (GAM), 36
Generalized linear model (GLM), 19
Generalized spectral density, 66
Generalized spectrum, 263
Geometrically ergodic, 101, 104, 117, 118
Global dependence functional, 61
Goodness-of-fit, 148, 151, 178
Goodness-of-fit test, 105, 150, 153, 154, 157, 159
Granger causality, 5, 366, 368, 369, 374
Gumbel copula, 144, 145, 157–159

H

Heatmap plot, 281, 282, 291, 292
Hellinger distance, 78, 319, 321, 371, 374
Hidden Markov chain, 201
Higher-order kernels, 26, 31, 415, 417
Higher-order spectra, 263
Hilbert–Schmidt information criterion, 74
Hilbert–Schmidt norm, 73
Hilbert–Schmidt operator, 73
Hoeffding functional, 65
HSIC measure of dependence, 68, 72

I

In distribution, 12, 71, 75, 332, 364
In probability, 117, 234, 306, 327, 348, 372, 389, 394
Index model, 39, 40
Indicator function, 24, 37, 65, 97, 149, 215, 289, 306, 356, 388, 405
Integrated relative squared error (IRSE), 319

J

Jensen's inequality, 330, 351
Jump processes, 197

K

k-nearest neighbor, 314
Kendall rank correlation, 54
Kernel density estimator, 24, 25, 27, 43, 78, 315, 318, 407, 417, 422
Kernel estimator, 3, 27, 30, 32, 122, 302, 318, 319, 336, 343, 345, 349, 408, 416
Kernel function, 24–26, 35, 42, 74, 78, 96, 97, 101, 103, 104, 118, 129, 130, 217, 233, 234, 236, 241, 266, 274, 278, 306, 309, 311, 313–315, 340, 342, 361, 364, 386, 393, 400, 407, 410, 417
Kernel of RKHS, 72
Kolmogorov–Smirnov distance, 65
Kullback–Leibler information, 78
Kurtosis, 114, 168, 175, 184, 189, 190, 206

L

Lasso, 18, 19
Level of test, 152, 155, 231, 373
Limit theorem, 71, 75, 99, 416
Linear discriminant analysis (LDA), 406
Linear regression, 8, 17, 19, 50, 92
Linear transformation, 107, 131
Ljung–Box statistic, 218, 231

Local bootstrap, 373
Local dependence, 3, 80, 88–90, 94, 122, 136, 144, 156, 166, 201, 362
Local Gaussian autocorrelation, 213, 224, 264, 265, 270–273, 282, 286, 288, 290, 294
Local Gaussian correlation (LGC), 4, 62, 94, 163, 165, 265
Local Gaussian cross-correlation, 99, 214, 236
Local Gaussian density estimation (LGDE), 302, 337, 412
Local Gaussian Fisher discriminant, 5, 403, 408, 425
Local Gaussian partial correlation (LGPC), 353
Local Gaussian partial correlation matrix, 378
Local Gaussian regression, 386, 388, 394
Local Gaussian spectral density, 264, 265, 270
Local independence testing, 219
Local likelihood, 41, 89, 95, 97, 98, 100, 105, 108, 121, 143, 150, 151, 232, 303, 313, 326, 327, 336, 349, 360, 411, 412
Local likelihood estimate, 97, 99, 100, 132, 140, 152
Local log likelihood, 11, 41, 99, 116, 215, 236–238, 267, 410
Local parametric, 5, 8, 9, 26, 43
Local polynomial estimation, 31
Local spectrum at diagonal points, 293
Locally parametric, 2, 4, 40, 337
Logarithmic returns, 59, 113, 115, 121, 173, 204, 206, 207, 249, 250, 316, 368, 370
Logistic regression, 36, 200
Logspline approach, 274, 305, 308, 339
Logspline estimator, 305
Long only positions, 184
LOWESS, 33

M

m-truncated version, 272
Marginal empirical distribution function, 4, 305
Marginally Gaussian pseudo observations, 312, 342
Markov regime, 162
Markov switching model, 197
MARS, 37
Maximal correlation, 63, 64, 72, 73
Maximal information coefficient, 80
Mean integrated squared error (MISE), 152, 315
Mean-variance (MV) approach, 161, 182
Minimum variance portfolio, 184
Mixing, 125, 277, 339, 340, 351, 362, 363, 394
Mixture of distributions, 322
Monte Carlo cross-validation, 424
Monthly prices of oil and gold, 316
Monthly prices on the US and Norwegian total market, 316
Monthly stock index returns, 175
Multicolinearity, 18
Multivariate density estimation, 6, 365
Multivariate LGPC, 376
Multivariate normal distribution, 9, 14, 28, 41, 43, 52, 56, 187, 302, 338, 355
Multivariate *t*-distribution, 3, 13, 14, 53, 58, 319, 325, 347, 395

N

Nadaraya–Watson estimator, 29–33, 35, 385, 388
Naive Bayes classifier, 407
Nearest-neighbor estimation, 33
Network model, 40, 197
Neural network modeling, 19
Neural networks, 37
Non-normalized, 123, 229, 230, 241
Nonlinear regression, 19, 22, 39, 51, 385, 415
Nonlinear time series, 22, 51, 214, 373
Nonparametric, 4, 8, 9, 28, 125, 126, 150, 302, 372, 417
  density estimation, 2, 23, 24, 97
  kernel density estimation, 24
  regression estimation, 20, 29, 37, 385
  tests, 368, 370, 373, 374
Nonstationary, 19, 23, 40
Normal scores, 54, 58, 60

Normalized local correlation, 115
Normalized local Gaussian correlation, 141
np-package, 342

O

Oslo stock exchange, 368

P

p-dimensional case, 123
Pairwise estimation, 303, 423
Pairwise local dependence, 410
Pairwise simplification, 321, 362, 364, 366, 386, 412
Parametric bootstrap, 151, 152, 154, 156
Parametric regression model, 17
Partial correlation, 5, 89, 353–355, 357, 358, 360, 362, 364, 366, 368, 370, 376, 381
Partial correlation matrix, 353, 355, 369, 378, 379, 381
Partial covariance matrix, 356, 359, 378
Partially linear models, 39
Partition function, 16
Pearson correlation test, 222
Pearson product moment correlation, 49
Periodicities, 99, 272
Plug-in bandwidth, 33, 248, 315, 319, 343
Polynomial regression, 19
Portfolio allocation problem, 182–184
Positive and negative conditional relationships, 366
Power of test, 108
Prior probability, 404
Product kernel, 96, 103, 128, 131, 236, 308, 313
Projection pursuit, 28, 39, 40, 320

Q

Quadratic discriminant analysis, 406
Quantile regression, 37, 38, 200, 263, 386
Quantile spectrum, 264

R

Radial symmetry, 108, 109
Receiver operating characteristic (ROC), 418
Reflection symmetry, 108–110, 112, 219
Regime models, 201
Regime switching, 162, 163
Regression and conditional quantiles, 5, 89, 385
Regression trees, 37
Rényi criteria, 88, 106, 115
Reproducing kernel Hilbert spaces (RKHS), 72, 371
Returns, 59, 61, 98, 100, 120, 162, 164, 167, 168, 171, 172, 175, 178, 180–182, 186, 187, 192, 200, 207, 249
Ridge regression, 18
Rosenblatt (1952) transformation, 136
Rotation symmetry, 108

S

S&P 500, 59, 114, 115, 121, 168, 170, 173–175, 204, 249
Semiparametric, 2, 4, 7–9, 15, 17, 38, 39, 302, 342, 371, 372, 386, 417
shiny application, 283, 284
Short positions, 184
Simulated data, 112, 285, 318, 346
  with irrelevant variables, 347
  with relevant variables, 345
Skewed t-distribution, 320, 322, 323
Skewness, 162, 168, 175, 184, 189, 190, 206
Sklar formula, 135
Sklar's (1959) theorem, 56, 57, 304
Spearman rank correlation, 53
Spectral analysis, 3, 5, 52, 261, 263, 287
Spectral density function, 66, 99, 261
Spherical distribution, 12
Standard deviation, 26, 49, 79, 161, 168, 172, 182, 189, 191, 192, 204, 225, 287, 394, 422
Standard error, 120, 413
Standard normal density, 137, 228, 390
Stationary, 21, 23, 25, 168, 201, 203, 226, 238, 244, 245, 249
Stationary bootstrap, 243, 246, 248, 249
Statistical independence, 49, 113
Stocks, 178–180, 368
Strictly stationary, 21, 236, 265, 270, 276, 341

Strongly mixing, 130, 277
Sufficient statistic, 16
Symmetries, 107, 108

T

t-copula, 147, 148, 156
t-distribution, 3, 11, 13, 14, 16, 53, 58, 109, 110, 112, 113, 147, 220, 221, 319, 320, 325, 346, 347, 395
t(4)-distribution, 323, 346
Tail behavior, 140
Taylor expansion, 25, 42, 96, 98, 102, 103, 123, 124, 128, 129, 137, 241, 256, 330, 331, 349, 398
Tensor product, 73
Test statistic, 66, 67, 154, 203, 216, 218, 224–226, 228, 230–232, 234, 235, 240, 243, 245, 246, 371, 372
Testing for conditional independence, 5, 123, 353, 370, 373, 381
Testing for serial independence in time series, 224
Tests of independence, 61, 235, 240
Time reversible, 271, 273, 280
Time series, 5, 6, 19–22, 25, 27, 30, 51, 55, 65, 66, 71, 76, 79, 89, 100, 101, 118, 122, 164, 186, 213, 214, 218, 225, 227–229, 235, 237, 244, 245, 249, 250, 261, 271, 275, 276, 278, 285, 287, 289, 301, 335, 339, 342, 366, 418
TOPIX, 168, 175, 204
Training set, 404, 407, 413, 419
Transformation step, 303, 305
Transforming the marginals, 4, 89, 115, 313
Tri-spectrum, 56, 263
Tri-variate fit, 276
Trigonometric examples, 287, 289
Truncated correlation, 164
Truncation level, 282, 285, 286, 288, 292
Tukey–Hanning lag-window, 282
Two-class discrimination problem, 411

U

Uniform convergence in probability, 327, 348
Uniform pseudo-observations, 149
Uniform scores, 57, 59

V

Validity of the bootstrap, 151, 214, 218, 229, 231, 234, 244, 245, 372
Value at risk, 4, 8, 162, 200, 417
van der Waerden correlation, 58, 89
Vine copula, 60, 61, 136, 162
Visualization, 280

W

Weighted Kullback–Leibler distance, 96, 266, 310, 361

X

x-scale, 4, 324, 357, 359, 363, 365, 390

Z

z-scale, 4, 324, 357–360, 362, 363, 372, 390